OXFORD HISTORY OF
MODERN EUROPE

General Editors
ALAN BULLOCK *and* F. W. D. DEAKIN

Oxford History of Modern Europe

THE STRUGGLE FOR MASTERY
IN EUROPE 1848–1918
By A. J. P. TAYLOR

SPAIN 1808–1939
By RAYMOND CARR

THE RUSSIAN EMPIRE 1801–1917
By HUGH SETON-WATSON

FRANCE 1848–1945, Vol. I
By THEODORE ZELDIN

FRANCE 1848–1945, Vol. II
By THEODORE ZELDIN

GERMANY 1866–1945
By GORDON A. CRAIG

THE LOW COUNTRIES

1780–1940

BY

E. H. KOSSMANN

OXFORD
AT THE CLARENDON PRESS
1978

Oxford University Press, Walton Street, Oxford OX2 6DP

OXFORD LONDON GLASGOW
NEW YORK TORONTO MELBOURNE WELLINGTON
KUALA LUMPUR SINGAPORE JAKARTA HONG KONG TOKYO
DELHI BOMBAY CALCUTTA MADRAS KARACHI
IBADAN NAIROBI DAR ES SALAAM CAPE TOWN

© *Oxford University Press 1978*

British Library Cataloguing in Publication Data
Kossmann, Ernst Heinrich
    The Low Countries, 1780–1940. – (Oxford history of
    modern Europe)
    1. Netherlands – History   2. Belgium – History
    I. Title   II. Series
    949.2   DJ202   77–30291
    ISBN 0–19–822108–8

*Printed in Great Britain
at the University Press, Oxford
by Eric Buckley
Printer to the University*

PREFACE

IN the 1930s the late Pieter Geyl started a work in many
volumes on the history of the Dutch-speaking population
in the Northern and the Southern Netherlands, in South
Africa, and in the Dutch colonies: *Geschiedenis van de Nederlandse
stam*. His main innovation was that he included in his national
history the Dutch-speaking provinces of what is now Belgium;
of course he excluded the Walloon areas. His rightly famous
work ends in 1798, roughly the time when my book begins,
but I must emphasize that my work is in no sense intended as
its continuation. It was not my task to propound and defend
a specific thesis as Geyl did. I had to write about two states in
their entirety, that is, in the case of Belgium, about a community which, during most of the period studied here, preferred
to use French rather than Dutch for all matters considered to
be of general interest.

There is undeniably an element of arbitrariness in cutting the
histories of these two nations out of the whole of Europe in the
centre of which they have been living for centuries, and in
studying them in one book as though they belong together.
This is why I should like to present my work as primarily
a study in comparative history, although in some chapters
I have not described Belgian and Dutch affairs in separate
sections and have tried to show, without neglecting the differences, that in many cases the two nations reacted to political
and intellectual challenges in almost identical ways.

I have been inconsistent in my treatment of cultural history.
In fact, one single principle has guided me: I have totally
omitted the history of art and music. As far as literature is
concerned, I have not hesitated to touch the subject wherever I
thought this might clarify the narrative but at no time has it
been my ambition to write literary history. The same applies to
such disciplines as philosophy and theology which I took the
liberty of using for my purpose when I hoped that would be
enlightening.

There are two terminological points which I must briefly

mention. The word 'Flamingant' which I use frequently indicates a person who is prepared actively to support the cause
of Flemish emancipation. In the second place I have used the
term 'Prime Minister' anachronistically. Not until 1918 did
the Belgians confirm in written law the existence of the function
of Prime Minister and not until 1945 did the Dutch follow their
example. But long before that time the chairman of the Cabinet
had obtained sufficient authority to justify my usage of the
term.

The writing of this book has taken me more time than I had
planned and it has given me more pleasure than I expected.
I am grateful to a number of friends whose comments on parts
of the typescript encouraged me to persevere. I mention with
particular gratitude Professor Maurits de Vroede at Louvain.

I owe a large debt of gratitude to Lord Alan Bullock for his
most perceptive counsel and to the editorial staff of the Oxford
University Press for their efforts to improve my English style.

E. H. K.

GRONINGEN

CONTENTS

LIST OF MAPS

(at end)

INTRODUCTION

IN 1648 the independence of the Dutch Republic was recognized by Spain. In 1830 the Belgians seceded from the United Kingdom of the Netherlands to found their own monarchy. 'Dutch', 'Belgian', the 'Netherlands' as well as the 'Low Countries' in the title of this book are all terms which have needed historical explanation for as long as they have been in use. Only in English and Dutch is it possible to use both the name 'Low Countries' (De Lage Landen) and 'Netherlands' (De Nederlanden or Nederland). Only in English and Dutch, therefore, can one help the reader by reserving 'Netherlands' for the present-day Dutch state and 'Low Countries' for the Netherlands and Belgium together.

The word 'Dutch' is used in this book both for a native of the present-day Netherlands and for the language spoken in the Netherlands and in the northern part of Belgium.[1] 'Flemish', of course, is the adjective belonging to Flanders, that is the old county and the present Belgian provinces West- and East-Flanders plus Dutch Flanders (Zeeuws-Vlaanderen) and French Flanders. It is common practice now to call the whole Dutch-speaking section of Belgium Flanders and the movement striving for the emancipation of that area the Flemish movement. This is awkward, for in this manner not only Flanders proper but also Antwerp, Limburg, and part of Brabant are collectively known as Flanders, but it is difficult to avoid these ambiguities. It is, however, not advisable to distinguish between 'Flemish' as spoken in Flanders in the wide sense of the word and 'Dutch' as spoken in the Netherlands. Although there are undoubtedly differences in accent and vocabulary civilized 'Flemish' in Belgium is the same language as civilized 'Dutch' in the Netherlands.

The Low Countries form part of the North European plain and today do not possess natural eastern frontiers—although in the past such provinces as Groningen, Drenthe, and Overijssel were prevented from extending further eastwards and were

---

[1] For the name 'Belgium' see below, p. 118.

protected against foreign invasion by the large virtually inaccessible bogs and moors which surrounded them. However, the south-eastern part of Belgium with the hills of the Ardennes and their forests belongs to a different kind of landscape. The southern frontiers of both states—the Dutch–Belgian and the Belgian–French borders—show no geographical characteristics whatever; they have been drawn by political and military accident. Thus the only permanent natural limit to the territory of the Low Countries is the North Sea.

Just as there is little in the geography of the Low Countries, beyond the fact that they form the delta area of the rivers Scheldt, Meuse, and Rhine, to explain the emergence of independent states, so there is little in the ethnic origins of the inhabitants to account for it. The essential fact in the history of this area was the penetration of the Germanic tribe of the Franks who seem to have settled in the fourth century in the northern part of the Netherlands and then in the second half of the fifth century to have moved southwards. This long process of Frankish colonization became less effective in the region south of the linguistic frontier between Germanic and Romance dialects which established itself between the sixth and ninth centuries and still exists: a line running from Gravelines (south-west of Dunkirk) eastwards, south of Brussels, to the region south of Maastricht in Dutch Limburg and then sweeping abruptly southwards through Luxemburg to the Franco-German border. South of this linguistic boundary the denser population of what are now the Walloon provinces was to a much lesser extent absorbed by the Franks than was the population north of it; at any rate they retained their Gallo-Roman dialects. North of the rivers Rhine and Meuse other Germanic tribes found ground to settle on; their Saxon and Frisian languages still survive in the Dutch province of Friesland and the eastern part of Gelderland.

The sea and the big rivers determined the development of the Low Countries more than any external event; they broke the coastline, they transformed mainland into isles, and they also carried the sand and clay needed for creating new land. They have never ceased giving the area, specifically the Netherlands, new forms. Of the Netherlands as it now is only small parts in the east have subsisted in their present shape since the Ice

Age. In nearly all other regions the advance or regression of the sea and the ever-changing course of the rivers determined whether life would be possible there, or whether the area would become impassable bogs and flooded fields where immense organized effort would be required to transform it into land suitable for human exploitation. Today's coastline is quite different from that of the Middle Ages or even of the sixteenth century. Much land has been reclaimed since medieval times but much has been lost too. There has always been so much water in the Low Countries that it has naturally dominated their economy. Nearly all the provinces of the Netherlands have an age-long experience of river, coastal, and overseas trade and of fishing. For many centuries the rivers were more important than the roads for carrying merchandise and immigrants. In the delta into which the big rivers debouch cultural influences from many parts of the world converged, making the Low Countries from prehistoric times onwards a melting-pot of peoples and ideas.

As a result of the marked differences between the various parts of the Low Countries, agriculture has always been highly varied. In the areas where the ground level reaches hardly above the sea level, cattle-breeding has often been more profitable, although in some parts the heavy clay deposited by the sea at an earlier time made the land suitable for wheat-growing. On arid and sandy soil mixed farming—corn-growing combined with cattle-breeding—has always been usual. Obviously, the local agricultural systems were instrumental in shaping the way of life of the inhabitants, the construction of their farmhouses, the layout of their villages, the rules governing their common lands, the organization of their village communities in general, even such simple everyday things as cooking, drinking, and heating habits. But the origin of the inhabitants, descending from populations dominated, north of the linguistic barrier, by the Frisian, the Frankish, or the Saxon cultures, also produced local differences which persisted for many centuries. Such differences manifest themselves in the various dialects, in the systems of common law that remained operative until the end of the *ancien régime*, and in many other matters. However, the boundaries between the ancient cultural or ethnic groups in no way coincide with the boundaries of the provinces into which the Low Countries have come to be divided; these are due to the accidents of power and politics.

The complexity of the political history of the Low Countries during the Middle Ages was caused by both the formation and the collapse of the Frankish Empire, that is the Merovingian and Carolingian structure that brought together under one dominion highly diverse areas where Christianity was either introduced or forcefully supported and where a new distribution of power was inaugurated. By the end of the eighth century the whole area of the Low Countries had become Christian and the organization of the Church was making some progress, Utrecht in the north and Liège in the south having already been transformed into ecclesiastical centres. At the same time the population of many of the northern regions, which had held only tenuous connections with the Roman Empire, was for the first time in its history confronted with the conception and the reality of kingship. The land was divided into districts controlled by high officials called 'counts' who represented the king in all his capacities. Their personal loyalty to the monarch whom they served gave way, however, to a strong attachment to the region where they were striking roots.

The division of Charlemagne's Empire into three parts after the death of his son, Louis the Pious (814–40); the decision to allot the major part of the Low Countries to Lotharius who was given the imperial crown together with the central area of his father's realm (with the Rhine as its eastern and the rivers Rhône, Saône, Meuse, and Scheldt as its western boundaries); the breakdown of the Lotharingian Realm during the subsequent wars of succession—this whole process of decomposition, which led to anarchy and in the ninth century served as an invitation to Danish pirates to invade the coast areas and to plunder them, forced the inhabitants and their leaders to rely on their own resources and build up new power on the basis of the structure designed by the Franks. In the southern part of the Low Countries powerful dynasties of counts were seen to be developing in the tenth century, some of them—such as the counts of Flanders—primarily thanks to the energy with which they fought the Scandinavian raiders, others simply by taking advantage of the political chaos. When in 925 Lotharingia became definitely a part of East Francia (Germany), where the Carolingian dynasty had become extinct and was replaced by Saxon princes, ambitious lords in the Low Countries eagerly sought to promote their own interests. Even Flanders, though tied to France, joined the struggle and tried to use the deep hostility between Germany and France for its own profit.

Thus the results of imperial aspirations since the Frankish colonization were, firstly, that as a substitute for Roman rule and order a new form of political power was introduced which, though designed to keep the area together, prepared the way for its being broken up into a very large number of duchies (Limburg, Brabant, and Gelderland were more or less officially elevated to that dignity), counties, bishoprics, and seigniories; and secondly, that thanks to the division of the Carolingian Empire into three parts, the delta area of Lotharingia was initially so independent of both East and West Francia that it was not unnatural for it to remain relatively uninfluenced by their later development into the better-organized states of the German Empire and France. Until the end of the fourteenth century the Low Countries were free to order their affairs without much interference from outside. This period of their history makes a chaotic impression with the endless wars fought between them, the short-lived alliances, the marriage contracts constantly thwarted by death and murder. There is little, apart from economic factors, which shows a tendency towards greater unity. What unity there was seems superficial: for three centuries the counties of Holland and Hainaut were ruled by the same dynasty, and yet they had little in common apart from their administrative superstructure.

In marked contrast to this impression of disorder, developments within the states themselves strike the modern observer as full of promise for the future. There emerged forms of government, jurisdiction, taxation, and representation which, although mostly copied from structures first elaborated abroad, were adapted to the conditions prevailing in the Low Countries in a thoroughly individual manner. In each of these countries administrations were built up which, while corresponding with the general pattern of all medieval states, were nevertheless made to fit the circumstances of a specific area. The result was that the governmental systems in the various countries differed considerably. So did the social systems, one of the most striking and influential facts for the future being the absence of a powerful nobility in the county of Holland. Subsequently, the growth of parliaments from the thirteenth century onwards, though following a general pattern, also produced very varied results. In other words, thanks to the sophistication of the ruling élites, their systems of government and the structure of their representative estates tended to become increasingly idiosyncratic, thus making for division rather than unity.

There were, on the other hand, factors which made possible a sense of sharing the same destiny, but they were economic and cultural, not political. The geography of the Low Countries predisposed their population to engage in trade and navigation. From the early Middle Ages on there were characteristic, though still isolated, instances of ambitious trading enterprises such as those of the Frisians dating from the seventh century. Later on numerous towns in the eastern parts of the Netherlands, in Overijssel and Gelderland, took part in the trade of the German Hanse. Eventually, the western sea coast area turned out to provide by far the best opportunities for developing important centres of trade and industry. In the eleventh century Bruges and Ghent were already known for their connections with England and served as export harbours of the cloth produced in Flanders and Brabant. By the thirteenth century Bruges had become one of the major markets in Northern Europe where the German Hanse and Italian merchants and bankers set up permanent offices and where the English established their wool staple. In the fourteenth century it had a population of over 30,000. In the middle of the same century Ghent—with 50,000 inhabitants—was undoubtedly still the biggest manufacturing town in Northern Europe although the prospects of the cloth industry in Flanders were beginning to look gloomy. In Holland urbanization followed the same pattern much later. The counts of Holland favoured the development of towns, perfectly aware as they were of the political, economic, and fiscal advantages which could be derived from them. But the biggest town of Holland in that period, Leiden, had in the beginning of the fifteenth century no more than 5,000 inhabitants.

Not only in their economies but also culturally the states south of the rivers were considerably more advanced than the northern territories throughout the medieval period. The history of medieval Dutch literature,[1] which may be said to have started in the twelfth century, can be traced in Limburg, Brabant, and Flanders rather than in Holland, Utrecht, or Gelderland. In its first phase French influence was predominant as could be expected in areas such as Flanders where the dynasty and the nobility used to speak French. But in the thirteenth century more original poets appeared in Flanders and Brabant, one of them a mystic woman, Hadewijch, whose life we know virtually nothing about but whose poetry is outstandingly personal, passionate, and imaginative. Totally different but in its own fashion just as distinguished is the famous poem *Vanden Vos Reinaerde* (*Reynard the Fox*) which also dates from the thirteenth century but about whose author we know still less. In the fourteenth century the prose writings of Jan van Ruusbroec who spent most of his life in his abbey near Brussels were literary and intellectual achievements of great quality owing to the profundity of his mystic conceptions and the lucidity of his style. Ruusbroec exercised a direct influence on Geert Groote, born in Deventer in Overijssel, whose Devotio Moderna, organized in the movement called the Brethren of the Common Life, transformed the mysticism of the Brabant writer into more practical ethical and religious precepts. One of Groote's followers, Thomas à Kempis, who lived in a monastery near Zwolle, also in Overijssel, was probably the author of *De imitatione Christi*, the most widely read book in Christian literature apart from the Bible. Works of this stature, originating both from the northern and the southern parts of the Low Countries, are obviously products of a mature civilization which, although not 'national' in the modern sense of the word, was linguistically, intellectually, and spiritually different from the style and the traditions prevailing in France or the German Empire.

From the end of the fourteenth century the penetration of

[1] There are two outstanding recent works in English on the history of Dutch literature: Theodoor Weevers, *Poetry of the Netherlands in its European Context 1170–1930* (London, 1960) and Reinder P. Meijer, *Literature of the Low Countries: a Short History of Dutch Literature in the Netherlands and Belgium* (Assen, 1971).

Burgundy into the Low Countries totally altered the political situation. In 1364 the French King invested his younger son Philip, known as the Bold, with the Duchy of Burgundy. Through his marriage with Margaret of Flanders and his excellent relations with the Duchess of Brabant Philip obtained for his dynasty both these wealthy states. From that base his House was able to acquire, in the early fifteenth century, the whole of the west coast, with Zeeland and Holland as well as Hainaut, Namur, and Luxemburg. A century later Philip's descendant Charles V conquered the Duchy of Gelderland (1543) after having obtained all the other territories in the north-east. In 1548 he put the seal upon his achievements by granting the Low Countries, under the name of the Burgundian Circle, a privileged and virtually autonomous position in the German Empire. The Circle included Flanders and Artois whose ties with France were severed in the 1520s. It had by that time become usual to call the Low Countries 'the Seventeen Nether-lands', although it is not altogether clear why. But whatever the number seventeen may have indicated—seventeen coun-tries, seventeen sovereign titles, or nothing so precise?—the fact that a name, however vague and impersonal, was apparently needed shows that thanks to Burgundian policies the Low Countries had become much more coherent than they had ever been before. They were very far indeed from forming a single country, were still, broadly speaking, a number of semi-independent states brought together by the fact that all of them happened to have the same ruler, yet some institu-tional innovations (for example, the occasional calling-together of the local estates into one States General, the establishment of central judicial and financial bodies) as well as their common reactions to the perplexing consequences of Burgundian–Habsburg greatness taught them to unite both in praise of Charles V's lustre and in self-defence against his encroach-ments upon their ancient rights and privileges. Common pride at being the homeland of the greatest emperor since Charle-magne—Charles V was born at Ghent—and at having in Antwerp the most advanced business centre of the world, reflected the growing sense of unity as much as did the common distrust of endeavours on the part of their rulers to centralize government with a view to improving the fiscal system and increasing taxes so as to provide the capital required for carrying out policies of truly global dimensions.

The Low Countries were one of the most active parts of Charles V's Empire. If it is true, as has been suggested, that an economy tends to enter into the category which we may call modern as soon as 50 or 40 per cent of the population have taken up residence in urban communities, then some of the Low Countries were approaching that stage in the early sixteenth century.[1] In Hainaut, undoubtedly one of the most rural societies in the Southern Netherlands, at least 29 per cent of the population were living in towns. In the fifteenth century 35 per cent of Brabant's inhabitants were townspeople. Flanders reached a higher percentage although we have no reliable data. We know that in 1514 46 per cent of the population in Holland lived in towns. Moreover, in Flanders, Brabant, and Hainaut a good proportion of the rural population was employed in the textile industry while fishing and shipping had drawn many of the rural villages in Holland and Zeeland into the market economy of that age. Of course, the growth of Antwerp—with *c.* 5,000 inhabitants in 1374 and *c.* 100,000 in the 1560s—reflects the expansion of the economy in a striking way and the building of its famous Stock Exchange in 1531 *in usum negotiatorum cuiuscumque nationis et linguae* emphasizes the comprehensiveness of its ambitions. With Bruges still retaining much of its traditional business,[2] with various Dutch towns and especially Amsterdam rapidly learning to grasp the opportunities offered by the new economic developments, the Low Countries formed in the early sixteenth century a major centre of trade and industry. This fact was decisive for the later history of this area for it meant that the population—estimated to have totalled approximately 1,850,000 inhabitants in the 1520s—came to know at this early stage the whole ambiguous set of consequences deriving from capitalistic expansion: wealth, luxury, sophisticated but disruptive cultural and religious innovation, social disequilibrium, proletarization, serious social disturbances, controlled as far as possible by harsh repression

[1] For the following see R. van Uytven, 'What is new socially and economically in the sixteenth-century Netherlands', *Acta historiae neerlandicae*, vii (The Hague, 1974), 23–4.

[2] W. Brulez, 'Bruges and Antwerp in the 15th and 16th centuries: an antithesis?', *Acta historiae neerlandicae*, vi (The Hague, 1973), 1–26.

as well as by remarkably elaborate, but nevertheless inadequate, forms of poor relief.

Charles V abdicated in 1555 leaving his sovereignty over Spain and the Low Countries to his son Philip II. A few years later the Low Countries entered into the long and complicated series of wars and disturbances commonly called the Revolt of the Netherlands. The Revolt was so decisive for the development of the Low Countries that no student of Dutch and Belgian history can hope to understand the later modern period without having at least tried to define the meaning of these sixteenth-century disasters.[1]

The consequences of the Revolt were clear at the time of the Truce which the rebel provinces negotiated with the Spanish King in 1609. They were partly expanded and partly confirmed at the Peace of Münster in 1648 between the Dutch Republic and Spain: the Spanish King retained his sovereignty over the Southern Netherlands but recognized the independence of the so-called Seven United Provinces, often called the Dutch Republic. Present-day Belgium, although deriving from the Spanish Netherlands, is territorially not identical with the possessions left to Spain in 1648. During the late seventeenth and early eighteenth centuries Spain was forced to abandon numerous towns and lands to France: the ancient county of Artois, the districts and towns of Lille, Orchies, and Douai, parts of Flanders, parts of Hainaut with Valenciennes, the archbishopric of Cambrai, etc. On the other hand, Belgium now includes territory which never belonged to the Habsburg possessions, above all the bishopric of Liège. In the North the Seven Provinces were Holland, Zeeland, Utrecht, Gelderland, Overijssel, Friesland, and Groningen but the territory of the Republic was somewhat larger: Drenthe (now a normal province) was during the *ancien régime* considered a mere territory without representation in the States General while Dutch Flanders (now part of Zeeland) and Dutch Brabant (now the province of North-Brabant) were regarded as conquered territory and as such directly ruled by the States

[1] For recent attempts in English to analyse the Revolt see J. W. Smit, 'The Netherlands Revolution', in R. Foster and J. P. Greene (eds.), *Preconditions of Revolution in Early Modern Europe* (Baltimore and London, 1970), pp. 19–54, and E. H. Kossmann and A. F. Mellink, *Texts Concerning the Revolt of the Netherlands* (Cambridge, 1974).

General. By far the most complicated area is Limburg, now Dutch and Belgian, but before 1815, when the Congress of Vienna allotted most of it to the United Netherlands, divided in a most intricate way into Dutch, Spanish (later Austrian), and Prussian districts.

So much then is obvious: the Revolt of the Netherlands led to the secession of the Seven Provinces from the Spanish dominion and the creation of a new independent state. Even the most cursory glance at the course of the Revolt, however, shows that this was not an effect consciously willed by the participants. Calvinism, one of the great factors which propelled the Low Countries into rebellion and anarchy, spread first in Flanders and was prominent in Antwerp long before it achieved success in what were later to become its strongholds: Holland and Zeeland. The economic recession of the mid-century hit the most developed areas in the South undoubtedly harder than the North. It was, moreover, in the South that the activities of the nobility, led by the greatest of them all, William of Orange, first transformed the widespread disaffection of the population with the style of government favoured by Philip II into concrete and, in the beginning, not unsuccessful opposition. In other words, the religious, social, and political factors determining the outbreak of the Revolt manifested themselves first in the most advanced provinces of the Southern Netherlands.

The objectives of the various groups which rose in opposition were manifold: religious toleration, lesser taxation, greater influence of the local authorities in the decision-making process, all these and other causes were bitterly fought for with the result that the struggle adopted the most diverse forms. But one thing it was not for many years: a war of independence. Not until 1581 did the States General declare that Philip II had forfeited the sovereignty over the Low Countries and not until the late 1580s did the States of the provinces which had not been reconquered by Spain claim that they were themselves in the possession of sovereignty. At that time twenty years or more had gone by since the first serious difficulties had arisen.

During the Revolt the rebels attempted to transform the States General—in which representatives of the various provincial States met at the order of the rulers to discuss serious common problems and to channel government proposals, mainly about taxation, to the local States—into a kind of national and representative executive capable of taking decisions binding on all the provinces of the Low Countries. Thus the rebels sought to accelerate the process of unification which the Burgundian sovereigns had started in an effort to facilitate government in an area split by the traditional complicated system of local authorities. Yet the springs of their own power were fundamentally provincial and could be nothing else. Effective opposition to the Spanish sovereign could, as was shown again and again by events, only be organized within the provinces which thanks to the old-fashioned pattern of the so-called Burgundian state had retained the old institutions, regulations, instruments of government, and habits of mind allowing them to act efficiently and independently. Without this large degree of provincial autonomy the Revolt would have been utterly impossible. Consequently, it turned out to be illusory to try and draw together all the Low Countries into a common, federal, supra-provincial—or, let us use the word, national—effort to obtain freedom.

There is one other factor which needs emphasis even in the briefest survey: in the Southern Netherlands, where the Revolt started but failed, social antagonisms were much more serious and stubborn than in Holland and Zeeland where the Revolt came later but was successful. There are various reasons for this. It was of some importance that in the Flemish and Brabant towns economic expansion had since the Middle Ages been accompanied by a growing estrangement, occasionally developing into fierce hostility, between the patriciate and the lower middle classes organized in guilds. In the less advanced towns of Holland and Zeeland there was comparatively little of this kind of social tension with the result that it was more natural for the bourgeoisie there to associate with the lower classes. Moreover, in Holland and Zeeland the status of the nobility had been for many centuries, and still was, radically different from that in the southern and eastern parts of the Low Countries; in comparison with the grand tradition and wealth of the nobles in Flanders and Brabant, their equals in Holland were poor and politically impotent. As a result,

the two small maritime provinces were socially more homogeneous than any other provinces in the Low Countries.
This, next to political and purely military factors, helps to
explain why it was possible for them to continue revolutionary
policies which in other areas tended to be paralysed by numerous inner conflicts, and efficiently to use or transform for their
new needs the old provincial institutions which did not function so well in the other less stable societies.

From this rapid survey three conclusions may be drawn:
first, that in view of the fact that provincial autonomy contributed so much to the perpetuation of the Revolt, it was not
unnatural for the Revolt to have failed to create a nationally
coherent state encompassing the whole of the Low Countries;
the breakup of Charles V's Burgundian Circle should not be
seen as the dramatic and essentially accidental end to a long
historical process of unification. Yet, and this is the second
conclusion, owing—among other things—to the sophisticated
propaganda of William of Orange's party, all groups, however
diverse and antagonistic, had developed a feeling that somehow the Low Countries belonged together and that the outcome of the wars represented a split of the Netherlands and
was in a sense a tragedy. The third conclusion to be drawn is
of a different nature. The Revolt had come to be a fight
between areas ruled by Calvinists against areas ruled by
Roman Catholics, and it had turned out to be easier for the
Calvinists to grasp and retain power in Holland and Zeeland
than in the southern provinces where Protestantism had first
made its appearance. This does not mean that the population
as a whole adopted one particular form of religion. It is much
more realistic to assume that for most people to make a choice
between Calvinism and Tridentine Roman Catholicism was
initially both impossible and unacceptable. The religious situation was, as it were, pliable. But once a government in a specific
area had taken a definitive decision about which religious
denomination it wanted to support, it had to try and make the
population adhere to its preference. Hence the policy of Protes-
tantization in the North (which was only partly successful)
and re-Catholization in the South (the success of which was
virtually complete)—a policy which in the North was a far
cry indeed from the original demand for toleration, although

it was pursued with peaceful means, and which in the South differed fundamentally from the practice of Charles V and Philip II in no longer using violence for the purpose of creating uniformity.

This then was the situation in the early seventeenth century.[1] Its highly paradoxical nature is characteristically revealed by the violent polemics of southern Jesuits against northern Calvinists and vice versa, an immense literature in Latin and Dutch. It is evident that neither had as yet given up the idea that the North and the South fundamentally formed a unity which both sought to restore. However, both wanted this reunification to be brought about on their own conditions only, that is to say through the establishment of exclusive supremacy of their own particular creed in both parts of the Low Countries. Since this obviously could not be achieved by either group, both were by the sheer force of circumstances driven back into their own provinces. There their influence was unchallenged, or, in the case of the Calvinists in the North, was at any rate considerable. As the hope of reconquering the other part faded, both Jesuits and Calvinists developed a resigned hatred of each other, now regarded as irretrievably corrupted and as complete strangers. Religion, used as a means to stabilize society, caused North and South not only to drift apart but to develop contrasting proto-national conceptions. North and South seemed to form an antithesis of widely diverging principles. The North, a Maritime Power, governed by a bourgeoisie and its commercial interests, looked fundamentally different from the continental South with its Spanish court at Brussels, its Jesuits, its loyalty to the monarchy, its nobility growing in number and social importance.

The conspicuous economic development of the Dutch Republic owed much to the outcome of the Revolt. In 1585 Antwerp had been reconquered by the Spanish troops, a fact which in the North also was felt to be a major disaster. The northern provinces which continued the fight then 'closed the Scheldt',

---

[1] For the following see my somewhat more leisurely account in *The New Cambridge Modern History*, iv, ed. J. P. Cooper (Cambridge, 1970), pp. 359–84 and in vol. v of the same series (ed. F. L. Carsten, 1961), pp. 275–300. Excellent English books on the seventeenth-century Dutch Republic include C. R. Boxer, *The Dutch Seaborne Empire* (London, 1965); K. H. D. Haley, *The Dutch in the Seventeenth Century* (London, 1972); J. L. Price, *Culture and Society in the Dutch Republic During the 17th Century* (London, 1974); C. Wilson, *The Dutch Republic* (London, 1968).

that is they blocked the entry to the river and thus made it impossible for enemy ships to reach Antwerp by sea. After the war the Dutch continued their blockade and in spite of protests remained adamant. In the Peace Treaty of Münster Article XIV explicitly stipulated that the Scheldt as well as the rivers connecting Bruges and Ghent with the Western Scheldt were to be kept closed by the Dutch. In this way the Dutch were allowed to prohibit direct Spanish or 'Belgian' navigation between Antwerp, Ghent, Bruges, and the sea; in actual fact this prohibition also included the passage of foreign ships beyond Flushing in Zeeland. In the 1660s Antwerp was given an outlet through the canalization of the interior waterway system via Ghent to Ostend but this was much inferior to the Scheldt route. The decline of Antwerp was only too obvious. The Dutch merchants used Antwerp as a harbour from which their merchandise flooded into the whole of the Southern Netherlands. Whereas the Dutch ports had in the sixteenth century been dependent on the Antwerp market, the relationship was now reversed: Antwerp was a dependency of Holland. Its population had been dramatically reduced by the sixteenth-century wars, falling to 42,000 in 1589. Thanks to the stability of the seventeenth century it rose to 67,000 in 1699, but as a consequence of the wars of the late seventeenth and eighteenth centuries it sank again to 42,000 in 1755. Amsterdam, on the other hand, grew rapidly, from some 50,000 inhabitants in about 1600 to 100,000 in about 1620, 150,000 in 1650, and 200,000 in the middle of the eighteenth century. Even Rotterdam, in the sixteenth century incomparably less influential than Antwerp, had at the end of the eighteenth century outgrown the Belgian port.

A second most profitable factor for the Dutch was the influx of Calvinist immigrants from the Southern Netherlands (totalling, according to a modern estimate, 60,000) who contributed their fortunes, their skill, knowledge, and dynamism to the development of the Dutch economy and civilization. Although it is impossible to reach any firm conclusion in this matter, there is some reason to suppose that during the Revolt 90,000 inhabitants left the Southern Netherlands never to come back, that is about one-tenth of the total population. And many of these people were experienced and wealthy merchants or entrepreneurs whose capital and business acumen greatly benefited the foreign towns where they found refuge. It is characteristic that 38 per cent of the starting capital of the Amsterdam Chamber of the Dutch East India Company— founded in 1602 and in the middle of the century undoubtedly the world's largest business enterprise—was raised by immigrants from the Southern Netherlands. The growth of the Northern Netherlands into a nation which for a number of generations dominated world trade and developed advanced forms of business organization and a prosperous industry, thus taking over the function fulfilled by the Southern Netherlands in the later Middle Ages and the sixteenth century, owes a great deal to the physical presence of thousands of Southerners.

It is impossible to give an impression of the demographic development of the Southern Netherlands in the seventeenth and eighteenth centuries. The only figures available concern Brabant which had about 360,000 inhabitants in 1526, 373,000 in 1709, 445,000 in 1755, and 618,000 in 1784, of whom 39, 37, 32, and 24 per cent respectively were living in towns. By the end of the eighteenth century Brussels had become the biggest town in the area (74,000 inhabitants in 1784) but it was less than half as big as Amsterdam at that time and even smaller than Antwerp in the 1560s. For Flanders we possess some data about the population of Ghent (31,000 in about 1610, 52,000 in about 1690, 38,000 in about 1740) and of a few other towns but a general estimate is out of the question. The total population of the Southern Netherlands may have amounted to slightly over two million in the middle of the eighteenth century. Moreover, one thing is clear: the high degree of urbanization which had been characteristic of the sixteenth century tended to diminish, especially in the late eighteenth century when population growth was mainly a rural phenomenon.[1]

For the Northern Netherlands historical demographers have recently studied their material with such sophistication that it has been possible to make a general estimate.[2] It is worth

[1] See below, pp. 49 ff.
[2] This is taken from the authoritative synthesis by B. H. Slicher van Bath, 'De demographische ontwikkeling tijdens de Republiek', *Vaderlands Verleden in Veelvoud* (The Hague, 1975), 312–36.

while specifying the demographic development of the province of Holland because this may reflect something of the economic drama performed there. In about 1500 Holland had an estimated 275,000 inhabitants (28·9 per cent of the total Dutch population), 903,000 in about 1650 (48·2 per cent), and 783,000 in 1795 (37·7 per cent). In 1514 46 per cent of the

Population of the Dutch Republic, 1500–1795	
Year	Population
1500	900,000–1,000,000
1550	1,200,000–1,300,000
1600	1,400,000–1,600,000
1650	1,850,000–1,900,000
1700	1,850,000–1,950,000
1750	1,900,000–1,950,000
1795	2,078,000

population in Holland lived in towns, in 1622 this had risen to 54 per cent. But for most of the towns, apart from Amsterdam, Rotterdam, and The Hague, the later seventeenth and eighteenth centuries were disastrous, with towns like Leiden and Haarlem, once famous for their textile industry, losing almost half of their population and others stagnating. Although Dutch developments differed significantly from those in the Southern Netherlands, it is clear that in both countries the urban element had in the second half of the eighteenth century become somewhat less preponderant than it had been in the sixteenth and seventeenth centuries.

In the South the seventeenth century was perhaps not as disastrous as is sometimes suggested but it is beyond question that the country had lost the economic and political position it held in the sixteenth century and was made to suffer atrociously from the semi-permanent warfare on its territory, more than ever Europe's battlefield, During the second half of the century the French invaded with monotonous regularity the Spanish possessions which the impotent government at Brussels, badly led and without sufficient money, could not protect. It is one of the ironies of European history that, owing to Spain's inability to withstand French pressure, the task of preserving the integrity of the Southern Netherlands or, at least, of preventing the French from totally absorbing them, fell upon the United Provinces. For them it was vitally important that the Southern Netherlands be kept more or less in the state in which the Treaty of Münster had left them: with the Scheldt closed and with just enough resilience to serve as a barrier between the Republic and France. French occupation of these territories was feared, in all probability quite rightly, as a mortal danger to the Republic because it would undoubtedly entail the opening of the Scheldt and the development of Antwerp as a formidable competitor of Amsterdam; but, more seriously still, the Southern Netherlands would serve as a base, both territorial and maritime, for the French to destroy the defiantly wealthy Protestant Republic. This was one of the main reasons for the Dutch building up with such stubbornness and ingenuity the system of alliances which eventually thwarted French imperialism.

The Spaniards kept the Southern Netherlands in their possession until the death of King Charles II in 1700. Then the interminable War of the Spanish Succession resulted in their being transferred to Austria. The provinces did not even try to influence decisions which were of momentous importance to them. The inhabitants accepted all the rulers who were given them although they clearly preferred a 'natural' sovereign, that is a member of the House of Burgundy–Habsburg, to the French or Anglo-Dutch authorities whom they had been forced to obey during the war. For them the main point was that the sovereign should govern them in the traditional way, respecting their old privileges, avoiding any disturbance in the routine of the provincial dignitaries, and carefully abstaining from introducing any 'absolute' principle which they had come to abhor so intensely during the Revolt. In the second half of the century the Spanish indeed administered the country rather than ruled it, with the result that provincial autonomy tended to be confirmed and even expanded in matters not pertaining to the only questions which interested the Spanish plenipotentiaries: military affairs.

The Austrians started their rule under even gloomier auspices. When the Dutch at last handed over the government of the Southern Netherlands (which they had ruled in collaboration with the British since their success in the Battle of

Ramillies, 1706), they forced the new sovereign, the Emperor Charles VI, to accept extraordinarily unfavourable terms solemnly specified in the so-called Barrier Treaty (1715; ratified 1719). Since the 1670s the Dutch had been permitted to hold a line of fortresses in the Southern Netherlands; in 1715 their powers were greatly extended although even then less than they wanted. The Emperor was obliged to pay large sums of money for the upkeep of the Dutch military establishments, money which had to be provided by the inhabitants. In this way Charles VI was deprived of the normal privileges of sovereignty. Dutch troops occupied the strongholds of his new provinces, the best revenues were appropriated for payment of the subsidy, and commercial regulations were accepted which preserved all the advantages the Maritime Powers had in the course of time been able to procure for themselves. As a result the Southern Netherlands were felt by the Austrians to be a burden rather than a useful acquisition, while the population was deeply irritated at the situation into which they were driven and most reluctant to pay for what amounted to military occupation.[1]

For the Dutch the Barrier Treaty was less a cynical method of exploiting the Southern Netherlands than an attempt to construct a better defence line without having to expand their territory or spend much money on it. The fundamental problem for the Dutch in the seventeenth century was the exiguity of their state, in terms of both land and population, a state that thanks to its economic successes was elevated to the responsibilities of a Great Power. The tendency among many of the Dutch statesmen was to design their foreign policy in such a way that the Republic could reduce its involvement in international political affairs to the absolute minimum; this, they hoped, would make it unnecessary for them to expand at all. They wished to attain three somewhat contradictory aims and they succeeded for a number of generations in maintaining the delicate balance required for this. They wanted to preserve their status as a Great Power, out of sheer necessity rather than because they enjoyed it; they wanted to keep out of

[1] R. Geikie and I. A. Montgomery, *The Dutch Barrier 1705–1719* (Cambridge, 1930), p. 369. Interesting information also in Alice C. Carter, *Neutrality or Commitment: The Evolution of Dutch Foreign Policy, 1667–1795* (London, 1975).

international conflicts but, if involved in them, pertinently rejected the ambition to strive for conquests. The smallness of their
territorial basis was in their view a prerequisite of economic
prosperity—the whole state having to be transformed into one
busy town rather than into an empire in continental style—
as well as of sound and orderly government. To be a Great
Power, to be a small country, to opt out of power politics, these
were the basic aims of Dutch society in the seventeenth century.
Thanks to the Barrier Treaty the fundamental contradictions
between them seemed at last to be reconciled. Safely protected
by a line of fortresses in another country the Dutch, who were
well aware that they owed this happy state of affairs to their
influence in international politics, could now devote themselves
to the pursuit of happiness, that is prosperity, order, a life style
inspired by the solid virtues of the Protestant middle class.

The rhythm of Dutch history is punctuated by the alterna-
tion of regimes in which the Orange Stadtholder plays a
major part and others in which his office is left vacant. Up to
1672 the most important provinces, Holland included, refused
to appoint a successor to William II who had died in 1650.
In 1672 the aggression of France and Britain and the conquest
of half the country by the enemies made the demand for a
prince of Orange to save the fatherland so overwhelming that
William III was hastily made Stadtholder. But when he died
in 1702 it was thought possible to do without such a dignitary.
Only in 1747 did the invasion by a French army once again
persuade the population and the patricians that it was wise to
entrust the final responsibilities to a personality capable of
serving as the central political figure in the decentralized
Republic. William IV—who was descended from a younger
brother of William the Silent and who had, in accordance with
the tradition established in 1584 in this branch of the Nassau
family, been Stadtholder of Friesland since 1711, of Groningen
since 1718, of Drenthe and Gelderland since 1722—was now
elevated to that dignity in the other provinces as well, with
the result that for the first time all the provinces had the same
Stadtholder. Thus the Dutch *ancien régime* had two periods
without a Stadtholder, the second lasting no less than forty-
five years: the longest period in the whole of Dutch history
up to the present day in which the House of Orange held no

function whatever in the main provinces of the Netherlands. There is no single explanation for this; one factor, however, was undoubtedly the desire of the patricians in Holland not to carry on indefinitely the foreign policies adopted by William III. Certainly, the War of the Spanish Succession had to be fought, whatever the cost, but with the purpose of not pursuing beyond the peace ambitious plans for future involvement. There was no question of altering the direction of William III's foreign policy. There was, however, the firm will not to make the Republic a permanent centre of European politics.

The Barrier failed to serve its purpose. Although the Dutch enjoyed thirty years of total peace this was due to French exhaustion rather than the defence line. When its strength was finally tested in the 1740s during the War of the Austrian Succession the French encountered little resistance and conquered the fortresses in a short time. The Dutch re-garrisoned them after the Peace of Aix-la-Chapelle in 1748, but the Austrian subsidy was no longer paid. In fact, the Barrier had come to have only symbolic value. The Dutch statesmen of the late eighteenth century were not only as reluctant as many of their predecessors to participate in international conflict, they now allowed the country to abandon even the means of taking part in war by allowing their defences, both territorial and maritime, to deteriorate to the point of becoming useless. This was a system (if system it may be called) of unarmed neutrality that could only be maintained as long as the other Powers tolerated it; it is interesting in so far as it indicates the degree to which the Republic had ceased to act as a real state. In 1782 the Dutch withdrew their garrisons from the Southern Netherlands at the request of the Emperor Joseph II. But Joseph did not succeed in reopening the Scheldt. It was the French who put an end to the closure of the river. On 21 November 1792 a French squadron sailed up the estuary and there was nothing the Dutch Republic could risk doing against the decision of triumphant revolutionaries not to respect a privilege infringing the 'natural right' of free navigation.

What, then, was the situation at which the Low Countries had arrived by the middle of the eighteenth century? In the Southern Netherlands the pattern of economic specialization was not fundamentally different from what it was to be in the early twentieth century, although the scope was of course incomparably smaller and the preponderance of agriculture still unchallenged. Generally speaking, the soil of Belgium was in the hands of large landowners[1] but in the most prosperous agrarian areas it was split up into small parcels cultivated by tenant farmers. This was the case in the northern part of the country, in Flanders especially, where on the loamy soil it made possible intensive husbandry of high quality and modern outlook, as is shown by crop rotation (not yet practised in the Walloon provinces), improvements in livestock breeding, the use of new fertilizers, and the successful introduction of new crops such as potatoes and tobacco. The second half of the eighteenth century was probably the only period in Belgian history when the country was self-sufficient in cereals, barley, oats, and forage.[2]

In the Walloon areas the land was much less divided. One of the major points in late eighteenth-century discussion was whether this was more or less progressive than the small-scale exploitation in Flanders; however, practice showed that it was at any rate less productive. The soil was less fertile; the method of exploitation was more old-fashioned (in many leases the three-course system was prescribed); the right of common pasture had not yet disappeared. It caused the Austrian Government, which in the second half of the century made some efforts to further economic expansion, much trouble to eliminate these traditions which were felt in physiocratic circles to be highly unprofitable.

Closely connected with agriculture were the domestic rural industries in which Flanders specialized; it is estimated that almost half of the rural population in that province made a living in the textile industry, spinning flax and weaving linen. Most of them were still independent, though very poor, workers who bought and raised their own raw materials and

[1] See below, p. 48.
[2] According to the studies of Slicher van Bath, Belgium and the Netherlands, together with Britain and Ireland, formed a group of countries where the yield ratios, that is the proportion of yield to seed, were much higher than in all the other parts of Europe: 'De oogstopbrengsten van verschillende gewassen, voornamelijk granen, in verhouding tot het zaaizaad, ca. 810–1820', *A.A.G. Bijdragen*, ix (1963), 29–125 and 'Yield Ratios 810–1820', ibid. x (1963).

sold their products to the wealthy capitalist merchants in
Ghent and Bruges. It was as yet rare for these merchants to
rationalize production itself by providing the rural workers
with materials and tools and paying them wages. The linen
was cheap enough to find ready buyers at home and abroad,
Spain being traditionally one of the main foreign customers.
In the last decade of the century Ghent—and some other
towns: Antwerp, Brussels, Mechlin, Tournai—saw the rise of
a new textile industry, cotton, organized from the start in
specially built factories with hundreds of workers. As to the
draperies, the areas in southern Flanders where in earlier
times they had flourished had been annexed by Louis XIV.
However, on the other side of the country, in Belgian Limburg,
the drapery industry was revitalized in an interesting way along
the River Vesdre by developing a system of factory production
that was still totally alien to the linen-weavers in Flanders.

The industrial development of Hainaut and Namur which
was to dominate the Belgian economy in the nineteenth
century had not yet outgrown the stage of small-scale enterprise lacking capital and technical refinement. The coal-mines,
blast-furnaces, and iron-forges between the rivers Sambre and
Meuse were for the major part owned by abbeys and nobles
and rarely did these invest sufficient in their businesses to
make it possible for them to expand. A blast-furnace may
on average have employed seven or eight workers, a forge five
times more, but even if one adds to these men the much larger
numbers of wood-cutters who provided the charcoal for the
blast-furnaces or miners who dug the coals for the forges, the
whole enterprise remained small and archaic. Iron was not
much in demand although in Liège it was required for the arms
factories. It is true that coal-mining expanded much more
than metallurgy, especially during the last three decades of
the century and partially thanks to the mechanization made
possible by the fairly large investments of a few enterprising
nobles, but this was by no means sufficient to change the
economy radically. Apart from rural industry the major part of
industrial output was produced by countless small enterprises
in all the Belgian towns: glassworks, paper-mills, potteries,
sugar-refineries, silk-factories, and many others working
without much capital and mainly for the local market.

A special case in all respects was Liège. Its prince bishops were independent rulers not subjected to the Austrian Government. Its economic equipment struck eighteenth-century travellers as more advanced than anything they saw in the Austrian provinces; its interest in cultural innovations has often been contrasted with the old-fashioned taste even of Brussels where the opera, patronized by the Court, drew large audiences but bookshops were rare. Of course the difference should not be exaggerated; Liège was after all a bishopric and the numerous clergy were understandably distrustful of the Parisian intellectual and moral fashions admired by the French-speaking élite of the city. Yet a number of factors explain why the principality was able to attain a level of intellectual and economic development beyond the reach of the Austrian provinces. The political impotence of the elected prince bishops, who had to subject themselves to the authority of an intricate system of representative assemblies, allowed a degree of freedom unthinkable in the Austrian territories. Moreover, with the exception of the region called the Hesbaye, west of the city of Liège, the soil of the principality is not suitable for agriculture. Forests, heath, and waste lands cover and surround the tiny country, long since forced to concentrate on industry and, not hampered by the economic restraints put on the Austrian Netherlands by the Dutch tariff policy, with easy accesss to the Dutch market by way of the Meuse. And of course coal was abundant around the city itself and somewhat further along the river. At the end of the century there was a tendency for the mines to expand; a few of them then employed up to 600 workers. But in Liège no less than in the Austrian Netherlands capital for industrial investment was scarce with the result that the scale of industrial development was bound to remain small. That is equally true of the arms manufactories for which the city of Liège was famous and of the production of nails for which the Dutch shipyards were ready customers. Nevertheless, it is clear that Liège was in many respects a more modern town than Brussels; with its 83,224 inhabitants it was larger than the capital of the Austrian provinces and, spreading out into the countryside along streets bordered by houses and workshops, it adopted the aspect of an industrial society, busy, noisy, and grimy. Although much smaller, Verviers (about 12,000 inhabitants) also showed the external signs of a manufacturing town. Its streets ran into the surrounding open space along the River Vesdre and the canal, full of houses, factories, and the large decrepit buildings where the badly paid workers in the town's major industry—drapery with all the small workshops serving it: the pressers', the shearers', the dyers'—found a dark, wet, airless shelter.

Life in the Austrian Netherlands and Liège cannot have been particularly exciting in the late eighteenth century. It was by no means a backward area but nothing in the civilization of that time reflects the intellectual adventurousness of the French and the Germans or even the spontaneous responsiveness to foreign innovation of the Dutch. In the Austrian provinces the influence of the Enlightenment was imposed from above by foreign dignitaries, especially Count Charles of Cobenzl who was appointed as Maria Theresa's minister plenipotentiary in 1753, an erudite *philosophe* and patron of the arts. The government no longer heeded ecclesiastical advice about scrupulous censorship; French books were circulated more freely than before and the number of bookshops increased. So did the number of printers who made a profitable job out of reprinting the works of French celebrities. In Brussels appeared one of the most enjoyable editions of Rousseau's complete works, in Liège Voltaire's writings and even the *Encyclopédie* were reprinted. In Bouillon, an independent duchy in the Ardennes near the French border, Pierre Rousseau published his *Journal encyclopédique* (founded in 1756), the only literary journal of some importance in the area, financially supported by the Austrian Government in Brussels which welcomed the editor's positive appreciation of a mitigated form of enlightened absolutism.

The government's tolerance towards new ideas and its cautious support for some of them provoked traditionalists to react by expressing their radically different views in a more systematic way. In 1774 the Jesuit F. X. de Feller—his order had been abolished in 1773—started in Luxemburg his *Journal historique et littéraire* for which he found no less than 3,000 subscribers. He became a formidable conservative publicist and it is characteristic of the cultural situation in the Southern Netherlands that his work, although less distinguished than that of Burke, which he used, or that of De Maistre, who was influenced by him, should have shown more native originality than that of the epigones and propagandists of the Enlightenment. Equally characteristic is the fact that the government's attempt to reorganize secondary education (which until 1773 was entirely controlled by the Jesuits) and to adapt it to modern needs failed miserably. Moreover, the Enlightenment did not penetrate into popular culture. In Flanders the people continued to enjoy the spectacles performed by innumerable amateur companies in all the towns and even the smallest villages. The repertoire was strictly traditional, in many instances directly derived from medieval religious mystery plays, in other cases renewed by the many simple writers able to rhyme contemporary versions of old themes in a primitive style. The upper classes tended to look down upon such activities and even on the language used. The Flemish nobility was taking to speaking French and sometimes reading or writing it badly. The upper middle classes started to imitate their example, first of all the women for whom it became a serious ambition to equal French elegance in dress and speech. Yet in a general way it is clear that French captivated the Flemish bourgoisie not, as it did the Flemish nobility, as a language to speak but as a language in which to read books. One of the major influences exercised by the Enlightenment in Flanders was to inspire the upper middle classes to regard French as the sole really cultured language, French books as the only ones worth reading, French art and architecture as the true models of modern taste.

By the middle of the century the Dutch Republic was both culturally and economically much more active than the Southern Netherlands, although seventeenth-century grandeur was gradually withering away. Whilst the early seventeenth century had been for the Dutch economy a period of enormous expansion the hundred years from 1650 to 1750 saw consolidation at the high level already reached. But this was not enough. Holland's seventeenth-century greatness was due to the fact that the Dutch market provided services not available elsewhere; it provided an entrepôt where European business men found the wares and the capital they needed and where they could take decisions on the level of prices; moreover, it provided the ships and the men for transporting these wares to all destinations. Only one element in this structure was permanent: the geographical position of the country in the delta of great rivers. But in all other respects the country was extremely vulnerable, depending as it did on the necessity to locate the international exchange of goods and capital in one particular place able to function as a centre for commercial and banking transactions as well as for transport. As long as Southern Europe was obliged by the growth of its population and the poor state of its agriculture to import large quantities of grain from the Baltic, Amsterdam had the means to deliver the goods: its merchants bought the stocks, brought them to Amsterdam, stored them in their warehouses, and shipped them to their customers at the appointed time. But when Spain and Italy or any other country started to grow rice or maize as adequate substitutes for grain, it was the Dutch market and all the economic functions dependent on it that suffered. Or, to take an example which illustrates another side of the problem, when the Baltic countries needed salt the Dutch were able to serve both as financiers and transporters for the exchange of Baltic grain or wood asked by France and the French and Portuguese salt needed in northern Germany or Sweden. However, as soon as the organization of the economy and of transport in Königsberg or Stockholm had improved sufficiently for merchants to establish direct contact with the French and Portuguese ports the intermediary function of Amsterdam was no longer necessary. As a result the staple market was in danger of losing much of its value. What made this situation so grave was not only the undermining of Amsterdam's market position but the high degree to which the urban economy of the Netherlands in general had come to be dependent on the function of Holland as an entrepôt. Dutch export industry, for example, was in large part a finishing industry which worked up the materials brought to the Amsterdam market. In other words, even if Holland managed for a long time to maintain the economic level reached in the early seventeenth century, its economy was fatally weakened by the growing tendency of other states to bypass the staple market, allowing it to survive but not to increase its importance in the same proportion as the European economy generally was expanding. In a growing European economy the Dutch saw not only their supremacy being reduced, which it would not have been hard to accept, but their role in international business and thus the structure of their system becoming increasingly obsolete.

The centre of the system was the province of Holland and in that province Amsterdam, the city that in the eighteenth century had nearly twice as many inhabitants as agrarian provinces like Friesland or Overijssel (with 130,000 and 122,000 inhabitants respectively). At present Holland, despite the vicissitudes of nineteenth- and twentieth-century development, still has about 40 per cent (5·3 millions) of the total Dutch population (13·6 millions in 1975), whereas the northern provinces of Friesland and Groningen together have approximately the same number of inhabitants as the conurbation of Rotterdam and only slightly more than that of Amsterdam. From the point of view of Holland the rest of the country (with the exception of Zeeland and of the geographical centre, the province of Utrecht) belonged to the Outer Provinces, politically important in so far as they were officially considered sovereign and could not be overruled in the States General at The Hague but economic, social, and cultural dependencies rather than equal partners in the alliance of the Seven United Netherlands. As a result the differences between the various provinces were so fundamental that no broad generalization can do justice to the facts. The interests, the power, even the language of the cattle-breeding gentlemen farmers in Friesland, or the nobility of Gelderland, still in the eighteenth century in possession of semi-feudal rights, were hardly comparable to those of the urban patricians in Holland; nor did the misery of crofters or peat-diggers in Drenthe, of flax-spinners and linen-weavers in Overijssel or Northern Brabant, spring from the same causes as that of the unemployed fishermen or workmen in the towns of Holland. The tenant farmers of Gelderland and Overijssel, living in sparsely populated areas and working in the first place to supply their personal needs, had problems different from those of farmers in Holland who specialized in the cultivation of commercial crops for industry or in horticulture but did not grow corn.

Yet there was one general phenomenon observable in all

provinces and directly influencing the whole character of social life: the growth during the seventeenth century of an urban patriciate with great power and a peculiar life style.[1] These 'regents' formed the ruling aristocracy of the Republic. Since the middle of the seventeenth century they had tended to move away from active involvement in trade and industry, to invest their capital, earned in years of hard labour and risky initiatives, in land, stocks, and government funds, to educate their sons for a career in politics rather than in business by sending them to the university to study law and then on the grand tour through Europe. It is impossible to estimate the total number of persons qualifying to be considered members of the ruling group. The number cannot have been particularly small in view of the fact that there were so many offices of one kind or another to fill. If it is true, as has been suggested,[2] that over 2,000 men occupied political posts giving them the privilege of belonging to the regents' group—having seats in the provincial states and the States General, or in the urban administrations, as burgomasters or council members, as members of the provincial law courts or the administrative councils of the East and West India Companies—then the aristocracy cannot be said to have been exceedingly narrow with thousands of families in a population of approximately two million people participating in government. This may help to explain its remarkable tenacity even after the storms of the eighteenth-century revolutions. But that the regents had to disappear as a ruling group is in retrospect hardly surprising. In the eighteenth century they developed idiosyncrasies which clashed strongly with the precepts of orderly and honest government put forward and sometimes even obeyed by their parents and grandparents. The possibility for newcomers to enter the oligarchy became increasingly smaller. Although the group was too large for it ever to become completely closed, abuses were rampant in the eighteenth century. Offices were

[1] D. J. Roorda, 'The Ruling Classes in Holland in the Seventeenth Century', in J. S. Bromley and E. H. Kossmann (eds.), *Britain and the Netherlands*, ii (Groningen, 1964), 109–32.
[2] S. J. Fockema Andreae, *De Nederlandse staat onder de Republiek* (Amsterdam, 1961), p. 37. As pluralism was a distinctive feature of the Dutch aristocracy a mechanical enumeration of public posts is not meaningful; the figure mentioned is therefore exceedingly tentative.

divided among the ruling families according to 'contracts of correspondence' (i.e. agreements to remain on good terms with one another) and this did not exclude the nomination of a baby to a financially most rewarding postmastership. What had originally been an attempt to attenuate the sometimes fierce struggle between the regents for profit and power came in the late seventeenth and eighteenth centuries very close to the conception of public offices as private, more or less negotiable property.

Much in all this did not differ fundamentally from what was happening in other European countries, but in Holland the universal progress of aristocratic rule for which the eighteenth century is known was far less extreme than elsewhere. Even when adorning themselves with semi-noble titles and with highly coloured clothes instead of the black velvet of their ancestors, and when spending much of their time in their elegant homes and gardens along the River Vecht, the regents remained with all their stilted pride thoroughly bourgeois. And what else could they have been? Apart from Frederick Henry in the early seventeenth century, the Stadtholders had never succeeded in building up a court even remotely resembling those of Spain, France, or England. If The Hague, where the Stadtholders lived and the States of Holland as well as the States General met, was the place where high officials, diplomats, and the nobility of Holland worked and entertained their guests, it was not there but in Amsterdam that the regents, immensely wealthy and feeling far superior to those who controlled the style of The Hague, defined the true model of Dutch life; and for all their airs of *bourgeois satisfaits* or *bourgeois gentilshommes*, bourgeois they were and nothing else. It was they who set the standards and determined the meaning of private and social life not merely for their own caste but for their inferiors who imitated their example and repeated their professed ideals. The phenomenon pervading Dutch society as a whole in the seventeenth century, but more still in the early eighteenth century, was, next to the aristocratization of the oligarchy, the *embourgeoisement* of the entire population. Orderliness,[1]

---

[1] K. W. Swart, 'Holland's Bourgeoisie and the Retarded Industrialization of the Netherlands', in F. Krantz and P. M. Hohenberg (eds.), *Failed Transitions to Modern Industrial Society: Renaissance Italy and Seventeenth Century Holland* (Montreal, 1975), p. 46.

respectability, material success, and quiet family life formed the main elements of the Dutch eighteenth-century concept of happiness and the Dutch valued the Enlightenment, or much in the Enlightenment, for stressing these practical virtues.

It is generally assumed that in the middle of the eighteenth century Dutch prosperity was not much less than in the seventeenth and that wealth was more evenly distributed in the Netherlands than in any other European country.[1] The sources of Dutch welfare at the time were, probably in this order of importance, trade, industry, the colonies, and agriculture, but only in agriculture is it possible to discern the reality or the prospect of expansion. The scene was highly varied. On the wet soil of North-Holland and parts of South-Holland the farmers specialized in cattle-breeding, butter- and cheese-making (with Gouda cheese as one of its great products), and horticulture, whereas the fertile marine clay of the islands of South-Holland and Zeeland allowed the cultivation of wheat, madder, flax, pulse, and colza. Zeeland madder was one of the major export articles of the Republic, prepared in workshops employing about ten men and needing much capital. The most important agricultural areas outside Holland were situated in Friesland and Groningen. In the course of the century various epidemics of rinderpest led the cattle-breeders who had prospered in the seventeenth century to lay part of their land under the plough and start growing corn; in the nineteenth century grain, not livestock, was to become the main product of Groningen. In the other parts of the country it was considerably more difficult to make a decent living out of agriculture. In the eastern part of Overijssel (Twente) the growth of the population caused bitter poverty for nearly half of them. The soil was so poor that the crofters were unable to grow sufficient food and the day-labourers, finding shelter in the ignominious turf huts for which both Drenthe and Overijssel remained notorious until the early twentieth century, were undoubtedly the most wretched members of Dutch society. The domestic linen-weaving introduced in Twente during the second half of the seventeenth century was gradually being

[1] J. G. van Dillen, *Van Rijkdom en Regenten: Handboek tot de economische en sociale geschiedenis van Nederland tijdens de Republiek* (The Hague, 1970) is a mine of information but weak in analysis.

concentrated in urban communities but it was only in the
nineteenth century that the textile industry was developed on
a large scale. In North-Brabant with its sandy soil, heath, and
forest the situation was much the same. The growing population survived precariously by growing rye and flax, by keeping
sheep, and, mostly to the orders of textile manufacturers in
Amsterdam and Haarlem, by spinning and weaving linen or
woollen cloth. But here also it was only in the nineteenth
century that the textile industry began to further economic
growth.

Until the second half of the eighteenth century industry
remained a major element of the Dutch economy. The variety
and quality of its products were highly appreciated by contemporaries and many of them were exported through the
Amsterdam market. It was mainly concentrated in Holland
and constituted one of the best examples of *ancien régime*
technology based on windmills, canals, peat fuel, and wood
mechanisms. Its scale was small. Only in such industries as
glassworks, potteries, or pipe-factories was it necessary to
employ as many as thirty or forty workers in buildings specially
constructed for the purpose. Even the shipyards—one of the
most active centres was the Zaan area north of Amsterdam—
cannot at this time have employed more than forty men on
average, although there were exceptionally big yards in
Rotterdam with more than a hundred employees. This labour-
intensive sector of industry which worked up the raw material
and produced finished articles—apart from those already
mentioned, the textile industry and the breweries are among the
most important of this type—is usually carefully distinguished
in Dutch historiography from the capital-intensive industry
dependent on the staple market not only for its exports but
also because it finished or improved semi-manufactured goods
imported from abroad: sugar-refineries, saltworks, tobacco-
factories, etc. Throughout the eighteenth century the second
form of industrial activity remained in fairly good shape, with
profits still being made from the monopolistic, if no longer
expanding, staple market. However, labour-intensive industry
was almost totally ruined. The main cause of this disaster,
which wrought havoc in the lives of thousands and made some
of the formerly neat and healthy towns look gloomy and im-

poverished, was the competition of France and Britain, now able to close their markets to Dutch products. An additional reason may have been the high wages which Dutch industrialists had to pay as a result of the heavy indirect taxation and the resulting high prices of food, clothing, and housing—wages in Holland were two or three times as high as in the Southern Netherlands or England.[1] That the textile industry in Leiden, once prosperous and well organized, should not have been able to compete with Verviers becomes understandable if one realizes that in 1741 wages in Leiden were twice as high as in Tilburg in North-Brabant and three times as high as in Verviers in Liège.

Whether the setbacks in this sector of the economy were compensated by the growing value of East Indian trade and the steadily increasing importance of Amsterdam as a financial market,[2] it is impossible to say, but the weight of these factors should make one wary of the view that from being great and central the Netherlands declined in the eighteenth century into becoming backward and peripheral. This is not the way to describe the development of a state which, though losing its advanced position, retained much of its wealth and continued to participate actively in European culture.

[1] In *Industrialization in the Low Countries, 1795–1850* (Yale U.P., 1976), pp. 193 ff., J. Mokyr suggests that the large-scale charitable relief may have provided a floor for wages higher than many employers could pay for certain types of jobs; this factor may have been more decisive than taxation.

[2] M. G. Buist, *At Spes Non Fracta, Hope & Co. 1770–1815: Merchant Bankers and Diplomats at Work* (The Hague, 1974).

I

THE REVOLUTIONARY BACKGROUND, 1780–1795

1. *The Dutch Republic in the 1780s*

EARLY seventeenth-century monarchical Europe had no confidence in the viability of the new Republic of the Seven United Provinces. In the middle of the century, however, the proudest kingdoms, France and England, were themselves disrupted by crises which threatened them with ruin. The Republic, on the other hand, though suffering several *coups d'état*, and apparently changing its form of government every thirty years, did not experience such bloody civil wars and found more sedate ways of solving its problems. Perhaps its very imperfections were a help. The republican constitution was sufficiently vague to be extremely flexible and it could be adapted to changing circumstances without breaking. Or perhaps it was the result of its prosperity, for amidst all the economic troubles of the seventeenth century the Republic remained an island of wealth. Perhaps it was due to its religious divisions; only a minority of the population was Calvinist and in a position to aspire to a place in the government of this officially Calvinist state, whereas the numerous dissenters, Roman Catholics as well as Protestant sectarians, not only disagreed with the ruling parties but also among themselves about the fundamental problems of life. Whatever the reason, during the *ancien régime* the political history of the Republic was relatively stable.

Then quite suddenly this well-balanced state fell a prey to a crisis which was to last for many decades. Between about 1780 and the middle of the nineteenth century the Dutch did not succeed in drawing correct inferences from their experiences or in properly defining their individuality and their desires. During the 1780s a civil war broke out which now seems to have been the prelude to the French Revolution. In 1795 the French invasion followed, inaugurating a long period of revolutionary rule. In 1813 the liberated state resumed only a few of its traditions and did not recover its former strength; in 1830 it shook off the South, its partner in a short-lived union, expecting that it could now devote itself again to its own problems. Yet so much of its vitality had gone that representative Dutchmen felt grave doubts about the wisdom of perpetuating the isolated existence of an independent but third-rate Dutch state. Only in 1848 did the Northern Netherlands succeed in accepting its fate. Only in 1848 did it overcome the profound crisis originating from the 1780s, a crisis that (unlike the seventeenth-century English and the eighteenth-century French revolutions which were growing pains, violent adaptations to widening possibilities) was a crisis of decline, a slow and exhausting adjustment not to the growth but to the diminution of wealth and power.

The consciousness of eighteenth-century Dutchmen showed curious contradictions. No other literature can be more self-complacent than that of the Dutch during these years. With carefully cherished smugness they treasured their ancestors' achievements, counting what they possessed and others were still passionately seeking: liberty, tolerance, civil order, and a classical literature that, in their view, equalled or surpassed that of the Ancients. At the same time, however, they noticed that the outside world was beginning to look down upon them. In foreign politics the Republic, once an arbiter in matters of war and peace, degenerated into a passive object of other countries' craving for power. The Peace of Utrecht which, it was thought in Holland, gave the English the fruits of the victory gained by the Republic, remained a painful memory. Humiliation followed humiliation. Britain had difficulty in forcing its old ally to play an active part in the diplomatic conflicts of the early eighteenth century. The War of the Austrian Succession once more brought the French across the frontiers and they met hardly any resistance. The navy and army deteriorated. This was seen and deplored by all, but who could find a remedy? And was not the country best served by a policy of neutrality? What were the decisive conflicts in Europe and in the colonies that could affect this self-satisfied society? During the Seven Years War the Republic did indeed remain neutral and benefited from being able to carry on its trade in time of war. But though its wealth seemed to increase, the merchants complained more loudly. In a society given to self-complacency and pretentious displays of prosperity there was under the surface resentment at an easy-going policy, and the alarming feeling began to gain ground that the country had lost its place, belied its past, and gambled away its future. Long before Dutch society was disrupted by the troubles of the 1780s, many were convinced that Holland's wealth was declining.

Complaint and opposition are closely related. There is a clear connection between the pessimistic views on the economic decline of the Republic and the rise of the reformist party of the so-called Patriots. Not only the Patriots, however, pointed out the decline of trade; among their opponents, the adherents of the House of Orange, there were those who did the same. Thus one of the most convinced followers of the Prince of Orange, Elie Luzac, argued (quite wrongly, of course) that Dutch trade and navigation were in a worse way in 1780 than they had been in 1570;[1] this, however, did not prevent him from declaring with emphasis that this decline had not affected Dutch economic supremacy.[2] The Patriots were more pessimistic.[3] If, wrote their opponent Van de Spiegel in 1782 (afterwards Grand Pensionary of Holland and the leader of the Orangist restoration regime from 1787 to 1795), only half of what we are reading day after day is true, the fall of the Republic must be imminent.[4] The Patriots were disturbed by deep anxieties, which transformed a vague national consciousness into a really modern but wounded nationalism and made them ask for political reforms capable of restoring their country to its former wealth and power.

The tragedy of this attempt at political and economic recovery was that it started from a false premiss. Objective economic factors were reducing the Republic to a humbler

---

[1] Elie Luzac, *Hollandsch Rijkdom* (4 vols., 2nd edn., Leiden, 1801), ii. 338. The first edition appeared in 1780–3.

[2] Ibid. iii. 6–7.

[3] J. de Vries, *De economische achteruitgang der Republiek in de achttiende eeuw* (Amsterdam, 1959), p. 4.

[4] L. P. van de Spiegel, 'Schets tot een vertoog van de intrinsique en relative magt van de Republijk', published by J. de Vries, *Economisch-Historisch Jaarboek*, xxvii (1958), 87.

state, and reform designed to retrieve glories irrevocably lost was doomed to failure. The symptoms of decline which were so deeply resented were not brought about by accidental psychological factors—laziness, luxuriousness, weak policies—but pointed to a fundamental change in the economic and political position of the Republic. There was decline, and it was inevitable. The seventeenth-century development had been made possible by a combination of fortunate circumstances which no longer existed. Its basis was Holland's, and especially Amsterdam's, function as a staple market. The whole economic structure of the Republic rested on this. It was precisely the staple market which in the eighteenth century was crumbling away. Better means of communication by land and sea, the aggressive competition of Britain and France, innovations in the method of fixing prices and in the commission business made the world's economy less dependent on a central staple market and enabled business men to send goods directly from seller to buyer, thus avoiding the expensive port of Amsterdam. The Dutch merchants, or rather a small group among them, found an economically correct answer to the challenge. Thanks to their financial strength they were able to enlarge their banking and commission business at a time when expansion of the goods trade was no longer possible. But naturally this development of financial alongside commercial capitalism had serious social consequences: with a growing population, it probably led to a reduction of available employment and a narrower concentration of prosperity.

At the end of the eighteenth century the situation had become paradoxical. Contemporaries, convinced of a sharp decline, were hoping for a recovery. They were as misguided in their pessimism as in their expectations. No recovery was possible since the seventeenth-century need for a staple market had vanished. But at the same time they did not properly understand the decline which they were complaining about. For there was no serious quantitative decline; the number of ships and the total of imports and exports did not greatly fall. Only relatively, compared with Britain whose imports and exports trebled, or with France where they rose to a figure five times greater than before 1700, was Dutch trade in decline.[1] It is

[1] De Vries, op. cit., pp. 28 ff.

easy enough to see why contemporaries were mistaken in their interpretation of the country's economic development. But this error had an immense psychological effect in forcing upon the Patriot party a wrong starting-point and illusory objectives. While a realistic policy would have advocated adaptation to possibilities which had been relatively reduced, the irritated nationalism of the Patriots strove for the complete restoration of a position explicable only by the very special circumstances of the seventeenth century, and lamented over a decline that was, in fact, not so much decline as an aspect of the natural growth of the rest of Europe.

Although before 1780 or 1795 there was no absolute quantitative decline of Dutch trade and navigation and the total wealth of the Republic does not seem to have shrunk, the structural changes in the economy caused acute crises in certain branches of industry and resulted in a new distribution of wealth. The technically backward industry could not, even in the home market, compete with its foreign rivals. Its dependence on the staple market—it was mainly a finishing industry—increased its vulnerability. Moreover, prices were inflated by high wages, themselves an inevitable result of the heavy indirect taxes on the primary necessities of life. Almost the whole of industry collapsed. Fishery and whaling also suffered from a depression that could no longer be checked. As a consequence, Dutch society was confronted with the problem of serious unemployment. It was unable to solve it. Only fundamental reforms might have been of some avail to industry. But the state with its empty treasury was unable to provide any financial help and the political paralysis of these years prevented a revision of the fiscal system which might have cleared public finances and, by lowering indirect taxation, made possible a cut in wages.[1] There was nothing left but poor-relief. But this was insufficient. Especially after 1770 the number of paupers seems to have grown alarmingly.[2] They lived in great misery in the towns or fled from these to roam the countryside (for, unlike the development in the Southern Netherlands, the population of the Dutch

---

[1] De Vries, op. cit., p. 119.
[2] Ibid., p. 170; J. de Bosch Kemper, *Geschiedkundig onderzoek naar de armoede in ons vaderland* (Haarlem, 1851), pp. 108 ff.

towns apparently decreased even during the second half of the century).

The distress of the poor contrasted sharply with the growing prosperity of small groups profiting from the activities in the financial sector. Dutch capital found advantageous investments, especially abroad, and foreign investments were estimated at 1,500 million guilders in 1780.[1] The increasing concentration of commercial and financial business in Amsterdam, an important late eighteenth-century development, contracted still further the circle of prosperity. Lack of information makes it difficult to assess the influence of these factors on the various classes of the population. But probably the regents and big bankers prospered, while the less important bankers, the merchants, the lower middle classes were seriously affected by the economic decline and the structural changes in the economic system. The lower classes certainly suffered acute distress, although the peasants were doing well.[2] As a result social tensions increased considerably during the second half of the century, and it seems that it was precisely the declining middle class of merchants and industrialists that constituted the dynamic force in the political conflicts of the 1780s. It was this group that aspired to the ancient greatness. Looking back over a magnificent and wealthy past, it now found inspiration in an over-excited nationalism.

The political atmosphere was thoroughly corrupt. Attempts made in the 1780s to improve the situation resulted in dismal failure, partly because the Great Powers (Britain, France, Prussia) were all actively interested in the internal troubles of the Republic and impeded natural development. But it was also partly because the hostile parties themselves involved these Powers in their conflicts and lacked sufficient creative vision and perseverance. Many traditional elements are to be found in the struggle between the two parties. The whole history of the Republic is characterized by conflicts between sections of the urban patriciate and the House of Orange, and this conflict was once again at the centre of the civil war. The composition of the Prince of Orange's party was much the same as it had been a hundred years before. William V, Stadtholder

---

[1] Luzac, op. cit. iv. 310. Cf. De Vries, p. 66.
[2] Ibid., p. 150.

of each of the seven provinces (he held these functions from 1751 to 1795), wielded a badly defined but quite extensive power. It was not based on a single clear principle but sprang from a chaos of special rights, privileges, usurpations, and abuses. His party (or rather those groups that depended on him for their livelihood and success) was far from forming a unity. But all the components together make an impressive list: the officers of the mercenary army, the provincial and urban authorities in Utrecht, Gelderland, Overijssel, Zeeland, and the countryside of Groningen, a number of sometimes very influential individual adherents here and there in the Republic. The party had no specific social colour and was composed of widely different interest groups. It also lacked leadership: William V was good-natured and knowledgeable but totally incompetent as a statesman—irresolute, without vision, hampered by obstinacy and a dogged concentration on details and formalities. Could such a party have any other purpose than to protect a *status quo* which allowed small cliques of profiteers to enjoy power for power's sake?

Some authors tried to adapt the old Orangist slogans to eighteenth-century taste. They made very efficient use of the generalization—for many years a commonplace—that the Princes of Orange, who incurred the hostility of the urban patricians especially in Holland, were the protectors of 'the people' against the oligarchies. Experience had in fact shown that it was relatively easy to raise a mob against the urban regents, and loyalty to the House of Orange seemed to come quite naturally to some groups of the lower classes. The Calvinistic elements in the lower middle and working class, the Jews of Amsterdam, the peasants in Holland in so far as they were Protestants, were amongst those on whom the Orangist party could count with some confidence. Strong sentiments, which in the last two centuries had several times manifested themselves in violence, tied the conservative masses of Holland to the illustrious House, the traditional defender of liberty and religion. It is true that the Orangists had never used this as anything but a slogan. Nobody had ever developed a rational theory of Orangist policy until at the end of the eighteenth century a few authors tried to draft one. Although their hastily concocted notions were almost valueless as an intellectual system, they possessed some significance in providing the constitutional monarchy of the early nineteenth century with a basis on which it could comfortably rest.

Elie Luzac (1721–96) was the best Orangist publicist of his time. An admirer of Locke and Montesquieu, his greatest discovery was that he could praise the Dutch Republic as a perfect example of Montesquieu's state. There was the Frenchman's principle of the division of power, with the representative bodies of the States as the legislative and the Prince of Orange as the executive; his balance of social groups (was not the Prince the defender of the lower classes?); his mixture of the three forms of government, monarchy, aristocracy, and democracy—all this the natural but unintended outcome of a highly fortunate historical development which made the Republic the best possible state.[1] In long, facile arguments full of brilliant ideas Luzac tried to render plausible these palpably incorrect theses. He found a follower in the person of the young, ambitious Gijsbert Karel van Hogendorp (1761–1834), who during the late 1780s attempted to put a new façade on the ancient edifice of the Orangist party. In the letters and memoranda which he wrote down for his own use he toiled at the construction of a political doctrine. The Prince of Orange as mediator between the patrician oligarchy and the people, as personification of the constitution, as the executive, as the representative of the state's unity, all these sometimes complementary, sometimes contradictory notions had to find a place in his system.[2] He had no success at the time. But the reflections collected in this period with such assiduity were the starting-point for the task which he undertook in the years of the French Revolution and which, after the fall of the Empire, resulted in his greatest achievement: the definition of constitutional monarchy in purely Dutch terms.

There were among the adherents of the Orangist party certainly other intellectuals, but they were relatively few.

---

[1] Luzac, iii. 325 ff. Cf. P. Geyl, *De Wittenoorlog. Een pennestrijd in 1757* (Amsterdam, 1953), pp. 64, 67 ff., 97 ff.; W. Gobbers, *Jean-Jacques Rousseau in Holland* (Ghent, 1963), pp. 189 ff., 213 ff., 307 ff.; and E. H. Kossmann, *Verlicht conservatisme: over Elie Luzac* (Groningen, 1966).

[2] G. K. van Hogendorp, *Brieven en Gedenkschriften* (7 vols., The Hague, 1866–1903), i. 442 ff.; ii. 57 ff.; L. G. J. Verberne, *Gijsbert Karel's leerjaren* (Amsterdam, 1931), pp. 204 ff.

The Press was largely controlled by their opponents; most students, professors, and jurists supported the fashionable opposition and called themselves Patriots. Patriotism had become synonymous with anti-Orangism and, although the phenomenon was short lived, the nomenclature points to a characteristic aspect of Dutch history: the fact that the House of Orange, for two centuries a symbol of the will of the Dutch to remain independent, was no longer considered by the best-educated sections of the public to be the representative of the national idea. It had ceased to give guidance. It now seemed to be a supine instrument of English policies.

The conflict between the Patriots and the Prince of Orange had basically the same cause as previous conflicts between regents and Stadtholders: foreign politics with which all Dutch *coups d'état* were closely connected. This was true in 1618, 1650, 1672, and 1747; it was also true during the 1780s. The new feature in 1780, however, was that on this occasion it was not the Prince of Orange but his opponents who took the offensive. The Republic tried to remain neutral during the American War of Independence. William V himself was outspokenly pro-British in accordance with the traditional policy of his House. But the merchants, understandably resenting British competition as well as British actions against neutral ships carrying contraband, were willing, if not to provoke a war with England, at least to risk it. In this situation William's weakness became very apparent. He did nothing to prevent the open war into which the mutual irritations were bound to degenerate, and when in 1780 the British Government actually declared war (Fourth Dutch War, 1780–4) he accepted it unwillingly but without resistance. To his enemies the struggle in which the Republic fought its old ally and rival at the side of France and the United States seemed an excellent opportunity to settle accounts with the Dutch Anglomaniacs and in particular with William V himself. The British Empire, the greatest power concentration since the Empire of Louis XIV, appeared to be on the verge of dissolution, and the Dutch accomplice of this robber state would be ruined by its fall.

Paradoxically enough, the anti-Orangists did indeed manage to undermine William V's position, not, however, because

Britain suffered any damage from the military actions of the Dutch, whose army and navy were equally impotent, but because the weakness of the Republic was so unbearably humiliating. It was easy enough to hold the Stadtholder (who was after all the military leader) responsible for the total inertia of army and navy, and this the urban patricians, organized in the States of Holland, did not hesitate to do at once and with the greatest possible vehemence. There was nothing new in their attitude, as their opposition to the House of Orange was one of the traditional pivots of Dutch politics. But there was one entirely new element in the situation. The nearly traditional struggle was this time complicated by a democratic movement which originated outside the province of Holland and opposed the House of Orange not in order to hand over power to the patrician regents but to claim it for a broader stratum of society. Initially, the anti-British and anti-Orangist 'patriotism' of the regents ran parallel with the pro-American and democratic 'patriotism' of more modern type, but in the end the two trends inevitably clashed.

From either a geographical, a social, or an intellectual point of view Patriotism is a complicated phenomenon. Its intellectual contents were ambiguous. The regents hardly attempted to give new significance to their old slogans; no vigorous aristocratic–republican ideology sprang up in these years. The so-called democratic wing, on the other hand, which developed beside this old group did put forward a sort of political programme and even began in some places to carry it into effect. This was full of quite remarkable paradoxes. They were embodied in the man who might be called the father of this Patriotism: Joan Derk van der Capellen (1741–84), a nobleman from Overijssel. The force driving him was the sentiment of nationalism. His democratic notions sprang from this predominant emotion. Yet he hardly succeeded in giving his nationalism a concrete political form. He wanted a democratization of the town governments. But no attempt to break through the federalist, extremely particularist system of the Republic (a juxtaposition of seven provinces more or less united through the person of their common Stadtholder) was ever made by this enemy of the Stadtholder. His nationalism, if it had been effective, might well have resulted in the breakup of the nation into local patriotisms.[1] The Patriotic 'system' was enfeebled by the organization of the Republic. It is difficult to make a revolution in a state without a centre. There was no adequate enemy to fight, nor was there an elevated point from which reforms could penetrate into the corners of the flat countryside. The democratization of the urban governments would automatically have led to the democratization of the provincial States and consequently of the States General. It would have eliminated the influence exercised by the Stadtholder on the appointments of the urban magistrates. But it would have broken the state, for the government of the regents, so extremely cumbersome despite long experience, was to be replaced by a government of politically inexperienced, until recently quite indifferent, and unpaid bourgeois.[2]

Patriotism was fashionable. Most intellectuals were Patriots. The better-off dissenters also supported it because its democratic-nationalist aims seemed to entail the end of their political exclusion.[3] But although it was to some extent affected by the Enlightenment, it did not spring from it. English theories were referred to—Locke, Price, Priestley were quoted: why not seventeenth-century Dutch ideas that would have served the same purposes?[4]—but, with the exception of Montesquieu, French authors were hardly used for political ends. Abstract principles played a lesser role than the history of purely Dutch institutions. Patriotism, therefore, although it employed enlightened terms, was in fact the very denial of systematic abstraction rather than its expression. It failed to put forward a guiding principle for the general reform of the whole state; it tried instead to replace stone after stone in the decrepit building of the Republic without changing its basic construction.

The social contents of Patriotism were equally determined by the organization of the state. In all provinces the economically declining middle classes, suffering from a feeling of insecurity, doubtless constituted the dynamic factor. This group

[1] M. de Jong Hzn, *Joan Derk van der Capellen* (Groningen, 1921), pp. 16 ff., 195, 215, 219, 507 ff., 668 ff.

[2] H. T. Colenbrander, *De Patriottentijd* (3 vols., The Hague, 1897–9), iii. 163–4.

[3] For the attitude of the Roman Catholics see M. J. M. van der Heijden, *De dageraad van de emancipatie der Katholieken* (Nijmegen, 1947), pp. 55 ff.

[4] Cf. E. H. Kossmann, *Politieke theorie in het zeventiende-eeuwse Nederland* (Amsterdam, 1960), pp. 69 ff.

was, of course, strongest in commercialized Holland. There, however, Patriotism was socially narrower than in the other provinces because the lower middle class and the mass of the people traditionally sought the protection of the House of Orange against the regent aristocracy, which now found among the upper middle classes support for its guerrilla war against the Stadtholder. Consequently, in Holland collisions between the bourgeois Patriots, organized in free corps, and the urban proletariat were frequent. In Utrecht, Gelderland, Overijssel, and some other provinces the situation was radically different. There the Stadtholder had exercised since the days of William III a decisive influence on the appointment of the urban and provincial governments. Thus the ruling patricians were Orangists and feelings of social aversion among the lower middle classes and the popular masses were directed both against them and the House of Orange, with the result that the bourgeoisie could count on the lower strata of the population when attempting to introduce democratic reforms in the town governments. Although in these provinces the Patriotic movement had fewer opportunities than in Holland because the regents were opposed to it, there was a chance for its democratic tendencies to become broader and more radical. It was not by accident that the democratic action started in Overijssel and not in Holland.

From about 1782 until 1787 democratic Patriotism was able to establish itself as a major force in parts of the Republic and to create a party organization. From 1783 onwards representatives of the movement from various provinces met in assemblies of about seventy members.[1] The free corps organized by the Patriots in the towns also kept in touch with each other; in 1784 they held their first national meeting.[2] It soon became clear that a real centralization of the movement was impracticable and that the central body would have to confine itself to co-ordinating the essentially provincial or even urban activities. But at critical moments the free corps (totalling probably about 28,000 volunteers)[3] actually co-operated in a national, not a local context. In Holland and Utrecht the democratic Patriots succeeded in getting hold of some town

---

[1] Colenbrander, op. cit. i. 275; ii. 251 n. 1.   [2] Ibid. i. 279; ii. 224.
[3] Ibid. ii. 218 n. 2.

governments. William V lost important powers. For although he commanded the army, the greater part of which remained loyal to him, he was too much of a formalist to ignore those constitutional rules which in an emergency made him dependent on the very bodies—the States of Holland in the first place—that were opposed to him.

What made the Patriotic movement powerless in 1787 when at last the Orangist party took sharp measures? There were two main factors. In the first place it was weakened by inner contradictions. The campaign of the patricians against William V had made it possible for a democratic Patriotism to develop. But when the democrats also turned against the urban regents, the latter sought the help of the Stadtholder who was eager to take them under his protection. This of course isolated the democrats. Moreover, the King of Prussia, who was William V's brother-in-law, found in an affront which his sister suffered at the hands of the democrats an excuse for sending an army to the Republic in order to demand satisfaction. The English Ambassador at The Hague, Harris, had done much to help organize the Orangist party and his government willingly gave the Prussians a free hand. France, though siding with the anti-British Patriots, disliked democracy and was moreover becoming involved in domestic difficulties, so it lent no effective support to the Dutch revolutionaries. Those who were most compromised went into exile: between 5,000 and 6,000 persons in all, some of whom were men of great wealth.[1] They formed emigrant committees in the Southern Netherlands and in France but never exercised very much influence on the course of events.

After its victory the Orangist party organized a restoration regime which, notwithstanding the talents of the new Grand Pensionary of Holland, L. P. van de Spiegel, was a serious failure. The Orangists who had not even had the courage to use Dutch forces against the Patriots lacked vision. Persecution of the Patriots (especially the less well-to-do Patriots: the smaller merchants, the shopkeepers, the artisans),[2] solemn guarantees

[1] H. T. Colenbrander (ed.), *Gedenkstukken der algemeene geschiedenis van Nederland, 1795-1840* (10 vols. in 22 parts, The Hague, 1905-22), i, pp. xxxi ff.

[2] Letter from Gogel, 21 Feb. 1794 in *Gedenkstukken* p. 378; Van Hogendorp, op. cit. ii. 19; P. Geyl, *Geschiedenis van de Nederlandse stam*, iii (Amsterdam, 1959), p. 186.

of the constitution, the inexpert purge of the urban governments, were not followed by measures of a more positive
character. A reform of the fiscal system proved to be impossible
despite being urgently needed at a time when the province
of Holland spent millions of guilders to keep the East India
Company going and the big bankers and merchants, who were
both Patriots and opposed to monopolies, categorically refused
to co-operate with the new government. The debt of Holland
increased at an alarming pace. Public loan after public loan
failed dismally. With the French approaching the frontiers
there was no money to strengthen the hopelessly weak army.
Yet taxation was very heavy. It is estimated that a family in
Holland with an annual expenditure of 2,000 guilders paid
about 600 in mostly indirect taxes.[1] But the collection was
badly organized, the budget badly planned. The other provinces contributed hardly anything at this time to the federal
treasury and nobody possessed sufficient authority to make them
meet their liabilities. A feeling of impotence permeated the
state. There was no one capable of checking the decline which
the Patriots, now expelled or forced into submission and sabo-
tage, had tried to stem. 'I see the weakness, the smallness of the
Republic', Van de Spiegel wrote in 1794 to the wife of William
V, 'and the whole disorder staring us in the face . . .'[2]

2. *The Austrian Netherlands in the 1780s*

Passing from the Republic to the Austrian Netherlands around
1750 was like stepping from modern times into an earlier
period. The Southern Netherlands were not ruled by an oligarchy of bourgeois descent which, although degenerating into
an isolated and parasitic group, still represented something
very different from the old division of society into distinct
estates. On the contrary, the South was dominated by the
traditional and seemingly well-established powers of nobility,
clergy, and corporations. The economic and social strength of
the nobles was unbroken. They possessed greater wealth than
any other social group except the clergy, and thanks to the

---

[1] A. J. van der Meulen, *Studies over het Ministerie van Van de Spiegel* (Leiden, 1905),
p. 415.
[2] *Gedenkstukken* i, p 331 (11 Feb. 1794).

increase in the output of landed property their fortunes were growing in the eighteenth century. Moreover, they could, because of their simple, provincial way of life, place their increased profits in mortgages and other safe investments and thus strengthen their position.[1] Of course, the nobility did not have the same predominant influence in all provinces. In Brabant and Hainaut it was stronger than in Flanders. But even in this province where the nobility was not represented in the States and where the small but independent peasant free-holder was perhaps most typical of the economic and social structure, the nobles dominated society and inspired the rising class of the industrial bourgeoisie with the ideal of being accepted in the old aristocratic group.[2]

The clergy were undoubtedly as influential in social, economic, and cultural life. They owned immeasurable wealth. According to evidently very exaggerated contemporary estimates, they controlled three-quarters or half of the country's real estate.[3] Thanks to the low rents imposed by the monasteries and the prosperity of the mostly well-to-do farmers who tilled their soil,[4] they were ensured of the loyalty of the economically strongest groups of the rural population; they protected the poor, and their educational system left its mark on the civilization of the whole people. They were also numerous: of a total population estimated in 1784 at 2,272,962 inhabitants (the independent bishopric of Liège with approximately 400,000 people not included) over 17,000 men and women belonged in some way to the clergy.[5]

The third estate was organized in an intricate system of guilds and corporations. In the seventeenth and eighteenth centuries these had spread from the towns, where they had

[1] Suzanne Tassier, *Les Démocrates belges de 1789* (Brussels, 1930), p. 15.

[2] H. Coppejans-Desmedt, *Bijdrage tot de studie van de gegoede burgerij te Gent in de XVIIIe eeuw* (Brussels, 1952), pp. 155 ff., 163 ff.

[3] H. van Houtte, *Histoire économique de la Belgique à la fin de l'Ancien Régime* (Ghent, 1920), p. 426; Tassier, op. cit., p. 19. Ecclesiastical property was of course not everywhere equally large. In South West Brabant it amounted to 50 per cent of the fields, in parts of Flanders to 7 per cent. Cf. L. van Buyten, 'Grondbezit en grond-waarde in Brabant en Mechelen, volgens de onteigeningen voor de aanleg der verkeerswegen in de achttiende eeuw', *Bijdragen voor de geschiedenis der Nederlanden*, xviii (1963), 108-9.

[4] Van Houtte, op. cit., p. 427.

[5] H. Coppejans-Desmedt, 'Economische opbloei in de Zuidelijke Nederlanden'. *Algemene geschiedenis der Nederlanden*, viii (Utrecht, 1950), 265; Tassier, p. 20.

their roots, into the countryside and now also dominated the industries (especially the textile industry), which in the sixteenth century had tried to disentangle themselves from their deadly grip by leaving the old urban centres like Ghent and Bruges. As everywhere else in Europe the corporations had long since ceased to be organizations which promoted the interests of the employees and the consumers as well as those of the employer; they were now dominated by the masters and were typically petty bourgeois in outlook. They were often an impediment to the growth of the economy. But they seemed doomed, not only because government and public opinion demanded their abolition or reorganization but also because after their hypertrophic development during the *ancien régime* there was no longer room for all of them. They exhausted their finances in endless lawsuits about their respective rights and duties.[1]

The Northern Netherlands no longer experienced such problems. Although in the course of the last century life in the Republic had become more hierarchical, its society was certainly less stable than that of Belgium. But whereas in the North with its stagnating economy it proved impossible to break through the social structure of the seventeenth century, the older social pattern of the Southern provinces permitted a quick and startling economic development without being affected by it. The bourgeois society of the Republic ruled by the regents was in decline; its crisis provoked the Patriot movement but at the same time prevented this from realizing its programme. Belgium was stirred by an economic dynamism sharply contrasting with Dutch lethargy and yet, though stimulated by a despotic and levelling government, by no means incompatible with the old structure of the society.

The Belgian economy was indeed developing. Its growth should not be compared, however, with the rise of the Dutch Republic in the early seventeenth century: it was much more like the development of France since the end of the seventeenth century. It was a development within the traditional framework and it did not hollow out or break the old social forms. Progress was most remarkable in agriculture. In Brabant the country population grew in the three decades from 1755 to

[1] Van Houtte, p. 23.

1784 by 44 per cent, the urban population by 25 per cent.[1]
In the Flemish towns the increase in the population, after the
rise of the seventeenth century and the fall of the early eighteenth, was slight in comparison with what was happening in
the countryside. Bruges, for example, had 35,156 inhabitants
in 1699, 27,821 in 1748, and 30,846 in 1784. In Ghent and
Antwerp a similar phenomenon can be noted.[2] It is difficult
to establish whether this demographic development, which is
typical of the whole of Western Europe, followed or stimulated
the growing output of agriculture. Both facts, in any case, are
unmistakable and the Southern Netherlands constitute one of
the most striking examples. Thanks to the opening-up of
uncultivated land, to the more effective agricultural methods,
and to better manuring, agricultural production rose sharply.
But it is not at all likely that the whole population benefited
from this increasing prosperity. On the contrary, the conditions
of the proletariat, the small farmers, and the factory workers
probably deteriorated, even though in Belgium corn prices
were going up rather slowly in comparison with the rest of
Western Europe where their rise after 1756, unaccompanied
by any increase in wages, caused such unspeakable misery.[3]
Moreover, the gaping wound of the *ancien régime*, the pitiful
pauperism, was past recovery in this densely populated,
mainly agrarian country. Contemporaries estimated that after
1770 the number of those receiving poor-relief grew steadily.[4]
Insufficient industrial and commercial expansion, structural unemployment, quite inadequate schooling (in 1789 the majority
of the children in Flanders never went to school)[5], a well-
intentioned but extremely inefficient poor-relief, all these factors
caused the insoluble problem afflicting in general the under-
developed societies of this period and, notwithstanding its rapid
economic progress, Belgium too.

The development of commerce and industry was considerable

[1] Cf. Coppejans-Desmedt, *Algemene geschiedenis der Nederlanden*, viii. 264.

[2] Cf. *Revue du Nord*, xlii (1960), 133.

[3] B. H. Slicher van Bath, *De agrarische geschiedenis van West-Europa* (Utrecht,
1960), p. 249; P. Deprez, 'De boeren', *Flandria Nostra*, i (Antwerp, 1957), 157 ff.;
C. Verlinden, *Dokumenten voor de geschiedenis van prijzen en lonen in Vlaanderen en
Brabant* (*XVe–XVIIIe eeuw*) (Bruges, 1959), p. xvii.

[4] P. Bonenfant, *Le Problème du paupérisme en Belgique à la fin de l'Ancien Régime*
(Brussels, 1934), p. 31.

[5] Ibid., p. 65

but remained relatively restricted. Enclosed as it was by protectionist neighbours and without recent experience in navigation and overseas trade, the country possessed only few
possibilities for commercial expansion. The parochial character of this society was made apparent by the spasmodic but in
the end always unsuccessful and never properly sustained efforts
to break the spell of an agricultural, continental economy. It is
true that the government did its best and achieved at least
some results. Ostend, connected with the interior by an am-
bitiously planned network of roads, rivers, and canals, became
a port of national importance, unaffected by the closure of the
Scheldt. Moreover, the nature of trade with the Republic
changed during the last decades of the century. Since the early
seventeenth century the Southern Netherlands had been the
victim of the commercial imperialism of the Northern provinces; now they were recovering and their economic dependence on the declining Republic decreased.[1] In industry also,
and especially the textile industry, innovations promoted by
the protectionist government were introduced and helped to
widen the structure of the economy. But the opportunities for
grand-scale capitalist enterprise were severely limited by the
lack of funds. The nobility and the clergy were both incomparably better provided with capital than the merchants and
industrialists (it is estimated that they possessed in Brussels
five times as much as the bourgeois, and the five most important abbeys of Ghent had the same revenue as all the
wealthy local bourgeois together); neither of them, however,
was willing to invest in these enterprises.[2] Banking and the
credit system were still in their infancy. But there was a
development of some kind and in various towns there emerged
a group of rich entrepreneurs, interested in technical improvements, which at least opened up the possibility of carrying
through the industrial revolution. There was no such group in
the Northern Netherlands.

Thus the Southern Netherlands may be described as a
counter-reformation and agricultural state, developing a
remarkable prosperity and constituting the very opposite of

---

[1] Van Houtte, pp. 268 ff.; Coppejans-Desmedt, *Bijdrage*, pp. 35 ff.
[2] J. Lewinski, *L'Évolution industrielle de la Belgique* (Brussels, 1911), pp. 107 ff.

the Protestant bourgeois republic of the North whose lop-sided commercial economy was stagnating and declining. Yet only some aspects of the situation can be illuminated by such clear-cut formulas. For it was precisely during the 1780s that important sections of Southern society seemed to turn to the North, metaphorically as well as literally. Indeed it is most remarkable that opposition to the enlightened despotism of the Emperor Joseph II should have led some leading and representative members of the Southern aristocracy to empha-size the historical background which they shared with the Republic. Of course, it was not a new phenomenon that dis-satisfaction with the foreign ruler induced groups of Southern Netherlanders to look for support from the free Northern neighbour. This had happened in the 1630s and again in 1706 when Brabant and Flanders rose in revolt against the French occupation. The Republic was so closely interested in what was happening in the South that it was logical to expect help from that quarter. Yet such opportunist motives were not the only factors; in times of crisis the Southern Netherlands, eager to defend their individuality against foreign governments, would obviously become more sharply aware of their affinity with the North where much of the common Burgundian heritage was still being preserved. Or, if affinity is too strong a term, there was at least a fresh appreciation of common historical origins. These became particularly apparent when the forces of federalism and particularism which both states had in common, and the conservatism of the North as well as of the South, gave a certain similarity to the revolutions which affected both areas in the 1780s. Though aimed at totally different situations, they derived from comparable traditions and tendencies.

From the time of the Burgundian dukes onwards the foreign rulers of the Southern Netherlands always respected the individuality of the provinces. They maintained the covering authority of the central government but interfered as little as possible with local customs and powers. Within the provinces the States met regularly, more often than in the Republic where, dominated by the oligarchy of the regents, they were administrative councils rather than representative bodies. In the South they still represented the old estates. Their power, based on all sorts of privileges regarded as constitutions—the most famous, of course, being the *joyeuse entrée* of Brabant—was considerable; in matters of taxation their decision carried weight. In the administration of justice also the central governments had confined themselves to building a superstructure of new tribunals above the time-honoured courts so that under the protection of the central state there survived the intricate forms of an infinitely articulated federal community.

Some opposition to these traditions had sprung up among the Southern Netherlanders themselves. In the 1750s progressive personalities in Flanders succeeded in reforming the provincial administration and in improving the provincial finances. But as their work, although strongly influenced by Montesquieu and the Enlightenment in general,[1] was primarily concerned with the technique of administration and not with politics proper, they were able to carry out their purposes without making any alarming attack on the old principles. The Emperor Joseph II, who on his study tour as a young ruler through Belgium in 1781 was shocked by the apparent chaos of the administration and jurisdiction, was unable to proceed so inconspicuously. His reforms, which hit the Netherlands in the 1780s painfully, were always prompted by genuine abuses and discrepancies.[2] But this complicated man, who suffered—as he remarked himself—throughout a miserable life because of his inability to spread happiness,[3] did not respect everyday routine in the same way as the Flemish radicals thirty years earlier. He failed to understand the difference between administrative innovations and revolutionary political measures affecting the population's day-to-day life. But above all he mistook the character of his Belgian subjects. They liked a certain measure of warm-hearted paternalism but felt repelled by the cold paradoxes of Joseph II's policies. And indeed, what could they make of so meddlesome a benefactor who, while busily transforming all the institutions of their country, told them publicly that he would gladly exchange it for Bavaria?[4]

[1] P. Lenders, S.J., *De politieke crisis in Vlaanderen omstreeks het midden der 18ᵉ eeuw* (Brussels, 1956), pp. 36, 47 ff., 131.
[2] E. Hubert, *Le Voyage de l'empereur Joseph II dans les Pays-Bas* (Brussels, 1900), pp. 137, 153. [3] Ibid., p. 36.
[4] H. Schlitter, *Die Regierung Josefs II in den Oesterreichischen Niederlanden*, i (Vienna, 1900), p. 121.

From 1781 onwards his edicts were fired off in rapid succession. Each one in itself was well considered and well intentioned. Religious matters came first: in 1781 toleration, and the independence of the Belgian monastic orders from their generals, most of whom resided in Rome. In the next few years 163 'useless' monasteries were closed and regulations restricting religious feasts and fraternities were published. All this was not meant as an attack on the Church according to enlightened principles, but as a purge. In 1786 general seminaries under government control were established at Louvain and Luxemburg and all who wanted to take holy orders were obliged to study there; the old episcopal seminaries had to disappear. In 1783 the Emperor started reorganizing the state administration and at the same time reforming the judicial system. This activity culminated in the two edicts issued on 1 January 1787 which completely remodelled the system of government and jurisdiction. The old law courts were replaced by a well-planned hierarchy of new ones; the provincial boundaries were cut through by a new division of the country into districts administered by intendants; and the authority of the provincial States, whose permanent deputies were attached to the central government, was weakened.[1]

All this was not designed as an attempt to make the ruling classes powerless; it was intended as a purely technical reform of an admittedly chaotic situation. The measures would doubtless have strengthened the Austrian Government, but they were not in the interests of the new classes or even an expression of new ideas. The Emperor was fully responsible for them. His Belgian advisers had repeatedly warned him against this reckless radicalism. In 1787 he was honestly astonished at the unrest which his edicts caused.[2] He was no revolutionary; he never wanted to disturb the existing order. He thought that his reforms were based on the constitution or at any rate that with a modicum of goodwill it could be made to support them. In the eyes of his Belgian subjects this was an appalling error. Not only the ruling classes but representative elements of the

---

[1] The edicts of 1 January 1787 in F. X. de Feller (ed.), *Recueil des représentations, protestations et réclamations faites à sa Majesté Impériale par les représentants et états des provinces des Pays-Bas autrichiens* (17 vols., Brussels, 1787-90), i, pt. I, 1, pp. 90-103.

[2] Schlitter, op. cit., p. 84.

whole people felt Joseph's activities to be an attack upon their autonomy and dignity; they were ready to take up arms against a despot.

Three years of general bewilderment followed. In 1787 the States of Brabant, driven on by the formidable demagogue Hendrik van der Noot, drafted the ground-plan of a rebellion which was not, after all, to be carried out before the autumn of 1789. Much in these revolutionary activities brings to mind the Patriot troubles in the Dutch Republic. In the first place they were both nationalist in character. As in the North, this nationalism was based on nostalgia; it was retrospective and closely related to a profound feeling of humiliation. It sprung from a crisis. But whereas in the North it was essentially the awareness by one economically threatened group of its own difficulties, in Belgium it was the psychologically less complicated reaction of large parts of the population to foreign innovations thought to be unnecessary. It was not constructive. Its simplistic mythology is characterized by indignation at the pedantry of a sovereign who treated the Netherlands—the Netherlands, beaming with prosperity, glorying in a magnificent past, Europe's master in matters of commerce, agriculture, arts, and literature[1]—just as arbitrarily as he did his hereditary Central European lands which still groaned under the feudal yoke. It is characterized by boisterous pride in the ancient Belgian freedom, which generation after generation had shed blood to defend.[2] It was limited, on the other hand, by a deep satisfaction with the existing order.

Language had not yet become a problem for the Belgians. Dutch held its own as the everyday speech of the majority of the people, even at Brussels, but French increasingly penetrated among the nobility and the upper middle classes of the Flemish-speaking provinces. It became the fashionable language, the language of social and cultural prestige, the language of the élite. Belgium assimilated the Enlightenment through the medium of French. Yet it was rather badly taught at the secondary schools. Its greatest competitor was not Dutch but Latin, still the language of Louvain University and, thanks

[1] *Recueil* i, pt. I, 1, p. 226 (petition of the States of Flanders, 5 May 1787); ii, pt. I, 4, p. 232 (*idem*, 27 June 1787).

[2] Ibid. i, pt. I, 2, pp. 73–4.

C

to the clergy, capable of preserving its hold on Belgian civilization. Flemish, since the seventeenth century quite isolated from the Dutch of the Northern provinces which developed into a very articulate language, seemed in this period to degenerate into a local patois, although there was still a relatively high output of books: devotional books, exercises in verse, some scientific works, and even a scientific periodical.[1] The revolutionary situation after 1787 made only a few nationalists aware of the possible connections between language and nation. In 1788 J. B. C. Verlooy published in Dutch a short 'Treatise on the neglect of the native tongue in the Netherlands' in which he compared the glorious past to the miserable present and related the decline of the Netherlands language in Belgium to the decline of the nation. Dutch, however despised and neglected, was the tongue of freedom, natural to both North and South and linking them as one people and one civilization. Verlooy (1746–97) was a lawyer from Brussels; he played an important part in politics as lieutenant to the leader of the more or less democratic resistance movement. His erudition was French and in later years he welcomed the French invaders because they brought the revolution. His book showed that he had but a scanty knowledge of Dutch culture.[2] Yet at this moment in his life a modern national sentiment awoke in him. It was shared by only a small number of his Belgian contemporaries.

The extreme conservative wing of the anti-Austrian Patriotic party also made a contribution, though a rather paradoxical one, to the literature on the linguistic problem. F. X. de Feller (1735–1802) was a former Jesuit who developed into a vehemently conservative journalist. In his *Journal historique et littéraire* he carried on an immoderate polemic against the abstractions of the Enlightenment, which contrasted so sharply with the venerable realities of Church and tradition. He naturally became involved in the political conflicts of his age, resolutely taking up the defence of the reactionary States of Brabant against the Austrian regime. He spoke and wrote in French. Nevertheless, he glorified in his writings the Flemish

---

[1] M. Deneckere, *Histoire de la langue française dans les Flandres (1770–1823)* (Ghent, 1954), pp. 124 ff.

[2] Geyl, *Geschiedenis van de Nederlandse stam*, iii. 114–19.

language, the 'national idiom', the 'langage antique et négligé de nos bons habitans de la Belgique' because it protected the Belgian people, uncorrupted by the new fashions and the hard rationalism of the time, from the 'follies and vices of foreigners'. Flemish, with its 'rather hard sounds and its uncivilized turns', became in the eyes of this French-writing polemicist a kind of protection of 'the masses of the people' against infection by the foreign Enlightenment.[1] This notion, too, was to grow in the course of the nineteenth century into a more generally accepted romantic doctrine.

It was not so much the language but the national past which during these critical years drew the attention of the Southern provinces to their Northern neighbours. For there was one obvious precedent for the rebellion against Austria: the six-teenth-century revolt against Spain, successful only in the North. It was, of course, not easy for Roman Catholics to recognize that both situations had something in common and to put Philip II, the protector of the true religion, on the same level as Joseph II who found no favour with the Church. Yet sometimes they went so far as to do this and the national motive prevailed over religious considerations.[2] More im-portant, however, was the political structure of the state which, once the revolution had done away with the all-embracing central government, showed a close affinity with the framework of the Dutch Republic and seemed to develop in the same way. It was especially the conservative wing of the Patriotic party that now attempted to carry through the revolt which had failed in the sixteenth century.

The leader of these conservatives was a Brussels lawyer, Hendrik van der Noot (1731–1827), a popular and rough man from a noble family, with much influence in the States of Brabant. He was the organizer of the resistance that arose in 1787 against the reforms of the Emperor but which did not at that time develop into open rebellion. In 1788 he fled from the

---

[1] *Recueil* vi, pt. XV, pp. xxi ff. (1790). Cf. J. Smeyers, *Vlaams taal- en volksbewust-zijn in het Zuidnederlands geestesleven van de 18de eeuw* (Ghent, 1959), pp. 367–71.

[2] *Recueil* i, pt. I, 1, p. xxi. In 1787, probably in August, a pamphlet was pub-lished (*Discours adressé par Charles-Quint à Philippe Second*) in which Joseph II was compared with Philip II. Cf. *Recueil* i, pt. I, 3, p. 9 and E. Hubert, *Correspondance des ministres de France accrédités à Bruxelles de 1780 à 1790* (2 vols., Brussels, 1920–4), i. 266.

country and tried to awaken interest in the cause of Brabant's liberty in England, the Republic, and Prussia. Only Prussia, just after defeating the Dutch Patriots in 1787, was inclined to come to the aid of the Belgian Patriots—because they were anti-Austrian. Van der Noot achieved little with the Grand Pensionary of Holland, Van de Spiegel, although, when talking to him in May 1789, he stressed the sixteenth-century precedent. The Dutch statesman felt no sympathy at all with his plan to proclaim William V's younger son Stadtholder of a free Belgian Republic; to him the idea of reuniting the Burgundian provinces looked like a fantastic dream. It was out of the question, not so much because of religion perhaps but because of trade—in other words, Dutch commercial imperialism and the closure of the Scheldt.[1] Van de Spiegel certainly expressed the feeling of the whole of Dutch society, Orangists and Patriots alike, although Van Hogendorp, the young, conservative, but independently minded Orangist, admitted that the matter constituted a painful moral problem.[2]

This chilly reception did not prevent Van der Noot making the town of Breda in Dutch Brabant the centre of his agitation, and he remained faithful to its sixteenth-century form. In the autumn of 1789 his Breda committee took the lead in the revolution. In the meantime the liberal lawyer J. F. Vonck (1743-92) in Brussels had started with the utmost secrecy a well-planned action against the Austrians. The clergy supplied the necessary money. Vonck depended much less than Van der Noot on foreign aid; the Belgians themselves, he thought, should wage war against the despot and were capable of winning the victory. His call was successful. Some thousands of young men from all strata of the population and all parts of the country emigrated and, properly armed and equipped, formed at Breda the Patriotic army. This army remained small.[3] But the Austrian forces dispersed as the Belgian soldiers

---

[1] *Gedenkstukken* i, pp. 137 ff.

[2] Van Hogendorp, iii. 12. William V even thought that Van de Spiegel was going too far when in January 1790 he considered the possibility of an extremely loose confederation. Belgium should be restored to Austria. Cf. *Gedenkstukken* iii, 2, p. 1043.

[3] In 1790, when the rebels had established their rule, the army still remained small, totalling probably not more than about 20,000 men. In much more difficult circumstances and with a smaller population, the Dutch Patriots had a larger number of volunteers at their disposal. Cf. *Gedenkstukken* iii, 2, p. 936 and P. Verhaegen, *La Belgique sous la domination française* (5 vols., Paris, 1922-9), i. 40.

serving in them deserted by the hundred. When Van der Noot, after some initial hesitation, gave his blessing to the activities of the volunteers whom he himself had not called upon, the revolution started: in October 1789 the Patriotic army invaded Belgium, took Ghent in November, and thus brought the whole of Flanders on to the side of the rebellion. In December the Brussels population drove the Austrian troops and authorities out of the town; all their possessions, even the treasury, were left to the rebels.

On 24 October, the day of the first invasion of Belgium, Van der Noot, the self-styled 'plenipotentiary of the people of Brabant', published (in French) a manifesto said to be issued by the States of Brabant, and in fact acknowledged by those members of the assembly present at Breda who could be considered representatives of the three estates. It is a very remarkable document. It explains in high-flown style why the people of Brabant have the right to renounce their allegiance to a ruler who has violated the agreement sworn by him at the time of accepting the sovereignty. Sonorous phraseology, proclaiming the will of the nation to be the highest law, lends it an eighteenth-century flavour. But in fact it is not eighteenth-century at all; it is only an adaptation, partly even a literal translation, of the resolution by which in 1581 the States General at The Hague set forth the reasons why Philip II could no longer act as the sovereign of the Netherlands. Van der Noot simply adjusted the framework and the argumentation of the famous sixteenth-century document to the circumstances of 1789 and translated almost word for word into French the long conclusion in which the States deposed the Prince.[1]

As soon as the Patriots had laid hands on Brussels, they were obliged to draft a free Belgian constitution. They had quite a number of examples to choose from. In the end Van der

---

[1] The document is published in *Recueil* v, pt. XIV, pp. 258–92. The Flemish version of the document which must have existed is unknown. Was it published in both languages at the same time? The language of the States of Brabant was Flemish. Cf. L. Picard, *Geschiedenis van de Vlaamsche en Groot-Nederlandsche Beweging*, i (2nd edn., Antwerp, 1942), pp. 61–2. In the preamble to the Manifesto Van der Noot simply copied some passages from Holbach's *Politique naturelle*: cf. J. Vercruysse, 'Van der Noot, Holbach et le manifeste du peuple brabançon', *Revue belge de philologie et d'histoire*, xliv (1968), iv, 1222–7.

Noot's group preferred the American constitution. At the beginning of January 1790 fifty-three representatives of the various provincial States met at Brussels. These States General adopted on 11 January a draft constitution proclaiming the union of the provinces and the institution of a Sovereign Congress of the United States of Belgium.[1] It was a rather unimpressive document. Yet the way in which the new constitution attempted to resolve the painful problems raised by the sixteenth-century forms of the revolution was not ungraceful. The Belgians did not directly copy the constitution of the Dutch Republic. Their source was the American Articles of Confederation of 1776,[2] which in their turn, however, were an improved version of the Dutch Union of Utrecht of 1579—a fact well known in the North[3] and probably also in Belgium. Thus the new constitution was based on the Dutch as well as on the American precedent and resulted from a compromise between Flanders, which on breaking with Joseph II had borrowed much from the American Declaration of Independence,[4] and Brabant, which made use of the Dutch Verlatinge.

During the greater part of 1790 this new constitution was put to the test. It turned out to be unworkable. The reason was not only its particularist structure but also the peculiar development which took place in Brabant and exercised an increasing influence on the course of the revolution. The groups which had at the end of 1789 collaborated for a short moment, Vonck's more or less liberal reform party and Van der Noot's conservatives, came into conflict about the composition of the provincial States, a conflict for which no peaceful solution existed. Vonck, believing that the doctrine of popular sovereignty had now triumphed, wanted to apply this principle in elections through which the upper middle classes were to get a strong vote in the States, traditionally dominated by the nobility and the clergy. But the States of Brabant themselves took the line that, after the deposition of the ruler, sovereignty did not revert to the people but to the States; they had the

[1] Reprinted in L. P. Gachard (ed.), *Documens politiques et diplomatiques sur la révolution belge de 1790* (Brussels, 1834), pp. 113 ff.

[2] T. K. Gorman, *America and Belgium. A study of the influence of the United States upon the Belgian Revolution of 1789-1790* (London, 1925), pp. 206 ff., 275 ff.

[3] De Jong, op. cit., p. 211.

[4] Gorman, op. cit., p. 157.

well-known 'Short Exposition' of 1587, by which the States of Holland claimed supreme power, translated into French.[1] They carried the day. Vonck's socially rather narrow party was helpless against the united forces of the lower classes, the greater part of the clergy, the nobility, and the corporations. Already in March the Vonckists were forced to leave Brussels. But even after the departure of most of them there was still boundless exasperation in the capital. And in the first days of June the peasants of Brabant, armed with rifles, sticks, scythes, and spades, marched in groups through Brussels, under the command of their priests on horseback, some of them carrying large crucifixes, to give expression to their loyalty to the States and their hatred of the Enlightenment: the Vonckists, on the quite wrong analogy of what was happening in France, were suspected of anti-clericalism. The number of peasants taking part in these crusades totalled perhaps 100,000.[2] Brussels witnessed the spectacle of the Brabant revolution receding further and further into history, through the sixteenth century into the Middle Ages.

Governing was difficult in these circumstances. Moreover, in some of the other provinces, in wealthy, densely populated Flanders, in Mechlin, Tournai, and Hainaut, the development appeared much more favourable to the Vonckists. There liberal reforms, designed to end the political supremacy of the privileged estates, were taken into consideration.[3] It is not surprising that the States General and Congress, whose composition was just as badly defined as their function, should never have obtained any real power, being totally unable by their homely and pedantic admonitions[4] to induce the provinces to make substantial contributions. The new federal government was thus weakened by the pronounced particularism of the provinces; and its authority was also undermined by widespread criticism of what was happening in Brussels. And what, after all, could be the sense of a revolution made possible by the absence of a strong Austrian army and the

<hr />

[1] *Recueil* vi, pt. XVII, pp. 49 ff.

[2] Tassier, op. cit., pp. 389 ff. Cf. Hubert, *Correspondance* ii. 459 ff.

[3] Tassier, pp. 319 ff. See also J. Craeybeckx, 'De Brabantse omwenteling een conservatieve opstand in een achterlijk land?', *Tijdschrift voor Geschiedenis*, lxxx (1967), 303–30.

[4] Cf. the numerous documents in Gachard, op. cit., pp. 201 ff.

hesitations of the Austrian Government in Belgium which executed the orders of a sick Emperor with remarkable reluctance and clumsiness? On 20 February 1790 Joseph II died and his successor was known as a liberal.

This indeed may help to explain the development of the Brabant Revolution, which started as a struggle against the despotic Joseph II but soon found that it was fighting his successor's liberalism. It did not prove difficult to crush the revolt. The Great Powers did not support the cause of the Belgians. Nor did the Dutch seriously consider the projects of a dynastic union with Belgium which were still being circulated in January and February when a great many people in Brussels were seen wearing Orange cockades.[1] Prussia, which at first had sent a small army to aid the Brabant revolutionaries, withdrew in July under Austrian and British pressure. In September Leopold II, having concluded an armistice with the Turks, was able to send 30,000 men to make the Belgians see reason. By November Hainaut had recognized Leopold II as its legitimate sovereign; the other provinces soon followed. In December the Austrians entered Brussels and met with no resistance. Van der Noot fled to Holland. His party disintegrated: his adherents, though not entirely unwilling to collaborate with Leopold II during his short reign—because in reaction against the French Revolution he became increasingly conservative—were no longer in possession of any considerable power. Only after the Great Revolution could they attempt to recover their former position. And it is highly paradoxical that the very groups which were so eager to associate themselves with the Dutch Republic and to copy its form of government, thus making the Brabant Revolution of 1789 and 1790 a re-enactment of the sixteenth-century revolt of the Netherlands, were after 1815 strongly to oppose the United Kingdom of the Netherlands. Some of the heroes of the anti-Dutch Belgian Revolution of 1830 were heirs of the Van der Noot group.

The Brabant Revolution, in the end dominated by Van der Noot, had originated from the initiative of his opponent Vonck. It is not altogether easy to determine by what forces this ailing lawyer was driven and what kind of people he was

---

[1] Hubert, *Correspondance* ii. 228, 254.

representing. He wanted to acquire more influence for groups until then excluded from politics: the industrialists and merchants, the intellectuals and the small landowners. He was inspired by the French Enlightenment in its most moderate form. He was neither anticlerical nor, in principle, anti-aristocratic. It is remarkable that his party, whose natural language was Dutch as opposed to the mainly French-speaking aristocratic group of Van der Noot, had no contacts with the North except, perhaps, with the Dutch Patriots who in 1787 had sought refuge in Brussels.[1] Vonck found his main support in Flanders, intellectually and socially more emancipated than Brabant. But this support was hardly effective. Indeed there was no reason to expect that any large group of the population would take sides with Vonck in an attack on the dominating position of the estates. For many years the bureaucratic, enlightened Austrian Government had been undermining this position, whether intentionally or not, and there was no real conflict between the Austrians and, for example, the Belgian industrialists. The economic policy of the Enlightened Despot seemed sound enough. For a short moment Vonck could make use of the general exasperation at the excesses and the clumsiness of the Austrian Government and start an action at that time more nationalist than democratic in character, but he was unable to mould into a party of any importance the small groups of wealthy bourgeois who might blame the government for injuring their honour but certainly not for interfering with their purses—and who as a group remained loyal to the standards of the old-fashioned society in which they were living.

This explains why the Belgian Revolution of 1789 and 1790 developed quite differently from the struggle of the Patriots in the Northern Netherlands. In the Republic the attack on the Stadtholder was opened by the regent aristocracy which was soon overrun by the torrent of nationalism and, especially outside the province of Holland, popular radicalism. In Belgium the liberal Vonck took the initiative but the aristocracy finally got control and founded a new state of a kind that would have had the approval of the Patriotic regents of the North. They created a republic similar to that of the United

[1] H. T. Colenbrander, *De Bataafsche Republiek* (Amsterdam, 1908), pp. 12–13.

Provinces but based upon the American example, because the United States of America had not adopted one of the striking features of the Dutch constitution: they had no Stadtholder. In the end the conflict in both countries petered out in the same way: the Prussian army met in the Dutch Republic with as little resistance as the Austrians did in Belgium. And just as the restored Orangist rule transformed the democratic Patriots into pro-French extremists, the Vonckists living in exile in France forgot the nationalist origins of their movement and welcomed the moment when the foreign revolution crossed the Belgian frontiers. The important fact of the following years was the denationalization of the reform party, which had once been primarily nationalist and only in the second place democratic.

II

THE GREAT REVOLUTION, 1792–1813

1. *A Contrast: North and South during the French Revolution*

IT cannot be proven with any precision, yet there is no reasonable doubt that at the end of the eighteenth century there were many more people in the Northern Netherlands interested in politics and culture generally than there were in the South. The urban character of the North's society, the standard of teaching which even in the popular schools was not particularly low for this period, the traditional but still amazing productivity of journalists and pamphleteers, provided broad groups of the Dutch population with an opportunity to acquire some insight into questions of public interest and thus to take part in political discussions. According to the estimate of the local pensionary, during the Patriot crisis one-quarter of the male population of Rotterdam was politically involved in one way or another, being prepared either to take up arms or to sign some petition.[1] Whether the situation was the same in the rest of the country is doubtful. Nevertheless, many thousands of men (the male population totalled about 400,000) certainly had a sufficiently mature philosophy of life to make them aware of its implications in the political field. In the Southern Netherlands the case was very different. At least half of the men were illiterate and among the female population the proportion was probably much higher.[2] Moreover, the federal constitution of the state had not granted the provinces a vote in the States General as was the case in the Dutch Republic—the Belgian States General never met—or entrusted them with any responsibility for major political decisions: on the contrary, it confined their attention to parochial affairs, leaving

[1] Van Hogendorp, *Brieven en Gedenkschriften*, ii. 252.
[2] In the Northern Netherlands the situation, though bad enough, was certainly far better. Interesting data concerning the rural population in 'De landbouw-enquête van 1800', *Historia Agriculturae*, i–iii (Groningen, 1953–6).

the foreign authorities in Brussels to take care of matters of national and international importance. This explains why the Patriot conflicts found much less response in Belgium than in the Republic and why the political literature they gave rise to was much less voluminous than in the North—although some of it was of a fairly high standard.

The same contrast is to be seen during the Great Revolution. The North produced sufficient men and ideas of distinction to make a more or less original contribution to the Revolution. Belgium was unable to do this. It offered resistance; it resented the French domination, and at times its anger burst into open revolt. But the Belgian counter-revolutionaries and the adherents of the French regime were alike incapable of adding new elements to what existed before the arrival of the French or to what they brought. And just as the Belgians were themselves unable to make the Revolution, so they were unable to drive it away. Of course, external circumstances partly explain this contrast between developments in North and South, for the French allowed the Dutch a degree of liberty which they did not dream of granting the Belgians. But this is not a complete explanation. Thanks to their centuries-old independence the Dutch, although lamentably weakened and uncertain, still possessed an intellectual and emotional power of resistance unknown in the Southern Netherlands. Perhaps the available evidence on the growth of the population also allows the conclusion that the Dutch took the crisis much more seriously than the Belgians. From 1795 to 1813 the Dutch population, probably totalling about two millions, did not grow at all. The population of Belgium, Liège included, rose with an annual increase from 1784 onwards of about 22,500 people to 3,379,000 in 1815. From 1815 to 1830, however, the Northern Netherlands, with their independence restored but their economy not much improving, grew at an average annual rate of at least 40,000 people.[1] Thus psychological factors may have contributed to the stagnation during these tense and difficult years when the future of the nation was in doubt. Belgium,

---

[1] I. J. Brugmans, *Paardenkracht en mensenmacht* (The Hague, 1961), pp. 58 and 188. In 1829 the population totalled over 2·6 million. Cf. also B. D. H. Tellegen, *De wedergeboorte van Nederland* (2nd edn., Groningen, 1913), p. 112 n. 1 and H. T. Colenbrander (ed.), *Ontstaan der Grondwet* (2 vols., The Hague, 1908–9), ii. 334.

already by 1795 annexed by its immense neighbour, did not experience such anxieties nor such uncertainty about the future.

This sharp contrast between the fate of the two countries led to paradoxical results. After obstinately seeking and to some extent finding new ways of life, the Dutch in 1814 had after all not recovered from their eighteenth-century backwardness and, exhausted by their revolutionary adventures, relapsed into a languid enjoyment of their freedom. In Belgium conditions were different. The masses were probably still living and thinking in much the same way as before the Revolution; perhaps they were even more exclusively absorbed by the routine of their narrow existence, for during the French period popular education, bad enough already under the *ancien régime*, deteriorated. It was, moreover, the lowest classes which were the most painfully affected by the economic depression after 1810. By 1815 the number of paupers in Belgium was probably, in proportion, considerably larger than in the Northern Netherlands. A strong public opinion was certainly lacking. Nor was there a political élite capable of moulding a new state. But a small group of people had been able to take advantage of the economic opportunities offered by the incorporation into France. And thanks to their activities in the industrial sector, however adventurous and romantic these may have been, they opened a way to a new, more realistic, less stable society. In the North there was hardly anything to suggest the development of such a modern outlook.

2. *The Southern Netherlands under French Rule*

The history of French domination in Belgium is a story of strange errors, great misery, and total failure. Neither the Belgians nor the French succeeded in attaining any of their objectives. Self-government, which during and after the Brabant Revolution seems to have been the ambition of the leading groups in Belgium (a distinct desire for independence should not be attributed to them), proved as impossible to achieve as the assimilation and absorption into the French nation which the foreign rulers sought to bring about. Nor did the turmoil of these years provoke emotional reactions which might at least have served as a starting-point for a future development in one of these directions. The French rulers could neither awaken Belgian nationalism nor win over public opinion. During the twenty years of the occupation political and public life seemed to be stagnant. The parties, which in the 1780s had divided Belgium and broken the monotony of its existence, made some efforts to re-establish themselves, but in vain. There was no opportunity and no desire to found new parties. The opposition failed to discover positive ways of expressing itself and exhausted its energy in sterile outbursts of anger.

Especially during the first years of the occupation it is very difficult to determine what kind of independent political opinions, among the grey misery and the daily vexations provoked by the French army, were still lingering on in the town halls, the villages, the presbyteries, the palaces of the nobility, the offices of the bourgeoisie, and the workshops. In April 1792 France declared war on Austria. In November 1792 the French armies, strengthened by about 2,500 emigrants from Liège and the Southern Netherlands, outnumbered and beat the Austrian troops near Jemappes and soon occupied the whole of Belgium. During the first few weeks the Belgians lived in hopes of recovering the independence of which the Austrians had deprived them in 1790. '*Viva* the French! *Viva* our liberators!' the population of Brussels cried (in Dutch) when on 14 November the armies triumphantly entered the city.[1] But when on 24 March 1793, eight days after the defeat at Neerwinden, they left again, the populace ransacked the houses of the pro-French citizens and set fire to the tree of liberty on the Great Market.[2] And when, after the great French victory of Fleurus on 26 June 1794, the revolutionary troops once again occupied the country and expelled the Austrians, now for good, tens of thousands of Belgians emigrated while the rest passively resigned themselves to the large-scale robbery that followed. From that day until the end of 1813 there was only resentment, despair, and apathy: after five years of illusions the people were forced to accept the bitter reality of their tutelage.

In fact, in November 1792, when Belgium fell a prey to the

---

[1] L. Galesloot (ed.), *Chronique des événements les plus remarquables arrivés à Bruxelles de 1780–1827* (2 vols., Brussels, 1870–2), i. 94.   [2] Ibid. 140.

Revolution, independence seemed to be a possibility. The commander of the Northern army was Dumouriez, backed by the French Minister of Foreign Affairs, Pierre Lebrun, who in 1785 had founded at Liège a radical *Journal général de l'Europe* and who felt a genuine interest in the Southern Netherlands. Both men were deeply involved in the activities of the Comité des Belges et Liégeois réunis, a committee of emigrants from Belgium and Liège which was established in Paris in January 1792. After Jemappes it was charged with the task of revolutionizing the conquered territories. In October and November Dumouriez, first from Valenciennes and then from Mons, sent proclamations to the Belgians inciting them to elect new rulers. Immediately the Comité started organizing elections of provisional representatives who would serve as municipal and provincial administrators, but its zeal was so excessive that the General had to check it. Yet on 12 December Dumouriez decided to hold general elections with the intention of calling a National Convention of Belgium and Liège at Alost in January 1793.

It is impossible to determine how much support the democratic activists found among the masses of the people. Probably the basis of their activities was considerably narrower than that of the Patriots in the Northern Netherlands when they in their turn, in January 1795, filled the urban and provincial governments with their adherents. In Brabant the resistance of the conservatives proved so tenacious that after the old States suspended their meetings in the middle of November it was impossible to appoint a new and representative provincial government. During the first weeks committees of provisional representatives of the provinces were acting in Hainaut, Tournai, Namur, and Flanders on behalf of the people by whom they claimed to be elected.[1] Liège was regarded as by far the most revolutionary town in the Southern Netherlands, yet when in December elections were held for the National Convention (it never actually met) no more than 43 per cent of the electorate troubled to take part in the poll.[2] In the other towns and in the country people were even less interested.

---

[1] S. Tassier, *Histoire de la Belgique sous l'occupation française en 1792 et 1793* (Brussels, 1934), pp. 127 ff.
[2] Cf. P. Harsin, *La Révolution liégeoise de 1789* (Brussels, 1954), p. 159.

The revolutionaries were disastrously divided among themselves. The new leaders during these passionate weeks were
moderate lawyers and merchants who, like the leaders of the
Dutch revolutionary movement in January 1795, made it
their task to abolish the old order with its privileges and its
feudal duties without provoking revolutionary disturbances
and terror.[1] However, many members of the Comité and some
dozens of commissioners sent by the French Government to
Belgium were fanatic Jacobins. They found support in the
clubs which had sprung up in some towns of Flanders and
Hainaut and were dominated by members of the petty bourgeoisie, by young men without means, and occasionally even
by people of proletarian origins.[2] Their radicalism made them
champion a complete social revolution and a political union
with France. They advocated terrorism.[3] But they had only
a few adherents and their activities, looked upon with deep
disgust by Dumouriez as well as by some Vonckists, drove the
members of the old States party, who had dreamt of re-
enacting the Brabant Revolution of 1789, back to the Austrians.

From 15 December 1792 the whole discussion about Belgium's future was in fact meaningless. The famous decree by
which the National Convention in Paris carried through the
revolution in the conquered territories, confiscating all the
property and capital of the defeated rulers, admitting only
those to the franchise who swore allegiance to the Jacobin
principles, and refusing to recognize the provisional representatives, led inevitably to the annexation of Belgium. Dumouriez's
plan turned out to be an illusion. Might it have materialized
if the National Convention had given him support? It is
unlikely. The total failure of the loan which Dumouriez had
been trying to get from the clergy, the categorical refusal of the
States party to help establish or even admit a democratic
independent state, the inertia of the masses, and the disunity
among those on whom the revolution and the cause of independence had to rely (in most towns the bourgeoisie was
unquestionably conservative) are incontestable facts and they
explain the frantic hurry of the annexationists. On 31 January

[1] Tassier, *Histoire*, pp. 174 ff.   [2] Ibid., p. 69.
[3] Cf. e.g. Publicola Chaussard, *Mémoires historiques et politiques sur la révolution
de la Belgique et du pays de Liége en 1793* (Paris, 1793), p. 76.

1793 the Belgians were asked to decide whether or not they wanted to be united with France. The plebiscite, which wherever possible took place in February and March, was a failure. Although various constituencies dominated by French troops pronounced for annexation, the victors themselves recognized that only very small groups took part in the poll. Even in the former bishopric of Liège, incomparably more pro-French than the Austrian Netherlands, no more than 21 per cent of the male population voted in favour of annexation.[1] It is, however, remarkable that in Belgium generally the country districts took a larger part in the plebiscite than the towns.[2] In the Northern Netherlands, too, radicalism grew more deeply in some of the agrarian provinces than in the urban centres.

The annexation proceeded slowly and it had hardly been started when Dumouriez, defeated on 18 March 1793 at Neerwinden, had to leave the country. From March 1793 till the Battle of Fleurus in June 1794 the Austrians once more ruled Belgium. They had no difficulty in establishing themselves. Though the French had abolished a number of institutions and stolen many properties, the structure of a new state had not yet been created. About 10,000 Belgian and Liègeois Jacobins left the country for Paris[3] thus making it easy for their opponents to resume their former posts. But the Austrians met immediately with the old problems and the old pretensions. Once again the privileged classes claimed for Belgium some measure of independence, demanding a national army and even a national bank, as they had in 1790. Once again the Austrians refused to make concessions. Consequently, the government obtained only very small sums of money from the clergy and nobility, and the bankers and merchants did not open their purses at all. The provincial States whose credit, owing to the uncertainties of the situation, was strictly limited, were just as little prepared to grant important subsidies.[4] In April 1794 the Emperor Francis II himself came to Brussels in a last attempt to win the Belgians over to the

[1] That is, 19,401 votes in favour of annexation (Harsin, op. cit., p. 165) out of a total population of about 400,000 (ibid., p. 20).

[2] Tassier, *Histoire*, p. 306.

[3] Verhaegen, *La Belgique sous la domination française*, i. 184.

[4] Ibid. 281 ff.

Austrian Government. He was inaugurated as Duke of Brabant, but what should have been an occasion for unparalleled jubilation—never since Philip II had a Duke of Brabant actually taken the trouble to make his *joyeuse entrée* into Brussels— was in fact a cold, spiritless ceremony. In June the Emperor left Belgium. His departure indicated that the Austrians were no longer willing or able to defend the country against French attacks.

When in the same month the French took Belgium again it was not clear what they intended to do with the country.[1] To begin with, they treated it as conquered territory and sought to get as much out of it as possible. But the war contributions which they levied, the military requisitions imposed on the population, and the activities of the *agence de commerce* which was commissioned to bring large quantities of the most varied articles—from cattle to works of art—to France produced much less than expected. The whole exercise was extremely badly organized but in spite of its harshness and abuses it was carried out in a not unfriendly way. At the end of 1794 the French started to change their policies. From June to November they had made no effort at all to provide for a central administrative system. In November they began to build one up. By then the thousands of Belgians who had left the country in June were already returning. In February 1795 it was evident that still greater changes were to be expected: Belgium would cease to be conquered territory, it would become part of France and be treated accordingly.

Disorder was such that any estimate of the Belgian losses remains purely arbitrary but they should not be exaggerated. The annexation in October 1795 which the population passively accepted meant for the majority at least the return of a safer existence. And notwithstanding the impassivity of the population, the next year was doubtless the most fruitful one of the whole occupation. The excellent French official L. G. de Bouteville, who ruled Belgium in 1796, succeeded where Joseph II had so miserably failed and created a new administration and new law courts to replace those which the Brabant Revolution of 1790 had resolutely abolished. Indifferent to

---

[1] For the following see the exhaustive study by R. Devleeshouwer, *L'Arrondissement du Brabant sous l'occupation française, 1794–1795* (Brussels, 1964).

Belgian objections and to their refusal to take office in the revolutionary institutions, he achieved the division of the country into nine *départements* (not coinciding with the former provinces but none the less built round the old capitals). He established departmental and municipal governments and introduced some French legislation. The population very soon got used to this efficient and sound organization. It was, thanks to its simplicity, much easier to understand than the *ancien régime*, and because it needed fewer officials it was also cheaper.

But though in the long run certain institutions proved acceptable, the style of French radicalism remained completely alien to the Belgians. They were still attached to the homely rhetoric of their former order; astonished at first, they soon received the literary extravagances of the French Revolution with complete indifference, and only a few attended the severely stylized revolutionary festivals. In the first years after the French conquest the Dutch were given the opportunity to carry through their revolution in their own way, to create their own national versions of revolutionary lyrics, and their own solemn style of revolutionary polemic, in form and tone strongly reminiscent of the Protestant sermon. In Belgium, on the other hand, the contrast between the ways of expression of ruler and ruled remained absolute. The French were well aware of this: they complained of the apathy and slowness of the Belgians and accused them of hating all foreigners and liking none but themselves.[1] To the French nationalism was a dynamic conception. They regarded the resistance which they encountered as the expression not of nationalistic Belgian emotions but of short-sighted egotism and dragging routine and they had as little patience with them as with the Vendée rebellions. In a way they were right. Belgian national consciousness had not yet risen above the level of a conservative and complacent self-sufficiency. Moreover, the Belgians did not so much react to the demolition of their national past, as this had survived in the structure of their state and in their language, as they did to the destruction of the Roman Catholic Church.

Only after reorganizing the administration did the French

[1] See the remarkable quotation in C. Pergameni, *L'Esprit public bruxellois au début du régime français* (Brussels, 1914), p. 97.

introduce their ecclesiastical legislation. In September 1796 they abolished most of the religious orders and monasteries and confiscated their properties. This measure made about 10,000 religious homeless and yielded up a property of which the value was estimated at 511 million francs.[1] By the end of 1796 it was put on the market. In 1797 the attack on the secular clergy followed; they were asked to promise loyalty to the laws and to declare that they approved of the dogma of popular sovereignty but, like the French clergy, only a minority complied and most of them suspended their work.[2] After the radical *coup d'état* of Fructidor (September 1797) the situation grew still more tense; the required promise was now replaced by an oath of hatred for royalty and anarchy which almost all Belgian priests refused to take. Then the persecutions started; 585 Belgian priests were sentenced to death in 1798, though all but one hundred were able to escape. Where possible religious services were carried on in private dwellings, in churchyards, or in the woods.[3] There can be no doubt that Belgian public opinion categorically rejected the French measures.

Yet possibly the ecclesiastical problem alone would not have driven the Southern Netherlanders to the point of taking up arms any more than the destruction of their old institutions had. What caused thousands of men to burst into desperate resistance in 1798 was the introduction of conscription. At the end of September the first Belgians were called up for military service. At the beginning of October riots took place in East-Flanders; a few days later the whole countryside of the department was under the control of rebellious peasants. But before the month was out the French had restored order and in early November they made short work of the rising of West-Flanders which followed. In the meantime the revolt had penetrated Brabant; in November a peasant army amounting to nearly 10,000 men was roaming that area, moving back from municipality to municipality in face of the French troops, until thousands were surrounded in Hasselt and forced to submit. This was the end of the revolt.

---

[1] Verhaegen, op. cit. ii. 298.

[2] Ibid. 320; L. de Lanzac de Laborie, *La Domination française en Belgique, 1795–1814* (2 vols., Paris, 1895), i. 84 ff.

[3] Lanzac, op. cit. i. 199 ff.

To the French, who had thought their hold on Belgium so secure that few troops were needed, the peasant rising came as a surprise. But they needed only relatively small reinforcements to beat the not very warlike rebels. They dealt with them with the utmost severity. There is an appalling contrast between this bloody suppression and the remarkably moderate behaviour of the peasants, who in the villages through which their march led them burned the archives in the council halls, destroyed the houses of the pro-French inhabitants, but abstained from pillage or murder.[1] The Belgian revolt was indeed quite different from those of the Vendée or the Tyrol.[2] But it is far from easy to determine its objectives or its implications. A national rebellion, carefully planned, carefully led, and backed from abroad, it certainly was not, though some historians have tried to prove this.[3] It was a revolt of the rural population; among the rebels it was not the peasants themselves who were predominant but the petty bourgeois. These were so deeply shocked by conscription that once again—for the last time, in fact—the conservative, patriotic enthusiasm of the Brabant Revolution awoke in them.[4] However, they had no leaders among the higher classes. It is true that some Belgian *émigrés* tried to direct the rebellion from their exile in Germany and the Northern Netherlands but this was completely unsuccessful. Many months after the French repression it was said that thousands of rebels, badly equipped and very undisciplined, were still lurking in the woods of Flanders, Brabant, and Liège, out of reach and unemployable.[5] But though Britain unquestionably supplied the rebels through the Northern Netherlands with arms and money, and though the presence of the British navy raised the hope of foreign intervention,[6] there was never any question of the enemies of France making a serious attempt to take the lead in the movement and fit it into an international pattern.

The revolt was almost entirely confined to the Flemish-speaking parts of Belgium. Yet it is dangerous to deduce from

---

[1] Lanzac, op. cit. i. 230 ff., 262 ff.   [2] Pirenne, *Histoire de Belgique* vi. 115.
[3] Verhaegen tries to do this (iii. 283 ff.).
[4] H. J. Elias, *Geschiedenis van de Vlaamse gedachte* (4 vols., Antwerp, 1963–4), . 63–4.
[5] Cf. the letter from the Bishop of Ypres, 9 May 1799: *Gedenkstukken* iii, 2, p. 934.
[6] Verhaegen, iii. 307 ff.

this that on the whole the Flemings offered more stubborn resistance to the French than the Walloons. Undoubtedly, the language bar rendered the French measures still more incomprehensible in the Dutch-speaking areas than they were to the Walloon peasantry; but there is no reason to suppose that the Walloon provinces were much more pro-French and revolutionary. When the estates of the monasteries were put up for sale, religious motives prompted most of the Walloon peasants not to buy them; they reacted exactly like the Flemings. And though ultimately more Flemish than Walloon farmers persisted in ignoring the auctions, it is unnecessary, by way of explanation, to bring in ethnic differences. After all, the tenants of the large farms in Hainaut were financially much stronger than the small East-Flemish peasantry.[1] In Wallonia and even Liège the conscripts, of course mostly peasant boys, do not seem to have obeyed the order to join the army with greater willingness than in Flanders or Brabant; most of them tried to escape.[2] Nor did the bourgeoisie react differently in the south of Belgium; in Flanders, whenever possible, it shut the town gates to the approaching peasant army and docilely allowed itself to be Frenchified. The bourgeois of Hainaut were just as ready as their Northern neighbours to take advantage of circumstances to buy national properties, but apart from a small minority they remained hostile to the revolution. It is noteworthy that when Bouteville was putting into effect the new organization of government in 1796, he praised Dutch-speaking Ghent as well as the French-speaking towns of Liège and Mons, and censured the recalcitrance of Antwerp as well as Namur.[3] In this matter the linguistic difference does not seem to have exercised much influence. But the position of the Dutch-speaking regions in relation to the Northern Netherlands, whence arms and money were arriving, and to the sea, where the British navy lay waiting, lent a stimulus to the revolt which was absent in the geographically more isolated Walloon parts of Belgium. Perhaps this explains why in

---

[1] I. Delatte, *La Vente des biens nationaux dans le département de Jemappes* (Brussels, 1938), p. 64; H. van Werveke, 'Vestiging van het nieuwe regime in het Zuiden', *Algemene geschiedenis der Nederlanden*, ix (1956), 60.

[2] Cf. Lanzac, i. 271, 365 ff.; ii. 70 ff.

[3] E. Hubert (ed.), *Correspondance de Bouteville* (2 vols., Brussels, 1929-34), i. 123, 129 ff.; ii. 88, 153 and *passim*.

Wallonia a more or less co-ordinated movement supported by specific groups like the Peasant Revolt did not emerge, even though for many years it had been troubled by discontented elements whose activities bordered on highway robbery.

Immediately after crushing the revolt the French started a violent campaign against the Belgian priests, but of the 7,500 they wanted to imprison they captured less than 500. Their attempt to carry through conscription rigorously met with just as little success. By the end of 1799 they had at their disposal only a quarter of the 22,000 men Belgium was ordered to supply. Then, paralysed by its hesitations, the Directoire collapsed. Yet Napoleon's *coup d'état* of 18 Brumaire (9 November 1799) was greeted by the Belgians with complete indifference and they hardly participated in the plebiscite on the new constitution, by contrast with France proper where more than half the electorate took the trouble to cast votes in favour. By 1800 it was clear that the notabilities, the big land-owners, the industrialists, the merchants, fearing to compromise themselves, were still unwilling, under the Consulate, to serve in the unpaid departmental and municipal offices. Consequently, the regime did not yet rest upon a broad basis of native collaborators:[1] it retained the character of a foreign occupation and with a few exceptions all Napoleon's prefects in Belgium were French.

From about 1800 the political and economic situation in Belgium improved, if only slightly. Belgian development followed the French rhythm. However, the scattered and not very reliable information does not convey a clear picture of the growth of prosperity, nor of the resignation with which French domination was now accepted as permanent. About the misery during the years from 1795 to 1800 there can be no doubt. The complaints are much too numerous to be ignored: the peasants were unable to export their produce, industry was in decline, and the workers' plight was desperate; high tariff walls were closing traditional markets to Belgian commerce (for instance, the Northern Netherlands); there was depopulation of the big towns; and there were organized gangs of robbers, who added to the dangers and bad conditions of the roads. Some groups were of course directly hit by

[1] Lanzac, i. 327 ff.

the heavy financial demands of the French, by the inability of the nationalized monasteries and guilds and the refusal of the revolutionary urban governments to pay interest on their old debts. They also suffered to a lesser degree from the abolition of the remaining feudal duties. All this must have caused a fairly general impoverishment; but its extent cannot be calculated and it should not be exaggerated. The new general taxes, too, were much lamented. The Belgian historian Verhaegen has tried to establish that the burden on the population rose from 16 francs per head under the Austrian regime to 25 under the French.[1] Yet even if this is true, the increase cannot be considered very onerous in view of the rise of prices and to a certain extent of wages, or in view of the greater activities and responsibilities of the modern state.[2] At any rate a French satellite state like the Northern Netherlands had to pay much higher taxes: about 40 francs per head, not including extraordinary levies and loans.[3]

Under the Consulate and the Empire the economy seems to have expanded a little. It was still almost exclusively an agrarian economy and in this time of constantly rising corn prices and rising rents agriculture was very profitable to landowners and big tenants. But the wages of the urban and rural workmen followed the rising costs of living slowly and inadequately, so that the contrast between the economic circumstances of the various social classes became even sharper than at the end of the eighteenth century. In this regard Belgium did not differ from the rest of Western Europe. Nor was the rapid emergence of a group of merchants and industrialists, capable of taking advantage of the situation, in itself a very remarkable phenomenon. By buying valuable national properties at low prices petty bourgeois, adventurers, or foreigners settling in the Southern Netherlands were able to acquire the capital to set up new enterprises. Most of these did not survive, but such varied activities certainly strengthened the position of the bourgeoisie. The land of the Church (the Belgian nobility did not emigrate, so that the national domains consisted mainly of ecclesiastical property) passed chiefly to the Belgian bourgeois who felt no religious, moral, or political

---

[1] Verhaegen, ii. 182, 186.   [2] Van Werveke, loc. cit. 40.
[3] *Gedenkstukken* iv, 2, p. 486 n. 1 but cf. p. 439.

qualms about purchasing it. Especially during the period from 1797 to 1799 prices were exceptionally low. In Hainaut, where one-sixth of the land was Church property, 75 per cent of it was ultimately acquired by the bourgeoisie.[1] In the Namur area the same class benefited most.[2] In East-Flanders, where one-twelfth of the land was put up for auction, they obtained about 50 per cent.[3] The remainder was bought by the nobility, by foreigners, by big farmers—although by means of some complicated manipulations part of it was kept by the Church. Thus the whole operation, originally designed to help the peasantry, achieved very little in the way of a social revolution.

Bourgeois strength and success manifested themselves most clearly in the development of some highly modern industries, and in the triumphant penetration of the French language amongst the Flemish social élite. Industry benefited from the opening of the huge French market and the Continental System. Production in the coal-mines of the Borinage, where steam-engines came into use, was greatly increased.[4] Until the crisis of 1810 the textile industry of Verviers in the former principality of Liège developed at a hectic pace. Thanks to mechanization, introduced after 1801 by the English engineer Cockerill, it could satisfy rising demand; between 1808 and 1810 its production was 88 per cent higher than under the *ancien régime*.[5] Ghent became one of the largest industrial centres of the Empire. The tanner Lieven Bauwens, who had already in 1792 started a profitable career as a contractor for the French army, tax-farmer, and purchaser of national estates, had managed by 1796 to acquire parts of English spinning-machines and steam-engines and then established, first near Paris and 1801 also in Ghent, spinning-mills, engineering works, and other rapidly growing factories. Capitalism in the style of Bauwens and his friends at Ghent was still a very adventurous, reckless, and far too speculative business, as the

[1] Delatte, op. cit., pp. 79, 86.

[2] I. Delatte, *La Vente des biens nationaux dans l'arrondissement de Namur* (Namur, 1933), p. 232.

[3] Cf. J. Lambert, 'Inbeslagname en verkoop van de nationale goederen', *Handelingen der Maatschappij voor Geschiedenis en Oudheidkunde te Gent* (Ghent, 1960), 131 ff.

[4] See R. Darquenne, *Histoire économique du département de Jemappes* (Mons, 1965).

[5] P. Lebrun, *L'Industrie de la laine à Verviers pendant le XVIIIᵉ et le début du XIXᵉ siècle* (Liège, 1948), p. 338.

catastrophic financial crisis of 1810 was soon to prove.[1] But this rapid industrial development transformed the Ghent of the *ancien régime* with its orientation towards Habsburg and Spain, its guilds, and its handwork into a centre of capitalist enterprise; the number of workmen employed in the cotton industry grew from nearly 1,300 in 1806 to nearly 12,000 in 1816.[2] It was a sign of the times that the nobility also began to invest money in this industry.[3] Tendencies already apparent under the Austrians were thus further developed and broadened by a group of industrialists who linked their fate with the French regime and together with their economic activities assumed certain administrative responsibilities.

The success of these groups of industrialists, merchants, and civil servants seems almost tangible when one sees how little resistance Dutch as a language of civilization and administration offered to the new influences. The bourgeoisie, spurred on by economic motives and largely indifferent in matters of culture and politics,[4] readily submitted to Frenchification. The French Government, quite unlike the Austrian, had a purposeful linguistic policy and just as it combated the dialects of France proper so it drove Dutch, which until 1795 was always used in the local administration of Brabant and Flanders, out of public life. By about 1800 only the most backward rural municipalities still continued to write their official correspondence in Dutch.[5] Jurisdiction was entirely in French. The theatre and the Press eschewed Dutch, though Dutch books were still being published for use by the lower classes. The children of the higher urban population were increasingly taught only in French; popular education, initially taken away from the clergy, was neglected by the Directoire because it was incompetent and by Napoleon because he was unwilling to build it up. In this way French became the language of all public life and also of the well-to-do middle classes, which were rapidly gaining more social prestige than they had possessed under

[1] J. Dhondt, 'L'industrie cotonnière gantoise à l'époque française', *Revue d'histoire moderne et contemporaine*, ii (1955), 263.

[2] Ibid. 266–7.   [3] Ibid. 276.

[4] Cf. the well-known *Rapport à l'Institut national . . . d'un voyage fait à la fin de l'an X, dans les départemens du Bas-Rhin, de rive gauche de ce fleuve, de la Belgique . . .* (Paris, an X) by the scholar A. G. Camus, p. 95.

[5] Deneckere, *Histoire de la langue française dans les Flandres*, p. 270.

the aristocratic *ancien régime*. They now made a point of distinguishing themselves linguistically from the masses of small peasants and labourers, who lacked all education and because of the fall in their real income were living in great economic distress.

Only in the Church did Dutch remain the predominant language. The village priests in Flanders and Brabant spoke little or no French.[1] But the clergy were the only group of people in Belgium after 1799 who were still being made to suffer from the new regime. Reconciliation between the upper classes and the French authorities was gradually becoming a possibility, though high society, in Tournai and Antwerp for example, refused to invite French civil servants and military officers to its dances and parties.[2] The nobles were often prepared to accept official appointments and after 1801 they served as mayors of the villages and towns where they had their untouched estates.[3] But Napoleon's attempts to find a compromise between the interests of his state and the Church failed time and time again. So after his fall only the Church could claim a record of constant hostility to the tyrant. It was very much weakened; the major part of its properties had been sold, its priests had been persecuted and it was difficult to replace them: after 1802 fewer priests per diocese were ordained in Belgium than in France.[4] But the Belgian clergy was counter-revolutionary, anti-Gallican, and ultramontane; it was not anti-French. It did not, and never wanted to, represent a national idea. Thus there can be no doubt that when in 1815 the Empire finally broke down and all possibility of restoring French power in Belgium was excluded, no strong body of political opinion of any kind existed in the country. The future lay open. Napoleon had failed to turn the population of the Southern Netherlands into Frenchmen. But twenty years of submission had not inspired in any of them a belief in Belgian nationalism. They were still pursuing their own conflicting and irreconcilable interests.

[1] Even from the pulpits at Brussels the priests continued to speak Flemish. Cf. *Gedenkstukken* viii, 2, p. 579 n. 2.

[2] Comte de Mérode-Westerloo, *Souvenirs* (2 vols., Brussels, 1864), i. 255.

[3] J. Lefèvre, 'De Adel', *Flandria Nostra*, iv (Antwerp, 1959), 398.

[4] Lanzac, ii. 113.

3. *The Batavian Revolution in the Northern Netherlands*

On 1 February 1793 the French declared war on the 'tyrants' George III and William V, the Dutch Stadtholder. In the same month Dumouriez marched into the Republic and occupied some areas in the South. But in March, after the Battle of Neerwinden, he had to retreat not only from the Northern Netherlands but from Belgium as well. Only after the Battle of Fleurus in June 1794 was the Republic once more in danger. In December Pichegru took North-Brabant and Dutch Flanders. At the beginning of January 1795 he crossed the frozen rivers and marched northwards; on 16 January he captured Utrecht. Two days later William V left for England. The Dutch army offered little resistance; it melted away and York's undisciplined English army, which had not put up much of a fight either, retreated to Hanover, ransacking the country on the way. Everywhere in the Republic revolutions broke out. At last the reform party, so miserably defeated in 1787, was able to start carrying out its programme.

At first sight the situation did not seem unfavourable for revolutionary action. Initially the French, who in principle allowed the country to make its own decisions and did not impose the reforms they thought necessary, were relatively tactful. Until 1798, moreover, quite a large number of people were actively interested in political events. In 1798, when all Orangists and conservatives were deprived of the franchise, two-fifths of the male population made use of their right to vote and declared themselves in favour of the revolution. And in the light of French experience since 1789 it was certainly much easier in 1795 than it had been ten years earlier to define a programme of reform, a revolutionary method, a political end. The grave economic situation may well have helped to convince many people that reforms were urgently needed.

However, there were at the same time factors at work which retarded and, in a sense, prevented the revolution. The attitude of the French themselves rendered a social revolution impossible: the only benefit we can derive from the Netherlands, wrote the French Minister at The Hague in 1795, is the credit of its capitalists.[1] It was thus in the French interest to make sure that

[1] *Gedenkstukken* ii, p. 17.

this was not jeopardized by radical projects. Again the economic depression, which in 1795 was already more serious than in 1785 and in the course of the next few years assumed alarming proportions, meant that many radical bourgeois could not afford to devote themselves, unpaid or badly paid, to public affairs. For this reason the petty bourgeois in the towns soon withdrew from the revolutionary councils.[1] The situation was far from promising, moreover, for political opportunists: it was a small country where people kept a strict eye on their neighbours and where traditions of careful bookkeeping were so deeply rooted that to do violence to them was to ask for trouble. So it is understandable, though still remarkable, when compared with what happened in France, that very few political careers were made between 1795 and 1813. The revolutionary group remained small; it did not contain men of great talent and, after the *coups d'état* that in this period formed the almost inevitable track along which the revolutionary process moved, it was in fact totally exhausted. Furthermore, many revolutionaries were Roman Catholics or Baptists, and as dissenters had not been allowed to take office before 1795 they completely lacked experience in government.[2]

Finally, though in the Northern Netherlands interest in public affairs was fairly widespread, the Dutch people remained deeply divided, with a sharp contrast between the parties of the *ancien régime*, the federalist structure of the old Republic, the strict isolation of the various religious groups, and the independence of urban and rural communities. The country was intersected, as one French observer put it, by as many social barriers as there were ditches.[3] It is difficult in such a society to generate national and revolutionary enthusiasm. Repeated interference by the French added to the complexity and ambiguity of revolutionary events. In 1798, in 1801, in 1805, 1806, and 1810 they abruptly put a stop to developments which they themselves had started. Napoleon's cynical whimsicality left the Dutch statesmen no scope for consistent policy or political ideals, forcing them into opportunist compromises

[1] K. M. van der Sterre, 'De Bataafse Republiek in wording', *Algemene geschiedenis der Nederlanden*, ix (1956), 4.

[2] Cf. *Gedenkstukken* iii, 1, p. 20 and iv, 1, p. 132.

[3] Marmont in a letter to the Emperor, Nov. or Dec. 1804: *Gedenkstukken* iv, 1, p. 125. Cf. ibid. pp. 74 and 98.

which they accepted with the resignation of thoroughly disillusioned reformers. Even so, in spite of the rapid changes
and the innumerable unfinished initiatives, it is possible to
trace throughout the whole period certain continuous themes
and tendencies.

In 1795 it soon became clear that the French, who only
annexed Belgium on 1 October of that year, were not planning
to incorporate the Republic as well. They recognized the individuality of the Dutch people. As a historical motive for sparing
the Dutch nation they could point to the Dutch form of government—an ancient, respectable republicanism, after all, though
one corrupted by the tyrannical Stadtholder. They could
recall the sixteenth-century revolution and the great acts of
the seventeenth-century heroes who had successfully fought
England as well as the Bourbons. Moreover, the theory of the
natural frontiers came up against the big rivers; it encompassed
Belgium, partly French-speaking anyway, but not the Northern
Netherlands. The North was not a merely continental state;
it was foreign to France. What was the use of incorporating
it? The French could not as in Belgium annex rich monasteries and fertile fields, only ditches and lakes; and the Dutch
ships and the Dutch capitalists would seek refuge elsewhere,
taking with them the national wealth, their money, securities,
and credit. A seafaring nation cannot be annexed; it escapes
over the water.

Thus it was possible in 1795 for the Dutch to carry out their
revolution in a leisurely manner within the boundaries set
by France, without anarchy and without restoring Orangist
rule. The revolutionaries started by dismissing the Orangist
town governments and appointing instead provisional representatives of the people; they in their turn nominated new members of the various provincial States, who finally elected the
States General. In March 1795 this process was completed
and all the posts of the former regents were held by Patriots; the
generosity and naïvety of the revolutionaries had made it an
extraordinarily quiet development. In January 1795 the Amsterdam provisional representatives, wishing to show how magnanimous Liberty could be,[1] promised the regents complete

---

[1] C. Rogge, *Tafereel van de geschiedenis der jongste omwenteling in de Vereenigde
Nederlanden* (Amsterdam, 1796), p. 283.

safety of life and property; there was no echo of the Terror, no reference to the systematic plundering of Belgium. A former orthodox court *predikant* declared in the summer: 'This revolution is from the Lord';[1] a professor of theology at Groningen traced in it 'the footsteps of Divine Providence'.[2] The United Committee of Revolution in the Netherlands, established in February, thought that quiet and order were the characteristics of the true popular revolt.[3] Everywhere the ordinary salaried civil servants were retained until further notice and the prosecution of members of the former government was stopped when no grounds for an accusation could be found within traditional law.

Though proud of the mildness of the Patriotic revolution, which unlike the Orangist revolts of the past ran its course without bloodshed or violent popular outbursts, the radicals were nevertheless often irritated by the fact that the regents were not obliged to make special financial sacrifices in order to redeem their moral and political guilt. This irritation soon found more positive expression, leading the moderates to summon a National Assembly elected on the basis of universal male suffrage and intended to replace the States General and draft a new constitution. In December the States General finally decided to call elections, but at the same time tied the planned Constituante to a set of regulations governing the processes of discussion and decision which were clearly intended to prevent it making any radical changes. In January 1796, after an incomplete census, the elections were held at two removes. All the male inhabitants over twenty years who declared themselves in favour of the doctrine of popular sovereignty and received no poor-relief were entitled to vote. Many of them, however, seem to have stayed at home. On 1 March the National Assembly was opened at The Hague, but only 90 of its 126 members were present. They were, of course, all Patriots, and the majority belonged to the higher middle classes—advocates, merchants, industrialists, professors, clergymen, and priests.

---

[1] J. Heringa, *Godsdienstige redenvoering* (The Hague, 1795); see W. P. C. Knuttel, *Catalogus van de pamflettenverzameling berustende in de Koninklijke Bibliotheek* (9 vols., The Hague, 1882–1934, no. 22472), p. 14.

[2] P. Chevallier, *De voetstappen der Godlijke Voorzienigheid in Nederlands Staatsomwenteling* (1795; Knuttel, 22688).

[3] Rogge, op. cit., pp. 330–1.

Even so, some members came from former regent families and there were a few noble and petty bourgeois representatives. Their position made demands on their time and money: on top of their daily compensation of 10 guilders each of them spent about 2,000 guilders a year out of his own pocket.[1] The meeting was certainly not fully representative of Dutch public opinion. All Orangists were excluded and thanks to the electoral system the moderate wing of the Patriots was unduly well represented.[2] This became apparent on 8 August 1797 when the anti-radical draft that the Assembly produced after innumerable meetings was rejected by the electorate. About 33 per cent of the male population took part in the referendum; the majority (26 per cent of the male population) voted against the proposals.[3] .The numerous adherents of the House of Orange were naturally not allowed to go to the polls.

In view of the result of the plebiscite the work of the National Assembly must be called unsuccessful. Yet the meeting was a highly important event. It forced the Dutch population to make a choice between various political possibilities and obliged the parties to define their positions. There were two extremes— the federalists and the unitarists, as they were called in the awkward jargon of the time. In between was a middle group tending towards federalism without accepting its main principles. The federalists were anti-Orangist, rejected the *ancien régime*, and adhered to the doctrine of popular sovereignty. But they were anxious to avoid a radical break with the past and remained faithful to the programme of the Patriots in the 1780s when the ideal of a unitary state had not yet been put forward. In their view the state ought to protect itself, through a careful system of balance, against despotic abuses. Only by retaining some measure of independence could the rural or urban communities prevent the provincial administrations from becoming tyrannical. The natural tendency of the central government to increase its power could, in its turn, only be checked by leaving the provinces, as in the past, a well-

---

[1] Geyl, *Nederlandse stam* iii. 380.   [2] Cf. *Gedenkstukken* ii, p. 191.

[3] Figures in C. Rogge, *Geschiedenis der staatsregeling voor het Bataafsche volk* (Amsterdam, 1799), p. 402. As the radical draft of 1798 was accepted in the various provinces with about the same majorities as rejected that of 1797, the unfavourable results of 1797 must have been caused by irritation at the anti-radicalism of the constitution.

defined sovereignty, whereas within the spheres of local, provincial, and federal government the separation of powers had to
be worked out precisely. Obviously, the federalists were attempting to apply Montesquieu's concepts to the new republic.[1]

There was, no doubt, a certain affinity between the federalists
and some sections of the Orangist party now excluded from
political life. It was often practical rather than theoretical
issues that divided the two groups. Even before 1795 various
Orangists had regarded Montesquieu as an inspiring example,
and in the writings of others after 1795 it is possible to trace
his influence as well as that of Burke.[2] The political tempera-
ments of both parties, or at any rate important representatives
of both, were congenial; it was only the starting-points of
their arguments that differed. The Orangists kept to the guiding principle of loyalty to the national dynasty, the federalists
to that of popular sovereignty. But many of their conclusions
were not incompatible. For in the course of the next few years
the Orangists also began to see that a new constitution might
be an efficient means not of expressing popular power but of
guaranteeing the liberty and independence of individuals and
groups. Some of them were actually readier than the federalists
to emphasize the necessity of a strong executive power, to be
exercised by the Prince of Orange, and so to recognize the real
needs of the modern state.[3]

The quality of their nationalism was also comparable. In
neither party was there to be found any trace of the exuberant
hope of the Patriots in the 1780s that the Republic might re-
emerge as a Great Power. They resigned themselves to the
humble position of their country, only wishing it to stay independent, carrying on its trade freely, and avoiding the obligations and dangers of international diplomacy. This was an
attitude quite often taken in the past by important sections of
Dutch society. In fact, in the time of their greatest success the
patricians in Holland had advocated such a policy, and during
the seventeenth century the Princes of Orange were repeatedly

---

[1] Cf. ibid., pp. 21 ff., 206 ff.
[2] e.g. Charles Bentinck in *Gedenkstukken* ii, pp. 430 ff.
[3] Orangist constitutional ideas in *Gedenkstukken* ii, pp. 839 ff. (1795); iii,
pp. 369 ff., 547, 1100 (1799). But the House of Orange itself still wanted to restore
the old regime with only very slight modifications; cf. ibid. iii, pp. 400, 942, 1037 ff.,
1076. See also Colenbrander (ed.), *Ontstaan der Grondwet*, i, pp. xxx ff.

forced by the resistance of the regents to abandon their expansionist schemes. Stadtholder William V, however, followed
the traditions of the seventeenth-century regents rather than
those of the Orangists. And in October 1795 one of his most
representative adherents declared that the Republic must give
up its pretensions to being a great power and drastically reduce
its army, fleet, and diplomatic service to the minimum needed
for keeping up a few garrisons and providing jobs for young
aristocrats. The status of the Republic was similar to that of
Denmark, Venice, or Genoa.[1] In the course of the next few
years both the federalists and the Orangists were confronted
by vague plans for aggrandizing the territory of the old
Republic; both parties reacted hesitantly. To both the idea
was probably as repellent as it would have been to a seventeenth-century regent in Holland.[2] They loathed the dynamic
of the authoritarian, continental state and thought it foreign
to Dutch traditions.

The federalists constituted the conservative, more or less
aristocratic, wing of the Patriots. Their most important
representatives came from the more backward provinces like
Overijssel and Gelderland where, because of their lack of
political experience and influence, the masses of the peasantry
failed to get men of more radical intentions appointed to the
National Assembly in 1796. In political discussions the federalists confined themselves to resisting the wishes of their opponents. They combated the proposal that in the forthcoming
unitary state the ancient debts of the provinces should be
amalgamated, protecting the smaller provinces which, charged
with a total debt of 155 million guilders, were understandably
very reluctant to share the responsibility for the interest payable
on the province of Holland's debt of 455 million.[3] They were
equally opposed to the project of levying general taxes because
this too would jeopardize the privileged position of the smaller
provinces. In Holland taxes amounted to more than 25 guilders

---

[1] A. J. C. Lampsins to the hereditary Prince, 13 Oct. 1795. *Gedenkstukken* ii,
p. 876.

[2] Cf. the reaction of the Agent for Foreign Affairs Van der Goes (almost a
federalist at that time) to the possibility of territorial expansion in 1801 (*Gedenkstukken* iii, p. 653) and the views of the Orangists living in the Netherlands on the
plans of the hereditary Prince concerning Belgium (1799) (ibid., pp. 972, 1010–11).

[3] According to a statement by Canneman: *Gedenkstukken* iv, 2, p. 472.

per head of the population, in Gelderland to 8 guilders, in Overijssel to 6·7, and in Drente to less than 5.[1] During the debates on these problems the federalists at times found support among some radical representatives of the small provinces, which naturally confused the discussions in a most embarrassing way.

A number of so-called moderates shared the federalist party's dislike of revolutionary measures, its fear of social disturbances and violence, its aversion to the dynamic of radical nationalism—according to their leader, the Amsterdam advocate R. J. Schimmelpenninck (1761–1825), people should forget about the time of De Ruyter and Tromp.[2] But, on principle as well as for practical reasons, they were in favour of a unitary state, the amalgamation of the debts, and a system of general taxation. They were pre-eminently realists. Thanks to their leaders' talents they exercised not only on the National Assembly[3] but on the revolution generally a much larger measure of influence than the number of their adherents warranted. An additional explanation of their success is that their leaders were all Hollanders who could rely on support not from the Orangist masses or the former regents (who after a time went to live in their country houses and muse on their days of glory) but from the bankers, the big merchants, the higher bourgeoisie of Holland. If one group during these confused years may be considered to represent the interests of the bourgeoisie of Holland it was this one.

The party of the radicals—they were called unitarists or Jacobins or democrats—was much more complex and its programme more paradoxical than that of the other groups. Especially outside Holland it found larger support than its rivals, the Orangists perhaps excepted. But the quality of its followers was generally not outstanding and its leaders, most of whom did not come from Holland, lacked the political suppleness and the cool realism of the sceptical moderates. The party's theorists and intellectuals had unoriginal minds; they simply adopted the slogans of their French colleagues and

[1] According to a statement by Gogel: ibid., p. 516. When assessing the implications of these facts it should be taken into account that in Holland wages were much higher than elsewhere.

[2] Ibid. ii, p. 377.

[3] Cf. Vreede's remark in *Gedenkstukken* ii, p. 635 n. 1.

seemed willing to act as the revolutionary élite of the quiet and declining Republic. Their nationalism was Janus-faced. The Patriotic exuberance of the 1780s was not alien to them and during the dark years from 1787 to 1795 they tried, exaggerating Dutch political and economic strength, to convince the French revolutionaries of the enormous benefit that they would derive from the conquest of the Northern Netherlands: united with the Dutch Republic and with the help of Dutch money and the Dutch navy, France would have no difficulty in beating Britain.[1] Dynamic cosmopolitanism and over-excited national pride strangely intermingled in their programmes and their emotions. After 1795, disappointed at seeing the French *élan* diminished, they returned to a fiery nationalism, asking for an energetic government capable of stemming the decline by means of a thorough reform of the state;[2] nor were they averse to territorial aggrandizement. To them the democratic ideal no longer seemed, as it had to the Patriots of the 1780s, subordinate to nationalist emotions; it had grown independent. They were eager to respond to the possibility of an international revolution, but when France closed its frontiers, withdrawing inside its own *raison d'État*, their democratic enthusiasm quite naturally narrowed, being once again exclusively directed towards the national community and absorbed by the aim of establishing a strong, united, and indivisible Dutch Republic.

In the National Assembly (1796-7) the radical party under the leadership of Pieter Vreede (1750-1837), the wealthy owner of textile works in North-Brabant and an *homme de lettres* in his spare time, exercised great and stimulating influence. The radicals not only championed the complete merger of provinces and towns into one solid block but made a plea, sometimes with success, for such ideals as the admission of the Jews to the National Assembly, the dissolution of the guilds, the separation of Church and State (the State no longer subsidizing any religious community), and the abolition of the slave trade. But after interminable discussions the Assembly, crippled by the regulations the States General had devised for it, finally drafted an extremely complicated and timid constitution, containing over 700 articles, which took no account at all of radical wishes. This was rejected in the

---

[1] Ibid. i, pp. 341, 377, 381.   [2] Ibid. ii, pp. 493 ff.

plebiscite of August 1797 despite the intensive propaganda of federalists and moderates. New elections, however, did not sensibly modify the composition of the National Assembly and it seemed likely that the second Constituante would be just as incapable of producing an acceptable draft. This is why in January 1798 the French backed a radical *coup d'état*. After the federalists were driven out of the meeting by armed force, the French Ambassador dictated to the radical rump a new unitarist constitution. On 23 April 1798 the electorate, purged of all federalists and Orangists, gave its opinion; of course the voters accepted the proposal almost unanimously.

The results of the April plebiscite provide some interesting data about Dutch public opinion. Altogether 165,520 men (40 per cent of the adult male population) took part in the referendum; only 11,597 of them voted against the proposal. In comparison with France, where in 1793 not more than about 30 per cent of the electorate troubled to go to the polls, the turn-out was high. And the fact that almost two-fifths of the male population accepted the radical constitution, after rejecting the federal version in August 1797 by about the same majority, gives a clear indication of the mass following of the radical party. But the figures also reveal its qualitative weakness. For it was less popular in Holland, where 26·9 per cent of the male population voted in favour of the draft, than in provinces like Zeeland (27·3 per cent voting affirmatively), Gelderland (27·5 per cent), Overijssel (43·1 per cent), and North-Brabant (67·2 per cent).[1] This was not a new phenomenon. In the 1780s, too, democratic Patriotism found a weaker and socially much narrower support in Holland than in some of the more backward provinces. The dangers inherent in this situation are obvious. Although the poor peasants and Roman

---

[1] The results per province in Rogge, *Staatsregeling*, p. 561. Figures about the provincial populations in R. Metelerkamp, *De toestand van Nederland* (2 vols., Rotterdam, 1804), i. 27–8. I have estimated that one out of 4,512 inhabitants was a man. This produces a total of 416,444 men. In 1801 with no one any longer deprived of the franchise, 416,419 men were registered (Colenbrander, *De Bataafsche Republiek*, p. 236). In Drenthe (21 per cent), Utrecht (16·7 per cent), Friesland (18·1 per cent), and Groningen (14·3 per cent) still fewer than in Holland voted affirmatively. As far as Friesland and Groningen are concerned, the strong particularism of these provinces, hostile to the unitary character of the constitution but not necessarily to its democratic contents, must be taken into account. Army and navy also voted. They produced about 27,000 affirmative votes.

Catholics in Overijssel, Gelderland, and North-Brabant might in a referendum give expression to their dislike of the ruling classes and doctrines, they possessed neither the means nor the ability to sustain the radical party, which in Holland constituted only an isolated minority among the moderate high bourgeoisie and the Orangist or politically indifferent masses. Accordingly, it is not surprising (especially when its leaders' lack of political perspicacity is taken into account) that in spite of this undeniable success the party soon lost ground.

In June 1798 a new *coup d'état* put an end to radical power, and the moderates of Holland took over the government. Though glad to preserve the unitary constitution they were, however, so apprehensive of revolutionary experiments that they spent their forces combating the Jacobins and neglected to take the measures to reform public finance, taxation, education, the Church, the law courts, and municipal administration that were required by the new constitution. Moreover, the characteristically radical-Patriotic articles obliging the government to interfere actively in the national economy in the interest of general prosperity (in sharp contrast to the traditional view in Holland, the main emphasis was laid upon industry rather than trade)[1] were allowed to fall into oblivion. Neither the guilds nor the feudal duties, abolished by the constitution, actually disappeared. The moderate government lacked the energy about which Vreede, the leader of the short-lived radical regime, used to speak and write so much— in the apologia which he published soon after his fall the word, printed in italics, occurred ten times[2] though never in his active political life did he succeed in summoning its reality. As long as renewed democratic activity seemed imminent, the few members of the moderate government with radical ties and intentions found so little support among the bourgeoisie of Holland that they were unable to put any of the democratic decisions embodied in the constitution into effect. Only when democratic radicalism, which after Napoleon's *coup d'état* was

---

[1] Cf. art. 51 of the General Principles which form the first part of the constitution of 1798. See also H. F. J. M. van den Eerenbeemt, *'s-Hertogenbosch in de Bataafse en Franse tijd* (Nijmegen, 1955), p. 20 and L. G. J. Verberne, *Het sociale en economische motief in de Bataafse tijd* (Tilburg, 1947), pp. 17 ff.

[2] J. van der Poel, 'Leven en bedrijf van Pieter Vreede', *Verslag . . . Historisch Genootschap . . . te Utrecht, 1951* (Utrecht, 1952), p. 34 n. 5.

deprived of all support from France, had disappeared as a popular movement were they given the opportunity to realize some of their ideals of reform. But these, though highly important in themselves, were by then reduced to matters of administrative technique.

Yet it was shown in the autumn of 1799 that in spite of the revolution's lack of purpose and its queer contradictions public opinion in the Netherlands had certainly not become anti-French. The landing of British troops in North-Holland in August 1799 (in October they embarked again) was, to the great disappointment of the coalition and the House of Orange, not greeted by a rising of the Dutch people; even the Orangists living in the Netherlands made no move. But this negative success hardly reinforced the government, and in 1801 the French swept away a regime which, however moderate it might actually be, was based upon a Jacobin constitution and as such seemed fundamentally alien to Napoleon's syncretism, which transcended or rather ignored the parties. Many changes were made; both the powers of the representatives and the franchise were greatly limited, whereas the executive was given stronger and more independent power. The democratic principles of 1798 were replaced by the authoritarian principle provisionally embodied in a government of no less than twelve persons but soon concentrated in the hands of one dictator.[1] This system pretended to be national and even the Orangists were allowed a place in it. But it had no national appeal. Dutch interest in political developments decreased alarmingly; in 1801 only 69,000 out of more than 400,000 entitled to vote took part in the polls, and when in 1805 the dictatorship of the moderate R. J. Schimmelpenninck was established no more than 14,000 voted. The turn-out in Holland was proportionally smaller than in the other provinces.[2]

All the same, Schimmelpenninck's rule (1805–6) achieved some very useful results. These were due to the radical collaborators of the short-lived dictator, in the first instance to I. J. A. Gogel (1765–1821). It was he who proved capable of accomplishing in one year what had been left undone since 1798, by drafting a system of general taxation that turned out to be

---

[1] L. G. J. Verberne, *In den spiegel van het verleden* (Utrecht, 1947), pp. 178 ff.
[2] *Gedenkstukken* iv, 1, p. 277.

eminently workable. It is surprising to see so excellent a representative of radical Patriotism concentrating on this one aspect of Dutch life and doing so with such passionate energy that the history of radicalism during the first decade of the . nineteenth century can only be described in fiscal terms. He no longer expected Holland to have a great future and in 1806 resignedly accepted King Louis Napoleon when the Emperor thrust his brother upon the Northern Netherlands.[1] Gogel's radicalism, wounded and humiliated by twenty years of disillusionment, was reduced to the determination to organize the Republic's Finance Department efficiently; his nationalism, which in 1795 had wavered between grandiose visions of Franco-Dutch revolutionary imperialism and the restoration of the great Dutch past, now withdrew behind the narrow frontiers of his fatherland—his fight against Dutch foreign investments[2] was fairly representative of the autarchic and minimalist character of early nineteenth-century Patriotism. Far from being inspired by revolutionary ideals, it showed only a desire carefully to look after one's own.

The need to reform Dutch finances was, of course, urgent enough. By 1795 the public debt was already large and in the course of the next eight years it grew from 760 million to 1,126 million guilders.[3] It was calculated that from 1795 to 1804 the Republic raised about 230 million guilders to meet French claims.[4] The interest payable on the national debt increased from 24 millions in 1795 to 34 millions a year in 1804,[5] that is (by way of comparison) to 40 francs per head of the population against 16 francs in the France of 1789, where the weight of the debt was used as proof of the untenable financial position.[6] The taxes, though exceptionally heavy (40 francs per head compared with 15 francs in France), were far from adequate. The balance was provided by extraordinary levies and forced loans; from 1795 to 1804 sums totalling 30 per cent of capital and 53 per cent of income were raised in

---

[1] *Gedenkstukken* v, 1. p. lvii.

[2] See, e.g., *Gedenkstukken* ii, pp. 780 ff. and cf. Brugmans, op. cit., p. 20.

[3] *Gedenkstukken* iv, 2, p. 472.   [4] Ibid., p. 541 n. 2.

[5] J. A. van Sillem, *De politieke en staathuishoudkundige werkzaamheid van I. J. A. Gogel* (Amsterdam, 1864), pp. 173 ff.

[6] Interest on the French public debt amounted in 1789 to a good 300 million francs.

this way at relatively low rates of interest, not including loans to the urban governments.[1] It was to be feared that in spite of its strength. Dutch financial power would finally collapse. For the financial situation was also seriously disturbed by the wars; income from foreign loans seems to have fallen in the period from 1795 to 1813 from about 40 million guilders a year to 25 or 30 million. This was partly because payment of interest was stopped, but also because the Dutch were forced to withdraw capital—probably about 500 million guilders—from foreign funds to place it in the Republic, thus contributing to a marked decrease in the prestige of the Amsterdam financial market.[2] Notwithstanding this accumulation of Dutch capital in the Netherlands it became increasingly difficult for the government to get its loans fully subscribed and often the extraordinary levies yielded less than expected. Harsh inquisitorial procedures, heavy penalties for tax evasion, confiscation of houses because of arrears in the payment of land-tax (in the big towns of Holland with their declining populations many of them were bought at low prices by demolition contractors who were said to sell the building materials to prosperous Belgium,)[3] these constituted the external symptoms of the emergency.

The system of taxation introduced by Gogel in 1806 was designed in such a way as to lower the pressure on the poor by the abolition of the excise on many foodstuffs, whilst charging the middle classes and the rich more heavily than under the *ancien régime* by means of progressive direct taxation on the basis of prosperity, for which the house-rent, the number of domestic servants, horses, and hearths, and the value of the furniture were taken as criteria. Thanks to the abolition of innumerable urban excises and tolls commerce benefited from the free flow of traffic and the middle classes were expected to find some compensation for the higher sums they had to

---

[1] According to Gogel's calculations: *Gedenkstukken* iv, 2, p. 516. Cf. ibid. v, 1, p. xxvii.

[2] Brugmans, p. 19. Also Van Hogendorp, an expert in this field and obliged to make as favourable an estimate as possible, thought (in 1815) that income out of foreign funds amounted before 1795 to 40 millions (Colenbrander (ed.), *Ontstaan der Grondwet*, ii. 237, 242). See also Metelerkamp, op. cit. i. 61 and cf. below, Ch. III, p. 133.

[3] H. T. Colenbrander, *Inlijving en opstand* (Amsterdam, 1913), p. 93.

pay in direct taxes.[1] Gogel's hopes for an increase of 18 million guilders in the tax yield were soon fulfilled; in 1807 it rose to 47 million. The rise was partly due to cuts in the cost of administration made possible by curtailing the number of officials. Yet the new system with its unmistakably democratic and radical intentions was only welcomed with any warmth by the capitalists of Holland, and it cannot be doubted that it was their collaboration which gave Gogel the opportunity to accomplish his reforms. For the system involved a great increase in the taxes payable by the middle and lower classes outside the province of Holland, which before 1806 was charged so disproportionally. It is not surprising that this act, drafted and put into operation by a radical, was regarded by many people as an attempt to help the rich *rentiers* and capitalists who had been exhausted by the torrent of extraordinary levies, and to spread the burden under which they were in danger of collapsing among less wealthy sections of the population.[2] The levies from 1795 to 1806 had in practice amounted to a heavy capital tax and one of the purposes of the new system was to render these unnecessary. Thus, under the direction of the dictator Schimmelpenninck who himself belonged to the party of the moderates, Gogel's democratic radicalism ultimately furthered the interests of the higher bourgeoisie in Holland.

Of the other reforms drafted between 1805 and the annexation by France in 1810, the Education Act of 1806 was by far the most important, for this was really put into operation and provided an excellent basis for building up a system of public primary schools. Most of the other plans were not carried out. Later in the century, when complete independence was restored, they were able to serve as preparatory studies for more fortunate reformers. The most remarkable aspect of the whole period was that provincial and urban autonomy, which survived for the most part until 1806 despite the unitarist constitution of 1798, was at last abolished, without any protests being raised against the destruction of these tenacious traditions. Federalism was dead. The Dutch finally surrendered

---

[1] H. T. Colenbrander, *Schimmelpenninck en Koning Lodewijk* (Amsterdam, 1911), pp. 47 ff.

[2] Cf. *Gedenkstukken* iv, 1, pp. 144, 288 ff.; v, 1, p. xxxi.

just as docilely as the Belgians to the practice of the unified state, which they had so long despised as despotic and alien, although it took some time before the still numerous civil servants abandoned the slow routine of the old order. Even in 1810, when Napoleon put an end to the experiment of a Dutch monarchy under his brother Louis and incorporated the country into France in order to complete the blockade of Britain, the Dutch remained quiet. They submitted without resistance and without enthusiasm; though seeing some advantages (for instance, French taxes were lower), they soon learned that the disadvantages were greater, only one-third of the interest on the national debt being paid. But the Napoleonic regime in the Netherlands was too short to affect permanently the structure of the state, the economy, or Dutch civilization; it was after all no more than an unpleasant incident endured with resignation. But certainly the Dutch did not resist the abolition of their independence any more vigorously than the Belgians had in 1795. On the contrary, unlike the Belgian conservatives who categorically refused in 1795 to play any part in the new government, many Dutch civil servants, who owed their career to the 1795 Revolution (for example, Gogel), were willing to keep their posts and to serve as French officials. A comparison between the circumstances of 1795 and 1810 is, however, meaningless. During the last years of his reign the Belgians also respected the Emperor: to mention but one instance, before 1813 they complied with conscription as readily as the Dutch; more readily, as a matter of fact, than the inhabitants of France proper.[1]

Napoleon's government in the Northern Netherlands did not solve any of the outstanding problems. It only exacerbated the economic problem. The whole revolutionary period, a period of almost uninterrupted war, was naturally unfavourable for the Dutch economy, and especially for Holland itself. The colonies, all of them gradually taken by Britain, no longer yielded profits to compensate for the losses incurred by the Dutch Government when, as an inevitable consequence of the new order, it nationalized the old East and West India Companies with their enormous debts. The war with Britain, into which the new

[1] Lanzac, ii. 305 ff.; J. Haak, 'Van inlijving tot bevrijding. Het Noorden van 1810–1814', *Algemene geschiedenis der Nederlanden*, ix (1956), 137–9.

Dutch Republic was drawn from the moment of its establishment, created disastrous difficulties for Dutch overseas trade; the number of ships entering ports in Holland fell from a yearly average of 4,180 in the period 1785-9 to 2,713 in 1797; after the recovery of the peace year 1802, it again fell steadily, especially after 1806, until in 1811 the total was 15.[1]

Trade did not decline in exactly the same proportion. Part of it chose other routes, carrying the goods which no longer arrived directly by sea over land from North-West Germany, for many years the centre of European overseas trade. With France too it was mainly by the overland routes that economic relations were maintained. Anglo-Dutch trade continued to be important, British goods being imported into the Northern Netherlands from North Germany and also directly by means of extensive and more or less officially tolerated smuggling. Only after the annexation did it virtually collapse. But in 1809, admittedly a peak year, approximately 5 per cent of total British exports went to Holland against approximately 10 per cent of total Dutch exports going to Britain. The value of the British exports to the Northern Netherlands totalled £2,458,000, the imports from the Northern Netherlands £1,722,000;[2] during the 1820s and even in the middle of the nineteenth century Anglo-Dutch economic relations did not rise much above this level.[3] Thus, in spite of the Continental System, the Northern Netherlands remained until 1810 a relatively important commercial power whose total imports and exports still averaged about one-third of those of Britain. Compared with the seventeenth-century situation when the roles were reversed (Dutch trade was then three times that of England), this evidently amounted to a disastrous decline but, in view of the size of the two states (the British population was after all more than six times that of the Republic), it indicated that Dutch trade was by no means negligible.[4] Commerce during the revolutionary period until 1810 may be estimated at about 80 per cent of what it had

[1] Brugmans, p. 24.

[2] Figures in F. Crouzet, *L'Économie britannique et le blocus continental (1806-1813)* (Paris, 1958), p. 447, to be compared with those in Brugmans, p. 30.

[3] Figures in R. Demoulin, *Guillaume Ier et la transformation économique des provinces belges (1815-1830)* (Liège, 1938), pp. 424-5 and Brugmans, p. 135.

[4] English figures in Crouzet, op. cit., pp. 883 ff., Dutch in Brugmans, p. 30.

been in the mid-eighteenth century:[1] in other words, the slow decline, which had started nearly a century earlier, continued after 1795 without taking a very dramatic turn. Only the annexation in 1810 caused a more or less complete interruption of trade, but it was so short lived as to be no more than a regrettable incident.

Yet a fairly general decline of the Dutch economy is unmistakable. High finance and industry suffered losses so heavy that the repercussions were felt by large sections of the population. Shipyards and related industries, factories making luxury products and those depending on the staple market—such as the sugar-refineries—or on materials imported from overseas, were in an evil plight which many of them did not survive. Foreign markets were gradually becoming unattainable, partly because harsh French protectionism broke off old relations—with Belgium in the first place—and partly because it was physically impossible to reach them over the closed seas. In complete contrast with the development in Belgium, which after 1795 was allowed to enter the huge French market, circumstances rendered the badly needed renovation of Dutch industry virtually impossible. There was no use for steam-engines in Dutch factories.[2] And though the small factories working for the local market suffered less from the isolation of the Northern Netherlands, they had no great economic or social importance, employing very few people.

The province of Holland especially showed the symptoms of a deeply wounded economy. However, it is not at all clear whether the revolutionary period itself constituted a rupture. Certainly the population of some big towns was decreasing (Amsterdam had 215,000 inhabitants in 1798, 201,500 in 1811) but this seems to have been true already before 1795. The number of paupers was unquestionably very large (in 1799 there were 80,000 people in Amsterdam receiving outdoor relief), but here again it remains difficult to determine whether the situation was actually deteriorating when compared with the pre-revolutionary period. It should also be

[1] Brugmans, p. 31.

[2] Brugmans (p. 47) states that only two steam-engines were used for industrial purposes. For the draining of polders, however, steam-engines were already used in 1787. According to Crouzet (pp. 227–8) the Dutch imported a steam-engine for this purpose in 1807 in spite of the Continental System.

taken into account that Holland possessed a great tradition of
charity and was able to spend much more money on relief
than was available in Belgium with its lower living standards
and its larger numbers of paupers. Experiments with certain
forms of unemployment relief work did not achieve economic
success but they provided a means of existence for some sections
of the proletariat. Although the impoverishment of the masses
is, accordingly, a fact established beyond any doubt by a vast
array of evidence, the question whether this must be explained
by the decline which the new regime inherited and by the
general European price rise, or by the special circumstances
of the revolutionary period, remains unanswered. It is equally
impossible to estimate how far the distress of the maritime
provinces was compensated for by the relative prosperity of
the agrarian provinces where agriculture was flourishing. But
one thing is certain: after fifteen difficult years the annexation
of 1810 brought the ultimate catastrophe. Only in 1812 did
the French open their home market to the Dutch. This was of
no avail, and after recovering its independence in 1813 Dutch
society was still saddled with an obsolescent economic system.
Though working with more flexibility than before 1795, as a
result of the newly won unity of the state, it still suffered from
the fundamental defects that had been crippling it for so long
and had been responsible for the decline from which in the
1780s the Patriots had in vain attempted to rescue the country.
The revolutionary period accelerated this decline; it did not
change its course. And it greatly increased the economic difficulties of the lower middle classes who in the view of contemporaries were hit just as severely as the workers.

4. *The Results*

Under the threat, the pressure, and the stimulus of the same
foreign influences the Northern Netherlands and Belgium lived
totally separate lives. Each turned away from the other. Only
after 1810 when Belgian officials, considered to be bilingual,
were preferred as prefects in the Northern Netherlands did the
two countries resume some of their contacts. Before that date
the North worked in isolation at its own individual experiments,
its population often reacting in a way which was the very

opposite of the Belgian response. The attitude of the Roman
Catholics was perhaps the most surprising example of this.
For though the plight of the Roman Catholic Church in
France and Belgium was well known in the Republic and some
Dutch priests issued very clear warnings against revolutionary
ideology,[1] the strong Catholic minorities in the North nevertheless backed the 1795 Revolution and in 1798 approved a
radical constitution derived from the French regime of 1795.
It was this French constitution that in 1798, the very year of the
radical victory in the North, served as a basis for the persecution of the Belgian clergy. The degree of Catholic support is
shown by the high percentage of affirmative votes in a homogeneously Catholic province like North-Brabant or in a province like Overijssel where the Catholics formed 34 per cent of
the population, lived in closed groups, and probably suffered
acute economic distress.[2] Dutch Catholicism was politically
radical because only radicalism was expected to accelerate
Catholic emancipation (after the fall of the radicals in June
1798 most of the Roman Catholics were indeed driven out of
government) and because there was no danger of anticlerical
excesses in the quiet Dutch society: Dutch Jacobinism, though
not in principle pro-Catholic, was certainly not anticlerical.

It is easy enough to explain the somewhat parochial character of the Dutch Revolution in terms of the exceptional Dutch
past. This enhanced the estrangement from Belgium, which
was in any case absorbed into an enormous continental
empire, in whose adventures it participated, and forced to
direct its attention towards Paris. The Revolution opened the
southern frontiers of Belgium; it closed all the Dutch frontiers.
But it can be argued that nationalist resistance to French
influence was the driving force of the Europe now emerging
and that the absence of it in Belgium was proof of its political
backwardness. This is possibly true. Yet one should immediately add that Dutch nationalism did not grow in depth or
extent either. It became a carefully cherished emotion stemming
from the 1780s, and even among the radicals gradually lost its
earlier fervour.

[1] Van der Heijden, *De dageraad van de emancipatie der Katholieken*, pp. 113 ff.
[2] Cf. B. H. Slicher van Bath, *Een samenleving onder spanning. Geschiedenis van het
platteland in Overijssel* (Assen, 1957), pp. 104 ff., 358 ff.

Only on one level were Belgian–Dutch relations maintained. From the first years after the catastrophe the few Dutch Orangists who sought refuge abroad and the small group of Belgian *émigrés*—mainly members of the Brabant States and the high clergy—discussed the possibility of resuming Van der Noot's project of a Dutch–Belgian confederation. The son of Stadtholder William V—the future King William I—was much in favour of these schemes, and in 1799, when the English landed in North-Holland, they seemed to be not unrealistic. But his father resisted them; at any rate he claimed with no less emphasis than the Belgian *émigrés* that the projected federal state must rest upon a strictly conservative basis and restore all the powers of the *ancien régime*. Amid the hubbub of political reform in the Northern as well as the Southern Netherlands all such plans were like echoes of the old-fashioned and miserably inadequate programmes of the 1780s.

III

THE GREAT NETHERLANDS
HYPOTHESIS, 1813–1830

1. *The Liberation of the Low Countries*

SOME weeks after the Battle of Leipzig small numbers of allied troops crossed the frontiers of the former Dutch Republic; on 12 November 1813 they captured Zwolle, on 15 November Groningen. The French commander-in-chief concentrated his forces in Utrecht and when on 15 November the garrison of 1,800 men left Amsterdam, popular disturbances against the occupying authorities immediately broke out. The sentry-boxes of the French customs officers went up in flames. But the new Amsterdam government formed by the city's notabilities on 16 November set itself the task of crushing the riots rather than fighting the French; and it did not yet break off relations with the foreign authorities. On 17 November, however, The Hague, left by the French officials fleeing southwards, rose in revolt and there both the masses of the population and the few notabilities constituting themselves their leaders called for independence under a Prince of Orange. It was not known in The Hague where he was to be found, so complete was the rupture between country and dynasty. The former Stadtholder William V had died in 1806. His son, now soon to be known as King William I (1772–1843), had survived the Revolution in various roles: as an admirer and as an enemy of Napoleon, acquiring possessions and losing them; but since April 1813 he had been in Britain soliciting Castlereagh's support for what, after Napoleon's Russian débâcle, he was once again able to consider a reasonable political objective: the restoration of his House in the Northern Netherlands. Messengers from The Hague discovered him in London. On 30 November he sailed for Scheveningen. Once in Holland he found not without amazement and some embarrassment that he was looked upon as the symbol and the repository of Dutch liberty and he was overloaded with power.

The Hague revolt was a risky adventure. But its leader, the Orangist and former Pensionary of Rotterdam, Gijsbert Karel van Hogendorp, now living in The Hague, was with all his solemn dignity a reckless rather than a brave man. He was, however, successful. The French, thoroughly demoralized in spite of having 9,000 men at their disposal, made no attempt to reconquer their lost positions, and thus allowed the revolt to take a calm and unexciting course. Its purpose was obvious. Van Hogendorp wanted to make the Allies press forward the liberation of the Northern Netherlands and recognize Dutch independence immediately and without discussion. This indeed they did. The initiative of The Hague was extremely well timed. It reinforced the international position of Holland, showing that, though the country had not actually contributed much to its own liberation, it was willing to make heroic sacrifices. Moreover, it allowed the nation, restored to its former sovereignty, to decide for itself upon its future form of government. Probably the Allies would have left that decision to the Dutch in any case for they could hardly refuse them the freedom which the French had granted in 1795. But thanks to Van Hogendorp's action the question was settled before it arose.

In the name of the Prince of Orange Van Hogendorp on 21 November formed a provisional General Government. An attempt of his on 18 November to strengthen the legal basis of the new regime failed because the frightened ex-regents, whom he invited to resume the sovereignty they had lost in 1795 and, as it was vaguely formulated, 'to proclaim the Prince', refused to collaborate. But on 1 December, immediately upon his arrival, the Prince was offered the sovereignty by the General Government. William accepted it, at the hands of the people as he declared in his proclamation of 2 December, and on the condition that a constitution guaranteed their freedom. The various proclamations issued in the course of these tense weeks made only one thing clear, namely the determination to establish a constitutional monarchy. There was no mention of any alternative. Yet the way in which this monarchy was created, its legal foundation, the question of whether the constitution was freely granted by the new sovereign or whether it was a condition imposed by the people on transferring their sovereignty, such and other awkward problems were left unsolved by the deliberately vague formulas chosen. Perhaps at that moment it did not matter much. Support for William I was universal enough to enable him to take up actual government himself on 6 December. Who could doubt that he submitted to the national will when accepting the sovereignty? The only possible doubt is whether there was a national will at all and whether Dutch unanimity was not due to weariness rather than conviction. In fact there was only one man with a coherent view of the future. He organized the revolt. He also determined the form of the new state.

Gijsbert Karel van Hogendorp could not live without his pen. From 1795 to 1813 he was out of office, and an attempt to establish himself as a business man ended in failure, but his life-long ambition was to play a grand role in politics. He was endowed with an acute intelligence, a great though somewhat disorderly erudition, and immense vanity, being both disturbed and fascinated by what was going on in himself. He did not yet belong to the Romantic movement. His introspection was cool and rationally controlled. It was due to his need to know and master himself that paper became the most faithful companion of this man thirsting after great deeds.[1] There was no thought that he did not write down, no idea that was not immediately noted. And when in December 1813 the Sovereign called a commission to draft a constitution, Van Hogendorp had one ready. He had been working on it since 1799. At first he had simply wanted to revise the Union of Utrecht of 1579; then he came to the conclusion that an entirely new constitution was needed. In 1812 he assembled his scattered notes and ideas into the 'Draught of a constitution for the monarchy of Holland', which after being slightly revised, partly in consultation with the Prince, was put before the commission. The 'Draught' is a quite exceptional document. It proposed a state which was to be the synthesis of all Dutch history as interpreted by the late eighteenth-century Orangists. In 1801 Van Hogendorp carefully

[1] For his character see the fine portrait by J. Romein, 'Gijsbert Karel van Hogendorp: lof der eerzucht', *Erflaters van onze beschaving* (4 vols., 5th edn., Amsterdam, 1946), iii. 207 ff.

noted down an important turn in the development of his ideas. He argued, as he had done frequently in his youth,[1] that the meaning of the monarchical principle in the Northern Netherlands was not only to guarantee a measure of unity but also to protect the 'common people' against the aristocracy. A written constitution, he thought in 1801, would give the Prince sufficient power to do what William V had failed to do—to fight the regents. Thus constitutional monarchy was to be the confirmation of the Stadtholderate's anti-aristocratic principle.[2] In the history of the Dutch state this episode in Van Hogendorp's meditations constitutes an essential link, connecting the partisan and materially incorrect interpretation of the Republic by the eighteenth-century Orangist propagandists with the nineteenth-century monarchy. At the same time, however, Van Hogendorp regarded the royal authority he wanted to establish as the continuation of the centralized Burgundian system preceding the sixteenth-century Revolt of the Netherlands.[3] In this way, despite its all too obvious defects, the 'Draught' became a grandiose attempt to transform the new start of 1813 into a synthesis of all the contradictions in the country's tumultuous history. It is true that much in it closely resembled the English system of government, but Van Hogendorp emphasized that this was not imitation but a result of the common origin of the old Nordic tradition.[4] Within that general framework the 'Draught' sought to be as purely national as possible.

The commission for drafting the fundamental law instituted in December 1813 consisted of seven members of the pre-revolutionary nobility, six ex-regents, some of them not ill disposed towards the new ideas, and two Patriots. It was mainly a conservative group. The 'Draught' was accepted without discussion as the basic document and it was considered article by article at innumerable meetings. The constitution drafted in this manner and presented to the Sovereign in

[1] See Ch. I, p. 41.
[2] Van Hogendorp, *Brieven en Gedenkschriften*, iii. 195 ff.
[3] Cf. his 'Discours sur l'histoire de la Patrie' (1810–13), *Brieven en Gedenkschriften*, iii. 317 ff. and his 'Aanmerkingen op de grondwet' published in Colenbrander (ed.), *Ontstaan der Grondwet*, i. 56 ff., 159. See also J. W. Smit, *Fruin en de partijen tijdens de Republiek* (Groningen, 1958), pp. 78 ff.
[4] *Ontstaan der Grondwet*, i. 57.

March 1814 differed radically on some points from Van Hogendorp's original, but it did not pretend to be more than a revision of this. The commission's labours in fact simply introduced more order into the draft, eliminated some rather old-fashioned ornaments, and appealed with greater emphasis for the reform of such bodies as the provincial States. It was no new system of its own with which the commission replaced Van Hogendorp's ideal; the composition of the commission was so heterogeneous and the political convictions of its members so vague that it was incapable of original thought. The majority wanted to establish a limited monarchy with a Parliament whose power would be considerably less than that of the British Parliament. It was the former revolutionaries in particular, the radicals of the French period, who persuaded the commission to adopt the generous definitions that enabled William I to govern in a more autocratic way.

The draft was full of reminiscences both of Burgundy and of the system of the Dutch Republic. Although the States General was no longer a meeting of deputations from the Provincial States but an assembly with independent authority representing the whole nation, it was still the Provincial States that appointed its members. And although the Provincial States were no longer sovereign, as they had been under the *ancien régime*, they were none the less given much greater executive responsibilities than the departmental administrations of the revolutionary epoch had possessed. In the whole pre-revolutionary history of the Netherlands, which was quite unlike the English and French experience, popular influence, in so far as there was any at all, could not make itself felt in the process of electing the central assembly. It could express itself only in provincial elections. So the representative principle was dependent on the way in which the Provincial States were elected and on how they were composed. The commission struggled for a long time with this problem,[1] but finally left the whole question for the Prince to decide. In this manner, completely uncertain about what it was going to create, the commission abandoned its responsibility for the most vital point of the fundamental law. As far as the competence of the States General was concerned, it followed Van Hogendorp. The assembly, consisting of one chamber only,

[1] Ibid. i. 157 ff.

was made strong enough to exercise some control over the government. But the principle of the political responsibility of Cabinet ministers was not introduced and the Prince was not granted the right to dissolve Parliament.

On 29 March 1814 this draft was accepted by 448 to 26 votes (most of those against were Catholics)[1] at a meeting in Amsterdam of notabilities, chosen by the provincial governors: 126 of those originally appointed did not take the trouble to travel to the capital and hardly anyone made use of the right to object to the selection, a right granted to all adult men in order to give the meeting a certain representative character. When the Prince was solemnly inaugurated by this assembly the next day, he could consider his position firmly established. This time even the right to appoint the members of the States General and Provincial States (they were to sit until 1817!) almost automatically fell to him, as nobody was able to contrive a more innocuous way of putting the government in train.

Before the commission started its discussions, Van Hogendorp stressed the need to design the constitution in such a way that it could if necessary also encompass Belgium,[2] and this indeed the members always bore in mind.[3] In 1789 the Prince and his mother seem to have felt some sympathy for the idea of federation put forward by Van der Noot.[4] Yet at the end of 1813 it was by no means certain whether William's old desire was at last to be realized. The Allies captured Brussels in February 1814 and the first thing they did was to appoint a government council of an outspoken counter-revolutionary character, all the members of which hoped that Belgium would revert to Austria.[5] Even the old Van der Noot now regarded Austrian rule as essential because he was convinced that only the *ancien régime* authorities were likely to re-establish the old order.[6] The policy of the Allies, who tried to stimulate anti-

[1] J. de Bosch Kemper, *De staatkundige geschiedenis van Nederland tot 1830. Letterkundige aanteekeningen* (Amsterdam, 1871), p. 471. Cf. *Gedenkstukken* vii, pp. 99–100.

[2] *Ontstaan der Grondwet*, i. 60, 62.

[3] Ibid. i. 121; ii. 58.

[4] *Gedenkstukken* ii, p. 892 n. 2.

[5] Ch. Terlinden, *Guillaume Ier, Roi des Pays-Bas, et l'Église catholique en Belgique, 1814–1830* (2 vols., Brussels, 1906), i. 5 ff.

[6] Cf. his pamphlet dated 6 June 1814, *Observations historiques, critiques et impartiales . . .*

French feeling, seemed for a time to suggest that the Emperor was still interested in his former territory. In 1789 and 1799 the old Estates had seriously wanted a federation with the North on a strictly conservative basis; all their pro-Austrian inclinations of 1814—the clergy were also toying with the idea—show how feebly developed their political thought still was. The possibility of national independence was never realistically considered. At the same time they showed perhaps a clearer insight into the development of their Northern neighbour, no longer the reactionary state of the late eighteenth century but a more modern construction. This current of thought, however, did not prevail. Agents of William I, immediately after the allied occupation of Belgium, busily tried to win adherence to the idea of associating the Northern and Southern Netherlands, and were welcomed not only by some industrialists and merchants (who were afraid of a restoration of Austrian rule which would force them to make restitution for the nationalized Church property) but also by liberal elements among the noblemen and notabilities of Brussels.[1] But there was no strong pro-Dutch party in 1814. Public opinion, which had resigned itself to French rule without supporting it, was not aware of any attractive alternative. Belgium's most vigorous minds were either absolutely reactionary (as, for example, part of the clergy) or pronounced liberals, that is anticlerical and pro-French. There was no basis for an initiative in Van Hogendorp's style. In a society with so little self-confidence only the right- or left-wing extremists held opinions which were at all definable.

Of course the international position of Belgium was weak. It was a conquered territory whose destiny the Allies were entitled to determine arbitrarily. But though there was no doubt that Belgium must be severed from France—this was a *conditio sine qua non* of British diplomacy—it took much time before Castlereagh finally acquired his allies' approval for the proposal to unite the Northern and Southern Netherlands into a strong bastion against France. In the Paris Treaty of 30 May 1814 the articles promising the Northern Netherlands territorial expansion were still vague. The question was decided only in June; on 21 June 1814 the Great Powers signed the protocol

[1] See *Gedenkstukken* vii, p. 547.

by which both the principle and the form of reunion were established. William I, whose minister Falck had written the eight articles of the protocol defining the nature of the 'amalgam', hesitated a month before signing it, as some of its financial clauses made him nervous. But then at last the question was settled. Ten days later, on 31 July 1814, William took over the government of the Southern Netherlands. And in August 1814 the problem of the Dutch colonies, about which many negotiations had already taken place, could also be solved. Britain from the very start of these negotiations had been quite ready to cede to the Northern Netherlands the greater part of the former Republic's overseas possessions, the future of which it could decide at will since it had from 1803 onwards conquered them in open war. On the condition that the new state would be strong enough to play a political role as its continental outpost, Britain retained only the Cape and in the West Indies Demerary, Essequibo, and Berbice. Though William was not entirely satisfied, because his ambition to expand his south-east territories was ultimately thwarted, he had in fact through British support succeeded in acquiring the government of a large state the foundations of which were mainly laid by himself.

The eight articles stipulated that North and South were to be equal parts of a unitary state. Belgium would be reasonably represented in the common States General but was charged with the same financial liabilities as the North. This excluded the possibility of a looser federal connection. The ideas of the Prince of Orange had indeed greatly developed since the late eighteenth century. The unitary tendency of the eight articles is one among many indications of the way in which he was departing from his father's traditions; and he was well aware of the radical, not to say Patriotic, character of his sovereignty which he owed ultimately, as his sister admitted in January 1814, to former Patriots who had elevated him in the face of Orangist opposition.[1] But it was the international situation that made the establishment of a completely united state imperative; it was the common opinion that a federal state could not accomplish the great task of serving as a bulwark against France. Historical influences were not decisive in the

[1] Ibid., pp. 471–2.

creation of this new kingdom. Naturally its advocates liked to
refer to Burgundian tradition but such reminiscences carried
little weight in international negotiations. The question of
linguistic unity was [touched upon only by the Germans;
Dutch diplomacy objected to this criterion which would have
caused the Allies to attribute Wallonia to France (and Alsace
to Germany).[1] It was only after the establishment of the United
Netherlands that the government sought to arouse a new
nationalism common to North and South on the basis of history
and language.

On 16 March 1815 William, who until then had been
provisionally called Sovereign Prince, took the title of King of
the Netherlands. Belgium had been greatly impressed by
Napoleon's adventure of the Hundred Days and the King
hoped, by his action, to stifle any possible doubt about the
future. In April a Dutch–Belgian commission began to consider the constitutional modifications made necessary by the
reunion. The eight articles set strict limits to their freedom of
action; even so the twelve Dutch members, most of whom had
also sat in the 1814 commission, were prepared to accept
fairly radical changes. The twelve Southern Netherlanders,
on the other hand, formed a very heterogeneous group which
could not agree on a common policy. A minority was ultra-
conservative, though it was recognized that in the present
circumstances the ideal of integrally restoring the *ancien régime*
was unattainable; there were also some more moderate conservatives and a number of anticlerical liberals. At least five
of them had in the past experienced moments of nationalist
exultation: they had participated in the anti-Austrian agitation of 1789 and 1790, one as a Vonckist, the others as adherents
of the conservative Estates. During the discussions neither the
Dutch nor the Belgians generally acted as representatives of
particular countries or particular political tendencies. It was
no more a confrontation of liberals and conservatives than it
was of North and South. Only when the strength of the
Northern and Southern representations in the States General
had to be determined did the Belgians present a united front:
they claimed the greater number of seats but even then the
reconciliatory attitude of two among them made possible the

[1] Ibid., pp. 532, 538.

compromise of equal representation—fifty-five seats for each group.

The problem of where to establish the capital—according to the 1814 constitution it was to be Amsterdam—was solved by not mentioning it at all and deciding that the government would alternately reside in The Hague and Brussels. On the question of the States General both the conservative and the liberal Belgians turned out to be strongly in favour of splitting it into two houses by creating a Chamber of Peers. Apparently the conservatives regarded this as the confirmation of aristocratic privilege, whereas the liberals wanted to follow as closely as possible the British system. Yet when it became clear that the Dutch were not opposed to bicameralism in itself but horrified by the prospect of hereditary peers, a concept alien to their bourgeois and republican past, it was decided to degrade the existing States General to the status of a Second Chamber upon which a First Chamber of notabilities appointed by the King was to be superimposed. Thus the Belgian initiative finally reinforced the position of the King. This was paradoxical, for the Belgians really wanted to reduce royal power; the pre-revolutionary state with its powerful Estates was the conservative ideal, the purely parliamentary system the liberal one. Yet the constitution of 1815 was more monarchical than its predecessor.

The draft agreed by the commission was intended to establish a moderate form of monarchy which would be a mean between the British system and that of the Central European restoration regimes. It was a synthesis of traditional but contradictory tendencies rather than a compromise between old and new. Neither the conservatives nor the liberals at first seemed dissatisfied with the result. Even the reactionary theorist from East-Flanders, the member of the drafting commission, J. J. Raepsaet, found much to admire in it;[1] his colleague in the commission, Count de Thiennes de Lombize, regarded it in the manner of Van Hogendorp as a modern summary of the rights and liberties of Charles V's still undivided Netherlands which in Belgium had survived until the French Revolution.[2] Even E. C. de Gerlache, who was to develop into a bitter enemy of

[1] *Ontstaan der Grondwet*, ii, pp. xxxix ff.
[2] Ibid. 87, 120, 306–8, 550; Terlinden, op. cit. i. 93.

William I's rule, recognized its merits.[1] Its weak spot was the organization of the Provincial States. No adequate solution was found to the problem of how to preserve the variety of pre-revolutionary institutions without jeopardizing the state's unitary character.

In comparison with other European states the electorate was by no means small. The two representative members of the Provincial States (in addition to the nobility, the countryside and the towns were represented, just as Vonck had wanted in 1789)[2] were indirectly elected by the urban administrations and in the countryside by electoral colleges. The number of Belgians entitled to vote was estimated at 60,000,[3] of Dutch at more than 80,000.[4] But the government exercised a strong influence both directly and indirectly upon the composition and the proceedings of the States. This weakness vitiated the whole system; the possibility of further development was greatly reduced by the frightened caution of the Dutch representatives in the provinces and the States General who shrank from attacking the royal government because, in their view, it was protecting the North against Belgian opposition.[5]

2. *William I's Political System*

A vein of triumphant pride runs through a long memorandum of January 1829 in which the Foreign Minister J. G. Verstolk van Soelen (1776–1845), a Dutchman, described the situation of the new state and tried to determine its place in the European community. Verstolk was an old-fashioned patriotic Hollander. According to the ironic British Ambassador Sir Charles Bagot he was 'perfectly convinced that the old flap-hatted fellows in black cloaks and ruffs who hang in the town halls of most of the cities in Holland were among the bravest and wisest men in history', and that Jacob Cats was superior

---

[1] É. C. de Gerlache, *Histoire du Royaume des Pays-Bas depuis 1814 jusqu'en 1830* (3 vols., 2nd edn., Brussels, 1842), i, p. xxiii.

[2] J. Gilissen, *Le Régime représentatif en Belgique depuis 1790* (Brussels, 1958), p. 62.

[3] Ibid., p. 65.

[4] *Gedenkstukken* x, 2, p. 540; J. de Bosch Kemper, *Staatkundige geschiedenis van Nederland na 1830* (5 vols., Amsterdam, 1873–82), v, *Letterkundige Aanteekeningen*, p. 269.

[5] Cf. W. F. Prins, 'De Restauratie', *500 jaren Staten-Generaal in de Nederlanden* (Assen, 1964), p. 180.

to John Milton, Meindert Hobbema to Claude Lorrain.[1] Yet in his view the United Netherlands of 1828 were more prosperous, more vigorous, and healthier than the old Republic, whose strength grew from Europe's weakness. In his erudite and very intelligent report[2] he emphatically advised the King to withdraw from the guardianship exercised by the five Restoration Powers and to pursue a policy of strict independence. The conservative members of the alliance were not prepared to concede the Netherlands its legitimate place among the Great Powers although its wealth, its economic development, its culture, and colonies made it the equal of Prussia.[3]

About the same time the famous Belgian statistician A. Quetelet was working on optimistic calculations which showed how fortunate the new state was in comparison to other countries. Mortality was low, primary education much better than in France, proportionally more newspapers were being published than anywhere else, civilization generally was more widely spread than even in Britain, charity was better provided than in any other country.[4] With some astonishment the foreign diplomats reported that the state whose disintegration they had prophesied with monotonous gloom in the years of crisis 1816, 1817, and 1818 and about which they had not been much more encouraging later,[5] seemed by 1825 to be firmly established.[6] Occasionally it showed its pretensions in a challenging style. When in 1826 the Austrian Government stated in a clumsy memorandum that Holland had been given to the House of Orange in 1813 by the four Allied Powers, the Netherlands Minister of Foreign Affairs vehemently protested and defended the essential independence of the state in an article which was printed together with the Austrian document and sold by the official Netherlands newspaper, the profits being intended for the heroes of the Greek War of Liberation.[7]

---

[1] *Gedenkstukken* ix, 1, p. 8.   [2] Ibid. 2, pp. 442–513.
[3] Ibid., p. 483.
[4] A. Quetelet, *Recherches sur la population, les naissances, les décès, les prisons, les dépôts de mendicité, etc., dans le Royaume des Pays-Bas* (Brussels, 1827), pp. 30, 62 ff. *Idem, Recherches statistiques sur le Royaume des Pays-Bas* (Brussels, 1829), pp. 9 ff. (less optimistic about mortality), 21 ff., 26, 29.
[5] See, e.g., *Gedenkstukken* viii, 1, p. 207.
[6] Ibid. 691; ix, 1, p. 215.   [7] Ibid. ix, 1, pp. ix, 251, 256.

During these most successful and contented years of the United Kingdom—they may be dated from 1825 to 1828— government seemed to settle down into a firm and dependable system, and it looked as though the initial hesitations whether it was possible to reconcile the interests of North and South had given way to the certainty that through cultural, economic, and social action on a grand scale the two countries could be absorbed into a single national unity. Such optimism was premature. Much of what the government had carefully built up it destroyed itself in the following years, and in 1830 a fairly weak shock sufficed to bring the whole edifice down. In fact the government never achieved a precisely defined system. The King was as abrupt, obstinate, and as slow to forgive slights as his father; he was more industrious and intelligent, but basically was like him a waverer, easily hurt, given to outbursts of sudden anger and cantankerous despair. His was the temperament of an autocrat with as little confidence in his advisers as in himself. He has been characterized as a belated enlightened despot[1]—already in 1817 the Austrian Ambassador at The Hague, Binder, an active counter-revolutionary theorist, had described his system of government as 'despotisme libéral'.[2] But one might just as well regard him as the prototype both of Louis Philippe and Napoleon III, a bourgeois-king and business man like the former, a would-be social reformer and nationalist like the latter. He never knew quite who or what he was; the role of king, which he took very seriously and loved to play, did not really suit him. When, realizing the failure of his work, he decided in 1840 to abdicate, he said: 'Ne veut-on plus de moi? On n'a qu'à le dire; je n'ai pas besoin d'eux';[3] and indeed, in this way, though in much more dramatic circumstances, Louis Philippe and Napoleon III also abandoned power, like sulking civil servants.

Sometimes the King fell into meditations about himself, his task, his lot. 'I was born a republican', he said in 1840;[4] 'I am, like my ancestors, a man of the people', he declared shortly after coming to the throne.[5] Though often taken for a liberal, an

---

[1] A. Goslinga, *Koning Willem I als verlicht despoot* (Baarn, 1918).
[2] *Gedenkstukken* viii, 1, p. 515.
[3] H. T. Colenbrander (ed.), 'Gesprekken met Koning Willem I', *Bijdragen en Mededeelingen van het Historisch Genootschap*, xxxi (Amsterdam, 1910), 292.
[4] Ibid., p. 288.   [5] *Gedenkstukken* vii, p. 658.

innovator, an heir to revolutionary Patriotism, he was always aware of the traditions of his House and of historical precedent. He compared his position to that of medieval counts and dukes who, when the States refused subsidies, governed without their help.[1] The Netherlands monarchy is a tempered monarchy, he said in 1819 when the States General objected to the proposed budget; it is not a constitutional one and the States General which reject a budget and thus prevent me from governing constitutionally destroy themselves because they owe their existence to the constitution, but not me, the Sovereign who is prior to it.[2] He was prone to bizarre irritations: 'I much preferred to have Holland alone', he exclaimed in 1823, angered by Belgian opposition but forgetting that the association of North and South was one of his major ambitions. 'I was a hundred times happier when I governed only the North'.[3] If the Dutch nation does not abandon me, he casually stated in 1833, 'I shall not abandon her either. In that case we must, if necessary, perish together. . . .'[4]

This difficult, lonely man was capable neither of delegating power nor of collaborating with other people. The decisions he was unable to take no one took on his behalf. He regarded his ministers as his servants; only in 1823 was a Cabinet council established, but it was not allowed to take decisions nor to consider any questions except those which the King himself put on the agenda. Consequently, the ministers, lacking almost all information about each other's tasks and purposes, acquired no insight into the wider aims of government. The King soon found himself surrounded by ministers of only mediocre quality. Gijsbert Karel von Hogendorp, who had chosen himself for major assignments but whose theatrical pride estranged both his subordinates and his Sovereign, was not maintained; nor was the more supple Falck. The most important of his ministers was and remained C. F. van Maanen (1769-1849), the Minister of Justice, who tried to mould

---

[1] Colenbrander, 'Gesprekken', p. 266. Cf. Finance Minister Beelaerts van Blokland's speech in the Second Chamber, 20 Dec. 1839: De Bosch Kemper, *Staatkundige geschiedenis* iii. 87.

[2] *Gedenkstukken* vii, 2, pp. 234-5. Cf. the King's meditations in 1829 in C. Gerretson (ed.), 'Gesprekken met den Koning 1826-1839', *Bijdragen en Mededeelingen van het Historisch Genootschap*, lvii (Utrecht, 1936), 157.

[3] *Gedenkstukken* viii, 1, p. 298. [4] Gerretson, op. cit., p. 207.

domestic policy. After 1795 he had, as a moderate unitarist, taken part in all the revolutionary governments. He was pre-eminently a jurist who did not much care which sovereign he was serving so long as he was able first to impose upon the pre-revolutionary chaos the order of general codes of law, and then to translate these French codes into a purely national system.[1] Lacking political intuition, his reaction to the hatred which the Belgian opposition showed for him was one of absolute disregard or short-sighted contempt; in the tense years preceding 1830 this former revolutionary shamelessly used in his official correspondence the most extravagant counter-revolutionary rhetoric.[2]

His Southern Netherlands enemies hated Van Maanen as the embodiment of Dutch Calvinism. But as a Remonstrant,[3] he was far from being a typical representative of Holland's idiosyncrasies. It is true that he felt little respect for the Belgians, that he expressed in 1814 his doubt about the wisdom of closely uniting North and South, forcibly defended the supremacy of Holland, and was as vehement in his opposition to Roman Catholic extremism as he was stubborn in his fight on behalf of the Dutch language. Yet this was not in the least characteristic of the general attitude of the North. On the contrary, such a cold zeal was radically alien to the traditions of Holland, where he was rather indifferently allowed to toil on among his papers. He rightly complained in 1820 that the attorneys and judges in Belgium were readier than their Northern colleagues, on his suggestion and contrary to the inclinations of William I, to take measures against the newspaper Press.[4] Yet it is due to him that the policies of the United Kingdom achieved some degree of consistency. In an altogether different field Johannes van den Bosch (1780–1844), who served the King in a variety of capacities, did much to lend the system a character of its own. He was not a bureaucrat like Van Maanen but a former soldier

---

[1] See the splendid portrait by C. Gerretson, 'De grote justicier Cornelis Felix van Maanen', *Gerretson de Strijdbare* (n.p., n.d.), pp. 73 ff.

[2] Cf., e.g., *Gedenkstukken* ix, 2, pp. 382, 532.

[3] In the seventeenth century Remonstrants or Dutch Arminians came into conflict with the orthodox Calvinists called Contra-Remonstrants. Eventually they formed a separate Church which was dogmatically more liberal than the Dutch Reformed Church.

[4] *Gedenkstukken* viii, 2, pp. 494, 501; cf. p. 530 and ix, 2, p. 543.

full of exuberant energy and endowed with a deep originality
which can only partly be explained by his lack of erudition;
to him the government owed some decisive innovations in the
organization of poor-relief and colonial policy.

The state which seemed to be firmly established in 1825
was meant to be a national state, a political and economic
unity kept together by the feeling of solidarity which the
common language, historical background, and civilization were
supposed to have engendered. This was certainly not yet the
case, but it seemed that the consciously nation-forming policies
of the government were beginning to show some results. These
policies sprang from different traditions and took various forms.
Perhaps they are best characterized as Burgundian and humanist, superficially coloured by the Enlightenment. They were
Burgundian because the sixteenth-century unity, the Netherlands of Charles V, was officially regarded as the prototype
of the new community. The King opened the first session of
the United Kingdom's States General by declaring that 'the
close and lasting unification of the Seventeen Provinces was
already three centuries earlier the aim of a Prince who, unlike
many of his ancestors and successors, had the privilege of
being born and educated in this country . . . Charles V was
convinced that in order to be happy and independent the
Netherlands ought not only to obey the same Sovereign but also
to be governed according to the same general laws'. The
King did not discuss the Revolt; he simply stated—and quite
rightly—that William the Silent, Charles V's pupil, also wanted
this close association of North and South, and the parting of
their ways he called a 'sad split'.[1] This set the key. In official
documents sixteenth-century usage was adopted. An inhabitant
of the new state was called a 'Netherlander'; in the French
translation this became 'un Belge' and the monarchy of the
Netherlands was referred to as 'la monarchie des Belges'. This
was quite in the humanist style, for the Latin word 'Belga' did
often mean in the sixteenth century and later an inhabitant of
the seventeen Netherlands, both the Southern and the Northern provinces. But it was in complete contradiction to ordinary practice, because for decades 'Belge' had come to indicate

[1] *Verslag der Handelingen van de Tweede Kamer der Staten-Generaal* (1815–16), ed
J. J. F. Noordziek (The Hague, 1862), p. 3.

the Southern Netherlander only.[1] In 1826, when the state was at its most prosperous, the government asked historians for ideas for writing a history, based upon original documents, of both parts of the Kingdom. In true Renaissance manner the scholar who submitted the best suggestion was to be appointed as official Historiographer of the Realm. The idea was not followed up. Yet here again the wish to provide the United Kingdom with a historical basis was apparent.

Unfortunately, the Great Netherlands movement both in the North and the South failed to come to terms with or derive support from the Romantic movement. Most Romantics were in fact opposed to the Great Netherlands idea. There were only a few notable exceptions. J. R. Thorbecke (1798–1872), who from 1820–4 studied in Germany, was deeply influenced by the conceptions of Eichhorn and Krause and it was as a Romantic that in 1825 he returned to the Netherlands and was appointed to the chair of political and diplomatic history in the University of Ghent, which William I had founded. But he did not have many pupils and though his reticence and stiff manners had not prevented him feeling at home in the world of German scholarship he remained an outsider in the rather different atmosphere of Ghent. And in many respects his romanticism was limited by his loyalty to the state of William I. Despite some minor misgivings he preferred to continue the custom of lecturing in Latin, thought it wise to keep the University closed to the working class,[2] and generally supported the King's school policies.[3] His friend G. Groen van Prinsterer (1801–76), a high civil servant in the King's Cabinet since 1827 and not without some influence on his policy, also discovered the Romantic movement. In 1822 he read the famous book by F. C. von Savigny, founder of the German school of historic law, *Vom Beruf unsrer Zeit für Gesetzgebung und Rechtswissenschaft*.[4] This book, which had been published in 1814, played a paradoxical role in the Netherlands. About the time when Groen was studying it, Guizot was making use of it in his seminal Sorbonne lectures (1820–2) on the origins of

[1] Elias, *Vlaamse gedachte* i. 184 ff.

[2] P. Frederick, *Thorbecke voor 1830* (The Hague, 1906), pp. 71, 73.

[3] Cf. L. W. G. Scholten, *Thorbecke en de vrijheid van onderwijs tot 1848* (Utrecht, 1928), pp. 68 ff.

[4] J. L. P. Brants, *Groen's geestelijke groei* (Amsterdam, 1951), pp. 27, 31, 41.

representative government in Europe,[1] and these were instrumental in forming a Romantic liberal-doctrinaire party in
Belgium which in its turn contributed to the 1830 Revolution.
In the case of Groen, however, Romanticism strengthened his
anti-liberal views. Like Thorbecke he too was limited by his
adherence to the policies of William I, as well as a certain lack
of discernment and a confusing eclecticism which allowed him
to accommodate many contradictory ideas at the same time.

It is more difficult to determine the place of the poet and
philosopher Johannes Kinker (1764–1845). From 1817 to
1830 he fought with perseverance and *esprit*, as the professor
of Dutch language and history in French-speaking Liège, for the
principle of Great Netherlands cultural unity. He was a Kan-
tian who in 1801 wrote a symbolic play in verse in which
Reason taught virtue and beauty to a humanity which for
centuries had been blinded by passion; and in 1823 he defended Kant's doctrine of law in a book which inspired Thorbecke to his first great work—the *Bedenkingen aangaande het
regt en den staat* of 1825.[2] But although he remained faithful to the
Enlightenment, his thought later moved in the direction of
Schelling's Romantic philosophy of identity.[3] This paradoxical
man, famous as a witty parodist of many minor and major
poets as well as of his own serious work, sent his friend Van
Maanen detailed reports on the backwardness and fanaticism
of the Belgian Roman Catholics,[4] and at the same time earned
the gratitude of his pupils at Liège, themselves educated in the
style of a stale French Classicism, by introducing them to the
great German Romantic authors.[5]

Romanticism was equally rare among the Belgian adherents
of the Great Netherlands ideal. Jan Frans Willems (1793–
1846) was the only full-blooded Romantic nationalist of his
time. His poems on historical themes, his studies in the history
of Flemish literature and philology, the eloquent panegyric,

[1] E. Kossmann, 'De doctrinairen tijdens de Restauratie', *Tijdschrift voor Geschiedenis*, lxiv (1951), 146, 165–6.

[2] W. J. A. J. Duynstee, *Geschiedenis van het natuurrecht en de wijsbegeerte van het
recht in Nederland* (Amsterdam, 1940), pp. 74 ff.

[3] F. Sassen, *Geschiedenis van de wijsbegeerte in Nederland tot het einde der negentiende
eeuw* (Amsterdam, 1959), p. 278.

[4] See e.g. *Gedenkstukken* ix, 2, p. 535.

[5] G. Charlier, *Le Mouvement romantique en Belgique*, i: *La Bataille romantique*
(Brussels, 1948), p. 397.

inspired by Herder, of fatherland and mother tongue—the sources of life and thought, the essential unity amid the endless diversification of the world—by which he opened his 'Treatise concerning Low Dutch Philology and Literature, especially in the Southern Provinces of the Netherlands' (1819, 1820-4), are all permeated with Romantic Great Netherlands nationalism. Willems was not isolated; a whole group of kindred spirits grew up around him. But these men were even younger than he and the romanticism of poets like K. L. Ledeganck (1805-47) and Pr. van Duyse (1804-59) only revealed itself as a movement after the Revolution of 1830 when it became a Flemish opposition to the supremacy of French in an independent Belgium. William I's advisers did not often seek help from among such people.

The official nationalism of the new state was humanist in character.[1] It was a nationalism of scholars, historians, and classicists, who sought their inspiration in the early sixteenth-century Burgundian state and in the precepts of the sixteenth-century educationalists and patriots. It was neither Romantic, liberal, nor bourgeois. Because it was so much in the spirit of the Renaissance it was entirely in keeping with the traditions of Dutch civilization. D. J. van Lennep and A. R. Falck were sophisticated representatives of this kind of humanistic nationalism. Van Lennep (1774-1853), from a patrician family in Amsterdam, was professor of belles-lettres and history from 1799 in the Athenaeum, a semi-academic institution in Amsterdam. He was an excellent classical scholar and experienced Latin poet. He was not greatly interested in politics; during the revolution he was glad to have a safe refuge in his professorship. In 1812 he made a journey to Ghent where he met several scholars,[2] and in 1813 he was full of enthusiasm for the idea of restoring Burgundian unity. His patriotism fed on classic examples.[3] And as a good humanist he devoted himself not only to the interests of university education but also to those of the popular primary school, one of his most cherished functions being his curatorship of schools for the poor in Amsterdam.[4]

---

[1] Cf. the brilliant pages of Picard, *Geschiedenis van de Vlaamsche Beweging* i. 105 ff.

[2] J. van Lennep, *Het leven van Mr Cornelis van Lennep en Mr David Jacob van Lennep* (4 vols., new edn., Amsterdam, 1865), iii. 314.

[3] Ibid. 118

[4] Ibid. 226.

His social feeling was classicist. In a speech of 1816 he demonstrated through an exposition of 'the measures of the Ancients concerning pauperism' that the poor could be given work and livelihood by making them reclaim waste land, an idea put into practice by the Society of Charity.[1] He looked upon the theatre, which the administration was hoping to use to spread the Dutch language and civilization in Belgium, as the 'popular entertainment under governmental supervision and patronage' that it had been in Greece and Rome.[2] His Belgian correspondents were in complete agreement; in their letters Burgundy and literature loom large. As a Great Netherlander from Ghent wrote to him in 1815 in his poor French, let us indeed speak about literature and history, for however vehement the conflicts between North and South they will always form our *point de réunion*.[3]

A. R. Falck (1777–1843) acknowledged Van Lennep's great influence on him. It was only after hearing his friend's account of his short summer journey to Ghent in 1812 that Falck finally adopted as his own the great idea of restoring the old Burgundian state, an idea which had first occurred to him in 1799 and which both men had often discussed.[4] Falck was an amiable and witty person, a sensitive nationalistic Hollander who enjoyed travelling and living abroad, an erudite connoisseur of contemporary, but above all classical, literature. His philosophy —he vaguely followed Kant—his educational ideals, and his tolerant attitude towards religion revealed his eighteenth-century background. In 1817 he married a Roman Catholic woman of a noble Walloon family; it is perhaps symbolic that the German adventurer Eckstein who introduced counter-revolutionary Romanticism into Belgium had been turned down by her in 1814.[5] Falck favoured the reunion of Holland and Belgium in the first place because he thought it would strengthen the North. In 1813 William I became very dependent on him, a young man who knew the country well and was

[1] Van Lennep, op. cit. iv. 76.
[2] Ibid. 150.
[3] Ibid. 47.
[4] *Brieven van A. R. Falck, 1795–1843* (2nd edn., The Hague, 1861), p. 208; *Gedenkschriften van A. R. Falck*, ed. H. T. Colenbrander (The Hague, 1913), pp. 136, 147. For Falck on Burgundy see Van Lennep, iii. 11.
[5] *Gedenkschriften van A. R. Falck*, p. 759.

good at making friends. From 1813 to 1818 his personality and his position as Secretary of State gave him control over the foreign and domestic policies of the Netherlands, and it was under his influence that the Prince found the courage to impress upon the Great Powers the merits of his ambitious plan to unite the two states.[1] But Falck was not inflexible. In 1830 he was one of the first to recognize that the experiment had failed; the dream, he realized, had evaporated and it was imperative that the Dutch should bring about a complete separation as soon as possible.[2] He was a cool classicist; for Thorbecke and Groen, affected by Romanticism, the Great Netherlands ideals were less eradicable and they abandoned them later and with greater reluctance.[3]

Although the humanist policy ended in failure it doubtless achieved some results. The decrees concerning the use of the Dutch language exercised a profound influence in Belgium. A cautious start was made by the royal decree of 1 October 1814 whereby Flemish was recognized as an official language but without making its use compulsory.[4] During the next five years the government, while trying to reinforce the position of Dutch in the South, abstained from compulsory measures. It was realized, for example, that the prohibition of French in the law courts of Flemish-speaking areas would be meaningless as long as the Belgian lawyers did not possess an adequate knowledge of Dutch. But on 15 September 1819 the government took a further step, deciding that after a transitional period use of the Dutch language would be compulsory in administration and in the law courts of Limburg, Antwerp, and Flanders. On the whole the difficulties encountered were not insurmountable. It soon became clear that there were enough Dutch-speaking judges in Belgium to allow the courts to co-operate reasonably well.[5] The plight of the advocates, especially the younger ones who had gone to school and university during the French period, was, however, often awkward.[6] But even among the advocates there was no immediate vehement reaction. In 1823 the state seemed to be gathering strength and the general

[1] Ibid., pp. 136, 143.   [2] Ibid., pp. 307, 309, 733.
[3] Cf. C. C. ter Haar, *Nederland en Vlaanderen* (Santpoort, 1933), pp. 13–19.
[4] A. de Jonghe, *De taalpolitiek van Koning Willem I in de Zuidelijke Nederlanden (1814–1830). De genesis der taalbesluiten en hun toepassing* (Brussels, 1943), p. 48.
[5] Ibid., pp. 148 ff.   [6] Ibid., pp. 158 ff.

policies of the government were not unpopular with the Belgian liberals who included a significant number of barristers.

The most obvious way to 'Dutchify' Belgium was through the schools. The task of the government had been made easier by Napoleon's neglect of primary education. For in its humanist zeal and in accordance with Holland's traditions the government was interested above all in the primary schools. It was in a position to make virtually a fresh start. But it took its time. Only in 1821 did it make the Dutch law of 1806 more or less applicable in the Southern provinces, and then it did not attempt to put all its articles into effect. There can be no doubt about the relative success of this building-up of a primary school system. Illiteracy slowly decreased. Whereas in the French period 60 per cent of the Belgian population may have been illiterate or, at any rate, unable to write, the fifteen years of William I's rule brought the percentage down to 50.[1] In 1825 89 out of 1,000 inhabitants in Belgium went to school; in the North where the situation was particularly good, 123 out of 1,000.[2] With pride the government pointed out in 1820 what it had already achieved in Hainaut, where the primary schools were attended by twice as many pupils as in 1817.[3] Not only was the scale of education greatly expanded but thanks to the careful training of teachers it was also possible to raise its standard. As far as the linguistic issue was concerned the results were indeed of great importance. Primary school teaching in the Flemish areas was entirely in Dutch; French had lost its supremacy.[4]

There was some resistance in Belgium to the governmental school system but no sharp and effective opposition. The clergy watched uneasily the development of this new form of education, which in principle was neutral but in fact by no means irreligious. The municipalities were at times reluctant to bear the financial burden the system entailed. But the traditional indifference of the South towards the primary school was so deep

[1] A. Sluys, *Geschiedenis van het onderwijs in de drie graden in België tijdens de Fransche overheersching en onder de regeering van Willem I* (Ghent, 1912), pp. 394 ff.

[2] C. de Keverberg, *Du Royaume des Pays-Bas sous le rapport de son régime, de son développement et de sa crise actuelle* (2 parts in 3 vols., The Hague, 1834), ii. 128–9.

[3] *Handelingen van de Tweede Kamer* (1820–1), *Bijlagen*, pp. 824–5.

[4] De Jonghe, op. cit., p. 183. Cf. R. Demoulin, 'Noord en Zuid onder Willem I', *Algemene geschiedenis der Nederlanden*, ix (1956), 284, who agrees with this view.

that in this field the government had its way without much trouble. Moreover, it acted very cautiously, and did not in practice try to prevent the schools from becoming Roman Catholic.[1] Secondary education was a more serious problem. But it is characteristic of Dutch society that the government, following in this respect the traditions of Holland, was less interested in secondary than in popular education, whereas in Belgium with its more highly developed bourgeoisie it was the secondary schools that became the object of profound dispute. This contrast occurs again and again in the course of the nineteenth century. In the next decades the religious and political battle over the schools in the Northern Netherlands concerned mainly the primary schools; in Belgium mainly secondary education. In the North it was not the education of the numerically small and exclusive higher classes that caused the trouble but the education of the politically and culturally mute masses; in the South the character of the growing élite was at stake. Consequently, it came as a complete surprise to the government when its policy on secondary education met with such opposition. But even so it could claim some important achievements. The grammar schools (*athenaea*) which it founded were very well attended, much better in fact than their Northern equivalents, the *gymnasia*. The number of pupils in the South rose from 2,400 in 1818 to 5,498 in 1825, but dropped to 4,791 in 1828. In the North the figure grew from 1,000 in 1818 to 1,550 in 1825. In other words, whereas in 1825 8·9 per cent of the Belgian population attended a primary school and 0·15 per cent an *athenaeum*, in the Northern Netherlands 12·27 per cent went to a primary school but only 0·067 per cent to a *gymnasium*.[2]

The Belgian *athenaea* and boarding schools were influenced by a Voltairian attitude; anticlericalism, scepticism, religious indifference created an atmosphere that the clergy could only

[1] M. de Vroede, 'Het openbaar lager onderwijs in België onder Koning Willem I: de katholieke school', *Bijdragen en Mededelingen van het Historisch Genootschap*, lxxviii (1964), 38 ff.

[2] Calculated from Keverberg, op. cit. i. 197. Cf. *Handelingen van de Tweede Kamer* (1829–30), *Bijlagen*, p. 787. Of course there were also private schools offering a form of secondary education. In the Northern Netherlands they were called 'French schools'. As they were expensive only the well-to-do attended them. The number of pupils is unknown but probably did not exceed a few thousand. Teaching was often rather poor. In these schools the Dutch entrepreneurs were brought up.

regard as repulsive.[1] The government was aware of this but, accustomed in the North to an easy compromise between enlightened ideals and a not very dogmatic Protestantism, it underrated the vehemence of the Southern conflicts and got hopelessly entangled in them. Immediately after 1815 it was struck by the growth of so-called *petits séminaires*, institutions for secondary education founded by the bishops which were originally intended for future priests but were also attended by boys without clerical ambitions.[2] As soon as the government felt strong enough it launched a frontal attack on these schools, much to the delight of the Belgian liberals. Its arguments and its motives were many sided. To start with it pointed out that under the *ancien régime* the bishops had never possessed the right to establish such schools, which had developed only in the nineteenth century and were thus innovations.[3] This line of attack was important. Until 1825, when the government closed the *petits séminaires*, the clergy always insisted on its ancient rights and sought to restore its traditional position. During the struggle over the seminaries it became apparent that the bishops were in fact pretending to something more than, or at least something different from, the privileges they had had under the *ancien régime*. As a consequence they radically altered their tactics, though without altering their aims. After 1825 they no longer claimed their traditional powers; they asked for freedom in the new state. Such a fresh approach was all the more necessary because it was difficult to deny the correctness of the government's second argument: it was indeed true that the clergy withdrew from governmental supervision an important section of the school system without being prepared to give any guarantee as to the character and standard of their teaching. The debate now centred on whether the constitution of 1815 allowed such behaviour, for it was clear that the Austrian regime before 1792 had not. In other words, the clergy who had previously refused to recognize the constitution now entered into a discussion of its interpretation.

Yet the motives of the government were equivocal. As far as

[1] This is Van Ghert's view: *Gedenkstukken* viii, 2, p. 621; viii, 3, p. 263.

[2] Cf. e.g. *Gedenkstukken* viii, 3, pp. 253–4.

[3] Ibid. 2, p. 413; viii, 3, pp. 174–5; Terlinden i. 358. Cf. J. de Bosch Kemper, *De staatkundige geschiedenis van Nederland tot 1830* (Amsterdam, 1868), pp. 618 ff., 623–7.

the schools themselves were concerned it is understandable that the government, in its attempt to create a general and efficient system of education, should feel unable to accept this encroachment upon its responsibility. However, there were also genuine religious issues involved that raised the problem to an altogether different level. But William I's religious policy was particularly confusing and paradoxical. He himself was deeply influenced by late eighteenth-century German theories about the relations of Church and State that assured the latter wide powers.[1] Some of his ministers agreed, others held different views. Influential Roman Catholics among them thought that it was the state's duty to introduce at least some 'enlightenment' into the Belgian Church. Even Hegel's doctrines played a part.[2] The situation was not improved by the King's consultations with Roman Catholic advisers of strictly anticlerical persuasion who were eager to enlist the services of the liberals in their struggle against what they regarded as the backward Belgian clergy. In this way the government became a party in discussions which were really outside its province. It should therefore be emphasized that the conflict between Church and State which the latter could not avoid being involved in was, notwithstanding occasional suggestions to the contrary by the Belgian clergy, in no sense a conflict between the Protestant North and the Roman Catholic South. Internal Belgian conflicts lay at the bottom of it. It was a struggle between Belgian anticlerical liberalism on the one hand and Belgian ultramontanism on the other, complicated by theological disputes within the Church.

By royal decree of 14 June 1825 all 'Latin schools' founded without royal permission were closed. This meant the end of the *petits séminaires* and other boarding-schools supervised by the clergy. Some thousands of boys suffered from this measure.[3] It would be difficult to deny that the standard of teaching in most of these institutions was very poor;[4] not only its enemies[5]

---

[1] For the views which William I picked up when ruling Fulda cf. J. A. Bornewasser, *Kirche und Staat in Fulda unter Wilhelm Friedrich von Oranien 1802–1806* (Fulda, 1956), pp. 133 ff.

[2] L. J. Rogier, *Het tijdschrift 'Katholikon' 1827–1830* (Amsterdam, 1957), pp. 11 ff., 32 ff.   [3] Terlinden, i. 422 n. 2.

[4] See, e.g. A. F. Manning, *De betekenis van C. R. A. van Bommel voor de Noordelijke Nederlanden* (Utrecht, 1956), p. 38.

[5] *Gedenkstukken* viii, 2, p. 218 and *passim*.

but also priests as well as Roman Catholic laymen[1] knew that the Belgian and above all the Flemish clergy, mainly recruited from the peasantry, was not conspicuous for its erudition. The government now made it compulsory for the bishops to admit to their *grands séminaires*, where they trained students for the priesthood, only pupils who had completed their secondary education at a state school or a school recognized by the state, and taken a two-year course at the Collegium Philosophicum, established in 1825 at Louvain.

The archbishop of Mechlin was invited to act as supervisor of this Collegium, which was to be linked to the University, and to put forward names of suitable candidates for the new chairs. He not unnaturally refused the invitation and the whole Belgian clergy followed his example. Thus the government was forced to look for professors abroad. Some were found in Germany; the institution founded for the purpose of educating the Belgian clergy in a more 'enlightened' way was decried as anti-Roman Catholic, pagan, and even Protestant. In the ensuing conflict the government's position was extremely weak. The number of pupils remained minimal. The Belgian bishops refused to admit to their *grands séminaires* former students of the Collegium; and although it gave some consolation to the wounded pride of the government that the bishops of Trier and Cologne and even the papal seminary at Rome were willing to provide them with the proper theological instruction,[2] this made practically no impact on Roman Catholic Belgium, still parochial in its views. Already in 1825 and 1826 it was quite clear that the government's initiative was going to fail. Soon the King was ready to acknowledge his defeat. In June 1829 he declared that study at the Collegium Philosophicum was no longer compulsory; in January 1830 the whole institution, for many months entirely empty, was closed down. In May the government repealed all restrictions on secondary and higher education but preserved, characteristically, the precise regulations relating to the primary schools.[3]

---

[1] Terlinden ii. 221 n. 3, 238-9.

[2] J. A. Bornewasser, 'Duitse bemoeienissen met de strijd om het Collegium Philosophicum 1827-1830', *Bijdragen voor de Geschiedenis der Nederlanden*, xiv (1960), 279 ff.

[3] J. H. J. M. Witlox, *De Katholieke Staatspartij in haar oorsprong en ontwikkeling geschetst*, i ('s-Hertogenbosch, 1919), pp. 250 ff. See also S. Stokman, O.F.M., *De*

Governmental policy on higher education was equally humanist. The six universities of the Netherlands were tied to the use of Latin, thus becoming unique Renaissance bulwarks in Europe, and to a syllabus carefully purged of all modern subjects. The system was grafted upon French Classicism; it lacked the spirit of adventure and the vitality of the German universities.[1] Even so it did not work too badly. It is, incidentally, typical of the social differences between North and South that in the Northern Netherlands almost all the pupils of the grammar schools, members of the élite, completed their education at a university, whereas in Belgium less than one-third did so. Yet neither in the North nor in the South did the universities play an important part in the cultural life of the nation. Shortly before 1830 a whiff of liberal political Romanticism from France reached the undergraduates in anti-Dutch Liège; shortly after 1830 it reached the North where it inspired the students to their anti-Belgian crusade. Generally speaking, the government's educational programme, although not properly carried through, was well designed and successful. But it utterly failed as a means of forming a new unitary nation. Owing to clumsy mistakes and embarrassing misunderstandings it contributed in the end to the estrangement between the two parts of the country.

William I's economic policies had more positive effects. The state's cohesion seemed to be linked directly to the level of prosperity. Thus the unquestionable political *malaise* of the early 1820s resulted from unsatisfactory economic conditions imputed by the Belgians to the King's pro-Dutch policy and by the Dutch to his pro-Belgian policy. The Kingdom's heyday was a period of economic expansion, which seemed, however, to have passed its peak by 1829 or 1830. But this phenomenon does not so much indicate the primary importance of economic issues as the slackness of political and cultural life. North and South looked like being irremediably torn apart by their desperate attempts to defend their own supposedly contrary

Religieuzen en de onderwijspolitiek der regeering in het Vereenigd Koninkrijk der Nederlanden (1814–1830) (The Hague, 1935), pp. 289 ff.

[1] J. Huizinga, *Geschiedenis der Universiteit gedurende de derde eeuw van haar bestaan, 1814–1914 (Academia Groningana, 1614–1914)*, *Verzamelde Werken*, viii (Haarlem, 1951), pp. 56 ff.

interests. Yet there was no objective reason for this. Both countries were mainly agrarian; both could very well develop without injuring the other. In about 1825 43 per cent of the Kingdom's total exports consisted of agrarian, 34 per cent of industrial products.[1] The towns were growing only slowly. In 1815 23·3 per cent of the Belgian population were living in towns, in 1830 24·5 per cent. The development in the Northern Netherlands was just as insignificant, with the percentage rising from 37·5 in 1815 to 39·3 in 1830. On the whole the population figures indicate (if they indicate anything at all) a certain euphoria. The Belgian figure rose from 3,380,000 to almost 4,070,000, that is by 20 per cent, an increase more rapid than in the preceding decade and much more rapid than in the decade to come. The Dutch population also grew from about two millions to 2,600,000 in 1829, that is—if these figures are correct—by no less than 30 per cent.[2] Even in comparison with Britain this was a considerable expansion.

The Dutch probably still maintained their economic lead over Belgium although reliable statistical material is nonexistent. At any rate, pauperism was less widespread in the North. In 1817 11 per cent of the Dutch as against 12 per cent of the Belgian population were receiving public assistance but by 1828 the figures were 9 per cent and 14 per cent respectively.[3] Moreover, Northern poor-relief was better provided with funds,[4] though comparisons in this field are difficult because of the higher Dutch price level. Proportionally, and during

---

[1] H. J. M. Witlox, *Schets van de ontwikkeling van welvaart en bedrijvigheid in het Verenigd Koninkrijk der Nederlanden* (Nijmegen, 1956), p. 104.

[2] See the figures in Demoulin, *Transformation économique*, p. 400; Lewinski, *Évolution industrielle*, p. 58; and Brugmans, pp. 188–9. The Dutch figure covers the territory of the Northern Netherlands as constituted in 1839, the Belgian includes the whole of Limburg and Luxemburg, from 1815 to 1830 regarded as parts of the Southern provinces. Thus the total population of the Kingdom was almost 200,000 (that is, the population of the part of Limburg alloted in 1839 to the Northern Netherlands) less than in the total given above.

[3] Calculated from material in Demoulin, *Transformation économique*, p. 420. See also De Bosch Kemper, *Armoede*, Table I ff. All these figures were taken from the governmental statistics later published by Noordziek in the annexes to the *Handelingen*. They are difficult to study because no distinction was made between the various categories of the destitute but provide all the same interesting data.

[4] Cf. e.g. the table in *Handelingen* (1817–1818), *Bijlagen*, p. 378 and ibid. (1829–1830), *Bijlagen*, pp. 850–1. See also H. R. C. Wright, *Free Trade and Protection in the Netherlands 1816–1830* (Cambridge, 1955), pp. 51, 93.

most of the period absolutely as well, the Dutch paid more in direct and indirect taxes than the inhabitants of the Southern provinces. Roughly the annual *per capita* contribution of the Belgians amounted to about 11 guilders, that of the Dutch to 17.[1] By comparison with the French period this represented for both parts of the country a reduction of fiscal charges (even without taking into account the fall of prices): from over 25 to 22 francs in the South, from about 40 to about 34 francs in the North. The licence fee—that is, the French *impôt de la patente* levied on all kinds of businesses and professions—might perhaps have served as a basis for comparing the two economies if it had been correctly assessed. It was, however, very badly defined. Even so it is interesting that of the $2\frac{1}{2}$ million guilders which it produced in the early 1820s more than half was paid by the Dutch.[2]

It must have been a deep disappointment to the Belgians that after 1815 they did not rapidly surpass the North. They had expected to be able to and they were not alone in thinking so. The Flemish jurist and historian J. J. Raepsaet (1750–1832), a former collaborator of Van der Noot, a member of the committee of 1815 for drafting the constitution, and an ultra-conservative member of the ecclesiastical party, thought that the reunion of North and South would bring Belgium the greater profits. Already strong thanks to its incomparable agriculture and its developing industry it would, in his opinion, not be difficult for the South to re-establish the centre of trade where it belonged: in Bruges and Antwerp. In the past Amsterdam had seen its wealth grow like weeds from Belgium's ruins; now the Northern Netherlands would have to confine itself to coastal trade in the service of the South.[3] The spirit of the Belgians was fiercer and more obstinate than that of the refined and submissive Hollanders whose energies had been exhausted for many centuries.[4] The liberals in Belgium did not use historical but rather statistical and psychological arguments.

---

[1] Cf. Keverberg, i. 366 ff.

[2] *Handelingen van de Tweede Kamer* (1821–2), *Bijlagen*, p. 112; ibid. (1822–3), ii, *Aanhangsel*, p. 12.

[3] J. J. Raepsaet, *Œuvres complètes* (6 vols., Mons, 1838–40), vi. 15 ff. Some years before Raepsaet's Dutch friend Van de Spiegel, the former Grand Pensionary of Holland, had put forward similar arguments. Cf. *Gedenkstukken* iii, p. 1053 (1799).

[4] Raepsaet, op. cit. vi. 200.

According to the fantastic arithmetic of Dotrenge in 1815 at a meeting of the constitutional commission, the South was twice as rich and powerful as the North.[1] The North, wealthy and saturated, stagnated, said one of his colleagues; Belgium, however, was rapidly growing and to Belgium belonged the future.[2] There was little in the way of counter-arguments that the Dutch felt inclined to raise against such excited reasoning; on the contrary, they encouraged it with the purpose of rendering the reunion more attractive.[3] But they probably actually did think that Belgium was likely to surpass the Northern Netherlands.[4] Foreign observers had the same impression. The French Ambassador at The Hague predicted in 1816 that it would be impossible to bring about a reconciliation between the old, immovable, conservative North and the young, versatile, vigorous Belgium which was certain to acquire supremacy.[5]

It is not difficult to understand why Belgium's place in the United Netherlands was so much overrated. For several decades the Northern Netherlands had been haunted by the impression that they were continuously declining, whereas since at least 1790 many in Belgium had taken pride in their progress and dreamt of future power. The North was still looking backwards to its great past. Even men like Gogel, the former radical who had already under Schimmelpenninck's short rule identified himself with the interest of Holland, or G. K. van Hogendorp, were under the illusion that the days of Holland's vigour could be recovered by restoring freedom of trade. Yet many in the Netherlands realized that times had changed and that the staple market had become an anachronism. In 1824 it was calculated that only one-tenth of the imported products were afterwards exported—in the eighteenth century it had been two-thirds.[6] No one, however, seemed to be able to think of an alternative solution and thus the Dutch lived on, not displeased with themselves despite their lamenta-

---

[1] *Ontstaan der Grondwet*, ii. 334.

[2] Ibid. 236, 238, 242.   [3] e.g. *Gedenkstukken* vii, p. xxiii.

[4] William I himself predicted this in a conversation with the British chargé d'affaires in August 1815: *Gedenkstukken* vii, p. 264. A similar observation dating from 1829: ibid. ix, 2, pp. 912 ff.

[5] Ibid. viii, 1, p. 220; cf. p. 252.

[6] W. M. F. Mansvelt, *Geschiedenis van de Nederlandsche Handel-Maatschappij* (2 vols., Haarlem, 1924–6), i. 34.

tions and wistful dreams of being free again to work and think according to the old routines of early capitalism. Of course, trade recovered slightly after 1813. But in the late 1820s the number of ships entering Dutch ports was not much higher than in the late 1780s.[1] No important commercial expansion took place.[2] The North German towns maintained the supremacy they had acquired in the Napoleonic period, and although Amsterdam's link with the Zuiderzee was improved by the digging of the North Holland Canal (1824) the port did not recover its former prosperity. Dutch industry continued to be on a small scale, often employing fewer than ten workmen in its factories, although efforts were made by G. M. Roentgen in Rotterdam and Paul van Vlissingen in Amsterdam to lay the basis for big capitalistic factories—the shipyards and engineering works of Feijenoord (1823) and Werkspoor (1825). Steam-engines were little used in Dutch factories; in 1837 there were only 72 of them with a total of 1,120 horsepower.[3] Dutch capitalists were still reluctant to invest in national industry. In spite of governmental attempts to make it impossible they preferred to place their money in foreign funds producing, it was estimated, just as much interest as in the period from 1795 to 1813, about 27 million guilders per annum.[4]

Of course conditions were not altogether different in Belgium. There, too, small enterprises were predominant, and modern capitalism was still an isolated phenomenon. But pauperism affected the agrarian provinces more than the towns in which industry had been developing, whereas in the North it was worse in the economically stagnating urban centres. The fall in the prices of agrarian products to their pre-war level was not serious enough to cause a general crisis but it prevented agricultural expansion.[5] Moreover, agriculture was

[1] Cf. the tables in Wright, op. cit., p. 165 and Brugmans, *Paardenkracht*, p. 24 and see also De Vries, *Achteruitgang*, p. 29.

[2] See Wright's calculations, pp. 30–1.

[3] I. J. Brugmans, *De arbeidende klasse in Nederland in de 19e eeuw (1813–1870)* (4th edn., Utrecht, 1959), p. 52.

[4] *Gedenkstukken* ix, 2, p. 475. According to Witlox (*Schets*, p. 174), Van Hogendorp estimated foreign investments at one milliard guilders. In 1825 British foreign investments were of the same size. They totalled about £100 million (J. D. Chambers, *The Workshop of the World. British economic history from 1820 to 1880*. London, 1961, p. 89).

[5] Slicher van Bath, *Agrarische geschiedenis*, pp. 250 ff.; Witlox, *Schets*, pp. 143 ff.

indifferently treated by the government whose tariff policy was designed to help industry by low grain prices and to please the Amsterdam market by low import duties. Yet in 1815 and after Belgian industry looked like being the more tragic victim. As a result of falling prices and excessive, financially irresponsible expansion it had been fighting against formidable difficulties since 1810. When English products which were both better and cheaper appeared on the market in 1814 it seemed hardly possible to avert a catastrophe. The bad harvests of 1816 and 1817 and the rise in grain prices that followed worsened the economic crisis and ruined the industrial towns. Disturbances directed against the government because it allowed speculation in grain and because Amsterdam prospered as it had done so often in times of dearth threatened to undermine the new state.[1] Only after 1820 did the depression slowly recede—thanks to the recovery of the British economy. Then it became apparent that in the new circumstances it was possible for Belgium to prosper as well, to continue along the lines of progressive development that had begun to reveal themselves at the end of the eighteenth century.

Production in the collieries of Hainaut and Liège doubled between 1819 and 1829. Thanks to the steam-engine they began to grow into big industries, though by British standards they remained technically backward.[2] The metal industry, although still more backward, also expanded.[3] Cloth manufacture, largely concentrated at Verviers, grew at a quieter pace, the entrepreneurs being able to develop the innovations introduced during the French occupation and gradually to increase production. No longer admitted to the French market, they found sufficient customers in Germany and Italy, in North and South America. Notwithstanding its greatly increased production (rising from 693,310 tons in 1810 to 1,719,600 in 1826) and its modern equipment (10 steam-engines in 1820, 26 in 1826, and 40 in 1830), the Flemish cotton industry suffered from much more violent shocks and did not achieve lasting stability.[4] Thus it is clear that industrial expansion which had

---

[1] Witlox, *Schets*, pp. 65 ff.   [2] Demoulin, op. cit., pp. 300 ff.
[3] Ibid., pp. 316 ff.
[4] Ibid., pp. 322 ff. The total number of steam-engines in Belgium about 1830 was estimated at 400 with 12,000 horsepower.

been going on for many years continued slowly but not at a
pace rapid enough to bring about profound social changes.
Nor did Belgian commercial expansion, considerable though
it was, have any marked social effect. Antwerp, however, certainly took advantage of the new circumstances. In 1828 the
port was equal in importance to Rotterdam, and half as
big as Amsterdam,[1] a fact which seemed to prove the prophets
of 1815 correct. Unhampered, as Amsterdam was, by antiquated methods and the restrictive practices of long-established
vested interests and free from the obsession that the staple
market could and should be restored, Antwerp was able to
devote itself to the real tasks of the future and organize an
efficient and cheap transit trade.[2] Moreover, as a port for
exporting industrial products it had a function that no Dutch
town was called upon to fulfil. But above all, it once again
became a centre of trade in colonial products, as it had been
before the rise of Amsterdam in the early seventeenth century.[3]

The King, always interested in economic matters, tried
through his personal initiative to further economic expansion
generally and the economic amalgamation of both parts of his
realm in particular. But in this field also it was only after
much hesitation that he decided upon a definite course. The
first seven years of his reign were taken up with skirmishes over
tariff policy, which the compromise of 1822, levying an average
import duty of 10 per cent, finally succeeded in ending. Shortly
afterwards the economy of the Kingdom began to pick up,
partly as a result of British activities following upon the recognition of the South American states. William I was not slow
to see his chance. His aims were simple and straightforward
enough. Industrial expansion should be accelerated by generous credits. Commerce could only benefit from this, and the
King thought that it was possible to reconcile the interests of
Southern industry and Northern trade by means of a great
common effort; the inhabitants of his realm should send their
own manufactures, mainly textiles, in their own ships to the
colonies, whence they would return bearing valuable colonial

[1] Ibid., p. 337.
[2] See the opinion of the Amsterdam merchants in 1823: *Gedenkstukken* viii, 2,
pp. 328 ff. and Brugmans, *Paardenkracht en mensenmacht*, pp. 131–2.
[3] Th. P. M. de Jong, *De krimpende horizon van de Hollandse koopman* (Assen, 1966),
p. 247.

products to the Amsterdam staple market; such transactions would serve as the natural link between the Southern and Northern economies. In this way his national, economic, and colonial policies would become the elements of a single finely balanced system. His economic policy has been characterized as late-mercantilist.[1] It was an innovation for Belgium in so far as it took account of colonial factors, and for the Northern Netherlands because it was relevant to industry.

But although its aims were relatively simple, the means chosen for carrying it out were extremely complicated. Various institutions, all created by the King himself (the Fund for the National Industry of 1821, the Amortization Syndicate of 1822, the General Society for furthering the National Industry— Société générale—established in Brussels in 1822, the Netherlands Trading Company of 1824), were intended to serve the interests of the great system but at times conflicted with each other. These policies were the more confusing because they were also being used at the same time to help fight pauperism. In the North the problem of poverty was being seriously studied. But an objective analysis of the phenomenon was difficult to achieve: confronted by physically weak paupers, wasting away through excessive drinking, miserably housed and miserably subservient, no observer could draw a clear distinction between the victims of low wages or structural unemployment, and the asocial or disabled workers. 'The poor' was a term used to describe totally different categories. We may perhaps assume that about half of those receiving poor-relief were unemployed or badly paid workmen.[2] If this is true, about 5 per cent of the Dutch population belonged to this group. In 1816 it was estimated that what was called the 'class of the workmen'—certainly also comprising the peasants and agricultural workers—represented more than 83 per cent of the Dutch population.[3] Of course these figures are extremely tentative. Yet they seem to indicate that the problem of involuntary unemployment was only a relatively minor aspect of

[1] Brugmans, *Paardenkracht en mensenmacht*, pp. 136 ff.
[2] This was Van den Bosch's opinion. Cf. A. C. J. de Vrankrijker, *Een groeiende gedachte* (Assen, 1959), p. 8.
[3] *Handelingen Tweede Kamer* (1815-16), p. 204. Cf. I. J. Brugmans, 'Standen en klassen in Nederland gedurende de negentiende eeuw', *Verslag Historisch Genootschap*, lxxiv (Groningen, 1960), p. 32.

a much broader social problem—that is, the misery of many tens of thousands with enough work and income to stay out of the category of the poor but nevertheless forced to live a life of blind degradation on the verge of absolute poverty. This was the lot of at least half the Dutch workmen.[1] Some of those who studied the problem explained the social evils in an almost Marxist way. Johannes van den Bosch sought to demonstrate that the wealth of the capitalist consists of the sums deducted from the workman's wages; that the final cause of poverty is property; that capitalism tends to reduce wages to the lowest possible minimum.[2] Willem van Hogendorp, Gijsbert Karel's son, saw that the concentration of capital in a few hands, a phenomenon which started to manifest itself in the fifteenth and sixteenth centuries and had developed much more rapidly in modern times, had reduced the standard of living of the nineteenth-century workman to a level far below that of a medieval serf. And he, a Calvinist pessimist, thought that there was nothing that could be done about it.[3] Thorbecke too examined and analysed these phenomena and warned against their social consequences.[4] Malthus and Ricardo were obviously studied carefully in the Netherlands.

Yet these men did not conceive the idea of purposeful social reform; they confined themselves to combating pauperism in the narrowest sense of the word. Neither social utopianism nor democratic radicalism penetrated into the stagnating and placid Dutch society of the 1820s. Dutch poor-relief was paternalistic and philanthropic. But the form chosen for it was interesting enough. The Society of Charity (Maatschappij van Weldadigheid), established in 1818 and supported by the state, tried to use urban paupers for cultivating waste land and to train them to become agricultural labourers or small farmers. The initiator of this semi-official society, Johannes van den Bosch, hoped to solve in this way the problem of poverty in only a few years.[5] But even an institution like the Netherlands

---

[1] Van den Bosch stated in 1842 that only one-third of the population earned more than half of what they strictly needed: J. J. Westendorp Boerma, *Johannes van den Bosch als sociaal hervormer* (Groningen, 1927), p. 45.

[2] Ibid., p. 223.

[3] *Gedenkstukken* viii, 3, p. 317.

[4] K. H. Boersema, *Johan Rudolf Thorbecke* (Leiden, 1949), App. III.

[5] The Society was studied with interest abroad. Both Fourier and Owen wrote

Trading Company accepted, in spite of all its other tasks, the vocation of fighting pauperism. When Belgian industry was cut off from the Indonesian market after 1830 the Trading Company founded textile schools and weaving-mills in Twente where the 'poor' could get some training and employment. Thus, somewhat paradoxically, one tried to transform urban paupers into farm-labourers and rural paupers into factory-workers.

So it appears that during the 1820s the government succeeded in designing policies for the economy, poor-relief, education, and the colonies which not only included both North and South but actually linked them together in a closer interdependence. These policies were more cautious than William's initiatives relating to the language problem and the schools. As they did not represent comprehensive programmes for reform they gave rise to fewer tensions and conflicts. But support for them remained tepid. In Belgium, where generous government credits enabled courageous industrialists to put their projects into execution, they certainly met with most success. In the North they were less successful and the attempts of the government to persuade Dutch capitalists to invest in Southern industry largely failed. Consequently, many Belgian entrepreneurs may have felt some attachment to the government but not by any means to their Dutch compatriots. In other words, the government met with opposition to both its cultural and its economic policies in Belgium but also found influential support, whereas in the Northern Netherlands it was paralysed by the indifference of an élite which was only prepared to help the government as long as it seemed to act as the defender of specifically Dutch traditions and interests.

3. The Opposition to William I's System

Romanticism arose as a reaction against this humanist, paternalist, mercantilist system. Romantic literature and philosophy reached the North much earlier than Belgium, where they were not known before 1814. Romantic political theory, however, penetrated to both parts of the realm at about the same

comments on the experiment: H. P. G. Quack, *De Socialisten*, ii (5th edn., Amsterdam, 1921), pp. 223, 268.

time although it was only in the South that it developed during this period into a doctrine with practical political consequences. This is true in both its conservative and its liberal manifestations. Both caught on much more rapidly in the South and it was only in the 1840s that the Dutch began to understand what the Belgians discovered in the 1820s—Romantic liberty. But at the time of the Restoration neither the Dutch nor the Belgians added much to foreign thought, merely adapting it to suit their own circumstances.

To begin with, Dutch Romantic politics bore the character of innocent eccentricity. The formidable poet and dilettante Willem Bilderdijk (1756–1831)—Orangist, exile, admirer of Napoleon—who could not get a position at the University, opened a private seminar in Leiden in 1817 for the study of history and public law. His Romantic and egocentric nationalism was hostile to the state of King William. It was, in the first place, rigidly Calvinist. Moreover, this passionate and reactionary neurotic preached a counter-revolutionary absolutism which was totally unreasonable as far as the Netherlands was concerned and the very opposite of constitutional monarchy. His best-known disciple, the Jewish poet Isaäc da Costa (1798–1860) who became a Christian in 1822, also developed a form of reckless absolutism and messianic nationalism on the basis of his studies of Calvinism. Among Da Costa's friends were the sons of Gijsbert Karel van Hogendorp, who had inherited their father's power of self-willed meditation and his conspicuous lack of pliability. This circle of intellectuals and patricians affected a formalized Calvinist orthodoxy, an almost sentimental fanaticism, and a kind of coquettish pride in their own spiritual nobility, if not in the nobility of their ancestors. Contempt for the bourgeoisie[1] and belief in their own calling (the Van Hogendorp family was not only highly aristocratic but also in the Calvinist sense *elected*)[2] were coupled with resentment against a world that failed to give them their due. Their aversion to William I and his policies induced curious fantasies about the Crown Prince—the future King William II—whom they expected to restore the Dutch nation

---

[1] See Willem and Dirk van Hogendorp's letters, *Gedenkstukken* viii, 3, p. 417; x, 2, p. 940.

[2] Ibid. viii, 3, pp. 454–5.

to its former greatness, to make it the seat of the true Church, and the centre of Europe.[1]

Political Romanticism in Belgium did not inspire the same exaltation or such violent absolutism. For it was much easier to become a Romantic conservative in Belgium after 1815 than it was in the North. The Dutch conservatives' difficulty was that they were unable to ground their romanticism in eighteenth-century traditions, largely because Gijsbert Karel van Hogendorp had already employed these in devising the constitution of 1814, which they opposed. But Belgian conservatives hostile to the constitution of 1815, which derived, whatever its supporters might say, from Dutch and not from Belgian history, could justifiably make their own traditions the basis of their political doctrines and nationalism. Indeed the 1815 constitution immediately gave rise to violent conflicts between conservatives, some of them already interested in the Romantic movement, and the so-called liberals. Yet it was not the Romantic conservatives who first joined battle. The signal was given by the Bishop of Ghent, a French nobleman called Maurice de Broglie (1766–1821), a man of great but obstinate courage who was unable to adapt himself to a Europe dominated by Metternich and Castlereagh.

To the surprise of the government and the Allies he started in 1815 a lonely campaign against those articles of the constitution that guaranteed religious liberty and the protection of all existing Churches. He considered these incompatible with the legitimate pretensions of the Roman Catholic Church. For according to him religious liberty was not to be permitted and toleration of dissenters was only conceivable if it were granted by Roman Catholicism itself as the religion of the state—or at least the recognized dominating religion; it could not be granted by a state which was neutral. He therefore ordered the notabilities, who following the Dutch example but on a much larger scale were asked to give their opinion of the constitutional draft, to reject it. He was successful: 1,323 of the 1,604 invited actually voted; 796 of them opposed the proposal. No less than 554 of the negative votes came from the Flemish-speaking areas, where the government had only 272 supporters,

[1] M. E. Kluit, *Het Réveil in Nederland 1817–1854* (Amsterdam, 1936), p. 130 and cf. e.g. *Gedenkstukken* viii, 3, p. 416; ix, 2, pp. 291, 924.

whilst in Wallonia the proposal was accepted by only a small majority.

Although the result was so favourable, it did not improve De Broglie's case. The government, bound by the eight articles of 1814 in which religious liberty was explicitly guaranteed, could not have satisfied De Broglie's requirements even if it had wanted to. So the government declared that the proposal had been accepted, which was misleading but not totally untrue because the States General—representing only the Northern Netherlands before the 1815 constitution came into effect—had subscribed to it and thus a majority in the whole Netherlands could be held to be in favour of it.[1] The Bishop, however, absolutely refused to accept this and continued his agitation. But although it created serious difficulties for the government and caused it to make tactless mistakes, his action was doomed to failure. In 1817 De Broglie left the country, shortly before he was condemned in the Brussels law court to deportation, and at once the more conciliatory elements in the Belgian Church became predominant. It was now expected that the King would negotiate a new concordat and consequently allow the Church to be reorganized and appointments to the numerous vacant episcopal sees to be made. It was not, however, until 1827 that a concordat was signed and no attempt was made to act upon it until just before the fall of the Realm in 1830.

The conflict between the conservative Romantics and the Great Netherlands state dates from 1815. In that year Léon de Foere (1787–1851), a priest at Bruges, started his periodical Le Spectateur belge, of which twenty-four volumes were published by 1824. De Foere was a young man greatly interested in the arts, music, and history. He wrote in French but only reluctantly and without distinction. Dutch was his mother tongue and the language of his nation, but the readers to whom he addressed himself and whose national feelings he wanted to awaken were the very people who were unable to understand it.[2] He was by no means an enemy of the North. On the

---

[1] H. T. Colenbrander, *Willem I, Koning der Nederlanden* (2 vols., Amsterdam, 1931–5), i. 348 ff.

[2] *Le Spectateur belge, ouvrage historique, littéraire, critique et moral* (Bruges, 1815–24), i (1815, 2nd edn. 1825), 12, 20.

contrary, just before the discussions concerning the constitution began, he called upon his compatriots to look for inspiration not in the frivolous and degenerate French literature but in the Dutch.[1] Nor was he a particularist. He opposed the contention —which is indeed gratuitous—that Flemish is a language radically different from Dutch in strong terms.[2] As early as 1816 he grew impatient at the government's procrastination in introducing Dutch as the official language of Flanders.[3] De Foere possessed a fair knowledge of German Romanticism and could quote with ease from such authors as Schelling and Schleiermacher. German nationalism rising in opposition to France was to him a praiseworthy example.[4] But he was not an original thinker, and although rightly considered De Feller's successor as a conservative journalist,[5] this courageous yet rather weak man lacked his predecessor's caustic wit. His most striking achievement was to lend the support of his Romanticism to De Broglie's agitation, thus greatly enlarging the issues. His Flemish origins made him better fitted than the Bishop, whose ideal and fatherland was Bourbon France, to put forward practical ideas. He was in favour of a Belgian–Dutch federation which would leave the Southern Netherlands in possession of its pre-revolutionary, aristocratic, and Roman Catholic tradition. This had been the ideal of De Feller and Van der Noot in 1789, but it became more intense and purposeful under the impact of Romanticism. De Foere cherished Belgium with much less complacency than the Patriots of the 1780s. His conservatism was dynamic. He wanted to impart to his people a new emotion through which they would be able to understand again their free past as well as their true nature.

De Foere tried to combine ecclesiastical ultramontanism on the one hand and political and conservative nationalism on the other. He found powerful support among both the clergy and the nobility. Curiously enough, however, the Romantics of noble birth (most of them Walloons and all French-speaking) reacted differently from De Foere, a priest whose ultramon-

---

[1] Ibid. ii (1815, 2nd edn. 1825), 57–8; cf. i. 17.
[2] Ibid. iii (1815, 2nd edn. 1825), 34, 255 ff.
[3] Ibid. iv (1816, 2nd edn. 1825), 191.
[4] Ibid. ii. 56.
[5] H. Haag, *Les Origines du catholicisme libéral en Belgique (1789–1839)* (Louvain, 1950), p. 49.

tanism was, as it were, subordinated to his nationalism. For the nobles had fewer ties with their country and their people, and were so impressed by ultramontanism that they considered the national question of only secondary importance. In fact their nationalism did not rise above the level of old-fashioned Belgian particularism. Count Henri de Mérode-Westerloo (1782–1835) was one of the most articulate writers of this group. In 1814 he came to know a young adventurer, Ferdinand Eckstein, of Danish-Jewish origin who as a member of the occupying forces at Brussels paraded a German noble title. It was this man who initiated a number of rigidly Roman Catholic nobles into the mysteries of German Romanticism. Before long they were themselves writing and publishing exercises in conservative theory. They meditated on the true Christian society, that of the Middle Ages, and De Mérode soon discovered that the French ultra-royalists of Bonald's kind whom he had at first admired really entertained in their adulation of French absolutism ideals totally foreign to Belgium.[1] Thus ultramontanism and the old Estates became the basis upon which they tried to rest their system. Their aversion towards the Great Netherlands state had no limits, for they despised both its policies and its Dutch character. Ignorant of the North and of its language, they looked down even on the Dutch Roman Catholics and gave them no support—although according to the census of 1829 there were more than a million of them (almost 39 per cent of the Dutch population) as against $1\frac{1}{2}$ million Protestants. They were afraid that they might introduce the Dutch language into Belgium, the language of heresy.[2] These theorists had not yet formed any practical political aims, which was not surprising. Since the sixteenth and seventeenth centuries the Belgian nobility had moved strictly within a limited provincial or local framework, and that the Restoration philosophy should even have prompted some of them to write down a few individual ideas was itself remarkable enough.

In the course of the 1820s the conservative concepts of the Belgian Church underwent a profound crisis. This was partly due to the influence of the Romantic nobility which from the start did not really advocate a return to the *ancien régime* but

---

[1] Mérode-Westerloo, *Souvenirs*, ii. 6 ff.

[2] See Witlox, *Katholieke Staatspartij* i. 101 ff.

rather to a largely illusory medieval system. Of no less importance was the attitude of the clergy of the Northern Netherlands who, considerably more cultivated than their Belgian colleagues and without their nostalgia for the old order, realized that the policies of De Broglie and his Flemish priests were reactionary as well as sterile. Finally, events during this period made a change in the Church's tactics inevitable. As a result the Roman Catholic opposition in Belgium which rejected the constitution in 1815 because it guaranteed freedom of religion and the Churches, ten years later appealed to it for protection from interference by the state.

The writings of the French ultramontane Lamennais, much studied both in Belgian and Dutch seminaries after 1815, acquired wide popularity when the Master urged that all links between Church and State should be severed. He was himself inspired by the example of Belgium. Mérode's group got in touch with the Paris priest and propagated his anti-Gallican and anti-absolutist ideas. Freedom, freedom of the Church, of education if necessary, even of the Press, became the means through which these so-called liberal Catholics now tried to realize their purely conservative aims, namely the restoration of the Church's predominant influence and, in the manner of the pre-revolutionary Statists, the suppression of the monolithic power of the state.[1] This, of course, did not make the liberal Roman Catholics any more kindly disposed towards the Great Netherlands Kingdom; nor did the government develop any sympathy for them. It suspected that though their tactics might have changed their purposes had not. Moreover, the freedom now required by and for the Church was so unconditional that the state, which was expected to continue to support the clergy financially, could hardly be expected to grant it in this form. It became still more difficult for the government and the King to understand what was happening when Belgian liberals suddenly declared themselves in favour of much of the Roman Catholic programme. For not only were the Roman Catholics passing through a phase of unusual development; Belgian liberalism too was adopting new atti-

[1] For this see Haag's excellent work (op. cit., *passim*) and K. Jürgensen, *Lamennais und die Gestaltung des Belgischen Staates* (Wiesbaden, 1963). A. Simon, *Rencontres mennaisiennes en Belgique* (Brussels, 1963) contains some interesting material.

tudes, and the evolution of the liberals was, in fact, much more radical than that of the Catholics.

The term 'liberal' had no precise meaning in 1815. It was used to indicate a vaguely modern outlook, a certain degree of anticlericalism and anti-aristocratic tendencies. In this sense quite a number of Belgian bourgeois were liberals, especially in Wallonia where advocates, writers, purchasers of national property, civil servants, and all kinds of semi-intellectuals applauded the 'liberal' policies of the government, which appeared to be against the Church and the nobility and which calmly allowed the Belgian Press, entirely in the hands of French revolutionaries after 1815, to campaign against the Bourbons. The numerous strictures on the government made by these liberals and aired in the States General in eloquent French bore almost exclusively on economic matters. When the King at last started formulating a clear economic policy and prosperity generally increased, this particular form of opposition stopped. Thus by about 1825 the government had substantial support among the Belgian bourgeoisie, the anti-clericals, and industrialists. But at the very moment when the old form of liberalism—a somewhat diminished inheritance from the Great Revolution—looked like winning the ultimate victory, a new and in theory completely different liberal doctrine emerged. This neo-liberalism was of French origin too. It was the system of men like Royer-Collard, Barante, Cousin, and Guizot. It too was Romantic in inspiration. The aims of the neo-liberals—it would perhaps be better to call them neo-conservatives—were just the opposite of those of the old liberals. They repudiated the French Revolution and the Enlightenment. They objected to the idea of popular sovereignty as well as to rationalism. They felt no confidence in constitutions ingeniously put together, believing in the free development of free institutions. Above all they devoted their energies to fighting the principle of sovereignty. To them the state was a living and moving unity of tensions and contrasts. Never again should it become what conceptions of both monarchical and popular sovereignty had made of it: a Leviathan, a massive body of concentrated, despotic power.

In April 1824 a new liberal daily, the *Mathieu Laensbergh* was started at Liège. Its founders, among others the brothers

Charles and Firmin Rogier, Joseph Lebeau, and Paul Devaux, had barely finished their academic studies. In 1825 the paper first committed itself to the Romantic movement.[1] In 1826 the *Journal de Bruxelles* was also converted to Romanticism; its literary editor, a Frenchman, explained that liberalism and Romanticism, meaning the emancipation of politics and of literature, were fundamentally linked.[2] These newspapers tried to do in Belgium what the most famous periodical of the liberal-romantic movement, the *Globe*, did in France—to fuse politics and literature into a general philosophy of liberty. The Belgians did not attempt to make an original contribution to the movement; at this stage Belgian literature in French found neither new forms nor new emotions, and in political matters the younger generation was equally obedient to the French example. Just as the French doctrinaires demanded by way of a practical political aim the correct application of the Charte— 'la Charte', said Royer-Collard in 1824, 'est maintenant toute notre histoire, elle est le fait unique et suprême'[3]—so the constitution of 1815 became for the Belgians the token of the liberty they wanted to create, the guarantee of representative government. And like their French masters the Belgians propounded the same anti-revolutionary principles. Public liberties—the individualistic principles of the Revolution—were to them no more than forms of resistance to the state's sovereignty, the means by which the proper forces of social life could be protected and allowed to grow and work together in organic harmony.

This neo-liberalism was opposed to the government. For when looked at closely the United Kingdom of the Netherlands turned out to provide remarkably little liberty. The Press was not entirely free and Belgian judges in particular enforced the Press laws very strictly. Education was not free either and in official business or in the law courts French-speaking people in most provinces were not even allowed to use what they considered to be their mother tongue. French was relegated to Wallonia which had approximately 1·5 million inhabitants out of a total population of about 6·5 million. It was not difficult to transform grievances of this kind into an opposition

[1] Charlier, op. cit. i. 174.   [2] Ibid. 212.
[3] A. de Barante, *La Vie politique de M. Royer-Collard* (2 vols., Paris, 1861), ii. 233.

programme. But it is not at all clear how the liberal agitators actually envisaged the reform of the state. The loudly praised freedom was, in fact, most selfishly defined. If, to take an example, the Walloon or Flemish bourgeois who refused to learn Dutch were admitted to all offices in the provinces outside Wallonia, or to the central institutions, this would mean that for the sake of efficiency and good order the Dutch-speaking civil servants and lawyers ought to learn and use French. Moreover, the neo-liberals were only interested in politics, ignoring as yet social and economic problems. They wanted parliamentary government on the basis of direct elections to the Second Chamber and ministerial responsibility. Like the French doctrinaires their ideal was the British system. The nucleus of the group consisted of journalists, Walloon students, or graduates eager to start a career and bitterly hostile to a civil service in which the Dutch preponderance was overwhelming, and young Romantics in search of a purpose in life. But among the Belgian members of the Second Chamber they found some supporters. It was they who continued the opposition which the old liberals had begun in 1815 but which in 1825, more or less satisfied with what they had achieved, they tended to abandon.

It is understandable that the Roman Catholics who changed their tactics after 1825 and the Belgian liberals who found new contents for their doctrines should have been able to collaborate under the umbrella of Romanticism. In December 1825 the Belgian Roman Catholic leader in the Second Chamber, E. C. de Gerlache (1785–1871), offered an alliance with the liberals; the *Mathieu Laensbergh* at first reacted hesitantly.[1] Only in 1827 did this periodical itself propose such a 'union' and in 1828 some influential Roman Catholic papers accepted the invitation. The old-liberal *Le Courrier des Pays-Bas* soon followed suit; its most eloquent contributor, Louis de Potter (1786–1859), a brilliant but all too versatile publicist, changed sides in anger over the proceedings of the (Belgian) law courts against the newspaper Press and henceforth devoted his polemic talents to fighting the government instead of the Jesuits. Charles de Brouckère (1796–1860), like Potter from Bruges,

---

[1] Haag, pp. 100 ff. Already in July 1825 Kinker thought that liberals and Catholics at Liège might finally decide to collaborate: *Gedenkstukken* ix, 2, p. 11.

a member of the Second Chamber and closely associated with the *Courrier* group, also maintained contacts with the neo-liberals—his ambition was to write for the *Globe*.[1]

In the autumn of 1828 De Brouckère formally proposed the repeal of all restrictions on the liberty of the Press. In December the States General defeated this by 63 votes to 44; the Liège neo-liberals, however, had by that time drawn public attention to the matter by inviting signatures for a petition addressed to the government. By the beginning of 1829 the petition movement was gathering momentum; the Roman Catholic nobility of Brussels drafted a petition advocating freedom of education, and ultramontanes and liberals decided to co-operate with each other. In March their efforts resulted in an unprecedented agitation: the Second Chamber was flooded by hundreds of petitions, signed, it was estimated, by approximately 40,000 people. The points most frequently referred to were freedom of the Press and of education.[2] There can be no doubt that the great majority of the signatories were Roman Catholics. Indeed the clergy, though hesitantly, agreed with and supported the movement.[3] The Dutch Roman Catholics took part in it too, but on a much more modest scale.[4] In May the government suffered a defeat at the hands of the Second Chamber which by a large majority voted against the following year's budget, the Dutch members being so worried by financial matters that they overcame their scruples about backing the Belgian opposition, even though the latter was only using the right to reject the budget in order to exercise political pressure.

The situation looked dangerous. The Belgian parties began to build up some kind of political organization. With the intention of publicizing their policies among the electors of the Provincial States they founded so-called 'associations constitutionnelles', largely dominated by the local nobles and the clergy.[5] Their success was manifest when the elections turned out to be unfavourable to the government. But at the same time William I made a journey through Belgium, and wherever he went he was warmly acclaimed; the King himself was not the object of

---

[1] *Gedenkstukken* ix, 1, p. 144.   [2] De Jonghe, pp. 322 ff.
[3] A. Simon, *Le Cardinal Sterckx et son temps (1792–1867)* (2 vols., Wetteren, 1950), i. 113.
[4] Witlox, *Katholieke Staatspartij* i. 185 ff.
[5] *Gedenkstukken* ix, 1, pp. 151, 155, 158; ix, 2, pp. 590–1, 631.

Belgian resentment. It was his ministers and, above all, Van Maanen who were being attacked. The opposition scrupulously kept to its starting-point, emphasizing that it was solely concerned that the government should fully apply the constitution, interpreted of course in the most liberal manner. The possibility of cutting the ties between North and South, or merely of making the relationship more rewarding for Belgium, was hardly mentioned; on the contrary, the opposition seemed confident that the constitutional liberties, if at last properly applied, would automatically result in what many Belgians, both reactionaries and liberals, had been expecting since 1815: the absolute supremacy of Belgium. The government hesitated. In May it finally consented to an urgent request from the Church; by means of a compromise with Rome, the appointments to three episcopal sees were approved. In June the obligation for student priests to attend the Collegium Philosophicum was withdrawn; in August the use of French in some official documents and in criminal cases was allowed in the Flemish-speaking areas.

But the petition movement was shortly resumed in West-Flanders and this time the clergy itself gave it such an impetus that it grew into a massive agitation. From December 1829 to February 1830 more than 350,000 people, most of them from the Flemish countryside, by putting their signature or— as in thousands of cases—just a cross under the petitions, manifested their desire to free the Press which they could not read, the schools which they did not attend, and a language which they did not understand.[1] Once again the government attempted to reinforce its position. On 11 December 1829 the King accompanied a fairly restrictive Press bill with a strongly worded message to the nation lauding his own achievements, repudiating ministerial responsibility, and declaring his indifference to petitions. Duly impressed by such vigorous language the States General in May 1830 passed the Press bill. Yet at the same time the government was preparing far-reaching concessions. In May all conditions governing secondary and higher education were dropped, in June the language decrees applicable in the South were repealed and the Collegium Philosophicum was closed. But although the government

[1] De Jonghe, pp. 342 ff.

seemed willing to abandon, or to moderate, its Great Netherlands policies, it still refused to recognize Belgium's supremacy,
tenaciously clinging to the fiction that its leading principles were
based upon Dutch traditions.

Notwithstanding all the gloomy predictions of 1815 and the
following years, there was in fact no particular reason why the
great experiment of a Dutch–Belgian reunion should fail. In a
century that saw the unification of North and South Italy, of
North and South Germany, why should the few million Dutchmen and Belgians be unable to form a common state? It can admittedly be argued that unification came too early. In the
Restoration period, not a notably creative period, nationalism
devoted its energy to attacking old states instead of establishing
new ones. Yet the fundamental weakness of the United Kingdom was that it did not possess a strong centre. The Northern
Netherlands were neither able nor willing to do what Prussia
and Sardinia were destined to do. Not only were they too
weak but they were also naturally opposed to policies whose
dynamism they felt contradicted their traditions. Although the
government and the civil service, to the great indignation of
the Belgian liberals, were for the most part composed of
Dutchmen, this did not mean that Belgium was being 'Dutchi-
fied'. On the contrary, one of the most striking facts is that the
government's policies came increasingly to be determined and
absorbed by the old Belgian conflicts, those of the Vonckists
and the Statists, the ultramontanes and the febronians, that is
the adherents of the German bishop Febronius who was
prepared to subject the Church to state control. The Southern
part of the Realm was justified in complaining that its inhabitants had a grossly inadequate share in public offices;
on the other hand, all the policies the government was capable
of putting forward seemed to be Belgian in origin. Even in the
States General the Dutch, who often spoke French but with
difficulty, were mostly on the defensive, and although they
assumed exasperatingly superior airs they were in fact driven
from the field by their pugnacious colleagues. At the beginning
of 1830 it was obvious that the concessions made by the
government had been insufficient and that a new struggle for
mastery in the United Kingdom was bound to follow.

IV

IN SEARCH OF NATIONAL
PRINCIPLES, 1830–1848

1. *The Belgian Revolution*

IT was not easy to determine the meaning of the disturbances taking place in August and September 1830 in some of the Southern provinces. An echo of the Paris July Revolution was to be heard in them. They seemed to result from the vehement agitation for a liberal application of the constitution. They were made possible by the violent action of the proletariat, directed by the bourgeoisie, who had been the initial target of their anger, against the government. A small group of liberal journalists and advocates tried to take the lead but they were pursuing an ideal of liberty of which they were as yet unable or unwilling to define the terms. Some of the clergy backed the rebels. No objective observer could decide whether the revolt was aimed at the Great Netherlands state, Protestantism, the constitution, the system of government, the government itself, or the dynasty. But neither the Dutch ministers nor Dutch public opinion hesitated for a moment before giving their opinion: it was an attack by Belgium on Holland. The Dutch had been fearing this for years. Now, they thought, the liberal and Roman Catholic opposition which for so long had kept up the pretence of legality revealed itself in its true colours: the passions of mutinous Belgium had finally burst out. This was the only clear response in a chaotic situation, and it gave direction to the course of events. The rebels overcame their uncertainties; the contradictory nature of their actions was resolved by the nationalist purpose so thoughtlessly placed at their disposal. The paradoxes did not disappear but they ceased to hamper the progress of a revolution upon which the Dutch themselves had imposed the character of a single-minded national war of liberation. It was the government and the North generally that supplied the revolt with its nationalist identity, and to that it owed its success.[1]

By 1830 the economic prosperity of the Kingdom seemed to be waning. The winter was severe and long; agriculture was in a bad way. Overproduction in southern industry caused bankruptcies, contraction, reduction of wages, and unemployment. Thus there was tension and discontent which the extremists could exploit at any time. On the evening of 25 August 1830 a large and threatening crowd first gathered in Brussels. It was roused against the government—it is not known by whom— and attacked the houses of various dignitaries, who were all, with the exception of Van Maanen, Belgians. During the next few days the proletariat in the Brussels suburbs and in the Liège area attacked factories, smashing machines. On 26 August the Brussels bourgeoisie quickly responded by proposing to set up a civil guard to subdue the revolt. The governor of Brussels could only approve; he also had to admit well-known opponents of the government to important functions in the guard, which worked very efficiently. By 27 August, when still only a mere thousand men strong, it had quelled the disturbances. Henceforth it was itself in possession of power. For the government, which was slowly and cautiously taking strategic measures in connection with the situation in France, had few troops at its disposal, no more than about 30,000 men in the whole country.[2] The army commanders were in any case happy to leave the dirty work to the civil guard. How favourably events developed for the Walloon liberals is shown by the fact that from 28 August onwards the minutes of the Brussels city council were no longer drawn up in Dutch but in French.[3]

[1] There is a vast literature on the Belgian Revolution. My interpretation owes much to the following publications: A. Smits, O.S.B., *1830: Scheuring in de Nederlanden*, i: *Holland stoot Vlaanderen af* (Bruges, 1950), and the exchange of views with J. Dhondt in *De Vlaamse Gids*, xxxv (1951); R. Demoulin, *Les Journées de septembre 1830 à Bruxelles et en province* (Liège, 1934); *idem* and H. van Werveke, 'De Omwenteling', *Algemene geschiedenis der Nederlanden*, ix (1956), 289 ff.; R. Demoulin, 'L'influence française sur la naissance de l'État belge', *Revue historique*, ccxxiii (1960); Elias, *Vlaamse gedachte* i. 357 ff. Additions to Colenbrander's *Gedenkstukken* are to be found in C. Gerretson, *Muiterij en Scheuring* (2 vols., Leiden, 1936) and A. Smits, 'Instructies aan en rapporten van gouverneurs uit 1830', *Bijdragen en Mededelingen van het Historisch Genootschap*, lxvii (1948), pp. 157-358.

[2] *Gedenkstukken* x, 1, p. 52; x, 3, p. 153.

[3] Smits, *Scheuring*, p. 113.

But on the whole the liberals kept to the pattern of nineteenth-century revolutions, asking for the lawful redress of grievances. The King who was staying in his Het Loo palace gave way; he decided to call an extraordinary session of the States General on 13 September. At the same time he sent his sons William and Frederick south with some troops.

In September the rebels were able to break the pattern of a proletarian social action exploited by the bourgeoisie in the interests of liberal intellectuals. Early in the month their hope of liberalizing the Realm and thus attaining what they considered their legitimate supremacy vanished into thin air when Dutch public opinion made it abundantly plain that it would tolerate no such development. During the next few weeks they resigned themselves to a compromise solution, namely administrative separation of the two parts under the Orange dynasty. Thanks to this formula, dynamic Belgium, no longer obliged (as the young Liège doctrinaire Devaux put it in not unfamiliar terms[1]) to drag its stagnating, reactionary partner along like a heavy weight, would be free to develop progressively in the French fashion but still retain the North as a natural field for expansion.[2] The North wavered. When the King's elder son—the future King William II—arrived in Brussels, he agreed on 3 September to administrative separation as the best solution. On 4 September public opinion at The Hague also seemed to favour this.[3] But the King, weak and vacillating, looked like refusing. On 3 September he dismissed Van Maanen, on 5 September he ordered the States General, called for 13 September, to decide on the need for administrative reforms. Only on 29 September did the States General vote in favour of administrative separation. But by then the liberals in Liège and Brussels, totally disillusioned and in complete disarray, had already abandoned this claim too and pronounced for secession. After striving for supremacy in the United Kingdom, they now had to resign themselves to the Realm being broken in two.

[1] Quoted by E. Discailles, *Charles Rogier (1800–1885) d'après des documents inédits* (4 vols., Brussels, 1892–5), i. 195.

[2] Cf. the quotations in J. C. Boogman, 'Achtergronden en algemene tendenties van het buitenlands beleid van Nederland en België in het midden van de 19e eeuw', *Bijdragen en Mededelingen van het Historisch Genootschap*, lxxvi (1962), 69.

[3] *Gedenkstukken* x, 3, pp. 6–7.

The fundamental reasons why the liberal revolution developed in this way were the vehemently anti-Dutch attitude of the Catholic masses, especially in Flanders, where the revolution would have been impossible without their support, and Dutch public opinion. In August and September Holland was seen to be identifying itself with the government and the government, pushed northwards, as it were, by the Southern revolt, was obliged to accept this as a fact. But it was by no means the natural result of fifteen years of unity. For fifteen years the government had been merely administering the North whilst pursuing active policies in the South. When in 1829 and early 1830 it met with serious opposition to its old liberalism, it made important concessions to the liberal and Roman Catholic Romantics. Once again it redesigned its policies to meet Belgium's needs. But in the summer the North, less weakened by conflicts and disorder than the South, acquired new influence and forced the Southern opposition to abandon its ideas of liberal, Southern supremacy, and to accept first administrative separation and then secession. Yet the only contribution the North was able to make to the government was negative. It wanted to punish the rebels, not, however, with the purpose of preserving Belgium as part of the Kingdom but simply because in a well-ordered state rebellion was intolerable. On 23 September Prince Frederick marched into Brussels at the head of his troops. He came as the representative of the Northern Netherlands with which the government had identified itself. The reaction of the rebels was inevitable. Secession, the minimal claim of a small group of extremists who had abandoned all hope of better things, assumed intense emotional significance, and was transformed into the ideal of national independence and liberty.

The attack on Brussels began too late and was half-heartedly carried out. The picked troops of ten thousand men encountered stubborn resistance, which was backed rather than led by the secessionst Commission administrative which proclaimed itself on 26 September the provisional government of the whole of Belgium. During the following night the army left the town. The losses of the armed forces and the resistance fighters ran into hundreds. Shortly afterwards the army began to disintegrate; Belgian officers and soldiers, lured by national enthusiasm and the possibility of rapid advancement in a career, abandoned their regiments. Soon the government's power in the South collapsed completely. The disorganized troops withdrew behind the old frontiers of the Republic of the United Provinces. The Flemish areas wavered for a time, partly out of loyalty to the Church which made them anxious not to be involved in a re-enactment of the godless July Revolution, and partly because of the presence of strong garrisons. But now influential groups associated themselves with the revolution which had been transformed into a national war. Indeed the government and Dutch public opinion did not leave them with much choice. Although many people realized that Flanders was slow to react, slower than Wallonia,[1] even the Prince of Orange made no attempt to use the Dutch-speaking Belgians against the Walloon liberals. When he stayed in Antwerp for a few weeks in October and tried to master the situation he got little support, was finally publicly disowned by the King, and saw his adventure end in total failure. One day after the Prince's arrival in Antwerp the King issued a proclamation calling upon his loyal Dutchmen to protect their native soil against the mutineers.

From all parts of Belgium patriots flooded into Brussels, and with remarkable speed started to build a new state. It was no longer only Romantic liberals who devoted themselves to the revolution, but also Romantic Roman Catholics—with so much enthusiasm that a Frenchman characterized it as 'boiling holy water'.[2] Brussels, at any rate, swarmed with priests.[3] On 4 October the central committee of the provisional government[4] declared that the Belgian provinces, forcibly torn from Holland, constituted an independent state.[5] Two days later

[1] Cf. Smits, *Scheuring, passim*; *Gedenkstukken* x, 1, pp. 43, 52, 104; x, 2, p. 14; x, 4, pp. 105, 204, etc.

[2] J. Lebeau, *Souvenirs personnels et correspondance diplomatique* (Brussels, 1883), p. 134.

[3] *Gedenkstukken* x, 2, p. 32. Cf. Simon, *Le Cardinal Sterckx* i. 127.

[4] It consisted of Louis de Potter, Charles Rogier, Sylvain van de Weyer (1802–74), an ambitious, Romantic, and liberal philosopher, follower of Victor Cousin, and soon also Félix de Mérode (1791–1857), an ultramontane, supporter of Lamennais who up to 1830 had been living on his French estates but now arrived to help the cause of Roman Catholic nationalism.

[5] 'Les provinces de la Belgique, violemment détachées de la Hollande, constituent un État indépendant.'

they appointed a commission to draft a new constitution and on 10 October they called elections for a Constituante which they christened National Congress in memory of the American influence on the late eighteenth-century Brabant Revolution. But even before Congress met the government, headily wielding arbitrary power, decreed in rapid succession the numerous new liberties of the Belgian nation—among others, freedom of education, of the Press, of the Church, and of association. Elections took place on 3 November. Unlike the pre-revolutionary ones they were direct. Moreover, the franchise was not only granted to people paying a certain amount of taxes but also to those considered sufficiently educated to exercise it. Thanks to this system the influence of the electorate was much greater than before 1830. But in comparison with the situation under the United Kingdom, its size was reduced (as Rogier, for example, had expected and wished),[1] falling from about 60,000 to 46,000, of whom less than 30,000 actually voted.[2]

On 10 November Congress began its session. It had 200 members, most of them bourgeois, and in many cases petty bourgeois. Very few came from industry or high finance. Young and poor intellectuals, journalists, lawyers, and large landowners acquired greater influence. Nearly half the members were under forty. There were about twenty Orangists, some reactionaries, a few anticlerical republicans, a number of people wishing to see Belgium absorbed into France which they considered their fatherland, and thirteen priests mostly of very democratic persuasion.[3] The great majority, whether liberal or Catholic, were hoping to establish, on the basis of the Romantic Catholic-liberal Union of 1828, a state in which liberty would be supreme. On 22 November Congress determined Belgium's future form of government: it was to be a parliamentary monarchy. During the next few weeks the machinery of government was assembled: ministerial responsibility, direct elections to both the Chamber of Representatives consisting of 102 members and to the Senate consisting of 51 members, a franchise made dependent on payment of direct taxes between 20 and 100 guilders (accord-

---

[1] Cf. his *Dissertatio inauguralis juridica de electione administratorum provinciarum et municipiorum in regno belgico* (Liège, 1826), pp. 16–19.

[2] Gilissen, *Régime représentatif*, pp. 82–4.

[3] Simon, *Le Cardinal Sterckx* i. 136.

ing to the various regions), the guarantee of important liberties to boroughs. On 3 March an electoral law defined the composition of the electorate more precisely. The result was a system favouring the countryside over the towns and giving the franchise (as in 1830) to about 46,000 men. This gave Belgium one voter out of 95 inhabitants compared with one out of 160 in France, and made Belgium the most democratically governed state in Europe. In the Netherlands where the franchise was enjoyed by more than twice as many people, elections were indirect until 1848 and extremely unrepresentative, and Parliament had nothing like the same power.

The text of the constitution nearly half of which was borrowed from the constitution of 1815 and more than a third from the French constitution of 1830,[1] hardly expresses its main characteristics; it is the vehement and excellent discussions in Congress that indicate how its articles were to be interpreted. The delegates made use of French, English, and American formulas to build a neo-Gothic construction. Their passionate progressiveness took as its starting-point the medieval achievements of urban liberty and Church life. Yet at the same time Congress carefully looked after the individual liberties of man and citizen. It is to this fascinating harmony of historical reminiscence and enthusiastic individualism that the constitution owed its great success. The state, the monster of modern times, was tamed. It was even incapable of imposing silence upon its enemies; indeed the most fervent foes of an independent Belgium, the Belgian supporters of William I, were allowed to publish in their Orangist newspapers the most odious slanders against the new regime. In such a manner the state gave way to the individual. But it equally gave way to the respresentative self-government of the boroughs and to the influence of the Church (subsidized by the state) to which, for example, it virtually surrendered all control over education.

When in February 1831 Congress voted this proud constitution into existence, the nation to which it had succeeded in giving a new form was confronting seemingly insoluble problems. It was difficult for the government to raise money. Taxes

[1] J. Gilissen, 'La Constitution de 1830: ses sources, ses influences', *Res Publica*, x (1968), 107–41.

were often not paid; in October 1830 a loan issued by the government failed, and help from some Paris banks came all too slowly and remained insufficient.[1] The economy stagnated. There was as yet nothing to prove that Belgium's new liberty was awakening new energies. The great industrialists of Ghent and Liège, the merchants of Antwerp who as a result of William I's efforts had been able to create important centres of modern life, despised revolutionary Belgium and fought against it. After the withdrawal of the Dutch behind their old frontier, the army soon disintegrated. At the beginning of 1831 bad mistakes by Congress, apt in its naïve and impassioned self-exaltation to forget European realities, seriously impaired the international position of the young state. It might look in Brussels as if Europe's future was being shaped by the revolutionary idealism of Belgium; in fact Belgium's future was entirely dependent on the goodwill of the Great Powers.

At the end of September 1830 William I appealed to Great Britain, Prussia, Austria, and Russia to support his fight against the revolution and to rescue the state built by them in 1815. The international situation, however, was such as to prevent any of the Powers from giving assistance. In October it was decided to call a conference in London of the Great Powers and of France. Its task was clearly defined; it was to ensure that a general war did not result from the revolt. Soon the Belgian Congress and the London Conference seemed to be engaged in a struggle for the diplomatic initiative. First Congress set the pace: it proclaimed Belgium's independence on 18 November 1830, and the Conference followed suit on 20 December. On 24 November Congress declared that it would never accept as sovereign any member of the House of Orange, with the result that the British were ultimately forced to abandon their attempt to make the Prince of Orange King of Belgium. But then Congress ran into difficulties. In January 1831 the Conference decreed that Belgium should be permanently neutral and allotted to the Netherlands all territories which had been governed by the Dutch Republic in 1790 whilst Luxemburg was also in future to belong to its Grand Duke, William I. The Belgians, however, wanted both

---

[1] Cf. B. Gille (ed.), *Lettres adressées à la Maison Rothschild de Paris par son représentant à Bruxelles*, i (Louvain, 1961), p. xvii.

Limburg and Luxemburg (and explicitly laid this down in the constitution) and it was an indisputable fact that generally speaking these areas were strongly in favour of the revolution. Moreover, Congress did not meekly accept the financial regulations of the Conference. When, however, in February 1831 it made the mistake of electing as sovereign the son of the French King—a candidature hastily declined by Louis Philippe—it was obvious that the Belgians had lost the initiative. The decision of Congress (24 February) to appoint as regent their own president, the Liège baron Surlet de Chokier, an amiable, simple man but one without energy and even without much confidence in the viability of a Belgian state, characterizes the apathy that followed so much violent emotion.

In 1830 the inflexibility of Dutch public opinion had transformed the liberal revolt in the South into a successful national revolution. In 1831 William I's obstinacy freed the Belgian nation from its dangerous isolation. The King's prospects, bright at the beginning of 1831, grew weaker in the spring when the Belgians realized that, as only British support could help them out of the deadlock, it was imperative for them to accept the British candidate for the Belgian throne, Leopold of Saxe-Coburg. Their reward was a new set of articles drawn up by the Conference (the eighteen articles of June 1831) which despite their vagueness were more favourable than the January protocol and consequently were turned down by the Dutch King. In theory William's decision was entirely legitimate. Why, after all, should he obediently follow the Conference's tergiversations? He was not obliged to resign himself to the election of Leopold as the Belgian King (4 June 1831) nor to accept his nomination on 26 June. Even his armed invasion of Belgium in August 1831 was, no doubt, justified juridically as well as militarily: to the great astonishment of the Dutch leaders, not to mention the Belgian politicians who had not yet grasped the realities of the situation, the Belgian army turned out to be virtually non-existent. Yet in political terms all this hardly made sense. The French reacted to the Dutch attack by promptly sending an army and the Dutch immediately withdrew. It is true that as a result of his short military campaign William obtained from the Conference more equitable conditions (the twenty-four articles of October 1831) but he took no advantage of them. They were, however, accepted by the Belgians. As William rejected them the Netherlands was driven into complete diplomatic isolation, soon losing the support of even the conservative Powers.

2. The Netherlands in the 1830s

From 1831 to 1838 William I's negative attitudes determined Dutch political development. He refused peace. Expecting Belgium to revert to him in the near future he did not want to compromise his position by abandoning his sovereign rights over his Southern provinces. This is perhaps not surprising. The King did not believe that the Great Powers, which after only fifteen years had betrayed the careful arrangements of Vienna, would be able to uphold the shaky and artificial equilibrium of 1830. In one form or another, he thought, the war, so laboriously avoided in 1830, would still come.[1] The Belgian state was obviously not viable. And could anyone really be confident that Europe, deprived of leadership, direction, and purpose, had found a durable shape? It seemed to him (and to others in the North) that the concept of a monarchical Netherlands deprived of its continental identity and without a clear role in international politics was equally illusory.[2] Only in a strong continental state did monarchy make sense; in a Netherlands reduced to its republican frontiers it could not survive. In 1832, in one of his outbursts of brusque negativism, William I said to a personal envoy of the Tsar: 'Je ne suis roi que d'occasion. I am aware of being the son of a Stadtholder. If I am unable to defend my kingdom, I can follow the example of William III by flooding Holland and then go to the Dutch East Indies . . .'[3] For many years he persisted in this kind of attitude. At the end of 1832 Britain and France tried to force him to subscribe to the twenty-four articles. A French army drove the only Dutch troops still remaining in the South from the citadel of Antwerp. But the King, though accepting an armistice, once again refused to agree to a definite settlement. And by this time even Belgium

[1] Cf. Gedenkstukken x, 2, pp. 267–8, 361–2, 389, 523.
[2] Ibid., p. 466; x, 4, p. 533; x, 5, p. 94.   [3] Ibid. x, 3, p. 573.

no longer wanted one. For as long as the Netherlands did not sign the twenty-four articles Belgium need not evacuate the parts of Limburg and Luxemburg which had been allocated to the North by the Conference, had taken part in the revolt, and were still ruled by the Brussels government. When in March 1838 William I finally declared himself willing to accept the articles, Belgium was most indignant, for peace now appeared more disadvantageous and humiliating than the *status quo*.

On the Dutch domestic scene the impact of the King's single-minded policies was great. There was very little opposition, and early in 1831 it became apparent how weak Roman Catholic resistance still was. Only relatively small groups, particularly in Overijssel and Gelderland, the radical provinces of 1798, refused to obey the King's order to mobilize against liberal-Roman Catholic Belgium and it did not take much trouble to crush occasional riots.[1] Nor did the almost entirely Roman Catholic province of North-Brabant show much inclination to fight the Sovereign; it was in any case closely supervised by the army guarding the frontiers.[2] The liberals were just as incapable of opposing royal policies. In 1830 and 1831 some Dutch liberals insisted on the necessity of revising the constitution in a liberal sense so as to meet the requirements of what was left of the United Kingdom. But the government was so strong that it did not even have to reject these claims; it could safely ignore them. In 1833 the more or less liberal Amsterdam newspaper, *Het Handelsblad*, and other dailies strongly advocated the cause of peace; the government, however, quickly put an end to this campaign. The States General was docile, although some members raised their voices against the financial consequences of policies that required an expensive and idle army of some 75,000 men, that is one-tenth of the adult male population.

But the Dutch public did not support the King's policies

---

[1] J. van Beekum, 'Gouverneur mr. Jacob Hendrik Graaf van Rechteren van Appeltern, 1787–1845', *Overijsselse Portretten* (Zwolle, 1958), pp. 244 ff. and R. Reinsma, 'De houding van de Rooms-Katholieken ten noorden van de grote rivieren tijdens de eerste maanden van de Belgische Opstand', *Archief voor de geschiedenis van de Katholieke Kerk in Nederland*, iii (Utrecht, 1961), pp. 50 ff.

[2] L. G. J. Verberne, 'Noord-Brabant in den status-quo tijd', *In den spiegel van het verleden* (Utrecht, 1957), pp. 229 ff.

because they wanted to have Belgium back. On the contrary, especially in Holland which was once again the proud and firmest bulwark of the government, the great majority of the population was delighted that the Netherlands no longer needed to sacrifice itself for the benefit of Europe as it had between 1815 and 1830,[1] but could now resume its old traditions. The Netherlands, though small and weak, must, however, fight for its honour and, from time immemorial the refuge and sanctuary of virtue, it could never allow itself to be humiliated by the frivolous opportunism of the Great Powers. It found some compensation for its wounded *amour propre* in the awareness of being the only honest country in a world corrupted by power. It was not concerned to recover foreign territories gladly enough abandoned but it did want to be recognized as honourable and patriotic.[2] The government's ingenious propaganda stimulated these feelings, carefully hiding the real aims of the King. Self-glorifying, slightly xenophobic, and very inflated rhetoric rendered the people for many years obedient to what were in fact irredentist policies, although at the same time it raised the expectation that soon cynical Europe would understand the full nobility of the Dutch cause and pay homage to a nation that only wanted, as in its great days, to serve as a loyal servant of God and the law behind its old and cherished frontiers.

Holland felt itself again. And such was the success of this masterly propaganda that from 1830 Dutch national consciousness came increasingly to be characterized by the illusion that the Netherlands, despite or perhaps because of its weakness, was the world centre of justice. Holland felt itself again in another way too. The heavy charges imposed on top of a badly balanced budget caused alarming financial difficulties and it was only through loans that the government could hope to avoid bankruptcy. This brought much work to the

[1] Thus wrote the *Bredasche Courant* in Feb. 1833, quoted in *Gedenkstukken* x, 1, p. c.

[2] On 15 Oct. 1832 the Dutch Foreign Minister addressed the States General in these terms: 'When we consider how, because of the strange times, the foreign Powers treat the Netherlands, full of respect for the sanctity of treaties and scrupulously meeting all its obligations, then we think of the lot of Aristides who was ostracized by the Athenians because they disliked hearing him called the just'; quoted by De Bosch Kemper, *Geschiedenis van Nederland na 1830* i. 285.

Amsterdam financial market and revived the banking business. Many people were affected by a fever of speculation but it
was of course the bankers of Holland, and above all of Amsterdam, who profited most. Not surprisingly they were among the
most obstinate champions of William I.[1] In 1837 they even
founded a newspaper to defend the *status quo* against liberal
attacks.[2] By then the situation had become paradoxical to the
highest degree. For the only result of these policies ultimately
designed to win back Belgium was in practice the Belgian
occupation of Limburg and Luxemburg, and they were financed
by people who were bitterly opposed to the re-annexation of
the South.

Even the Dutch financial market, however, was unable to
give sufficient help. The government, forced to look for money
elsewhere, found it in the Dutch East Indies. For half a century
the colonies had brought nothing but losses to the Dutch state
which, when nationalizing the old East India Company in
1798, took over a debt of 140 million guilders and for some time
to come received nothing in return. Only after the departure of
the English in 1816 did the Dutch recover control of these
regions, but for the next ten years they found no way of
making a profit out of them. Indeed a number of setbacks,
including the war from 1825 to 1829 with the tragic Javanese
leader Dipo Negoro (1785–1855), forced them to contract
new debts to the order of 35 million guilders. These losses
(although indeed negligible in relation to the value of the
territories acquired by the state in 1798 for a ludicrous sum)
were thought so heavy that the financial question dominated
colonial policy entirely. In 1829 Johannes van den Bosch,
who had won William I's respect by his energetic attempts to
combat pauperism, drafted a plan for a steep increase in East
Indian production in the interest of the Netherlands. From
1830 to 1834 he himself, as the all-powerful Governor-General,
put the scheme into operation and during the next five years
he closely supervised, as Colonial Minister, the work of his
successor. His so-called 'culture-system' required the Javanese

[1] *Gedenkstukken* x, 1, pp. 315, 324, 346, 418, 447; x, 2, pp. 308, 374, 399, 468.
[2] De Bosch Kemper, *Geschiedenis van Nederland na 1830* iii. 29 and A. J. C. Rüter
(ed.), *Rapporten van de gouverneurs in de provinciën 1840–1849* (3 vols., Utrecht, 1941–
50), i. 105 n. 2.

population to pay very little in money taxes but instead to put at the disposal of the government one-fifth of its soil and working hours (though it soon became much more) for the purpose of growing coffee, sugar, and indigo. These products were transported in Dutch ships to Amsterdam by the Trading Company which also marketed textiles, manufactured in Twente (Overijssel), in the East Indies. Soon it became apparent that in this way Van den Bosch was taking incomparably greater advantages of the Indian riches than his predecessors. By 1834 he could boast an annual profit of almost 10 millions, a figure which soon rose to 20 millions. The King, who had supreme power over the colonies, arbitrarily disposed of these sums without rendering account to the States General. With them he financed his *status quo* policy abroad and its corollary—stagnation at home.

3. Belgium in the 1830s

When the Lutheran Leopold I (1790–1865) made his entry into Belgium in July 1831, he was received with great emotion, especially in the Flemish countryside and also by the clergy,[1] which for so long and so obstinately had fought the Protestant William I. Although a German conservative who felt more affinity with Metternich than with Palmerston, he was welcomed as the protector of Belgian independence and the restorer of the old Belgian nationality. He was expected to put into effect the constitution that had been drafted with such lyrical enthusiasm; but he found it, as he later said, an absurdity.[2] He was never very popular, and although a king brought in by a popular revolution, he did not look for popularity. He felt contempt for the Romantic progressives and was, when necessary, more inclined to back the neo-conservative doctrinaires. It would have been hard to predict this in 1831. For the doctrinaires had opted for the monarchical form of government not only out of respect for and fear of monarchical Europe, but also because they thought that Belgian public opinion, with its primitive feudal-agrarian love of royalty, was simply not mature enough to accept the ideal of a republic.

---

[1] Lebeau, op. cit., pp. 147 ff.
[2] Cf. Pirenne, *Histoire de Belgique* vii. 50 and Haag, *Origines*, p. 210.

They could not see that it was they who needed the monarchy to combat the progressive claims of the lower, and largely religious classes, as well as the episcopacy, which risked to bring about the state's disintegration.

All these contradictions, however, did not greatly embarrass Leopold I. He possessed to a high degree what the Orange King lacked: he was tactful, albeit haughty, and this made him cautious; he had common sense, which protected him from mistakes of the kind that the more original and creative William I made; and he had self-confidence, a quality his predecessor had never known. He was indeed a much more balanced personality. Moreover, he had the advantage of feeling so little attachment to the country he was governing that he gladly left domestic policy to his ministers, reserving for himself the vital problems of foreign policy in which his subjects were not greatly interested. His close relations with Britain, and his marriage in 1832 to one of Louis Philippe's daughters, secured a firm position in Europe not only for his own person but for his kingdom as well. In Belgium he remained a withdrawn, somewhat mysterious figure whose influence was not easy to determine although it could be seen that it was constantly increasing. His nearest collaborators were Baron Stockmar and Jules van Praet (1806–87), the Romantic historian whose *Histoire de la Flandre* of 1828 introduced into Belgium the style of Guizot and Barante and who after 1831 made a long career as the King's secretary, confidant, and spokesman. They did not often move in public either. Thus, despite a constitution intended to make government transparent, there was still in Belgium an impenetrable centre of partly hidden power.

It might be said that William I's *status quo* policies facilitated the consolidation of the Belgian state because they paralysed the strong centrifugal forces existing in the country. As long as the young fatherland was living under the threat of attack, Belgian policies were bound primarily to serve national unity, and the maintenance of a large army (it was rapidly built up after the disaster of 1831 and soon totalled 80,000 men) was clearly a patriotic prerequisite. Thus the period until 1839 is characterized by so-called Unionism, that is the continuation of the 1828 liberal–Catholic Union which claimed the credit for the revolution's success—an unintentional, but none the less serious, falsification of history. Unionism had a much stronger emotional appeal and a deeper national significance than any matter-of-fact parliamentary or governmental coalitions could ever hope to acquire.[1] For it was supposed to express the permanent revolutionary purpose of the Belgian people. From 1831 to 1839 three successive cabinets derived from this remarkable sentiment the strength which they would have sought in vain among the whims and passions of a Chamber without organized parties.

One of the merits of Unionism was that the reconciliation of liberalism and Catholicism led to a division of political opinion between progressives and conservatives. For under the cover of Unionism left-wing Catholics and liberals were free to join against right-wing Catholics and liberals without endangering national unity. If Unionism had not made this unity a first priority it is not at all unlikely that soon after 1830 liberals and Catholics would have clashed, and thus prevented the development of liberal Catholicism. At any event, in this period political life in Belgium adopted the classic pattern of two parties not embarrassed by religious factors and disagreeing over purely political matters. Just as in France and England, it was not so much liberals and Catholics but progressives and moderates who found themselves confronting each other.[2] But this was to last only so long as William I's policies and the mood of the period linked Belgian statesmen and bishops together in the Romantic Union. When in the 1840s the Union was undermined by the increasing security of the state and the emergence of positivism, it became clear that the great antithesis was after all not between Right and Left but (as in the eighteenth century and under William I) between liberal and Catholic.

It is difficult to determine the numbers and importance of the progressives. Their influence seems to have been greater in the Chamber than in the country. They formed only a minority

---

[1] Colette Lebas, *L'Union des catholiques et des libéraux de 1839 à 1847* (Louvain, 1960), pp. 48 ff.

[2] See Rogier's address to the electors in 1833 (Discailles, op. cit. ii. 265), Devaux's excellent article in the *Revue nationale de Belgique*, i (Brussels, 1839), 302 ff., and Haag, op. cit., pp. 202 ff.; Haag, 'De Belgische buitenlandse en binnenlandse politiek van 1831 tot 1840', *Algemene geschiedenis der Nederlanden*, ix (1956), 376 ff.

in the National Congress but during the first years of independence their number grew so sharply that at times they held
nearly half the seats. One of the reasons for this curious fact
was that only very few moderate politicians were available for
Parliament. The young men who dominated the developments of 1830 and 1831 and learned the profession of statesman during these years received with the creation of Belgium
the most important posts in administration, the diplomatic
service, and the law courts. As the government itself tried to
keep its civil servants out of the Chamber (in the 1840s this
was no longer so), it was not at all easy to find suitable candidates, with the result that enthusiastic idealists, often somewhat
older and largely indifferent about their own careers, got their
chance.[1] What distinguished them from the moderates was their
temperament, rather than their doctrines or social origins.
Apart from an isolated republican like A. Gendebien (1789–
1869), they were in favour of parliamentary monarchy and a
franchise restricted by financial conditions; and the left-wing
Catholics were, like their right-wing colleagues, solemn bourgeois dressed in the black suits so despised by Balzac as the
uniform of Anglomaniac French doctrinaires.[2] In fact, terms
like 'progressive' and 'democratic' which they and others used
to indicate the aims of this group are somewhat misleading.
The feature most clearly characterizing them during the 1830s
was their revolutionary passion for freedom and nationalism.
Their boundless confidence in the vigour of the Belgian
people and their contempt for Europe's old states made them
arrogant and reckless in the field of foreign policy. What was to
prevent Belgium from crushing its foes—the Netherlands, of
course—in the first place? What was to prevent a nation,
unbeatable because of its army and the readiness of its generous
population to make sacrifices, from forcing the Dutch garrisons
out of Antwerp? What was to prevent it from keeping Limburg
and Luxemburg and taking the Prussian Rhineland, which
was so near to Belgium and Catholic, so that their peoples
could enjoy Belgian liberties? In this way left-wing nationalists,

---

[1] Cf. *Revue nationale* i. 303.
[2] See the remarks made by F. du Bus in the 1830s (C. du Bus de Warnaffe, *Au temps de l'unionisme*, Tournai, 1944, pp. 321 ff.) and J. Kamerbeek, jun., 'Une intempestive de Balzac', *Neophilologus* (1962), 1 ff.

unable to resign themselves to the narrowness of the state of
1830—no less unhappy than Verlooy had been in 1788 within
the frontiers of the then Austrian Netherlands—became revolutionary expansionists.

Yet their expansionism did not imply any desire to increase
the power of the state. On the contrary, the left wing wanted
the state to be as weak as possible. When in 1833, on the insti-
gation of the King himself, the government initiated a Municipal Corporations Bill through which it hoped to acquire
decisive influence on the composition of the municipal administrations, the democratic liberals and Catholics opposed
this in the most vigorous terms and forced the doctrinaires in
1836 to accept a compromise far from satisfactory to them [1]
After 1839, moreover, they thought it unnecessary for Belgium
to maintain an army of any significance. Spontaneous mobilization in times of crisis seemed to them a much better instrument than the dangerous institution of a large standing army.
They believed only in moral forces, the moral forces of the
uncorrupted people. It is not surprising that the Catholics particularly, Walloons as well as Flemings, should have tended to
regard the latter, less affected by civilization and content to
live the simple life of an agrarian community, as the nucleus of
the nation.[2] But naturally such feelings, however genuine,
impeded rather than furthered Flanders' cultural and social
development. In relation to purely economic matters also the
Left was, on the whole, fairly conservative. It regarded
anxiously and with some revulsion the activities of industrialists
and financiers, and was by no means convinced of the wisdom
of building railways or establishing limited companies.[3] Yet
some of the Left were in touch with socialist ideas, vague
though these still were. Sometimes, as in the case of the remarkable anticlerical Flemish leader Jacob Kats (1804–86) who

[1] H. Haag, *Les Droits de la cité. Les catholiques-démocrates et la défense de nos franchises
communales 1833–1836* (Brussels, 1946), p. 129.

[2] Haag, *Origines*, pp. 204–5; L. Wils, *Kanunnik Jan David en de Vlaamse beweging
van zijn tijd* (Louvain, 1957), pp. 211 ff. The left-wing Catholic *Journal des Flandres*
(just as Feller during the Brabant Revolution) wanted the clergy to protect the
Flemish people against the French language, a language of a corrupted civilization; cf. Th. Coopman and J. Broeckaert, *Bibliographie van den Vlaamschen taalstrijd*
(10 vols., Ghent, 1904–14), i. 115–16, 118.

[3] Discailles, ii. 320 ff.; B. S. Chlepner, *La Banque en Belgique* (Brussels, 1926),
pp. 391 ff.

wrote very primitive plays in good Dutch to be performed by workmen, the arguments were not even directed against the bourgeoisie but against priests and nobles.[1] And an impatient and democratic republican like Louis de Potter, who after helping to create the state of 1830 grew to despise it for its timidity—to such an extent that he sought contact with the adherents of William I—had no insight at all into the social and economic problems of his time.[2]

Left-wing Catholicism was threatened by the encyclicals of 1832 and 1834 which condemned it, but owing to the balanced attitude of the Belgian episcopacy its plight did not immediately become desperate. However, the King and the right-wing groups had no intention of sparing the left, and in 1839 it suffered such a crushing defeat that it was a long time before it recovered. This defeat was inevitable. The right wing, liberal as well as Catholic, was simply much more powerful and, moreover, got support from Leopold I. It should, however, be emphasized that in some respects the term 'right wing' or 'conservative' in relation to many of them is just as misleading as the term 'progressive' in relation to the numerous adherents of Lamennais.

The so-called right-wing liberals who acquired great influence, men like Charles Rogier (1800–85), J. B. Nothomb (1805–81), Joseph Lebeau (1794–1865), and Paul Devaux (1801–80), had accepted and furthered the transformation of the liberal revolution into a nationalist revolt in 1830, albeit reluctantly. They were no less Romantic than the Mennaisians, and they worshipped freedom just as passionately as the extremists. They, too, were fascinated by French utopian socialism (until 1848 Rogier kept in contact with the disciples of Charles Fourier)[3] and were anxious to pursue dynamic foreign policies. But their enthusiasm encountered its natural limit in their ambition. Their revolution had originated with their determination to win supremacy in the United Kingdom.

[1] Jacob Kats, *De vyanden van het Licht, of de tegenwerkingen van den Maetschappy der Verbroedering* (Brussels, 1836), p. 25. See Julien Kuypers in J. Dhont (ed.), *Geschiedenis van de socialistische arbeidersbeweging in België* (Antwerp, 1960–7). The author studies Kats' role in the Belgian Charbonnerie.

[2] L. Jottrand, *Louis de Potter* (Brussels, 1860), pp. 79–80.

[3] L. Bertrand, *Histoire de la démocratie et du socialisme en Belgique* (2 vols., Brussels, 1906–7), i. 188 ff.; Discailles, iii. 232.

When this proved impossible, they had built a state of their own in which they were holding high positions. Now, they thought, it was imperative to consolidate the state, to extend its power, to increase its safety. They failed to understand whither and against whom the Left wanted to continue the revolution. Opposition seemed to them a 'strange and dangerous anachronism'.[1] It was prudent diplomacy, the careful application and cultivation of what had been gained in 1831 that was required, not reckless extremism; they must devise domestic policies on the basis of previous achievements. They were quite right, of course, but on the other hand most of these Walloon, or at any rate French-speaking, liberals were so egocentric that they ignored certain matters that soon turned out to be of major importance. The subjectivity of their love of liberty and of their nationalism led to the political, cultural, and also the social subjection of the Flemish majority to the French-speaking minority.

However, there is no more reason to suppose that the state of 1831 and the statesmen who learned to rule it were anti-Flemish than that the Flemings were anti-Belgian. Of course, the revolution immediately entailed the collapse of the language policies which William I had introduced but which he had already begun to withdraw himself. The new state allowed everyone to use in the law courts, the schools, or wherever he had to express himself the language of his preference. The government of 1830 thought that French was the language spoken by most people in Belgium,[2] and no doubt it expected that linguistic liberty, such a completely natural thing in its opinion, would establish or reinforce the natural supremacy of French. And this was a correct assessment, provided one gave a sufficiently narrow definition to the term 'natural'. After all, no force on the part of the government was needed to make the dominant class use French in the courts, in the schools, and in the administration. The fact that four-sevenths of the population—according to the census of 1846 there were 2·4 million Flemish against 1·8 million French-speakers[3]— were unable to understand the language in which they were

---

[1] Lebeau, p. 164.   [2] Picard, *Geschiedenis* i. 157.
[3] Ibid. 160; E. van Bemmel (ed.), *Patria Belgica* (3 vols., Brussels, 1873-5), iii. 404-5.

being governed and tried did not constitute a problem to this generation. Concepts like liberty and the nation were still so vague that brute facts could hardly mar their beauty: if a state in which one in 95 inhabitants possessed the franchise and one in seven was in need of poor-relief[1] could gain a proud reputation for liberty the fact that hardly one out of two knew the language in which the administration expressed itself was not likely to cause undue embarrassment. In local administration and in primary schools—indeed, until some years after the revolution even in secondary schools[2]—Flemish was still much in use. Moreover, no one prevented the Flemings from learning French. In 1847 Charles Rogier, with that boundless naïvety of the French-speaker unwilling himself to learn foreign languages (the Latin of his dissertation was poor), seriously and benevolently advised the illiterate paupers of Flanders to devote themselves to the study of French.[3]

The tendency of the ruling groups to regard French as Belgium's national language was so strong that they placed Flemish on the same level as Walloon, an interesting and touching but doomed dialect. It was against this patronizing attitude towards their language that various groups of intellectuals, especially in Ghent and Antwerp, rose in opposition. Their claims seemed modest enough, for in fact they were prepared to recognize French as the state's language. Yet in the circumstances of this period their claims were so radical that for many years to come it was quite impossible to realize them. A Flemish petition of 1840, which had only very limited popular support, asked that the administrations of Flemish provinces and municipalities and of the Flemish law courts should as far as possible use the native language, as they had before 1794. Most of the 'Flamingants', as the men who wished to preserve the Flemish or Dutch language in Belgium were called, felt no attachment to the Northern Netherlands. Only very few, like J. F. Willems, continued to deplore the split of 1830; but Willems found so little encouragement among his Dutch

[1] X. Heuschling and Ph. Vandermaelen, *Essai sur la statistique générale de la Belgique* (Brussels, 1841), p. 53.
[2] L. Wils, *De ontwikkeling van de gedachteninhoud der Vlaamse Beweging* (Antwerp, 1955), p. 36.
[3] Discailles, iii. 219.

literary friends that he soon resigned himself to the necessity of an independent Belgian state.[1]

Many of his younger admirers and followers, however, men of letters and philologists who tried hard to create a genuine Flemish Romantic literature, sedulously lined up with the eulogists of the Belgian people, an old nation which the 1830 Revolution had brought to new life and unity.[2] The best of them, Hendrik Conscience (1812–83), had in 1830 even joined the anti-Dutch volunteers and it was only after many years that he decided to write in Flemish—son of a French petty bourgeois and a woman from Antwerp, it was in a strict sense his mother tongue. He said that he found in the language 'something truly romantic, naïve, wild'.[3] These adjectives are certainly applicable to his first novels, *In the Year of Wonders 1566* (1837) and *The Lion of Flanders* (1838), which were written in still far from perfect Dutch. But this hardly mattered, for the principal aim and the *raison d'être* of the whole movement was not to realize an aesthetic ideal but to awaken what they liked to call Flemish nationality, which represented the core of the Belgian nation and the Belgian state, the true expression of the ancient Belgian *Volksgeist*. This Romantic Flemish-Belgian patriotism, always anti-French and sometimes also anti-Dutch, was undoubtedly an unexpected result of William I's linguistic and cultural policies. That these made possible the surprising revival of Flemish literature and art can be seen from the age of its protagonists: many of them had been at school under the United Kingdom.

The Flemish movement was petty bourgeois. It neither sought nor obtained support from the masses of the Flemish population, and the French-speaking élite was totally indifferent. It was primarily interested in historical, literary, and artistic matters. When at times members of the group felt that they ought to side with one of the Belgian political parties, they tended, so it seems, in spite of their Romantic individualism and occasional anticlericalism to opt for the Catholics, who were intimately linked with Flanders and more respectful

[1] M. de Vroede, 'Noord en Zuid na 1830', *Bijdragen voor de Geschiedenis der Nederlanden*, xii (1957), 297–300.

[2] Wils, op. cit., pp. 43 ff.; Elias, op. cit. ii. 107–43.

[3] E. de Bock, *Hendrik Conscience en de opkomst van de Vlaamsche Romantiek* (Amsterdam, n.d.), p. 51.

towards the Flemish language than the liberals.[1] In many ways the Flemish movement in its infancy was antithetical to the strong Orangist elements in the Belgian community. The Belgian Orangists sought to undermine the state of 1831. They remained loyal to the Orange dynasty, hoping either that the pre-revolutionary unitary state would be restored or that the Prince of Orange (the future King William II) would come to rule the Southern parts of the realm. Their attachment to the United Kingdom was dynastic; it was not inspired by Great Netherlands nationalism. The group had little cohesion. Resentment dominated it but its adherents nursed highly differentiated grudges. The movement was predominantly upper middle class or aristocratic, the motives of its most influential members being largely economic in character. The great industrialists and merchants, grateful for William I's constant and generous support, felt no sympathy whatever for the young Romantics of 1830 and 1831 and their adventurous experiments. In Ghent, Antwerp, and the Liège area they vehemently opposed the government; in Brussels it was, above all, the nobility which enjoyed demonstrating its contempt for the new rulers. Old-liberal, anticlerical, anti-Romantic, French-speaking, these are adjectives which indicate some of the more striking features of Belgian Orangism. Both William I and his son, the Crown Prince, helped the Orangists financially,[2] but public opinion in Holland was such that they could make no overt gesture of support. Resentment also brought the Orangists some support from left-wing groups, which was readily accepted. Republicans, embittered Mennaisians, socialists, all occasionally appeared under this improbable banner.

As an active political movement Orangism collapsed along with left-wing Unionism in 1839 when the Belgian Government finally accepted William I's decision of March 1838 to abandon his *status quo* policies. For this decision meant that the King was ready to agree to Belgium's independent existence and that he now wanted to take possession of the parts of Luxemburg and Limburg allotted to him in the twenty-four

[1] L. Wils, *De politieke oriëntering van de Vlaamse Beweging (1830–1857)*, (Antwerp, 1959), pp. 8 ff.; Elias, ii. 145 ff.

[2] *Gedenkstukken* x, 4, p. 423 and *passim*; x, 5, pp. 167, 709 and *passim*.

articles. Belgium had subscribed to these, but as long as William continued to decline the articles Belgium kept the provinces. The bitter disappointment of the Orangists gave a kind of moral support to the government which was taken aback by William I's volte-face. To the left-wing nationalists, many of whom were fervently Catholic and full of an expansionist crusading spirit, the idea that Limburg and Luxemburg might be seized by the national Protestant enemy was intolerable. Both provinces were represented in the Belgian Parliament and there is little doubt that the majority of their inhabitants preferred to belong to Belgium rather than to the Netherlands.[1] The nationalists implored the government to start a holy war.[2] The episcopacy and the professors of the Catholic University of Louvain (opened in 1834) protested in the strongest terms against giving up their brothers.[3] It looked as if the spirit of 1830 was reawakening, the spirit of revolutionary solidarity. The Prussian Rhine provinces, too, were stirred and in February 1839 inflammatory posters appeared in the streets of Brussels: 'Mort aux Prussiens protestants . . .'[4] The Unionist Government, led by a moderate Catholic and with only one doctrinaire among several extremists, was in a rather weak position. It was clear enough to Leopold I and his most important advisers that it was out of the question for Belgium to start a war, if only because of the twenty-four articles to which it had already subscribed. The country, moreover, was still highly dependent financially on Rothschild who had been granting enormous loans to the young nation since December 1831; his representative at Brussels, who had easy access to Cabinet ministers and was informed of all political manœuvres, tirelessly warned the government against such adventures.[5] Probably, therefore, there was never any real danger of war, but it was nevertheless over a year before the government signed the treaty with the Netherlands (in April 1839). The

---

[1] M. de Vroede, 'Voor of tegen België. De openbare mening in het huidige Nederlands-Limburg in de jaren 1830', *Bijdragen voor de Geschiedenis der Nederlanden*, xv (1960), 39; J. C. Boogman, *Nederland en de Duitse Bond 1815–1851* (Groningen, 1955), pp. 14 ff.

[2] *Gedenkstukken* x, 2, p. 455.

[3] L. Wils, *Kanunnik Jan David en de Vlaamse Beweging van zijn tijd* (Louvain, 1957), pp. 81 ff.

[4] *Gedenkstukken* x, 1, p. 517.   [5] Gille, op. cit., pp. 70 ff.

delay did, it is true, bring some advantages. The portion of the
United Kingdom's national debt payable by the Belgians was
much more fairly assessed in 1839 than it had been in 1831.
But the territorial regulations of 1831 remained valid. Belgium
lost the German-speaking part of Luxemburg and the major
part of Limburg.

In 1839 a vital period in the history of Belgium and the
Netherlands ended. After that year there was, for a long time to
come, no one to pursue active policies with a view to reuniting
the two countries. Yet in both the North and the South
there were statesmen who continued to deplore the events of
1830 because they had split a vigorous empire into two small,
weak states. Considerations mainly of power politics caused
some highly representative personalities in Belgium (among
them Charles Rogier)[1] and the Netherlands (an original
thinker like Thorbecke)[2] to seek some means of restoring, in
one form or another, the situation of 1815. In the nationalist
conception of Belgium particularly, the traditions of the Burgundian realm, revived by William I with such single-minded
perseverance, remained a factor of importance. In their diplomacy the Belgians could not of course translate these inclinations into a realistic programme, but they kept insisting that
somehow the areas lost in 1839 should be won back, and
after the First World War Belgian irredentism manifested
itself once again in extreme and dangerous forms.[3] However,
such claims were never backed in the nineteenth century by
military power, for the army was generally neglected by a
country which considered itself sufficiently protected by the
very treaties that so irritated it. In Belgian foreign policy the
second essential link with the Netherlands, the Flemish movement, played no part. But it is obvious that the Flemish question, the Flemish humiliation, and the Flemish revival can
only be understood in the framework of the history and culture
of the Low Countries as a whole. Flemish owed its ability to
develop as a vehicle of civilization to the Dutch language,

[1] Boogman, 'Achtergronden', pp. 63 ff.; for Lebeau's views in 1840 see Elias,
ii. 115.

[2] For Thorbecke's opinion in 1839 see E. Cantillon, 'Thorbecke en Europa
1851–1853', *De Gids* (1944–5), 16, and for his views in 1847 J. Michelet, *Journal*,
ed. P. Viallaneix, i (Paris, 1959), p. 670.

[3] Boogman, 'Achtergronden', p. 48 and *Nederland en de Duitse Bond*, p. 52.

which was already fully established. Although the decision of 1839 finally confirmed the breakup of the United Kingdom, during the nineteenth and twentieth centuries Belgian history was much more closely connected with Dutch history than in the seventeenth and eighteenth centuries.

The diplomatic and political crisis of 1838 and 1839 was followed by a more threatening crisis in the very sector of the economy in which hitherto rapid and psychologically important developments had been taking place, in finance and heavy industry. In 1830 the economic situation had been difficult. Thrown back upon its own resources, without colonies, with an agriculture on which more than half the dense population depended but which covered only a relatively small area, the country was probably poorer than its neighbours.[1] Political uncertainties, the abrupt termination of William I's help, and the closing-down of the markets in the Netherlands and the Dutch East Indies, the anti-Belgian agitation of the leading Orangist industrialists, all these and other factors made the prospects gloomy. Yet in fact the 1830s saw the transformation of the Belgian economy, and the first years of independence were characterized by restless activity and sometimes reckless enterprise. It was as if Romantic nationalism, frustrated politically, could only express itself fully in the sphere of economics. Belgium did not owe its growth to Europe's economic climate. On the contrary, in this period industrial prices were falling.[2] Nor did it owe it to foreign encouragement. The enormous expansion was a strictly national development, an expression of Belgium's long-felt pride in the creative powers of its bold young people.

It should be emphasized, however, that it was only the iron industry and the collieries—of major importance, of course, but still inferior economically to the small industries and agriculture—that expanded so impressively[3]. Railway construc-

---

[1] This is the not unchallenged opinion of F. Baudhuin, 'Histoire économique de la Belgique' in Jean Deharveng (ed.), *Histoire de la Belgique contemporaine, 1830–1914* (3 vols., Brussels, 1928–30), i. 336. Cf. E. H. Kossmann, 'België en Nederland, 1780–1830', *Bijdragen en Mededelingen van het Historisch Genootschap*, lxxvii (Groningen, 1963), 36–8.

[2] P. Schöller, 'La Transformation économique de la Belgique de 1832 à 1844', *Bulletin de l'Institut des recherches économiques et sociales*, xiv (Louvain, 1948), 531.

[3] Ibid., p. 540.

tion was the most spectacular achievement. In 1834 Parliament decided that the state itself should take the initiative in building a network of railways. The doctrinaire Cabinet ministers, Rogier and Lebeau, impressed by Saint-Simon's doctrines, emerged as the eloquent champions of the project against many doubtful members. Such a grand, such a national monument, Rogier exclaimed, must be built by the country and could not be abandoned to the whims and greed of private interests.[1] The 'moral effect' of the railways, that miracle of the time, that invention unequalled in all history, was thought by many, most of all by the doctrinaires, to be overwhelming.[2] Mechlin became the centre from which tracks spread out to Germany, Ostend, Antwerp, and France, enabling transit traffic to move rapidly and safely through the country. In 1840 Belgium had a network of 336 kilometres (against Germany 549, France 497, and the Netherlands 17!). Soon the iron industry and the mines started benefiting from this grandiose initiative.

After agriculture, the coal industry was the major economic enterprise; it grew rapidly from 1834 onwards. In the ensuing decade the number of men working in the Mons mines increased by 23 per cent, the number of tons produced by 43 per cent. In Charleroi these figures were 55 per cent and 209 per cent, in Liège 38 per cent and 72 per cent respectively. In Hainaut and Liège the iron industry also prospered. Now the steam-engine triumphed, and total horsepower grew from 12,000 in 1832 to 25,000 in 1838 and 37,000 in 1844.[3] Lively financial development made possible relatively large investments, even though the public was still reluctant to use its money for this purpose. Banking business expanded. The Société générale, which William I had established in 1822, was ahead of its time because it not only acted as banker for the government but on a limited scale granted industrial credit;[4] after 1834 it flourished vigorously. It gave increasingly large credits to industry and founded investment trusts which

[1] L. Hymans, *Histoire parlementaire de la Belgique de 1831 à 1880* (5 vols., Brussels, 1877–80), i. 211–12.

[2] *Revue nationale* i. 103, 384.   [3] Schöller, op. cit., p. 575.

[4] Julienne Laureyssens, 'Le Crédit industriel et la Société Générale des Pays-Bas pendant le régime hollandais', *Belgisch Tijdschrift voor Nieuwste Geschiedenis*, iii (1972), 119–40.

actively furthered industrial growth.[1] In 1835 the Banque de Belgique was established, partly because the Société générale was suspected, in all probability unjustly, of Orangism. Mainly dependent on French capital,[2] the Banque de Belgique also provided considerable industrial credits. Others soon followed. It is estimated that in the period from 1833 to 1838 more than 350 million francs were invested in industry.[3] The limited company became more popular. There were no more than about fifteen in 1830, nearly all insurance companies. From 1833 to 1839 151 such companies were founded.[4]

With the political crisis of 1838 and the danger of war there was some loss of confidence. In December 1838 the Banque de Belgique had to stop payments when it appeared that its liquid resources were totally inadequate to meet the demands of its clients, who were anxious to take out their deposits and to change their paper money into coins. The Société générale managed to keep going only with great difficulty. A real panic broke out in Antwerp and Liège. As a result the credits on which heavy industry especially was dependent were abruptly withdrawn or, at any rate, greatly reduced. The government hesitated to intervene, but in January 1839 it provided the Banque de Belgique with sufficient means to reopen its paying-counters. Although confidence was slowly restored when the Chamber decided to cede and declared once again in March 1839 its willingness to accept the twenty-four articles, the first *élan* of economic optimism had gone. The banks learned from the experience that they ought to cut back their activities.[5] Fortunately, light industry and agriculture, still in the whole framework of the Belgian economy more important, were so far removed from capitalism that they did not feel the disturbance of 1838 to any great extent. Yet the sudden crisis in the heavy industries which hit the financiers, merchants, and entrepreneurs persuaded the statesmen in power, who did not realize how ephemeral it was, that war might entail catastrophic economic consequences and thus contributed to the peaceful settlement of the Belgian–Dutch conflict.

---

[1] Chlepner, op. cit., pp. 69 ff. [2] Ibid., pp. 63 ff.
[3] Schöller, p. 567. The calculation was made by N. Briavoinne, *De l'industrie en Belgique* (2 vols., Brussels, 1839).
[4] Chlepner, p. 68. [5] Ibid., pp. 155–200.

4. *The Netherlands in the 1840s*

In the 1820s the Belgians had moulded their political concepts into forms more modern than those of the Dutch and in the 1830s they also surpassed their Northern neighbours economically. Only after 1840 did the Dutch, under constantly deteriorating economic circumstances, start trying to develop their political system. In 1848 they at last succeeded; by that time their economy too was being adapted to international conditions. This transformation was not a gradual process; it came about as a result of unexpected developments abroad and of the kind of resigned despair at home that sometimes induces seemingly reckless decisions. Until 1848 it seemed highly unlikely that the Romantic liberals would ever be allowed to alter the structure of Dutch political life. The period starting with the 1839 treaty and ending with the liberal revision of the constitution in 1848 was characterized by a widespread and growing desire to escape from the atmosphere of William I's government and to recapture the freedom of the past. At no moment during these years would it have been possible to foresee a radical reform at least as modern in its conception as the 1831 constitution of Belgium.

William I was isolated in Europe and threatened in his own country by an opposition which had grown conscious of the absurdity of Dutch attitudes and forced the States General to tread more cautiously in financial matters. In March 1838 he decided to end his feud with Belgium and a year later the final treaty was signed. It was then necessary, of course, to revise the constitution of 1815—the constitution of the United Kingdom—in the light of the new situation. It was no longer possible to avoid discussions which, it was feared, might subject the whole political framework to a painful and perhaps fatal re-examination. However, not only the government, but also the major part of the opposition was afraid that radical changes would release uncontrollable forces.[1] This explains why the government succeeded in hurrying through the revision of the constitution and in keeping the discussions as brief as possible. In December 1839 the government itself made the first proposals; in the spring of 1840 further proposals followed. Most

---

[1] *Gedenkstukken* x, 2, p. 563.

were accepted almost unanimously by the States General. According to the 1815 constitution a revision had to be sanctioned at a meeting of the Second Chamber supplemented by the Provincial States with an equal number of extraordinary members. This double meeting took place from 4 August to 2 September. It accepted most of the proposals by large majorities.

The revision was reduced to mainly technical matters of little political relevance. But at this time the Dutch people were shocked to learn that the King, whose wife had died in 1837, was proposing to marry a Roman Catholic court lady of Belgian family. In March 1840, when it appeared that this might cost him what remained of his popularity and become a dangerous weapon in the hands of the radicals opposing the limitations set upon the constitutional debates, he undertook to abandon his plan. But once the revision had been passed, he decided to carry it out and on 7 October abdicated, the embittered victim of public opinion that for years had been encouraged to detest Popish Belgium, and which now considered the marriage of its King to a Catholic an act of treachery. Moreover, one series of articles in the new constitution was so repulsive to William I that he thought he would be unable to govern under it.[1] For it was stipulated that in future Cabinet ministers themselves would be prosecuted if they were suspected of violating the constitution or the laws in their official capacity and, in order to show that they now bore a certain amount of personal responsibility, they were to countersign all royal decrees. Not without justification did the old King consider that his traditional system of government, under which ministers acted only as the King's servants, could no longer be continued; the States General would certainly regard this as contrary to the spirit of the constitution. Although the system of 1840 did not amount to the Cabinet's collective political responsibility, it did away with purely royal government, as the French Minister immediately realized.[2] And so William I, the best of the three Dutch kings, the most original of all European princes in the Restoration period, abdicated.

His son William II (1792–1849) succeeded him. He had

---

[1] J. A. Bornewasser, 'Ministeriële verantwoordelijkheid onder Koning Willem II', *Tijdschrift voor Geschiedenis*, lxxv (1962), 440.

[2] *Gedenkstukken* x, 2, p. 575.

inherited his father's impressionability but it manifested itself in a very different way. Weakness had made his father stubborn, hesitation had made him brusque. But work, the daily responsibility of government and the daily task of taking initiatives, had become the *raison d'être* of this inexhaustibly active man. The son's weaknesses took the form of a desire to please, and what creative powers he possessed dissipated themselves in wild vagaries. As Crown Prince he had been involved in impossible situations; often his relations with his father were strained. He did not know the country he was now going to rule very well. His Dutch was defective. He thought and spoke—with an English accent—in a princely French. When in 1848 he exchanged some letters with Leopold I, the Belgian King wrote in German, the Dutch in French.[1] His attitudes were so unclear that liberals, Catholics, Calvinists, and conservatives, all took him, on occasion, for their exclusive champion. It has been calculated that he changed his political persuasions eight times during his life.[2] Yet he possessed something which was not often to be found in his father: a certain largeness of spirit and gesture, that undoubtedly often sprang from lack of principle but could also at times amount to open-mindedness and magnanimity. His character influenced both his foreign and his domestic policies. His natural, dynastic conservatism, his wish to be popular with the Dutch liberals, and his hope of winning back Belgium were the three contradictory elements confusing his relations with Europe.[3] His conduct of domestic affairs was also complicated by his hesitations and lack of self-knowledge. In 1840 he announced a new era: 'il faut marcher avec son siècle, il faut franchement entrer dans la voie constitutionnelle. . .'[4] But after seeing the practical implications of constitutional government, even though it was still so insecurely based on the constitution's ambiguous articles relating to ministerial responsibility, he found that he was not a liberal at all and was opposed to constitutionalism.[5]

[1] Published by M. Huisman, 'La crise révolutionnaire de 1848 et le rapprochement hollando-belge', *Bijdragen voor Vaderlandsche Geschiedenis en Oudheidkunde*, 7th ser. iii. 21 and vi. 3.
[2] J. C. Boogman, 'The Dutch Crisis in the Eighteen-Forties', in J. S. Bromley and E. H. Kossmann (eds.), *Britain and the Netherlands* (London, 1960), p. 195.
[3] Boogman, *Nederland en de Duitse Bond*, pp. 63 ff.
[4] *Gedenkstukken* x, 3, p. 665.   [5] Bornewasser, op. cit. 443.

At the start of his reign the new King did not meet with much opposition on matters of principle. In fact financial rather than political issues caused the most concern. In the decade from 1829 to 1839 the interest-bearing public debt increased by 408 million guilders. In 1842 payment of interest devoured nearly half the budget; in 1844 it totalled 43·9 millions, that is 14·60 guilders per head of the population. Although this was not yet as catastrophic as it had been (for example, in 1804), compared with the situation under the United Kingdom when the Belgians were also paying their share (in 1830 it was 3·85 per head for the whole population, both in the North and the South) it represented an intolerable burden.[1] Repeatedly the parliamentary opposition protested against the manipulations of William I's ministers which flouted all the rules of honest accountancy. They demanded that the figures should be made public and justified. After getting some insight into the difficulties, they asked for redress, and their wishes were fulfilled in 1842 when the Minister of Justice, Van Maanen, a symbol of William I's autocracy, made way for the barrister Floris van Hall (1791–1866), who was regarded as a liberal. He was indeed a liberal,[2] in the restricted sense typical of the province of Holland. He was neither a radical nor a Romantic. Under the Batavian Republic he would have been a moderate, an adherent of Schimmelpenninck. He disliked the Romantic doctrinaire views of Thorbecke and his followers which were alien to Holland's mood. But his practical mind and matter-of-fact suppleness made him eminently capable of finding his way through the labyrinth of public finances when in 1843 he exchanged the Department of Justice for that of Finance. Without trying to bring about profound reforms, he managed by means of a loan at 3 per cent to redeem the old debts with interest at 4½ or 5 per cent, or to convert them into new ones at 4 per cent. He thus saved annual interest of 4 millions and reduced the national debt by 51 millions. By 1847 the budget was well balanced for the first time for

[1] I. J. Brugmans, 'De financiële crisis van 1844', in his *Welvaart en Historie* (The Hague, 1950), pp. 64, 68, 73.

[2] See the remarks of C. W. de Vries, 'Politieke invloeden op de grondwetsherziening 1848' *Tijdschrift voor Geschiedenis*, lxxi (1958), 51 ff. and J. C. Boogman, 'De Britse gezant Napier over de Nederlandse volksvertegenwoordiging' (in 1860), *Bijdragen en Mededelingen van het Historisch Genootschap*, lxxi (Groningen, 1957), 196.

many years; in 1848 interest had sunk from nearly 44 to 36 million guilders or from 14·60 to 11·85 guilders *per capita*.[1] Thanks to his influence on the capitalists of Holland, whom he had persuaded to make a not-inconsiderable sacrifice after the profitable 1830s (it was estimated that total losses of interest amounted to 30 million guilders),[2] Van Hall had succeeded in averting the threat of state bankruptcy.

It is characteristic of the situation that the financial problem attracted greater attention than the economic and social difficulties which were in fact more serious. After twenty relatively favourable years pauperism once again became an acute danger during the 1840s. About 10 per cent of the population had been receiving poor-relief in 1830; in 1847 it was at least 16 per cent. In North-Holland almost a quarter of the population was in need of support.[3] It is true that in other parts of Europe, and certainly in Belgium, conditions were probably worse. But there the problem of the proletariat was an aspect of economic expansion. In the Netherlands, with its slow industrial development, pauperism was a result of economic stagnation. This was the opinion of Gerrit de Clercq, who in a controversial article on social utopianism, mainly that of Louis Blanc, published by the liberal monthly *De Gids* in 1846, asked himself why socialism found no support in the Netherlands.[4] Indeed it is easy enough to quote figures indicating Dutch backwardness. Between 1839 and 1849 the number of people living in towns decreased from 39·30 to 38·86 per cent of the total population.[5] Apart from a few exceptions—such as the shipyards and engineering-works in Rotterdam and Amsterdam, the textile industry in Twente, the glassworks and potteries of Regout in Maastricht—Dutch industry was organized in small businesses hardly or not at all mechanized. In 1853 the Netherlands could put only 7,000 horsepower against the 40,000 of the Belgian steam-engines in 1846. Railway construction was slow. The banks were considerably more conservative

---

[1] Brugmans, 'Financiële crisis', 73.
[2] De Bosch Kemper, *Staatkundige geschiedenis na 1830*, iv. 281.
[3] See the tables in De Bosch Kemper, *Armoede*.
[4] Reprinted in *Mr G. de Clercq herdacht* (Amsterdam, 1887), p. 59. This interpretation has been accepted by both I. J. Brugmans and Henriette Roland Holst-Van der Schalk, *Kapitaal en Arbeid in Nederland* (4th edn., 2 vols., Rotterdam, 1932), i. 89.   [5] Brugmans, *Paardenkracht en mensenmacht*, p. 189.

than the Belgian banks and did nothing to stimulate indus-trialization. Yet the economic traditions of the Netherlands were such that, although in many respects the country appeared to be in a state of decay, it was still in 1850 certainly not back-ward all along the line. The number of limited companies (137 in 1850) was proportionally not much smaller than in Belgium (191 in 1852).[1] The Dutch merchant fleet, the fourth biggest in the world, was of course much larger than the Belgian, and so was its foreign trade generally. But the Nether-lands had not yet known the tensions experienced by the expanding societies of England, France, or Belgium. The country was perhaps not much poorer than its neighbours, but it was undoubtedly much more old-fashioned and conser-vative in its economic policies.

In consequence, the most serious opposition of these years remained, even after Van Hall's successful manœuvre, that of the financial specialists. They were in favour of free trade (if not immediately, at any rate in the near future)[2] and were liberals as far as the economy was concerned. In the political field, however, their liberalism was largely confined to an insistence upon a closer examination of the government's financial opera-tions. Of course the States General ought to have been capable of providing this, and it was mainly in order to facilitate their task that a new revision of the constitution was called for. Their ideal was the British constitution which the liberal financiers, unlike the Belgian doctrinaires, praised not for what it granted but for what it left unsaid. In their opinion a consti-tution ought to be vague, so that the legislator could at any time adjust the state to the requirements of the moment without the need for any fundamental discussion of principle.[3] In their view too government involved little more than a cautious susceptibility to situations which were forever changing and often moving in totally unexpected directions. They did not suppose that the state, or political action, could accomplish anything positive. Hence their aversion to Thorbecke and to anti-revolutionary principles. They preferred a government

[1] Brugmans, *De arbeidende klasse*, p. 71 and Baudhuin, op. cit., p. 245.

[2] J. Zwart, *A. J. Duymaer van Twist. Een historisch-liberaal staatsman, 1809–1887* (Utrecht, 1939), p. 42. L. C. Suttorp, *F. A. van Hall en zijne constitutioneele beginselen* (Amsterdam, 1932), pp. 25 ff.

[3] Suttorp, op. cit., pp. 81 ff.; Zwart, op. cit., p. 56.

that could be called liberal because, in contrast with the government of William I and his vacillating son, it might modestly
leave both the individual and society[1] alone and allow the
representatives of the higher classes in the States General to
scrutinize more carefully the activities of the executive. This
group of moderates, spiritual descendânts of the moderates
of the Batavian Republic, was important. In the Second Chamber it had a number of highly influential supporters who drew
their strength from Holland and from Amsterdam in particular.[2] Their dependence on Holland implied that moderate
liberalism was limited by the traditions of Holland. It was
opposed to giving the lower middle classes or the lower classes
generally a larger share in politics. It was Protestant and anti-
Romantic, and though perhaps not actually hostile to freedom
of education it was not greatly in favour of it either.

The small, still almost powerless group of self-styled anti-
revolutionaries, on the other hand, was Romantic, if not in the
absolutist fashion of the 1820s. After 1830 an evolution started,
similar in many respects to that of the Belgian Catholics during
the Restoration period, although it did not lead to comparable
extremes. It was a highly complicated process and it threw
both supporters and opponents, theologians and politicians,
into confusion. Isaäc da Costa drifted away from Bilderdijk's
apocalyptic visions; his theology remained quite orthodox but
he adjusted and simplified it according to his interpretation of
the scholarship of the period.[3] He also brought his political
conceptions up to date.[4] In the manner, but without the passion,
of the Catholic democrats of Belgium, he became interested in
the social question and in the 1840s the royalist absolutist of
the 1820s could even approve of Thorbecke's doctrinaire
liberalism.[5] He did not become a liberal himself, however, but
dreamed of a Christian-historical political theory which he was
unable to draft.

[1] Zwart, p. 43.
[2] See also Th. van Tijn, 'Tien jaren liberale oppositie in Amsterdam', *Bijdragen
voor de Geschiedenis der Nederlanden*, xvii (1963), 184 ff.
[3] D. A. de Graaf, *Het leven van Allard Pierson* (Groningen, 1962), pp. 26–7.
[4] See his remarkable letter of 1837 to Willem de Clercq in M. E. Kluit (ed.),
Briefwisseling tusschen Willem de Clercq en Isaac da Costa (Baarn, n.d.), p. 40.
[5] J. C. van der Does, *Bijdrage tot de geschiedenis der wording van de Anti-Revolutionaire of
Christelijk-Historische Staatspartij* (Amsterdam, 1925), pp. 67 ff.

His follower, the jurist and historian Groen van Prinsterer, went beyond Da Costa's meditations. After 1830 he detached himself from William I's government and in 1834 was put in charge of the Royal Archives, becoming the editor of the *Archives de la Maison d'Orange-Nassau*. By then he had already adopted rigidly Calvinist views. But he was not a dogmatist. His religion was emotional like that of the German Romantics rather than intellectual in the manner of the great seventeenth-century Calvinists. But just as his passion was hidden under the smart manners of the wealthy son of a doctor who moved among the Hague aristocracy as an equal without actually belonging to it, so in his writings he concealed the hesitating, tentative sensibility of his thought behind a severe intellectualism. His disquisitions, however, were rarely strictly logical, not even in his masterly work of 1847 *Ongeloof en Revolutie* (*Unbelief and Revolution*) in which he sought to demonstrate, in a fascinating and original way, that there is a necessary development from irreligion to revolution and from there to dictatorship and communism. None the less, he succeeded in finding a starting-point for his political ideas in the late eighteenth-century Orangism that once inspired Van Hogendorp. He visualized a monarchy which would allow great independence to the provinces, towns, and other historically founded corporations; he thought deeply about the fundamental liberties due to individuals, and approached the position of the Romantic Catholics. But he never went the whole way. The state remained for him a means, given by God, of limiting the chaos resulting from the Fall. He wanted to preserve and to use its authority. In this respect the Protestant Romantics of Holland differed radically from the left-wing Catholics in Flanders and Brussels.

The reverence they felt for the pre-revolutionary past of the Netherlands and for the independent existence of the Protestant sects made the anti-revolutionaries much less afraid than the other groups of forming a political party. The Dutch generally stuck to the view, dating from 1813, that the revolution had done away with the divisions of the *ancien régime*, which had led the Dutch Republic from catastrophe to catastrophe. The Catholics, too, were still anxious not to be called a party and there were in any case reasons why they were not yet capable of forming one. They reacted like a more or less oppressed minority to such an extent that their political sympathies seemed to be almost exclusively determined by their assessment of what they could hope to obtain from the government in power. They expected no good from William I and thus the Catholic newspapers of North-Brabant were soon converted to Lamennais's liberal Catholicism. William II, however, was thought to be well disposed towards them. He entertained a curious friendship with a Catholic priest at Tilburg, where both as Crown Prince and as King he liked to stay, and indeed shortly after his accession he mitigated various measures which had prevented the growth of monasteries and congregations. This sufficed to turn the Mennaisian leaders of William I's period into royalists painfully loyal to King and state.[1] It was a reaction that did not make much sense, but there were other reactions too. During the 1840s some Roman Catholic newspapers, mainly in North-Brabant, took part in a violent agitation together with a group of irreligious democrats. The journalist Adriaan van Bevervoorde (1819–51)[2] was one of these: he was a member of Marx's Association démocratique at Brussels but can hardly be called a genuine revolutionary for he preferred to address himself in French to the educated Dutch.[3] In the province of Holland the Roman Catholic Press adopted a different attitude again. There a relatively small but active group of younger Catholic members of Parliament and intellectuals discovered that political reforms rather than royal gestures were required to improve the lot of the Catholics. The Revolution of 1830 was now so obviously past history that these men no longer felt obliged loudly to proclaim their loyalty to the nation lest they were suspected of being in league with the Belgian mutineers. Men like the priest F. J. van Vree (1807–61) from Gelderland, and Judocus Smits (1813–71) from Brabant who in 1846 established the newspaper De Tijd (Time) at Amsterdam (where there were 50,000 Roman Catholics in a population of 220,000), or the brilliant doctor

[1] L. J. Rogier, Katholieke herleving. Geschiedenis van Katholiek Nederland sinds 1853 (second edn., The Hague, n.d.), pp. 23 ff.

[2] G. A. M. Beekelaar, Rond grondwetsherziening en herstel der hiërarchie. De Hollandse Katholieke jongeren 1847–1852 (Hilversum, 1964), pp. 37 ff.

[3] C. T. de Jong, 'Portret van een pamflettist: Adriaan van Bevervoorde', Streven, ix (1956), 532.

and journalist of West German origin, J. W. Cramer (1817–84), also a writer of importance on *De Tijd*, made the Western provinces the centre of liberal Catholicism, although none of them was himself a Hollander.[1] In the monthly *De Katholiek* of 1842, under the celebrated priest and philosopher Cornelis Broere (1803–60), another attempt was made to provide Dutch Roman Catholicism with a broader intellectual and political basis.[2]

Thus it might seem that during the 1840s a development took place in the Netherlands that had occurred twenty years earlier in Belgium: Romantic Catholics and liberals came together in the hope of founding a free state. In theory this is true. But in actual fact there were great differences, the most striking one being that Dutch Catholic liberalism made no claims at all to originality. Neither in the political nor in the ecclesiastical sphere did it seek to be creative. After the difficulties encountered by Lamennais in the 1830s it is easy to see why it did not experience the lyrical ecstasies of its Belgian co-religionists. It was just a means for achieving certain ends, a tactic to obtain greater independence. Its importance lies in the fact that it enabled Thorbecke and his followers to revise the constitution in 1848, and to re-establish the Catholic hierarchy in 1853. This proved the Catholic-liberal method right but it proved nothing else. Because of the lack of self-confidence of early nineteenth-century Dutch Catholicism the liberal Catholics, unlike their Belgian predecessors in 1831, gave the new constitution their support but contributed nothing to its contents.

Only in the 1840s—twenty years after it was born in France and adopted by Belgium—did doctrinaire liberalism take shape in the Netherlands. Of course this tardiness can be explained by political and social conditions. There was little room for innovation in a society drawing its strength from tradition, with an economy living on the past, and a civilization well informed of foreign achievements but submitting these all too distrustfully to the test of what were called essentially Dutch principles. In the Netherlands, with its rigid, classicist

---

[1] Rogier, *Katholieke herleving*, pp. 33 ff.
[2] G. Brom, *Cornelius Broere en de Katholieke emancipatie* (Utrecht, 1955), p. 234 and *passim*.

universities intended for an élite, there were no groups of young, ambitious intellectuals who learned to use Romanticism as their weapon; nor were there rising middle classes, still striving after a place in society, whose representatives they might have claimed to be. Compared with France and Belgium where doctrinaire liberalism seemed to express itself naturally and spontaneously, the Dutch variant looks studied and affected. The literary leader of the Romantic liberals, E. J. Potgieter (1808–75)—an Amsterdam business man born at Zwolle in Overijssel, and author of some highly ambitious poetry—wrote in a style as consciously conceived as that of the political leader Thorbecke, also from Zwolle, whose prose impressed his contemporaries not only by its vigorous conciseness but also by its deliberate originality.

The literary revival preceded the political. In 1837 Potgieter founded the monthly *De Gids* (*Guide*) and soon got support from the versatile historian R. C. Bakhuizen van den Brink (1810–65). During the first decade of its existence this periodical, which had set itself the task of purging Dutch literature, dedicated itself mainly to criticism. It was certainly Romantic, although the Belgian doctrinaire-liberal *Revue nationale de Belgique* founded in 1839 by Paul Devaux had by then moved beyond Romanticism and was often hostile to it.[1] On the other hand, a comparison of the two periodicals shows how much richer and more original Dutch civilization still was. The Belgian review suffered from a fatal anaemia. Probably its excellent editor had to fill most of it himself, but in the end long quotations from foreign publications made it a sort of reader's digest for the half-educated. *De Gids*, however, became a really influential review. Whereas Devaux's work had primarily a political, even a party political, character, it is typical of Dutch conditions that *De Gids* started to defend political liberalism only after 1839.[2] The two periodicals also differed in their approach to nationalism. Devaux did not seek to draw his national concepts from the past, but rather from the future, which if doctrinaire principles were obeyed would mould the

---

[1] Charlier, *Le Mouvement romantique*, ii: *Vers un romantisme national* (Brussels, 1959), pp. 356–7.

[2] De Bosch Kemper, *Geschiedenis van Nederland* ii. 427, *Letterkundige aanteekeningen*, p. 199.

nation into a unity.[1] *De Gids* and Potgieter wanted to reform the Dutch national consciousness as it then was. For it was corrupted, complacent, and egocentric. He and Bakhuizen confronted their contemporaries with the energetic spirit of the seventeenth century. Only by introducing that spirit into the present could the Netherlands hope to recover. The word 'national' possessed doubtful overtones for the liberals. During the 1830s it had been used both by the government and the public in the narrowest possible sense, as a synonym for a kind of plaintive pride in Dutch righteousness and rigid conservatism. As late as 1862 Thorbecke still boasted that he had always managed to avoid the term.[2] Some of the doctrinaires were not even sure that the Netherlands deserved a place of its own in Europe. During the gloomy years of crisis after 1844 both the liberal *Arnhemsche Courant* and *De Gids* published articles advocating the absorption of the Netherlands in Germany.[3] It is true that similar ideas had sometimes been propounded in the 1830s.[4] But it is remarkable that such defeatism found its way into liberalism, which was after all by definition fundamentally nationalist; it shows how tense and intricate were the emotions of the Dutch doctrinaires.

There are at least two other factors that explain the slow evolution of Dutch liberalism. Thorbecke, to whom Dutch Romantic liberalism owed some of its most idiosyncratic features, was a highly complicated personality. His development was slow as well as erratic. The first crisis in his life occurred on a long journey through Germany when he came into contact with the Romantic movement. In the course of a few days in May 1821 the pedantic young classicist from Leiden University suffered a conversion.[5] However, he did not yet draw political conclusions from his experience. He deplored the Belgian Revolution. Only after the catastrophe—he soon became professor of later modern history at Leiden—did he

---

[1] See e.g. *Revue nationale* i. 26; iii. 424.

[2] Cf. W. Verkade, *Overzicht der staatkundige denkbeelden van Johan Rudolph Thorbecke (1798–1872)* (Arnhem, 1935), p. 36.

[3] De Bosch Kemper, *Geschiedenis van Nederland* iv, *Letterkundige Aant.*, p. 208 and Boogman, *Nederland en de Duitse Bond*, pp. 95 ff.

[4] See e.g. *Gedenkstukken* x, 1, p. 378; x, 5, pp. 179 ff.

[5] Cf. his most remarkable letters in J. Brandt-van der Veen (ed.), *Het Thorbecke-Archief 1798–1872*, ii (Werken Historisch Genootschap, 4th Ser., no. 7, Groningen, 1962), pp. 47 ff.

start critically to study Dutch politics. In 1839 he published his *Comment upon the Constitution* in which he indicated where, in his view, cautious improvement was necessary. The 1840 revision did not at all meet his requirements. Then the 42-year-old scholar, who had supported William I's autocracy, became the leader of the liberal opposition to the much less articulate system of William II. The second edition of his *Comment* (appearing in 1841 and 1843 in two volumes) was more radical than the first. Now Thorbecke declared himself in favour of truly constitutional government, of ministerial responsibility, and of various other points in the classic liberal programme. In 1844 he went so far as to state in a magnificent lecture on 'Contemporary Citizenship'[1] that a universal franchise was the logical consequence of the state's development and that it should be introduced in stages, despite the tragic fact that capitalism with its fatal tendency to increase the power of the wealthy at the cost of a constantly growing proletariat contradicted the evolution of political equality in the most extreme way. This lecture represents a climax in Thorbecke's thought. It is characteristic of his type of doctrinaire liberalism that here, in offering a theoretical justification for what he was later allowed to do as a practical statesman, he examined the dangerous tensions and the insoluble contradictions within his own concepts with sagacity and resigned pessimism.

Thorbecke was not a Hollander. He came of a German family established in the province of Overijssel, where in the eighteenth century the Patriot party was born and in 1798 the radical party counted a larger number of adherents than anywhere else north of the great rivers. When in 1844, as a member of the Second Chamber, he and eight friends—most of them not from Holland either—made a proposal (quickly rejected) for a radical revision of the constitution, the Dutch public certainly did not react impetuously. But it seems that in Groningen, Zeeland, and Overijssel people showed some interest in it,[2] whereas in Holland, and especially North-Holland, there was almost total indifference.[3] For Holland was

[1] J. R. Thorbecke, *Historische Schetsen* (The Hague, 1860), pp. 84 ff.

[2] Rüter, op. cit. iii. 151, 208, 343, 219. G. W. Vreede (*Levensschets*, Leiden, 1883, p. 274) declares that the proposal might have found support 'in small towns or in the countryside in Holland, Gelderland, Overijssel etc.'.

[3] Rüter, ii. 186 ff.; iii. 139, 152–3.

either moderate or conservative.[1] And although doctrinaire liberalism cannot be said to have been hostile to Holland, its romanticism, its relative radicalism, and its desire to be politically creative were alien to it. In other words, the strongest opposition to tradition came, as it had half a century earlier, from outside the country's economic and cultural centre and was, more or less, directed against it. This imposed a strain on the movement and withheld from it the dynamic, rhetorical optimism of the French and Belgian doctrinaires.

Thorbecke's victory in 1848 was largely a result of a number of accidents. In the Second Chamber of which he himself was no longer a member, his group consisted of only seven or eight men as against more than twenty-five moderates and only a few less conservatives.[2] It was, fundamentally, William II's autocratic character that enabled him to carry the day. For it was the King who suddenly decided on 13 March 1848 to have the constitution thoroughly revised, and he commissioned the doctrinaires to draft a new one. Not only that but he allowed them to prevent the radical-democratic agitation of Van Bevervoorde and his companions, of which initially he had seemed in favour, from developing into a popular movement. Finally, he saw to it that the States General agreed to the doctrinaire proposals. Why William II should have made so radical a volte-face is difficult to explain. Of course, it represented a reaction to the great events taking place in France and Germany. The revolutions of February and still more those of March obviously worried him desperately. But other factors combined to make the capricious and impressionable King change course. There were mysterious communist activities in Amsterdam at the beginning of March, and a financial crisis as a result of which many people in Amsterdam and The Hague went bankrupt; there were his odd relations with the few radical-democratic journalists to be found in the

---

[1] The moderate chairman of the Second Chamber, Boreel, told Thorbecke in 1849 'that one should not deny that a large part of the nation, especially in Holland, and more particularly in Amsterdam, was very conservative . . .': 'Herinneringen van Jhr. Mr. W. Boreel van Hogelanden, voorzitter der Tweede Kamer der Staten-Generaal', ed. J. de Louter, *Bijdragen en Mededeelingen van het Historisch Genootschap*, lii (Utrecht, 1931), 377.

[2] Cf. H. T. Colenbrander, '1848' in his *Historie en Leven*, ii (Amsterdam, n.d.), p. 198 and Boreel, op. cit., p. 344.

Netherlands, his serious physical exhaustion, and his anxieties about what would happen to the autocracy when the Crown Prince, generally considered incapable and very unpopular, succeeded him.[1] Not only did this persuade him to alter his domestic policies, it also influenced his foreign policy. For long years William II, like his father, had been expecting chaos in Europe. For long years he had been hoping, though with increasing misgivings, to win Belgium back, when anarchy, so laboriously overcome in 1830, raised its head again. By the end of February 1848, however, the King made it clear to the Belgians that he regarded their country as a bulwark against the revolution and in March he wrote appreciative letters to Leopold I whom he had for so long despised.[2] Thus after nearly a decade of quarrelling, mainly for economic reasons, the year of revolution unexpectedly brought the two countries closer together.

In this way Thorbecke, as the recognized leader of the doctrinaires, was given the opportunity to draft a new constitution. The States General, and to begin with the government as well, tried to obstruct his plans. But the King supported him although he disliked the professor and kept considering other possibilities. Fear of the consequence of failure, however, and the absence of any positive initiative from the opposition, finally made Thorbecke indispensable. It was Thorbecke himself who drafted the constitution, his colleagues on the commission appointed on 17 March being quite ready to subscribe to his suggestions. On 11 April the commission had finished; in June the Second Chamber started discussing the proposals. Only heavy pressure by William II and the vigorous help of the Catholics prevailed upon the States General to accept them, though in a slightly modified form. On 3 November the new constitution could be solemnly proclaimed. Just as the 1813 constitution was mainly due to Van Hogendorp, so that of 1848 was largely the individual achievement of Thorbecke. Thorbecke's work was by far the more successful: it still stands. For it was less stubbornly personal than that of his predecessor.

[1] F. J. Duparc, *Willem II, België en Luxemburg* (The Hague, 1933), p. 92. Cf. Baud's letter quoted by Zwart, p. 51 n. 1 and Boogman, *Nederland en de Duitse Bond*, p. 273 n. 1.

[2] Huisman, op. cit. iii. 17 ff.; Duparc, op. cit., pp. 88 ff.

Its formulas and style differ greatly from those of the Belgian constitution, but its content and purpose are, generally speaking, similar. A Second Chamber directly elected, a First Chamber of notabilities elected by the Provincial States, a system of government with full political responsibility of the Cabinet to the representative body, together with a careful concern for the autonomous characteristics of the lower political bodies, all these matters were defined in a way not fundamentally at variance with the Belgian precedent. Yet it is remarkable that (on the initiative of the States General) the new constitution also emphatically committed education to the care of the government, and that the election law which Thorbecke himself carried through in 1850 granted the franchise to no more than 75,000 men out of a population of three million. This represented a reduction of the electorate in comparison with the 90,000 entitled to take part in some stage of the indirect elections before 1848; but, when put against the Belgian electorate—in 1848 enlarged to nearly 80,000 out of a population of about 4,360,000—it shows how relatively prosperous and democratic the country still was.[1]

The events of 1848, though in some respects unexpected, are of fundamental importance in Dutch nineteenth-century history. Since 1780 the Dutch had been uncertain about their own nature and destiny. It was difficult for a nation which had reached the summit of its wealth, power, and influence almost as soon as it had emerged to live in the much humbler circumstances of the late eighteenth and early nineteenth centuries. The constitution of 1815 was designed for a middle-sized continental state with a proper function to perform in the European balance of power. Seen in this perspective, the constitution of 1848 appears as a recognition of Dutch weakness. Thorbecke,

---

[1] Yet the electoral qualification (the *cens*) was, on an average, higher in the Netherlands than in Belgium. According to the act of 12 March 1848 each Belgian man paying at least 20 guilders or 42·32 francs in direct taxation was entitled to vote (cf. Gilissen, *Régime représentatif*, p. 97) whereas in half the Dutch municipalities a considerably higher *cens* was required. None the less, about 10·7 per cent of the adult male population in the Netherlands and 8 per cent in Belgium obtained the vote. Obviously the cause of this was that, although in both countries the United Kingdom's system of taxation was still in force, Dutch taxes were higher than the Belgian. About 1840 the Belgians paid per head of the population 19 francs in direct and indirect taxation, the Dutch 32 francs. It is true that after 1844 Dutch taxes became less oppressive, yet they remained higher than those of Belgium.

who before the secession of Belgium was wont to emphasize the international significance of the United Kingdom, was after 1840 silent about the place of the Netherlands among the nations. Although occasionally praising the small state in fairly conventional terms as the seat of peace and freedom, he never did so with particular reference to his own country.[1] There can be no doubt that there is a connection between the liberty acquired in 1848, the establishment of a state which 'does not know one absolute will' (as Thorbecke put it at the end of his life with an unmistakable reminiscence of Guizot's formulas dating from the 1820s),[2] and the idea that the Netherlands, powerless and deprived of any great task, could afford to be weak. Thus the importance of 1848 is not only that the new domestic arrangement brought hitherto excluded groups into politics and was flexible enough later to bring in still others, but also that it effected a reconciliation of liberty and weakness. The Patriots of the 1780s wanted freedom in order to restore their vision of a democratic and powerful past. The radicals of the 1790s wanted freedom in order to found a vigorous revolutionary state. Van Hogendorp sought to establish a harmonious compromise between freedom and international greatness. In 1848, for the first time, liberty was seen as a luxury made possible by the very lack of power. Not only did men resign themselves to the country's reduction to the status of a small power, they eulogized its advantages. The feeling of *malaise* which had been disturbing the Netherlands since the late eighteenth century gave way to a positive appreciation of the narrowness of its national existence. At last, after a crisis, at times acute, at times latent, lasting some seventy years, the Dutch succeeded in adapting themselves to reality. They found a new equilibrium that was to endure for nearly a hundred years.

5. *Belgium in the 1840s*

The Belgian doctrinaires assumed government a year before their Dutch colleagues. Their victory, much more than Thorbecke's, was the natural product of their social and intellectual

[1] See Verkade, op. cit., pp. 199, 209, 213.

[2] In his 'Narede', *Parlementaire Redevoeringen* (6 vols., Deventer, 1867–70), vi, p. xv.

awareness.[1] The task of revising the constitution fell to Thorbecke because of extraordinary circumstances; the Belgian doctrinaires grasped and organized power. Thorbecke and his followers did not want the Netherlands any longer to play a role in international affairs; their Belgian counterparts, in a totally different position, quite rightly considered as vitally important the consolidation of the young state and of the dynasty, which implied energetic diplomatic activity on behalf of neutral Belgium. Their nationalism was more orthodox than that of the Dutch liberals. What a magnificent task we have to perform, exclaimed the *Revue nationale* in 1840. Everywhere in Europe there is *malaise* but we dedicate ourselves to the noblest work the human spirit is capable of, the creation of a people, and our ideal fertilizes our intelligence, elevates our character, warms our soul.[2] Again and again the periodical attempted to indicate in what fields the Belgian people were able to achieve excellence, how they could grow to greatness and make a contribution of their own to European civilization. And here becomes apparent the extent to which the Belgian doctrinaires had already left Romanticism behind. For it was Belgium's common sense and seriousness, its positive attitude towards life, that they regarded as the peculiar characteristics of the nation. Belgium ought not to try and emulate French literature. The Belgian is neither a poet nor a man of imagination. He must concentrate on the solid study of history, political science, philosophy, and general education.[3] There, incidentally, lies not only his own future but that of Europe. With inexhaustible admiration the *Revue nationale* wrote about the country of common sense *par excellence*, almighty, imperialistic Britain whose ambitions, it declared, would always benefit mankind. The world owed to Britain modern industry, something so tremendous that no intellectual development in antiquity could stand comparison with it.[4]

Such views were naturally closely related to the social background of the Belgian doctrinaires. In the Netherlands where the government had always (in theory at any rate) been made

---

[1] For an interesting analysis of the rise of political parties, especially the liberal party, in the main towns see E. Witte, *Politieke machtsstijd in en om de voornaamste Belgische steden* (2 vols., Brussels, 1973).

[2] *Revue nationale* iii. 424. [3] Ibid. iv. 153–4; v. 227 and *passim*.

[4] Ibid. ii. 216–17.

up of unprivileged bourgeois, it was difficult for the liberals to derive much enthusiasm from the generalization that they were acting as champions of the rising middle classes. But in Belgium the situation was different. There (undoubtedly under French influence) doctrinaire liberalism was emphatically proclaimed a class movement. Rogier proudly announced that his party represented the bourgeoisie.[1] The *Revue nationale* was no less outspoken in this respect. The point and purpose of the bourgeoisie was materialistic. In the liberal election manifesto of 1845 it was explicitly stated that the doctrinaires would never renounce the middle classes to which they belonged and, in the interest of the material welfare of the country, would forcefully advance their claims.[2] In this way the Belgian doctrinaires in the course of the 1840s arrived at what might be called a classic definition of mid-nineteenth-century liberalism. They wanted to be both nationalist and materialist. They enjoyed using lyrical prose in praise of the army[3] and of the great ideal of social order. They did not ignore the social problems of the period but thought that these would solve themselves. They were also relativists, conscious of their time being only an episode in the stream of history. For soon the middle classes would cease to exist; they would lose their characteristics and become absorbed in the emancipated masses.[4] But at this unique moment in history it was the task of the doctrinaires to push society forward towards a brilliant future. Karl Marx, who lived in Brussels from 1845 to 1848, must have felt more at home in the intellectual atmosphere of Belgian doctrinaire liberalism than in that of the Dutch.

The evolution of Belgian liberalism was in many respects strongly influenced by the support which it received after 1839 from numerous former Orangists.[5] A number of elements, which had not originally belonged to the neo-liberal set of values, passed from Orangism into the doctrinaire outlook. In the 1820s the doctrinaires were opposed to giving the state strong power; in the 1840s they insisted on the creative work that could be done by government and on the primary importance of politics. In the 1820s they associated themselves

---

[1] Discailles, iii. 146.   [2] Ibid. 98–9.
[3] See e.g. ibid. 95 and *Revue nationale* i. 432 ff.
[4] *Revue nationale* viii, p. 190.   [5] Pirenne, vii. 104, 110–11.

with the Roman Catholics; now, however, they abandoned Unionism. Although the Orangist legacy—protectionism, vehement anticlericalism, a certain Voltairian rationalism—was not officially adopted by the serious, moralizing, and religious doctrinaires, it certainly helped them to detach themselves from Romanticism and to form an independent party of their own. At the same time, the connection with the generally wealthy Orangist industrialists, financiers, and nobles gave to the group an upper-middle-class character which it decidedly did not possess in 1828; the Dutch doctrinaires who were specifically opposed by the highest strata of the conservative bourgeoisie establishment did not possess it either. It is not surprising, therefore, that resistance to this identification of nation, state, middle classes, and liberals should have arisen from within liberalism itself.

The radicals drew their inspiration from the left-wing Unionism of the 1830s. Like the men of 1828, they were deeply distrustful of the state, the dynasty, and the ruling classes. But they were no longer so fervently nationalist as they had been ten years earlier; more than any other group in Belgian history before them they were preoccupied by the social question. They tried, still without much success, to enlarge their influence through such organizations as the Association démocratique (of which Marx was a vice-president) and the Alliance and through numerous and usually ephemeral periodicals— after the abolition of stamp-duty on daily newspapers in May 1848 many were founded and soon disappeared.[1] Their aims, largely borrowed from French utopian socialism, were far from precise. But writers like Édouard Ducpétiaux (1804–68), with his detailed, statistical research on the Belgian proletariat, made an original contribution to pre-socialist radicalism.[2] Even more so did Lucien Jottrand (1804–77)—a Walloon disciple and admirer of Kinker at Liège in the 1820s[3]—who entertained

[1] Cf. Bertrand, op. cit. i. 414.

[2] R. Rezsohazy, *Origines et formation du catholicisme social en Belgique 1842–1909* (Louvain, 1958), pp. 10 ff. and the study of F. Delhasse, *Écrivains et hommes politiques de la Belgique* (Brussels, 1857), pp. 177 ff.

[3] Jottrand told about his relations with Kinker in his book, written in Dutch, *Nederduitsche gewrochten van den Nederlandschen Waal* (Brussels, 1872), pp. 19 ff. See also his follower Delhasse, op. cit. and J. Kuypers's study in *Biographie nationale*, vol. xxx (1959), 471–87.

interesting illusions about the creation of a Great Germanic or Great Netherlands federation of free peoples, hated France vehemently, admired Flanders, and was hot in the pursuit of social justice. But these very examples show the insecurity of the radical position. For in the second half of the century both writers tended to be more in sympathy with social Catholicism than with socialism.

The influence of liberalism increased when it began to resist the growing power of the clergy in Belgian society. The liberties of 1831 and Unionism had helped to strengthen the Church in the first place, and in 1830 the neo-liberals had overrated their forces. They failed to acquire supremacy in the United Kingdom; but the severance of the links between North and South did not lead towards liberal hegemony in independent Belgium either. Only after 1839, when the Orangists lost hope in a restoration and gave their support to the neo-liberals, did it become possible for them to study the situation critically with a view to planning an offensive against episcopal pretensions. It was still many years before they were ready for action, however, and before then they were obliged to make heavy concessions. The Church grew rapidly after 1830. Membership of monasteries and convents increased from under 4,800 in 1829 to almost 12,000 in 1847.[1] In 1834 a Catholic University was founded at Mechlin and moved to Louvain a year later. By 1839 it had more students (489) than the State Universities at Ghent (396) or Liège (331) or the liberal Free University of Brussels (354), which was also established in 1834.[2] (It should, however, be noted that the three Southern State Universities of the United Kingdom together had more students in 1827 than the four universities of Belgium in 1839.) Liberal attempts to gain some state authority over the secondary schools, which were largely dominated by the Church, failed both in the 1830s and the 1840s. Innumerable free schools and seminaries competed with the state schools in which the clergy also possessed a large measure of influence. In 1850 only 24 secondary schools were supervised by the

[1] Deharveng, op. cit. ii. 504; at the end of the eighteenth century it had totalled nearly 10,000: Tassier, *Démocrates belges*, p. 20.

[2] Heuschling and Vandermaelen, *Essai*, p. 353. Greyson in Van Bemmel, op. cit. iii. 308 gives somewhat lower totals.

state as against at least 53 over which it had no control what-ever.[1] The situation was so chaotic that it is impossible to give even a rough estimate of the number of pupils attending second-ary schools, though it was probably higher than before 1830. Teaching standards, however, seem to have fallen.

Conditions in primary schools were still more confused. The number of pupils grew,[2] but according to liberal experts like Ducpétiaux teaching had badly deteriorated. Although the Catholics denied this, the archbishop and some of the bishops realized that primary education needed to be put in some sort of order,[3] and that they did not have sufficient funds at their disposal to assume the whole task themselves.[4] By the law of 1842, the work of the Unionist Cabinet of Nothomb, the state prevented primary education becoming the exclusive responsi-bility of the Church, but it allowed the clergy, in the capacity of supervisors and teachers of religion, access to all schools. It is difficult to assess the achievements of this system, but it seems fair to say that during the whole of the nineteenth century Belgian primary education remained backward in comparison with countries such as Germany, the Netherlands, and, in the second half of the period, also France. In 1860 almost 33 per cent of Belgian recruits for the army were illiterate[5] as against 18 per cent in the Netherlands.

Liberals had no choice but to acquiesce, though reluctantly and provisionally, in the compromise of 1842. However, they let it be known immediately that they were not prepared to subscribe to a similar compromise bearing on secondary education. And the very fact of their being confronted, in 1842, with the *fait accompli* of such overwhelming ecclesiastical power was sufficient inducement for them to consider their position carefully. Indeed Paul Devaux had for three years been busily emphasizing the vital necessity of parties in a representative

[1] W. Theuns, *De organieke wet op het middelbaar onderwijs (1 juni 1850) en de con-ventie van Antwerpen* (Louvain, 1959), pp. 8 ff.

[2] É. Ducpétiaux, *De l'état de l'instruction primaire et populaire en Belgique* (2 vols., Brussels, 1838), i. 100. More pessimistic figures are quoted by V. Mallinson, *Power and Politics in Belgian Education 1815–1961* (London, 1963), p. 33.

[3] A. Simon, *L'Église catholique et les débuts de la Belgique indépendante* (Wetteren, 1949), pp. 100 ff. and idem, *Sterckx*, i. 365 ff.

[4] Simon, *Sterckx* i. 399.

[5] Van Bemmel, iii. 309.

monarchy—a regime, he declared in 1842, not of concord but of contrasts.[1] The Catholics as well as Leopold I were sharply hostile to this; they realized that they were the main beneficiaries of Unionism. For the Catholics, Unionism meant that they, the representatives of a large majority of the Belgian people, were not confronted by a closed, combative minority. For the King it meant the maintenance of national unity, and of his own authority as an indispensable prerequisite. But these factors did not prevent the liberals arming themselves. The fact that the franchise was made dependent on fiscal conditions provided, for all the smallness of the groups backing them, the opportunity to enlarge their influence in the Chamber of Representatives. It is true that in the beginning the number of liberal members of Parliament hardly increased at all. They were still in the minority; yet after 1843 they drew more closely together and stuck more strictly to their principles.[2] In June 1846 384 liberals from all parts of Belgium gathered at a congress in Brussels. This, in itself a triumph of Belgian liberties (for in what other country on the Continent would the opposition have been allowed such a demonstration?), greatly increased their cohesion and clarified their programme. The meeting asked for cautious reduction of the *cens*, especially in the towns, and the organization of state education free from all supervision by the clergy, although the clergy would be invited to give religious instruction. Moreover, the congress drafted precise plans for the elections to be held in June 1847 (every two years half of the members of the Chamber of Representatives lost their mandate). These were at last to give the liberals a majority, though of only two seats. The King had no choice but to charge Rogier with forming a Cabinet, and his liberal government ruled from 1848 to 1852.

But Rogier met with unexpected difficulties. The 1848 revolutions threatened both Belgium's international position and its internal order. In the 1840s the relations between France and Belgium were cool. From 1836 French statesmen sought to negotiate a Franco-Belgian customs union which it was hoped would give France, at the cost of economic concessions to the small neighbour closed in by high tariff walls, overriding political influence and serve as the first stage of

[1] *Revue nationale* vii. 280.   [2] Lebas, op. cit., pp. 228–9.

a general effort to counterbalance the Zollverein. Owing mainly to the opposition of the very protectionist French industrialists of the North and the lack of interest in the scheme on the part of the Belgian nationalists, it came to nothing and after 1842 was no longer seriously considered.[1] Commercial treaties with the Zollverein (1844), France (1845), and the Netherlands (1846) provided the Belgian economy with outlets and confirmed the country's independent stability. When in February 1848 the revolution in France started again, it seemed possible that Belgium, which had felt the impact so deeply in the eighteenth century and in 1830, would once again be flooded by the waves of this tremendous disturbance. Yet, in spite of the fact that for a moment Leopold I lost all his self-confidence,[2] the government was so sure of itself and the country reacted on the whole so quietly (in March incursions by revolutionary Belgian proletarians working in France failed ludicrously) that there was no question of a panic as in Germany or even the Netherlands.

Rogier succeeded in taking the wind out of the sails of the progressives. With a swiftness reminiscent of the cascade of edicts through which, in October 1830, the provisional government of revolutionary Belgium had proclaimed the new liberties, he persuaded Parliament to reduce the *cens* to a much lower level than even the liberal Congress of 1846 had wanted, to abolish the stamp-duty on newspapers, and to support industries and banks hit by the crisis. But the government's, in fact very moderate, proposal to reform the system of taxation was decried by the Chambers as an attack on property and amended out of recognition.[3] Because of the reduction of the *cens*, the Chambers had to be dissolved. The elections in June turned into a triumph for the doctrinaires, forcefully backed by the conservatives, and a crushing defeat for the progressives who suffered from the tide of reaction spreading over Europe after the June revolt in Paris. In August a tribunal at Antwerp opened a gigantic lawsuit against forty-three democrats, sentencing seventeen of them to death. But they were all re-

[1] See H. Th. Deschamps, *La Belgique devant la France de juillet. L'opinion et l'attitude françaises de 1839 à 1848* (Paris, 1956), pp. 105 ff. and *passim*.

[2] B. D. Gooch, *Belgium and the February Revolution* (The Hague, 1963), pp. 27-8.

[3] B. S. Chlepner, *Cent ans d'histoire sociale en Belgique* (Brussels, 1956), pp. 36 ff.

prieved. Thus the result of the year of revolution in Belgium was ambiguous. It forced the government to initiate reforms more democratic than the liberal Congress of 1846 or the Parliament of 1847 had dreamed of. Yet at the same time it consolidated the doctrinaire party as a bulwark of the social order, hostile to the democratic ambitions and the social progressiveness that some years before had not yet become entirely alien to it.[1]

The successes of the liberal party were achieved in a period of tragic economic and social difficulties, especially in the Flemish provinces. There is not necessarily a causal connection between these two phenomena, in the sense that it was the decline of Flanders which enabled the Walloon bourgeoisie to grasp power. After all, liberalism was no more an exclusively Walloon movement than the Catholic party was exclusively Flemish. But Belgium's industrialization benefited Wallonia, which possessed the raw materials, and not Flanders which for so long had been the economically leading area of the Southern Netherlands. The freedom of 1830, the nature of the parliamentary system, the character of the emerging parties entailed the supremacy of people who expressed themselves in French, whether they came from Flanders or Wallonia, whether they opted for the liberals or the Catholics.[2] The increasing political tensions within the ruling classes reduced the significance of the Flemish movement, which represented so little that it could not hope to constitute an independent political party, and which, unable to make itself heard by either of them, could not even choose between the two big groups. Thus there were liberal as well as Catholic Flamingants, and even progressives, who especially in Flanders formed small centres of social agitation, were in some cases also Flamingants.[3] How conventional the reactions of most Flamingants still were became apparent in 1848 when they loudly praised the Belgian state and the stability of the Belgian people. They were so obsessed by their

---

[1] See the excellent analysis by J. Dhondt, 'De sociale kwestie in België', *Algemene geschiedenis der Nederlanden*, x (1955), 314 ff. and A. J. Vermeersch, 'L'opinion belge devant la révolution française (1848)', *Revue du Nord*, xlix (1967), 483–508.

[2] Picard, *Geschiedenis* i. 246–7; Wils, *Politieke oriëntering*, p. 43.

[3] Cf. Dhondt, op. cit. 321 ff. and E. Willekens, 'De taalstrijd in België 1840–1884', *Algemene geschiedenis der Nederlanden*, x (1955), 357.

fear of France and her social revolution that the Central European national movements left them, unadventurous provincials after all, wholly indifferent.

The economic distress of the Flemish provinces was not the result of Walloon supremacy but rather of the methods of production which the innumerable Flemish flax-spinners and linen-weavers (in 1840 they were estimated to total 278,000, that is one-third of the working population) and the Flemish entrepreneurs who dealt in their products still employed. Many peasant families were dependent for their livelihood on this handicraft, localized in the countryside and partly organized in the form of home industry. During the 1840s the industry was unable to compete with the cheaper and more fashionable products of the British factories, and in 1830 it was shut out of the Dutch and soon also out of the French markets; as a result it completely collapsed, notwithstanding attempts by the government to save it through premiums and protectionist policies.[1] Flemish backwardness was emphasized by the misery that followed this catastrophe. In spite of the Ghent cotton industry, which had succeeded in overcoming the difficulties of 1830 when it lost its market in the Dutch East Indies, and in spite of the growth of Antwerp, East- and West-Flanders became during the 1840s an area of great poverty. It had been relatively prosperous under the United Kingdom: in East-Flanders 11·6 per cent of the population received poor-relief in 1828, but by 1847 28 per cent were receiving it. There was much suffering during the famine which resulted from the potato disease. And the great mass of the people were also intellectually inferior to the inhabitants of Wallonia, where more children went to school and more money was available for educational purposes.[2]

In 1848 no one could have predicted that the Flemish problem was to become the major disintegrating factor in Belgium. In 1848 people in Belgium as well as in the Netherlands were proud about the dignified calm with which they had solved the problems of this year of international crisis. Without revolu-

---

[1] See the standard work by G. Jacquemyns, *Histoire de la crise économique des Flandres (1845-1850)* (Brussels, 1929).
[2] Picard, *Geschiedenis* i. 181. Cf. also *Bibliographie Vlaamschen Taalstrijd*, i (1904), 255.

tionary unrest they had been able to adapt their states to the new situation and by doing so had shown how successful they had been in establishing the national principles which the Belgian Revolution of 1830 had forced each of the two populations to search for.

V

LIBERALISM AS A SYSTEM
1848–1879

1. *The Character of the Period*

IN September 1880 a curious celebration took place at The
Hague. The indefatigable publicist Dr. Johannes van
Vloten unveiled a statue of Spinoza after delivering a speech
resounding with principles and fine phrases. For two centuries
Spinoza's philosophy had been treated by the Dutch with fear
and caution, if not ignored altogether. When in the late eighteenth century the Germans began to take an interest in the
Dutch philosopher there was no one in the Netherlands to
share their admiration. On the contrary, Protestant mistrust
was so deep that the young Thorbecke, who had been drawn
to the system when travelling through Germany in the 1820s,
subsequently abandoned his intention of writing a book about
him for fear that it would ruin his chances of obtaining a chair
in a Dutch university.[1] Not until the 1860s did it become
possible for the Dutch openly to praise Spinoza.[2] One of the
first and most vigorous manifestations of this new admiration
was Van Vloten's book of 1862, *Baruch d'Espinoza*, with its
characteristic sub-title 'His life and works in relation to his
and our times'. The relationship was, in fact, more with the
nineteenth century than with the seventeenth, for Spinoza appeared as the rationalistic, materialistic atheist who Van Vloten
rather than Spinoza was. Yet what is a book? Only by erecting a
statue can posterity express its gratitude. For many years Van
Vloten exerted himself for this purpose. In 1880 at last he
achieved his aim. And so successful had been the collection
of funds that Van Vloten was left with more money than he had
hoped for. He made good use of it. After enabling the common

---

[1] Brandt-Van der Veen (ed.), *Thorbecke-Archief*, ii. 249 (1823).
[2] Sassen, *Geschiedenis van de wijsbegeerte in Nederland*, pp. 364 ff.

man to look at Spinoza's statue, Van Vloten published the first complete edition of Spinoza's works for the benefit of those who could read Latin.[1]

For understanding the character of progressive liberalism during the 1870s the history of the Spinoza statue is perhaps more revealing than all liberal theories, laws, and economic achievements. Spinoza was honoured as the 'glad messenger of an adult humanity' (to quote the title of Van Vloten's speech),[2] as the man who had raised true wisdom above religion and its conflicts, who had completed the Reformation, and whose spirit called upon the Dutch people of the nineteenth century 'to ennoble society by moving beyond all religious disunity and social prejudices'. It is as if that generation's left-wing liberalism found its most characteristic expression on this occasion. Although squarely facing reality it was abstract and schematic. It did not construct memorials in honour of its own experience or to remember the joys and disappointments of the present day; it cast history, which it studied with a curious mixture of self-absorbed egocentricity and a passion for objectivity, into a lasting monument for its own glory. It was nationalist. And although it was a highly sophisticated doctrine of a social and intellectual élite capable of understanding the complicated civilization of the nineteenth century, it was at the same time democratic, for it brought its historical heroes to the people in the form of statues. The liberal statues of this period, which adorn countless towns and villages in the Netherlands and Belgium, were to carry to the illiterate masses the joyful tidings not only of a glorious future but also of a national past during which centuries ago the emancipation of mind and people had already begun. With unwavering pride the liberals sought for their predecessors in history and placed them among the people in the market-place. Flemish intellectuals welcomed the great anticlericals of the sixteenth century into their own family, and would name not only their streets and squares but also their sons after Marnix of Saint Aldegonde.[3]

In this way the Jew Spinoza who wrote in Latin became the

[1] Mea Mees-Verwey, *De betekenis van Johannes van Vloten* (Santpoort, 1928), pp. 214 ff.

[2] J. van Vloten, *Spinoza, de blijde boodschapper der mondige menschheid* (The Hague, 1880).

[3] F. Vercauteren, *Cent ans d'histoire nationale en Belgique* (Brussels, 1959), i. 178.

symbol of Dutch progressiveness; the withdrawn, almost incomprehensibly abstract mystic found a place in the streets just when the liberals, both in the Netherlands (1878) and in Belgium (1879), determined to introduce the masses to liberal concepts by a reorganization of primary education. The education laws were the most vehement challenge which this liberalism, detached from its Romantic origins and developed into a system, had to offer. And yet it aroused in both countries such aversion that its triumph turned into defeat. The confirmation of liberalism in the 1850s, the growing resistance to it and the polarization of life in the 1860s, the aggressiveness of liberalism and its attempt to win over the masses in the 1870s, are the themes which dominate Belgian and Dutch history during the third quarter of the nineteenth century.

There is a remarkable similarity between the development of liberalism in the two countries. Although doctrinaire liberalism and radicalism took different forms, they still seemed on the whole to obey the same evolutionary laws. But what do these terms mean? 'Doctrinaire liberalism' generally refers to the liberalism that came into existence under the Restoration. Liberals like Royer-Collard and Guizot were, not without irony, called doctrinaires and they accepted this as a compliment. At that time the term was not yet applied to the Belgian liberals. Only after they had established themselves as political leaders did their opponents call them to account for their stubborn 'doctrinairianism'. In the Netherlands the term was less common; generally speaking, the word kept its original meaning and indicated a man who maintained in too dogmatic a fashion his arbitrary principles.[1] A name, of course, does not signify very much and this particular label is too convenient not to be used as a *terminus technicus*. Yet it should always be remembered that the liberals of the 1820s were not called doctrinaires because they had a solid body of doctrine at their disposal but because the French aristocrats could not help smiling at their ponderous theories and their displays of

---

[1] The Austrian minister determined the political parties with some precision in 1840. He saw the difference between Thorbecke, 'le chef et naguère l'oracle des doctrinaires' and the 'parti radical' of Van Dam van Isselt and De Kempenaer. (*Gedenkstukken* x, 3, pp. 387–8.) Cf. the view of the Prussian minister who called Thorbecke in 1840 'le Royer-Collard de la Hollande', one of the great men 'du parti doctrinaire' (ibid., p. 133).

erudition. The doctrinaires did not have a doctrine. And when from the 1840s onwards both in France and in Belgium the Left bitterly criticized doctrinaire liberalism the main point of their attack was not so much the positive contents of a system which was hardly a system at all, but its narrow limitations. They criticized the doctrinaire liberals for being far too evasive about questions of primary importance, for not supporting and furthering democracy, for failing to give the state its due and crush the Church, for leaving, in short, so much undone. It was contempt for what they regarded as the vagueness of their liberal predecessors that inspired the opposition to construct a real system, to attempt at least to put their social, political, and historical views into some kind of logical unity. This was anti-doctrinaire, left-wing liberalism.

In both countries the great period of the doctrinaire governments ended at almost the same time. Rogier's Cabinet fell in 1852, that of Thorbecke in 1853. Both men had to give way before the wave of anti-liberalism sweeping across Europe. But in neither country were the conservatives allowed to take the helm. From 1852 to 1855 the Belgian government was still liberal, although it was more moderate than under Rogier and tried to keep aloof from party conflicts. In the Netherlands liberals of the same colour came to power in 1853. The Belgian and the Dutch moderates were not successful for long, however. The movement to the Right continued. In 1855 a Roman Catholic Cabinet took over in Belgium; in 1856 a member of one of the Protestant parties became Prime Minister in the Netherlands. Both remained in power for two years. In 1857 the Belgian Roman Catholics were succeeded by a new doctrinaire government; in the Netherlands the situation was complicated by the King's aversion to undiluted doctrinairianism and developments were rather different. A number of weak and colourless liberal–moderate coalitions appeared with the sole purpose of keeping Thorbecke out. Only in 1862 was he able to form a new Cabinet. Then, with the exception of five years (1866–8, 1874–7) the liberals remained in power until 1878. In Belgium the liberals survived, although not without terrible crises, until 1870. At that point they had to give way to a Roman Catholic Cabinet, but they returned in 1878. On the whole, therefore, the developments in both countries were strikingly similar: between 1848 and 1878 they were governed by the liberals for exactly seventeen years.

Even when out of power the liberals remained at the centre of the political and cultural movements of the time. It was their initiatives, their opinions that forced the conservative and the progressive oppositions to define their views more clearly and more coherently. But whereas in Belgium radicalism was already a force in the 1850s—though not yet dangerous it had acquired some sort of independent existence and was represented in Parliament by 1858—the first Dutch radical did not enter the Second Chamber until 1869. The transformation of the right-wing parties started earlier in Belgium too. In the 1860s certain Roman Catholic groups considered the possibilities of drafting a programme that was not based on the constitution of 1831, hitherto so unanimously praised: they criticized liberal conceptions much more sharply than their predecessors and did not entirely exclude the possibility of social legislation and a measure of democratic reform. In the Netherlands it was not until the 1870s that some members of the Protestant parties began to work along similar lines. Yet although opposition to doctrinaire liberalism matured a decade later in the Netherlands than in Belgium (at the beginning of the century the Belgian opposition had a start of two decades on the Dutch) the turning-point in both countries occurred in the vital 1860s.

The international position of the two states was of course different, but their foreign policies, largely determined by the dramatic complications which occurred in Europe, were broadly similar. The condition and the guarantee of Belgium's existence was its neutrality as defined on 21 January 1831 by the London Conference. No doubt the average inhabitant of Belgium resigned himself to this imposed status with indifference or even with gratitude. Did it not give him the certainty of a carefully protected life and the opportunity to devote himself to the furtherance of his own interests? He lived in a country without extra-European possessions and without as yet much ambition to acquire them, a country whose European irredenta (Limburg, Luxemburg, and, at some stretch of the imagination, Dutch Flanders) might occasionally cause a sweet patriotic pain but need never become a dangerous problem, for they did nothing after all to shake off the supposedly tyrannical Dutch yoke. Such a community was naturally inclined to spend its energy on improving the domestic situation and not on playing a role in world politics. In Parliament the parties took care not to start sharp discussions on foreign affairs; rarely did questions of this nature divide them. During the entire period from 1850 to 1870 the Ministers of Foreign Affairs never experienced any difficulty in having their budgets accepted by the Chamber of Representatives. In all those years not even as many as forty members voted against their budgets, whereas their colleagues responsible for domestic affairs were confronted by about 90 and the Ministers of Justice by more than 270 dissentient votes. Of course, not all Belgians had the same views on foreign affairs. The establishment of the Second Empire, for instance, was as welcome to the Roman Catholics as it was unwelcome to the liberals; even so, this fundamental difference of opinion did not entail any discussion about what Belgium's policies should be. There was complete agreement about the necessity and the beauty of neutrality. Moreover, national independence seemed so often and so seriously threatened that for this reason alone it was considered highly dangerous to make foreign policy an object of party conflicts.

The position of the Netherlands was different. Economically it was more directly connected with the outside world. Its exports and imports were considerably larger than those of Belgium—to the value of 103 guilders *per capita* in 1850, 206 in 1875, 1,138 in 1913 compared with the Belgian figures of 46, 217, and 546 guilders respectively.[1] It possessed ships— 527,000 tons in 1876 against Belgium's 48,000—as well as its own outlets. Dutch diplomacy was not bound by an international treaty and was in theory completely free to act as it wished. Moreover, the Netherlands had huge colonies which the Dutch considered were the only factor that raised the country above the diplomatic and economic status of a third-rate

---

[1] See the figures in J. A. van Houtte, *Economische en sociale geschiedenis van de Lage Landen* (Zeist, 1964), pp. 264–5. According to Chambers (*Workshop of the World*, p. 111) British exports and imports rose from £9 *per capita* in 1842 to £18 in 1872— a pound was worth about twelve guilders in the 1870s.

Power.[1] Thus it is not surprising that problems of foreign and, to a much higher degree, of colonial policy were included in the party programmes and discussions. During the Crimean War, for instance, the doctrinaires were vehemently opposed to the moderate government because of its 'hesitating, cringing neutrality'; they deplored the lack of the brave, honest, morally vigorous, though equally neutral, policy demanded by Thorbecke.[2] During the 1860s the Chambers were not above voting down a budget for foreign affairs and on one occasion this led to a serious constitutional crisis. But although the parties were ready enough to see foreign policy as a matter to disagree about, in actual practice the Dutch state often did freely what Belgium was obliged to do. It withdrew into a neutrality which, partly in order to distinguish it from the Belgian situation, was called a 'policy of independence' and was widely appreciated as such.

Not only in international law but also in international power politics the position of Belgium was generally thought to be weaker than that of the Netherlands. The vague, half-hidden aspirations of some German annexationists towards the Netherlands were never taken as seriously as the threat represented by the more blatant French imperialism towards Belgium. Moreover, it was not altogether inconceivable that the other Great Powers might allow France entry into Belgium. After all, they had left Denmark without protection, they had agreed to the sacrifice of Savoy, and given the impression of accepting the fact that the existence of small states had been made hazardous by modern developments in Europe. Of course, such fears were also felt in the Netherlands. Yet whereas it was easy to speculate on the ways in which by common consent Belgium might be taken over or divided, it was unimaginable that, if Germany were to annex the Netherlands, any such agreement could be achieved when the future of the Dutch colonies had to be decided. In other words, the Dutch problem was incomparably more complex. With good reason and sensible arguments intelligent Dutch commentators tried

[1] Robert Fruin, 'Nederland's rechten en verplichtingen ten opzichte van Indië' (1865), *Verspreide Geschriften* (10 vols., The Hague, 1900–5), x. 292.
[2] W. J. van Welderen baron Rengers, *Schets eener parlementaire geschiedenis van Nederland* (4th edn., ed. C. W. de Vries, The Hague, 1948), i. 129.

to calm Dutch public opinion after the alarming Prussian successes in the 1860s and the frightening rumours that ensued. It was pointed out that the Prussians had more important things to do than to annex the Netherlands; and even after the establishment of German unity, what sort of profit could they hope to gain from such a foolhardy enterprise?[1] About French ambitions and French interests in relation to Belgium, however, there could be no reasonable doubt in spite of all official denials. Moreover, notwithstanding its political hostility to France, Belgium was culturally dependent on that country to a much higher degree than the Netherlands ever was on Germany. It is true that Germany made a deep impression on Dutch civilization and that nearly all political groups found their inspiration in German examples or German doctrines— a Romantic Protestant like Groen van Prinsterer learned from Stahl; a radical like S. van Houten looked to Schopenhauer; a Christian democrat like Abraham Kuyper owed some of his ideas to Stoecker. Even so, the Germans never really dominated Dutch culture. In Belgium, where French was used for state affairs and for the higher forms of civilized intercourse, the French impact was so great that it might reasonably be doubted whether the Belgian way of life was more than a variant of the French one. This certainly made Belgium appear more vulnerable than its Northern neighbour.

Even more serious and fundamental was the uncertainty about Belgium's role in Europe, when the basis and justification of its nationalism came under scrutiny. Paradoxically, the naïvely nationalist convictions which, despite terrible tensions and the stubborn resistance of the Orangists, had characterized the first years of independence and gained in strength when order and unity had been so easily maintained in 1848, were increasingly questioned in the second half of the century, even though the state itself was more firmly established than before. In Parliament and among the people who belonged or felt loyal to the ruling groups the old hypotheses of 1830 were still uncritically repeated. The foundation of the Belgian state was still represented as the logical outcome of a long and

[1] Cf. e.g. J. T. Buys, *Studiën over staatkunde en staatsrecht*, ed. W. H. de Beaufort and A. R. Arntzenius (2 vols., Arnhem, 1894), i.173 ff. (1867) and *Nederland tegenover Duitschland . . . door een ongenoemde* (Utrecht, 1873), p. 3.

venerable development. In 1859 the Roman Catholic statesman A. Dechamps, a most prolific writer of pamphlets, expounded the view that the Belgian state had grown out of
three hundred years of assimilation and crystallization, out of a
long and patient process of 'nationalization', and that because
of this it was more deeply rooted in history than, for instance,
Poland or Lombardy.[1] The historian Théodore Juste (1818–88),
whose talents were well suited to the unsophisticated Belgian
bourgeoisie for whom he wrote, sought to prove in the 40,000
pages of his massive work that Belgian independence was the
result of an age-old process of maturing and that it deserved
everyone's deepest respect.[2] All Belgian historians thought that
although the Belgian nation had two languages at its disposal
it nevertheless constituted a unity. For the nation was purely
Germanic and owed to France only the language in which its
civilization could best express itself. The national character
was alien to the Latin—because Belgium was religious and
opposed to the Revolution, according to the Roman Catholics;
or because it was permeated with German individualism and
love of freedom and deeply hostile to Roman Catholic authoritarianism, according to the liberals.[3] Curiously enough, such
theses were propounded by historians who wrote exclusively
in French and few of whom had any knowledge of the German
language or of German historiography.

But this façade of historical fictions began to show dangerous
cracks. The party struggle assumed such proportions that it was
sometimes difficult to maintain national unity. No longer as in
the early part of the century were village and town, belief and
unbelief, Fleming and Walloon, represented as threads in the
great fabric of Belgian solidarity; they came to be, politically
and morally, profoundly hostile elements. With the reckless
intellectual ambition characteristic of the late nineteenth century, the leaders of the various groups demanded exclusive
rights for themselves and their followers. But what was the
point of calling oneself a Belgian and a patriot if one begrudged
one's neighbours their schools, their cemeteries, and their
churches? What could keep the Flemings and the Walloons,
the faithful and the unbelievers, the peasants and the towns-

---

[1] A. Dechamps, *Le Second Empire. Dialogues politiques* (Brussels, 1859), p. 66.
[2] Vercauteren, op. cit., p. 139.   [3] Ibid., pp. 190 ff.

people together? Nationality might matter, but there appeared to be other things that mattered more. Of course, in many other countries clericals and anticlericals were at odds; nowhere, however, was the conflict quite so hysterical as in Belgium, a small, previously homogeneous Roman Catholic country without great problems to solve or great ideals to pursue which could devote most of its political energies to this sole controversy. And because the nineteenth century with its rather simplistic sociological views tried to understand life by bringing as many phenomena as possible under one common denominator, inevitably the anti-national idea that Roman Catholic and rural Flanders differed from urbanized and agnostic Wallonia in spirit, language, way of life, and origins, was given much emphasis. In some circles it became common to speak of a Flemish 'people' which, without any justification, was believed to possess a long and glorious existence in history. In the Netherlands, also deeply divided, the conflicts between clericals and anticlericals, Roman Catholics and Protestants, town and country, never grew so vehement as to endanger the essential feeling of national unity.

But although Belgium may have stood somewhat lower in the hierarchy of states and although it was exposed to more serious domestic troubles than the Netherlands, its economic superiority was triumphantly maintained. Even in that section of the economy which had for centuries been Holland's greatest pride, its trade, Dutch growth—from a total value of imports and exports of 783 million golden francs per annum in the 1850s to 2,186 million in the 1870s—was less than that of the Belgians, which increased from 729 to 2,511 million in the same period.[1] Although the population rose more slowly in Belgium (by 14·9 per cent from 1850 to 1870 as opposed to 16·7 per cent in the Netherlands), it remained considerably higher (5,100,000 in 1870 compared with 3,600,000).[2] Mortality in Belgium, which in 1830 was about the same as in the Netherlands, fell rapidly in the third quarter of the century, whereas in the Netherlands it did not start to fall until 1875. The quicker population growth in the North was caused by the higher birth rate, which hardly changed between 1830 and

[1] Van Houtte, op. cit., p. 264.
[2] Ibid., p. 218.

1880 (36 per thousand in 1830, 35 per thousand in 1880); in Belgium it fell from 33 per thousand to 31 per thousand.[1] These and similar figures indicate the measure of Belgium's economic lead. Not until the end of the century did the level of Dutch social and economic life reach that of Belgium, with a larger proportion of the working population engaged in industry (33·4 per cent in the Netherlands in 1910; in Belgium 46 per cent) than in agriculture (27 per cent compared with 23 per cent in Belgium) and with about 60 per cent working in enterprises employing more than fifty men.[2] It would appear that only in the 1880s was the demand for labour balanced by the supply, a situation that had already occurred in Belgium in the 1850s.[3] And mortality rates did not improve very perceptibly in the Netherlands until the twentieth century when infant mortality and mortality generally were lower than in Belgium. By the Second World War the populations of the two countries were about the same, and almost equally divided between the various professions, although the Dutch interest in trade and freightage continued to dominate as did the traditional Belgian interest in industry.

During the third quarter of the nineteenth century neither country showed much inclination to establish more intimate contact with its former partner. Although in this time of rapidly expanding trade economic relations between them inevitably became closer, those which linked each of them to the economies of other European states grew more extensively.[4] Nor is there much evidence of more intimate cultural or political ties. This is easy enough to understand. France, Britain, and Germany could provide examples and inspiration; there seemed little to be gained by pondering the achievements of another small country. Generally speaking, the Belgians tended to be rather more interested in Dutch affairs than the opposite. Although the Dutch now accepted the existence of the Belgian state as an obvious necessity they found it hard to take their

[1] Van Houtte, op. cit., pp. 221–2. Cf. J. A. de Kok, *Nederland op de breuklijn Rome-Reformatie* (Assen, 1964), pp. 118 ff.

[2] Van Houtte, p. 242. Cf. Brugmans, *Paardenkracht en mensenmacht*, p. 385.

[3] J. A. de Jonge, *De industrialisatie in Nederland tussen 1850 en 1914* (Amsterdam, 1968), p. 269; Van Houtte, p. 244.

[4] Some figures in *1830–1880. Le Développement intellectuel et matériel de la Belgique depuis 1830* (Brussels, 1880), p. 39.

neighbours altogether seriously. During the diplomatic negotiations between the two countries which took place in this
period, the Dutch attitude was so reserved as to be haughty.
As compared with the autochthonous French culture it did
not seem to the Dutch that Belgian culture was deserving of
much attention. And Flemish literature and philology remained in the opinion of the Dutch so naïve that, although in
sentimental moments they might be touched by their inno-
cence, they could not regard them as genuine contributions to
the civilization of the Netherlands. It is true, however, that
some Flemish authors, notably Conscience, found a relatively
large audience among the more unsophisticated sections of the
Dutch reading public.

Dutch influence, on the other hand, was surprisingly small,
even on those Flemish leaders and agitators who in the 1860s
saw their movement as drawing its inspiration from the
cultural and linguistic unity of the Great Netherlands, and
highly valued their connections with the North.[1] It is quite
true that in comparison with other European countries the
Netherlands had very little to offer. It is equally true that in the
Netherlands even men who took an interest in Flemish emancipation, and they were few enough, resented and feared all
attempts to establish closer links and all forms of Great Netherlands idealism: for a Flemish secession from Belgium or even
an exacerbation of the Flemish–Walloon conflict would fatally
weaken Belgium, and only so long as it was strong and united
could Belgium fulfil its traditional function as a barrier against
France.[2] Even so the reaction of some Belgian radical liberals,
who wrote in French but were both pro-Flemish and pro-
Dutch, was astonishing. They deplored the Revolution of 1830
and hoped to wean the Belgians from their inveterate Catholicism by substituting an unorthodox form of Protestantism.
For them the Dutch Republic was a major argument in favour
of their thesis that in modern history economic and political
progress was due to Protestantism—a thesis which Max
Weber was to put forward in a more scholarly way. But they
were apparently quite unaware of the modern, ultra-liberal
theology developing in the Netherlands during the 1850s and
1860s, although it would have served their purpose extremely

[1] Eli s, iii. 162 ff.   [2] Ibid., p. 173.

well.[1] Even their Protestantism sprang from French,[2] English, or American sources, rather than Dutch.

In spite of this fundamental ignorance of each other, Belgian interest in the North was still greater than Dutch interest in the South. One important consideration was the natural but far from constant tendency of some pro-Flemish intellectuals to look for support from their brethren in the North who spoke the same language. Another was the fight against clericalism. Émile de Laveleye, the remarkable radical economist who later became a professor at the University of Liège, published in 1858 a booklet in which he warmly recommended the Netherlands to his compatriots both in general terms and more specifically because the Dutch education laws in his view best upheld the cherished principle of the separation of Church and State.[3] And in the late 1870s Belgian liberals often defended their educational policies by referring to the Dutch situation, which proved, according to them, that religiously neutral education was both possible and beneficial.[4] Their influential Ligue de l'enseignement of 1864 imitated and was inspired by the old Dutch society *Tot Nut van 't Algemeen*.[5] Still greater, however, was the consolation that some Belgians found in the study of Dutch history under the Republic. The liberals took part in the cult of the sixteenth-century Sea Beggars. On 1 April 1872 Flemish liberals even found their way to Den Briel, where the heroic events of 1572 were enthusiastically commemorated.[6] The seventeenth century taught how a small progressive people could become a world Power, and the colonial history of the Dutch could appear extremely attractive. King Leopold II, who admired the culture-system and was

[1] See, e.g., the articles of Émile de Laveleye and Eugène Goblet d'Alviella, who was from 1884 professor of the history of religion in the University of Brussels, in the *Revue de Belgique*, xix (1875), 5 ff.; xxii (1876), 5 ff.; xxiii (1876), 209 ff.; and esp. Goblet's study, 'Le Protestantisme libéral et la question religieuse en Belgique', ibid. xxvi (1877), 225–56.

[2] It was fashionable amongst French intellectuals in the 1870s to praise Protestantism, cf. K. W. Swart, *The Sense of Decadence in Nineteenth-Century France* (The Hague, 1964), p. 132.

[3] Émile de Laveleye, *Débats sur l'enseignement primaire dans les chambres hollandaises* (Ghent, 1858).

[4] See the protests against this view by Ch. Woeste, *Vingt ans de polémique* (3 vols., Brussels, 1885), ii. 66 ff., 261 ff.

[5] Cf. *Revue de Belgique*, iv (1870), 232.

[6] Elias, op. cit. iii. 73, 191.

fascinated by Dutch East Indian profits,[1] constantly impressed on his stay-at-home compatriots that their Northern neighbours, though such a tiny nation, had in the seventeenth century acquired enormous prestige, wealth, and power by their colonial enterprises. And one of the very few instances of direct Dutch influence on Walloon Belgium was the admittedly rather feeble imitation of a famous Dutch novel about Java—Multatuli's *Max Havelaar*.[2] Thus, although the group of Belgians who felt some sympathy for the Netherlands was, during this period, much smaller and much less influential than in the time just after 1830, when Orangism was rampant, there still existed in the South some interest in and admiration for the North which was not reciprocated. The situation had not essentially changed: the Dutch, with their confined, rather conservative and complacent national consciousness, largely ignored the Belgians; the latter occasionally looked northwards with interest and respect.

In its foreign policy the uncertainties of Belgium's international position, the self-confidence of its very prosperous and active population, and the unlimited ambitions of King Leopold II[3] manifested themselves simultaneously. When under pressure from radical idealists the doctrinaire government slightly reduced the costs of defence and the diplomatic service in 1848, it did so with much hesitation and reluctance. In an impassioned speech in the Chamber of Representatives the Minister of Finance, Frère-Orban, attempted to prove that even a neutral country like Belgium needed a powerful army

---

[1] J. Stengers, *Belgique et Congo: l'élaboration de la charte coloniale* (Brussels, 1963), p. 58. Idem, *Combien le Congo a-t-il coûte à la Belgique?* (Brussels, 1957), pp. 144 ff.

[2] It was written by an accountant in Brussels, Jules Babut (1827–95), and published in two volumes in 1869 under the title *Félix Batel ou la Hollande à Java*. In it Babut stressed the imperative need for colonial possessions, and at the same time severely criticized Dutch colonial policy. He urged that Belgians should penetrate into, and even occupy, parts of the Netherlands East Indies (i, pp. vii ff., 194 ff.; ii. 97 ff., 138 ff.). Cf. *Revue de Belgique*, ii (1869), 249 ff.; iii (1869), 193–223.— Multatuli regarded this work as a parody and shameless plagiarism. See his 'Aanteekeningen en ophelderingen by de uitgaaf van 1875', *Max Havelaar* (1875 edn.), n. 53.

[3] It is difficult to determine with any precision the influence of Leopold II, but it cannot be a coincidence that Belgian expansionism increased after his accession in 1865. At a time when he was still Duke of Brabant he once wrote to Prince Albert that Belgium was small but that Rome, Carthage, Austria, Prussia, and Russia also had started as small states (Windsor Royal Archives, Q 8/1; 27 Jan. 1857).

and distinguished diplomats, and he went so far as to suggest that in the mid-nineteenth century circumstances were at least as favourable for Belgium assuming a world role as they had been for Holland in the seventeenth century.[1] He can hardly have believed this. And yet his optimism was more than a facile illusion for it gave expression to something that constituted an essential part of Belgian self-awareness. Although only a small neutral state, Belgium was, according to this view, more than just an industrious country without weight or influence. She was growing. Her neutrality should be her strength, commanding respect; it was Belgium's duty to see that, far from being merely a restriction, neutrality was a positive act to be proudly recognized as the basis of European order.[2]

The most idiosyncratic form of this thesis was presented by Émile Banning (1836-98), the son of a man born in Amsterdam who had in 1830 established himself in Liège. Banning first worked for the almost blind doctrinaire leader Devaux. Devaux introduced the able but physically seriously handicapped young man to the Minister of Foreign Affairs, Charles Rogier, who appointed him to a post in his ministry. Soon his talents, and the reliability with which he drafted important memoranda, procured him real influence. He was a nervous, passionate worker who exhausted himself by his researches, his vehemence and idealism causing him to identify himself with the views which it was his professional task to expound and defend. He was not an original thinker but he had the inimitable gift of endowing the ideas of his masters with the vigour and logic of a systematic argument. He gave substance to the vague dreams of Rogier; he helped Leopold II, whose real purposes he was slow to understand, to draft an idealistic justification for his Congo policies. But Banning, who spent his life writing patriotic imprecations to his fellow countrymen, urging upon them a leading role in Europe and Africa, died in the deep pessimism of the *fin de siècle* period, when he forecast

---

[1] Paul Hymans, *Frère-Orban* (2 vols., Brussels, 1905-7), i. 241.

[2] Howard, the British minister in Brussels, wrote on 6 May 1859 to the Foreign Secretary Malmesbury: 'it is difficult to inspire [the Belgian ministers] with sufficient or invariable self restraint to prevent allusions to the weight of Belgium in the balance in any struggle between France and other great Powers' (P.R.O., FO 10/219, 59).

the reign of the masses and their leaders, the liberal middle classes having weakly and shamefully gambled away all their influence and responsibilities.[1]

In the 1860s he wrote curious memoranda about the nature of Belgium's neutrality.[2] In these he expresses views which he must have found in other texts but which had never been so excellently and so systematically put together. He made two points. First, Belgian neutrality was steadily becoming stronger because it triumphantly passed one difficult test after another—in 1840, in 1848, during the Crimean War, in the troubled 1860s. Second, it constituted a kind of mission. It was only Belgium's carefully defined, vigorously maintained, and well-armed neutrality that prevented such formidable fighters as France and Germany from an immediate confrontation that could lead to war. In 1866 Banning wrote a splendid piece on Belgium's essential task as a buffer state, a buffer state, however, which, if it were adequately to fulfil its function for the benefit of Europe, ought to be given more territory.[3] This was the style in which he elucidated for Belgian diplomats a concept of neutrality that made Belgium the corner-stone of Europe. In a memorandum circulated on 12 August 1868 even the fact that Belgium consisted of two different peoples was used as a justification for its national existence. For whatever changes the Continent might experience, it was argued, Belgium's independence would always remain not only a political but also a social necessity. On the borders of large nations there were always populations in which two elements approached one another and mixed. This intermediate territory was the natural domain of secondary, neutral states.[4] In such a way Belgian diplomacy tried to formulate for itself a meaningful national task, just at the time when the Netherlands, alarmed by contemporary events, confined itself to hoping that it would be allowed humbly to continue in existence. It was some

[1] See Émile Banning, *Réflexions morales et politiques. Précédé d'une notice biographique par le Général Brialmont* (Brussels, 1899).

[2] Idem, *Les Origines et les phases de la neutralité belge*, ed. A. de Ridder (Brussels, 1927).

[3] Idem, *Les Traités de 1815 et la Belgique* (Publications du Comité de politique nationale, Brussels, 1919).

[4] P.R.O., FO 10/294, 140 (Lumley to Clarendon, 2 Apr. 1869). Cf. J. Willequet, *Le Baron Lambermont* (Brussels, 1971), p. 47.

decades before the Dutch too elevated their neutrality, which they called independence, to the status of a mission. It was not as a buffer state that they saw their country, however— rather as a haven, a refuge for the peaceful and virtuous.

Lack of confidence in their national identity and the insecurity of their frontiers may well have caused Belgians to compensate by exaggerating their own importance. Diplomacy, still in any case conducted largely by the revolutionaries of 1830, was certainly more active and dynamic than in the Netherlands, where it remained as aristocratic and stiff after 1848 as it had been before. Diplomatic relations between the two nations were polite but cool. The reconciliation of 1848 was maintained; it did not, however, inaugurate a period of closer collaboration. After the *coup d'état* of Louis Napoleon, Thorbecke made some moves to safeguard Belgium's independence which he considered of vital importance to the Netherlands. He projected an alliance between Belgium, the Netherlands, and Britain, in which Prussia ought also to join. But this fall in 1853, for which, among other factors, French intrigues and the admiration of the King for Napoleon III may have been responsible, put an end to this initiative. Moreover, Franco-British understanding during the Crimean War reduced the danger that France might encroach upon the North. Neither Belgium nor the Netherlands allowed itself to be involved in the war in any way, and had at least this much in common in their foreign policies. But they criticized each other bitterly at times. In 1851 the Belgian–Dutch draft of a new commercial treaty which was to replace that of 1846 was seriously challenged by the Belgian Chamber of Representatives. And in 1858, when both governments wanted to improve their economic relations by lowering the customs barrier, the Dutch Second Chamber defeated the bill to the great irritation of the Belgians. Generally speaking, the Dutch Parliament stubbornly resisted the government's attempts to find solutions to Belgian–Dutch problems. Some compromises in the early 1860s were immediately followed by the fruitless bickering that had for so long characterized relations between the two countries.

Yet those solutions which were found were useful enough. In 1863 and 1865 customs duties between the two countries were lowered. More important was the agreement of 1863 for the redemption of the Scheldt duty, which had been a painful problem since 1839.[1] It had been agreed then that the Dutch should be responsible for keeping that part of the river that passed through their territory in good order and open to navigation; in return they acquired the right to levy a toll of one and a half guilders per ton on all ships sailing to Belgium. The Belgian Government responded by freeing ships bound for Antwerp from this duty by paying it for them. Because of the rapid expansion of trade the sums involved grew considerably. In 1840 the Belgian state paid about 600,000 francs; in 1862 it had to provide more than two millions. Between 1839 and 1862 it paid a total of 28,500,000 francs. From 1853 onwards the Belgian Government was trying to put an end to this situation; it was not only inconvenient but also humiliatingly reminiscent of the period before 1790 when the Scheldt was kept closed by the Dutch.[2] A new agreement took a long time. First the government had to persuade the states that had profited from Belgian willingness to pay the toll for so long that this was not a duty but a favour that might well be withdrawn. Thanks to negotiations conducted by the Belgians with considerable mastery, and to the useful precedent of the abolition of the Sound toll in 1856, Britain was prevailed upon to provide the sum of 9 million francs for the redemption of the Scheldt duties. Many other states had already promised to collaborate. The Dutch Government, though still suspicious, declared that it was prepared to sell its rights for over 36 million francs, more than one-third of which was to be paid by Belgium. Henceforth navigation to Antwerp was completely free, and the final, hateful remnant of Holland's old supremacy disappeared. At last, the Minister Rogier solemnly told the Chamber, relations with the Netherlands, so long disturbed by this anomaly, could become closer and more lasting.[3]

How close and how lasting? It is a complicated question.

---

[1] See, e.g., S. T. Bindoff, *The Scheldt Question to 1839* (London, 1946), pp. 219 ff.

[2] In a conversation with the British minister Howard, Rogier talked about an 'act of hardship and humiliation'. Quoted by C. A. Tamse, *Nederland en België in Europa (1859–1871). De zelfstandigheidspolitiek van twee kleine staten* (The Hague, 1973), p. 217. I owe much to this work and am grateful to its author for providing me with the archive material quoted.

[3] Hymans, *Histoire parlementaire* iv. 143.

During the following years relations between the two countries were confused in a most peculiar way. Belgian attitudes fluctuated bewilderingly, at times openly hostile, at others inviting new forms of intimate association. Rogier, who was responsible for foreign policy, sometimes gives the impression of being infected by the poisoned atmosphere in Europe and the ambitions of the leading statesmen. He might try to imitate the reckless style of Napoleon III or Bismarck only to run up against the unmoving, haughty level-headedness of his colleagues in the Netherlands.[1] He grimly contested Dutch plans, first drafted as early as 1846, to build a railway from Flushing in Zeeland to Venlo in Limburg, on the grounds that this would affect the structure of the Zeeland waterways. The railway was intended to run over bridges or even dams which would prevent ships from using the waterways between the islands of Walcheren and Zuid-Beveland, as well as between Zuid-Beveland and the continent. Of course the Dutch proposed alternatives, as they were obliged to do according to the treaties of 1839 and 1842. In order to ensure that navigation from the Scheldt to the Rhine remained possible they planned to dig a canal through Zuid-Beveland and Walcheren which would connect the West Scheldt with the waterways in the North. The whole question was allowed to remain dormant until 1860 when the Dutch state assumed responsibility for the construction of railways. The Belgians expressed serious objections to these projects. They feared that the new canal would turn out to be an insufficient substitute for the old waterways and that the hydrographical situation in the West Scheldt would deteriorate if dams were built. Moreover—but for obvious reasons they could not use this as an argument— they were afraid that if it were connected by railway with Germany Flushing would prove a dangerous competitor to Antwerp.[2] A fruitless discussion dragged on for years. It was not unnatural for the Dutch to oppose the Belgian claims, for the corollary seemed to be that the Belgians possessed a

[1] For a detailed study of these and other matters see Tamse, op. cit., pp. 257–310. See also Jules Garsou, *Les Débuts d'un grand règne. Notes pour servir à l'histoire de la Belgique contemporaine* (2 vols., Brussels, 1931–4), ii. 32 ff.

[2] A. Brialmont expressed this fear in his *Complément de l'œuvre de 1830. Établissements à créer dans les pays transatlantiques. Avenir du commerce et de l'industrie belges* (Brussels, 1860).

sort of co-sovereignty in relation to the Dutch part of the Scheldt which obliged the Dutch to consult them before making modifications in the waterways. The question led to much acrimonious comment both in the Parliaments and in the Press, and revived memories of 1830. In the end the Dutch got their way, the Great Powers refusing to support the Belgian point of view, and Belgium had to resign itself to a *fait accompli*.

Curiously enough, at the same time as this probably unnecessary squabbling Belgian diplomacy, or at least Charles Rogier, was making repeated attempts to restore the unity of the two countries in some form or another. Rogier remembered with obvious nostalgia both the strong state of 1830 and his attempt in that year of revolution to establish Belgian supremacy in it through liberal reforms. In 1860, when he was still Minister of Home Affairs, he composed a new national hymn to the tune of the Brabançonne in which he first declared that Belgium, led by King, Law, and Liberty, was going forward from strength to strength, and then urged her to open her ranks to her old Dutch compatriots and to draw the fraternal ties tighter.[1] Some years later, in 1866 and 1867, Rogier—who became Minister of Foreign Affairs in 1861—frequently discussed with the Dutch Envoy at Brussels a possible restoration of the United Kingdom, either in the form of a federation or of a unitary state.[2] The excessively unpoetical Dutch Government, however, left both his verses and his suggestions unanswered. In fact, the whole conception did not make sense from the Dutch point of view. An independent Belgium could remain a useful barrier whereas a restored unity, far from strengthening the North, would make it more vulnerable, for the Netherlands, although economically weaker, was internationally more firmly established and seemed less prone to foreign attacks. It was, moreover, clear

---

[1] Discailles, *Rogier* iv. 134. In 1860 the legal requirement for members of the municipal and provincial councils to swear that they would never allow a prince of the Orange dynasty to become king of the Belgians was dropped. The doctrinaire J. Lebeau applauded this in an eloquent speech in the Chamber of Representatives (Hymans, *Histoire parlementaire* iii. 549).

[2] C. Gerretson, *De Tusschenwateren 1839–1867* (Haarlem, n.d.), pp. 195 ff., 330, 381. For what follows see Boogman, 'Achtergronden' 63 ff. Leopold II too hoped that Belgium would be able to establish very close political and commercial relations with the Netherlands and its colonies: Tamse, pp. 290 ff., 309.

that Rogier regarded Belgian supremacy in the new state of which he dreamed as both natural and welcome. It is not difficult to see why nothing came of his fantasy.[1]

In any case in 1867 his attention was distracted by another exciting possibility: the acquisition of the Grand Duchy of Luxemburg. This was a two-sided affair. Rogier, the man of 1830, had never been able to accept the cruel decision of 1839 to sever Luxemburg from Belgium, even though Luxemburg had taken part in the Revolution and sent deputies to the Brussels Parliament. For his closest collaborator, Banning, the matter had wider significance. Banning envisaged the creation of a large and strong neutral buffer state or federation of states centred round Brussels. Deep in the Middle Ages he discovered the roots of a magnificent future,[2] and the possibility of establishing some form of federal connection with the Netherlands and the Rhineland, or of straightforward Belgian expansion, became a part of his elaboration of history. Was it not rumoured in 1866 and 1867 that the Netherlands would ask to be declared neutral?[3] If this were true (incidentally, it was not), it could be fitted very harmoniously into the grand design. But to begin with, Belgium, the core of a large neutral bloc, should recover its lost territories. It should be strengthened by the acquisition of Dutch Limburg, the Grand Duchy of Luxemburg, and, perhaps, also the Scheldt bank, that is Dutch Flanders.[4] In such a way Rogier's emotional attachment to Luxemburg was placed in the framework of Belgium's mission as a neutral state, and his pro-Dutch sentiments

---

[1] An anonymous Dutchman published in 1868 a pamphlet entitled *La Confédération des Pays-Bas Unis* (Brussels and Liège, 1868) in which he drafted a project for a Great Netherlands state. He regrets the weakness of the two minute kingdoms, emphasizes the historical and natural unity of the two nations, and thinks that the time for a federation has come. In his view a unitary state should be the final purpose of the development. He takes it for granted that Dutch will be the national language of that unitary state. Obviously, the ruling groups in Brussels were far from happy with this version of their federative ideas.

[2] Boogman, 'Achtergronden', pp. 64–5.

[3] Cf. Boogman, 'Achtergronden', p. 69 n. 2.

[4] Similar ideas in memoranda written in 1864 and 1868 by a high civil servant, called E. L. F. Fisco, in the Ministry of Finance at Brussels. In 1864 he wrote (Affaires étrangères, Brussels, 4714, Escaut, notes et documents, numéro 26): 'Pour que la Belgique eût la force indispensable à l'accomplissement de la mission d'intérêt européen que la Conférence de Londres lui a donnée, elle devrait comme sous les rois francs, avoir la Moselle et le cours du Rhin jusqu'à la mer pour limite à l'Est et au Nord . . .'

reflected Belgian expansionism. In this same context Belgian diplomacy hoped briefly in 1865 and 1866 that Belgium would be allowed to take over, or to enter into, some of the Dutch colonies which, it was thought, were too heavy a burden for the North to bear alone.[1]

To such aspirations Dutch territorial indifference provided the sharpest possible contrast. When in 1848 relations between Dutch Limburg, a member of the German Confederation, and Germany were becoming troublesome, a leading minister suggested at a Cabinet meeting that the whole province should be abandoned.[2] After the creation of the North German Confederation in 1866 the position of Limburg as well as of Luxemburg was ambiguous and again there were Dutch statesmen who were quite willing to give up these territories if this would avoid risks. The Grand Duke of Luxemburg, King William III, was himself prepared to sell his duchy to Napoleon III, but on 1 April 1867 Prussia declared that she would not tolerate this and William III immediately withdrew. This had hardly become known when Rogier began the campaign to acquire Luxemburg for Belgium.[3] But he encountered vehement opposition from his own colleagues, especially the powerful Frère-Orban, who strongly opposed what he regarded as a dangerously adventurous policy. According to Frère-Orban the acquisition of Luxemburg would bring no material benefits and only increase Belgium's difficulties, for the territory was coveted both by France and Prussia. Conflict between the two men dragged on, and Rogier did not in the end find an opportunity to state his ambitions in official terms. To his deep distress—so deep that he resigned—and to the distress of King Leopold II, who was only too keen to see the plan materialize, but who distrusted Roger's clumsy tactics,[4] this dream too evaporated.

[1] Gerretson, op. cit., pp. 143, 145, and the message from the Belgian minister at The Hague (Affaires étrangères, Brussels, 12192, 27 Feb. 1866).

[2] Boogman, *Nederland en de Duitse Bond*, pp. 423 ff., 640. See also W. H. de Beaufort, *Nieuwe geschiedkundige opstellen* (2 vols., Amsterdam, 1911), i. 217, who in his youth was often told that it was to be regretted that Limburg had not remained a Belgian province.

[3] Garsou, op. cit. ii. 74 ff.

[4] See the most interesting article by R. Demoulin, 'Léopold II et le Grand-Duché de Luxembourg au printemps de 1867', *Mélanges offerts à G. Jacquemyns* (Brussels, 1968), pp. 163–89.

In 1869, however, Frère-Orban continued Rogier's policy
of reconciliation towards the Netherlands, although in a more
pragmatic and concrete way: he suggested (as Rogier had
already done before in his vague manner)[1] the possibility of a
customs union. His fall in 1870 put an end to this initiative
for the time being, but for the next few years the idea was
repeatedly discussed in the Press and in some trade circles, so
that public opinion was not entirely unprepared when immediately after his return to power in 1878 Frère-Orban
raised the question again.[2] He too wanted more than economic
advantages and pursued a political aim, hoping that through
a common commercial and even a common defence policy[3]
the two countries would restore the unity of 1815 in so far as the
national identity of both (which was to be preserved) would
allow.[4] Such suggestions were embarrassing to the Dutch
Government. In July 1880 it proposed calling a meeting of
specialists to consider ways of harmonizing some indirect
taxes[5] but this did not satisfy Frère-Orban at all. When the
Dutch Foreign Minister told the First Chamber that he did
not feel hopeful about the project (January 1881), his Belgian
colleague abandoned it.[6] The Dutch remained extremely
cautious. In August 1880 Belgium celebrated its fiftieth anni-
versary. The Dutch Government studied the course of the
festivities with suspicion and reprimanded its minister at
Brussels for taking too much part in celebrations in honour of
a revolt against the House of Orange.[7]

The importance of these years does not lie there. It lies in the
fact that certain aspects of Belgian foreign policy and a significant interpretation of the Belgian national consciousness were
closely defined. And for the first time for three decades the
fundamental solidarity of the two countries, split off from the
Burgundian Empire and situated in the centre of European

[1] Tamse, pp. 263–4.
[2] Cf. De Beaufort, op. cit. i. 225 ff.; Karl Hampe, *Belgien und Holland vor dem
Weltkriege* (Gotha, 1918), pp. 12 ff.; J. Woltring (ed.), *Bescheiden betreffende de
buitenlandse politiek van Nederland 1848–1919, tweede periode*, ii: *1874–1880* (R.G.P.,
Grote Serie, vol. 118, The Hague, 1965), p. 877, and cf. p. 593.
[3] Woltring, op. cit., p. 584.
[4] Ibid., p. 643.   [5] Ibid., p. 760.
[6] J. Woltring (ed.), *Bescheiden . . . tweede periode*, iii: *1881–1885* (R.G.P., Grote
Serie, vol. 122, The Hague, 1967), pp. 18, 51.
[7] Woltring, ii. 792–5, 809, 831–5, 845, 849.

civilization, was if not finally confirmed, at least more or less officially recognized.

2. Belgium, 1848–1879

François Laurent was more than a doctrinaire. His passionate character, his immense erudition, his radical conclusions appeared at times to put him in a different category, to make him less pragmatic, less restricted in his ideas. Yet it may be said that if the doctrinaires had possessed sufficient intellectual courage and curiosity, they would have revered Laurent as their most eminent theorist. For although he carried their opinions and sentiments to extreme conclusions, he refused to pass over into the 'socialism of the academic chair' and the atheism of the bourgeois radicals. He developed doctrinaire liberalism to such an extent that he sometimes ran the risk of undermining it altogether; but he never abandoned it.

Laurent (1810–87) was the son of a wig-maker in Luxemburg. In the late 1820s he was just old enough to take part in the student protests against Van Maanen. In 1836 he became a professor of law at Ghent. He wrote his main work under the rule of the great doctrinaire Cabinets: the 18 volumes of his *Études sur l'histoire de l'humanité* appeared from 1850 to 1870. They were immediately succeeded by the 32 volumes of his *Principes de droit civil* (1869–79).[1] In his *Études* he put together what might be called a system, although it remained somewhat shapeless. It is a doctrine about progress and religion. God, he thought and tried to prove, leads mankind, though sometimes with the most improbable detours and contradictions, through various stages of emancipation towards the coming golden age of individualism. With the unflinching self-confidence of a nineteenth-century system-builder and in the restless, careless style of a preacher of the truth, Laurent indicated God's purpose in each development, in each great event in history. He could have entitled his book 'God in History'.[2] But this God was not the God of the Roman

---

[1] See Ernest Nys, 'François Laurent. Sa vie et ses œuvres', *Revue de droit international et de législation comparée*, xix (1887), 408–23; R. Warlomont, *François Laurent* (Brussels, 1948); Robert Flint, *History of the Philosophy of History* (Edinburgh, 1893), pp. 680 ff.

[2] F. Laurent, 'Dieu dans l'histoire', *Revue de Belgique*, xxv (1877), 34.

Catholics. In the sharpest, most challenging way, Laurent was an anti-papist and saw the task of a strong, enlightened, liberal state in humiliating and containing the Church, as the state of the French Revolution had done. He detested the liberal–Catholic Union of 1828 and the Primary Education Act of 1842. He repudiated the constitution of 1831. Nothing but the deepest misery and oppression could come from any pact with the ultramontane foe. He fought for the future of which he knew the ground-plan: the future of religion as a liberal, undogmatic form of Protestantism.

All this went further than the doctrinaires were usually prepared to go. Rogier never altogether abandoned his Romantic ideals. Frère-Orban himself did not become a Protestant; only his son did. To a certain extent the liberal voters and their wives remained loyal to the old religion. And yet the Act of 1842 which favoured the Catholics was abrogated, the Freemasons' lodges frequented by the liberals developed a more violent anti-Catholicism than they had ever shown before, the whole liberal party spent itself in its fight against the Roman Catholic Church. Laurent drew extreme conclusions from such premises, but the premises themselves were not fundamentally different from those of the practical politicians. He may also be said to have led the way in the field of social policies. He realized earlier than the other doctrinaires the desperate seriousness of what was later called the social question, and sought a solution for it. State education, savings banks, co-operatives, were the weapons with which this scholarly recluse, who was as generous as he was compassionate, tried to alleviate the misery of the workers in his own town. But as an impassioned individualist he rejected all forms of state intervention, and he strongly disapproved of labour organizations and of the class struggle. Only by educating the workers and teaching them to become morally mature people could the responsible bourgeoisie solve the social problem. Laurent pushed back the frontiers of doctrinaire ideology but he did not cross them.

The practical application of doctrinaire ideas was attempted by Frère-Orban. Walthère Frère (1812–96) was of the same generation as Laurent. Like him he came from a lower-middle-class family. He studied in Paris and in his native town Liège, where in 1832 he set up as a barrister, and a few years later married the daughter of Orban, a prosperous industrialist. In 1840 he entered politics as a follower of what was called by radicals the 'coterie aristocratico-métallique'.[1] This characterizes Frère-Orban. Frère did not, as Rogier had done, start out by being a Romantic. He belonged to the second phase of doctrinaire development, when it was dominated by ex-Orangist and anticlerical ideas. Yet he was decidedly in favour of the conception of the United Kingdom which, in his view, had perished because the Belgians had not been allowed a sufficient share in its administration.[2] The liberal programme of 1846 was mainly his work; it was his influence that persuaded the Liberal Congress not to ask for an important reduction of the *cens*. This, too, was characteristic. Unlike the Romantic and sensitive Rogier, who was perhaps willing to postpone the arrival of democracy although he did not fear it, the younger man repudiated it on the strength of his principles and sense of priorities. His fight was primarily against the Church, and his liberalism was both socially and intellectually much more restricted than that of Rogier. At the same time, it was also more precise and more aggressive.

Violent in words, a formidable antagonist who enjoyed challenging his opponents not only by his majestic, fluent, if unoriginal oratory, but also by his deeds, Frère-Orban remained nevertheless a spokesman of the bourgeoisie, offering practical solutions to practical problems. He was not the man to adhere to a system. His economic ideas were typical of his policies in general. As for many other countries in Europe, the third quarter of the century was for Belgium a period of rapid expansion, particularly, of course, in industry and in the export of industrial products. The energy consumed by industry and the railways increased by ten times; coal output trebled, and so too did the network of railways. Naturally many of those who profited from these developments accepted the ideals of free trade. During the 1840s an Association belge pour la liberté commerciale had served to spread the doctrine but it had not lasted very long. In the middle 1850s, however, the movement acquired new vigour when a periodical, *L'Économiste belge* (1855), and two societies began to preach the great

[1] Hymans, *Frère-Orban*, i. 87   [2] Ibid. 132.

ideal in its most extreme form.[1] It was the task of Frère-Orban to realize it. At this stage, however, it is useful to inquire whether free trade was really a liberal policy. The answer can only be in the negative. Although it is true that in the 1840s the Roman Catholics enjoyed the role of defenders of agrarian interests and made it their aim to reduce corn imports, none the less as soon as the tariff was lowered many of them wanted to abolish industrial protection too and thus exerted themselves on behalf of free trade.[2] In fact the Roman Catholic Cabinet of De Decker (1855-7) found it easier to carry out a liberal tariff policy than its doctrinaire successor which was dependent on urban electors, many of whom were far from enthusiastic about the prospect of seeing their carefully protected businesses exposed to international competition.[3] The leaders of the sugar industry and the cotton-factories at Ghent were particularly strong protectionists.

During the first doctrinaire government Frère-Orban followed the example set by Britain, as the Netherlands had already. He reduced the duties on many different products. But he did not do this by national legislation, as the two maritime nations had done, but by a number of bilateral treaties concluded in 1852 after careful negotiations.[4] In the second phase of doctrinaire power, after 1860, the development was much more rapid. The commercial treaty of 1861 with France, a consequence of the Cobden treaty, set the precedent for a whole series of such treaties, the first of which was with Britain (1862). During these negotiations it was apparent that Belgian free trade policy was practical rather than doctrinaire. The extent to which Frère-Orban kept his distance from the extreme wing of *laissez-faire* idealists, who repudiated all state interference in the economy, became clear in 1860 when he combined the abolition of the urban right to impose duties on wares brought into the towns (*octrois*), a decision which ruined urban finances, with a brilliantly planned and original

---

[1] Chlepner, *Cent ans*, pp. 57 ff.; L. Wils, *Het ontstaan van de meetingpartij te Antwerpen en haar invloed op de Belgische politiek* (Antwerp, 1963), pp. 72 ff.

[2] Wils, *Meetingpartij*, p. 82. Cf. É. de Moreau, *Adolphe Dechamps (1807-1875)* (Brussels, 1911), pp. 196 ff.

[3] Howard to Russell, P.R.O., FO 10/226, 28 (17 Feb. 1860); ibid. 10/233, 71 (2 May 1861); ibid. 10/234, 167 (4 Oct. 1861).

[4] Hymans, *Frère-Orban*, i. 382.

institution, the Crédit communal, that enabled the municipalities to borrow from the state on very advantageous terms. In various other ways Frère made the state, after the demolition of the old protectionist structure, an active participant in the economic life of the country. It would be wrong, therefore, to say that he refrained from interfering with the economy; on the contrary, his policies can be regarded as a continuation, although in a very different form, of those of King William I.[1] It was, consequently, his *étatisme* rather than his free trade policies that was stubbornly fought by the conservatives on the Roman Catholic side.

Frère also believed that the state should play a positive part in the intellectual life of the nation: education, the acceleration of intellectual progress, and the creation of a new order of freedom were among its tasks. This freedom, of course, was by definition well ordered and for that reason could only be based on Christian ethics. In the late 1840s Frère-Orban said: 'In my view it is just as impossible to understand the world without God as it is to understand society without religion'.[2] In 1856 he said: 'I find absolute freedom both of political and religious doctrines unacceptable and I refuse to admit in the state school the teaching of atheism, materialism, or any doctrine harmful to general morality.'[3] Intellectual and spiritual emancipation did not, in the eyes of the doctrinaires, mean de-Christianization; it meant, in the manner of François Laurent, no less than a complete transformation of the Christian religion itself which, because of the inherent logic of progress and the dispensation of Providence, would cease to be organized and dogmatic in character and become a higher morality, with mature and intellectually independent men submitting of their own free will to the fundamentally religious ethics implied in all social life. There could be no doubt that the core of this ethic was individualistic; its purpose was to confirm each individual's freedom of conscience and security of property.

There was nothing, after all, very new or shocking about such opinions. For decades to come most of the Catholic bourgeoisie must have held social and moral views that did not

---

[1] Chlepner, *Cent ans*, pp. 78 ff.; Pirenne, *Histoire de Belgique* vii. 167.
[2] Hymans, *Frère-Orban*, i. 514.   [3] Ibid. 498.

differ fundamentally from those of the doctrinaires. Even the liberal terminology was not in itself unacceptable to Belgians who had grown up in the atmosphere of liberal Catholicism. Was not Belgium still regarded as the free state *par excellence*? Did not Roman Catholics fight as stubbornly as their opponents for freedom of conscience? The bitter discussion between Roman Catholics and doctrinaires, a discussion which could almost have led to civil war, was conducted within the confines of one particular system of values. It was a discussion between men with roughly identical social and moral attitudes, unlike the conflicts of the late eighteenth century with their much deeper antitheses. What was peculiar about it, and perhaps characteristic of the nineteenth century, was the fact that the fight was not about the present but about the future. Neither the doctrinaires nor the Roman Catholics saw the need for reforming society as it actually was. In this sense both were strictly conservative. But both were convinced that in one way and another their society was rapidly changing and both felt the urgent need to secure for their own convictions a safe place or a greater authority in the profoundly different social and intellectual circumstances of the future. So it was the duty of the Roman Catholics to make sure that future generations would not go beyond the bounds and reject religion altogether; it was the duty of the liberals to protect the Belgian people against the danger of remaining dependent on a Church predestined to disappear but obviously capable of showing great resilience in its decline. As both parties were blind to the acute social problem that actually existed, as both felt safely established in the social order of the present, they could devote all their energy and ingenuity to vehement discussions about the type of man which Providence had decided to create.

This explains why the school question became an obsession with this generation. The discussion was opened in 1850, and at that time it concerned secondary education. University education had occasionally been the object of controversy in the past, in 1849, for instance, when teachers at the liberal Free University in Brussels too were allowed to supervise the state examinations that students of all four universities had to sit at the end of their courses. And in 1842, when the law relating to primary education had been passed, there were liberals who insisted on changing it. But in this period secondary education was a problem much more hotly debated. It concerned the future not of the élite, which was mature enough to look after itself, nor of the masses which nobody was as yet greatly worried about, but of the broad rising middle class. Moreover, this form of education was in a chaotic state. There were at least 77 secondary schools but the government could exercise supervision only over 24 and of these 6 were controlled by the clergy.[1] According to the bishops the system that gave them decisive influence in by far the largest number of secondary schools ought to be extended to cover them all.[2] On top of this they wanted general legislation that would make the numerous and confusing local arrangements for individual schools superfluous and establish their authority on a legal basis.[3] However, in 1850 Rogier's solidly liberal Cabinet introduced a bill of a totally different character. It was a clear attempt to expand and improve secondary education and it would be difficult to deny that this was both necessary and beneficial. But at the same time Rogier's bill sought to reduce clerical influence. The minister proposed to increase the number of state grammar schools from 8 to 10, to found 12 new secondary schools, and to reform 38 of the existing ones. All of these would be closely supervised by the state, although it was proposed to invite the clergy to give religious instruction without granting them any authority over syllabuses or teachers.

It is remarkable that the Dutch doctrinaires waited thirteen years before they too ventured into this field; only in 1863 did Thorbecke introduce legislation that would lead to the creation of 50 secondary state schools. It is equally remarkable that the Dutch bill of 1863 met with no opposition whereas Rogier's proposal led to passionate conflicts. This shows that the Belgian liberals were still far ahead of their Northern colleagues, and also that in Belgium it was still the future and the *Weltanschauung* of the middle classes that divided statesmen and public opinion. In the 1850s the Dutch did not quarrel about the secondary but about the primary schools, and although

---

[1] Theuns, *De organieke wet op het middelbaar onderwijs*, pp. 8 ff.; Discailles, *Rogier* iii. 314.

[2] Theuns, op. cit., p. 26.   [3] Simon, *Sterckx* i. 440.

there are other important reasons for this it nevertheless illustrates a concrete difference between the two nations in the whole atmosphere of their political life, as well as in their social conditions. It is also significant that in this period, as under William I, there were far more children at secondary schools in Belgium than there were in the Netherlands.[1]

Rogier's bill which was passed by the Chamber of Representatives by 72 to 25 votes caused a rupture of relations between government and episcopacy. The clergy refused to teach religion in the secondary state schools, which consequently got the reputation of being irreligious or even anti-religious. Although after 1854 compromises proved possible in particular cases, these remained shaky and were often dangerously short lived. The Roman Catholic schools continued to attract large numbers of children and in the 1870s the liberals were shocked to find that the number of Roman Catholic intellectuals, doctors, and lawyers was constantly increasing. The situation was explosive. Once again, it was said, Church and State, those old and bitter foes, were at war. Was the struggle the Church had waged against Joseph II and William I to be resumed? Did the Church, the triumphant survivor of so many defeats, once again have to resist the ambitions of the amoral State? But in fact the situation of 1850 was not strictly comparable with anything that had gone before. Roman Catholics hated Joseph and William because they tried to reform the Church itself, and, whatever their true intentions,

---

[1] It is difficult to compare the Belgian and the Dutch situations because Dutch secondary education was intended for a socially slightly higher group. The schools of 1850 with their two- or three-year courses were obviously designed for the lower middle classes and the upper strata of the working class. Thorbecke's so-called 'higher burgher schools' with a three- or five-year course were intended to draw their pupils from the best-paid groups of the lower middle class. Thorbecke's project to open 'burgher schools' for the children of artisans, peasants, and similar groups failed. In the 1870s, 14,000 children in Belgium attended some form of secondary state-controlled education (Van Bemmel (ed.), *Patria Belgica*, iii. 308); in the Netherlands the figure was 4,000 (A. Bartels, *Een eeuw middelbaar onderwijs 1863–1963*, Groningen, 1963, pp. 281 ff), that is respectively 0·27 and 0·11 per cent of the total population. It should, moreover, be remembered that Belgium possessed countless free schools not supervised by the state. In the Netherlands there were the traditional so-called French schools, private enterprises of often rather doubtful quality attended by some thousands of pupils. The Dutch state grammar schools, excluded from the above-mentioned totals, had about 1,500, the Belgian state *athenaea* about 3,500 pupils. As far as university education is concerned Belgium, with 41 university students out of 100,000 inhabitants, was not so far ahead of the Netherlands.

their efforts were regarded as an outright attack. But this the liberals of 1850 hardly did at all. They made little attempt to extend their influence over fields already securely occupied by the Church and its institutions. They did not seek to obtain influence in the seminaries, the free schools, the monasteries, the bishops' palaces. What they attempted was in some ways more serious. Their programme of secularizing society meant the construction of new institutions, and the introduction of state influence into fields hitherto uncultivated. The important thing about their school policy was that they planned new schools where none had been before. If they attempted to secularize society it was not so much by driving the Church from institutionally protected positions as by insinuating the authority of the state into the whole of social life. This the Roman Catholics well understood and they accused their opponents of socialist methods and intolerable, despotic centralization. Undoubtedly, these were clumsy and inadequate terms, yet they showed that the Catholics had some insight into the expansive force of liberalism. They were slower to grasp the fact, however, that the liberals were cautiously and hesitantly trying to give direction to irreversible processes already occurring in social life itself. The improved means of communication and the increasing complexity of the economic structure were gradually making society so homogeneous that the social enclaves of the pre-industrial period, the more or less autonomous social or administrative entities like the family, peasant communities, or municipalities, were bound to lose some of their independence and to conform to the general pattern of development. The Roman Catholics refused to accept the reality of this process. They still held to the illusion that state and society could remain neatly separated and that, whatever the state might be or do, society remained the Church's exclusive domain.

In 1852 Rogier's Cabinet resigned. It had been exposed to vehement attacks from its domestic opponents, but its authority was more dangerously undermined by the unceasing hostility of Napoleon III. For the next five years the King attempted to rule through conservatives of various shades. With great reluctance, however, he entrusted power once again to the doctrinaires in 1857 and they managed to survive until 1870.

They went through several profound crises—threats from foreign Powers, the death of Leopold I in 1865 (many people, especially abroad, predicted that the state would perish with the King who had founded it), and fierce party strife. The Cabinet was undeterred by such alarms. Convinced of its own intellectual superiority and secure in the loyal backing of the social élite of the towns, it challenged its Catholic foes again and again on carefully selected points and defeated them. A number of laws, such as those concerning poor-relief (1859) and student grants (1860), to name only two, enabled the liberals to restrict Catholic influence and define more precisely relations between the neutral state and the Church. But in 1870 the Cabinet was forced to resign. Rogier had already left, and at the 1870 elections the party was seen to have lost some of its popularity.[1] The radicals refused to give further support to a policy that seemed to exhaust itself in sterile anticlericalism, or to a wealthy bourgeoisie indifferent to social problems. In this year of war the King was obliged to give power to the Roman Catholics, although he profoundly distrusted the antimilitarism of some of their leaders. In 1871 he replaced this Cabinet by another equally Roman Catholic but led by a moderate, Jules Malou, whose caution was such that he stayed on until 1878. Then the elections once again brought the liberals back to power and Frère-Orban was able to form the last doctrinaire Cabinet (1878–84). In 1879 he turned on the Catholics. Forced by the radicals, who had made this an essential condition for their much-needed support, he reorganized primary state education in such a way that Roman Catholic influence was finally eradicated. At last the doctrinaires made an attempt to win over the masses to liberalism.

Essentially this was left-wing liberal, not doctrinaire, policy. Belgian left-wing liberalism is an interesting phenomenon. It drew its inspiration from the intense humanitarianism of the 1840s, which had seemingly perished in 1848 in ugly confusion but which soon revived. It was democratic; it

[1] The defeat was partly due to the electoral system which was highly advantageous to the Catholics. Although the total of liberal votes increased, more Catholics were actually elected as members of Parliament. This was often sharply criticized by the *Revue de Belgique*: v (1870), 252; xii (1872), 49; xxiii (1876), 300 and *passim*.

aimed—according to a definition dating from the 1840s—at making as many people as possible as happy as possible but at the smallest possible cost.[1] This was vague and unoriginal enough, yet it is an excellent definition in so far as the most contradictory wishes of the Young Liberals of the 1850s and 1860s can logically be deduced from it. They despised the state and what they regarded as the *étatisme* of the doctrinaire authorities. The old aversion to power, coercion, and an institutionalized élite that inspired the Belgian Left of the 1830s now aroused in their heirs a positive enthusiasm for free trade and the withdrawal of state interference. They opposed Frère-Orban's policies, asking for the demolition of the expensive state apparatus, the dissolution, or at any rate the reduction, of the useless army, the total freedom of the workers, and consequently the abrogation of such Napoleonic remnants as the ban on strikes and unions. Thus 'cheap administration' became an ideal with some social significance, for it was expected that as a result the life of the workers would greatly improve. Yet, in spite of their deep distrust of the state, the left-wing liberals wanted to strengthen it for certain specific purposes. Although they criticized the doctrinaires for their centralizing policies they were themselves in favour of compulsory education and legislation regulating female and child labour.[2] Like John Stuart Mill, the Belgian radicals combined the individualist's contempt for the state with the interventionist reforming zeal of democrats and social progressives. Indeed, Belgian left-wing liberalism both in its aims and in its contradictions was a version of English utilitarianism.

It was, of course, a doctrine adopted by young intellectuals of bourgeois origin. Among the masses of the people it neither sought nor achieved success, but among the electorate in some of the big towns, especially Brussels, it found sufficient support for two radicals to be sent to the Chamber of Representatives in 1858. During the 1860s the doctrinaires were sometimes obliged to take the left wing seriously and in the 1870s there were seven representatives of the left wing in Parliament. The influence of these liberals as a pressure group was much broader than these figures suggest. They forced upon the

---

[1] Hymans, *Frère-Orban* i. 94.   [2] See Wils, *Meetingpartij*, pp. 70 ff.

attention of the doctrinaires problems they would have preferred to ignore. In their various periodicals they raised, and
sought solutions for, urgent and dramatic questions. One of the
outstanding progressive liberals was Émile de Laveleye, who
became professor of political economy at Liège in 1863, and
one of the outstanding reviews was the *Revue de Belgique* (1869),
of which he became an editor in 1874 and which had 2,000
subscribers.[1] Towards the end of his life De Laveleye (1822–92)
declared that he felt he belonged to the extreme left wing of
Katheder-socialism, yet that at the same time he had always
managed to remain loyal to the programme of even doctrinaire
liberalism.[2] He was after all an individualist opposed to
collectivization and to the enfranchisement of the uneducated
Roman Catholic masses, a latitudinarian Protestant who
identified Protestantism with progress and self-realization and
thought that agnosticism was alien to man's essentially religious nature, an admirer of the parliamentary system of government which, although in need of reform, was the only one to
grant sovereignty to reason. But at the same time he was
tireless in promoting the cause of reform. He was full of contempt for the plutocracy of his age with its vulgar, useless
luxuries in the midst of the wretched misery of the proletariat.
He considered agrarian states happier than industrial ones
and admired the Netherlands, in his view one of the most
progressive agrarian countries of the world.[3] In book after
book he examined new methods for dealing with real problems.
Would it be wise to redistribute property and to allot to each
individual his share? Would such a plan be meaningful enough
to resolve the mortally dangerous conflicts in modern society?
In such speculations the character of his work and his group
shows itself most clearly. These men saw vividly and without
dismay that society was exposed to violent shocks; but they
hoped to moderate the changes they foresaw and to create
some kind of stability. It was no Utopia but a useful and more
or less durable compromise that they were seeking. To a much
higher degree than their acid polemical style and their fearless

[1] E. Goblet d'Alviella, *Émile de Laveleye* (Brussels, 1895), pp. 176–7. During its
greatest years (1885–92) the Dutch radical periodical *De Nieuwe Gids* had never
more than 800 subscribers.

[2] Quoted by M. Wilmotte, *Trois semeurs d'idées* (Paris, 1907), p. 179.

[3] É. de Laveleye, *Études d'économie rurale. La Néerlande* (Paris, 1865), pp. 256 ff.

criticism suggest, the real aim of their progressive liberalism was harmony and reconciliation.

On many points the left wing adopted positions for which the doctrinaires could feel no sympathy whatever, and frequently the *Revue de Belgique*—an excellent periodical illustrating the improvement in Belgian intellectual standards since the days of the *Revue nationale*—savagely criticized the liberals' lack of vision, courage, and consistency. Yet generally the review remained loyal to the liberal system, simply trying to broaden its social framework—for instance, by a wider but by no means universal franchise.[1] It also sought to reduce Belgium's cultural dependence on France. It wanted to be truly international and carried much information about English, German, and Swiss experiments. It was, of course, vehemently opposed to Napoleon III but expressed admiration for Bismarck's fight against the Roman Catholic clergy. Its editors had a keen and sympathetic understanding of Flemish problems and aspirations, but curiously enough, in spite of the best of intentions, displayed an almost total ignorance of developments in the Netherlands. There were no Dutch contributors, apart from the rather eccentric G. W. Vreede, and apparently none of the editors, some of whom knew Dutch—not even De Laveleye who loved the Netherlands and regretted the Belgian Revolution as a dismal mistake—was able or willing to study Dutch developments closely enough to write about them.

Most progressive liberals did not want to do permanent damage to liberal unity. In 1874 one of the leading personalities in the *Revue de Belgique*, Count E. Goblet d'Alviella (1846–1925)—a follower of De Laveleye and later a celebrated professor of the history of religion at Brussels—showed that although it was impossible to reach agreement about certain problems such as the franchise and army organization, on other equally important points perfect harmony already existed. Thus he urged all liberals to collaborate in order to achieve compulsory education free from Church influence and legislation to regulate child labour. Finally, he called on the doctrinaires to help in the heroic fight against the ultramontane enemy.[2] In his view it was anticlericalism that cemented the unity of the liberal

[1] See, e.g., *Revue de Belgique*, xxviii (1878), 51 ff.
[2] *Revue de Belgique*, xviii (1874), 295 ff.

party. In 1879 the day of reckoning came. Inspired by French ideas, on which even the progressive liberals remained dangerously dependent, they drove the Catholics out of the public schools. It is true that they tried to justify some of their moves by reference to Dutch rather than French examples, but because of the religious divisions and the relative weakness of Roman Catholicism in the Netherlands the situation there was too dissimilar for such comparisons to be really meaningful. Even so, liberal school policies failed in Belgium as they did in the Netherlands, whereas they succeeded in France. Why was this so?

The primary Education Act of 1879 sought to exclude religion from the public schools, where it had held a place of honour since the beginning of the century, a place that had been officially guaranteed in 1842. But the Catholics reacted promptly and successfully. In the next few years 2,253 out of 7,550 teachers left the public for the free Catholic schools. By December 1879 the free Catholic schools, according to calculations made by the Roman Catholic party, already had 379,000 pupils whereas the public schools had only 240,000; by 1881 60 per cent of Belgian children were attending Catholic schools.[1] Although the Act of 1879 was the result of admirable intentions and showed a clear enough insight into the needs of modern society, it was doomed to failure. The unparalleled difficulties to which the legislation gave rise, and the conflict with the bishops, weakened the Cabinet to such an extent that in 1884 it had to resign. Political liberalism was defeated. After 1884 the liberals were never again able to form a Cabinet. Even the small electorate of bourgeois origin was split, the majority refusing to support liberals who wished to impose their own individual conceptions on the unwilling masses. In 1850, when the doctrinaires had built new schools where none had previously existed, they had enjoyed the loyal support of the electorate. When the liberals tried to drive the Church from positions it had held for so long, no such support was forthcoming.

Obviously the transformation and defeat of liberalism can only be understood in relation to developments that took place

[1] G. Guyot de Mishaegen, *Le Parti catholique belge de 1830 à 1884* (Brussels, 1946), pp. 169 ff.

within the Roman Catholic party and the Church. The liberals were appalled by the flourishing condition of a Church which they kept confidently predicting was near to disintegration. No doubt they exaggerated. From 1846 to 1866 the number of monasteries increased from 799 to 1,314, though the number of nuns and monks rose less rapidly (from 12,000 to 18,000), and in comparison with the French experience under the Second Empire this could be regarded as disappointing. Yet they did not exaggerate when they complained so bitterly about the power of the clergy, particularly in the countryside. Year after year the electors from the Flemish villages were seen to be conducted in groups by their local priest to the polling stations in the main towns. It was obvious that both the nobility, almost totally Roman Catholic and determined not to admit liberals to the high society, and the large landowners of bourgeois origin, obliged their tenants to vote for the Roman Catholic party. Everyone was aware that the courts of law were unable to prevent the growth of property in mortmain although it was forbidden by law to bequeath property to the Church.[1] And where was the wise fatherly village priest of the good old days? The seminaries of the third quarter of the century were accused of training rigid zealots who kept the masses submissive by means of extraordinarily ugly prints, images, and churches, by sugary stories about improbable miracles, and by monstrous threats. Even among intellectuals the liberal Press spotted an alarming increase in Roman Catholic power. Louvain attracted more students than any other university. Still more serious was the unmistakable success of ultramontane doctrines in a state founded on liberal-Catholic principles.

By 1850 little was left of the liberal-Catholic enthusiasm that had prevailed in the 1820s and 1830s. The ideal of freedom which had inspired a whole generation boldly to accept the liberal and neutral state inclined its successors to conservative and passive caution. They remained loyal to the heritage of the 1830 Revolution; they ignored none of the great Romantic hypotheses; they defended with sincere conviction the principles

[1] É. de Laveleye, 'Le parti libéral et le parti catholique en Belgique', *Études et essais* (Paris, 1869), pp. 86 ff.; idem, *Le Parti clérical en Belgique* (Brussels, 1874), pp. 20 ff.

of the constitution. But they did not bother to build on foundations laid with so much passion; they did not create a system or a policy, nor did they adapt their vision of the future to the profound social changes which were taking place. It is not surprising that they should have been conservatives, for they continued to live in the essentially conservative tradition of the Union of 1828. But it is surprising that they lacked all intellectual and political ambition. Their conception of the state was almost entirely negative. In order to survive, the central power must govern as little as possible, wrote the Roman Catholic leader Charles Woeste (1837–1922), using one of those haughty, tart, and unimaginative formulas in which this arch-conservative master of acrimonious prose excelled.[1] Distrust the state, he said later when the Roman Catholics themselves were in power.[2] 'I am afraid of the state, I hate Caesarism'.[3]

But this was all. It was assumed that society was Roman Catholic and the process of de-Christianization, if noticed at all, was dismissed as little more than an aspect of liberal policy. If it were possible to curb the state and defeat the liberals, the position of Roman Catholicism, protected by constitutional liberties, would be safe enough; and so too would the social classes which determined Catholic policies. It is interesting, however, that this negative attitude towards the state and the doctrinaires made conservative Roman Catholics receptive to some radical views. This could be seen, though in an absurdly confusing way, during the long and exhausting conflict that arose about the vexed question of the Antwerp fortifications. From 1848 the King and successive governments had been determined to eliminate the useless frontier fortifications and to concentrate the national defence on Antwerp. The argument was, of course, that the small Belgian army would never be able to protect the frontiers but that in the event of a French invasion Antwerp could keep open the way to Britain. It was a strictly logical plan. The Dutch, somewhat later, took a similar strategic decision when they made the province of Holland, which thanks to the water defence line was difficult to penetrate, the national bastion.

---

[1] Charles Woeste, op. cit. ii. 24.
[2] Idem, *A travers dix années. 1885–1894* (Brussels, 2 vols., 1895), i. 94.
[3] Ibid. 382.

But it seemed as if the interests of Antwerp, the commercial centre of the country, were being cynically sacrificed to the interests of Brussels which, although the national capital and the royal residence, was not required to submit to the building of fortifications and the dangers of warfare. Brussels could continue to build houses and parks whereas Antwerp was to be girded tightly by forts. During the 1850s, when the first serious steps towards the realization of this plan were taken, a vociferous opposition arose and the so-called Meeting party was formed to contest the scheme. At the start-only those directly concerned protested: house-owners who feared that the value of their property would decline if it were situated within the field of fire, and landowners who objected to the use of their property being restricted by military needs. But soon all sorts of local and general resentments became associated with the objects of the Meeting party.

Eventually the Meeting succeeded in winning important concessions. In 1870, 1873, and 1893 laws were passed which, although Antwerp was maintained as the national bastion, respected the town's interests and gave decent compensation to the injured parties.[1] Yet after what excitement, after how many claims and threats! The Flamingants were particularly active: was government policy not patently anti-Flemish? The progressive liberals protested: these were doctrinaire methods at their most extreme, centralist, indifferent to local interests, militarist, despotic, anti-democratic, showing no respect at all for the masses of the metropolis who were to be enclosed within narrow walls, exposed to epidemics, guns, and untold misery. The Roman Catholics supported the whole campaign and in the end dominated it. This is not hard to understand. For a long time Roman Catholic leaders had been in the habit of attacking *étatisme* and militarism; decentralization and care for the needs of Roman Catholic Flanders were an important part of their programme. Not unnaturally, therefore, they took advantage of the excitement to fight the government. Yet in the long run the radical–Catholic coalition was difficult to maintain, partly because of the intransigent anticlericalism of the progressive liberals but also because, though both radicals and Roman Catholics professed to stand for

[1] F. Lehouck, *Het antimilitarisme in België 1830–1914* (Antwerp, 1958), p. 163.

democratic reform, they were by no means agreed upon what this should amount to. As the progressive liberals gradually withdrew from the Meeting the Roman Catholics came to master it completely.

The Meeting arose out of grievances and hopes that sought political expression but were much too diffuse and undisciplined to serve as the basis for a political programme or a political party. Yet because the movement reflected such fundamental dissatisfaction with existing society it acted as a catalyst; moreover, it influenced in at least two ways the actual political situation. It forced the government to grant generous concessions to Antwerp. Secondly, it persuaded the Roman Catholic party, which was slowly and gradually acquiring a measure of coherence, to take some interest in democratic ideas, an interest that was not yet profound nor always genuine but that later made it easier for many Roman Catholics willingly to move into the democratic era. However, the history of the Roman Catholic party in these years is something of a paradox. For in fact the Catholic leaders were far from eager to build up a political party. Politicians whose dearest aim was to break the state or to reduce its influence as much as possible, and whose starting-point was the hypothesis that society would remain Roman Catholic so long as the state did not interfere, felt little inclination to form a party, indeed regarded the very existence of political parties as a danger. As late as 1865 their leader, Adolphe Dechamps, claimed that the Catholics had done all they could to prevent the emergence of a Roman Catholic party.[1] But already at that time the party unmistakably existed. During the 1850s some very cautious steps had been taken in developing a 'conservative party'— conservative in the sense that its aim was to preserve the constitution of 1831. After the disappointing election results of 1857 a number of Roman Catholics realized that there was a need for serious organization. They established an action committee, the task of which was to maintain permanent contact with the electorate, but this did not last for more than five years.[2] About 1860 the commotion caused by the Meeting

---

[1] A. Dechamps, 'Situation politique de la Belgique', *Revue générale*, i (1865), 43, quoted by De Moreau, op. cit., p. 283.

[2] Guyot de Mishaegen, op. cit., pp. 113–15.

and the initiatives of a small group of young Roman Catholic conservatives indicated that a clearer and more positive programme was urgently required. Ducpétiaux, who started as a fairly radical liberal, quarrelled with the doctrinaires in 1857, and became a supporter of Catholic policies, inspiring some younger men to study those social problems which he had always considered most important. Prosper de Haulleville, whom Rogier dismissed in 1857 from his professorship at Ghent, founded a short-lived periodical in which, as a liberal Catholic by nature and by intention, he tried to persuade his coreligionists to give new content to the old conservative principles. His ideas were moderately radical; he was in favour of freedom on a constitutional basis, of rigorous separation of Church and State, of free trade, decentralization, franchise reform, and of all those other ways of solving the social problem in an individualist manner of which the radicals approved.[1]

It was on Ducpétiaux's initiative that the first Roman Catholic Congress met at Mechlin in 1863. It was an international congress, dominated in fact by the French, although some Germans and British and one Netherlander, who did not feel at ease in such surroundings, also attended.[2] Contrary to Ducpétiaux's original intention the Congress assumed the character of a liberal-Catholic demonstration, at which the French enthusiast Montalembert, who was not allowed to speak freely in his own country, was able to extol in high-flown and prolonged rhetoric the merits of liberty, of aristocracy—he was himself a count and son-in-law of the Belgian count Félix de Mérode—and of the propertied classes generally. Only religion, he explained to his captivated audience, could effectively protect society against democracy and attacks on property.[3] These, obviously, were not the principles on which to establish a political party. But other opinions were expressed as well, and the very fact that Belgian Roman Catholics, inspired by the German and Swiss, accepted that it might be useful to define or explore the Catholic point of view publicly at such gatherings, expressed an inclination not fundamentally different

---

[1] Rezsohazy, *Catholicisme social en Belgique*, pp. 81 ff.; K. van Isacker, *Werkelijk en wettelijk land. De Katholieke opinie tegenover de rechterzijde 1863–1884* (Antwerp, 1955), pp. 134 ff.

[2] Van Isacker, op. cit., pp. 21 ff.   [3] Ibid., p. 43.

from the desire to found a party. In 1864 the doctrinaire Cabinet, which had the support of only a very small majority, offered its resignation, and Leopold I reluctantly invited the Catholics to put forward a programme. Adolphe Dechamps produced one that was characteristic, both in what it said and in what it left unsaid. It was the first Roman Catholic political programme in Belgian history and that it could be drafted at all is proof enough of the Roman Catholics' emerging political ambitions. It was by no means a religious or confessional programme; it was not suggested that the state should become Roman Catholic again. It was, in the end, cautiously democratic. Dechamps wanted to grant more authority to the local boards; he wanted to lower the tax qualifications for electors of the provincial and municipal governing bodies; he proposed to change the character and reduce the strength of the army; he wanted to reduce taxes.[1] Undoubtedly, the concessions to radicalism—in the form of decentralization, antimilitarism, and democratization—were the most prominent features of the programme which Leopold I foreseeably rejected, to the relief of the large conservative wing of the Roman Catholic parliamentary party. Yet although in some respects radical, the programme was none the less within the conservative tradition of liberal Catholicism. It is obvious that Dechamps felt no sympathy with the potentially important radical desire for state interference in order to achieve democratic and social reforms: his aim was still to protect society against the neutral state.

Among the liberal Catholics there was little genuine interest in social problems. It was against this passive attitude that their co-religionists and foes, the ultramontanes, protested. During the 1860s and 1870s ultramontanism became so vociferous and attracted so much more attention than the cautious liberal Catholics that it became the perfect target for anticlericalism, even though the liberal catholics remained politically more powerful and more numerous. The ultramontanes were, of course, following the lead of Pope Pius IX. They thought that the Pope's campaign against liberal freedom implied an attack on the Belgian constitution—wrongly, for they misinterpreted

[1] Discailles, *Rogier* iv. 226 ff.; cf. A. Simon, *Le Parti catholique belge* (Brussels, 1958), p. 80.

Vatican policies. They had no patience with Parliament and the basic principles of the Belgian state. They passionately fought a constitution that allowed a totally unrepresentative group of anticlericals to take power in a country which was and wished to remain Roman Catholic. Their influence was considerable. After the death in 1867 of the Archbishop of Mechlin, E. Sterckx, who first as Vicar-General and after 1831 as Archbishop had firmly adhered to the Union of 1828 and the constitution of 1831, there was considerable uncertainty about the personal views of his successor and most Belgian bishops began to take up ultramontane positions. Although the ultramontane group was small, and although the Roman Catholic statesmen in Parliament as well as in the governments from 1870 to 1878 followed very moderate and conciliatory policies, the whole spirit of the Church and of its paladins was clearly changing and it looked as if ultramontane zeal was the flame which was to set the country on fire.

The nature, style, and theory of Belgian ultramontanism was most articulately expressed in the writings of Charles Périn.[1] Yet was this really a Belgian view? Périn (1815–1905) came from a French emigrant family and although until 1881 he held the chair of public law and political economy at Louvain his intellectual background was entirely French. He was a keen partisan of the Count of Chambord and believed that legitimism would be the world's salvation, for it was France's mission to carry out God's great designs.[2] It is much more difficult to distinguish national characteristics in this ultramontane theorist than it is in a doctrinaire like Laurent or a radical like De Laveleye. Was Belgium anything more to Périn than a place of residence where French was spoken? Probably he never asked himself such questions, for he lived in a world of abstraction. His ideas soared above reality and were expounded in a seemingly precise though monotonous and pedantic style. His reasoning gives the impression of being strictly logical but in fact is both dogmatic and incomplete, neither sufficiently sustained to be coherent nor sufficiently supple to be even moderately persuasive. Yet his views were

---

[1] See Van Isacker, p. 81 and *passim*.
[2] Charles Périn, *Les Lois de la société chrétienne* (2 vols., Paris, Lyons, 1875), ii. 384, 406, and *passim*.

taken seriously, much appreciated by Pius IX and, for instance, by the unbalanced bishop Dumont of Tournai, who later went mad. According to Périn it was impossible to envisage a reconciliation of, or even a compromise between, truth and error; both were total, both absolute.[1] Thus liberal Catholicism was nonsense both in logic and in practice. Périn flatly rejected the attempts of the liberal Catholics to solve the dilemma of how to make Church and State coexist; he scorned their ingenious distinction between thesis, that is the unchangeable, lasting, absolutely superior and true doctrine of the Church, and hypothesis, that is actual reality which must make allowance for modern liberties and the toleration of modern errors. There is only one relation between belief and unbelief: antithesis. They will fight each other to the death. In the state, which must be built on truth, error cannot be tolerated. This state should be ruled by a sovereign prince obedient to papal commandments[2] who will also heed the humble advice offered by a parliament representative of interests and not of individuals.[3] Roman Catholic charity would permeate the whole of society and reconcile the social classes, none of which would ever try to move out of the place that God had given it. If this ideal were to be ignored or denied, rationalism would inexorably destroy bourgeois supremacy and give rise to Caesarism and communism.[4] Only by reverting to Roman Catholic solidarity[5] was it possible to avoid the fatal but logical consequences of revolutionary principles.

Périn's theory is considerably thinner than that of his Dutch Calvinist predecessor Groen van Prinsterer, who decades earlier had pronounced similar views with, of course, Protestantism as the guiding principle; it is less flexible than that of the younger Dutch Calvinist Abraham Kuyper who appreciated Périn's work. To a greater degree than these Dutch writers Périn, in spite of his intense aversion to contemporary society and the state of the times, defended what he saw around him

[1] Charles Périn, op. cit. i, pp. viii, 141, 143, and *passim*.
[2] Charles Périn, 'Les libertés populaires' (1871), *Mélanges de politique et d'économie* (Paris, 1883), p. 110; *Lois* ii. 368 ff.
[3] Idem, 'Libertés', pp. 114 ff.; *Lois* ii. 360 ff.
[4] Idem, *Les Doctrines économiques depuis un siècle* (Paris, Lyons, 1880), pp. 10, 125, 169, and *passim*.
[5] Idem, *De la richesse dans les sociétés chrétiennes* (2 vols., Paris, 1861), i. 40 ff.

against the perils of socialism. Private property was declared almost sacred;[1] the worker was condemned to eternal submission to his betters but might find comfort in Périn's respect for his noble sacrifice and thrift;[2] bourgeois society, built up by Christians, was praised and considered morally pure enough if it showed itself sufficiently charitable.[3] And yet in some respects his work is a positive contribution to the study of social problems. It was at least to his credit that Périn recognized the social problem as a problem and was more genuinely concerned about it than the liberal Catholics.[4] No doubt his solutions were not very imaginative. His corporatism[5]—that is, the restoration of the guilds under the direction of the employers —his paternalism, his insistence on the moral improvement of the workers, were unoriginal and unrealistic devices. But they helped the Belgian Roman Catholics of the third quarter of the century in their search for an answer to the threat of socialism. In this sense Périn's was essentially a transitional position, reflecting the importance of ultramontanism generally. Although the ultramontanes failed to develop coherent and practical propositions they were clear-sighted enough to abandon liberal-Catholic optimism, according to which all would be well so long as social life remained untouched.

Thus ultramontanism probably served a purpose in a country that was later than its neighbours in embarking upon a social policy. For, notwithstanding the activities of a few progressive liberals, the Belgian Parliament remained a bastion of social conservatism. Until 1873 the economy and the population were rapidly expanding but the composition of Parliament did not change. Indeed proportionately the franchise became if anything more restricted, for direct taxation did not greatly increase—yielding thirty million francs in the 1830s and forty million in the 1870s—whereas indirect taxation more than doubled.[6] There was, moreover, after the débacle of the 1848 revolutions a remarkable feeling of safety among the upper classes. Throughout the *ancien régime* and in the early nineteenth century fear of the populace and of social upheavals had preoccupied statesmen and thinkers alike. In the third quarter

---

[1] *Doctrines économiques*, pp. 210 ff.   [2] 'Libertés', p. 91.
[3] *Lois* ii. 311.   [4] *Doctrines économiques*, pp. 172 ff., 201, and *passim*.
[5] Ibid., pp. 229 ff.   [6] *Revue de Belgique*, xxiii (1876), 284.

of the century this was no longer so. Nevertheless, after the great report on social conditions which the Ministry of the Interior published in the late 1840s the misery of the people was better known than ever before, even though none of the various governments could draw any conclusions from it. It was assumed that somehow the workers would benefit from the general increase in prosperity.

This assumption was, of course, not altogether unwarranted. By about 1873 when the great period of expansion ended the workers were perhaps slightly better off than they had been in 1850.[1] Yet how insecure and temporary this improvement was became apparent during the difficult years that followed and was clearly shown by the second large-scale social inquiry in 1886. Only then did the ruling classes in Belgium come to realize that not only Britain but also less industrialized countries such as France and even the Netherlands were engaged upon social policies deserving of emulation. During the third quarter of the century this had been simply denied. Such indifference can be partly explained by the fact that the Belgian workers themselves showed little initiative, rarely putting their claims forcefully enough. Although Belgium was the oldest, most mature industrial nation on the Continent, trade-unionism and socialism had developed more slowly there than in other European countries. There seem to have been at least three reasons for this. In the first place, Belgian industry was mainly an export industry serving different markets with highly variegated demands; as it did not develop standardized mass production methods, the typical Belgian factory remained small or medium sized.[2] Secondly, the small size of the country itself, with its dense population and its numerous industrial centres in different areas, prevented the growth of the massive concentrations known in Britain. It is true that Belgian industry also drew its workers from the countryside but most of the rural population that worked in the factories did not have to move into the towns. They stayed in their villages, travelling each day to and from work, a habit which later became even more widespread with the introduction of cheap season tickets

[1] Cf. Denise de Weerdt's sceptical conclusion in 'Arbeiderstoestanden van 1850 tot 1876', in Dhondt (ed.), *Geschiedenis van de socialistische arbeidersbeweging*, p. 225.
[2] B. S. Chlepner, *Belgian Banking and Banking Theories* (Washington, 1943), p. 4.

on the railways.[1] Finally, the intellectual as well as the economic standing of the Belgian, and especially the Flemish, workers was undoubtedly much lower than that of their English, French, or German comrades. It is, for obvious reasons, impossible to indicate with any precision the impact of religion. Yet undeniably the Church continued to preach the virtue of submission and patience and did what it could to keep the Flemish proletariat quiet. This must have been a factor of some importance in an area still so predominantly Catholic.[2]

Nevertheless, this period is a crucial one in the history of the Belgian labour movement, not for what was achieved but for what was being projected. In the 1850s two societies of freethinkers (L'Affranchissement of 1854 and Les Solidaires of 1857) connected their rational atheism, which far transcended traditional anticlericalism, with socialist ideas and through all the confusion, all the false initiatives and failures which the labour movement experienced, the atheist organizations in various towns, especially in Wallonia, remained the solid and permanent centres out of which each time the situation became more favourable new socialist organizations could grow.[3] During the 1860s in particular groups of workers—artisans, naturally, but also some of the proletariat in the textile factories at Ghent—showed signs of developing a form of class-consciousness and solidarity. The First International met with a surprisingly widespread response; it is stated that 70,000 Belgian workers supported it but this figure indicates the total number of members of organizations which associated themselves with the International; obviously only a minority took part in the activities.[4] But undoubtedly the First International did inspire the Belgians, not only in Ghent and Brussels but also in Antwerp, Hainaut, Verviers, and Liège, to build up new organizations and explore new fields of action. In relatively large numbers workers began to think in more contemporary terms. They no longer fought simply for higher wages but took

[1] L. Delsinne, *Le Mouvement syndical en Belgique* (Paris, 1936), p. 24.
[2] Cf. F. Broeckaert, O.F.M., *Predikatie en arbeidersprobleem. Onderzoek naar de sociale opvattingen van de seculiere en reguliere clerus in Vlaanderen, 1800-1914* (Mechlin, 1963).
[3] Dhondt, *Geschiedenis*, pp. 229 ff., 304-5.
[4] L. Delsinne, *Le Parti ouvrier belge des origines à 1894* (Brussels, 1955), pp. 47 ff.; Dhondt, 'De sociale kwestie in België', pp. 340 ff.; idem, *Geschiedenis*, p. 239.

an interest in such issues as universal suffrage and the restriction of working hours. Despite the split in the International, its final collapse in the early 1870s (like the Dutch, the Belgians took Bakunin's side), and the disappearance of the numerous small trade unions which had owed their existence to the International, the movement continued, although it was not until the 1880s that socialism acquired a more or less permanent form.

In the vital 1860s the Flemish movement also experienced profound changes. Until about 1860 it was mainly a literary romantic movement; after that date it took part in politics. This presented the Flamingants with problems they were unable to solve and may have weakened the movement as a whole; at the same time these problems were a challenge, demanding a positive response. The Flamingants achieved some concrete successes. In 1857 the generation that had dominated the movement since 1830·wrote its last will and testament. The Catholic Flemish minister P. de Decker had appointed a committee to study Flemish grievances and propose ways of redress,[1] and in that year the committee's report was completed. De Decker, however, did not have time to draw practical conclusions from it. His Cabinet fell and the doctrinaires under Rogier devoted their energies to demonstrating how nonsensical the Flemish demands were. But the report is a valuable document[2] and reveals the modesty of Flemish pretensions. The committee clearly did not take seriously the possibility of restoring in the near future the Dutch language as the medium of instruction in the secondary schools or the universities in Flanders. It was also very cautious with regard to the linguistic equipment of the higher civil servants, for if knowledge of both languages were made a requirement the Walloons would be obliged to study Flemish, a concession which they would refuse to make and which even most of the Flamingants considered unreasonable. The only principle they put forward was that in Flanders itself where the majority of the population knew only Flemish—in 1880 there were about two and a half

---

[1] A detailed study on the origin of this commission in De Vroede, *De Vlaamse Beweging in 1855–1856*, pp. 27 ff., 44 ff.

[2] See Picard, *Evolutie*, ii. 91 ff.; Wils, *Ontwikkeling gedachteninhoud*, pp. 72 ff.; and esp. Elias, ii. 283–98.

million people who spoke no other language and only 420,000 who were bilingual—the administration and the law courts should use both languages. This was far from being a radical claim, especially as it was by no means exceptional for the provincial and municipal governments to use Flemish. Moreover, the committee, representing the feelings of the patriotic generation of 1830, did not consider any form of separatism or federalism and never called in question the unitary character of the Belgian state and nation. And yet the committee's programme was impossible to realize in the circumstances of the 1850s. The government rejected it, as it was bound to. The enfranchised Flemish bourgeoisie felt no sympathy with such aims although they were not necessarily hostile to the language and habits of the people among whom they were living in quiet comfort; the Flemish masses not only did not have the vote, they had no opinions either.[1]

It is difficult to explain, therefore, why fifteen years later it had become possible actually to pass laws in protection of the Flemish language and Flemish-speakers. Various factors combined to bring about such a fundamental change. Firstly, the two big parties, approximately of equal strength and engaged in a conflict of rare bitterness, were both desperately anxious for extra support and were prepared to seek it by courting the Flamingants. The agitation of the Meeting also undoubtedly increased the willingness to make concessions. Finally, France's defeat in 1870 was a terrible blow to French prestige.[2] It did not affect the cultural influence of France on Belgium, but it must have made the bourgeoisie wonder whether French was still and would forever remain the obvious universal language. The language legislation itself did not have any immediate effect. The important thing was that it was passed at all. In fact, the principle of linguistic freedom had failed. It had led to the subordination of Dutch to French but the expectation of the legislators of 1830 that the Dutch-speaking population would use its freedom to give up Dutch and change over to French had turned out to be totally unrealistic. Clearly, it was

[1] De Vroede, *De Vlaamse beweging*, pp. 94 ff., 130–1; cf. also M. C. G. Lamberty, *Philosophie der Vlaamsche Beweging en der overige stroomingen in België* (Bruges, 1933), p. 71. This last book is now obsolete.

[2] Lamberty, op. cit., p. 101.

necessary to recognize that at any rate for the time being two languages were being spoken in the Flemish provinces. In 1873, 1878, and 1883 Parliament decided by big majorities that Dutch ought to be allowed a larger part in jurisdiction, administration, and secondary education. These laws were never fully applied, not so much because they were ignored or sabotaged by the government but because the Flemings themselves were not yet mature enough to find them acceptable. It is typical that in the secondary state schools the law of 1883 was put into execution and the Dutch language was indeed increasingly used, whereas in the much more numerous free Roman Catholic schools which were more dependent on parental desires Dutch was very often strictly excluded.

Limited Flemish successes, the slowness and incompleteness of the new legislation, together with the withering-away of Romanticism and of unionist ideals, caused the Flamingants to detach themselves from the patriotic inspiration that was still characteristic of the 1857 report. During the 1860s and 1870s Belgium lost its emotional appeal: it was accepted as an administrative framework within which the Flemings were prepared to live, but it was not a nation. A Flemish nationalism began to emerge.[1] No longer was it thought sufficient to obtain a measure of recognition for Dutch in Flanders, no longer was a bilingual regime the main aim of Flemish aspirations; now it was claimed that Flanders should become exclusively Flemish. This did not immediately have any practical consequences. Although many praised decentralization in lyrical tones no concrete scheme for reconstructing the state of 1831 emerged. Moreover, Flemish nationalism had very narrow limits. The popular classes and the bourgeoisie hardly supported it or did not support it at all. There was, furthermore, no adequate foe.[2] The Walloons might be foreigners in theory to the Flemish nation, but they were still, none the less, beloved brothers. The government might not be a national government, but it was certainly not felt to be an alien, hostile, oppressive power. And the whole development of the Flemish movement during this period undeniably

---

[1] I use this term here merely to indicate that from now on more emphasis was laid on the homogeneity of Flemish culture.

[2] De Vroede, *De Vlaamse Beweging*, pp. 68 ff.; Elias, iii. 259.

proves that political unity was a far greater practical force than any Flemish nationalist conviction. Flemish nationalism was unable to acquire an independent political influence. It was obliged to seek association with the existing political parties which encompassed the whole country and for which the Flemish question remained, after all, an issue of secondary importance. The result was that the dichotomy that split Belgian intellectual and political life in the 1860s also broke the Flemish movement. Yet liberalism was so powerful that at one time it looked as though the movement which had hitherto generally depended on Roman Catholic and conservative sympathy would follow the pattern of so many other national independence movements in Europe and adopt a liberal or left-wing character.

In the end this did not happen. Neither liberalism nor socialism absorbed Flemish nationalism, although some excellent Flemish leaders fervently tried to bring this about. Liberalism always turned out to be too much of a bourgeois phenomenon and the Flemish bourgeoisie spoke French. Socialism, on the other hand, was international and anti-nationalist, and in any case drew its most solid support from the Walloon proletariat. In spite of all attempts to point out a certain parallellism between liberal and Flemish demands (for was not the true solution for Flanders' troubles more and better elementary education?) or between socialist and Flemish ideals (for was not the emancipation of the Flemish 'people' essentially the emancipation of the Flemish masses?), ideological and social differences ultimately proved too strong. The majority of the Flamingants were Catholic; and both the leaders of the Flemish movement and their followers were lower-middle-class people who had no insight into the social-economic needs of the proletariat. A curious Flemish-nationalist revival in West-Flanders, an ultramontane, economically and politically backward area, showed on the other hand how natural the connection between Catholicism and the principles of Flemish nationhood still appeared to be, as well as what excitement and what brilliant results it could produce. In the 1850s the young priest Guido Gezelle (1830–99) from Bruges became a teacher at a Catholic school in West-Flanders, where he converted a group of pupils to his own extreme views. Gezelle scorned the two civilized languages available to him, both the rigid and alien language of the Hollanders and conventional, lifeless French; he favoured the living, idiosyncratic reality of the West-Flemish dialect, which was indeed transformed by him, the greatest Dutch poet of his time, into a lyrical language of refined melodiousness. Gezelle was a priest and a poet; he was neither a theorist nor a leader. His ultramontane political journalism was narrow-minded. His religious, mystical exaltation of nature was perhaps medieval or perhaps Romantic; it was at any rate old-fashioned in comparison with the realism and positivism of the Flemish liberals. But his poetry showed a complete mastery of his instrument and a spontaneous, entirely personal originality. In a literature such as that of the Netherlands, which in spite of magnificent individual achievements remains fundamentally second rate because it draws its inspiration from foreign sources,[1] Gezelle's work is exceptional.

None of his pupils, nor his pupils' pupils, reached the master's level, but they widened the scope of West-Flemish inspiration. Gezelle's West-Flemish nationalism, almost identical with West-Flemish Catholicism, his love for what he regarded as the nature of the Flemish people and his aversion to what he felt to be 'unnatural', all these and other Romantic simplifications were transformed by the young student Albrecht Rodenbach (1856-80) into an ethical and political programme. As an adolescent poet—who, incidentally, rejected ultramontanism[2]— he dreamed of a resurrection of the Flemish people and called upon Roman Catholic youth in school and university to awake to their heroic destiny. His life was filled by feverish activity inspired by Wagner, the German *Burschenschaften*, eclectic and false historical interpretations, as well as by Gezelle's great example. Although after his early death Rodenbach's practical achievements were soon forgotten, it was his spirit that was later to characterize the Flemish Roman Catholic student movement and through it to dominate the whole Flemish movement for a long time to come.

For the French literature of Belgium these years of Flemish

[1] As is rightly pointed out by R. F. Lissens, *De Vlaamse Letterkunde van 1780 tot heden* (3rd edn., Brussels, 1959), p. 69.

[2] Albrecht Rodenbach, *Verzamelde Werken*, i: *Het leven, de persoonlijkheid* by F. Baur (Tielt, 1960), pp. 310 ff.

reorientation are a period of preparation. The country's intellectual life was still sleepy; intellectual curiosity was limited. Brussels with its twenty bookshops was backward compared with Amsterdam which boasted 129.[1] There was little interest in French-Belgian literature. When the radical pro-Flemish Charles de Coster (1827–99) published his *Ulen-spiegel* in 1867, the splendid and amusing tale of the Belgian *gueux*, symbol of the Belgian soul thirsting after freedom, he was hardly understood. In the same year the liberal-Catholic writer André van Hasselt (1805–74), who is sometimes regarded as a precursor of the Christian Democrats, published a long ambitious poem on a religious theme. Apart from these two authors there were many others who worked industriously enough and prepared the ground for the sudden flowering of the early 1880s.

3. The Netherlands, 1848–1879

Dutch culture has often seemed wanting in epic force and shown no great genius for constructive synthesis. It is not surprising, therefore, that doctrinaire liberalism in its literary expression was characterized in Holland by the form of the essay. Even so its modesty is striking during a period when in other countries there was an abundance of great intellectual systems and historiography on the grand scale. Thorbecke was without doubt intellectually superior to Rogier or Frère-Orban, more original, and the creator of a highly personal style of writing; his work, however, consists not of big books like that of Guizot, but mainly of commentaries, reviews, sketches, and speeches. The best liberal historians, Bakhuizen van den Brink and above all Robert Fruin (1823–99), the Leiden professor who dominated Dutch historiography for a long time, were excellent authors and wrote profusely, easily, and precisely, but they wrote essays, not books. C. G. Cobet (1813–89), who remained loyal to the liberal party, enriched classical philology with a wealth of emendations, editions, conjectures, and analyses; he did not produce a synthesis.

[1] G. Schmook, 'Het culturele leven in België 1840–1886', *Algemene geschiedenis der Nederlanden*, x (1955), 415.

Only the theologians attempted ambitious and original works, such as the Leiden Professor J. H. Scholten (1811–85), whose two heavy volumes—*De leer der Hervormde Kerk* (1848–50)—were much admired because of their generous proportions, their emphatic expression, and the harmonious grouping of the chapters.[1] But the theologian and man of letters who so deeply admired the work, Scholten's student Cd Busken Huet (1826–86), himself wrote brilliant essays in an elegant and supple style, and only one rather badly constructed book.

In other fields, in public law, economics, or political philosophy, the situation was no different. J. T. Buys (1828–93), also a Leiden professor, worked for many years on a commentary on the constitution, which finally appeared towards the end of his life; his influence, however, was due to his lectures and the lively and witty articles on Dutch politics which he published in *De Gids*. S. Vissering (1818–88), who was appointed to Thorbecke's chair when the great man became a professional politician and who was a leading economist, wrote an excellent text book[2] but never worked out a system of his own. The president of the Nederlandsche Bank, W. C. Mees (1813–84), propounded his economic views in a book published in 1866 which was praised as a masterpiece;[3] but he confined himself to treating in two hundred small pages and a highly abbreviated style only some 'chapters' of his field of research. Dutch liberalism was vigorous but short-winded. Compared with Belgium its literary output appears very large; yet despite all their advantages nobody in Leiden, which for a few decades was once again a brilliant centre of learning, attempted so bold a construction as François Laurent achieved in his relative isolation in Ghent.

This lack of creative power was not, of course, a new phenomenon in Dutch civilization; in the third quarter of the century, however, there are special factors which help to explain it. The Dutch language in which liberals thought and wrote reached only a small public which would accept the dogmatic generalizations of the liberal authors only on condition that they were

[1] Cd Busken Huet, *Verspreide polemische fragmenten* (Haarlem, 1864), pp. 93 ff.

[2] S. Vissering, *Handboek van praktische staathuishoudkunde* (2nd edn., 2 vols., Amsterdam, 1867).

[3] W. C. Mees, *Overzicht van eenige hoofdstukken der staathuishoudkunde* (Amsterdam, 1866). See N. G. Pierson in *Jaarboek Kon. Ned. Akademie van Wetenschappen* (1885).

not embodied in a rigid system. The groups in sympathy with liberal sentiments and ideas abhorred abstract speculation. Impartiality, practical common sense, critical prudence were the qualities in which the liberals hoped to excel. The systems proposed by their enemies on the Right and on the Left seemed to them as dangerous as they were nonsensical, intended for other, less-educated classes with different traditions. Moreover, the liberals had so much more to do. They spent their time studying their special fields, writing in their periodicals and dailies; and apart from this they used much of their remaining energy in endless polemics. They all knew one another personally; by nature and principle they were all individualists; they disagreed among themselves on innumerable matters. With a great display of erudition, vivacity, and an outspokenness bordering on the vulgar, they disputed in a state of almost total incoherence all the political, historical, constitutional, and theological problems of the day.

C. W. Opzoomer (1821–92) was a typical and interesting example of intellectual liberalism. It was rightly said of this combative, ambitious, and capricious man that like the salamander he could only survive in fire.[1] Polemics were his whole existence. Trained as a jurist at Leiden, he had already by 1846 been appointed to the chair of philosophy at Utrecht; later he developed as a theologian, political theorist, and a man of letters. In none of these fields did he produce profound or original work, but in whatever he did he was always ready to look for new openings. He was brought up in the orthodox Protestant tradition, rejected dogma, became deeply impressed by Krause's Romantic philosophy, which was so much admired by .Thorbecke as well, then sought refuge in Hegel but detached himself from this system too, and was finally converted to empiricism. This road he did not follow to the end, however. Although he was averse to abstract speculation and Romanticism he retained from his religious past what seemed to him essential: the religious sentiments on which he based a very liberal Protestantism. In one way and another he played a leading part in Dutch culture. Thanks to Opzoomer modern empirical philosophy took shape; thanks to him Darwin's

[1] After Van Oosterzee quoted in H. van 't Veer, *Mr C. W. Opzoomer als wijsgeer* (Assen, 1961), p. 61.

book attracted wide attention; in general his erudition, courage, and rather conceited pugnacity forced upon himself and his readers the contemplation of all sorts of fundamental problems.

He was of course a liberal. Despite his objections to Thorbecke's personality and to some of his actions the framework within which he moved was that of doctrinaire liberalism. In many of his reactions he resembles François Laurent: in his contempt for France's glittering but superficial and artificial culture, his belief in the future of Germany, racially akin to the Dutch, his admiration for Bismarck's foreign and religious policies.[1] He was like Laurent particularly in his anti-orthodox instincts which brought him near to the limits of doctrinaire liberalism. His faith in the state school and his active support for general compulsory education estranged him from Thorbecke. Yet he was firmly committed to the constitution of 1848, which seemed to him to be the same in its essentials as the constitutional doctrine he himself put forward.[2] This doctrine, called 'positive', can hardly be regarded as a creative theory, however, and in fact Opzoomer did not wish it to be so regarded. His attitude is typical of doctrinaire liberalism of the second generation. It is individualistic; yet Opzoomer also believes in the Romantic *Volksgeist* and in a constitutional system that can only lay claim to the title of popular sovereignty if the restricted franchise on which it is based is arbitrarily assumed to be the expression of public opinion.[3] His doctrine is 'positive' because it begins with the facts rather than some abstract idea, and calls only for such reform as is absolutely essential. Thus it may also be called a 'historical constitutional theory', a theory of which the only foundations are experience and the reality of history. Hence the statesman's art consists of

[1] C. W. Opzoomer, *Frankrijk's onrecht in den oorlog van 1870* (Amsterdam, 1870), p. 8; Sassen, *Geschiedenis*, p. 318. Opzoomer courageously opposed the strong anti-German tendency of Dutch public opinion. Although on different grounds, the radical S. van Houten did the same. He too was pro-German in 1870. See his *Staats- en strafrechtelijke opstellen* (The Hague, 1897), pp. 103 ff.

[2] C. W. Opzoomer, *Staatsregtelijk onderzoek* (Amsterdam, 1854), p. 11. It seems to me that L. J. Rogier's views on Opzoomer's alleged conservatism are incorrect, based as they are on an erroneous interpretation of the letters written by Opzoomer to Robert Fruin: Rogier, 'Robert Fruins verhouding tot Opzoomer' in his *Terugblik en uitzicht* (2 vols., Hilversum, 1964–5), ii. 278 ff.

[3] Both Thorbecke (Verkade, *Overzicht*, p. 16) and Buys (*Studiën* i. 41) were of the opinion that there was no popular sovereignty in the Netherlands.

carefully showing progress (or evolution) where to go, and of guiding the much-admired nineteenth century into the twentieth which is to be even more perfect than anything that has gone before.[1] Opzoomer revered Burke as such a statesman, the great empiricist of politics.[2] In an enthusiastic review of Opzoomer's book—*Staatsregtelijk onderzoek*—one of the editors of *De Gids* acclaimed the good fortune of the Netherlands in having acquired in 1848 institutions that were so fittingly designed to accommodate the realities of history. The Netherlands, he wrote, chose the 'scientific method' for reforming the state and it was one of the few nations that could boast that it needed neither revolutionary nor conservative doctrines.[3] In this way the doctrinaire victory of 1848 was interpreted by Thorbecke's young followers not as a triumph for Romanticism but for positivism.

There could therefore be no general theory, for no such theory could ever apply to the endless variety of history, no principles except for the single principle that the law must be maintained, no all-embracing speculations that would inevitably be shattered by the facts. Such negations and scepticism inspired doctrinaire policies. Opzoomer called them 'positive'. Vissering wrote a textbook on 'practical' economics. When Thorbecke formed his first Cabinet in 1849 and the Second Chamber asked him for his programme he answered, 'Wait for our acts', and he always sought to avoid parliamentary debates on matters of principle. With imperturbable sobriety Opzoomer showed how fruitless the interminable discussion about the limits of state interference in social life actually was; the state, he concluded, must help everywhere except where such help is unnecessary.[4] As the need for state intervention differs from place to place and from time to time, it is impossible to say anything more fundamental on the matter than is contained in this lapidary sentence.

Although it would be wrong to assume that Dutch doctrinaire liberalism accepted the dogma of non-intervention, in practice the Dutch state behaved more modestly than that of

---

[1] C. W. Opzoomer, *De Restauratie* (Amsterdam, 1854), pp. 37-8.

[2] Idem, *De staatkunde van Edmund Burke* (Amsterdam, 1852).

[3] *De Gids*, xviii, ii (1854), 265-91. The author, P. A. S. van Limburg Brouwer (1829-73), was a man in whom Thorbecke was greatly interested.

[4] C. W. Opzoomer, *De grenzen der staatsmacht* (Amsterdam, 1873), pp. 71 ff.

Leopold II and Frère-Orban. Thorbecke's laws of 1850 and 1851 gave more authority to the provinces and municipalities than was allowed to them in Belgium. On the problem of the municipal excises, that is the duties levied by the municipalities especially on food, the approach in the Netherlands was fundamentally different from that of Frère-Orban with his Crédit communal in 1860. The local duties which constituted the most important source of income of the municipalities were gradually replaced by direct taxes and finally, after innumerable difficulties, abolished altogether in 1865. No one was entirely satisfied with the law of 1865 but one thing was clear: the Dutch congratulated themselves on not having followed Belgian *étatisme*, which destroyed municipal autonomy.[1] Equally notable is the endless effort it needed to make the state responsible for railway construction. For a long time the Dutch persevered in their conviction that in a country served by such an admirable net of waterways railways were unnecessary. Only in 1860, that is twenty-six years after the Belgian Government had taken a similar decision on the initiative of the doctrinaire liberals, did the moderate Van Hall, largely against the wishes of the majority in the Chamber and of Thorbecke himself, get a law through Parliament permitting the state to build railways, leaving only their exploitation to private interest. And, to take one more example, whereas Belgium won international renown through the Commission centrale de statistique, founded by the state and resident in Brussels, a Dutch attempt in 1858 to copy it ended in failure after only three years. It turned out to be impossible to maintain such a centralized institution at The Hague, which provincial members of the committee could hardly reach in winter, and the Second Chamber soon refused to spend any more money on it.[2]

The primary aim of liberal economic policy was, of course, to destroy protectionism. The Dutch doctrinaires did nothing particularly original in this respect. The abolition of the British Navigation Acts in 1849 made some sort of action

[1] Cf. S. Vissering, 'Eene prinselijke rede' (1860), *Herinneringen. Politieke vertoogen* (Amsterdam, 1864), pp. 359 ff. and the literature mentioned there; idem, *Handboek* ii. 160.

[2] Idem, *Herinneringen*, p. xi. Not until 1892 was a new Central Commission for Statistics set up.

necessary, and so the government withdrew all measures for the protection of Dutch shipping in 1850. The British example and a certain degree of British pressure were apparently decisive.[1] In 1854 this was followed by a general reduction of tariffs; at that time, however, the government was no longer doctrinaire but moderate, for as in Belgium the introduction of free trade came largely in the period after 1852 when anti-doctrinaire influences prevailed. But the real triumph of free trade in both countries was due to the doctrinaires. The Dutch law of 1862, when Thorbecke was in power again, abolished all export duties and allowed only a few import duties on manufactures. No doubt Dutch trade benefited from this policy just as it benefited from the favourable economic trend of this period. And yet it did so to a lesser extent than Belgian trade. From about 1850 to 1873 Belgian imports and exports increased by 249 per cent, the Dutch by 179 per cent. Transit trade grew by 65 per cent but it became relatively less important than before: whereas in 1850 the value of transit trade averaged a quarter of the total value of imports and exports by 1870 this was reduced to one-eighth.[2]

Generally, between 1850 and 1875 economic expansion in the Netherlands proceeded at a more leisurely rate than in Belgium. The population increased more rapidly in the Netherlands (by 16·7 per cent as opposed to 14·9 per cent) but it is remarkable that both in the 1840s and in the decade after 1875 the growth rate was higher (17·6 per cent and 26 per cent). No massive drift into the towns was as yet distinguishable, although the small relative decline in urban population during the preceding years was compensated for and the proportion of urban to rural population was the same in 1870 as in 1830. Nor did the general social pattern, the distribution of the working population in the various jobs and professions, change appreciably. In the field of finance there was no great eagerness to exploit new economic conditions, as can be seen from the fate of some of the attempts made in the 1860s, by foreigners as well as Dutch, to follow the example of Péreire's *crédit mobilier* and to found credit banks to accelerate the pace of industrialization and commercial expansion. In 1856 the government

[1] Brugmans, *Paardenkracht en mensenmacht*, pp. 215–16.
[2] Cf. Van Houtte, op. cit., pp. 264–5.

showed itself hostile to such companies, but seven years later its attitude changed. Banks of this sort were then established in Amsterdam and Rotterdam, mainly with French and German capital. But either they quickly perished or remained relatively unused, not being asked to provide the vital services for which they had been created. Dutch capital was not made available for this form of expansion, the Dutch investor remaining loyal to his old preference for state funds and foreign investments. In other words, the means became available for creating a more modern economic apparatus, but they were not sufficiently taken advantage of.

Thus it is not surprising that industrialization was slow. Only a few new factories of lasting importance were built,[1] and the development of existing factories to meet the needs of large-scale industry was very gradual. Steam-power transformed the cotton-mills of Twente; the North-Brabant textile industry also expanded rapidly, and a similar development took place in other industries. There are no exact figures showing industrial growth but a comparison of the surveys made in 1857 and 1871 shows that there was at least some growth.[2] The shipyards, however, declined. The abolition of the various protectionist measures had a fatal effect on the Dutch merchant fleet, which had been kept artificially large and now dropped from fourth place on the world list of 1850 to eighth in 1874. This disastrous decline ruined the shipyards, already facing difficulties enough since sufficient capital to change over to the building of steamers had not been forthcoming. The establishment of some large enterprises—particularly the Koninklijke Nederlandsche Stoombootmaatschappij (1856) at Amsterdam mainly financed by local capital—made an important contribution to the modernization of Dutch shipping, but it was not enough to prevent the status of the Netherlands as a maritime nation from falling into relative decline. Nor did the New Waterway and the North Sea Canal built in this period to connect Rotterdam and Amsterdam with the North Sea have any immediate effect, because work on these gigantic enterprises met with too many troubles and

[1] Cf. K. D. Bosch, *De Nederlandse beleggingen in de Verenigde Staten* (Amsterdam, 1948), p. 66.
[2] Brugmans, *Arbeidende klasse*, pp. 39 ff.

delays. The Netherlands was by no means a poor country, but its prosperity was perhaps not so much due to the absolute increase in trade and industry as to agrarian production. The farmers benefited from extremely favourable circumstances; free trade made export to Britain, their chief customer, easier; the population increased; prices were rising and the means of communication were constantly improving. The prosperity was so great that no one saw any need for agrarian reform, with the result that the prosperity was largely based on an agriculture gradually becoming old-fashioned in its methods. In 1865 the Belgian radical, De Laveleye, noticed that the Netherlands had been unwittingly transformed from a commercial into an agrarian nation. No other European state exported so many agrarian products for its size as the formerly maritime Netherlands.[1]

And yet such a statement, though substantially correct, is also one-sided. It makes sense only if Dutch colonial production is taken into account together with the agrarian potential of the mother country; if that is done it becomes clear that the Netherlands could never have developed into a merely continental agrarian state. It was during this period of agrarian preponderance that the colonial problem and colonial trade made such a great impact on the Dutch economy, as well as on Dutch politics and culture. And it was the impulses and initiatives of the liberals that determined the situation, despite their failure to develop a coherent theory of colonial administration. Between 1848 and 1880 no less than twenty-five ministers, very often with diametrically opposed views, were in charge of the Department of Colonial Affairs; it is not surprising therefore, that colonial policies remained tentative, hesitant, and incomplete; this as much as liberal incompetence made it extremely difficult to work out a consistent point of view. The doctrinaires of 1848 were not themselves much interested in the colonial possessions. They did not know any more about them than their opponents, and no doubt joined in the laughter during colonial debates when the only specialist on the liberal side in the Second Chamber ventured to use Javanese terms and geographical names. Before 1848 liberal opposition to the government's colonial policies was directed against the

---

[1] De Laveleye, *Études d'économie rurale*, pp. 256, 280.

exclusive influence of the Crown. The fiscal and financial consequences of these policies could not be assessed by Parliament
because there was no reliable information available. The
Accountancy Law of 1864, introduced by Thorbecke's second
Cabinet, did make it possible for the States General to supervise the East Indian finances in detail. But there were some
liberals who were more imaginative when it came to the colonial
question. Under the influence of P. J. Veth (1814-95)—at
that time still a professor of Hebrew at Amsterdam but very
knowledgeable about the East Indies—the monthly *De Gids*
devoted much space to the history and problems of the possessions in the East. As early as 1848 and 1849 it was reminding its
readers of the moral debt that the selfish Netherlands owed to
its Eastern subjects.[1]

Thus the eloquence of the greatest and most active opponent
of the old colonial system, W. R. baron van Hoëvell (1812-79),
did not go unheard. After serving for eleven years as a minister
of the Reformed Church at Batavia, Van Hoëvell returned to
the Netherlands in 1849. He immediately became a member of
the Second Chamber and started his vigorous and courageous
campaign on behalf of the Javanese. His ideal was the very
opposite of the so-called culture-system. This system was
founded on a perhaps correct but certainly conservative insight into the static, unchangeable conditions prevailing in
Javanese society, with its rigid division into rulers and ruled
and its unformed notions of property and labour. On this
assumption the governments of William I and William II
endeavoured to isolate the Javanese from the West lest assimilation of European ideas ruin the basis of the existing system.
The Dutch refused to act as educators; according to these
principles not even the Dutch language and the Christian
religion were allowed to penetrate the native civilization. The
civil servants sent to the East Indies were only thought reliable
if they showed no interest in the Javanese population.[2] It was
against this shutting-off of the Indonesian empire that Van

---

[1] *De Gids*, XII. ii (1848), 72 ff.; XIII. i (1849), 245 ff.; XIII. ii (1849), 157 ff.
See also Potgieter, *De Gids*, XIII. i (1849), 21-2.
[2] R. Reinsma, *Het verval van het cultuurstelsel* (The Hague, 1955), pp. 37 ff., 51 ff.,
106 ff.; W. R. van Hoëvell, *Parlementaire redevoeringen over koloniale belangen* (4 vols.,
Zaltbommel, 1862-5), ii. 11.

Hoëvell fought his long and often bitter fight. He hoped to see the Netherlands and Indonesia fuse into one brotherhood united by Christianity and economic interest. Indonesia, for too long the exclusive domain of a few hundred civil servants, ought to be opened up to private individuals and the Christian missions so that the virtues of the Dutch lower middle classes, their commercial ability and their industry, could become shining examples for the natives. He did not deny, however, that the mother country was entitled to draw profits from its colonies, and he was not against maintaining the state plantations for as long as necessary provided that free labour was substituted for forced labour. During these first attempts of the liberals to influence colonial policy the reformers were indeed convinced that the Netherlands would benefit financially from adopting their proposals.[1]

But basically Van Hoëvell was guided and inspired by his interpretation of native interests. A strong feeling of moral guilt and responsibility lay at the bottom of it, and such a feeling was to be found in various circles. Thus one of the members of the Dutch Bible Society wrote in 1853 that through the completion of the translation of the New Testament into Javanese the Christian Dutch had made a start in paying off a great and heavy debt.[2] Either because of this or because of a sense of adventure many young intellectuals, impatient with the slow pace of life in Holland, were fascinated by the magnificent overseas empire whose doors were slowly opening. Even Buys, who in the end led a very quiet life as a professor of constitutional law at Leiden, was at one time on the verge of establishing himself in Java as a barrister-at-law.[3] In 1860 Eduard Douwes Dekker (1820–87), who wrote under the tearful pen-name Multatuli ('I have suffered a lot'), published his splendid novel *Max Havelaar*. Since 1838 he had been working his way up in the Indonesian administration until in 1856 he came into conflict with his superiors and resigned. His concern for the natives, who on the basis of the culture-system were being abominably exploited not so much by the

[1] Cf. e.g. D. C. Steyn Parvé, *Het koloniaal monopoliestelsel* (Zaltbommel, 1850) and Van Hoëvell, op. cit. i. 184 ff.; ii. 268–9; and *passim*.

[2] H. C. Milliës in *De Gids*, XVII. ii (1853), 161.

[3] Cf. S. A. Naber, *Vier tijdgenooten* (Haarlem, 1854), p. 93.

Dutch as by their own chiefs, combined with superb literary gifts, a biting wit, and an absorbing megalomania, enabled him to write the masterpiece of Dutch nineteenth-century literature. It was immediately successful. Although Multatuli did not attack the culture-system itself, he showed much more clearly than his predecessors and with incomparably greater skill—the abuses themselves had already been the subject of complaints many times before[1]—that the feudal foundation on which it rested and which the conservatives wanted to preserve at all costs was despicable and disastrous.

Yet only slowly and hesitantly did a liberal colonial policy take shape. Principles did not help much. The East Indian profits were large: until 1866 the culture-system was bringing the treasury an average of 19 million guilders, that is about one-fifth of the budget. If through a more moderate application of the system or its total transformation these profits were to be reduced, important tasks to which the liberal state was committed would either be left unfulfilled or have to be financed by the Dutch taxpayers themselves. These included not only the building of a new economic infrastructure, of railways and of canals, but also the emancipation of the West Indian slaves, which depended on whether the state was able to compensate the slave-holders.[2] To this generation it would still have seemed paradoxical for the liberals to increase taxes. Moreover, if they did it would mean the introduction of income tax—there was income tax on the municipal but not on the national level—and though many liberals theoretically approved of such a system[3] the Second Chamber as a whole, consisting as it did of representatives of the small group of people who paid enough in direct taxation to become electors, naturally disliked it. In any case such a measure would produce incalculable changes in the franchise and thus have unpredictable political consequences. On no less than six occasions during this period the liberals themselves—even including some

---

[1] Cf. Van Hoëvell, ii. 86 ff.

[2] There was almost no slavery in the Dutch East Indies. When all slaves in the areas under direct Dutch rule were emancipated in 1860, it turned out that they numbered only 5,000; most of these were house servants. In the West Indies 40,000 slaves were emancipated in 1863.

[3] Vissering, *Handboek* ii. 94 ff. Thorbecke was of a different opinion (Verkade, op. cit., p. 265).

who were said to belong to the left wing—prevented reform of the totally inadequate fiscal system.[1]

It took the war in Achin, in the western corner of Sumatra, to undermine the culture-system. The Dutch had had the greatest difficulty in establishing their authority there since 1873, and the war, which in 1884 was calculated to have cost already 150 million guilders, threatened to devour all Indonesian profits. After 1877, indeed, there were no longer any profits coming out of Indonesia, but losses for which the Dutch state did not hold itself responsible. In 1878 Parliament at last agreed to impose death duties. In 1889 all liberals in the Second Chamber supported a proposal to introduce income tax; in 1893 they brought it about.

Although it was a long time before the Dutch state finally ceased to act as an entrepreneur in the East Indies and confined itself to administration, during these years the colonies were increasingly opened up to private interests. Thorbecke's government in particular abolished many of the state plantations between 1862 and 1866. In 1870, when the state ended the obligatory cultivation of sugar, it retained a direct interest only in some coffee-plantations. As a result of these and other measures private entrepreneurs won a much larger share of Indonesian production. In 1842 government production accounted for 80 per cent, free enterprise for 15 per cent of the total agrarian production; in 1852 it was 70 and 29 per cent respectively; in 1862 57 and 38 per cent; in 1872 23 and 70 per cent.[2] Thus in this field too the liberals created the conditions for a new development: the development, on the one hand, of colonial capitalism and, on the other, of territorial imperialism, for it was after the state released its grip on the economy that it started in a systematic way to subject the whole colonial territory to its authority. However, two qualifications are needed. For of course it was not only liberalism that was responsible for the growth of private enterprise in Indonesia. To a certain extent the culture-system itself made this possible. It showed how much Java could produce and thus drew the attention of the Dutch, who in 1830 were as

---

[1] K. E. van der Mandele, *Het liberalisme in Nederland* (Arnhem, 1933), p. 95. Cf. Buys, op. cit. i. 475 ff.

[2] Reinsma, op. cit., p. 157. The statistics should be used with caution.

indifferent to the East Indies as they were ignorant, to the exciting opportunities awaiting them there. Moreover, it probably increased the prosperity of the natives, or if this was not the case it at least increased their needs, with the result that many among them were prepared to do regular wage work for the Dutch entrepreneurs, which they had not been prepared to do in the past.

Secondly, it should not be forgotten that even during the 1860s, when the liberals had at last adopted a colonial policy, they remained divided as to its aims and its method. One vital problem was landownership. The radical wing of the liberal party wanted to establish in Java a system founded on European conceptions, which would grant the Dutch entrepreneur sufficient security for him to take the risk of exploiting the land. In 1866 this idea was given concrete form in a vigorous bill introduced by the Minister of Colonial Affairs, I. D. Fransen van de Putte (1822–1902), an adventurous man who after a career as a mariner and a sugar-planter on Java in 1859 returned to the Netherlands and, free from financial worries, found in politics a fruitful outlet for his energies. By his bill the Javanese, released from all obligatory labour services, would be regarded as the proprietors of the land which they cultivated. The common land used by the whole village community might be divided among its members if that was the wish of the majority. These proposals would have meant the disintegration of the culture-system; they were much more radical than anything suggested by Van Hoëvell, for so long the only colonial specialist among the liberals. And Van de Putte also wanted the state to make available the waste land, which covered about three-quarters of Java, on long leases to private business men. But Parliament was reluctant to go so far. Thorbecke himself, who after a conflict with Van de Putte at the beginning of 1866 had resigned from his own Cabinet, now publicly turned against his former minister and opposed the introduction of private property into a society to which the concept was so alien. Fransen van de Putte in his turn resigned. The conservatives who succeeded him failed equally to find a satisfactory solution. But the problem was solved in 1870 when a liberal Cabinet (formed by Thorbecke, although he did not become a member of it) approached it more cautiously.

Characteristically, the new Minister of Colonial Affairs, E. de Waal (1821-1905)—a former Indonesian civil servant and expert on Indonesian affairs—tried, in the best doctrinaire style, to reduce a question that was in danger of growing into a profound moral issue to more manageable proportions. In his 'agrarian law' the relation between the Javanese and their land was defined as briefly and effectively as possible; an attempt was made to protect the natives against exploitation by the private entrepreneurs, a danger which would certainly increase, for the law also put the waste land at the disposal of the entrepreneurs on very advantageous terms.

In this way the States General finally adopted a colonial policy that for years to come was felt to be progressive enough. The long debates thus concluded were an interesting episode in Dutch political history for various reasons. They were conducted in a way that was characteristic of Dutch politics generally. It was widely agreed that the questions under discussion mattered enormously; indeed the time and attention that Parliament devoted to them indicate how important they were felt to be. Yet it was as though the members of Parliament were unable to raise their debates to a truly political level. Most of their attention was concentrated on the juridical aspects of the problem, and they often gave the impression of speaking as judges or barristers displaying their learning and ready wit rather than as statesmen trying to defend or to attack the principles behind a political decision.[1] Both members of Parliament and of the government were lacking in political spirit; they found neither the words nor the gestures to give political shape to the dramatic elements in the situation. It would be wrong to criticize them for this, for just as much as under the *ancien régime* the academic study of law was still regarded as the best preparation for a political career. In the First as well as in the Second Chamber the jurists prevailed. In 1850, for instance, forty-seven of the sixty-seven members of the Second Chamber had a law degree and boasted the title of Master in Law.[2] This not only gave them a preference for juridical arguments, it also ensured a common interest, a readiness to agree about priorities and the correct criteria to be

[1] Van Welderen Rengers, op. cit. i. 328.
[2] Cf. also Boogman, 'De Britse gezant Napier' 207.

used in judging a proposal; and this at the same time reduced the chances of parliamentary discussion becoming involved in fundamental political antitheses. The tendency of Parliament to confine itself to technical details, perhaps important in themselves but inhibiting deeper consideration, was exacerbated by the social exclusiveness of its composition. Political differences existed, but within such a relatively closed community the danger of these degenerating into petty personal feuds was very real. Of the one hundred ministers who served between 1848 and 1877 no less than 81 came from noble or patrician families.[1] In the Chambers the situation was, for obvious reasons, different. Yet of the 410 men who became members of Parliament during this period, 130 came from the traditional aristocracy, 70 were civil servants, 65 belonged to the magistracy, 13 were public notaries. Finally, there were the barristers, business men, rural entrepreneurs, and a few teachers.[2] So the overwhelming majority was directly dependent on the well-ordered functioning of the state, and on the traditional rules of social intercourse, with the result that whatever their personal views or inclinations it was natural for them never to allow their opposition to go beyond what was generally accepted.

The colonial legislation of 1870 was a major doctrinaire victory and it put an end to the remarkable attempts that had been made to create a conservative party. The word party must, of course, be used with caution, for during this period the Netherlands did not have organized parties along British or Belgian lines. In Thorbecke's view the very absence of political parties was an important feature of Dutch politics, giving the Dutch constitutional monarchy a form quite distinct from that of the British which he disliked. It could be argued that as there were no parties from which a Cabinet could emerge, it had necessarily to be created by the royal will. Consequently, a Dutch Government need never seek to be the faithful reflection of a parliamentary majority; it could behave as an independent body with an independent position between King and Parliament. As this was the outstanding characteristic of Dutch

[1] Boogman, 'Achtergronden' 57.
[2] S. J. Fockema Andreae, 'De grootburgers (1848–1879)', *500 jaren Staten-Generaal in de Nederlanden* (Assen, 1964), pp. 217–18.

constitutional monarchy it was essential for its preservation that parties should not be allowed to develop. Of course not everyone was so dogmatic on this point as Thorbecke, and even Thorbecke was forced to recognize that within Parliament there were parties or at least party opinions;[1] a modern party system, however, arising from activities outside the Chambers and from the political life of the constituencies, did not yet exist. The word party meant an unorganized group of men with broadly similar political views. They were not tied to a clear, detailed programme, and in Parliament they were free to vote as they liked. For this reason it was often extremely difficult to distinguish between the various political groups. But there were apparently certain political centres around which, in an interminable interplay of attraction and repulsion, individuals were constantly moving. Thorbecke himself was such a centre; his anti-revolutionary opponent Groen van Prinsterer was another. At the approach of elections they personally supervised the nomination of candidates[2] and in Parliament they could be sure of the support of a number of loyal collaborators. Among the conservatives, however, there was nobody with comparable prestige. Consequently, a conservative party was even less easy to identify than a liberal or an anti-revolutionary one. Yet it was impossible to deny the existence of conservative opinion, and it is interesting to see how from time to time the attempt was made to translate this into a party.

In 1848 many viewed the constitutional changes with consternation and horror, and they were not unimportant people: they were the men around the Crown Prince and the Crown Prince himself, who as King William III ruled from 1849 to 1890; the majority in Parliament; countless civil servants at the higher levels—in short, a large number of those who before 1848 had, in one way or another, been a part of the administration. These men did not simply constitute a court party: they may be regarded as broadly representative of the opinions of the patricians, the big trading firms, the former regents, and the aristocracy. For them, accustomed as they were to governing either at the local or the national level, the revision of 1848 was

---

[1] Verkade, pp. 98 ff.
[2] See e.g. the letters in C. W. de Vries, *De ongekende Thorbecke* (Amsterdam, 1950), pp. 186 ff., 191 ff.

a personal defeat, the more so when in 1850 and 1851 Thor-becke's vigorous legislation also reformed the municipal and provincial administrations. For many years to come these influential and experienced men kept hoping that the Nether-lands would follow the example set by the rest of Europe and that, as in France, Prussia, and Austria, there would be a move back towards conservatism.[1] In 1852 they believed (wrongly as it turned out) that public exasperation with the liberals was so universal that a humble petition to King William III to bring about a conservative revision of the electoral law would enjoy wide support.[2] Although their con-fidence was misplaced it was not altogether surprising that they should have felt it. The revision of 1848 had after all probably been due to the caprice of a king and the fear of falling a prey to the spirit of European revolution, rather than to the thoughtful preparations of the doctrinaires. Yet the new constitution remained in fact unaltered. Dutch conservatism, though robust and self-assured, failed to formulate a programme, and lacked creative inspiration. And this too is not surprising. Royalism, clericalism, feudalism, which served as adequate slogans in other countries, were quite alien to the Dutch past. What else had the conservatives to fall back on except the traditions of the old Republic, which the unsystematic regimes of William I and William II had to some extent allowed to survive, together with its regents, its proud and stubborn patriciate, its lack of principles? The most ingenious statesman could hardly be expected to find in these even a moderately coherent alternative to the liberal state of 1848. Moreover, getting or maintaining power on the strength of theories, constitutions, or political movements was something the Dutch ruling classes had never engaged in. Ever since the sixteenth century the real strength of the urban oligarchies had lain in their ability to adapt themselves to all changing circumstances. Thanks to their experienced and expert opportunism they had managed to remain in power under stadtholders and kings, in times of domestic peace and in times of wild commotion.

[1] Cf. L. J. Rogier, 'Schrikbeeld van een staatsgreep in 1853', Terugblik en uitzicht, i. 357 ff. and C. B. Wels in Bijdragen voor de Geschiedenis der Nederlanden, xvii (1962), 70 ff.
[2] See G. W. Vreede, Een twintigjarige strijd (Utrecht, 1869), pp. 103 ff.

It was not inconceivable that they could also survive the constitution of 1848.

The crisis of 1853 threatened all that had been achieved since 1848, and showed the adaptability of the old élite. It arose because of the re-establishment of the Roman Catholic hierarchy. This had been under discussion since 1795, but innumerable factors had combined to keep in existence the curious system of the *ancien régime*, so that in the Netherlands there were still the Catholic missions with archpriests North and apostolic vicars South of the big rivers, whilst the papal internuncio at The Hague (an Italian) acted as the vice-superior. The Concordat, which King William I had concluded in 1827 and which allowed for the appointment of two bishops, was never enforced. When in 1841, under William II, negotiations were started with a view to putting it finally into effect, Protestant reactions were so violent that the King had to abandon the project. But in 1848 the situation changed because the new constitution, loyally supported by the Catholics, emphatically granted the Churches complete freedom to organize themselves as they wished. Various groups of Roman Catholics sent petitions to Rome asking for the re-establishment of a normal episcopal hierarchy. Rome was slow in reacting. The Dutch Government, on the other hand, was repeatedly prevented by the King from discussing with Rome the whole issue of the Concordat and the appointment of bishops, with the result that, although the government's principles were clear enough, it remained for quite a long time difficult to see what attitude it would in practice adopt to the suggested innovation.[1] Finally Pius IX took the initiative. At the end of 1851 he informed the Dutch Cabinet, then under Thorbecke, of his conviction that the Netherlands was in need of a proper episcopacy; in March 1852 the Cabinet answered that it was prepared to regard the Concordat of 1827 as abrogated; in September 1852 the Pope concurred. Then at last all obstacles were removed. In March 1853 the Pope issued a brief in which he announced the establishment of an archbishopric at Utrecht and bishoprics at Haarlem, 's-Hertogenbosch, Breda, and Roermond. Although this was common knowledge the Dutch Government was not officially informed about the details,

[1] Beekelaar, *Rond grondwetsherziening en herstel der hiërarchie*, pp. 150 ff.

simply because the internuncio at The Hague, who feared serious complications, especially over the Utrecht archbishopric, thought it preferable to confront the Cabinet with a *fait accompli*. As it happened, however, this complicated matters unnecessarily and gave rise to lamentable discussions, recriminations, and confusion. Many Protestants in any case thought that Rome had announced its decision in a gratuitously insulting manner. For more than a century Utrecht, an overwhelmingly Protestant city, had been the seat of the Dutch separatist Jansenist Church which the brief called *monstrum ac pestis*; the Pope, who declared himself very satisfied with the growth (incidentally non-existent) of Dutch Catholicism, chose to write with deep disgust of the Revolt, and the violence and presumption of the Calvinist heretics.

A section of the Protestant community exploded in hysterical anger. From pulpits and other platforms, in petitions to the King (with a total of 200,000 signatures), in two hundred pamphlets, and in their weekly papers a large number of Protestants expressed their indignation in reckless, bombastic prose or miserable verse. They assured their readers that they could now expect tyranny, inquisition, censorship, the stake. Such a reaction was no doubt ridiculous, but however primitive and absurd, it was not altogether inexplicable. The re-establishment of the hierarchy meant that Roman Catholic emancipation, proclaimed in 1795 and maintained ever since without having many noticeable effects, was now to become a fact of daily life. In 1853 the age-old assumption that the Netherlands was a Protestant country in which the Catholics were a minority tolerated in a spirit of noble magnanimity needed to be thoroughly revised. Although obviously no one in 1853 could foresee that both in numbers and political power the Catholics would grow to such an extent that in the twentieth century they would have achieved a dominating position (38·15 per cent of the population in 1849, 35·38 per cent in 1889, and 40·43 per cent in 1960), the Protestants who reacted so furiously against Thorbecke's Cabinet were right in realizing that they could no longer regard themselves as the true masters of the nation. What to the Romantic liberals was a simple consequence of their liberalism seemed to these Protestants a betrayal of precisely those national ideals that had always been held to be characteristically liberal. Proud of the state that had been built upon their Protestantism, a state which they, like so many others, so often repeated, had for centuries been a bastion of freedom and peace, they felt utterly bewildered by the refusal of the doctrinaires to respect what had always been regarded since the sixteenth century as the national and liberal tradition.

An explosion such as this so-called 'April movement' is bound to be a complicated phenomenon. The emotions seeking expression were varied and contradictory. It looks as though the real consequences of 1848 became apparent only in 1853, as though it were only then that it was generally realized that the constitutional revision was in effect a drastic break with traditions that had survived even the French Revolution. Some people, of course, had known this all along; in 1848 not only direct elections but especially the freedom of association, of the Churches, and of the schools were attacked by the conservatives because they would favour the Catholics; ever since 1848 there was in the opposition to doctrinaire liberalism a hard core of anti-papism.[1] This does not mean that the whole Protestant community reacted in the same way. There was no lack of warning from Protestant authorities, including the Synod, against the anti-Catholic and anti-liberal movement. Although a man like Groen van Prinsterer, the orthodox political leader, was delighted to see these manifestations of Protestant zeal, he was at the same time genuinely worried about their possible implications; it was not after all inconceivable that the outcome of a successful campaign would be that all Churches, the Protestant Churches included, would once again be subjected to the state. Moreover, the Second Chamber generally approved of the government's conduct. And yet the doctrinaire Cabinet perished in the storm. The decisive factor in this highly complex interplay of sometimes contradictory elements and emotions turned out to be the attitude of the so-called conservatives, the 'aristocratic party', who were even accused by some doctrinaire publicists of having started and exacerbated what was only superficially a religious movement.[2] Although this view cannot be substantiated and is on

---

[1] See e.g. Vreede, *Levensschets*, pp. 318–19.
[2] D. Koorders, 'De Aprilbeweging', *De Gids*, XVIII. i (1854), 1 ff.

the whole rather implausible, it is none the less true that at the end of March 1853, when the campaign began in Utrecht, more than religious issues were involved.

Conservatism in Utrecht and in the Netherlands generally consisted of as many schools as there were conservatives. But it is possible to distinguish two dominant if discordant themes in the utterances of two Utrecht professors, G. J. Mulder and G. W. Vreede. Mulder (1802-80), from a family of surgeons and soldiers, studied medicine at Utrecht and in 1840 was appointed to the chair of chemistry there. A hot-tempered man, averse to theory and speculation but never completely satisfied by his own science through which he acquired an international reputation, he liked giving vivid expression to his views on politics, education, and life generally.[1] His Protestantism was rather old-fashioned, with a distinct eighteenth-century flavour. He was as indifferent to Protestant modernism as to nineteenth-century orthodoxy; without respect for dogma or theology he firmly believed in God's wisdom and man's eternal life. He hated the revision of 1848 both because it favoured Rome and because it transferred power from a Prince capable of being resolute to a Parliament split by partisan hatred, wasting its time in endless discussion and impotent legislation. Just when energetic, purposeful, and expert guidance was needed, especially in the field of education, 1848 brought government by jurists. The jurists refused to spend money on imaginative projects, and the spirit of materialism—what Mulder called commercialism, the pursuit of personal gain and ambition— was written into the new immoral constitution, ruining all natural social relations and respect for authority. Mulder was an Orangist; because the Netherlands was a monarchy he was also prepared to be a royalist. His ancestors had been Protestant Orangists and he himself enjoyed private connections at the royal court. But it is difficult to determine what precisely he imagined the ideal royal authority to represent. This anti-Catholic, anti-juridical, anti-parliamentary, and at any rate in colonial affairs decidedly conservative[2] royalism is very

[1] G. J. Mulder, *Levensschets* (2 vols., Rotterdam, 1881), ii. 10 ff.; cf. also W. Labruyère, *G. J. Mulder (1802-1880)* (Leiden, 1938).

[2] Mulder regularly advised the Colonial Office on chemical matters. His personal, scientific, and political friend G. Simons was director of the Koninklijke

curious. It had a chance of success, however, between 1854 and 1858 when two of Mulder's friends became ministers, both scientists and equally robust Protestant nationalists.[1] As a result of the April movement the development of a very mild form of despotism (which, absurd though it sounds, one is inclined to call Bonapartism) seemed, for a short while, possible. However, neither the King nor his friends, who were technicians and not statesmen, were able to harness these energies, and the so-called Great Protestant party remained a small and powerless group of political amateurs.

G. W. Vreede (1809-80) was an equally active anti-Catholic campaigner and a great admirer of his colleague Mulder. Yet he belongs to a different world. He was the grandson of Pieter Vreede, the revolutionary leader of the 1790s; he studied at Ghent and Louvain, but took his doctor's degree at Leiden. In 1841 he was appointed to the chair of constitutional and international law at Utrecht. During the 1830s he was a liberal opponent of William I's disastrous anti-Belgian policies; but when Thorbecke started giving liberalism a doctrinaire character in the 1840s he turned conservative. During and after 1848 his hatred of Thorbecke grew; in 1853 he was one of the first to open the fight against 'papo-thorbeckianism'. Like Mulder his Protestantism was undogmatic as well as illiberal, a strictly emotional religion which was probably less clearly defined than that of the Lutheran Thorbecke, who showed some interest in questions of dogma. Vreede felt only contempt for the collaboration between liberals and Catholics in 1848; it reminded him of the monstrous Union of 1828 in Belgium which had destroyed the prospering United Kingdom. He was a highly emotional man with innumerable principles but no system. He was a passionate foe of anything resembling Bonapartism, and this saved him from

Academie and of the training college at Delft for Dutch civil servants in the East Indies.

[1] A. Vrolik (1810-94) served as a minister from 1854 to 1858, G. Simons (1802-68) from 1856 to 1857. Simons's resignation was considered by Mulder to be the decisive defeat of his own ideals. For the views of Simons see some letters in G. Groen van Prinsterer, *Briefwisseling*, iii, ed. H. J. Smit (The Hague, 1949), pp. 947 ff. See also C. W. de Vries (*Ongekende Thorbecke*, pp. 87 ff.), who failed to see that Thorbecke could simply not avoid attacking such people and ideas with all his might.

Mulder's hot-headed Orangism.[1] But although he was a jurist, a very erudite historian, a much-travelled and prolific writer, deeply interested since his early youth in politics, he did not have the imagination nor presumably the urge to attempt a systematic exposition of conservative ideas. In his writings he expressed disgust for the society created by 1848, a society without coherence, confidence, or calm; for Thorbecke; for democracy; for the resignation which allowed the Netherlands to be regarded as a small second-rate state, an attitude which, as a nationalist in the style of Van Hogendorp and a specialist in diplomatic history, he fought with obstinate perseverance. But neither in his work nor in that of his friends—like the distinguished jurist, sociologist, and historian J. de Bosch Kemper (1808–76)—does one find an attempt to propound a rational, theoretically sound alternative to liberalism.

When the April movement weakened the Cabinet to such an extent that Thorbecke decided to resign—a resignation most readily accepted by William III—the ultimate sterility of Mulder's and Vreede's conservatism became apparent. Although they may have been instrumental in setting off the Protestant reaction it was not they who now dominated the situation but the moderates from Holland, who had held important positions in the administration before 1848 and were able to re-establish themselves. F. A. van Hall, the man of the financial reform of 1844, was delighted to be called back to power. But Vreede and Mulder soon realized that his policy was altogether different from what they had hoped for and they became his opponents.[2] Indeed, neither in 1844 nor in 1853 was Van Hall a real conservative. He belonged to the ruling classes of Amsterdam,[3] an adaptable, efficient, resourceful administrator without dogmatic principles. His objections to the constitution of 1848, against which he had written acrimonious pamphlets on the grounds that it threatened to eliminate the natural rulers of the Netherlands, were not such as to inspire him to revise it after he had kindly been allowed by it to return to power. The electorate generally supported him although

---

[1] This is Vreede's own term: *Levensschets*, p. 432.

[2] Vreede, *Een twintigjarige strijd*, pp. 137 ff. and a letter from Mulder and Simons to Van Hall in Groen, *Briefwisseling*, iii. 935.

[3] Th. van Tijn, *Twintig jaren Amsterdam* (Amsterdam, 1965), p. 147.

many did not even bother to vote. He and those of his successors who continued his policies avoided extremes and refused to challenge their opponents. Tactfully and delicately they respected all established interests, and recognized even the constitution and the episcopal hierarchy as irreversible *faits accomplis*. In 1856 an effort was made to draw more serious conclusions from the agitation of 1853 and a conservative Protestant Cabinet came to power; but this led to such confusion that the attempt was abandoned in 1858 and a more liberal government introduced. Only in 1862, however, was Thorbecke himself allowed to take up government again; only then did the antitheses, which in nine years of efficient moderate rule by compromise had lost much of their edge, recover political significance. In 1853 the conflict between Left and Right had not come clearly into the open because Protestant national feeling, so painfully hurt by Thorbecke, was anti-doctrinaire but not necessarily conservative; moreover, the old élite had emerged from that year's turmoil as the true victors. In the 1860s, however, the conflict was plain to see.

This was the decisive decade. On the colonial and constitutional issues that played so important a role in the 1860s the doctrinaires were at last able to win a definite victory; the half-way solutions, the policy of adaptation, evasion, and delay practised by the 'higher classes', the blurring of issues by the moderates, these were no longer acceptable. The problems of education and of the franchise might be left unsolved, although they were real enough; but to the colonial question an answer was urgently needed. This fact influenced the entire political and cultural history of the Netherlands. It meant the ruin of 'moderatism'[1] as a more or less independent movement, the end of a phenomenon that since the 1790s had shown a surprising tenacity. The moderates went back to the period of the French Revolution. They had always been 'enlightened', representatives not of the closed pre-1795 oligarchy but of the upper middle classes, the bankers, the big trading firms in Holland. Though owing their existence as a political group to

---

[1] The term 'moderate' was not a current one in this period. In 1851 Van Bosse, a liberal statesman, called them the party of the *moderados* (C. W. de Vries, *Het grondwettig koningschap onder Koning Willem III*, The Hague, 1946, p. 74).

the revolutionary situation and benefiting from it they were not themselves distinguished for their revolutionary spirit. They fought the House of Orange but in 1813 were quite happy to accept the establishment of a monarchy. It was expected to achieve what the moderates had always been working for: an enlightened unitary state with the province of Holland at its centre. For this reason they were hostile to the adventurous United Kingdom of 1815, rejoiced at its collapse in 1830, and got back into power again by their firm opposition to William I's *status quo* policy towards Belgium and its financial consequences. Even 1848 did not break their spirit. But in the 1860s 'moderatism' disappeared. Doctrinaire liberalism which originated outside the province of Holland and probably still found most of its support in the other provinces forced the moderates into the conservative camp and defeated them.

In the colonial controversy most moderates adopted the conservative standpoint. It is remarkable that in this field it was indeed possible to define the truly conservative position which in domestic matters proved so elusive. During the 1850s the arguments of colonial conservatives against dismantling the culture-system had been almost entirely opportunistic, the main one being that liberal reforms would inevitably reduce the profits drawn by the state from Indonesia. During the 1860s the manner of their reasoning if not its purpose changed.[1] They argued that the abolition of the culture-system amounted to a social revolution that would have disastrous consequences for the Javanese, who were not yet ready for a capitalist economy and would be helplessly exposed to ruthless European exploitation.[2] This was the first time the conservatives put forward an anti-liberal argument stemming from an awareness of social problems. It is not unreasonable to doubt whether it was altogether sincere. After all, such enlightened concern for the masses was never shown towards the Dutch proletariat. Indeed, with one notable exception, the conservatives seem to have been almost totally indifferent to the social question in the Netherlands. The exception was J. de Bosch Kemper. In the 1850s he wrote a *Historical Investigation into Pauperism in Our Fatherland* (1851) which is still much used; in the 1860s he

---

[1] Van Hoëvell, iii, pp. vii ff.

[2] Cf, S. L. van der Wal, *De motie-Keuchenius* (Groningen, 1934), pp. 32, 45- 6.

published his *Guide to the Knowledge of the Science of Society* (1863), intended as his *magnum opus* but far too nebulous and long, and very dull. Yet that De Bosch Kemper had the courage, among all the strictly analytical work produced by his colleagues, to venture a coherent synthesis in the badly neglected field of sociology was undoubtedly praiseworthy. Moreover, his serious attempt to show that organic society should be recognized as preceding and overruling the individual and individual interests was proof of his concern for those social relationships and obligations that were matters of indifference to so many liberals. He also devoted much energy and money to furthering popular education, among other things by writing and publishing a cheap newspaper. But he never exercised any real influence nor did he find concrete solutions to concrete problems. Even he was unable to help the conservatives to develop arguments of genuine political or scholarly significance.[1]

After long years of struggle colonial conservatism was defeated. It did not find much support in the Netherlands because only a small group of people benefited directly from conservative policies; in Indonesia itself it seemed already antiquated before it was abandoned by the mother country. In the early 1860s many civil servants in the East Indian administration realized the necessity of thorough reform and on the whole they gave the conservatives no backing. In addition, the conservatives made the mistake of defending constitutional principles fundamentally unrelated to their own policies. In 1866 they were in an excellent position. After four years of growing uneasiness the doctrinaires, confused and divided among themselves, abandoned power. The King, always happy to see a liberal Cabinet go out and worried too about the international situation, appointed a conservative government under the experienced diplomat J. P. J. A. Count van Zuylen van Nyevelt (1819–94), instructing him to ignore such difficult domestic questions as education and the franchise. But this attempt to establish national unity and a reconciliation of opposite interests through tactful inactivity—an attempt which in the 1850s had been not unsuccessful—failed. Within a few months the liberals, who still commanded a majority in

---

[1] See H. Th. Ambagtsheer, *Jhr Mr Jeronimo de Bosch Kemper* (Amsterdam, 1959) and H. P. G. Quack, *Herinneringen* (Amsterdam, 1915), pp. 43 ff.

the Second Chamber, had the opportunity to attack the Cabinet when it became apparent that the Minister of Colonial Affairs, P. Mijer (1812-81)—an authority on the East Indies—, had only accepted a seat in the government in order that, having disposed as quickly as possible of the most urgent legislation, he could become Governor-General in Indonesia. Mijer's behaviour was not unprecedented; and in later days it happened again that the Colonial Secretary resigned because he wanted to be made Governor-General. But in 1866 such a move was violently resented in the Second Chamber, and not only by the liberals. For Mijer, who had been expected to help to solve the colonial problem, gave the impression of being disdainful of parliamentary discussion. Van Zuylen too reacted violently, and persuaded the King to dissolve Parliament.

This was an extreme but not an unreasonable decision. Van Zuylen then made a serious blunder, however, which eventually ruined his party. The government argued that because the appointment of a Governor-General was made by the King, disapproval of the policy leading up to it must be regarded as a direct attack on the royal prerogative. As in 1853 the conservatives, supported by the King himself, attempted to use the monarchy for their own purposes. But neither constitutionally nor politically did the argument make sense, as a dozen professors of constitutional law immediately pointed out in a common declaration drafted by Buys. What was more important was the complete lack of interest shown by the general public. Despite some foolish pamphlets accusing the liberals of misinterpreting a still-born constitution, of transforming Parliament into a dissolute club, and of stifling the voice of the people,[1] and despite some heated articles in the newspapers, elections took place in the usual atmosphere of bored indifference. Although the anti-liberal groups won some seats, their victory amounted to a defeat, being much too small to justify the government's bombastic propaganda. Moreover, the difficulties were far from over. In 1867 William III, who like his wife and son admired Napoleon III, got involved in international controversies after declaring himself willing to sell his Grand Duchy of Luxemburg to France. Luxemburg

[1] R. W. J. C. Bake, *Oranje boven! is de leus van het bedreigde Nederland* (Arnhem, 1866).

together with Limburg had been a member of the German Federation since 1839 and its status had become unclear with the establishment of the North German Federation. It is well known how William III withdrew his consent to the sale as soon as the Germans protested. The London Conference set up to find a solution to the Luxemburg problem—made still more complicated by Belgium's desire to acquire the Grand Duchy— was attended by the Netherlands, which signed the protocol declaring it neutral. This agreement, unlike that guaranteeing the neutrality of Belgium in 1831, was given by all the signatories collectively and was thus much less dependable. From the Dutch point of view the outcome of the conflict was not unsatisfactory. William III had certainly manoeuvred dangerously, and there was no assurance that France's thirst would have been quenched by the acquisition of Luxemburg. Limburg too, though an integral part of the Dutch state, was closely involved in the whole matter and its status was equally ambiguous. Thus Van Zuylen's boast that his diplomacy saved the Netherlands from disaster was not altogether unjustified. It may well have been partly his ingenuity that saved the Netherlands from a crisis like that which ruined Schleswig-Holstein and from the danger of French imperialism.

Yet it was this diplomatic activity that gave rise to a new constitutional conflict. In November 1867 the Second Chamber expressed its disapproval of Van Zuylen's policy by voting down the foreign budget. They argued that the Netherlands, which had nothing to do with Luxemburg, should not have participated in the collective guarantee of its neutrality. Van Zuylen was accused of taking unnecessary risks and endangering Dutch independence. The argument may have been exaggerated, for the collective guarantee itself was almost meaningless; but it was not entirely beside the point and was certainly characteristic of Dutch anxiety to keep aloof from all international complications. Van Zuylen's rather ludicrous claim to have preserved the peace of Europe met with no response even from a nation that a few decades later was seeking inspiration from the messianic idea that history had entrusted to it the role of peacekeeper and promoter of international law. Once again the Cabinet showed itself violently angry at the criticisms expressed by Parliament. It offered to resign, but the King refused to accept the offer and dissolved the Chamber. The elections of January 1868 were presented, to an even greater extent than those of 1866, as a radical choice between royalism and republicanism. But once again the electorate and public opinion generally refused to be impressed by such a whimsical and unwarranted interpretation. Under the *ancien régime* Orange Stadtholder and regent patriciate had indeed provided the crucial antithesis, but that was long ago. The memory of 1813, when the pre-revolutionary parties became reconciled with each other and ashamed of their own past, and joined in praise of the monarchy as a glorious product of national history, was so tenacious that government propaganda raking over the old ashes and accusing the liberals of anti-monarchical tendencies was deeply distrusted. But although, as a result, the majority of the Second Chamber remained hostile to the government, the Cabinet did not resign. Inevitably, the Chamber repeated its action of November 1867 and voted down Van Zuylen's budget (April 1868). After long months of uncertainty William III finally allowed Van Zuylen to withdraw (June 1868). The conservative experiments with the constitution had failed. Indeed they had too obviously lacked any foundation in principle; they were, as all could see, no more than improvized attempts to save the skins of conceited ministers; and the people, roused in 1853 by a religious issue, showed no interest in the constitutional wrangle. Did the monarchy suffer from this defeat? Hardly at all, it seems. The fiction of 1813, that year of sentimental solidarity, assured the institution and sheltered the capricious King whose prestige in any case was not very great. Did the liberal victory mean that now at last a truly parliamentary form of government was established? The answer may be in the affirmative but it should be qualified. Dutch practice after 1868 often called for *cabinets d'affaires* not based on a clear majority in Parliament. And in fact it was hardly possible to build up such a majority when there were no real political parties or binding political programmes. The true importance of 1868 lies elsewhere. It showed that a compromise between conservatism and liberalism could no longer be envisaged; it also showed the purposelessness and lethargy of Dutch conservatism.

Although practical politics in the 1860s was largely determined by colonial and constitutional matters, new and deeper conflicts were developing under the surface. Disunity among the liberals had retarded their victory but after the victory their internal differences increased. The defeated conservatives made no attempt to act again as a 'party' but their defeat allowed the Protestant group to clarify its own, essentially conservative, doctrine and to enlarge the number of its adherents. The Roman Catholics, who for many years after 1848 had continued to associate with the doctrinaires, heeded the admonitions of the Pope and detached themselves from this alliance. As in Belgium it was the school question that most sharply divided the politicians and their followers; it was in discussing this problem that the positions of the political groups were more precisely determined. Of course the attitudes of the Belgian and the Dutch parties towards the issue were not the same, for they approached it from quite different premises. Whereas in Belgium the Education Act of 1842 had established the Catholic primary school, Dutch primary education had since 1806 been organized in such a way that, although positively Christian and broadly speaking Protestant, it was not in matters of dogma tied by any strict formula. The system had its merits. Its purpose was to provide enough instruction to make the 'people', still regarded as an amorphous, passive, but occasionally restive mass, aware of its precise duties in society. Moreover, popular education was a form of poor-relief. It was expected to supply the children with sufficient knowledge to prevent them from remaining or becoming paupers. Thus state education had fundamentally a conservative character. The public schools taught the children virtue, a sense of duty, willingness to submit to constituted authority, and to accept as God-given the consequences of the status into which they were born.[1]

Opposition to this system was primarily inspired by religious principles. The Protestant Réveil, a movement joined in the early nineteenth century by Bilderdijk, Da Costa, Groen van Prinsterer, and members of the aristocracy in Amsterdam and The Hague, was Romantic and orthodox as far as its aims were concerned, but in fact theologically vague, full of tears and fervent sentimentalism. The rationalism and moralism of

[1] Cf. e.g. Van Tijn, *Twintig jaren Amsterdam*, p. 298.

enlightened Protestantism were despised by these Romantics as barren and soulless. It is a paradox that men of this nature should have sought security in the hard dogmatism of seventeenth-century Calvinism, a paradox which can only be explained by the tensions disrupting the Restoration period and an extreme Romantic reaction to the moderation of the Dutch Enlightenment. This emotional dogmatism seems to have caused bewildering confusion in theology.[1] Yet historically it is an interesting and influential phenomenon. Groen van Prinstere in particular attempted to use his religion as the foundation for a political doctrine, and it soon became apparent that the school problem was to be the central factor in all his political activity. For in the 1830s the Dutch primary school came to be dominated by the unorthodox spirit of the so-called Groningen movement (Groninger Richting), a group of theology professors at the University of Groningen among whom P. Hofstede de Groot (1802-86) was the greatest fighter. These men also still lived in the atmosphere of Romanticism but it was no longer the Romanticism of the Restoration. They were not inspired by the tragic and the extreme, like Da Costa and Groen; theirs was a mild, lyrical belief, optimistic, extraverted, vague, conciliatory. They discovered a truly national Dutch Reformation, that of the Brethren of the Common Life and of Erasmus whose example they sought to follow, as opposed to that of foreigners like Luther and Calvin. Doctrinal differences did not matter much to them. They thought that they were bringing the Reformation to completion and hoped to see realized in the near future the sublime unity of the Church they were dreaming of, raised high above all religious division and linked together by common love of Jesus Christ. By indefatigable preaching and teaching they tried to achieve this ideal. They did not seek dramatic conversions in the Réveil manner; they wanted to teach men how to acquire that Christian humanism that was the goal towards which God wished to lead his ever-developing creation.[2]

Such ideals could serve very well as a justification for the primary schools on the 1806 pattern, which were Christian but

---

[1] K. H. Roessingh, *De moderne theologie in Nederland* (Groningen, 1914), pp. 44 ff.
[2] Ibid., pp. 26-44; J. Huizinga, *Geschiedenis der Universiteit gedurende de derde eeuw van haar bestaan. Verzamelde Werken*, viii. 139-63.

had to be acceptable to all sorts of Protestants and Roman Catholics. Thus it is not surprising that for some decades conservative school policy should have drawn on this body of thought.[1] The April movement of 1853 was also influenced by the Groningen theology, which created a common Protestant front, regardless of sectarian differences, against the limiting and exclusive dogmatism of the Catholic Church. Moreover, the promoters of the primary state school were impressed by the strong didactic element in the Groningen movement. During the 1850s, however, the power of Groningen was already on the decline; in the 1860s it collapsed, and its failure could be seen most clearly in the school legislation. Opposition came from various sides. Groen van Prinsterer rejected both the system of 1806 and the way in which it was interpreted by Groningen. He certainly wanted state education, but along denominational lines like the Prussian system: it should be possible for each creed—or at least for Protestant and Roman Catholic—to be instructed in the seclusion of its own school paid for by the state.[2] Thorbecke too, rejected the 1806 system, though for opposite reasons. Freedom was the main thing and he hoped that the state would gradually be able to withdraw from the field of education. Yet in 1848 he was compelled to make a concession to the conservatives: the clause ensuring that the state would continue to take care of popular education was added to his constitution by the conservatives. His first Cabinet (1849–53) was not able to draft the education bill that the constitution called for. Consequently, his successors and opponents, the moderates, took it up. However, they had no opinions of their own on the matter and the various tentative bills they drafted contained compromises so confused that they satisfied nobody. In 1856 William III tried a more strictly conservative policy, and indeed it proved possible in the following year to pass an Education Law acceptable both to the Second Chamber and to a large section of the Dutch population.

[1] Cf. e.g. Van der Does, *Bijdrage tot de geschiedenis . . . van de a.r. of c.h. staatspartij*, p. 232.

[2] Groen remained desperately vague in his definition of the ideal school. Cf. D. Langedijk, *Groen van Prinsterer en de schoolkwestie* (The Hague, 1947), *passim*.

This law was conservative in so far as it maintained some of the essential features of the 1806 system. Contrary to Groen van Prinsterer's wishes the mixed state school, the school attended by children of various religious denominations, was preserved as the normal institution. However, in accordance with the principles of Thorbecke, who was therefore in favour of the new law despite its conservative character, it was at the same time made somewhat easier to establish 'special' (*bijzondere*) or free schools, although these were not to be subsidized by the state. But the most important achievements of the new legislation were the raising of standards of teaching and teachers, the improvement of school buildings, and the assurance of adequate supervision by responsible authorities. This shows that Dutch ideas about the purpose of popular education were changing, for such expensive improvements could only mean that the children, equipped with greater knowledge, would rise above the social level of their parents. Whereas the system of 1806 fitted in with the at that time not unrealistic view of society as a largely unchanging structure in which each individual's place was fixed at his birth, the law of 1857 could serve to increase social mobility. The way in which the formula was reached, the effort that was made to do justice to all opinions expressed in the painful religious argument, indicated how far the Dutch had travelled since 1806. Then there had been nobody, not even among the Jews, who doubted that the schools should reflect the spirit of an enlightened but still positive and—to put it cautiously—not anti-dogmatic Christian belief. This was much less obvious in 1857. It is true that the primary school was still charged, as its main task, with impressing on the young 'the Christian and social virtues', but it was at the same time considered to be neutral in matters of religion rather than all-embracing. Although the new law was in many respects conceived according to the principles of the Groningen movement, it worked out in practice so differently from the system of 1806 that Hofstede de Groot was soon bitterly opposing it. In the schools of 1857 it seemed to him that his own brand of undogmatic but positive and biblical Christianity was allowed no chance to survive.[1] Thus the conservative

---

[1] D. Langedijk, *De schoolstrijd in de eerste jaren na de wet van 1857* (Amsterdam, 1937), pp. 4 ff.

law of 1857 eventually had an anti-conservative effect, although in regions inhabited by a religiously homogeneous population, such as the Catholic South or the Calvinist Veluwe, the primary school naturally tended to adopt, as it had done ever since 1806, the religious colour of its environment.

The law of 1857 did not terminate the conflict. On the contrary, only after 1857 did the various principles involved take definitive shape. In despair Groen and his followers abandoned their initial ideal of a state school system split according to denomination and concentrated on establishing free orthodox Protestant schools. This was a very slow process. In the early 1870s no more than about 200 of the 3,800 primary schools in the Netherlands—about 2,800 state and 1,000 free schools— were orthodox Protestant.[1] The situation in which the orthodox found themselves was difficult and paradoxical. The freedom which they now tried to take advantage of was to them no more than a *pis-aller*, accepted with desperate bitterness. Moreover, they were under the impression that they could only succeed in building their own schools if the traditional Protestant confidence in the state school was thoroughly undermined. This, of course, could only be achieved by insisting upon the strict religious neutrality of the state school, supposed to be abhorrent to truly Christian parents. As a result it was Groen and his followers who were most merciless in their attack on each positive assertion of Protestantism in the state school.[2] But at the same time they went further and questioned whether neutrality was in fact at all feasible. They were inclined to say that it was not. Neutrality and impartiality, they told their audience, in effect represent a choice; they are concordant with modernism. In this way their agitation developed into a fight against what they called the 'school of the modernist sect', although they did not prove that most teachers were in fact modernists.[3] Their indignation is not difficult to understand. Among the liberals, who increasingly determined the development of the educational system, there

[1] J. Waterink, 'Dr Kuyper en het onderwijs', *Dr. A. Kuyper Gedenkboek*, ed. L. W. G. Scholten (Kampen, 1937), pp. 171–3.

[2] Langedijk, *Schoolstrijd*, pp. 136 ff.

[3] R. W. Feikema, *De totstandkoming van de schoolwet van Kappeyne* (Amsterdam, 1929), pp. 14 ff.

was an undeniable tendency to adopt the conceptions of Protestant modernism.[1]

'Modern theology' originated in the 1840s in Leiden.[2] To a still greater extent than Réveil and Groninger Richting it was inspired by German examples. During the 1840s German philosophy, discarded earlier in the century with traditional Dutch condescension towards the eastern neighbours as 'extravagant nonsense concocted in unbalanced German brains',[3] was studied and discussed with great application. In the writings of Scholten, who soon became the leader of the modern movement, there are echoes of Hegel although he was never a true Hegelian. Opzoomer was deeply impressed by German authors, although also influenced by Burke and John Stuart Mill. His part in the movement was that of catalyst, his philosophical method enabling him to drive the theologians by a series of interminable questions into greater clarity and consistency. It is difficult consequently to determine to what extent the Dutch were original in their approach or in their conclusions. It is equally difficult, incidentally, to say to what extent this movement was 'modern' at all. Opzoomer in particular urged Protestant theology and Christianity to accept and absorb nineteenth-century civilization. But when it came to defining the problems which ought to be solved and suggesting the answers which could be derived from empirical philosophy, problems as well as answers turned out to be not fundamentally different from those discussed at length in the eighteenth century: the relation between revelation and reason, between Christian religion and rationalism, Bible and history, miracle and causality. The conclusions reached were certainly not startlingly new. In Scholten's impressive logical and intellectual system God becomes 'the idea of absolute causality', and the meaning of Christianity and history appears as the totally predetermined development of moral freedom. The optimism of Scholten and his liberal contemporaries was severe, almost authoritarian.

The originality of the modernists lies perhaps not so much

[1] A. Strang, *Eene historische verhandeling over de liberale politiek en het lager onderwijs van 1848 tot 1920* (Utrecht, 1930), pp. 30 ff.

[2] Cf. K. H. Roessingh, *Het modernisme in Nederland* (Haarlem, 1922).

[3] Quoted by Roessingh, *De moderne theologie*, p. 24.

in what they actually said as in the fact that they deliberately
set out to construct a Christian theology on the basis of modernity. They were soon confident that they had achieved their aim
and from about 1860 onwards the ministers produced by
Leiden University patiently explained in simple terms, in
lectures held outside the Church rather than in their sermons,
that it did not suit the modern Christian to believe in miracles,
the divine inspiration of the Bible, hell, original sin, or all the
other dualistic principles of ancient theology. By presenting
Christianity in a more highly developed form, adapted to the
world of the nineteenth century, they hoped to purify Christian
civilization. It was not their intention to make it possible for
people on the verge of becoming irreligious to stay within the
Church. That question did not arise, for the dechristianization
of society had not yet begun in the Netherlands. No precise
figures are available but probably the proportion of people
not belonging to any Church grew between 1859 and 1879
from 0·9 per cent to 0·33 per cent whereas it rose in 1899 to
2·5 per cent.[1] Thus modernism was not apologetic, not undertaken in self-defence against an unchristian world. It was an
attempt by means of a new theology to impress upon the morally
immature members of the Reformed Church the exalted
value of freedom.

The result was the exact opposite of what was intended.
Protestants from the upper and the more or less educated
middle classes who adopted modernism found themselves
aliens in the Reformed Church to which they still belonged
while ceasing to take much part in its activities. Initially the
Reformed Church showed considerable sympathy for modernism. The oligarchic upper-class elders and deacons on whom
the appointment of ministers really depended often nominated
modernists. But in 1867 the situation changed. It was decided
to deprive the oligarchy of its absolute power and to give
representatives of the lower bourgeoisie a say in the appointments. It then became apparent that the hard core of Church
members if not the majority were orthodox. Modernism failed
to bring about a religious reform within the Church itself.
But outside the Church it remained active. In the 1860s a
number of outstanding modernist ministers drew what seemed

[1] G. M. Bos, *Mr S. van Houten* (Purmerend, 1953), p. 165 n. 65.

to them the only logical conclusion from the new theology and resigned. Others who chose to stay within the Church waited in vain to be called to the ministry. Thus for the first time in Dutch history there emerged a small group of redundant intellectuals who were compelled to earn their living elsewhere, as publicists, school inspectors, and teachers. Some of them— above all Busken Huet and Allard Pierson (1831–96)—were among the best Dutch authors of the third quarter of the century. Modernism, which reflected, refined, and propagated the rationalist and optimistic elements in liberal civilization, became the sincere unbelief of a Christian élite.

Groen van Prinsterer and his party were, to put it mildly, hasty when they started accusing the state schools of being modernist and of forcing the young to adopt a modernist view of life. In the 1860s this was an over-simplification, with little to justify it except that liberal authors and statesmen were in favour of modernist theology. Yet it was undoubtedly true that liberal views on education were becoming increasingly radical, and that left-wing liberalism as a whole tended to take a latitudinarian or even hostile attitude towards religion, while adopting towards the masses, the object of popular education, a distinctly democratic point of view. Progressive liberalism in this period was an interesting phenomenon. As in Belgium it was anxious to work out something in the nature of a complete system with positive aims based on a coherent interpretation of reality. Such a system the doctrinaires did not possess. Thorbecke did not generalize in the manner of the progressives. He did not share the certainties the young liberals were so proud of. But doctrinaire liberalism, vague and unsystematic though its philosophical basis might be, acquired coherence because it managed to produce leaders—a Frère-Orban, a Thorbecke: neither in Belgium nor in the Netherlands was progressive liberalism able to produce comparable figures. As a political movement, therefore, it is quite different from doctrinaire liberalism or socialism, political Catholicism or Protestantism, all of which revolved round a central personality, a real leader, who claimed to express the convictions and the unconscious desires of the whole nation or of a large part of it. The progressive liberals did not pretend to represent semi-permanent interests or specific social classes; as a group they did not aspire towards perpetuity, they were indifferent towards their own future. Nor did they possess the will to rule. They did not originate from the families or the classes to whom governing was a traditional and natural activity. To them, moreover, politics could never be what it had been to their predecessors of 1830 or 1848: a means of creation, a form of self-expression. Very few became professional politicians; most remained outsiders, amateurs.

In the long run progressive liberalism was able to achieve more in the Netherlands than in Belgium. In the thirty years before 1914 Belgium was ruled by solidly Roman Catholic cabinets, whereas in the Netherlands progressive liberalism was in power from 1891 to 1901, and exercised some influence from 1905 to 1908 and from 1913 to 1918. Consequently, social legislation and the democratization of the state generally, which in both countries started in the 1880s and 1890s, bore the stamp of the liberal left wing in the Netherlands, of Catholicism in Belgium. It is noteworthy that the political history of both countries, which until 1878 ran broadly parallel, diverged after that date. As soon as the Catholic masses in Belgium were able to make themselves heard in the running of the state all forms of liberalism lost ground, and during the interminable years of liberal retreat many radicals moved towards socialism. After 1918 the liberals were once again called upon to join the government but by then the party had lost so much of its radicalism that it could be considered conservative. In the Netherlands both the eclipse and the return of liberalism took longer. This is not surprising for from the start the Dutch doctrinaires had rejected the Franco-Belgian habit of identifying the upper middle class with the nation, and so the class basis of their movement had been less manifest and less deliberate. They had also been able to show more caution in the matter of centralization. There was no equivalent in the Netherlands to Brussels, with its concentration of all political, social, and economic power. Amsterdam might be the official capital and to a certain extent serve as a cultural centre, but the government resided in The Hague, the biggest and most famous university was at Leiden, and Rotterdam was developing rapidly; the support for the doctrinaires came, to an important extent, from outside Amsterdam and even from outside

Holland. Because of these factors both doctrinaire liberalism and the progressive reaction against it were more moderate; the liberal left wing was less extreme in its views than its Belgian counterpart and probably in less danger of seeing its followers turn to socialism. The position of the religious parties, moreover, was much more difficult than in Belgium; they had no hope of obtaining power except by a coalition of Catholics and Protestants, and the great period of 'clerical' cabinets began only in 1918. Whereas the essentially conservative Belgian liberals took part in nearly all governments between 1917 and 1946, Dutch liberalism retained for a long time the character of an intellectual and progressive club that it had acquired in the late nineteenth century. At elections it was unable to compete with the efficiently organized mass parties of the twentieth century and was thus incapable of exercising a direct influence on the government.

In the third quarter of the nineteenth century Dutch left-wing liberalism was more austere and less emotional than the Belgian version. In Belgium it retained some of the intensity of the French humanitarian idealism that had found fervent adherents in the Southern and no support at all in the Northern Netherlands during the 1830s and 1840s. It would be difficult to think of anybody in the history of international progressive liberalism more hard-headed than S. van Houten (1837-1930), who was nominated to the Second Chamber in 1869 and was the first to express in his speeches and numerous publications a new, anti-Thorbeckian liberalism. This stubborn individualist nursed the illusion of being the only man in this capricious world able to preserve with perfect consistency a perfectly logical point of view, and he nursed it with such naïve conceit that it is impossible to regard him as representative of a group. But during the first period of his political activity in particular he undoubtedly managed to give expression to deeply felt desires among the progressives generally, and even succeeded in reconciling to some extent the contradictions inherent in utilitarian liberalism. His threefold criticism of doctrinaire liberalism may be unjust in many ways but it provides a very appropriate starting-point for his positive contribution. He began by refusing to accept that the economic laws which the liberal school had studied so carefully could ever actually

work in a society dominated by tradition, history, and prejudice. Although it may be meaningful academically to study
the economy *in vacuo*, the practical statesman must meet the
demands of reality rather than theory. Thus it is wrong to
dismiss, on principle, the possibility of state intervention in economic and social life.[1] Secondly, Van Houten attacked the pretension that Thorbecke's state was founded on the sovereignty
of impartial law or reason. He had learned from Schopenhauer that logic begins in self-interest and so it seemed to him
that the sovereignty of reason meant logically the sovereignty
of the educated middle class. Consequently, notwithstanding
the doctrinaire principles of non-interference the state regularly acted on behalf of a few vested middle-class interests.[2]
Thirdly, Van Houten rejected what he regarded as the absolutism and centralism of the liberal state, pleading for the
autonomy of the constituent parts in the name of popular sovereignty.[3]

At the same time he campaigned with equal vigour and even
deeper hostility against the wanton and frivolous irresponsi-
bility of the socialists who would use brute force to wreck the
delicate fabric of organic society,[4] and who by revolutionary
means would replace the disastrous hegemony of the enfranchised middle class by the certainly no less catastrophic
supremacy of the workers. There should be no question of
hegemony in a well-ordered society. The art of statesmanship
was not to allow supremacy to a single class but to determine
a perfect equilibrium of all social classes and interests. And
yet there can be little doubt that it was the social question
that prompted Van Houten to enter politics. Owing to his
courageous initiative the first Dutch law restricting child
labour was passed in 1874 (two years after the death of Thorbecke); although too limited to have much practical impact,
it showed that a liberal legislator could also initiate social
measures without being inconsistent. Other points on his

---

[1] Bos, *Van Houten*, pp. 22, 49 ff.

[2] S. van Houten, 'Over den invloed der wetgeving op de verdeeling van den
rijkdom', *Bijdragen tot den strijd over God, eigendom en familie* (Haarlem, 1878).

[3] Idem, *Liberale politiek op historischen grondslag* (Groningen, 1873) and *De
staatsleer van Mr J. R. Thorbecke* (Haarlem, 1872).

[4] Idem, 'Paus Leo XIII over het arbeidersvraagstuk' (1891), *Staats- en strafrechtelijke opstellen* (The Hague, 1897), p. 221.

programme were the repeal of the law forbidding workers to
form associations for the purpose of joint action against employers (this actually went through in 1872, six years later than
in Belgium), the revision of the electoral law and the fiscal
system, reduction of the army and the defence budget, birth
control, emancipation of women, new and freer legislation
relating to marriage and divorce—in short all the issues young
liberals had begun to take seriously in the 1860s and 1870s.
But Van Houten always emphatically denied that he was
moved by pity or sentiment. He refused to recognize any other
motives for his ceaseless activity than the promptings of a
strictly scientific logic and a perfectly sober concern for the
health of society. Useful results could be achieved in no other
way. On looking back he avowed with some shame that in the
1860s and 1870s he had too radically taken the side of the workers against the employers.[1]

In some respects Van Houten went beyond his friends—
he was an agnostic among liberal Protestants and a theoretical
republican among opportunist monarchists. In other respects he
remained more cautious and sensible, as can be seen from his
handling of the education problem. He was not slow to realize
that ultimately the task of progressive liberalism in this field
was to achieve a compromise; whatever logic or reforming
zeal might demand, the real need was for a reconciliation of
classes and opinions, for a new if provisional balance in an
ever-changing society. This Van Houten recognized more
clearly than those who after the death of Thorbecke in 1872
acquired most influence in the liberal party. The spokesman
of these 'young' liberals was J. Kappeyne van de Coppello
(1822–95), a famous barrister in The Hague, a highly learned
historian of law, a witty debater who gave the impression of
not taking politics very seriously. And indeed he lacked
political ambition and had little that was new to contribute.
In 1874 he delivered a speech in the Second Chamber[2] which
is our only source for the fundamental political conceptions
of a liberal leader who was a very competent and fertile author
of treatises on the history of Roman law. The object of
Thorbecke's liberalism, the constitutional state, having been

[1] Van Houten, 'Paus Leo XIII', pp. 227 ff.
[2] Van Welderen Rengers, op. cit., pp. 508 ff.

achieved, Kappeyne said, it was up to his successors to learn how to use this state in order to introduce new reforms in accordance with 'the modern view of life': a greater appreciation of the essential function of civil servants, reform of the courts of law, improvement of public health, and all the other matters with which the new state was now obliged to concern itself. Such work, however, presupposes a civilized and enlightened nation, and for that reason the educational problem was the most important of all. This speech made a deep impression on a Parliament more accustomed to discussing technicalities. Yet it was too vague to serve as a real party programme and it ended in a peculiarly sceptical peroration. For, Kappeyne concluded, we are living in bad times. Our predecessors completed the noble task of constructing a state; our successors will reform society. The only thing left for us is to fight with words and, by our impassioned polemics, to deliver the *coup de grâce* to clericalism which in its death-throes is wildly thrashing about.

Thus in order to enable the logic of historical development to work properly, the present generation, in no position to create something of its own, had the limited task of preparing for the future, that is of improving primary education and raising the mass of the population to the intellectual level at which the correctness of liberal concepts becomes self-evident. As soon as Kappeyne formed a Cabinet, in 1877, he applied himself to this work. In 1878 his Education Bill was accepted by both chambers. It did not satisfy all radical demands. Kappeyne thought that for practical reasons compulsory education could not yet be introduced nor did he consider it feasible to deprive the municipalities of all responsibility for local schools. His law, consequently, was not intended to be definitive; it was regarded as the first step on the road towards a school system that was to be universal, paid for and carefully inspected by the state. However, it was admittedly a very energetic step. By considerably raising the standard of the teachers' own training, by increasing their salaries, and by improving the quality of school buildings, Kappeyne made primary education so expensive that the state had to come to the assistance of the municipalities, which up to that time had been financially responsible, and to pay about one-third of the total cost. This meant centralization. At the same time the new conditions made the building or expansion of free Catholic and Protestant education, to which the liberals categorically refused to grant state subsidies, virtually impossible. This, of course, was intended. Moreover, the religious neutrality of the state school, which was supposed to have been established by the law of 1857 but which in fact had been by no means universally observed, could now be strictly enforced thanks to the increase in state authority and in spite of municipal resistance. It is true that Groen and his adherents had been asking for this for twenty years; yet because the free schools were at the same time threatened with extinction the result was (and obviously Groen had never wished this to happen) the total de-Christianization of all elementary education.

The 1878 law remained in force until 1889. Like its Belgian equivalent of 1879, which was repealed in 1884, it was not a success although after it was revised the state retained much more influence over education in the Netherlands than it did in Belgium. The failure of the liberals' educational policy was due to liberal disunity, weakness, and lack of courage as well as to the growth of the opposition, which began to realize and to prove that the constitutional state, although conceived by the liberals, did not exclusively belong to them. However, it was some time before the Calvinists learned to make effective use of the state. During the 1870s many among them were inclined, in truly ultramontane fashion, to regard the modern state and its entire constitutional apparatus as the devil's own work. Groen van Prinsterer did not go as far as this. Even in 1857 he had not altogether abandoned the hope that eventually a situation might arise in which it would become possible to interpret the state of 1848 in Christian terms. But Groen was growing old. When in the late 1860s a young minister, Dr. Abraham Kuyper (1837-1920), began to speak for political Calvinism, a totally different tone was heard. Kuyper, whose father was also a minister, came from a rather poor family. He studied at Leiden, the centre of modernist theology, but in his late twenties was converted to dogmatic Calvinism. His new radical beliefs changed him—according to his early portraits he was a mild, romantic young man—into a great fighter with rigid principles, a dictatorial ruler in his own tiny empire who even outside it wore the king's mantle and used a strangely pompous but imaginatively ornamental style of writing and speech. Nervous, capricious, once at least the victim of a serious breakdown, he became legendary in his role of leader and lived his life according to a consciously chosen image. Indeed he built everything with his own hands: his personality and his style, his Church, his university, and his political party, his theology, and his political philosophy.

His starting-point, however, was fairly traditional. Groen van Prinsterer had often enough taken the opportunity of pointing out, on the basis of Restoration philosophy, the unbridgeable gap between Christian truth and modern life. In Belgium the ultramontanes had pushed this antithesis to its extreme. Kuyper too started as a foe of the constitutional state of the liberals and of the society created, according to this theory, by the French Revolution. The difference between Groen and the ultramontanes on the one hand and Kuyper on the other was that whilst the theories of Kuyper's predecessors had been in political terms entirely negative, Kuyper himself was able to forge from them something positive and creative. In society, in the state, and even in the unorthodox Dutch Reformed Church he built up his own associations, his own organized political party, his own Church, and his own scientific institutions. In this way the 'antithesis' became much more than just a warning to the faithful not to allow themselves to be tarnished by sinful modernism; it was in Kuyper's mind the basis for a fundamentally different ambition. A new political and social doctrine, a new kind of scholarship and of science, a new state, followed from it. These were not intended —and this is another element of Kuyper's originality—either to serve as a substitute for liberal views, or as an imperious truth thrown into the fight against the intolerable misconceptions of the faithless. They were alternatives, competitors, independent, self-sufficient Christian realities. It was not his aim to reform or dominate modern civilization but to break it.[1]

---

[1] His writings are enumerated in J. C. Rullmann, *Kuyper-bibliografie* (3 vols., The Hague, 1923–40). Kuyper summarized his doctrine in his *Ons program* (Hilversum, 1879) and in his *Antirevolutionaire staatkunde* (2 vols., Kampen, 1916–17).

This was a manifestly conservative view. Allowing for the vigorous sense of national unity of the Dutch people—compared with the other political leaders of his time Kuyper was quite a strong nationalist—he wanted to see the emergence of a highly variegated society. He fought against 'uniformity, that curse of modern life'; where he found grey monotony, he wanted movement, contrasts, colour.[1] His slogan became 'sovereignty in one's own sphere' ('souvereiniteit in eigen kring'), for God, he thought, had granted to His creatures, both singly and collectively, their own inviolable principle of life. This was as true of institutions, whether a trade union, a political party, a Church, a university, as it was of the individual. So the 'antithesis', which originally called for a deadly fight against modernism, imperceptibly grew into this curious doctrine in praise of plurality and diversity. All this was far from being strictly logical. On the contrary, with remarkable energy and cheerfulness Kuyper entangled himself in brilliantly formulated contradictions. But the theory met with success and it was instrumental in giving Dutch society an unusually heterogeneous character. The origin of what in later years was disparagingly called *verzuiling*,[2] that is the system of institutionalized segmentation according to which each religious or quasi-religious group, Protestant, Catholic, or humanist, was encouraged and subsidized by the state to create its own social world, comprising the entire existence of an individual from nursery school via sporting club, trade union, university, hospital, broadcasting and television corporation, to the burial society, can be found in Kuyper's love of diversity.

Thus there grew in the 1870s a neo-Calvinist conservatism which became considerably more powerful than the less orthodox and socially more refined conservatism that had collapsed in the previous decade. It was fuller and more mature than its predecessor, one of its advantages being that, like ultramontanism, it developed some insight into the social problems of the time. Kuyper leaned to a much greater extent

[1] Cf. E. Kossmann, 'De groei van de anti-revolutionaire partij', *Algemene geschiedenis der Nederlanden*, xi (1956), 5 ff.

[2] *Zuil* means pillar. The *zuilen* are the pillars of Dutch society, Protestantism, Catholicism, etc. With a witty neologism the process by which the whole of Dutch social life was divided up into autonomous religious spheres of interest was called 'pillarization'.

than Groen van Prinsterer and his circle of aristocrats on the Calvinist lower middle class and in some orthodox areas on the peasantry. He felt no affinity, either social or intellectual, for the liberals, with their careless philosophy of non-interference, their upper-middle-class following and their so-called pluto-cratic policies. Occasionally his resentment became danger-ously acrimonious, even anti-Semitic, but neither in his work nor among his group did this anti-Semitism become really significant. His brand of anti-liberalism made it possible for him to adopt a relatively progressive attitude, one to which he remained loyal throughout his career despite the resistance and distrust that surrounded him. Under his leadership the extension of the suffrage, social legislation, a form of corporat-ism, and Christian trade unions became topics of discussion in the anti-revolutionary party. Of course, very little in all this was strictly new, nor were the solutions proposed by Kuyper strikingly original. Yet his version of Christian democracy was more than a hurriedly formulated answer to socialism. Although the social problem could never be of primary im-portance to him, both the social position of his party and the conservative character of his doctrine made him accessible to anti-doctrinaire views on society and social abuses. In this spirit he drafted, after Groen's death in 1876, a new party programme which he finished by the beginning of 1878. It called, among many other things, for decentralization, re-vision of the electoral and educational laws, abolition of the possibility of evading military service by paying for a sub-stitute, and legislation for the protection of the lower classes. This is the first party programme in Dutch history. The anti-revolutionary party became more than a parliamentary party; it was a genuine political party drawing its strength from the masterly organization of all Kuyper's sympathizers whether they had the vote or not.

In this way the right-wing opposition to liberalism acquired a modern form in the very year when the radicals presented their controversial school bill. It was the educational issue that finally allowed the Right to triumph. But for this they needed the help of the Roman Catholics, who had during the 1860s—and especially after the *Syllabus Errorum* (1864)—been abandoning their old liberal partners of 1848. The estrangement was confirmed and symbolized by the withdrawal of the Dutch diplomatic mission to the Vatican in 1871 on the initiative of the Second Chamber—a measure that Thorbecke's Cabinet did not try to prevent. The Catholics were still nervously seeking new political ideas, and it took a long time to find them. During the first few years after the establishment of the episcopal hierarchy most of their energy went into the cultivation of their own garden (which had been badly neglected) and the building of schools—the latter particularly after the Dutch bishops followed the lead of Rome and in 1868 declared state education absolutely unacceptable, a view which few Dutch Catholics would hitherto have been inclined to adopt. On the whole the atmosphere of the Catholic emancipation, occurring at a time when in proportion to the total population the Catholics were in decline, was not very cheerful. As for the Dutch orthodox Protestants this was politically as well as culturally a period of *malaise*. There were, of course, some celebrated Roman Catholic emancipators. J. A. Alberdingk Thijm (1820–89) was a prolific, courageous, and erudite man of letters (earning his living from his business in foodstuffs and later as a publisher and the owner of a bookshop), who wrote not only poetry and short stories but about many aspects of literary and cultural history. There was the country doctor W. J. F. Nuyens (1823–94), whose rewriting of the Revolt of the Netherlands in Catholic terms (in his *Geschiedenis der Nederlandsche beroerten in de XVIe eeuw*, 1865–70) was at least interesting. But it cannot be said that either of them made lasting contributions to Dutch civilization as a whole. Apart from their boundless devotion to their cause and the impressive bulk of their production, what is most striking about them is the narrowness of their apologetics, the parochialism of their views, and the strict limits they imposed upon themselves. They hoped to raise the cultural standard of Catholics in the Netherlands and to inspire in them some pride for former Catholic achievements. They were not narrow-minded men themselves; their intense interest in what their Flemish brethren were doing proves the contrary. But notwithstanding their display of self-confidence, their polemical aggressiveness, and their erudition they remained confined in the small, unadventurous circle of a cultural minority. Only after 1878 did the Catholic community begin to recognize a new sort of leader in Herman Schaepman. And it was only after Kuyper had drafted a political programme for his Calvinists that Schaepman designed one for the Catholics. Only then did the Catholics become a political power, and only after Protestant democracy had discovered the social problem did Catholics come to recognize its relative importance.

By then, however, it had become virtually impossible not to recognize it. The social movement of this period drew its strength from left-wing liberalism and was not, at this stage, in the strict sense of the word proletarian; it was dominated by lower-middle-class elements. The whole conception of a class struggle did not yet apply to Dutch society, in which there were rich and poor people but no sizeable class of industrial entrepreneurs. Most employers were, after all, small men whose economic circumstances were not particularly favourable. Until 1878, therefore, the whole movement remained extremely weak. It might have been possible in the Netherlands to foresee the growth of socialism, partly because it looked as if the objective conditions for it were gradually forming and because there was no reason to suppose that what was happening abroad would not also happen in the Netherlands. But for the time being nothing was organized and no course of action was clearly perceived.

After 1865 a number of trade unions began to appear, first of the typographers and the diamond cutters and then of other artisans, which in 1871 united in the federation called the General Dutch Workmen's Association (Algemeen Nederlandsch Werklieden Verbond: ANWV). It was radical, anti-socialist, and very reluctant to start a fight. Its aim, defined according to pure liberal principles, was to improve the workers morally, materially, and politically, by the reduction of working time to ten hours a day, and by better education. Very few thought in terms of independent action or organized strikes. The only instance of mass agitation occurred in 1874 when it was claimed that 86 trade unions representing 12,000 workers campaigned on behalf of the Child Labour Bill proposed by Van Houten—and this was on the initiative of progressive liberals.[1] The first real labour movement of any

---

[1] D. Hudig, jun., *De vakbeweging in Nederland 1866–1878* (Amsterdam, 1904), p. 178.

size—in 1876 the ANWV totalled about 5,500 members—began in Amsterdam, a city without much big industry, and it was in reaction against the International (some far from extremist groups of which had been established in parts of the country since 1869) as well as against the Commune which was thought to have been engendered by the International. A movement of this kind could not hope to survive for long. By 1887 membership had dropped to 2,730.[1] In 1878 the social problem was approached in a different and much more polemical way by a new group, the Social-Democrat Association (Sociaal-Democratische Vereeniging). Yet even the activities of the ANWV were considered too revolutionary by the Calvinist workers who in 1877 started an organization of their own called Patrimonium, which employers were also invited to join. Such was their distrust of social legislation, that is of interference by the state (and this is reminiscent of the ultramontanes), that they regarded even Van Houten's bill as an intolerable infringement of human freedom.

In the same period the free-thought movement, bordering on radicalism, was slowly acquiring coherence. During the 1850s a periodical and an association, both called The Dawn (De Dageraad), were founded with the major objective of asserting the supremacy of natural science over religious truth. The movement was lower middle class and tended to be amateurish and pedantic in its arguments; it was not yet ready to relate intellectual to social emancipation—unlike the Belgian free-thinkers who were socialists. Indeed, during the first years of their activities it was socially rather conservative.[2] But gradually the main interest shifted from science to moral and ethical questions. The men from De Dageraad came to lead the small and moderate Dutch sections of the International. At the same time more educated free-thinkers from socially higher classes who would not have dreamed of associating themselves with De Dageraad abandoned the realm of abstract speculation and turned to practical social problems. Thus in the 1870s atheism and radical liberalism came to be linked together by people

---

[1] A. J. C. Rüter, *De spoorwegstakingen van 1903. Een spiegel der arbeidersbeweging in Nederland* (Leiden, 1935), pp. 9-10.

[2] O. Noordenbos, *Het atheïsme in Nederland in de negentiende eeuw* (Rotterdam, 1931), p. 35.

like Van Houten. But only in the 1880s did atheism detach itself from the social and political tradition and identify itself, in the eyes of many, with social revolution.[1]

The forceful influence of free thought was not due to organization but to the talent of a few men of letters and thinkers. Multatuli, who started as the champion of the Javanese and went on to become an emancipator and leader in many spheres, shaped in fine prose his shapeless emotional atheism and by his idealism moved not only some professional intellectuals but a much larger group of primary school teachers, journalists, and through them the élite of the workers.[2] Busken Huet, the apostate modernist minister, the apostate liberal, the brilliant *homme de lettres*, was the author of *Het Land van Rembrandt* (1882–4), which is still valued as a badly constructed but splendid specimen of cultural history. His dissatisfaction with the present made him a conservative to taunt his compatriots with complacency, backwardness, and a disastrous indifference towards the misery of the lower classes; and he became an admirer of French-speaking Belgium out of spite. He may not have been a true atheist himself but he expertly undermined the religious beliefs of his readers. Multatuli and Busken Huet—less-distinguished writers than Nietzsche and Sainte-Beuve, with whom they may be compared, but within the limits of their national culture men of lasting importance—loyally fulfilled the mission of the great malcontents, and brought about an intellectual revolution outside and above professional theology, philosophy, and politics.

[1] Ibid., p. 76.
[2] F. M. Wibaut, *Levensbouw* (Amsterdam, 1936), p. 117.

VI

TOWARDS DEMOCRACY, 1879–1896

1. *Social Tension and the Franchise*

IN the history of the Netherlands the 1820s formed a turning-point more dramatic and more definitive than in most of the other European nations, for they led to the establishment of Belgium as an independent state. During the 1840s a new liberal form of government was introduced in Holland and it proved more lasting than the results of the revolutionary movements in the rest of the Continent. In the 1860s both the North and the South enjoyed an intellectual emancipation which characterizes the period as one of decisive importance. The paradox of the 1880s was that, whereas contemporaries were more than ever before under the impression that they were living in the most exciting decade of the century with great decisions imminent, in reality nothing very striking happened. Despite all the noise of these years, the serious incidents and unrest, the tensions which seemed to heighten to the point of revolution, and the passionate propaganda of liberal and social reformers, the decade actually showed merely the hesitant and troubled beginnings of what was, in fact, the slow and gradual process of democratization. The men of the 1880s were mistaken. Their view of the near future was wrong. The tragic crisis they were anticipating was as unreal as their conviction that they were able to reform the world. They overestimated both themselves and their era.

None the less the decade is of supreme importance. Although much less fundamental than the leading intellectuals had expected, there was political as well as cultural innovation. Moreover, the quality of life improved. This was shown most clearly in the arts and in literature. Modernist movements, new periodicals, young creative artists and men of letters raised the level of Belgian and Dutch civilization to a point not reached for a long time. It is remarkable that this happened in both countries at about the same time. The process may be defined in a slightly different way by stating that during the 1880s both Dutch and Belgian civilization had become sufficiently vigorous to be able to absorb the foreign examples by which they were inspired, instead of slowly imitating and cautiously adapting them as they had done before. As a result the quality of the work produced in both countries improved whilst it became more difficult to appreciate it as a national variation on a European theme rather than as an element of European culture in general. In other words, the better the Belgians and the Dutch learned to write in the style and on the level of their foreign models the more they abandoned the characteristics of their own traditions.

This is a wholly natural phenomenon, and much the same thing happened in other fields of social life. Socialism, for instance, took peculiar forms in both countries; it was, however, less original in spirit and achievement than the national variations of doctrinaire liberalism had come to be. The originality of Dutch socialism owed much to the eccentricity of one person—Domela Nieuwenhuis; that of Belgian socialism to the sobriety of its first, intellectually unadventurous leaders. In neither country did socialism acquire a new content. This presents the historian with a problem: the object of his study is less easily definable than in the preceding period and he cannot always escape the uneasy feeling that he is studying an arbitrarily isolated aspect of general European history. At the same time, however, he finds in the Netherlands as well as in Belgium a stronger sense of national unity and pride than hitherto and this is undoubtedly connected with the improved quality of their national achievements. So many conflicting factors determine the character of this period—cosmopolitanism and nationalism, strong influences from abroad as well as national messianism, modernism, or the participation in international fashions as well as the quest for the nation's soul and essence—that it can only be described with caution.

Perhaps Edmond Picard (1836–1924) embodied these ambiguities as clearly as anyone. His father, born in Paris, came from a Walloon family of farmers, his mother was of Dutch origin. He himself grew up in Brussels where his father was a barrister. In 1854 he escaped from this environment and went to sea as a sailor. But he soon returned, studied law at the Free University, and in the 1860s opened his own office. He was a most successful advocate and became a rich man and a celebrity. His activities were manifold and so varied that it is not at all easy to understand him. For many years he played innumerable roles in the social life of Brussels, always easily, generously, and with obvious enjoyment. He was a socialist, poet, novelist, dramatist, journalist, art critic, editor of interesting periodicals, author of long and important monographs, an indefatigable and perceptive initiator. Members of the French and Belgian *avant-garde*, poets, philosophers, painters, and sculptors, from Maeterlinck to Rodin, assembled in his magnificent and hospitable house and were sure of his help—a help which was vital to many artistic careers.[1] He supported all emancipatory movements, adopted all innovations. In the 1860s he was a radical liberal, in the 1880s he fought for universal franchise, in 1886 he became a member of the newly founded Workers' party. His conception of social art as opposed to the idea of art for art's sake prevalent in the 1880s and his sympathy with the Symbolist movement meant that he was still among the *avant-garde* in the 1890s. So did his personal connections. In his office young law graduates and *hommes de lettres*—among them Georges Rodenbach and Émile Verhaeren—were trained to become advocates but found it more rewarding to earn Picard's generous friendship. Yet although highly successful in so many spheres Picard failed in his ambition to play an important part in politics. Nor did he become, as he had certainly wished, a professor at the Free University. Being just outside the centre of real power and free of official responsibilities he could afford to enjoy his nonconformity: he remained an unrepentant freebooter loyal to his motto, 'Je gêne'.[2]

Although Picard did not represent anything very positive, his work was symptomatic of Belgium's uncertainties. As a well-informed member of all *avant-garde* movements, a sensitive follower of the latest international fashions, he sought to create in Belgium a nationalistic modernism which would exercise

---

[1] C. Lemonnier, *La Vie belge* (Paris, 1905), pp. 171 ff., 222 ff.

[2] F. Vermeulen, *Edmond Picard et le réveil des lettres belges, 1881–1888* (Brussels, 1935), pp. 85 ff.

some sort of lasting influence. It was a highly literary sort of nationalism he propounded, theoretical as well as rhetorical. In 1897 he published in the French *Revue encyclopédique* a four-page article that became famous. In it he described nothing less than 'l'âme belge',[1] the soul that had for so long been despised, ridiculed, or ignored. Picard believed in it, saw it as something that had developed over two thousand years of history. The Belgian soul was the daughter of the Germanic and the Latin souls, the two great members of the Aryan race. The fact that Belgium was bilingual now seemed to him to be something to be grateful for. As a French-speaking barrister deeply interested in the problem of nationality he had not always thought so: during the 1860s he had sometimes feared that to be truly himself a Belgian man of letters should write exclusively in Dutch.[2] But in 1897 the linguistic question no longer mattered so much, for he had discovered that language was of minor importance compared with race. Indeed modernism led Picard and his collaborators into racist doctrines which they presented to their readers as the latest truths of science. This shows how disastrously undiscriminating their eclecticism could be. Picard's anti-Semitic monographs[3] in the manner of Drumont, or statements by the writer Georges Rodenbach or the jurist Léon Hennebicq,[4] spring from a lack of insight which is symptomatic of the period—although anti-Semitism was certainly not symptomatic of Belgian society. Possibly Picard's political career was hampered by his anti-Semitism,[5] and the many who then and later believed in the existence of

---

[1] *Revue encyclopédique* (24 July 1897), 595–9.

[2] Vermeulen, op. cit., pp. 72–3.

[3] E. Picard, *Synthèse de l'Antisémitisme* (Brussels, Paris, 1892); idem, *L'Aryano-Sémitisme* (Brussels, 1899).

[4] F. Bournand (ed.), *Les Juifs et nos contemporains*, Introduction by Edmond Picard (Paris, 1898), pp. 27 ff. (Rodenbach's admiration for Drumont), pp. 273 ff. (Hennebicq (1851–1940) who was a brilliant barrister, the best collaborator, and in many respects the successor of Picard as a restless, almost revolutionary initiator and nationalist, though also a friend of King Albert. For his passionate and anti-democratic nationalist propaganda in the years just before 1914 see E. Defoort, 'Het Belgische nationalisme voor de eerste wereldoorlog', *Tijdschrift voor Geschiedenis*, lxxxv (1972), 524–42).

[5] According to L. Delange-Janson, *Paul Janson, 1840–1913* (2 vols., 1962), i. 271, Picard's political career was damaged by his anti-Semitism after 1882. However, no anti-Semitic writings by Picard dating from that period have come to my knowledge.

a Belgian soul—among them Henri Pirenne—cautiously eliminated the racist framework that Picard had constructed. Even
so the ambiguous influence of Picard, a fervent nationalist
infected by all European fashions, indicates the weakness
inherent in a national civilization that can only reach the
heights with the help of foreign inspiration.

The crisis of the 1880s may have been more superficial
than was thought by contemporaries but there was undeniably
good reason for them to suppose that something decisive and
dramatic was going to happen. Albert Verwey, the Dutch
man of letters, wrote in 1886: 'This is a time of passion rather
than of reflection. People have things to say that brook of no
delay and their movements are the movements of people proceeding to sudden action.'[1] In both countries, stigmatized by
radical Dutch critics as the two most backward states of Europe,[2]
big demonstrations of workers caused consternation and unrest. Social disturbances of hitherto unknown proportions
broke out in Belgium. In the Netherlands socialists preached
revolution with such passion that they amazed and frightened
even people who refused to listen to them. Although the government had little trouble in maintaining order, even the enemies
of revolution and democracy were forced to agree that the
system of 1848 with its limited franchise and its aversion to
social legislation needed to be reformed. In fact they succeeded
in rescuing the political system by means of relatively simple
changes. The revision of the Dutch constitution in 1887 and the
Electoral Act of 1896, together with the revision of the Belgian
constitution in 1893, apparently made sufficient concessions to
the radicals. This by no means solved the problems, but it
made it clear that no revolution was to be expected in states
flexible enough to allow for gradual reform.

The tension of the 1880s can be explained partly by political
but more especially by economic causes. The withdrawal of
Kappeyne van de Coppello's liberal Cabinet in 1879, and the
fall of Frère-Orban's paralysed Cabinet in 1884 seemed to

[1] Albert Verwey, 'Toen de Gids werd opgericht . . .', De Nieuwe Gids, i (1886),
ii. 190.
[2] M. C. L. Lotsy 'Laissez-aller', in De Nieuwe Gids, II. ii (1887), 257, and P. L.
Tak, 'Nederlandsche Politiek', ibid. III. i (1888), 477.

indicate the end of a coherent epoch. Liberalism, which by its
school laws of 1878 and 1879 had tried to imbue the democratization of society with a vigorous liberal spirit, had failed and
was threatened with ruin as a direct result of that failure. In
both countries right-wing cabinets followed, whose primary
aim was to abolish the liberal school legislation. So the decade
started with what seemed like a decisive turn: the end of
liberal supremacy and the possibility of a clerical and conservative counter-movement. This situation, highly threatening as far as the progressives were concerned, occurred at a
time of economic crisis. Holland was still not sufficiently
developed economically to be directly affected by the international depression from 1873 to 1895,[1] but even so it was
hampered for several years by an economic stagnation that
was very difficult to overcome. The period from 1882 to 1886,
the lowest point in the international depression, was particularly unpleasant.[2] It was characteristic of the Dutch economic
system that the *malaise* made itself felt initially only in agriculture, as a result of the fall in corn prices caused by the massive
imports of American grain. At the same time work was becoming more easily available, for there was some slight industrial
expansion in the towns after 1880, and roads and houses were
being built. Hence the migration from the severely hit agrarian
areas to the towns, inconspicuous before 1880 but now suddenly
assuming dramatic proportions. Soon, however, various factors—some of them external, such as foreign protectionism—
put an end to the small economic boom in the towns and the
number of unemployed grew alarmingly. Both the authorities
and the workers' associations were powerless. Various forms of
relief regulations and unemployment relief work were tried
out which though interesting—for such attempts had never
been made before on such a scale—nevertheless failed. Public
opinion was greatly concerned by the misery of the poor. In
1885 particularly, tension rose to such heights that many
doubted whether even armed force could still keep the situation under control.[3]

[1] Brugmans, *Paardenkracht en mensenmacht*, p. 430.
[2] A. J. C. Rüter, 'Hoofdtrekken der Nederlandse arbeidersbeweging in de jaren
1876 tot 1886' (1938) reprinted in his *Historische studies over mens en samenleving*
(Assen, 1967), pp. 108 ff.
[3] W. H. Vliegen, *De dageraad der volksbevrijding* (2 vols., Amsterdam, 1905), i. 112 ff.

In actual fact much less happened in the Netherlands than in Belgium. In July 1886 the badly paid, ill-disciplined Amsterdam police tried to prevent people in the Jordaan, the popular district of the city, from playing their cruel and stupid game called 'palingtrekken', a game in which eels were pulled apart. The result was the Eel Revolt (*Palingoproer*), which had no political purpose but showed the extent of popular hatred for a police force that for years had been busily chasing socialists and putting down demonstrations. Twenty-six people were killed, about one hundred wounded; several hundred were taken to prison. It tells us something about the Second Chamber that the matter was never discussed there until, many months later, lawsuits were started against some of the people regarded as ringleaders. Some members then protested against the action of the judicial authorities which they considered to be illegal. In other words, the Second Chamber took notice of the affair only after it had become a legal problem. Only a few people were sentenced and they were soon granted a pardon by the government. But the rebellion had made a great impression. The foreign Press devoted long and detailed articles to the disturbances, which were sometimes (but wrongly) imputed to the socialists, and compared them with the events of the same year in Belgium which, in the view of the foreign correspondents, was politically very similar to Holland.[1]

The long depression from 1873 to 1895 hit Belgium more directly than the Netherlands. Prices and wages fell and the increase in the total output of heavy industry, though on the whole maintained, became more irregular and spasmodic. The years 1877, 1885, and 1886 in particular were years of acute distress. Overproduction and the reduced purchasing power of the agrarian population, who were suffering from the crisis caused by the abundance of American grain, forced a number of factories to close down and others to reduce production. In the industrial centres unemployment and bitter poverty appeared once again. Generally speaking, the workers were probably living in better conditions than at any time in the nineteenth century[2] but for this very reason the new uncertainty, the sudden relapse from relative prosperity to misery, was so

---

[1] Vliegen, *De dageraad der volksbevrijding*, i. 189 ff.

[2] Workers' real wages rose from index-figure 100 in 1846 to 142·5 in 1876 and

intolerable that they were liable to react in the most violent fashion. On 18 March a meeting of anarchists at Liège, in itself a fairly uninteresting occasion, got out of control.[1] A few thousand demonstrators, many of them only young boys, marched through the streets, smashed windows, and shouted the usual slogans. Two days later a strike began in the neighbourhood of the city. It was not a political strike; the miners were only demanding better conditions. But the authorities, understandably worried about the situation, asked for troops to be sent. From 21 March a small army was stationed south of Liège uneasily performing a difficult task for which they were not trained and to which they were not accustomed. On 24 March the tribunal of Liège sentenced about forty of the rebels of 18 March and imposed stiff penalties. Soon after that the strike began to fizzle out.

But at that very moment another strike broke out in the mines of Charleroi and this spread with alarming speed. The blind, elemental force of discontent and despair showed itself on a scale never before seen in Belgium. On 26 March wild groups of striking miners, without any visible preparation, began marching through the countryside around the town and forced the workers of the iron and glass factories to join them. Incited perhaps by the beautiful spring weather, and by beer and spirits, they pillaged, ransacked the country, burnt factories and a castle built by a particularly unpopular manufacturer, a man hated because he had installed new machines. They celebrated their triumphs in a chaotic and drunken orgy. The next day the government called up twenty thousand men and appointed General Vandersmissen as their commander. The General showed remarkable strategic ability and in a few days managed to restore order. On 30 March the Prime Minister informed the Chamber of Deputies of the events. Cold, proud, showing neither fear nor pity, the Chamber declared its support for the government. At the beginning of April work was resumed. But whereas the miners of Liège

(thanks to the considerable fall in prices after 1876) to 220·8 in 1899. Cf. Denise de Weerdt in Dhondt (ed.), *Geschiedenis*, pp. 399–400.

[1] F. van Kalken, *Commotions populaires en Belgique (1834–1902)* (Brussels, 1936), pp. 80 ff.; J. Destrée and É. Vandervelde, *Le Socialisme en Belgique* (Paris, 1898), pp. 66 ff.; Bertrand, *Histoire de la démocratie et du socialisme en Belgique* ii. 382 ff.

had won some concessions from their employers, the strikers of Hainaut won nothing. On 7 April all but a few thousand were back at work again, completely beaten and poorer than before. They had had no pay for several weeks. Numerous rebels were sentenced.

It was obvious, and it was emphasized as much as possible by the socialists, that this was no attempt at revolution but only an outbreak of hatred and disgust, without plan or programme. Even so the movement had more political content than the Eel Revolt of Amsterdam. It started with a meeting of anarchists at Liège. During the few weeks of chaos a pamphlet, *Le Caté-chisme du peuple* by Alfred Defuisseaux (1843–1901), was published and met with enormous success. It is difficult to assess its importance. One thing is clear: it did not cause the revolt nor did it constitute its programme. But this does not necessarily prove that it failed to inspire the masses of people who were carried along by the dramatic events. During the next few weeks 200,000 copies of the booklet in French were sold and 60,000 in a Flemish translation.[1] The author who, if he can be called a socialist at all, was one of the pre-1848 vintage,[2] represented the authorities as profiteers shamelessly exploiting the treasury. His solution to the political and social problem was simple, even naïve: universal franchise.

Of course there was nothing new in this demand. Despite his scorn and loathing for political leaders and civil servants Defuisseaux did not want to dismantle but to develop the parliamentary system of government. He expressed views that had been put forward for many years by various groups in the Low Countries. During the 1880s universal male franchise became the highest aim of progressives, whether liberals or socialists, one which they threatened to achieve by revolutionary means if necessary. The eschatological spirit then permeating the labour movement gave the matter far greater significance than a merely political one. The letters SU (*suffrage universel*) obtained an almost magic function and represented for the illiterate Belgian workers what the ichthys sign had been for the early Christians and the cross for the crusaders.[3] When at last

---

[1] Bertrand, op. cit., 385–91, reprints its most important parts.
[2] L. Delsinne, *Le Parti ouvrier belge des origines à 1894*, p. 134.
[3] See the famous passage in Hendrik de Man's *Zur Psychologie des Sozialismus*

universal franchise came—though much later than they had expected—the men who had fought for it so tirelessly felt some astonishment when reminded of their old illusions, and some, disgusted by what they stigmatized as the inadequate, unbearably slow, and sometimes utterly wrong consequences of universal franchise, even felt shame for the errors of their youth. It was indeed difficult not to be slightly embarrassed by their juvenile enthusiasm when in maturer days they were faced with the fact that the parliamentary democracy they had helped to form and from which they had expected so much was a system of small compromises and often trivial discussions. In one way or another all of them were disappointed by the result of their great victory.[1]

This was inevitable. Expectations had been much too comprehensive. During the 1880s universal franchise was represented as the perfect instrument for totally reforming society in the shortest possible time. Indeed reform would be so rapid that it could just as well be called revolution. In this way universal franchise became, in the eyes of many agitators, the centre of a system of essentially revolutionary aims. Moreover, this drastic reform was often thought to be the only alternative to violent revolution, and sometimes socialist intellectuals suggested that it was a matter of complete indifference to the working class whether the new society which was to come in any case should be brought about by legal or illegal means. The decision rested with the ruling bourgeoisie. If they now granted the franchise to the proletariat they would at the very last moment be spared the revolution in which they and their property would be destroyed. Furthermore, it was a praiseworthy and generous concession on the part of the workers that they politely sought to impress upon the bourgeois the necessity to withdraw, to reduce their power, and to make society ripe for peaceful reform in a legal manner. In 1789 and 1848 the bourgeois themselves had not shown such tact in their dealings with the aristocracy.

(new edn., Jena, 1927), p. 118 in which he analyses the religious character of early socialist emotions.

[1] Maurice Wilmotte, *Mes mémoires* (Brussels, 1948), pp. 139 ff. is a good example of a deeply disappointed radical. The same attitude, though expressed more cautiously, in M. W. F. Treub, *Herinneringen en overpeinzingen* (Haarlem, 1931), pp. 202 ff.

Of course, the champions of universal franchise were to a certain extent right in regarding its introduction as more than just the expansion of the existing political system and the political nation. They did not think in the same terms as the liberals, who had long been saying that universal franchise was the natural end of a long gradual development and had made it dependent on mass education. They rejected the liberal proposition that the electorate should have sufficient intellectual capacity to make rational decisions. Had the doctrine of the sovereignty of reason and law ever been more than a bourgeois excuse for their ruthless preoccupation with their own interests? Universal franchise was to give the state a new basis. It was anti-rationalistic. Moreover, it was more honest: its advocates recognized that it was not the search for reason and law but naked interest that was the essence of politics. Because the proletariat formed the overwhelming majority, it would now be the workers' interests that would prevail. Thus universal franchise was to bring the rule of the proletariat: universal franchise was in fact the franchise of the proletarians, the way to bring their class to power.

Such ideas, however naïve, possessed a certain logical coherence. But they became slightly paradoxical as soon as the socialists in the Low Countries tried to imagine what should actually be done with universal franchise; for then it became apparent that it was expected to prepare the way for something infinitely more important than mere proletarian self-interest. The views of H. Gerhard were simple: he thought that in the new world created by universal franchise there would be no prisons, no prostitution, no war, no cholera, and no floods.[1] Gerhard (1829–86) was a simple though very attractive man, a Dutch tailor whose glory and tragedy it was to be the only workman in the first generation of Dutch socialists interested in theory. The views of an early socialist like the Belgian doctor Caesar de Paepe (1842–90) were more complicated and more characteristic. To him and to so many others socialism was a complete intellectual system. The new organization of labour and property and the just distribution of wealth among the population were only minor elements in its comprehensive

---

[1] Rüter, *Historische studies*, p. 62.

ideology. The main purpose was to transform the nature of man himself. Simultaneously there would be profound changes in learning and the sciences and not only in economic science but ethics and the study of law, criminology, philosophy, pedagogics, and history.[1] De Paepe seemed to think that in the socialist society the old irrational form of universal franchise dominated by class or self-interest would somehow be raised to an altogether different level. Perhaps he found inspiration in the visions of Saint-Simon. At any rate he expected that in the new world the general scientific laws which determine social life would be recognized as majestically objective and unchangeable by people now sufficiently educated to understand what previously they had been unable to grasp. In such a world, political discussions would no longer arise about the basis and the aim of legislation but only about the way in which it should be put into execution; there would be so much spiritual and intellectual certainty and moral unity that universal franchise would have lost all trace of the capricious and emotional character that in the old society it might well be suspected of possessing.[2]

The justification of universal franchise was radically changed by such arguments. Admittedly, De Paepe was exceptionally idealistic. Even those who shared his ideas were rarely as selfless as he was, for he exhausted body and soul in his fight for the Belgian workers. The attempt of some intellectual rebels to found a Université nouvelle in Brussels in competition with and opposition to the liberal Free University sprang from inspired modernism combined with resentment. It was an interesting experiment, closely connected with De Paepe's idea that in the new socialist society a well-ordered civilization could be expected to develop. The Free University had invited Élisée Reclus, the famous French geographer and anarchist, to deliver a course of lectures on comparative geography. But some months before his course was due to start in March 1894, the French Chamber of Deputies was disturbed by the explosion of a bomb thrown by the anarchist Vaillant. The university authorities then decided that it would be better to

---

[1] L. Bertrand, *César de Paepe. Sa vie, son œuvre* (Brussels, 1909), pp. 221 ff.

[2] C. de Paepe, *Le Suffrage universel et la capacité politique de la classe ouvrière* (Ghent, 1890), pp. 8 ff.

postpone the lectures of the anarchist Reclus. The students protested vigorously and found support among an intellectual élite with radical and socialist convictions. In October these founded the Université nouvelle with only one faculty—the Faculty of Law—and an Institut de hautes études. Famous novelists, among them Camille Lemonnier and Georges Eekhoud, brilliant barristers like (inevitably) Edmond Picard, who had not obtained a chair at the Free University, and the radical Paul Janson, the young socialists Émile Vandervelde and Jules Destrée and others acted as teachers. The number of students rose from 23 in 1894 to 170 in 1896, although the Free University did not suffer from this competition, having 1,316 students in 1894 and 1,419 in 1895.[1] The experiment was short lived. The Roman Catholic government refused to grant recognition to the diplomas issued by the New University which, compromising with the Free University, decided to give up its independent existence.

This had been, however, an ambitious enterprise. The liberal bourgeois style of the traditional university courses was scorned; the new teachers put their work at the service of the socialist future. They indicated how modern society must do justice to the needy and must create a new body of law to give direction to the inevitable and profound changes that would transform that society. More was needed for such a gigantic task than a mere sense of justice. New sciences and new syntheses of old sciences could provide the social reformer with the vision and the method he needed in order to act rationally. Thus the New University was to become a centre of pure scientific speculation, far above the scattered professional disciplines of the old universities but at the same time a centre from which the total reform of society could be promoted and guided. Janson praised the deep moral significance of this work.[2] Picard enjoyed its adventurousness.[3] Émile Vandervelde, who after his legal studies attended lectures in physiology, embryology, and psychiatry, used this new university as a place where he could experiment with his organic-

---

[1] E. Goblet d'Alviella, *1884–1909. L'Université de Bruxelles pendant son troisième quart de siècle* (2 vols., Brussels, 1909–10), i. 37.

[2] Delange-Janson, op. cit. ii. 52 ff.

[3] Destrée and Vandervelde, op. cit., pp. 223 ff.

social methods and seek to build a new science on the basis of sociology and biology.[1]

These were ideas of and for intellectuals. But within the framework of the workers' movement and the propaganda for universal franchise among the proletariat it is remarkable that the struggle against the despised petty interests and narrow rationality of the bourgeoisie was felt to transcend the class struggle and class-interests. Apparently at all levels of the agitation for the new order people were seeking objectivity and universalism, rather than self-interest and massive anti-intellectualism. Universal franchise, it was said, was urgently needed because the human dignity of the workers was no different from that of the bourgeoisie and demanded equality; it was needed because the worker possessed as many human and consequently political rights as members of the higher classes, because he must in the fullest sense of the word become a citizen taking part in the general life of the society into which he was born.[2] In Belgium, where such words as 'fatherland' and 'nation' used to be pronounced with greater exaltation than in the Netherlands, universal franchise even acquired the improbable aim of providing the workers with a fatherland. On 10 August 1890, after a long day of demonstrations for universal franchise, 100,000 men assembled in heavy rain in a Brussels park and swore to continue fighting until 'thanks to universal franchise the people shall have conquered a fatherland'.[3]

Thus universal franchise was advocated on many different and at times contradictory grounds, but its champions attached such overwhelming significance to it that, in whatever form it was justified or idealized, all regarded it as the main object of their reform programme. Even so the question was treated by Parliament with some indifference. It did not avoid discussion of the electoral system altogether, for its regulations were defective and all sorts of peculiar situations were created which

---

[1] Émile Vandervelde, *Souvenirs d'un militant socialiste* (Paris, 1939), pp. 25 ff. His *L'évolution régressive en biologie et en sociologie* (Paris, 1897), written in collaboration with J. de Moor and J. Massart, is a curious example of this method. J. Bartier shows in his 'Étudiants et mouvement révolutionnaire au temps de la première Internationale', *Mélanges offerts à G. Jacquemyns* (Brussels, 1968), pp. 43–4, that students of the Free University were already in the late 1860s deeply interested in such a form of socialism derived from positivism.

[2] Rüter, *Historische studies*, pp. 38 ff.

[3] Bertrand, *Histoire de la démocratie* ii. 475; Vandervelde, *Souvenirs*, p. 42.

the political parties enjoyed exposing whenever the anomalies worked in favour of their opponents. When this happened the government tried to push through modifications beneficial to its own party. In Belgium the *cens* could not be changed any more. According to the constitution it should not be lower than 20 guilders and in 1848 it had indeed been reduced to the minimum. But as the franchise was made dependent on the sum paid in direct taxes—in the absence of income tax, for example, taxes on land, houses, servants, fireplaces—it was possible to change the electorate through fiscal measures. Thus in 1872 the Catholics deprived publicans of the franchise because they used to vote liberal. The liberals reciprocated between 1878 and 1881 by disqualifying a large number of priests and farmers.

In the Netherlands, just as in Belgium, it was laid down in the constitution that to qualify for the franchise one must pay a certain sum in direct taxes; this sum Parliament was entitled to determine on condition that it should not be less than 20 guilders. Like the Belgians the Dutch had no income tax with the result that the same sort of direct taxes were involved: land, personal, and patent taxes, as they were called. The main difference between the two countries was that whereas the Belgians had reduced the *cens* everywhere in their country to the minimum allowed by the constitution there was still much variety in the Netherlands, where the tax requirements in the countryside were on the whole lower than in the towns. In 1874 the Dutch Parliament engaged in a remarkable discussion. The liberal government proposed to extend the minimum *cens* of 20 guilders much more widely, not yet generalizing it as in Belgium, but nevertheless spreading it considerably. Some liberal members of Parliament, however, were afraid of such democratic generosity and wished to stop at 28 guilders. As a result the government raised the proposed *cens* to 26 guilders. Then the Protestant anti-revolutionaries protested; the sum favoured by them was 24 guilders. One thing was obvious: there was no possibility of solving the franchise problem in such a manner, and indeed nothing came of it. The whole discussion is characteristic of the way in which the question was treated by Parliament. Although the anti-revolutionaries in particular claimed to base their point of view on solid principle, in fact they acted just like all the other parties in making their attitude dependent on complicated calculations about the practical effect which a modification of the *cens* would have on themselves.[1]

Not until the 1880s did a single courageous speaker venture to discuss the problem in the Belgian Chamber of Deputies, the famous Brussels barrister Paul Janson (1840–1913). Janson was a liberal of very radical persuasion who had been nominated as a candidate for the Chamber in 1877 by the liberals of Brussels, after he had declared that he was no revolutionary and that the fight against the Church should be the main object of liberal policies.[2] During his first years as a member of Parliament he loyally restricted himself to being an anticlerical, seeming to adhere to the doctrine that the unity and supremacy of the liberal party could only be maintained by opposing the Church and doing nothing else.[3] In 1881, however, he suddenly asked for an extension of the franchise for provincial and municipal elections. He did so very cautiously. He pleaded for a franchise dependent on capability and not on material property. In effect this meant that all men able to write and read should take part in local elections: because of the high proportion of illiteracy in Belgium more than a quarter of the male population would not meet his requirements. Even so the doctrinaires and their leader, Frère-Orban, called Janson to order in their haughtiest tones and, beating a hasty retreat to the safe refuge of anticlericalism, Janson withdrew his proposal.[4] In 1883 he tried again but only eleven members of the Chamber were prepared to consider the franchise problem and of course this was not nearly enough. Both the doctrinaires and the Catholics persistently refused to recognize the urgency of the matter.[5]

In such circumstances the radicals were understandably eager to mobilize public opinion against parliamentary conservatism. In Belgium especially this was an obvious step

---

[1] Buys, *Studiën over staatkunde en staatsrecht*, i. 552–3; J. A. A. H. de Beaufort, *Vijftig jaren uit onze geschiedenis, 1868–1918* (Amsterdam, 1928), p. 48. In his *Onze strijd in de Staten-Generaal* (2 vols., Amsterdam, 1927–9), ii. 75 ff., P. A. Diepenhorst tried in vain to prove that the attitude of the anti-revolutionaries was based on principle.

[2] Delange-Janson, i. 189.

[3] See P. Vercauteren, 'La place de Paul Janson dans la vie politique belge de 1877 à 1884', *Res Publica*, xi (1969), 383–404.

[4] Delange-Janson, i. 253 ff.   [5] Ibid. 280 ff.

to take. Since 1830 the political opposition had repeatedly appealed to the masses of the population in an attempt to set the judgement of the nation against the judgement of Parliament—if only by means of demonstrations and riots. But only the liberals and the radicals had ever been able to organize such demonstrations successfully. The reason is simple. Demonstrations had little or no effect unless they occurred at the centre, that is to say in Brussels, and Brussels was a liberal stronghold where the conservative Roman Catholic party found little support amongst the electorate or the population generally. In the Netherlands the situation was radically different. Political action outside and against Parliament was very uncommon, although some more or less organized demonstrations may have helped to convince King William II of the need for constitutional revision in 1848. But on the occasions after 1848 when such action was attempted it was organized by the conservatives and always related to matters of religion. Moreover, there was no question of mass meetings or demonstrations. The anti-liberal April movement of 1853 was a storm of words. When the liberal education bill was adopted by Parliament in 1878, the anti-revolutionaries drafted a petition to the King which was signed by more than 300,000 people and solemnly presented to him. But the King, refusing to repeat his mistake of 1853 and to involve himself publicly in political discussion, disregarded the document. The liberals condemned the uproar made by the anti-revolutionaries as unconstitutional and despised it as useless.

But in the 1880s the Dutch Left also started agitating outside Parliament. An association called Algemeen Stemrecht (Universal Franchise) was founded in 1876 in Amsterdam and organized meetings there and in other towns; and in 1879 there appeared a Comité voor Algemeen Stemrecht (Committee for Universal Franchise) which represented the left wing of the liberal party. In 1880 it published (though without much effect) a manifesto in which all the evils of the time, from the unjust tax system and high defence costs to the unsatisfactory standard of mass education and bad public health, were imputed to the restricted franchise. In 1882 the Committee declared itself in favour of universal male franchise. In 1886, however, it ceased to exist. It had refused to collaborate with the socialists but had found no substantial support among the liberals. Meanwhile, the Noord-Nederlandsch Verbond tot bevordering van Algemeen Stemrecht (Association of the Northern Provinces for the Promotion of Universal Franchise) was established in Groningen (1880), addressing itself especially to the workers, and in the same year De Unie (The Union) set out to mobilize support among the lower bourgeoisie, civil servants, primary schoolteachers, shopkeepers, and office clerks. In 1881 the higher bourgeoisie received its own organization called Kiesrechtshervorming (Franchise Reform). In 1882 the Bond voor Algemeen Kiesrecht (League for Universal Franchise) tried to introduce some unity into the socialist and radical propaganda, and indeed became remarkably active. From 1883 onwards all these groups tried valiantly to rouse the public and Parliament to an awareness of the urgency of the problem by means of publications, meetings, and demonstrations. Undoubtedly the socialists and those who sympathized with them were most active.[1]

The movement for franchise reform in Belgium was not characterized by the almost pathological dissipation of effort that had shown itself in Holland. In 1881 the radical liberals established a Ligue nationale pour la réforme électorale which many socialists joined. A year earlier one of the first demonstrations had taken place in Brussels and a year before that the socialists had started their campaign for universal franchise.[2] As in the Netherlands the whole agitation of the 1880s and after was in effect either a reaction or a concession to socialist demands. From the beginning in both countries it was the socialists who first asked for the immediate introduction of universal male franchise and rapidly succeeded in making the radicals adopt the same point of view. Paul Janson, who in 1881 had cautiously proposed giving the franchise to all literate men in the elections for provincial and municipal councils, committed himself in 1890 to claiming universal male franchise for parliamentary elections. This is a curious phenomenon for as a political group the socialists hardly counted; the radicals, on the other hand, although they had little popular backing, enjoyed excellent connections with the Press and the official

---

[1] Rüter, *Historische studies*, pp. 74–108.
[2] Bertrand, *Histoire de la démocratie* ii. 283.

world of government and Parliament and could exercise real influence where it mattered. But so firmly convinced were they that the growth of popular power was imminent and inevitable that they were prepared to serve as the vanguard of the socialists, even if they had their doubts about policies intended to grant power to the illiterate and the uneducated. In the mid-1880s the unrest in both countries increased. The Hague had its first demonstration for franchise reform on 20 September 1885. After a march through the city the mass meeting proclaimed itself the National Assembly and threatened the government with revolution if it refused its demands.[1] On 15 August 1886 Brussels was the scene of a similar demonstration in which, it was said, 30,000 people took part.[2]

2. *The Movements of the Eighties—and Radicalism*

Universal male franchise in the form demanded by the opposition did not come yet, however. Resistance to it was too stubborn. But undoubtedly the agitation in its favour helped to undermine the self-confidence of the ruling bourgeoisie. Of course they opposed universal franchise but not on grounds of principle. They restricted themselves to slowing down a development the inevitability of which they began almost unconsciously to accept. The great doctrinaire system was on the decline. Frère-Orban remained loyal to his ideas but support for them was steadily diminishing. The system had embraced two generations. There was no third generation to continue it. Even those who had fought on the extreme left wing of the doctrinaire party, Kappeyne van de Coppello and Van Houten, Laurent and De Laveleye, were overtaken in the 1880s both by events and by the young, who were doubtful of the validity of their predecessors' axioms. In the 1880s the cultural élites which won remarkably rapid success turned against doctrinaire intellectualism, moralism, and legalism. The starting-points of the modernists were not intellect, virtue, and law but passion, beauty, and self-interest.

The important modernist movement of the 1880s was prepared in Belgium by men like De Coster and in the Netherlands by Multatuli, who was in many respects superior to all later

---

[1] Vliegen, op. cit. i. 130 ff.   [2] Bertrand, *Histoire de la démocratie* ii. 435.

Dutch writers; he exercised some direct literary and political influence but even so remained somewhat isolated. The dynamic force of the movement came from abroad. The great slogans inspiring the young writers in the North and South were of French origin; so of course was Naturalism which was loyally adopted in the Low Countries and after some years was superseded as a literary fashion out of the same loyalty to French literature. For painting too, which expressed the new trends before they manifested themselves in literature, Paris was the obvious centre of attention and inspiration. Admittedly, the French monopoly was to some extent diminished in Dutch culture by the fact that some of the most important young writers discovered the works of Shelley and Keats and endeavoured to translate their romanticism into Dutch poetry. But however stirring such rhythms and forms may have been, and however exciting it was to use them in poetry, it was impossible to derive from them the force to start a new movement or new courses of action. This came from France.

In the 1880s Belgium always remained a few steps ahead of Holland. The two principles which were to form the basis of modernist theory had already begun to find support in Belgium by the late 1870s. The first was the thesis of *l'art pour l'art*, which originated in French Romanticism, the second was the new naturalism in novels and poetry which from 1875 onwards was highly valued by Belgian writers.[1] In 1881 the literary review *La Jeune Belgique* was started. This was less short lived than most such periodicals and became the centre of the whole literary movement in Belgium. It was also known in Holland and read by the champions of the Dutch literary revolution.[2] Various French influences penetrated to *La Jeune Belgique* and to the periodical *La Wallonie* of 1886: the Parnassians, Zola, decadent literature in the manner of Baudelaire and Villiers de l'Isle-Adam, Symbolism. But an older Belgian author too was greeted as a leader by the young: Camille Lemonnier (1844–1913) who as early as 1871 had won international fame with his book on the Battle of Sedan. He soon came to be considered a Naturalist, although his undisciplined and naïve mind

---

[1] G. Vanwelkenhuyzen, *L'Influence du naturalisme français en Belgique de 1875 à 1900* (Brussels, 1930), pp. 35 ff.

[2] G. Colmjon, *De Beweging van Tachtig* (Utrecht, 1963), pp. 109, 191.

and his love of detail made him fundamentally alien to all dogmatic theses about what the art of the novel ought to be.[1]

La Jeune Belgique catered for the intellectual élite. It did not represent a democratic movement. But the vulgarity despised by these men was not that of the masses, rather the vulgarity of the bourgeoisie from which the leaders themselves had come.[2] With their proud exclusiveness they rejected everything ever done, thought, or made by this bourgeoisie as inferior materialism. They sought isolation. Together in a small circle of kindred souls they cultivated their sophistication and their introspection, and infinitely refined their means of expression. They were unreligious and remained outside politics. In a world dominated by the bourgeoisie this meant that they were as full of contempt for liberalism as they were indifferent to the Roman Catholic party. But this élite (rapidly recognized to be such—liqueurs, ties, and cigars were called after *La Jeune Belgique*)[3] not only revolutionized literature but undermined the intellectual and moral authority of the ruling groups. To all those influenced by the review it did not so much seem wrong to be a liberal, as Frère-Orban and his followers were, as vulgar and ridiculous; it meant forsaking beauty and the transcendant purity of man's mind and individuality. The best, the most articulate, the most creative members of the well-to-do bourgeoisie gave the impression of turning against the political, economic, and intellectual system of the class on which they remained nevertheless financially dependent.[4]

They were not driven by social feelings. Their opposition was individualistic and aesthetic. It was their own souls not those of the masses which were at stake. These men, proud decadents, consumed by love of beauty, the last sons of a formerly powerful but now declining class, found inspiration in an exclusively egocentric reaction against their own origins. Edmond Picard deplored this. He too edited a periodical,

[1] P. Hamélius, *Introduction à la littérature française et flamande de Belgique* (Brussels, 1921), pp. 241 ff.

[2] Many of the French-writing Belgian poets and novelists of the 1880s came from well-to-do bourgeois families. Their Dutch colleagues, as well as the Flemish *avant-garde*, of this period were of lower-middle-class origin.

[3] A. J. Mathews, *La Wallonie, 1886–1892. The Symbolist Movement in Belgium* (New York, 1947), p. 15.

[4] Ibid., pp. 10–11; Pirenne, *Histoire de Belgique* vii. 262.

L'Art moderne, also founded in 1881, and it met with success. In the Netherlands this small weekly was read with great interest especially by the painters.[1] It soon found itself engaged in prolonged discussion with *La Jeune Belgique*. Picard scorned the egocentric, asocial aesthetics of the young rebels. He wanted a useful and a social art—although it turned out to be very difficult to define its form or content. Eventually he discovered that Henri Conscience who died in 1883 was an exemplary social novelist not only because of his popularity but also because he described the virtues of the people and the vices of the rich so convincingly.[2] The literature produced by *La Jeune Belgique* with its aspiration to transcend reality in pure lyrical exaltation seemed sterile to Picard. Literature must serve society; it must help improve social conditions and function as a substitute for the tired and dilapidated religion of the Churches; it must be a moral doctrine.[3] Obviously, this was still a fairly naïve conception of social art as essentially a form of propaganda. Not before the 1890s did still younger and vaguer idealists conceive of social art as an art of the community itself, drawing its inspiration from the people and finding its purpose in them. Yet Picard exercised an influence. Some of the individualists who in the 1880s admired the naturalism and the aestheticism of *La Jeune Belgique* were converted to socialism in the course of the 1890s. The most famous example is Émile Verhaeren (1855–1916) whose first collection of poems, *Les Flamandes* (1883), was naturalist albeit in a very unscientific form.[4] Another is the barrister Jules Destrée (1863–1936), who lived for a long time under the decadent influence of his friend J. K. Huysmans[5] but finally opted for socialism and became the greatest authority in the Belgian Workers' party on aesthetic matters.

Picard had a second serious objection to *La Jeune Belgique*: its dependence on France. The name of the review itself and of the group associated with it was an imitation of the Romantics in Paris who had started the art for art's sake movement in the

---

[1] Colmjon, op. cit., p. 129.
[2] Cf. Hamélius, op. cit., pp. 256–8.
[3] Vermeulen, op. cit., pp. 68–9.
[4] F. Vermeulen, *Les Débuts d'Émile Verhaeren* (Brussels, 1949), pp. 48 ff.
[5] See J. K. Huysmans, *Lettres inédites à Jules Destrée*, ed. G. Vanwelkenhuyzen (Geneva, 1967).

1830s and called themselves La Jeune France. Even when *La Jeune Belgique* tried to be true to its national origins, expressing suspicion of foreign models and adjuring writers to be 'themselves', Picard remained sceptical. What he hoped to see was a national art drawing its strength from Belgian scenery and the way of life of the Belgian masses, an authentic and independent literature. It was in keeping therefore that Picard, although he used to emphasize the Flemish character of Belgian art, became enthusiastic about the review founded in 1886 called *La Wallonie*—a successful neologism, for Wallonia was not at all a common term.[1] This review sought to express the 'Walloon' mind and soul, and its approach which also allowed it to function for some time as the leading review of the French and Belgian Symbolist schools appealed more to Picard than *La Jeune Belgique*.

Not only Belgian but Dutch culture as well was animated during these years by the heated discussions provoked by the deliberate eccentricity of the younger writers, by the various ways in which they tried to draw attention to their work, and by the alacrity with which they followed, and sometimes themselves initiated, the latest artistic fashions. Their activities were even reported in the newspapers. But the Dutch were somewhat slower: quite possibly Brussels acted in this period as an intermediary between Paris and Amsterdam.[2] Although the Dutch hardly needed any introduction to French literature —it was much read in The Hague and Amsterdam[3] and always had been—the way in which the Belgians embraced all French innovations may well have stimulated Dutch interest and helped to overcome resistance to them. It was surely no accident that the generation of the 1880s sometimes proudly called themselves Young Holland or Young Amsterdam.[4] But there remained a difference of some years between the successive phases of the Dutch and Belgian developments. The leading periodical of the new school, *De Nieuwe Gids* (*New Guide*), was started in 1885 and propagated a naturalism that the Belgian *avant-garde* had begun to criticize as no longer entirely

[1] The term 'La Wallonie' was used in 1858 for the first time: Elias, *Vlaamse gedachte* iii. 268.

[2] Colmjon, p. 105.   [3] Ibid., p. 138.

[4] *De Nieuwe Gids*, III. i (1888), 331, 460 ff. and *passim*.

up to date at least a year earlier.[1] By about 1890 the Dutch were beginning to understand that what they had continued to regard as *avant-garde* had for some time been considered old-fashioned in Paris and Brussels and was thus something that had to be superseded. In the 1880s Symbolism and decadent literature, highly fashionable in Brussels, had not yet made much impression in Amsterdam.

Notwithstanding many striking similarities, the Belgian and the Dutch Movement of the Eighties was different in several ways. What impresses one in the first place is the difference in the quality and durability of its influence. The most famous French-speaking representatives of the younger generation in Belgium, Verhaeren and Maeterlinck, wrote their best work in the 1890s and after. In Belgium the style of 1880 passed away relatively early, at any rate in the literature written in French. In Holland this was not so. In whatever form it chose, Naturalism continued to dominate Dutch literature for decades. Moreover, numerous writers remained loyal to the stylistic peculiarities that had become fashionable in the 1880s. They excelled in infinitely detailed impressionistic notes and used language as if it were a painter's palette, a language of forms and lines, crumbled to pieces, deprived of its music, its structure, its rhythm, and its logic. The difference between written and spoken language was heavily emphasized. The authors developed an 'écriture artiste', a sort of artistic language which had lost its value as a means of communication. Thus literature became totally estranged from the ordinary authors, the statesmen, scholars, and scientists, the journalists and others who wrote prose to be read. This was detrimental both to literature and to the quality of the language used in normal social intercourse. But however long lasting and in certain respects harmful the consequences of the Movement of the Eighties may have been, it cannot be denied that at the beginning some of the rare works in Dutch literature were written that can genuinely be called classical: the sonnets of Willem Kloos (1859–1938); *Mei*, the long mythological and symbolic epic in lyrical verse by Herman Gorter (1864–1927); the powerful, entirely subjective polemics of Lodewijk van Deyssel (Karel J. L. Alberdingk Thijm, 1864–1952), the son of J. A.

---

[1] Vanwelkenhuyzen, op. cit., p. 171.

Alberdingk Thijm, who replaced his father's name by a pseudonym and his father's loyal Roman Catholicism by Parisian and pagan decadence.

The programme for the revolution in poetry was written in 1882 by Willem Kloos,[1] who studied classics at the University of Amsterdam. Whereas the young men of *La Jeune Belgique* studied law by the special wish of their parents, the most active Dutch rebels came from the lower and not, like their Belgian colleagues, from the upper middle classes and chose classical studies, apparently as a preparation for the teaching profession. In his essay of 1882 Kloos expressed ideas and ambitions which were becoming the common property of European literature at the time and thus placed Dutch criticism of poetry firmly in a European framework at an early stage. However, Kloos did not refer to his contemporaries. His source was Shelley's *Defence of Poetry*. But he and his fellow poets lacked the idealism and the universalism of Shelley as world-reformer. Kloos has been well described as an 'aesthetic pietist'.[2] Thus he came very near to the asocial individualism of *La Jeune Belgique*, which may be called Romantic or Symbolist; it was at any rate a fairly common feature of the new poetic consciousness of the 1880s. Three years after publishing his text, rightly famous in Dutch literature, Kloos and his colleagues succeeded in acquiring a review of their own, which they called *De Nieuwe Gids*.

The title characterizes the position taken up by the periodical. The original *De Gids* was founded in 1837; it was the great review of opposition liberalism in the 1840s and of triumphant liberalism after 1848. In the 1880s it was still a well-edited and well-written periodical rightly regarded as the organ of the liberal establishment, rather haughty intellectually and politically, rather conservative socially. *De Nieuwe Gids* refused to accept the leadership of such a group and aspired to take over the role so long performed by its predecessor and foe. It was intended to be a 'guide', to indicate the direction in which society, literature, and the arts ought to go. At the same time it sought to do more than guide: it attempted to command. This,

---

[1] This essay served as an introduction to the first edition of Jacques Perk's poetry.

[2] J. C. Brandt Corstius, *Het poëtisch programma van Tachtig* (Amsterdam, 196 8), p. 53.

however, was a pretension that could not be made good. In the early 1890s dissension among the editors as well as writers had already become so fundamental that many of them refused to contribute to it any longer. *De Nieuwe Gids* dragged out its miserable existence for many decades as a lamentable monument to the magnificent early poetry and criticism of Willem Kloos, the young genius soon worn out with drink whose only function in later life was to continue to edit the useless paper and to rhyme innumerable bad sonnets. In fact even in its greatest period *De Nieuwe Gids* was not what it claimed to be. This generation did not 'guide'; it was unable and unwilling to do so. It represented neither an intellectual system nor a social group. Its task was rather to show, by the fury and brilliant irony of its criticism, as well as by its own creative work, that the presuppositions and the achievements of liberalism in its old form had become totally inadequate.

The authors of *De Nieuwe Gids* constituted a heterogeneous group and the ideals they were fighting for differed widely. The hyperindividualistic *l'art pour l'art* theories of Kloos, to whom poetry was the most individual expression of the most individual emotion, were the very antithesis of the naturalistic method, which at least in principle intended to establish the possibility of scientifically reproducing reality in all its appearances—although it degenerated in Holland into impressionism. In the early 1890s the political opinions of editors and contributors turned out to be equally divergent. Politically *De Nieuwe Gids* began by being 'radical'. Young Holland and especially Young Amsterdam refused to be either liberal, for that was considered bourgeois and banal, or socialist, for in this period the anti-intellectual and demagogic elements in socialism were too much for them. This generation attempted to create their own form of politics and explained their views in *De Nieuwe Gids*—which was backed financially by a group of progressive politicians.[1] They did not act as the bourgeois wing of socialism nor did they consider it their task to 'civilize' socialism and adapt it to society as it was. On the contrary, they, the generation of the 1880s, thought that dogmatic socialism was already

---

[1] J. Meijer, *Het levensverhaal van een vergetene. Willem Anthony Paap, 1856–1923* (Amsterdam, 1959), pp. 101–2. Cf. G. Stuiveling, *De Nieuwe Gids als geestelijk brandpunt* (Amsterdam, 1935).

on the way out. Nor did they regard themselves as an intermediary group between liberalism and socialism: they were a new political and literary *avant-garde*.

Radicalism acquired its own organization in Belgium and the Netherlands almost simultaneously in the late 1880s. If a political party needs to express a system, be it a system of ideas or of interests, the 'progressive' or 'radical' parties of this period are paradoxes, for radicalism did not have, and did not wish to have, a system. All systems, it was thought, slow down evolution, impede growth rather than direct it.[1] Realism, opportunism, a supple and rapid insight into what is required by the circumstances of the moment form the only sound basis for politics.[2] An impatient writer of numerous articles in *De Nieuwe Gids*, which clumsily attempted to provide a philosophical justification for radicalism, rejected even the possibility that a systematic and scientific study of constitutional law and economics could ever produce practical results.[3] The true statesman is like an artist who allows himself to be guided by his intuition.[4] But his aim is obvious: he must try to provide the greatest possible number of people with the greatest possible measure of happiness. The definition implies, however, that he must always remain within the bounds of what is possible at a certain moment and this restriction constitutes an essential part of the thesis. As possibilities were changing constantly, the statesman's aims must change accordingly.

By emphasizing the pragmatism and the unsystematic character of their politics, the radicals of the 1880s were able to distinguish themselves from those of the 1860s and 1870s who had attempted to make a system out of liberalism. But although the young radicals did not possess such a system, they were convinced of at least one elementary truth: the axiom that there is an evolutionary principle leading men towards complete equality. It was not altogether certain whether it might be called 'progress', but this did not really matter because a subjective value-judgement hardly made sense in face of the majestic inevitability of the process.

---

[1] Cf. Delange-Janson, i. 303.

[2] M. W. F. Treub, *De radicalen tegenover de sociaal-democratische partij in Nederland* (1891), *passim*; cf. also P. L. Tak, *De Nieuwe Gids*, III. i (1888), 488 ff.

[3] M. C. L. Lotsy, 'Humane politiek', *De Nieuwe Gids*, I. i (1886), 415–16.

[4] Ibid. 427.

In 1887 the Belgian radicals organized a congress that indeed decided to form a Parti Progressiste. This was to a certain extent an act of despair. Many members of the left wing of the liberal party were of the opinion that after the terrible riots of 1886 it was no longer realistic to expect the party to abandon its doctrinaire dogmas in time and they thus founded a new party, which at parliamentary elections often associated itself with the liberals, but frequently sought and found support among socialists at the elections for municipal councils.[1] Paul Janson was its leader and spokesman. His prestige was great. He was a celebrated barrister, a famous orator whose French eloquence could rise to the passion of grand emotions or to the dramatic anger of the resolute leader. Of course the desperate position of the liberal party, from 1884 constantly in opposition and with no hope of returning to power in the foreseeable future, made his fight with the doctrinaires easier, and it is improbable that he could have broken the unity of the party if it had been in power or had had some prospect of returning to office. But at the same time this, paradoxically, doomed him to the role of perpetual opposition.

The radical party hoped to solve the social problem by legislation—by the extension of the franchise, the gradual introduction of progressive income tax, the protection of the worker and his family, by controlling capitalism by nationalizing or municipalizing public utility services, by general military service, compulsory education, and several other reforms. Many of the demands at the various radical congresses on which the party programme came to be based showed it to be moving perceptibly to the Left, having much in common with the Belgian socialists. On the other hand, aspects of its policy became gradually acceptable to liberals who remained loyal to the old party. Under such circumstances it was inevitable that radicalism should disappear relatively early as an independent organization. Many radicals found a more solidly built foundation in the Workers' party; others returned to the liberals. After 1894 the radical party lost much of its influence and by the turn of the century it was reunited with the liberal party. This was far from being a tragic development. The radicals had no ambition to form a lasting popular party.

[1] Chlepner, *Cent ans d'histoire sociale*, p. 164.

According to the socialist leader Louis Bertrand, they even deliberately rejected the opportunity to win over the workers, not so much from fear of such support but because they did not want to compete with the newly created Workers' party.[1] But however ephemeral radicalism proved to be as an organized party, it disappeared in fact because it was so successful. It came to control the liberal party so long as the latter remained in opposition—once the party participated in government again it became more conservative. The radicals too provided the socialists with a cadre of intellectuals, an entry into the world of high politics, and some insight into the necessary limits of revolutionary idealism.

In the Netherlands the development was rather less simple, largely because the formation of properly organized political parties had not yet become a generally accepted practice. Consequently, a genuine radical party did not really emerge at all. It is true that the left wing of the liberal electoral association at Amsterdam decided in 1889 to withdraw from the main body and establish an association of its own;[2] it is also true that in various parts of the country radical candidates were nominated for election to Parliament who emphatically denied allegiance to the liberals. Even so there was never a national radical organization or a national radical congress. On the whole, however, the Dutch radicals resembled very closely the Belgian progressives. Their programmes were almost identical, with apparently only two major differences. The Belgian progressives, Janson included, wanted to extend the franchise in 1888 but did not want it to be universal—they accepted this consequence only some years later. The Dutch radicals were in favour of universal franchise from the start. Secondly, the Belgian radicals rejected the anticlericalism of the liberal party but pursued it themselves in the field of education; many of their Dutch colleagues, on the other hand, were prepared to allow state subsidies to the free Protestant and Catholic schools and thus to put an end to the conflict.[3] These differences can probably be explained quite simply: in a country less afflicted by illiteracy and where the standard of free primary

[1] Bertrand, *Histoire de la démocratie* ii. 521.   [2] Vliegen, ii. 3.
[3] Ibid. 224; Treub, *Herinneringen*, pp. 74, 80. See also F. van der Goes and P. L. Tak in various articles in *De Nieuwe Gids*.

education was undoubtedly much higher, universal franchise and support for the free schools were not so abhorrent to radicals as they were in Belgium.

The Dutch radicals disagreed among themselves about their attitude towards socialism. In the radical electoral association at Amsterdam there was vehement discussion whether socialists should be allowed to join and when finally the decision was in the negative, some members left the organization.[1] The chairman in particular, M. W. F. Treub (1858–1931), turned out to be hostile to socialist backing, and in due course wrote the first serious study and refutation of Marx's doctrines to appear in the Netherlands.[2] Such questions did not disturb the pragmatic Belgians, whose socialism was no more Marxist than their radicalism was anti-socialist. Even in the Netherlands, however, notwithstanding the native propensity to relate practical matters to fundamental philosophies of life, it was far from easy to distinguish clearly between radicalism and socialism. This became apparent in the 1890s when some important radicals were among the founders and pillars of the Social Democratic Workers' party, although there were no signs that they had undergone any dramatic conversions. It became apparent too in the curious history of the Frisian People's party which emerged in the course of the 1880s and for long hovered between radicalism and socialism.[3] The party constituted a federation of more than a hundred left-wing organizations in the province of Friesland—the League for Universal Franchise, the Social Democratic League established in 1881, workers' associations, social democratic youth clubs, and many others. It totalled about 5,000 members, more than the Social Democratic League had throughout the

[1] Vliegen, ii. 218–19; Meijer, *W. A. Paap*, pp. 150–1; Treub, *Herinneringen*, pp. 77, 81 ff.

[2] M. W. F. Treub, *Het wijsgeerig-economisch stelsel van Karl Marx* (2 vols., Amsterdam, 1902–3).

[3] Vliegen, i. 350 ff.; ii. 230 ff.; P. J. Troelstra, *Gedenkschriften* (4 vols., Amsterdam, 1927–31), i. 248 ff. In 1887 the Frisians founded a Frisian Committee for Universal Franchise. It was very active and collaborated with several other groups. In 1890 all of them federated into the Frisian Committee of the People's party: cf. D. J. Wansink, *Het socialisme op de tweesprong. De geboorte van de S.D.A.P.* (Haarlem, 1939), pp. 71 ff. and A. F. Mellink, 'Een poging tot democratische coalitie-vorming: de Nederlandse kiesrechtbeweging als Volkspartij (1886–1891)', *Tijdschrift voor Geschiedenis*, lxxxi (1968), 174–95.

whole country. That it was radically inspired was shown by its advocacy of universal franchise as well as by its belief in private property. But it went beyond radicalism in adopting the idea of land nationalization as propagated by the American Henry George—a reform, it was thought, which would be easy enough to enforce by legal means, with appropriate compensation to the landowners, after a Parliament had been elected on the basis of universal franchise. Although George's ideas looked attractive to a Belgian like De Laveleye and to the German *Katheder*-socialists, most Dutch radicals considered them reprehensible.

By the early 1890s the radical movement in the Netherlands, such as it was, had already exhausted itself. It had certainly achieved some remarkable local successes, especially in Amsterdam where the city's takeover of such monopolistic public services as gas and electricity and the telephone and tramway companies represented an important victory. But on the national level it lost much of its meaning in 1891 when the party of the old-liberals—the Liberal Union—drafted a programme that did not differ fundamentally from the radicals',[1] apart from the fact that it was not until 1899 that it accepted universal franchise.[2] The Frisian People's party became neither a national, a radical, nor a socialist party. In 1891 the Social Democratic League withdrew from it and this proved fatal to both.[3] Thus in the Netherlands too the attempt to revive political life by dissociating it from systematic political principles failed. Politics continued to be dominated by doctrine and political decisions could in practice only be reached by means of elaborate compromises between the various political dogmas. But though Dutch radicalism did not succeed in simplifying or rationalizing the political scene, it forced its vision of the future upon the liberal party, and when after the débâcle some of its champions joined the socialists, their experience and realism also proved a benefit.

3. Socialist and Confessional Parties

It was by no means obvious in the 1880s that Dutch socialism had a much stronger basis than radicalism. The number of

[1] Vliegen, ii. 216 ff.; Van der Mandele, *Het liberalisme in Nederland*, p. 129.
[2] Van der Mandele, op. cit., p. 136.   [3] Vliegen, ii. 244.

workers joining socialist organizations was relatively small and
the programmes put forward by the socialists, if they took the
trouble to put one forward at all, seemed either to consist of
wild utopian fantasies or to be dependent on, and indeed
subordinated to, the pursuit of universal franchise, which they
were not alone in asking for. But in both Belgium and the
Netherlands labour parties developed with a firm confidence
in their future and the firm intention of taking part in national
politics. The Parti Ouvrier Belge (POB, Belgische Werkliedenpartij) was formed in 1885 and rapidly acquired more
power than the Dutch socialists were to possess for a long time
to come. It is somewhat paradoxical that in Belgium where the
organization, unity, support, and the policies of both the radical
and the socialist parties were so much more developed than in
the Netherlands, Catholic cabinets continued to rule the
country until well into the First World War, whereas in Holland
the progressive liberals were several times in power and by 1913
the socialists had a chance to take part in a radical government, a chance they deliberately refused to take. But the
paradox is easily explained. The Dutch right wing was relatively weak because it consisted of a Protestant and a Catholic
group and because the Catholics, suffering from their age-old
drawback of civil inferiority, only very slowly managed to win
the political influence their numerical strength warranted.

The Parti Ouvrier Belge (POB) was not a creation *ex nihilo*.
Since 1879 there had existed a Belgian Socialist party which
itself owed its existence to the amalgamation of the Flemish and
the Brabant (that is to say the Brussels) Socialist parties founded
in 1877. The problem of the Belgian socialist leaders was not
primarily to win support and attention but to unite the workers
in one vigorous organization. Much resistance had to be
overcome and innumerable differences reconciled as best they
could before the goal was attained. The Belgian Socialist party
failed in so far as the Walloons were concerned: the representatives of the most industrialized area in Belgium did
not join it. They kept loyally to the French socialist and
anarchist tradition of Fourier, Louis Blanc, Proudhon, and
even Blanqui and felt no affinity with the Flemish socialists
who had learned to follow German examples and adopted the
Gotha Programme (1875), which seemed acceptable to many

of Marx's followers although the master himself criticized it sharply in his private correspondence.[1] The Socialist party met with little success. Its agitation in favour of universal franchise found some support but when the party tried to impress itself on public opinion by organizing a mass demonstration in Brussels in 1880, no more than a thousand people took the trouble to turn up. In 1882 the Brussels worker Louis Bertrand (1856-1943) and De Paepe attempted to further the agitation for the extension of the franchise by uniting socialists and progressive liberals in a common effort, but this too failed.[2] All this proved two things. It was impossible to form a popular party that drew its inspiration and support from radical *and* socialist sources simultaneously, simply because the progressive liberals refused to sever their fruitful connection with the conservative wing of the party. But if, secondly, it was indeed necessary to form a new party consisting of members of one social class only and sure of the backing of a representative section of the workers, this had to base itself not only on the small, politically active groups but even more on the much broader trade union movement. Thus for a vigorous labour party to emerge, the unions and the other non-political organizations of the workers had to agree on political action and to accept a political programme with all the serious risks that entailed for each of their members individually.[3]

This is what happened in 1885. Many trade unions had adapted themselves to the new economic developments, to mechanization and the diminished demand for highly skilled workers. Now that they were prepared to behave as representatives of a class and fight for class-interests, they gradually abandoned the apolitical and exclusive mentality characteristic of the traditional guilds and came to recognize that their interests could be served by state intervention. This also explains why from about 1880 on many trade unions were founded with one major political aim: universal franchise. Numerically the whole movement was still small: in 1898 less

[1] Delsinne, *Parti ouvrier*, pp. 57 ff.

[2] Bertrand, *Histoire de la démocratie* ii. 354 ff.

[3] Maxime Sztejnberg, 'La Fondation du parti ouvrier belge et le ralliement de la classe ouvrière à l'action politique, 1882-1886', *International Review of Social History*, viii (1963), 198.

than 14,000 workers were members of the socialist trade unions.[1] At the congress of 5 and 6 April 1885, when it was decided to establish the Belgian Workers' party, 59 workers' associations were represented. Despite the opposition of the vigorous organization at Ghent, Flanders' industrial centre, the conference avoided the term 'socialist' in the name of the new party because it was hoped to win Catholic members. As a result of its federated structure, the support it found among the trade unions, and its financial dependence on the co-operatives —which developed in Belgium more impressively than anywhere else in Europe—by 1886 the Workers' party could act as the political organ of about 40,000 members belonging to 160 workers' associations of widely divergent character.[2] The demonstration in favour of universal franchise organized in 1886 was an enormous success compared with that of 1880: at least ten times as many people took part in it. Then it became apparent that the Walloons too were influenced by the propaganda of the Workers' party. It is true that the followers of Defuisseaux, whose pamphlet on universal franchise had played such a curious role in the revolt of 1886, founded a revolutionary party in 1887, which was in effect a Walloon party, with syndicalist and anarchist tendencies. But this collapsed the following year as a result of its own adventurous naïvety.

After that the unity of the party was not again seriously threatened by doctrinal disputes. Of course the Belgian socialists had their theorists, but after the death of De Paepe the party hardly sought inspiration from abstract and scholarly speculations. The works of G. de Greef and H. Denis, followers of Proudhon rather than Marx, were received with great respect by the comrades, but left unread. The party made little effort to accommodate the intellectuals. Even its daily Press—the newspapers *Vooruit* of 1884 in Ghent and *Le Peuple* of 1885 in Brussels—was controlled by the workers themselves. Its leaders were artisans. Eduard Anseele (1856–1938) who grew up in Flanders in a purely Flemish environment and who became in 1884 the director of the big co-operative Vooruit at Ghent, was trained as a typographer; his friend and colleague

---

[1] Delsinne, *Mouvement syndical*, p. 14. At this time the industrial proletariat may have numbered about 840,000 people as against 400,000 in 1846: J. Kruithof in Dhondt (ed.), *Geschiedenis*, pp. 54 ff., 199.

[2] Sztejnberg, loc. cit. 211.

in Brussels, the French-speaking Louis Bertrand, started as a marble worker. The enthusiasm of such men was controlled by practical considerations. Their ideals may have been 'Marxist' but they did not find it difficult to sacrifice the subtleties of theory for immediate gains, whenever these appeared to be within reach.[1] So strongly did this pragmatism and sober eclecticism permeate the mind of the party that it preserved its unity even in 1893 when a group of young anarchists vehemently opposed the party's leaders for, as it seemed to them, making the despised cause of universal franchise the sole aim of its policies.[2] Again during 1911 there were debates between the young left-wing Marxists and the old reformist core of the party[3] which might have led to a tension similar to that which in the Netherlands eventually brought about a split within the party. But in Belgium the party held together. The programme agreed to at the Congress of Quaregnon in 1894 was characteristic.[4] One finds no 'scientific' theses and arguments here as in the famous Erfurt Programme mainly drafted by Kautsky (1891), but a statement of some simple principles nicely combining Marxism and French socialism, an exhortation to moral improvement (which was very un-Marxist indeed), and a relatively short list of realistic and concrete demands: universal franchise, proportional representation, decentralization, compulsory education, etc. With its emphasis on the idealistic rather than the theoretical and the realistic rather than the doctrinal, the programme was typical of the spirit then prevailing in the party.

During the 1880s Dutch socialism lacked the broad basis and the security which the Belgian party got from the trade unions and co-operatives out of which it arose. In 1878 a socialist Association was founded in Amsterdam; in 1879 some other towns in the province of Holland followed suit, and in 1881 all these associations, each with only some tens of members,

[1] Of course they wrote a great deal. Anseele even wrote two novels in Flemish: cf. M. Oukhow, 'Socialistische belangstelling in de Vlaamse letterkunde', in Dhondt (ed.), *Geschiedenis*, p. 166.

[2] Destrée and Vandervelde, pp. 131 ff.

[3] Peter Dodge, *Beyond Marxism: the Faith and Works of Hendrik de Man* (The Hague, 1966), p. 34 and below, pp. 505–6.

[4] Delsinne, *Parti ouvrier*, pp. 95–100.

amalgamated as the Sociaal-Democratische Bond (SDB: the Social Democratic League). This adopted the slightly modified Gotha Programme—the co-operative ideal was eliminated and a paragraph about women's emancipation was added.[1] In 1879 the socialists launched a weekly paper which became a daily, *Recht voor Allen* (*Right for All*), which was made over to the SDB in 1884 by Ferdinand Domela Nieuwenhuis, whose private property it had originally been. The rise of Dutch socialism is inconceivable without Domela Nieuwenhuis. But it may well have been his fault that it failed in its early stages. This strange character made the development of the SDB possible, and if at the same time he hindered its development, this can only have been because socialism came too soon to the Netherlands. Industrialization in the Netherlands only became really significant some ten years after the founding of the SDB. In the 1880s socialism had no real function to fulfil. It was virtually restricted to a few towns in the province of Holland, notably Amsterdam, and to the province of Friesland which was severely hit by the agrarian crisis and less religious than any other region.[2] Socialism was a marginal phenomenon imported from abroad, interesting enough if studied in its local context and with due respect for the remarkable personalities who endorsed it, but essentially little more than that.

Domela Nieuwenhuis (1846–1919) was a well-to-do Lutheran minister so strongly influenced by theological modernism that he resigned his post and devoted all his energy and financial resources to the promotion of socialist ideals.[3] In many respects he was the very opposite of his senior fellow cleric in politics, Abraham Kuyper. Kuyper often seemed pompous and vain, professing the strictest orthodoxy, but he owed his formidable confidence to his talent for improvization and his suppleness. Domela Nieuwenhuis, on the other hand, gave the impression of being rigid, unoriginal, and suffering from a dangerous

[1] Vliegen, i. 32 ff.

[2] In 1889 1·46 per cent of the total Dutch population did not belong to any Church but in Friesland the percentage was 7·07 and in Amsterdam 1·70: J. P. Kruyt, *De onkerkelijkheid in Nederland* (Groningen, 1933), p. 61 and idem, *Het Nederlandse volkskarakter en het socialisme* (Arnhem, 1934), p. 67.

[3] Cf. J. Romein, 'Ferdinand Domela Nieuwenhuis, de apostel der arbeiders', *Erflaters van onze beschaving*, iv. 209–39 and Albert de Jong, *Ferdinand Domela Nieuwenhuis* (The Hague, 1966).

form of self-glorification. But compared with any other contemporary statesman in the Netherlands they were genuine
popular leaders, worshipped as prophets by their followers.
Gifted orators who neither dazzled their audience with the
baroque brilliance of their rhetoric like the Catholic leader
Schaepman, nor lectured didactically to them like the liberals,
they induced a kind of transcendence by their booming eloquence and their devotional style, whether Christian or
secularized. But whereas Kuyper wanted to win his battles and
enjoy his victories, Domela Nieuwenhuis sometimes seemed to
prefer to sacrifice himself to his ideals and to represent the
suffering Messiah of the nineteenth century. Kuyper aspired
to be an individual of genius; Domela Nieuwenhuis strove to be
the type of a certain species of great man and is usually described in the same familiar terms—a tall martyr's stature with
a Christ-like head, and eyes burning like coals. Kuyper's grim
pride enabled him to lead men and have his way in the human
community; Domela Nieuwenhuis egocentrically sought the
loneliness of sacrifice and had no close associates.

Even so the history of the SDB seemed to become the history
of his person and his convictions. Its history was full of contradictions. Until about 1885 the SDB was foremost in the
fight for universal franchise, which still appeared to be the
most attractive way towards total and revolutionary reform.
The utopian and eschatological character of the movement[1]
was not yet felt to be alien to this practical political aim. It
was fine for the small group of Dutch socialists—the SDB never
had much more than 5,000 members and *Recht voor Allen*
no more than 2,100 subscribers[2]—assembled in meeting-halls
and bare rooms to talk about the imminent revolution, which
would strike as suddenly as a flash of lightning and at once
bring the proletarians the prosperity, comfort, and spiritual
security of the bourgeoisie—for the illusion that the proletariat
was to create an entirely new and better form of life was not yet
cherished by any of them.

But universal franchise did not come and when it was clear
that it was not going to in the near future, the SDB was at a

---

[1] Rüter, *Spoorwegstakingen*, pp. 21 ff.
[2] The socialist newspaper from Ghent, *Vooruit*, sold 15,000 copies in 1884, the
Brussels *Le Peuple* 12,000.

loss: there was no way in which it could force its attention on Parliament; no plans had been made. Yet Domela Nieuwenhuis was elected to the Second Chamber in 1889. He remained a member until 1891, a totally isolated man whose eloquence had no effect whatever in this environment and whose interest in legislative business was as small as his talent for it. During the late 1880s anarchism reached the Dutch workers—later than in the rest of Europe and possibly introduced from Belgium.[1] Domela Nieuwenhuis himself, who after his election found himself increasingly involved in bitter international disputes over the party discipline and dogmatism of German social democracy, gradually began to turn towards anarchism too. It was already too late for the SDB to benefit from the trade union movement, gathering strength after 1888, which the League regarded with suspicion. Domela Nieuwenhuis's isolation became complete: by 1891 he was fighting against the Germans and their powerful organization, against the Frisian People's party, and against the Dutch trade unions. In 1893 *Recht voor Allen*[2] disparaged with grim arrogance both the electoral successes of the Germans and the general strike organized by the Belgians in the cause of universal franchise. It was clear that the SDB had detached itself from the international movement and had nothing to offer apart from violent, though certainly lucid, criticism of the parliamentary system and foreign party bureaucracy. In the early 1890s the bankruptcy of the Dutch progressive parties was total. Radicalism and the Frisian People's party were on the point of perishing; the SDB preserved the loyalty of Domela Nieuwenhuis's admirers, but failed to achieve anything. When a number of intellectuals together with some workers who had broken with Domela Nieuwenhuis founded a new party in 1894, the Sociaal-Democratische Arbeiderspartij (SDAP: Social Democratic Workers' party) this looked like a foolhardy gesture: only a few hundred members of the SDB went over to the SDAP.

But it is clear from what happened later that Domela Nieuwenhuis and his SDB had played their pioneering part with considerable effect. Domela may have failed as the charismatic

---

[1] The Flemish anarchist paper *De Opstand* (1881) was widely read in the Netherlands: Wansink, op. cit., p. 36.

[2] Vliegen, ii. 343.

leader and saviour, yet his influence was far from negligible and it would probably have been much more difficult for the Dutch workers to learn to believe in the possibility of improving their lot and of dynamic changes in society, if they had not listened to his propaganda. His funeral in 1919 was attended by many tens of thousands, expressing their gratitude and the vividness of their memories of his achievements. Moreover, there is no doubt that the socialist agitation for franchise reform in the early 1880s was largely responsible for impressing upon public opinion the fact that the regulations of 1848 could no longer be maintained. Indeed it is abundantly clear that it was the left-wing liberals, the radicals, and the socialists, and not the 'official' opposition of the religious parties, who did most to undermine the theses of the doctrinaire liberals. The 'clerical' opposition was far too cautious. It understandably avoided tackling the franchise problem for as long as possible. The growing Roman Catholic and Protestant parties brought together all sorts of men who had little in common apart from their religion, and those conceptions stemming directly from their religions concerned morality rather than the general problems of democracy. In spite of the most industrious attempts to formulate either a Catholic or a Protestant doctrine regarding the franchise, it proved impossible. There was so much discussion and so little agreement among the members of the religious parties themselves about compulsory education, military service, progressive income tax, social insurance, and similar matters that a clear party programme seemed out of the question.

Yet it was probably wrong to consider the religious parties as unnatural phenomena, as the Dutch liberals and radicals often did. It is of course true that the religious parties were held together mainly by their fight for viable free schools, but it should not be forgotten that this represented only one facet, albeit a major one, of a more general principle which was not without political importance: their refusal to subordinate society to the state. In this period the real significance of 'religious' policies lay in the attempt to maintain between society and state intermediary organisms through which state power should be filtered before penetrating into society itself. If there is, in the late nineteenth century, a fundamental difference between the Left, whether liberal, radical, or socialist, and the Right, whether Roman Catholic or Protestant, it is this. The liberals wanted direct state authority over society in so far as it was necessary—and they held widely divergent views about how far it was—with the risk of increasingly subordinating society to state. Once the state, mainly as a result of liberal initiatives, had built an infrastructure—from railways and canals to primary and secondary education—facilitating economic growth and social mobility, it was possible to apply state intervention in social life still more directly, primarily to eliminate such abuses as child labour and later to prevent them from occurring again and to protect the workers by social legislation.[1] The Right, at last clearly recognizing the direction of events, accepted state intervention but sought at the same time to organize society so that it could offer some resistance to the centralized power, and hold its own in the face of constantly changing governments. When they were in power it was their policy to use the state itself for this purpose. The state must not only allow social organizations to develop freely but actually pay to make them viable. In Belgium this was called *liberté subsidiée*;[2] in the Netherlands the Christian democrats spoke of 'social decentralization'.[3] Although in the course of the years the principles may have become emaciated, they had their effect and helped to prevent the process, defined by sociologists as the 'osmosis' of state and society, from leading to a complete state monopoly.

It is of course evident that the liberals never deliberately wished to make the state dominant in all spheres of social life and when large co-ordinated social organizations developed in the Netherlands—whether big business, political parties, or trade unions—which could serve as counterweights to the central power, they supported them. But in the 1880s and 1890s the whole problem was essentially different from that which arose after the First World War. Only two questions mattered: education and social legislation to mitigate proletarian misery.

---

[1] The phases of state intervention in the Netherlands are intelligently analysed by P. E. Kraemer, *The Societal State. The Modern Osmosis of State and Society as presenting itself in the Netherlands in particular* (Meppel, 1966), pp. 51 ff.

[2] Chlepner, *Cent ans*, pp. 192 ff.

[3] Cf. W. H. Vermeulen, *Schets eener parlementaire geschiedenis van Nederland door W. J. van Welderen Rengers*, iii: *1901–1914* (The Hague, 1950), p. 80.

The liberals had no free schools and no philanthropic institutions. Nor had the socialists. If the state were to act in these fields it could only do so by direct intervention or through social institutions which were almost exclusively Roman Catholic or Protestant. In Belgium the policies of the religious parties were put into effect more consistently than in the Netherlands, where the Protestants, even those who belonged to the democratic wing of the anti-revolutionaries, did not fear the power of the state to the same extent as the Belgian Catholics. And in the Netherlands it was the Protestants who determined the policies of the religious parties. But being accustomed to regarding Dutch history and the Dutch state as essentially Protestant, they were prepared to allow the state greater responsibilities than the Belgian Catholics who in the long history of Belgian suppression had learned to keep the foreign regimes of pre-revolutionary times at a distance, as well as the liberal anticlerical regimes of their compatriots. Thus the Dutch system of social insurance, partly introduced by the Protestant party, was eventually more *étatist* than the Catholic system in Belgium.

4. *Dutch Domestic Policy, 1887–1896*

Although it was therefore possible, at least during these decades, to create a politically relevant distinction between the Right and the Left, the religious parties did not offer fundamental opposition to the ideas on the franchise put forward by left-wing liberals. The question was tackled first in the Netherlands, and in 1887 the constitution of 1848 was revised in such a way as to make a considerable extension of the suffrage possible. This happened after long years of hesitation and fruitless discussion and in fact the achievement of 1887 was entirely negative: the franchise of 1848 based on the *cens* was eliminated but universal franchise was explicitly refused. All men at the age of twenty-three were given the vote provided they could show some 'signs of capability and prosperity', and these signs were to be defined in a new electoral law. This meant that Parliament could, if it wanted, virtually bring about universal franchise by requiring the minimum of capability and prosperity. But straightforward universal franchise—as well as women's suffrage—was made dependent on the laborious and complicated procedure of yet another revision of the constitution. The constitution of 1887 was in fact intended as an obstacle to universal franchise rather than an alternative to it. Obviously it was impossible to conceive of a realistic as well as theoretically sound alternative at all and the only thing its opponents were able to do was to delay for as long as possible a development they recognized as inevitable.

How strong the desire to slow down the process was—a desire not altogether surprising in view of the absurdly inflated expectations of the champions of universal franchise— became apparent when an attempt was made to draft an electoral bill on the basis of the new articles in the constitution. It took nine years before the matter was settled. But something of direct practical importance was achieved in 1887. The Prime Minister, J. Heemskerk Azn (1818–97), might be called a conservative had he not served as Minister of the interior in the Cabinet which in 1866 and 1867 failed not only to carry through its anti-liberal policies but also to make clear what, if anything, it understood by conservative policies. In 1887 he managed to bring about the revision of the constitution with the help of his juristic knowledge and the tactful concessions by which he created a compromise acceptable to both Left and Right. Thus he persuaded Parliament to agree on three difficult points: on the fact that those liberals who claimed that the constitution of 1848 forbade the state to subsidize free schools[1] were wrong, that it was necessary to extend the franchise, and that it was necessary to make provisional arrangements for extending the vote even before a new electoral bill was accepted and put into operation. The electorate grew from 122,000 to more than 292,000 men, that is from about 6·4 per cent of the adult population to about 13·9 per cent. As had been expected, the elections of 1888 turned out to be a success for the religious parties who found support among the now partly enfranchised lower middle classes. The orthodox

---

[1] The anti-revolutionaries and Roman Catholics had refused to support any revision of the constitution unless their educational demands were met. However, it was impossible to revise the articles which were devoted to education in the constitution of 1848 in a way satisfactory to all parties. Finally, the liberals gave up their view that the 1848 constitution forbade subsidizing free schools; consequently, the relevant articles could be left as they were.

Protestants won 16, the Catholics 6 seats (in a Chamber with only 100 seats), and as they had together a small majority (54 seats) they were in honour bound to form a Cabinet. They succeeded in doing so although it was far from easy to find among them men both prepared and able to assume the responsibilities of government.[1]

This was the first Cabinet formed by what came to be known in Dutch history simply as 'the coalition', that is the coalition of anti-revolutionaries and Roman Catholics. In this government the ascendancy of the Protestants was still overwhelming. Yet the idea that Catholics and Protestants should collaborate in politics to drive the liberals out of power was first put forward by the Catholics.[2] The priest H. J. A. M. Schaepman (1844–1903) in particular saw this as the best way of making Catholics, still politically unorganized and insecure, formulate their aspirations more coherently. Moreover, only Catholic help could provide the religious parties both in the elections and in the Chamber with the numerical strength that the anti-revolutionaries as well as the Catholics needed in order to satisfy themselves on the school problem. Thus political necessity and the fundamental similarity of the developing Protestant and Roman Catholic Christian democrat parties made possible what theologically still seemed monstrous. That the coalition had no ecumenical corollaries was shown by the anti-popish polemics of Kuyper and the no less energetic anti-Protestant polemics of Schaepman. These two unnatural allies were well matched. Schaepman was a less original though more versatile man than Kuyper, but equally dominating and with the same bizarre style of expression. He was a most formidable publicist and a poet whose reputation was perhaps too cruelly wrecked by Willem Kloos in a characteristically witty *Nieuwe Gids* review of one of the priest's most ambitious epics.[3] He was an indefatigable agitator and initiator quite undisturbed by doubt, his emotions as exuberant as they were conventional. He could never stop thundering about his profound love for papal Rome and for his cherished Holland.

Schaepman was elected to the Second Chamber in 1880 and

---

[1] A. Goslinga, 'Het kabinet Mackay', *Antirevolutionaire Staatkunde* (1935), p. 6.
[2] J. Witlox, *Schaepman als staatsman* (3 vols., Amsterdam, 1960), i. 94; ii. 113 ff.
[3] *De Nieuwe Gids*, II. i (1887), 316 ff.

he was the first priest to appear in the Dutch Parliament. It soon became clear that he was somewhat isolated among the other Catholic members, who did not hold very firm opinions and were generally prepared to approve of right-wing liberal policies provided they were cautious and not anticlerical. In 1883 Schaepman made his first attempt to draft a Roman Catholic programme on the basis of which a real Catholic party might be built up. The programme itself was insignificant;[1] its importance was to show how determined Schaepman was to provide the Catholics with a political organization of their own. To begin with he met with no success. The small upper stratum of the Roman Catholic population which occupied itself with politics was very conservative; such people felt no need to challenge their compatriots with anti-liberal or anti-Protestant polemics, simply wanting the Catholics to live peacefully and quietly as they had always done. What could the Catholic upper middle classes hope to gain by calling attention to themselves? After a time Schaepman came to accept a number of Kuyper's democratic opinions. He wanted to extend the franchise, was prepared to abolish the practice that allowed young men to pay a substitute to do their military service for them, became a champion of social legislation—he attended the Catholic social congresses in Belgium and undoubtedly learned a lot there[2]—and even joined the left-wing liberals in their fight for compulsory education. But he met with furious opposition from his well-to-do co-religionists. The merchants from the province of Holland and the industrialists from Limburg and Brabant—who possessed much influence and helped the Church and its poor-relief funds financially[3]—the Catholic daily Press, and especially the priests and the bishops were against him. Yet he won: notwithstanding temporary setbacks the coalition established by him in 1888 survived and when in 1897 representatives of nearly all Catholic electoral associations accepted a programme based upon *Rerum Novarum* and drawn up by Schaepman in

[1] It is printed by Witlox, *Schaepman* i. 277–9. In fact it is no more than a very conservative interpretation of some themes of Kuyper's *Ons program* (1878). In 1878, however, Schaepman bitterly criticized Kuyper's programme: Witlox, i. 258.

[2] Jos. van Wely, *Schaepman* (Bussum, 1952), pp. 405, 457 ff.

[3] Rogier, *Katholieke herleving*, p. 296.

collaboration with his colleagues in the Second Chamber, it was clear that even if a Catholic party did not yet exist it was nevertheless possible to formulate a political programme that could be claimed as typically Catholic (but that—as was emphatically stated—had to further national unity as led and symbolized by the Protestant Orange dynasty!). In fact there was no alternative. What else could the Catholics do but unite in a political party, once the orthodox Protestants had done so? Even the Belgian Catholics had been unable to avoid it.

The coalition Cabinet of 1888 produced a new Education Act (1889) by which the free schools were allowed to pass on one-third of their costs to the state. This was an extremely important gain, especially when compared with the situation in 1878. Although the free schools were still subject to exactly the same regulations as the public schools, with regard to the quality of the teachers and the buildings, there was no longer any question of making it virtually impossible for them to meet the requirements, as was the case in 1878, and the state lost in consequence its best resource for keeping the mass of the population out of the clutches of the dogmatic Churches. The liberals resigned themselves to defeat in this matter. During the next few years the socialists too accepted the new system, primarily no doubt because they gave priority to social questions and did not want the school war to be resumed, but also because they had learned, like the progressive liberals, that it was time to abandon the intellectualism of 1878. There is a subtle and seldom recognized relationship between accepting free education as the equal of state education and accepting the need for universal franchise, for in both cases it means discarding the rigid system according to which the aim of education is the development of rational and independent thought, and the condition for taking part in government is the capacity to form a rational and independent opinion. In Dutch history the facts clearly show this connection: in 1917 the constitution was revised with the dual purpose of making as much money available to the free schools as was needed by the state schools, and of introducing universal male suffrage.

The coalition Cabinet introduced another bill of fundamental importance. The Labour Act of 1889, based on material col-

lected by a committee of inquiry set up in 1886 on the initiative
of left-wing liberals, was the first piece of social legislation
since the Child Labour Act of 1874. It was mainly concerned
with female and child labour. It cannot be a coincidence that
the Dutch committee which the government was asked to
appoint in August 1886 exactly paralleled a committee the
Belgian Government had decided to nominate in April 1886,
after the terrible spring riots. In Holland the results were seen
in the act of May 1889, in Belgium in that of December 1889.
The Dutch bill was a little more radical but both were essentially the same. The purpose was to prevent exploitation of
those categories of workers who were unable to protect themselves.[1] In the Belgian Chamber only a few of the liberals
upheld the doctrine of state non-interference and voted against
the bill; in the Netherlands no member of Parliament did so.[2]
It would seem that in both countries there was a measure of
agreement between the parties after the outbursts of despair
in 1886 that something had to be done to make life more
endurable for the proletariat and that only social legislation
could do it. But there was no attempt yet to eliminate the
fundamental abuses of the capitalist system most harmful to
the workers.

It is remarkable that after the wild agitation of the early
1880s the revision of the Dutch constitution in 1887 was regarded by the people with indifference. The noisy propaganda
of the anti-revolutionaries during the elections of 1888 aroused
more interest; the education and labour bills awoke few
passions outside Parliament. Yet the coalition Cabinet perished
in public tumult nevertheless, the vital issue proving to be the
question of military service. Kuyper firmly opposed the system
which made it possible for a young man chosen by lot for
military service—not all those available each year were needed
—to pay for a substitute. It was calculated that in the Netherlands about 18 per cent of the conscripts took a substitute—

---

[1] In both countries it was forbidden to employ children under twelve years in
factories. In the Netherlands several measures were taken to protect children from
twelve to sixteen years and women. In Belgium women older than twenty-one
were left unprotected. The working day for these protected groups was fixed at
eleven hours in the Netherlands and twelve hours in Belgium.

[2] Only Domela Nieuwenhuis rejected the bill which he considered totally
inadequate.

if this is correct it is a smaller proportion than in Belgium, where 25 per cent seems to have been normal. When the coalition Cabinet had been set up Schaepman had expected to be able to fall in with Kuyper's wishes. Thus it was by no means unexpected when the Catholic Minister of War, a professional soldier, proposed to abolish the system. Yet this led to insuperable difficulties. It became apparent that Schaepman had totally misjudged the attitude of his co-religionists. Catholic resistance to a measure which was praised as just from the social point of view and favourable from the military one—the army would improve qualitatively and cease being an army of the poor, the proletarians, and the illiterate—was so sharp and stubborn that the Cabinet lost its prestige, as well as the elections of 1891, and resigned.

As in Belgium defence was the object of interminable and extremely confused discussion in the Netherlands. It was of course true that the substitute system was characteristic of bourgeois rule and it was undoubtedly illogical; if it is every citizen's duty to defend his fatherland by what principle can he be allowed to buy his way out? What confused the issue, however, was that the radicals and socialists who attacked this plutocratic privilege most vehemently, acclaiming the virtue of personal service, also emphatically rejected what they called militarism. The Dutch Roman Catholics, on the other hand, like their Belgian co-religionists and no doubt under their influence,[1] opposed personal service as the most monstrous form of militarism—and not entirely without justification. Moreover, they refused to admit that it benefited only the rich. Belgians and Dutch were busily engaged in collecting figures and statistics to show that many different categories, artisans, shopkeepers, farmers, and others who needed their sons in their own businesses, were perfectly able and willing to buy them out of military service.[2] Whatever the merit of these different points of view, the remarkable thing is that this problem, which more than any other seemed to bring to the surface the real distinction between democratic and non-democratic conceptions, involved both the Left and the Right in irreconcilable inner contradictions. Only Kuyper gives the

---

[1] Witlox, *Schaepman* ii. 302.
[2] Ibid. 266; Wanty, *Milieu militaire belge*, p. 124.

impression of being consistent. His admiration for Germany and for brave manly vigour betrays a form of militarism, whilst his democratic sentiment and his aversion to what he stigmatized as plutocratic materialism led him to argue that boys from the upper middle classes should also enjoy the blessings of military duty and military discipline. However, he did not carry the day. After the Belgian Parliament rejected personal service in 1887, the Dutch one too proved to be not yet ready for it in 1891. But in nearly all continental countries apart from the Turkish Empire some form of personal service existed and the two small parliamentary monarchies were unlikely to be able to continue their opposition to it indefinitely. Indeed the possibility of taking a substitute was abolished in 1901 in the Netherlands and in 1909 in Belgium. This may have been a triumph for democracy but obviously the problem of defending small countries in a world ruled by the mass armies of Great Powers could not be solved simply by imitating them.

In 1891 the coalition Cabinet resigned after an election defeat which reduced the total number of anti-revolutionary and Roman Catholic seats from 54 to 45. Then the liberals once again took power and kept it until 1901. This was their last decade of undivided responsibility. It was very fruitful but it put an end to liberal supremacy. The paradox of the period is that by solving the problems of the franchise and military service at least provisionally, the liberals provided their Catholic and Protestant opponents with the means of restoring their own unity. After the liberals had eliminated the questions about which the coalition had been so deeply divided, the 'religious' parties seized power again and it turned out to be their interests that the liberals had served. Moreover, the liberals themselves were far from united. In their camp too there were progressives and conservatives, radicals and cautious men who disagreed about the pace of reform. Under the circumstances liberals showed courage and sometimes recklessness in venturing upon a policy of reform which the 'religious' parties carefully tried to avoid. It proved fatal to them.

The last liberal decade may be divided into three periods: the character of the first Cabinet (1891–4) was radical, that of the second (1894–7) more conservative; the third Cabinet (1897–1901), the best and most productive, was radical again.

The major achievement of the early 1890s was the reform of the tax system which dated from 1806 and had been only partially revised since. It was more or less taken for granted that it was unjust and indefensible, and for twenty years or so hardly anybody had dared to repeat the traditional theories that had once been used to prove that income tax was wrong.[1] No party in practice, however, had ever been strong enough or had vision enough actually to introduce income tax, although the matter had been endlessly discussed. The main objections to the existing system were obvious. Firstly, its excises and licence fees interfered with economic life in a totally arbitrary fashion; but secondly, it was inordinately hard on the poor because nearly half of the national and municipal tax yield was still drawn from excises and import duties on foodstuffs and other primary necessities.[2] Furthermore, although it was no longer possible to depend upon East Indian profits the system was much too rigid to produce the extra money the state needed to meet its growing responsibilities.[3] In 1892 and 1893 N. G. Pierson, the Minister of Finance, succeeded in bringing about some important modifications. Pierson (1839–1909) was an interesting figure, a self-taught man whose splendid career as a banker led him to become president of the Netherlands Bank in 1885. But he was perhaps even more distinguished as a scholar whose numerous works on economics and colonial matters were long considered classics because of their clarity and elegant style; they were also much appreciated abroad. Pierson hesitated a long time before agreeing to enter active politics with a view to revising the tax system. Ethical motives finally decided him to accept the task, for he was convinced that the system should not only be technically improved, but made more just and fair.

Pierson belonged to the left wing of his party. As an economist he felt an affinity with the Austrian school but he also

[1] A. C. J. de Vrankrijker, *Belastingen in Nederland, 1848–1893* (Haarlem, 1967), p. 108.

[2] The lowest classes of the population paid in 1823 37 per cent of the taxes, in 1848 40 per cent, in 1886 36 per cent. Cf. W. P. J. Bok, *De belastingen in het Nederlandsche Parlement van 1848–1888* (2 vols., Haarlem, 1888–95), i. 161.

[3] See above, pp. 270 ff. and Van Tienhoven's report printed by C. W. de Vries, *Schets eener parlementaire geschiedenis van Nederland door W. J. van Welderen Rengers*, ii: *1891–1901* (The Hague, 1948), p. 77.

appreciated the work and influence of the German academic socialist, Adolf Wagner. His eclecticism and the peculiarity of the Dutch situation kept him relatively independent. In one fundamental respect he opposed Wagner: according to Pierson taxation must not be used by the state as a leveller, forcibly to reduce financial inequalities between its subjects.[1] Probably most of his political associates shared his views on this matter.[2] The Dutch reformers were not attracted by the conservative and *étatist* elements in the social theory of the German academics, although their theories in general made a profound impression upon them. However radical their policy might be, it nevertheless remained liberal, and if they wanted taxes to be more 'just' this certainly did not mean that they hoped to reform society by fiscal legislation. Pierson's proposals were consistent with his starting-point. He did in fact succeed in moving part of the tax load from the poorer to the richer classes. He abolished the duties on salt and reduced those on soap, land, and mortgages. Instead of these he introduced a moderate progressive tax on income from private capital and a second one on income from business and other sources. This was an important step. Yet consumption taxes still predominated in the new system. In the 1890s income tax produced only 9 per cent of the total tax yield and by 1914 it was still no more than 13 per cent. Moreover, as capital itself was not taxed, as death duties remained low, and the progression in income tax was extremely gradual, the new system did nothing to prevent the building-up of capital or to reduce social inequality.[3]

Pierson was unable fully to develop his policy as he intended because the Cabinet ran into such opposition to its plans for franchise reform that it was obliged to resign in 1894. In September 1892 the Minister of the Interior, J. P. R. Tak van Poortvliet (1839–1904), introduced a bill that interpreted the constitutional articles of 1887 in so broad a sense that it gave the impression that he was virtually setting them aside. He wanted all men to be admitted to the franchise, apart from the illiterate

[1] De Vrankrijker, op. cit., p. 137.

[2] See also P. W. A. Cort van der Linden, *Richting en beleid der Liberale Partij* (Groningen, 1886), pp. 119 ff.

[3] De Jonge, *De industrialisatie in Nederland tussen 1850 en 1914*, pp. 315 ff. From 1851 to 1900 the total tax yield rose from 18·52 to 24·65 guilders per head, direct taxes from 6·18 to 6·70: Vermeulen, *Schets*, p. 17.

and those who received poor-relief, and he rejected the positive 'signs of capability and prosperity' required by the 1887 constitution. There can be little doubt that the opposition was right in accusing him of trying, albeit with some rather impracticable reservations,[1] to introduce the universal franchise that the constitution of 1887 had specifically rejected.[2] In June 1893 the debate on the bill opened in the Second Chamber. The opposition at once launched its attack under the leadership of S. van Houten, the most progressive liberal of the early 1870s, whose support for Pierson's tax reform had been indispensable. It soon became apparent that there were many in all parties who did not want to go as far as Tak—liberals, most of the Roman Catholics, and some anti-revolutionaries. When Tak saw that his bill had no chance of being accepted he modified it, and in 1894 declared that only those who had a fixed address and lived in a house should get the vote. The opposition was satisfied, for this stipulation was regarded as providing a sufficient 'sign of prosperity', and Tak's former principle that the vote belonged to every man unless there was a special reason for depriving him of it had obviously been abandoned. Yet the discussion on the correct definition of a home led to Tak's fall. When the Second Chamber agreed to a naïve amendment in which a one-room flat was not accepted as a sign of prosperity—the amendment would exclude many thousands of young working men from the franchise—Tak had had enough. The Queen Regent—Queen Emma, the very popular widow of the very unpopular William III, who acted as regent for her daughter, Wilhelmina, from 1890 to 1898—dissolved Parliament. But the elections turned out unfavourably for Tak: his followers among the liberals and in the other parties were in a minority and the Cabinet resigned.

In the new Cabinet Van Houten was effectively though not formally the leader. It was of course a liberal Cabinet, for the liberals as such had certainly not lost the elections and their 59 seats out of 100 constituted a relatively comfortable majority. But only about twenty-five members of the liberal faction belonged to the right wing on which Van Houten depended,

[1] People were expected to apply for electorship and to submit to an examination in the art of writing.
[2] De Vries, Schets ii. 58 ff.

with the result that he had to rely on the support of the Roman Catholics, most of whom had opposed Tak's bill, and the anti-revolutionaries, who were sharply divided. Abraham Kuyper was the leader of the democratic, 'Takkian' element in the party. His influence, however, was contested by A. F. de Savornin Lohman (1837–1924), a patrician, a jurist of author-ity, perhaps better suited than Kuyper to the work of a Parlia-ment still inclined to think in terms of law rather than of politics. He continued the aristocratic tradition of Calvinist politics which stemmed from the Réveil period and was widely respected for doing so, but he lacked (and personally distrusted) Kuyper's genius as an orator and his intellectual fertility. The Cabinet restricted itself mainly to the franchise problem. In 1896 Van Houten presented his solution. It was a highly complicated arrangement in which taxes, rateable value, the size of one's superannuation, wages, savings, the quality of one's diplomas, and many other items were used to distinguish those capable of voting rationally and independently from those who were not. This elaborate compromise was accepted by the Second Chamber although it obviously made sense only as a transitional measure. Nobody really knew how many voters it would produce but there was no doubt that it would be less generous than Tak's bill. In fact in 1890 the number of voters was 295,570, in 1900 it was 569,768, and in 1910 854,539—showing an increase from 13·9 per cent to 23·5 per cent to 30·7 per cent of the total adult population, figures which demonstrate that Van Houten's act was very cautious as well as very flexible. One thing was clear: it was viable only so long as the left-wing groups in the Netherlands remained in the state of confusion and decline in which they found themselves in the early 1890s. It was possible to defend Van Houten's electoral bill as the consequence of radical debility, but nobody could claim that it was a coherent system with a purpose or future of its own.

5. *Belgian Domestic Policy, 1884–1893*

It is no accident that the franchise reform in Belgium was accomplished somewhat later than in Holland nor that on the surface it was more radical (although it was possibly less so in effect). There was more opposition to it; the Belgian progressive liberals, however, were more vigorous and better organized. The Catholic party did not adopt a firm point of view and finally gave in to the pressure of public opinion as well as to its own left wing, and it was on the Roman Catholics that decisions depended. The Catholics came to power in 1884. The liberal regime had ended in a desperate fight with the Church. Although the Vatican warned the Belgian bishops against reacting too vehemently to the liberal School Act of 1879 this did not prevent them from totally breaking with the government. The liberals also refused to make concessions. They sometimes used rather underhand tricks in an attempt to make the clergy see reason, for instance withdrawing several forms of financial state support from the Church whilst continuing to build expensive state schools which, especially in Flanders, remained empty. For the parents sent their children to the hastily improvised Roman Catholic schools: in 1879 379,000 children attended free primary schools; in 1882 the number had risen to 622,000. In 1884 the electors had the opportunity to present their own opinions: as was required by the Belgian constitution half of the members of the Chamber of Deputies resigned, 69 in all among whom were 29 liberals. The verdict was clear. In the new Chamber the liberals had only 52 seats as against 79 in the old one, whereas the Roman Catholics, winning 11 seats, now had 70. Apart from this 16 Independents were elected and joined the Catholic ranks, giving them in consequence a majority of 33 seats. 'This is not a defeat', wrote Frère-Orban, 'this is a disaster'.[1]

In fact the decisive vote came from the Brussels constituencies, represented by sixteen members, which usually voted liberal but this time elected the Independents. If this had not happened, the Catholic majority would have been only two, not enough for them to form a stable government. The Independent party had been growing since 1879 in the Brussels constituencies as an expression of distrust of the ruling liberals. Roman Catholic leaders were quick to realize the importance of the phenomenon and soon attempted to organize the movement.

[1] Th. Luykx, *Politieke geschiedenis van België van 1789 tot heden* (2nd edn., Brussels, 1969), p. 179 n. 10.

At the 1884 elections they supported the Independent candidates with vigour and great effect. The Independents had no political system; indeed they could probably be called apolitical. Among their sixteen candidates were only three barristers —most political professionals in Belgium started their career as advocates; many of the others were established business men, moderate Catholics who stood for 'local and material interests', for cheap government, and were disgusted by the hysterical, ideological dissensions, for which they blamed the extremism and the democratic excesses of the progressive liberals. The slogans with which they defeated the liberals and totally changed the political situation were national unity, impartiality, and some modification of the Education Act (not its abolition as the Catholic party wanted).[1] From 1884 to 1917 all cabinets were solidly Roman Catholic.

In the long run the Roman Catholic party undoubtedly benefited from the schools conflict. Before 1879 the party was deeply divided between two radically hostile groups. The so-called liberal Catholics wished to preserve the tradition of 1830. They thought that Catholic interests were safest in the hands of a party that did not seek support among the masses of the people nor among the clergy and episcopacy but, as a cautious representative of the great landowners and sections of the higher bourgeoisie, calmly sought to realize parliamentary compromises with the moderate liberals. They were led by the Catholic members of Parliament who wanted to be free and independent of the voice of the people or the dogmatic pronouncements of the bishops. However, their comfortable opinions were vehemently attacked by the ultramontanes, who were only too anxious to fight. Their political ideals were simple enough: the state ought to become Catholic again and subordinate itself to Church authority. But by about 1880 it was clear that political ultramontanism had dismally failed. Pius IX died in 1878, and Leo XIII, his successor, rejected it. In 1881 Périn, its seriously compromised Belgian theorist, resigned from his chair at Louvain University. It was now possible to reconcile the embittered and exhausted groups, and not only was it possible it was realized to be urgent. The

[1] Massia Gruman, 'Origines et naissance du parti indépendant (1879–1884)', Cahiers bruxellois, ix (1964), 87–171.

liberal attack on the Catholic popular school reaffirmed Catholic unity.

This, however, was not a complete victory for the liberal Catholics. It is true that political ultramontanism disappeared and the illusion that a Catholic state would re-emerge went up in smoke. But the ultramontanes' hope that the Catholic party would take deep root in the solidly organized masses of the people, establish close links with the episcopacy, and develop a more or less clear programme especially in relation to the social problem, did not disappear. In the course of the schools conflict the strength of their idealism became apparent. The federation of Catholic groups in 1868, which was liberal-Catholic and covered a number of associations devoted to religious, social, or educational work or simply serving as clubs, united in 1883 with the equally liberal-Catholic Federation of the Constitutional and Conservative Associations which had often acted as electoral organizations. The school war, on the other hand, produced a Union nationale pour le redressement des griefs which was in effect a continuation of an organization founded by Périn.[1] This in its turn absorbed a federation of workers' associations dating from 1867 and started to collaborate with the liberal-Catholic associations. In 1884 one might regard the Catholic party as a popular party of which the hundreds of local associations served as subsections, each with its particular purpose and derived from its own special circumstances and needs. The clergy exercised great influence on the whole edifice. It was no longer possible for the Catholic faction in Parliament to deny that there was now a Catholic party which had to be taken into account and whose policies had to be defended.[2]

However, it was as yet far from clear what these policies actually were. It was not long after the glorious victory of 1884 before the party's divisions and uncertainties became manifest, despite the reconciliation effected between liberal-Catholics and ultramontanes. A new opposition to the conservative character of traditional Catholic policies sprang up which, although the ground for it had been prepared by the ultra-

[1] Van Isacker, *Werkelijk en wettelijk land*, p. 238.
[2] Simon, *Parti catholique*, pp. 106 ff. and Guyot de Mishaegen, *Parti catholique*, pp. 138 ff., 175 ff.

montanes of the previous generation, tended to be more worldly and more strongly influenced by social motives. It was the Christian democracy of a Catholicism now called social. Whereas Périn's ultramontanism of the 1860s and 1870s was hostile to everything modern, the social Catholicism of the 1880s and 1890s wanted to use and absorb modern culture. Social Catholicism adopted a slightly dandyish appearance; it was up to date, not only democratic and deeply interested in social questions but also nationalistic, imperialistic, and sometimes even militaristic[1]—entirely in the style of Abraham Kuyper who represented its Protestant variant. Henry Carton de Wiart (1869–1951), who came from a noble family and was elected to the Chamber in 1896, was one of the leading personalities in the history of Belgian Christian democracy. He was one of the young men who had trained as barristers under Edmond Picard and felt that they belonged to the intellectual and political *avant-garde*. He defended the new literature against the worthy citizens who were horrified by its modernism. In 1891 he and some of his friends founded *L'Avenir social*, a periodical which although short-lived greatly stimulated the growth of social thought among the Catholics.

The Belgian social Catholics were no more successful than their counterparts in the Netherlands, the Protestant Christian democrats, in formulating a really coherent system. Yet it would be wrong to regard their doctrines as only a hasty and somewhat frightened response to socialist theories.[2] No doubt there was this element too and it was not without significance: they familiarized the numerous and powerful conservatives in the Roman Catholic party with the idea of a state in continuous development, increasingly interfering with society. But essentially Christian democratic ideas expressed the desire of a young generation not only to reconcile its traditional beliefs with the modern world but also to work positively and creatively in that world because of its religion. The enthusiasm of these men was constructive even if their starting-point was negative: neither modern society with its atrocious injustice nor socialist ideals satisfied Catholic norms. But how was one to

---

[1] For a vivid description see Henry Carton de Wiart, *Souvenirs politiques (1878–1918)* (Brussels, 1948).

[2] Cf. Rezsohazy, *Origines et formation du catholicisme social en Belgique*.

build up a new society on the basis of a purified form of capitalism without resorting to revolution and without abandoning the
axiom of natural law that private property and social inequality are justifiable?[1] During the 1880s the Belgian Christian
democrats still remained loyal to the hope imported from
France and cherished by the ultramontanes that the ancient
guilds might be re-established. In various ways idealists experimented with the forms of a corporative society. People
of goodwill and sharp intelligence applied much energy in
attempting to cope with social abuses in such a way, and in his
encyclical *Rerum Novarum* of 1891 Pope Leo XIII still recommended it as the Christian solution of the workers' problem.[2]
However, *Rerum Novarum* also intimated that although the
Pope did not particularly favour it himself it might be useful
to organize Roman Catholic trade unions.[3] This was sufficient
reason for some Christian democrats to abandon their corporative illusions and to devote themselves to building up
Catholic trade unions which, unlike the guilds, excluded
employers and fought for the interests of the workers alone.

The party's unity was broken not only by sometimes bitter
discussions about the aims of social Catholicism but also by
disagreement over the franchise. There was of course a link
between the two matters. The corporatists argued that in a
society divided into interest groups universal franchise would
lead to a national Parliament representative not of individuals
but of social interests. In other words, in Roman Catholic
circles as well there were those who accepted a drastic extension of the franchise as long as the nature of Parliament
itself was modified. But once it became apparent that such a
modification was unrealizable,[4] the idea of extending the franchise turned out to be less abhorrent to the conservatives than
it had been in the past. Looking back on the fervent enthusiasm
of the young Christian democrats one may well ask if the
results were not disappointingly pedestrian. Did they not
return to the old track of cautious and moderate reform, after

---

[1] Victor Brants, *La Lutte pour le pain quotidien. Précis des leçons d'économie politique*
(Paris, 1885), pp. 18, 40, and *passim*. Brants was Périn's successor at Louvain
University.

[2] K. van Isacker, *Averechtse democratie. De Gilden en de Christelijke democratie in
België, 1875–1914* (Antwerp, 1959), p. 43 and *passim*.

[3] Ibid., p. 71.   [4] Ibid., p. 95.

their fruitless but brave attempts to mitigate the individualistic excesses of modern society by establishing organic connections between people and an organic responsibility for their lot? Of course this is true. On the other hand, not only Christian democracy but socialism too underwent the same experience. Socialism had to adapt itself to the structure of contemporary society. Although neither Left nor Right altogether lost the idealism of the 1880s both resigned themselves to the more matter-of-fact and more prosperous reality of the 1890s, by recognizing that individualistic society could be improved but not overthrown.

The first Catholic Cabinet after the victory of 1884 produced within a couple of weeks an education bill which was immediately accepted by Parliament. The Catholics released the schools from centralized control. Once again they were brought under the control of the municipalities, which were free to adopt or to subsidize free Roman Catholic schools. Both with regard to methods and curriculum the state refused to give binding directions and the local authorities thus acquired the liberties that were vital components of the Catholic system of decentralization. The state also relinquished most of its responsibility for providing teachers with a proper training. There can be no doubt that the results were unfortunate. Many municipalities, poor and small as they often were, had neither the money for nor interest in their schools; the standard of the teachers who needed to show no professional qualifications was generally low, especially in Flanders. Consequently, it was impossible to continue the fight against illiteracy which was still endemic in Belgium. It was estimated in 1905 that 14 per cent of the children received no schooling at all, and that 25 per cent of the adult men and 33 per cent of the women could neither read nor write.[1] Yet even this act was not radical enough in the eyes of some Catholics, for Catholic schools might still run into difficulties in municipalities which were dominated by the liberals.[2] But the government could not have gone further even if it had wished. The liberals expressed their indignation in violent street demonstrations and it was

[1] H. Charriaut, *La Belgique moderne. Une terre d'expérience* (Paris, 1910), pp. 123 ff.; Mallinson, *Power and Politics in Belgian Education*, pp. 104-5.
[2] Guyot de Mishaegen, op. cit., p. 187.

common knowledge that King Leopold II was urging the Roman Catholics not to increase the tension unnecessarily.

Probably Leopold II was just as bored as his father by the furious quarrels in his kingdom, but on the whole he was more successful in keeping himself at a distance. Leopold I had accepted it as his duty to build up a state which for many decades to come was to be threatened both by uncertainties in the international situation and by its internal dissensions. It was perhaps understandable that he made use of his own foreign connections to pursue a foreign policy that was to some extent personal, whilst he interrupted the free course of the parliamentary system whenever this seemed to exacerbate national disunity. But such a policy was no longer possible in the time of Leopold II. He was a more modern type of a ruler. Leopold I had been an old-fashioned paternalist; his son became notorious for a form of autocracy probably closer to that of an American millionaire than to that of an Eastern despot or a Renaissance prince. His conception of royal power seems to have been matter-of-fact and sober; it was a useful instrument. He used his royal position to acquire the Congo; he used his power over the Congo to acquire an enormous fortune. This utilitarian attitude made it easier for him than for his father to recognize with some resignation the limits of his power. In Belgium he kept himself within the bounds of the constitution and played his role of constitutional monarch with some satisfaction. Yet in two fields he not only stubbornly defended royal authority but wanted to increase it: in colonial policy and defence. And here he feared the resistance of the Roman Catholic Cabinet of 1884, the most influential members of which were known to be violent antimilitarists with no sympathy at all for newer conceptions about personal military service and the techniques of fortification. Deep distrust and contempt made the King decide to dismiss the Cabinet after only four months (June–October 1884) and with an excuse so flimsy that few could have been expected to take it seriously.

Of course the Catholic party disapproved of such high-handed conduct but it avoided making a constitutional crisis out of it. The idea that the King could choose his Cabinet and especially his Prime Minister was more than a constitutional fiction in both the Netherlands and Belgium. Situations might arise in which the royal authority was needed in order to prevent conflicts becoming too violent and party policies too extreme. Moreover, it was clear that the electoral victory of 1884 was not a result of massive support for extreme Catholic demands but was largely due to the Independents whose main aim was to lower the political temperature. Thus it was possible to argue that Leopold's decision was in accordance with the election results and that the new Prime Minister Beernaert, who was appointed in October and became a very close and trusted collaborator of the King, was an excellent representative of the will of the voters. August Beernaert (1829-1912) started as a highly successful barrister and entered politics rather late in life, becoming a minister in the Catholic Cabinet of 1873. Physically and intellectually he was a vigorous man, balanced, certain of himself, and flexible. The important reforms realized during his period of office—it lasted no less than ten years—were due to this flexibility rather than to any firm convictions. His policies resemble those of his Dutch colleague Heemskerk. Both men carried through revisions of the constitution, the Dutch minister in 1887, the Belgian in 1893, which, though compromises, turned out to be more democratic than they had really intended. Yet it cannot be said that they gave in to forces greater than any they could muster themselves. On the contrary, they gave the impression of having events fairly well under control, conscious of the inevitability of the policies they were pursuing and of their own indispensability. It was in effect a victory for them to achieve reforms which they did not in theory favour.

This paradox can be explained in two ways. First, as intelligent realists both men were convinced that franchise reform would have much less practical effect than was hoped for by the radicals and feared by the conservatives, and they considered it perfectly possible to define it in such a way that everyone would be more or less satisfied. But at the same time they obviously wanted to appear to be in the position of men simply acting upon other people's initiatives, administrators carrying out after careful examination what they thought valuable in plans put before them. This modesty gave them strength for it was highly realistic. In the 1880s and 1890s the situation was very different from that of 1830 or 1848 when problems were still so simple, options so few, and public opinion so weak that a small group of statesmen could put their personal principles into practice. Heemskerk and Beernaert belonged to a generation of politicians which recognized that the opportunity for such constructive personal policies was a thing of the past. Consciously or unconsciously they saw that democracy with its confusing and inexhaustible wealth of ideas, desires, and resentments had already begun before the franchise reform which they cautiously helped to achieve institutionalized it. They felt that in the democratic era it was impossible for a democratic government to build up a system of its own except perhaps in times of acute crisis or in the field of foreign policy, which, however, was regarded as relatively unimportant. Thus Beernaert had no political programme in 1884. In his first speech as a minister he behaved as an old-fashioned liberal. He promised to restrict state power—state power being always dangerous whether based on the people or on royal absolutism —to develop private initiative, and to promote the inspiring principle of individualistic liberty.[1] But he was faced with such complicated problems that the Cabinet, if it were to survive at all, simply had to make far-reaching decisions. The riots of 1886, the franchise, Leopold II's activities in the Congo, all had to be dealt with and when Beernaert resigned in 1894, after a conflict within his party, Belgium was more democratically governed than in 1884, some social legislation had been effected, and Belgian colonial responsibilities, however cautiously defined, were indisputably growing heavier.[2]

Beernaert started by trying to disarm the liberals by concessions with regard to the schools and he was not entirely unsuccessful, although he was obliged to maintain the detested system of 1884. In 1886 and 1887 he took advantage of international tensions—the Bulgarian question and French Boulangism—in order to improve defence. In 1887 Parliament adopted his proposal to construct at Liège and Namur the Meuse fortifications Leopold II had been asking for. But to the King's bitter indignation Parliament refused to make personal military service obligatory, although he and the generals had constantly

[1] É. Vandersmissen, *Léopold II et Beernaert d'après leur correspondance inédite de 1884 à 1894* (2 vols., Brussels, 1920), i. 23.
[2] For the Congo question, see below, pp. 375 ff.

emphasized the danger of allowing the situation of 1886, when an army of proletarians was used to quell proletarian revolts, to repeat itself. It had to be admitted, however, that the army had been efficient enough and that no proof of class solidarity between workers and soldiers had been provided by the events of 1886. But in spite of the fact that the government was busy, that it also occupied itself with the affairs of the Congo, introduced the first Belgian example of social legislation (1887), and maintained itself without difficulty, the feeling was widespread that these were the last messages of an expiring regime. Indeed what sense could there be in a system with an extremely restricted franchise (in 1892 about 4·4 per cent of the male population, boys included, had the vote) when the Prime Minister himself declared, as he did in 1887, that democracy had already begun and would soon prevail?[1] Yet in 1870, 1883, and again in 1887 the progressive liberals failed to persuade the Chamber to consider revising the constitution. Not until 1890 did the Chamber accept Paul Janson's proposal that such a revision should be considered, and not until 1892 did Parliament conclude that revision was indeed necessary. This meant that the King had to dissolve Parliament; the elections for a Constituante took place in June 1892. The assembly discussed the franchise problem from February to April 1893 when finally a solution was found which satisfied the necessary two-thirds majority in the Constituante. After that it was easy to arrange the other matters satisfactorily and in September 1893 the King proclaimed the new constitution.

There is little need to analyse in detail the endless and complicated meandering of parliamentary discussions on the franchise. In the end a great majority in the Constituante— 119 members against 14 doctrinaires and 12 abstentions —accepted a system which nobody wanted. If the debates proved anything it was that all points of view were arbitrary or one-sided. The British system of 1884, canvassed first by the Dutch anti-revolutionaries and now by the Belgian Catholics as an organic system, would have increased the number of voters from 130,000 in 1892 to 500,000 or 600,000. The Christian democratic project for the representation of interests, which was also adopted by progressives from other

[1] Vandersmissen, op. cit. i. 207.

groups, was equally regarded as 'organic'. The doctrinaire-liberal insistence on giving the vote only to those capable of exercising independent political judgement would, it was estimated, have created 400,000 electors. Leopold II's personal view was that the King should have authority in the coming democracy to hold referenda on whatever subjects and at whatever time he wished.[1] None of these suggestions had sufficient support. One alternative remained: that of universal male franchise, which only a small radical minority backed by some lonely Catholics positively favoured. But this alternative had behind it the support of the Belgian Workers' party and of the numerous spontaneous or organized demonstrations which alarmed the country during the long years of parliamentary debate. Whereas in Holland popular agitation diminished after the middle of the 1880s, because the franchise question was actually taken into consideration by Parliament and because radicals as well as socialists were paralysed by disunity, the Belgian crisis seemed to become increasingly desperate. The Chamber worked so slowly that it could well have given the impression of deliberately holding things up.

Only outside pressure, strikes, demonstrations, and threats by the leaders of the opposition succeeded in forcing the Constituante to make decisions. On 11 April 1893 the assembly rejected universal male franchise. After almost three years of totally fruitless discussion the assembly was faced with chaos: none of the proposed systems was acceptable. On 12 April the leaders of the Workers' party proclaimed a general strike which started the next day and was a success, although by no means a complete one. It was estimated that on 17 April 200,000 workers in heavy industry laid down their tools.[2] The principle of peaceful strikes as a means for obtaining political advantages was adopted by the Workers' party in 1890, more or less as a concession by the reformist leadership to the revolutionary and anarchistic aspirations of the workers in Wallonia. Of course the socialist leaders themselves did not believe that a general strike might serve as a starting-point for

---

[1] No one less than Émile de Laveleye was prepared to canvass Leopold II's ideas in the Press: ibid. ii. 94 ff.

[2] É. Vandervelde, L. de Brouckère, L. Vandersmissen, *La Grève générale en Belgique (avril 1913)* (Paris, 1914), p. 66.

revolution. But if this is true, what other purpose can such a strike serve? What can the masses of the strikers actually do if the political authorities refuse to give in to their demands or do not satisfy them completely? The problem became acute when under the impact of the strike and the acts of violence which despite all good intentions inevitably accompanied it (thirteen died)[1] the Constituante accepted a system of universal male franchise only to undermine it by wholly undemocratic provisos.

The system had been devised many years before by a professor at the University of Louvain, Albert Nyssens. On 9 April 1893, two days before the Constituante refused to admit universal male franchise as everyone expected it would do, Beernaert wrote to the King that Paul Janson was prepared to accept Nyssens's project and that the socialists at Brussels would probably support it too.[2] Leopold II did not at all approve of the system but Beernaert virtually forced both the King and the Constituante to adopt it. It was the only solution still open to them, if only because nobody until then had even thought of discussing it. Beernaert was rightly astonished that it found favour in the eyes of Janson and the socialists, for it was intended to mitigate universal franchise very considerably. Each man over twenty-four obtained one vote. Men over thirty-four with a family and living in a rateable home were given a second vote while those with some property or some professional qualifications obtained still another. The number of electors rose from about 136,000 to about 1,360,000 but the total number of votes rose to 2,090,000. Of these votes only 850,000 were cast by the poorest and youngest electors who had one vote at their disposal; the remaining 1,240,000 votes belonged to the 510,000 'plural electors' of whom 290,000 had two and 220,000 had three votes.

When the Constituante approved this on 18 April it was still not certain that the Workers' party would call off the strike, although Janson had given every assurance that it would. And indeed he was right, for what else could the workers do? Janson himself was such a recent convert to universal franchise that he cannot have had much difficulty in resigning himself to Nyssens's formula. Obviously, straightforward universal

[1] Ibid., p. 68.   [2] Vandersmissen, ii. 285 ff.

franchise was still unobtainable without revolution and neither Janson nor the socialists dreamt of precipitating themselves into such a wild adventure. Thus the socialists had to accept that a strike, successful and disciplined though it had been, did not produce the results which the workers had been fighting for. Of course it is possible to call the solution of 1893, elaborated in the Electoral Act of February 1894, a compromise if by this is understood that it represented a defeat for all parties and all groups in the parties. Even for Beernaert it was a defeat in one sense: both his party and Parliament rejected the principle of proportional representation which he defended tenaciously and courageously. The conflict arising out of this was so serious that he resigned in 1894. His project for reforming the Senate met with as little success. He was forced to give up his idea of copying the Dutch model—Beernaert repeatedly referred to Dutch precedents—and of having the Senate elected by the provincial councils. As a result the Senate remained essentially what it was although it became to a somewhat lesser degree the exclusive domain of the immensely rich.

VII

EXPANSION, 1880–1914

1. *Belgian Colonial Policy*

KING LEOPOLD'S quest for colonies has been described in innumerable books and in many different ways. To some this is the crowning glory of an energetic and idealistic genius who showed his complacent nation the mission she had to fulfil in the primitive world of Africa. To others it is a story of plunder, unlimited greed, and ambition. It is unnecessary to go to such extremes. Much can be said against Leopold II but his imperialism was more moderate than that of Cecil Rhodes; his colonial policies may be bitterly criticized but it should be remembered that it was a very traditional form of colonialism which, although it was much harsher than the so-called culture-system introduced by King William I in the Dutch East Indies, did not in theory differ from it very much. In the 1950s and 1960s it was often said that the glaringly unsatisfactory results of Belgian colonial policy must be explained by the origins of the Congo State. This is a truism. However, we need not conclude that the instability of the independent Congo State is particularly striking in comparison with other African states which have sprung from different colonial principles.

The most bizarre element of the whole enterprise is neither the form nor even the content of Belgian colonization but the fact that Leopold II forced his prosperous country into an imperialism it was not interested in and had no need for. Belgian entrepreneurs did not aspire after extra-European markets of their own. Belgium did not possess the discoverers, sailors, and adventurous business men who were found elsewhere and who were driven by their dynamism, idealism, or greed to assume new tasks and explore new possibilities. It is true that after the establishment of Leopold's colony there emerged the more or less closed groups of retired colonial officials, soldiers, and business men so well known in the capitals of other colonizing nations, and Belgium too had its lobbies of colonial specialists and capitalists. During the 1880s and 1890s, however, when the colony was gradually taking shape, nobody outside the narrow group of the King's most intimate collaborators was particularly interested.

The most important among the King's advisers was a military man, Henri-Alexis Brialmont (1821-1903). His father had been a formidable soldier, had taken part in Napoleon's campaigns, and remembered those years of triumph and defeat with nostalgia. He later served in the army of King William I, married a Dutch girl, but joined the Belgian patriots in 1830.[1] Henri-Alexis, born in that part of Limburg which to the bitter indignation of the Belgians was returned to the Netherlands in 1839, could find little outlet for his energies although he designed the fortresses round Antwerp and the line of defence on the eastern border—the fortresses along the Meuse of international renown. He also campaigned for Belgian expansion. In 1853 he published a work entitled *Utilité d'une marine militaire*—he wrote one hundred books and pamphlets— in which he argued that Belgium must build a fleet if it wished to develop its overseas trade. A second booklet on this subject in 1855 attracted the attention of Leopold I. The Crown Prince—after 1865, King Leopold II—may well have taken part in the preparation of still another publication, *Complément de l'œuvre de 1830* (1859), in which Brialmont proposed bold commercial expansion radiating from a Belgian free port in China. His outlook was not really imperialistic. He long advocated the principle of free trade, opposed projects for Belgian overseas settlements because he did not think his countrymen suited for them, and laid special emphasis on the economic advantages of sea-borne trade which he hoped would immensely increase the nation's strength and vigour.

A second loyal adviser of Leopold II was Auguste Lambermont (1819-1905). He was a very different type of man, coming from a peasant family in the province of Brabant. In 1838 he left for Spain to fight for a few months in the Carlist wars where he took the side of Queen Isabella and the liberals. His main purpose was to acquire military experience so that he

---

[1] P. Crokaert, *Brialmont* (Brussels, 1925), p. 358. As a boy he spoke better Dutch and German than French: ibid., pp. 364-5.

would be ready for the day when he would be called upon to fight for his own fatherland—a 'fatherland the future of which is a mystery', as he wrote himself.[1] Back in Belgium, he resumed his studies at Louvain University and then obtained a position in the Foreign Office where he rapidly rose to the top, becoming Secretary-General. In 1863 Émile Banning (1836–98) was appointed as librarian, translator, and researcher in the ministry. The two men understood one another well. Banning was the writer, scholar, dreamer; Lambermont the negotiator and man of action. They shared the same basic inspiration, nationalism. Expansion was in their view essential for the survival of their country, which they felt to be too tightly confined within its narrow borders. The national spirit, depressed by the atmosphere of provincial and petty party conflicts, would become strong and combative if it were to be exposed to the challenge of the outside world. They were not interested in mere power, and even economic factors, though vitally important, were subordinate to the nationalistic motives. Philanthropy and humanitarianism were also very secondary considerations. Of course they assumed that Belgian imperialism, especially in Africa, would benefit the indigenous population; but they defended the thesis that Belgium should take it upon herself to bring civilization to such primitive societies only in terms of the prestige that might accrue. As with territorial expansion in Europe (a topic on which Banning wrote long memoranda)[2] colonial expansion was thought of as an expression not of Belgium's surplus energy and wealth but of its international and internal weakness. The older collaborators of Leopold II belonged to the generation who thought that the creation of 1830 had to be strengthened by all possible means. Banning too, though much younger than Brialmont and Lambermont, felt at home in this atmosphere of late bourgeois intellectualism, which was composed of a belief in hard work, a fiery but somewhat puritanical patriotism, and a general anxiety about the future.

[1] A. de Robiano, *Le Baron Lambermont* (Brussels, 1905), p. 16. See also Willequet, *Le Baron Lambermont*.

[2] Above, pp. 220 ff. Colonies were sometimes regarded as a substitute for the provinces of Limburg and Luxemburg lost in 1839. Some years before becoming king Leopold II wrote to Brialmont (1 Dec. 1861): 'C'est au loin qu'il faut retrouver les demi-provinces perdues' (Crokaert, op. cit., p. 420).

In a small anonymous book published in 1882, which may well have been written by Émile Banning for it reflects very accurately his style of thinking,[1] this is fully elaborated. The Belgian population, the author argued, was growing so fast that its size would be doubled in a century. To feed all these people the Belgians must export more and thus expand their industry. This meant that the industrial proletariat, uneducated, desperately poor, deprived of any chance of escaping its miserable lot, would increase. At this level of society the demoralizing effect of industrialization would make itself still more widely felt, whilst at the top the degeneration of the bourgeoisie threatened to become even more damaging; the growth of the proletariat would reduce social mobility in this much too populous society and the élite would no longer be rejuvenated by new forces. There was only one way out, colonization; and only one virgin area, Central Africa. Obviously the Belgians would have to conquer this territory by war but was that necessarily a bad thing? Here the author hesitated. But the black race of course was inferior to the white and could only benefit from being ruled by Europeans. If it turned out to be necessary to fight some semi-savage tribes doomed to disappear sooner or later anyhow and never to contribute anything to mankind, was war then a risk to be avoided? However ugly it might be, it was essential to find opportunities, sustenance, and room for one's own population. The author also meditated upon the possibility of sending prisoners to the colonies and making them do useful work as in Australia, or of employing there the dissatisfied asocial groups of men who were a disturbing factor at home but might perhaps be a dynamic one abroad. The main argument, however, was that colonial possessions would change the Belgian national character; that, the author thought, was the vital condition for the survival of the unfinished nation of 1830.

King Leopold II (1835-1909) looked at the matter from a different point of view. For his propaganda he used every variety of argument, economic, humanitarian, nationalistic, in remarkable profusion. Many years before his accession to the throne in 1865 he advocated the establishment of colonies by

[1] E. B., *La Belgique doit être agrandie* (Brussels, 1882), analysed by A. Roeykens, *La Période initiale de l'œuvre africaine de Léopold II* (Brussels, 1957), pp. 180-205.

constantly pointing out the prosperity and glory that small states in particular—from the Greek cities to the seventeenth-century Dutch Republic—could acquire from them. Undoubtedly the Dutch colonies from which the Belgians had been excluded since 1830 constituted in his opinion admirable proof of the view that a small coastal state cannot be complete without overseas possessions. Not surprisingly, his colonial conceptions were strongly historical; in fact his thinking reflected the whole evolution of the Dutch colonial experience. At the start he wanted to restrict himself to establishing trading companies on the Dutch and English seventeenth-century pattern; later he adopted a system which had still been in force in the Dutch East Indies in the 1850s and 1860s but which had long since been abandoned when his own imperialistic meditations came to fruition in the 1880s and 1890s. In themselves the King's colonial ideas were not particularly cynical but they were inaccurate and easy-going. At first he thought that colonies were there to absorb the surplus of the mother country's population and so to help solve the acute social problem, but he became converted to the type of 'colonie d'exploitation' after having chosen Central Africa as his territory. He then presented the exploitation of primitive lands as a great and laudable task. In 1889 he wrote to his minister Beernaert in his hasty style, which used arguments as rhetorical rather than logical elements: 'By serving the cause of mankind and progress peoples of the second rank act as useful members of the great family of nations. An industrial and commercial nation like ours must exert itself more than others to conquer markets for all its workers, intellectuals, capitalists, and workmen. This patriotic concern has commanded my whole life. It is this that has determined the creation of the *œuvre africaine*.'[1]

As Crown Prince and during the early years of his reign, Leopold looked eagerly for territories suitable for Belgian expansion. He wondered whether British Borneo, the Far East, the Philippines, South Africa, Mozambique provided the proper opportunities. In the 1870s he toyed briefly with the idea of acquiring the Transvaal, which seemed to him particularly attractive because Flemish farmers could go and live there

[1] Quoted by A. Roeykens, *Les Débuts de l'œuvre africaine de Léopold II (1875–1879)* (Brussels, 1955), p. 29.

and, though themselves fervently Roman Catholic, would soon feel at home among their Calvinist brethren of the same race and language.[1] Naturally this foolish plan failed. Then Portugal, Spain, and the Netherlands refused to sell parts of their colonial empires (although the Netherlands ceded the African Gold Coast to Britain in the early 1870s). So finally the King decided on those areas of Central Africa that were only partly explored. From 1876, when he organized at Brussels a conference of geographers and other experts to study the problems of Central Africa, he set himself with all his bewildering energy, perseverance, and inexhaustible cunning to the task of acquiring in that region a domain that would belong to him personally.[2] After 1876 he no longer hesitated. He knew what he wanted: neither a Belgian colony nor a 'colonie de peuplement' but an African empire which would become for him what Java had been for King William I of the Netherlands.

In 1876 Europeans had not yet penetrated Central Africa from the mouth of the River Congo. None the less, some of the secrets of dark Africa were being revealed and the course of the big rivers more or less successfully traced by numerous expeditions. No Belgian, however, had yet ventured so far as these other explorers. Nor were there any Belgians settled on the West Coast, among the factories of French, British, Spanish, and Portuguese business men and especially of the Dutch, who with their thirty-five trading posts monopolized a large part of the trade with the indigenous population and claimed, perhaps rightly, to be the party most interested in the commercial aspects of Leopold II's affairs. However, the Afrikaansche Handelsvereeniging, founded in 1867 by two famous Rotterdam business men who had started trading with the African West coast in 1857, suffered serious losses; its breakdown in 1879 was a *cause célèbre* in Rotterdam's history.[3] Its successor, the Nieuwe Afrikaansche Handelsvennootschap, was more successful, finding the trade in spirits and weapons particularly

---

[1] A. Roeykens, *Le Dessein africain de Léopold II* (Brussels, 1956), pp. 29–119.
[2] Ibid., pp. 129 ff.
[3] The business was started by Lodewijk Pincoffs (1827–1911), a famous figure in the history of Rotterdam who in a very unorthodox and not altogether honest way did much for the expansion of the port. After the bankruptcy of the AHV he was allowed to flee to the United States: L. J. Rogier, *Rotterdam in het derde kwart van de negentiende eeuw* (Rotterdam, 1953), pp. 63 ff.

profitable.[1] Thus Leopold II found all sorts of people and institutions active in the areas he wanted to acquire but nobody at all from Belgium. Before the end of the 1880s not even Belgian missionaries were present in a region where French priests as well as British, American, and Scandinavian Protestant missionaries had been working for many years.[2]

Leopold II, never at a loss for an argument, asserted that the very absence of Belgians in Africa was a point in his favour; and in fact their absence made the idealistic façade for his enterprise look so impressive that it sufficed to persuade both the Belgians and the European Powers to allow the King virtually a free hand. The Association internationale africaine,[3] founded at the geographical conference at Brussels in September 1876 and presided over by Leopold, had been given a commission to explore the Congo basin and to fight slavery but it had been still-born. By the beginning of 1877 it was clear that none of the countries participating in the Association, and notably Britain, was prepared to spend money on it. In September of the same year it became known that H. M. Stanley had followed the course of the River Congo westwards from its upper course to its mouth. Leopold II reacted promptly by taking the British explorer into his service. On the advice and with the collaboration of the Afrikaansche Handelsvereeniging in Rotterdam, Leopold II created a Comité d'études du Haut-Congo financed by international capital. Its task was to supervise Stanley's next journey and to find means of improving communications with the mouth of the river. However, when the Afrikaansche Handelsvereeniging went bankrupt in 1879 Leopold II immediately exploited the enormous scandal that ensued to return the capital provided by the Handelsvereeniging and to dissolve the committee. Thus he was the only party left on what began as an international body, although he maintained the fiction that the committee liquidated by himself was still in existence. Several years after its disappearance Stanley was still under the impression that he was working on its behalf.

[1] Woltring ed., *Bescheiden* iii. 733–4, 737–9.

[2] Ruth Slade, *King Leopold's Congo. Aspects of the Development of Race Relations in the Congo Independent State* (London, 1962), pp. 146 ff.

[3] So it was generally called. Its official name was unusually pedantic: Association internationale pour réprimer la traite et ouvrir l'Afrique centrale.

After 1879 Stanley remained in the Congo for a long period with hardly a break. He found his way from the river's mouth to Stanley Pool and from there to Stanley Falls, nearly 1,250 miles from the Atlantic coast. He had been ordered to buy as much land as possible from the chiefs who were supposed to own it and to put it under the sovereignty of the Comité d'études or, after he had at last discovered that this no longer existed, of another largely fictitious institution called by Leopold the Association internationale du Congo. However, as time went on Leopold became aware that the situation was not without its risks for him. Some other states, Portugal, Britain, and also to a certain extent Germany, began to wonder whether they were not somehow concerned in what the King was doing, although they had no reason to feel that he was damaging their interests. France, on the other hand, was developing a positive appetite for the area itself. The European chanceries grew active. Various manoeuvres led to a conference at Berlin which opened in November 1884 with a view to resolving outstanding problems.[1] Of course Leopold II did not passively let matters take their course. He made use of all his personal connections, of which he had many, and of Belgian diplomats, in defence of his very private enterprise. It is remarkable that even those in Belgium who opposed Leopold's colonial projects made no objections to his using the Belgian diplomatic service for his purposes. In April 1884 he had succeeded in persuading the United States to recognize the Association internationale du Congo as the sovereign government, although the negotiations that led to this decision made only one thing perfectly clear: the Americans had not the slightest idea what Leopold was actually doing.[2] In the same month Leopold achieved a remarkable success when the French provisionally waived their claim to the Congo in return for a badly defined right of pre-emption (*droit de préférence*) if the Association was forced to sell its possessions. The French decision was mistaken in two respects. They supposed that the Association would soon collapse and that Leopold would have to abandon his ambitions; secondly, they thought that Britain

---

[1] A. J. P. Taylor, *The Struggle for Mastery in Europe* (Oxford, 1954), pp. 294 ff.

[2] R. S. Thomson, *Fondation de l'État Indépendant du Congo* (Brussels, 1933), pp. 147-62; P. van Zuylen, *L'Échiquier congolais ou le secret du roi* (Brussels, 1959), pp. 75-80.

wanted to take the territory. To Leopold this was very advantageous. After it was clear that France would benefit from a weakening of the Association and had recognized it as a state, albeit only implicitly, it became useful for the other Powers to support Leopold. On 8 November 1884 Bismarck gave his blessing to the activities of the Belgian King on condition that trade in the Congo should be absolutely free.

The Conference that started a week later in Berlin presented Leopold II with his colonial empire. At the invitation of Germany and France no less than fourteen countries took part. The Association was not officially represented but the United States, Germany, and Belgium graciously assumed the task of defending its interests, and the Belgian representative Lambermont, assisted by Banning, turned out to be an expert negotiator. They were of course in almost daily contact with the King, but Lambermont was in no position to act as the champion of Belgian expansionism. In June 1884 the Belgian Government had passed from the staunchly anti-colonial liberals into the hands of the Catholics and in October the cautious Beernaert took office. The new Cabinet did not oppose the King but it was neither able nor prepared to support him vigorously. Thus the Conference (November 1884 to February 1885) assumed a ghostlike appearance. It was summoned by France and Germany to obstruct Britain. Actually, however, Britain collaborated with Germany against France. It dealt with the Congo but the Association was not only not officially represented, it was hardly even mentioned, although it was soon quite evident that it was to acquire international legal status as a result of the Conference. Moreover, the fiction that Belgium had nothing to do with Leopold's private affairs was very carefully upheld. Yet the Conference of Berlin which was in the process of creating a neutral state in Africa to be ruled by Leopold II had an obvious precedent in the Conference of London which half a century previously had created the neutral state of Belgium ruled by Leopold I.

Leopold II had reason to be satisfied with the results. It is true that the French and the Portuguese finally prevented the other Powers from giving the Congo State adequate guarantees for the maintenance of its neutrality but generally he got what he wanted. The European Powers recognized his

Association as a sovereign state which was allowed to sign the Conference's final protocol. The French and Portuguese did not succeed in making their claims to large parts of the Congo delta effective and were forced to defer to the majority who wished to leave the enormous new state a free outlet to the sea. As far as the rest of the territory was concerned the diplomats accepted without discussion that the treaties made by the Association with more than 450 African chiefs were valid and included surrender of sovereignty. Nobody doubted that European occupation would mean bliss for the indigenous population and that Leopold II would bring civilization and light into their barbaric darkness. Free trade, vigorous action against slavery, and some form of neutrality were to be the principles upon which the exemplary young state would be based. From all sides Leopold was congratulated and praised for his virtuous and selfless idealism.

Leopold could now transform his so-called international association into an orderly kingdom of which he was naturally the sovereign, or rather the owner. However, this required Belgian support. According to the constitution, a Belgian prince was not allowed to accept a second crown without permission of a two-thirds majority in Parliament. For the first time the nation had to express its opinion about Leopold's colonial policy. But the nation's opinion was already quite clear: Belgium refused to accept colonial responsibilities. When Leopold organized a geographical and philanthropic conference at Brussels in 1876 no one in Belgium turned out to be interested in African geography or in action against slavery.[1] If in the course of the following years the political parties felt obliged to express views on the matter these were determined by internal resentments. The liberals feared that the Catholics were planning to spread their disastrous clericalism over the whole world, whereas the Catholics, after their initial outburst of enthusiasm for Leopold's philanthropy, soon discovered everywhere the unholy intrigues of Freemasons and atheists. For the socialists the problem was even simpler. They argued that it would be infinitely wiser for the King to exert himself on behalf of the innumerable paupers in his own country.[2]

[1] A. Roeykens, *L'Initiative africaine de Léopold II et l'opinion publique belge*, i (Brussels, 1963), pp. 30 ff.   [2] Ibid., p. 72.

Yet public opinion reacted positively to some elements of the royal initiative. In 1876 all kinds of groups, authorities, societies, newspapers, municipalities, and provincial administrations competed in professing loyalty to such a magnanimous prince and support for such a magnanimous effort.[1] In 1885 this phenomenon recurred. When—as it was said—the Berlin mandate had honoured Leopold with responsibility for so great a mission, congratulations were proffered by the whole country from the simplest private persons to the highest authorities, from the smallest hamlets to the most distinguished city dignitaries.[2]

Parliament, however, remained unmoved. It allowed the King, whom it could not repudiate, to take up his new crown in April 1885, but it did so without even attempting to show sympathy. The only thing it made abundantly clear was its refusal to accept responsibility, especially in the financial field. Leopold did not protest. He had always asserted that his private means would suffice and he certainly did not want any political interference in his affairs. Still his position was as false as that of Parliament. It was pure illusion that he could rule the Congo as a private absolutist and Belgium as a constitutional monarch. He owed his capital to his royal function and it was obvious that a private European millionaire was not in a position to found an African empire. Belgian public opinion was not entirely to be trusted either. The nation's enthusiasm, however loudly and widely expressed, had its limits. The people admired the King but contributed only words. The business men offered no money, the Churches no missionaries, the Belgians generally no energy. In 1889 there were 175 Belgians at work in the Congo State and 255 whites from other countries. When Leopold's private state was annexed by Belgium in 1908 there were still only 1,700 Belgians out of a total of 3,000 whites.[3]

Given the widely accepted nineteenth-century view that trade produces civilization and education, it is hardly even a criticism to say that Leopold's Congo policies were largely determined by his financial ambitions. The King needed a

[1] Ibid., p. 402.
[2] A. Stenmans, *La Reprise du Congo par la Belgique* (Brussels, 1949), p. 25.
[3] Slade, op. cit., pp. 71, 173.

great deal of money. From 1878 to 1885 he spent 10 million francs out of his own pocket,[1] but after that date costs rose steeply. The Berlin Conference had made it an explicit condition that the territory the state was allowed to acquire should be effectively occupied in the shortest possible time, but in order to achieve this expensive expeditions and much difficult organization were necessary. Very soon it was clear that Leopold's private capital (he had inherited 15 millions from his father and speculated profitably with them) was not sufficient for establishing a new state. In 1887 the Belgian Parliament gave the King permission to issue a loan in Belgium, but this failed. In 1889 it approved the government's request to appropriate 10 million francs for the construction of a railway in the unnavigable Congo delta. This, of course, did not suffice either. Leopold decided to attempt more radical measures. In November 1889 representatives of the European Powers met at a conference at Brussels to discuss further action against slavery. Leopold asked for and obtained a formal mandate to devote himself to this crusade, and was rewarded with the permission, withheld in Berlin five years previously, to levy import duties on goods entering the Congo State. Only the Dutch Government objected stubbornly in defence of the interests of the Nieuwe Afrikaansche Handelsvennootschap which monopolized 75 per cent of all trade to the Congo State, but it was finally forced by German and British pressure to give way.[2] Once Leopold's connections with the Arab slave-traders in the eastern part of his state, connections which had been far from idealistic but eminently practical, had become impossible to maintain, he did indeed start a campaign against the traders in 1892. But his action took the form of a war of conquest rather than a war against slavery[3]—although it naturally made an excellent impression in Belgium where people wished to see the King's work irradiated by high principle.

[1] J. Stengers, *Combien le Congo a-t-il coûté à la Belgique?* (Brussels, 1957), p. 29.

[2] Abundant documentation in J. Woltring (ed.), *Bescheiden* iv: *1886–1890* (The Hague, 1968). Generally speaking the Dutch were not hostile to the Belgian colonial venture. Initially the Afrikaansche Handelsvereeniging and its successor were anxious to collaborate with Leopold II but when the King began to monopolize trade to the Congo State conflicts became inevitable.

[3] Slade, pp. 106 ff.

Meanwhile Belgian relations with the Congo had undergone essential changes. Leopold was successful not only in the matter of import duties, he also managed to wring an important concession from the Belgian Parliament. It was after all obvious that the import duties would never yield enough to satisfy the state's needs and that other ways of raising capital must be found. What then was more logical, he asked, than to make the Belgian state provide the finance the Belgian public was not willing to lend him? Leopold's idea was simple indeed. He expected the Belgian state to make available to him a sum of money large enough to develop the Congo. After the Congo became a profitable enterprise further Belgian support would of course be superfluous, and Leopold could then at his leisure collect the profits and spend part of them on doing the things he liked to do: building grandiose public edifices and triumphal avenues. In the long run the Congo was intended for the nation and Leopold was prepared to draft a will in which he left the state to his country. It is extraordinary that Leopold who was always praised for his deep understanding of constitutional monarchy should not have seen that his proposition as it stood would be unacceptable to a Parliament with any self-respect. For Parliament was being asked to vote credits on behalf of an enterprise which it did not supervise and being promised a present of which it could not estimate the value nor define the nature. The project soon turned out to have no chance. The strong liberal opposition would certainly have objected to it if it had been officially put forward. Yet the liberal attitude was essentially different in 1890 from what it had been. The liberals were still indifferent towards colonies but they were now, or so it seemed, reconciled to the prospect of Belgium having them, on condition, however, that Parliament would be kept adequately informed and would retain ultimate control. What the King and the Beernaert Cabinet wanted was rather the opposite. They sought short-term Belgian support in order to make Congo affairs independent of further Belgian intervention until the King's death.[1] But under the circumstances it was necessary for the King to become rather more modest. He had originally asked for 150 million francs; he now asked for 25 million. And whereas he had originally mentioned the

[1] Stenmans, op. cit., p. 94.

day of his death as the moment Belgium would be given the Congo he now conceded that after the interest-free loan expired in 1901 Belgium had the option of asking for its capital back or of annexing the colony. Once again the compromise achieved was unsound, especially as Leopold had no intention of handing over his empire during his lifetime.

After 1890 Leopold II gradually introduced the system he had been striving for: exploration, occupation, and exploitation of the Congo by the state, that state being himself. The Congo was closed. To the great indignation of Beernaert, Leopold excluded Belgian and foreign trading companies as far as he could. At the same time he threw himself into new financial adventures which made the government shudder with apprehension. But what could be done about it? The answer was: very little. The revision of the constitution in 1893 made it possible to eliminate certain formal difficulties inherent in the 1831 constitution which might have made Belgian annexation of the territory legally objectionable. And two new articles were added which contained guarantees against the continuation of autocratic rule after annexation. The form of government of future Belgian colonies was to be decided by the Belgian legislature and Belgian conscripts could not be sent to the colonies against their will.[1] In 1894 both the Catholic Cabinet and the *éminences grises* of the Foreign Office, Lambermont and Banning, were embittered and frightened to such an extent that they advised immediate annexation. With his financial resources totally exhausted even Leopold could see no other solution. The situation was exceedingly complicated. In February 1895 the government introduced in Parliament a proposal to take over the Congo. A special committee of twenty-one members was appointed to study it, but the country was shaken by a discussion so vehement and so general that the government finally decided to leave the bill at the committee stage and not to bring it forward for parliamentary approval.

The Cabinet was probably well advised to act in this way. Although its majority in Parliament was strong enough at the time to take risks, there were uncertainties about the immediate future. In October 1894 democracy began to take shape in

---

[1] These articles were borrowed from the Dutch constitution.

Belgium when the first elections under the new system were held. The results were perplexing. In the Chamber elected in 1892 the Catholics had 91 seats and the liberals 61. In that of 1894 the Catholics increased their number to 104 whereas the liberals were reduced to 20. They now formed the smallest party of all, for the socialists had entered Parliament with no less than 28 members. The result was obviously not a true reflection of the nation's mood. The liberals, who received 537,000 votes against the Catholics' 962,000 and the socialists' 310,000, had suffered seriously from the majority principle that was still in force; their adherents were spread over the whole country and thus they were weaker than the Catholics concentrated in Flanders and the socialists in Wallonia. Because of the plural vote the number of counted votes did not, however, give a clear picture of the facts. As the socialists in all probability did not have second and third votes, and as the total number of electors was about 1,360,000, it may be assumed that from 20 to 25 per cent of the electorate voted socialist. Thus it was necessary in Belgium to recognize the fact that, as far as the number of socialist votes was concerned, the social democrats were nearly as successful relatively as in Germany, and with their 28 seats in a Chamber of 152 seats much stronger than their colleagues in any other country of Central and Western Europe.

In 1895 the socialists made it abundantly clear that they were not prepared to make concessions over the Congo. They nursed no illusions about the philanthropic purposes and propaganda of Leopold's enterprise and enlivened their fundamental opposition to all forms of imperialism by mordant criticism of the King's shameless greed. Obviously they were profoundly sceptical about the capacity of the Belgian nation or its leaders to eliminate the influence of King Leopold after annexation. The left-wing liberals and the radicals shared their point of view; the remainder of the liberal party, now nearly powerless in Parliament, was reluctant to support colonial experiments, especially since Belgian intervention had never been asked for in the past except for financial reasons. The Catholics were very uncertain. Most of them were convinced that the Congo would in the long run become a Belgian possession but under prevailing circumstances they preferred to postpone a decision. Moreover, there were elements in the situation they found highly attractive. The King had in his Congo affairs an outlet for his formidable energy; if he were deprived of this nobody could predict what he might try next. Finally, the Catholics as well as the liberals were afraid of the possible military consequences of annexation. They asked themselves whether Belgium would not be obliged to send a strong expeditionary force to these barbaric areas. The troubles the French had run into in Indo-China served as a warning; doubtless the sharp anti-colonialism of French public opinion also influenced Belgian reactions. Thus there was only one political group in Belgium that tried to think imperialistically: the democratic wing of the Roman Catholic party. Their motives were mixed. These young men endeavoured to be modern and progressive and they were under the impression that this was what imperialism stood for. They were afraid of the socialists. If the socialists should be in power in 1901 at the expiration of the ten-year loan of 1891—a possibility they did not consider at all unrealistic—there would be no question of annexation. Therefore they thought it imperative to take over the colony without delay. Perhaps the colonial riches would even enable Belgium to avert the revolution of the poor which in their opinion was almost inevitable.

Leopold II reacted tactfully to the vehement discussions in the nation and to the Cabinet's decision not to push annexation through. He showed the right measure of indignation at the questioning of his magnanimous aims but declared himself willing to continue on his own the great work he had started, provided Parliament helped him out of his immediate predicament. Parliament inevitably opted for this course. It was relieved to be able to postpone final decisions simply by presenting the King with the modest sum of 7 million francs. The King too was relieved not to have to abandon the Congo. And in the same year the colony at last started to yield profits. Rubber exports rose from 100 tons in 1890 to 500 in 1895, 1,300 in 1896, 2,000 in 1898, and 6,000 in 1901. In 1892 total exports were worth 11·5 million francs, in 1900 47·5 million. Much of this the King received himself. The so-called Domaine de la Couronne—that is, the territory reserved by Leopold for his own purposes as opposed to an area cultivated by the state and another in which private companies were allowed to work—was said to have made a profit of about 60 million francs between 1896 to 1906. By the turn of the century Leopold was beginning to embellish Belgium according to his own taste with monumental buildings and avenues. It has been calculated that by 1908 he had spent more than 30 million francs on this.[1] The idea that such profits ought to be used for the development of the colony itself did not occur to him. Throughout his life he remained loyal to the early nineteenth-century conception, which he knew well from the history of the Dutch East Indies, that colonial profits should benefit the mother country.

Criticism of Leopold's Congo policy was far from new in the mid-1890s. In particular his harsh treatment of private entrepreneurs had lost him much of the glory he had won through his action against the Arab slave-trade. But from 1895 the critics began to concentrate on the consequences of his monopolistic exploitation policy for the indigenous population. It is not surprising that criticism became more acid and general as the Congolese profits increased and that it grew into an international campaign which finally forced the Belgians to annex the Congo and to put its government under democratic control. But in Belgium events moved slowly. Radicals and socialists, relying on information from abroad, condemned the Congo scandals but they were not widely heeded. When at the expiration of the loan of 1891 in 1901 Belgium had another chance to assume responsibility for the colony it once again declined the honour. The Roman Catholic Cabinet understandably wanted to avoid a repetition of the confusion of 1895; the King was hostile to annexation and when his old friend Beernaert drafted a proposal that Belgium should take over the colony he was so bitterly and spitefully attacked by Leopold that he hastily withdrew it. Of course everybody realized that this passive approach could not continue indefinitely. Leopold was sixty-six and at his death the nation would have to decide what it intended to do. Nevertheless in 1901 the decision was postponed and the King was not even asked to return the 25 million francs he had received ten years before.

[1] Figures in N. Ascherson, *The King Incorporated. Leopold II in the Age of Trusts* (London, 1963), p. 241 and Stengers, op. cit., p. 211.

Seven years later the Belgian Government and Parliament at last assumed the responsibility thrust upon them. Undoubtedly, foreign pressure was instrumental in making them decide to take over the Congo even before the King's death. After 1901 criticism of royal policies assumed dangerous proportions. In 1903 the British Government took the matter up; in February 1904 the report of Roger Casement, British Consul at Boma, was published, describing his travels in the Congo from June to September 1903; in March 1904 E. D. Morel started the Congo Reform Association and by so doing gave a new impetus to the campaign. At the same time American missionaries, briefed and supported by Morel, brought as much pressure to bear on the United States Government as they could. Leopold II did his utmost to dam the flood. Many Belgians mistrusted British motives. The British were suspected of ulterior economic motives, now that the Congo had proved to be so profitable. Moreover, many were angry at the shamelessness of a people that criticized Belgian activities in Africa so self-righteously after depriving the Boers in the most cynical way of their freedom and their wealth. Leopold made use of his innumerable connections to defend his policies abroad. But in June 1904, a few months after the appearance of Casement's report, Leopold appointed a committee consisting of one Belgian, one Italian, and one Swiss to study the matter. The three distinguished gentlemen stayed in the Congo until March 1905 and published their report in October. This confirmed in essence all the criticisms levelled against the royal policy. It made a deep impression in Belgium. Up to November 1905 nearly all Belgians except socialists and radicals had considered it a patriotic duty to praise the King for what, in a parliamentary debate in May 1903, the Foreign Secretary had referred to as his 'noble initiative' and the 'miraculous development of the Congo under his wise rule'.[1] Now his policy was shown to have been disastrous for the African population, although the committee emphasized that by calling attention to certain abuses it was not launching a general attack on all Leopold's work; in spite of everything, Leopold's Congo State had, in its opinion, brought about substantial improvements when the reports of the explorers and missionaries

[1] Stenmans, p. 272.

who had visited the area before the arrival of Leopold's servants, and who on the basis of their nineteenth-century standards had represented the situation there as the ultimate in barbarism and inhumanity, were considered.

For one year more Leopold fought on. In June 1906 he published a series of documents written in collaboration with the ultra-conservative Catholic leader Woeste[1] in which he rejected the charges levelled against him, and announced a number of reforms. At the same time he launched a large-scale multilingual propaganda action. But it was to no avail. Not only Britain but also France, Germany, and America made it clear that they no longer intended to let Leopold have his way. Attempts by Leopold and his obedient government to suppress discussion in Belgium itself failed miserably. From 1906 to 1908 the Congo problem dominated Belgian domestic politics. And consequently the debate tended to go beyond the reforms required in the Congo until the whole question of the position of the monarchy itself was involved. The situation is reminiscent of events in the Netherlands during the 1860s. Then the abolition of the culture-system in the Dutch East Indies led to a serious constitutional crisis in the motherland; in the same way the necessity to put an end to Leopold's system of forced labour in the Congo made the Belgians reconsider the significance of constitutional democracy at home. However, the debate in Belgium, although it was tense enough and although the old King once again showed how intelligent and perplexingly supple an opponent he could be, was less portentous than the discussions in the Netherlands forty years before. The parliamentary system of government was so much more firmly established in Belgium at the start of the twentieth century than in the Netherlands during the 1860s that Leopold's defeat was achieved more smoothly than that of the Dutch conservatives. Moreover, his defeat could not signify, as it did in the Netherlands, the introduction, however tentative, of a

---

[1] Woeste was a very influential man, feared because of the icy causticity of his contempt but respected because of the asceticism of his religious practice. He was totally disinterested in colonial matters but thought that the Roman Catholics should allow the King to exhaust his energies in this meaningless enterprise. As a grateful and enormously busy man Leopold II would be obliged to let the Catholics have their way in Belgium. Cf. P. Hymans, *Mémoires*, ed. F. van Kalken and J. Bartier (2 vols., Brussels, n.d.), ii. 849.

new phase of constitutional development; it merely confirmed existing constitutional practice.[1]

Leopold lost. In 1906 the Cabinet forced him to accept the immediate Belgian annexation of the Congo. By the following year discussion was only about ways and means. The King attempted to reserve for himself and his dynasty enormous parts of the colony, asking for example that Belgium would recognize the so-called Fondation de la Couronne. He wanted this foundation to rule the gigantic Crown domain and to pay the profits into a fund out of which public works in Belgium were to be financed. Moreover, he wished to introduce a colonial government of a strongly absolutist nature which would leave him a great deal of influence. The Catholic Cabinet—from 1896 under Paul de Smet de Nayer with only a short interruption in 1899—was prepared to back the King but it met with serious opposition in Parliament. Having decided to give way to the latter, it then of course lost Leopold's confidence and in April 1907 De Smet resigned. After a period of sustained confusion Frans Schollaert at last formed a Cabinet early in 1908 that was strong enough to adopt consistent policies; it introduced a bill abolishing the Congolese Crown domain and drafted a governmental system for the colony which ensured close parliamentary control. Even so, by mysterious manipulations, Leopold managed to reserve the profits of his domain for the dynasty until his death although the Congo had become a Belgian possession. In August the Chamber agreed to annexation and to the proposed colonial charter. The Senate followed suit. On 8 October 1908 Leopold signed the bill which deprived him of his private business. His colonial adventure had ended.

He had started it many years ago with the purpose, as he said, of expanding Belgium outside Europe because it was unable to acquire more territory in Europe, of developing the national idea and the national spirit, of increasing prosperity, and of bringing his country into line with the Netherlands. The project had degenerated into a gigantic exploitation on behalf of his own treasury. Forced mainly by foreign protests the Belgian statesmen very reluctantly assumed responsibility for Leopold's Congo State. It seemed as if Belgium gloomily

[1] Above, p. 286.

decided in 1908 to pay for the recklessness of a King whom they had left alone too long. Indeed most Belgians probably looked at the situation that way. Obviously, it was a rather biased interpretation. In fact the Congo had not cost the Belgians a penny before 1908; on the contrary, it had yielded a substantial profit in the form of monuments and buildings. From 1908 the Belgian state spent more on behalf of the Congo and received less in return, but even so from the 1870s to 1950 it paid out only about 7 milliard francs (in the currency of 1950), which is an absurdly small sum in view of the enormous riches the Congo produced for the benefit of the mother-land.[1] In 1908 the attitude of Parliament was generally speaking responsible and sensible, yet it was partly determined by wrong premisses and there is something paradoxical in the rather tearful resignation with which it assumed under foreign pressure the responsibility of accepting the immense treasures of Leopold's state.

When the annexation bill was voted upon in the autumn of 1908 the political parties clearly remained loyal to their point of view of 1895, although circumstances obliged some of them to pursue different policies. Only the Christian democrats were convinced annexationists and one of them not unnaturally became the first Colonial Secretary of Belgium. Their influence in the Cabinet and in Parliament had been growing so much over the last few years that they played a more or less decisive role in the discussions of 1908. Both the socialists and the radical liberals remained anti-imperialist, as a matter of principle and because of a certain pessimism about the economic usefulness of colonies generally. These men—in 1908 there were 31 socialists and 21 radicals in the Chamber—were deeply convinced of the need to free the Congo from Leopold's rule but would have preferred to entrust it to some form of international authority.[2] Jules Destrée, the socialist man of letters, eloquently summed up all the socialists' objections to the bill. If the Congo yields profits, he said, the capitalists will benefit from them; if it makes a loss the Belgian workers

---

[1] Stengers, pp. 319 ff.

[2] Paul Janson said: 'Je dis que le Congo, internationalisé, apporterait les mêmes avantages que l'annexion et nous éviterait de nous engager dans une affaire trop vaste et périlleuse.' Delange-Janson, *Paul Janson* ii. 369.

will have to pay for it. The risks are enormous, and who will defend the colony against other imperialists? The socialists have no reason to soil their hands with the crimes inherent in all colonial policy and should refuse to accept the odious heritage of the Congo State. Even if a socialist like Vandervelde were to become Colonial Secretary, the party ought to say categorically that it is not prepared to allow Belgium, unwilling or unable to alleviate the misery of its own people, to assume responsibilities in such distant and foreign parts.[1] Destrée's flexible and puritanical arguments turned out to be convincing. Émile Vandervelde, the only socialist in Parliament in favour of annexation who believed that Belgium should take up the burden, failed to persuade his comrades that for the very reason of their anti-imperialism they must acquire a colony in order to rescue it. He was a close collaborator of E. D. Morel and one of the first in Belgium to understand that the British campaign was not motivated by national egotism or greed but by genuine humanitarianism. His interest in the matter was so deep that he did what nearly all the enemies and all the advocates of Leopold's politics omitted to do and what the King himself failed to do as well: he went to see the Congo for himself in 1908. He was an extremely sensitive man and experienced the atrocious misery he witnessed as a physical pain.[2] His attitude closely resembled that of the Dutch socialists who in spite of their anti-imperialist principles did not want to back out of their national and moral obligations towards the colonies.

Even before the socialists, the radical liberals had exposed the horrors of Leopold's system of forced labour, and in 1908 they followed the socialist line. As they were electorally dependent on socialist support they did not have much choice anyway. With only one exception all the Roman Catholics supported the bill, some with conviction, others with resignation, many with indifference. All of them, however, agreed that the problem must be solved as rapidly and efficiently as possible. Eight liberals joined them. Among them was the very active and in later days celebrated Paul Hymans,[3] who

---

[1] J. Destrée, *Discours parlementaires* (Brussels, 1914), pp. 408 ff.

[2] Vandervelde, *Souvenirs*, pp. 71 ff. Cf. his *Les Derniers jours de l'État du Congo* (Brussels, 1908).

[3] Paul Hymans (1865–1941) was a liberal and a Protestant. He started as a

spoke eloquently in favour of annexation. He and his friends were fervent royalists. In their eyes the King whom they admired profoundly was the dominating figure in the state, the highest expression of national unity. In this period when the liberal party itself was impotent, only his power and insight might form a barrier against Roman Catholicism and socialism.[1] Yet Hymans refused to support the King's plans for the Crown domain. Because of his royalism he was ideologically committed to the King's Congo policies, but his liberal interpretation of the constitution forced him to fight the royal projects vigorously and with great effect from 1906 to 1908. In his own party he was rather isolated. But after the Congo had become a Belgian colony men like Vandervelde and Hymans soon reconciled their parties to the idea of colonialism. It is remarkable how quickly anti-imperialism disappeared after 1908.

The colonial system of government introduced in 1908 was highly centralized; the colony was ruled from Brussels. Moreover, it was still strongly influenced by the King who together with the Minister of Colonies exercised an authority Parliament did not curb although it had the power to do so. Shortly before 1914 cautious proposals were put forward to give the colony more autonomy and to create political institutions with some responsibility of their own. But these suggestions were never taken up, so neither the whites nor the indigenous population had the opportunity to participate in government at any level. But of course the nature of the colonial regime changed rapidly. The state monopoly on produce was gradually abolished, the judicial system was improved, forced labour was replaced by a money tax, and the spirit running through these reforms worked in other fields, the spirit of a benevolent but unadventurous and unambitious paternalism. All this reassured the United States and Britain to such an extent that they decided in 1911 and 1913 respectively to recognize Belgian annexation. For four decades the Congo was henceforth held to be a normal, decently governed, reasonably happy, and profitable colony.

barrister, became professor at the Free University of Brussels in 1897, and entered the Chamber of Representatives in 1900.

[1] Hymans, *Mémoires*, i. 12 ff.

2. *Dutch Colonial Policy*

In 1870 the Dutch liberals won the battle over colonial policy; their principles triumphed. They abolished the state monopoly and made the East Indies more accessible to private entrepreneurs. Initially this seemed sound enough from an economic point of view; it was obviously in accordance with the spirit of the time and could also be considered the logical corollary of the opening of the Suez Canal in 1869. The following years were characterized by energetic activity. Many new plantations were started by business men who obtained the necessary capital from the hastily founded 'culture banks' which specialized in financing this sort of enterprise. The value of exports from the East Indies rose from 108 million guilders in 1870 to more than 175 million in 1880; total imports increased from 44·5 million guilders in 1870 to 141 million in 1890 and included many consumer goods for the Indonesian population such as rice and cotton.[1] New Dutch steamship companies—the Amsterdam Nederland (1870) and the Rotterdam Lloyd (1883) which together founded the Royal Paketvaartmaatschappij (1888) for transport in Indonesian waters—at last made an attempt to break through what was virtually a British monopoly and were not unsuccessful.

Yet liberal freedom did not by any means bring all the benefits expected of it. It is true that this freedom was defined in too narrow a manner.[2] In the mother country itself the liberal conception of freedom had more positive significance; it meant the free development of all national resources and of all members of the community. But even in the Netherlands this principle was of limited effectiveness, and it was totally irrelevant

---

[1]. See the figures in J. S. Furnivall, *Netherlands India. A Study of Plural Economy* (Cambridge, 1939), p. 207.

[2] The attitude of the Dutch liberals in the 1870s towards the migration of coolies from China and British India to the sugar plantations in Surinam and the tobacco plantations in Sumatra is characteristic. The British Liberal Cabinet allowed such emigration and employment only on strict conditions and under government supervision; the Dutch liberals objected to state interference and by so doing allowed the innumerable abuses following from uncontrolled immigration and employment of this foreign labour force. British liberalism was in this matter a step ahead of Dutch liberalism, as is rightly stated by F. van Dongen, *Tussen neutraliteit en imperialisme. De Nederlands-Chinese betrekkingen van 1863 tot 1901* (Groningen, 1966), p. 100.

in the colonies. In purely economic terms too free enterprise in its initial form soon proved unsatisfactory. From 1873 to 1895 world prices of colonial products tended to fall; in 1884 sugar, the most important product of Java, dropped to half its previous value. The crisis was aggravated by the cane disease.[1] But in any case the financial policy was unsound: the culture banks made capital too readily available without sufficient guarantees, and the planters took too many risks. In the mid-1880s a financial catastrophe seemed imminent; it was partly avoided by rapid help from other banks which gave rise to a healthier system. The structure of both banks and plantations was radically altered, the banks being made dependent on the big commercial banks in Holland and the plantations being transformed into limited companies. The small-scale individualism of the 1870s and 1880s was replaced by large-scale capitalism based in the Netherlands.[2]

It was inevitable, therefore, that the growing prosperity from which the Indonesian population had benefited during the first years after the introduction of liberalism in the East Indies should be followed by a period of stagnation or even decline. During the 1880s and 1890s it was gradually realized that the liberal principle of non-interference was causing fundamental changes in the social structure which might ultimately be damaging for the natives, unable to create for themselves a new framework within which they could find security. Moreover, politically, liberalism failed to provide an adequate basis for the solution of the many acute problems that arose. By far the most important was the Achin War and the whole question of the so-called Outer Possessions it provoked—that is, all Dutch possessions in the Archipelago outside the islands of Java and Madura. Although during the nineteenth century the Dutch administration had tried to confirm its rights, even through military expeditions, to most of the other islands, such as Borneo, Sumatra, Celebes, and Bali, effective occupation had not taken place and had not been attempted. The Dutch had no other ambition than to have their sovereignty formally recognized by the indigenous princes,

[1] G. Gonggrijp, *Schets ener economische geschiedenis van Indonesië* (4th edn., Haarlem, 1957), pp. 126 ff.
[2] Furnivall, op. cit., pp. 197–9.

hoping that such paper rights would sufficiently impress and deter other colonizing states, especially of course Britain. It was in Achin that it first became apparent how unsatisfactory this situation was. The Dutch were quite unable to guarantee the safety of the seas round Achin. Several times foreign ships, most of them British, were captured by Achinese pirates, and when with the opening of the Suez Canal the main route to the Dutch East Indies no longer ran via the Cape through the Sunda Straits but via Ceylon through the Straits of Malacca, more coherent action was considered imperative. The Dutch tried to solve the problem by bringing heavy pressure to bear upon the Sultan of Achin but they failed. In 1873 the Netherlands declared war on this small state, which had a population of some 550,000 inhabitants.[1]

It took the Dutch several decades to establish their power in Achin. In the 1870s and 1880s neither the geography nor the political and social structure of the area was sufficiently known. In 1873 it was hoped to subject the population by means of a single rapid expedition. This was unsuccessful. In the following years various new methods were attempted: blockade of the coast, reconciliation, concentration of the Dutch army in the north within a short line of fortified posts— all of them failed. Partly because of a genuine lack of funds, and partly for political reasons and a reluctance to get involved in an unattractive and unprofitable adventure, money for more ambitious projects was not made available. Until 1885 between 15 and 20 million guilders yearly were spent on Achin; after 1885 when the so-called concentration system was tried and the Dutch forces remained stationary within a circle of about three miles, costs were much lower (about 7 millions

---

[1] This became possible when Britain, which had obliged the Dutch by a treaty of 1824 to respect the autonomy of Sumatra, gave them a free hand in that area in 1871 on the condition that British trade would be treated in the same way as Dutch trade. For the way in which the treaty of 1871 was connected with the treaty by which the Dutch transferred the African Gold Coast to Britain see D. Coombs, *The Gold Coast, Britain and the Netherlands 1850-1874* (Oxford, 1963), pp. 71 ff.; P. van 't Veer, *De Atjeh-oorlog* (Amsterdam, 1969) describes in detail the misleading messages, intrigues, and misunderstandings by which the Governor-General was persuaded to force the liberal and by no means warlike Cabinet at The Hague to send a formal declaration of war. Conservatives and anti-revolutionaries were opposed to what they regarded as an unjust war of conquest, Kuyper denounced the 'liberal' war in strong terms: ibid., pp. 72-3.

a year) but for the twelve years during which this policy was maintained nothing whatsoever was achieved.[1] In the early 1890s the bankruptcy of traditional policies towards the Outer Provinces was glaringly apparent.

To solve their problems the Dutch evolved their own form of capitalist imperialism which in their political vocabulary was called 'ethical policy'. It was not the offspring of one specific political party; progressive liberals and some socialists were among its earliest advocates, but the Protestant Christian democrats were the first to give it a firm shape. It should be noted that, whereas the Belgian radicals differed from their Dutch colleagues by being anti-imperialist, the Belgian Christian democrats reacted roughly in the same manner as their Protestant brothers. In the form it took in the Netherlands in the 1890s modern imperialism was not initially prompted by economic motives, although no doubt its endorsement in the early twentieth century was very largely due to its economic success. The original inspiration, however, was ethical rather than economic, and it was initially carried through by idealistic scholars and statesmen and not by business men. The splendid report written by Dr. C. Snouck Hurgronje in 1892 about his investigations in Achin was essentially imperialistic. When Snouck (1857–1936) went to the East Indies in 1889 in the capacity of the government's adviser on Eastern languages and Islamic law he was already a famous man. In 1888 he had published (in German) his big book on Mecca where three years earlier he had managed to live as a Muslim in order to study the theory and practice of Islam. During the thirty years of his professorship at Leiden University, from 1906 until his death, he became recognized as the greatest international authority in Islamic studies. His colonial ideal, for which he found support in the East Indies at the start of his career but which was steadily abandoned after 1918, was called the policy of association. Through energetic Westernization, the native élite would, according to this theory, be rapidly educated and the East Indies would become an equal partner in connection with the motherland. But before this was possible it was necessary to bring the whole empire under effective

[1] F. W. Stapel (ed.), *Geschiedenis van Nederlandsch Indië*, v (Amsterdam, 1940), pp. 349 ff.

Dutch rule. From July 1891 to February 1892 Snouck travelled through Achin; in May 1892 he handed in his report, and some descriptive chapters from it were published in 1893 and 1894 in book form.[1]

With great intelligence and learning Snouck described the religious-nationalistic elements in Achinese resistance, which could in his view only be overcome by strong aggressive policies. However, it was not sufficient to restore authority by punitive expeditions; the Dutch should also try to convince the Achinese of their benevolent intentions. It was a most urgent task in this exhausted country to promote agriculture, industry, and especially trade.[2] Soon afterwards J. B. van Heutsz (1851–1924) published a series of articles in which he too advocated a more aggressive conduct of the war. Van Heutsz was a soldier and his views were undoubtedly less carefully worked out than those of Snouck.[3] But he was a cheerful man, an optimist who took difficulties and problems lightly. With his exuberant energy and his reckless, malicious way of talking he was a striking and original figure in the rather weightily conservative colonial society. After some years Snouck succeeded in getting Van Heutsz appointed civil and military governor of Achin in 1898 and he himself was associated with him in an advisory capacity. The new policy towards one of the Outer Possessions thus began and later Van Heutsz, as Governor-General between 1904 and 1909, extended it successfully throughout the whole empire. From 1898 Indonesia was gradually transformed into a single state governed from Batavia, a coherent colonial empire under effective (though by no means everywhere direct) Dutch rule. Although Snouck soon came into conflict with Van Heutsz, whom he criticized very pertinently for his abrupt, brazen way of doing things, his defective understanding of men, his lack of loyalty towards his friends and inferiors and of insight into Indonesian society and

[1] An English translation under the title *The Achehnese* was published in 1906. See also Harry J. Benda, 'Christiaan Snouck Hurgronje and the Foundation of Dutch Islamic Policy in Indonesia', *Journal of Modern History*, xxx (1958), 338 ff. and his article in *International Encyclopaedia of the Social Sciences*, xiv (1968), pp. 340 ff.

[2] The political chapters of the report were published by E. Gobée and C. Adriaanse (eds.), *Ambtelijke adviezen van C. Snouck Hurgronje, 1889–1936* (3 vols., The Hague, 1957–65), i. 47 ff.

[3] Ibid. 116–24. Cf. K. van der Maaten, *Snouck Hurgronje en de Atjeh Oorlog* (2 vols., Leiden, 1948), i. 105 ff.

mentality,[1] Van Heutsz's imperialistic policy was made possible and in major part inspired by the great scholar.

In the Dutch East Indies it was a practical problem that forced the administration to revise the liberal system of non-interference. The theory was developed in the Netherlands. In 1899 the liberal monthly *De Gids* published an article that may be considered a manifesto of the new ethical policy. Its author, C. Th. van Deventer (1857–1915) started his career in the Indonesian judiciary but made his fortune as a barrister at Semarang; in 1897 he returned to Europe. He was an erudite, artistically minded but not creative man, capable of lucid literary exercises if little more. His tastes and views were 'modern'; he was deeply devoted to Wagner about whom he wrote many articles in the Indonesian Press. Although origin-ally a liberal himself he developed such a contempt for liberal policy during his stay in the East Indies that he wel-comed the formation of the first Dutch 'clerical' Cabinet in 1888, believing that it would be particularly advantageous for the colonies. He admired Abraham Kuyper as 'the most skilful demagogue since 1848' and was fascinated by the Protestant political programme.[2] At the same time he was in sympathy with the socialists and the idea of land nationaliza-tion. Anything, it seemed to him, was better than the free entrepreneurship that had led to such intolerable abuses. He preferred a modernized culture-system to the liberal system, allowing the state to act as agricultural entrepreneur, provided the profits were used to develop the magnificent colony.[3] After his return to the Netherlands he started to sort out his ideas. His long article of 1899 was the first fruit of his labours and it attracted more attention than he had dared to hope for. In fact his main thesis was of a rather arbitrary kind.[4] Van Deventer argued that until 1868 the Dutch could justifiably use Indonesian profits for their own benefit. The victory of the liberals, however, had radically changed the situation. Never-theless, the Dutch state had continued for another ten years to collect money to a total of 151 million guilders. From 1876

---

[1] See Snouck's report of 2 Oct. 1903: *Ambtelijke adviezen* i. 320–56.

[2] H. T. Colenbrander and J. E. Stokvis, *Leven en arbeid van Mr. C. Th. van Deventer* (3 vols., Amsterdam, 1916–17), i. 153.

[3] Ibid. 161–2.   [4] Ibid. ii. 1–47.

the stream of money ran dry as the Achin War devoured huge amounts of capital. In Van Deventer's view it was the duty of the Dutch to return to Indonesia these 151 million guilders and also another 36 million they had misappropriated. This capital ought to be spent on building railways, harbours, and irrigation works in the colony. Henceforward Dutch and Indonesian state finances must be separated to prevent the possibility of further abuses. The democratic Netherlands had a mission to fulfil in the East Indies. Its task was to develop the colony, to work towards unity and ultimate independence, and to bring prosperity. Van Deventer conceded that a mature Indonesia might in some unforeseeable future wish to break the link with the Netherlands, but for the time being close connections should be maintained for the benefit of the native population.[1] Van Deventer joined those radical liberals who in 1901 founded a new party, the Vrijzinnig-Democratische Bond (VDB: Liberal Democratic Association).

There remained, however, a general consensus among the parties about colonial policy. The socialists hardly attempted to develop an original point of view. They had but one colonial specialist, H. H. van Kol (1852–1925), a technologist who had long worked in the East Indian government service and after his repatriation in 1892 had devoted himself to Dutch politics with the total dedication and enthusiasm that was characteristic of him. In 1894 he helped found the Sociaal-Democratische Arbeiderspartij (SDAP: Social Democratic Workers Party), and in 1897 he entered the Second Chamber where he naturally became the spokesman for colonial affairs. The policy he advocated did not differ essentially from that of Van Deventer: an ethical, humanitarian, paternalistic policy of slow emancipation within the framework of industrial capitalism. His only novel proposal came in 1903 when, deeply pessimistic about Dutch resources, he proposed to sell part of the Outer Possessions to bigger and richer states more likely to be successful in furthering development. His party did not accept the idea.[2] Van Deventer, too, who did not oppose the effective occupation of the Outer Provinces,[3] attacked Van Kol's proposal. In

---

[1] Colenbrander and Stokvis, op. cit., ii 88 ff.
[2] Cf. F. Tichelman, 'De SDAP en Indonesië, 1897–1907', *De Nieuwe Stem* (1968).
[3] Colenbrander and Stokvis, op. cit. i. 303, 317.

spite of this, the SDAP, a party committed in the 1890s to radical reform in domestic affairs but with little time to spare for colonial problems, allowed Van Kol to represent the party in an international context as the first European socialist with direct personal experience of colonial administration.[1]

The Protestant Christian democrats had a much more important contribution to make. In article eighteen of the antirevolutionary programme of 1878 exploitation of the colonies for the benefit of the mother country was condemned, irrespective of whether it was done by the state or by private entrepreneurs, and a 'policy of moral obligation' was advocated. The Netherlands was to act as guardian to the East Indian population which should be led towards independence and, as far as possible, Christianity.[2] This was a responsibility which, in Kuyper's view, the country should proudly and unhesitatingly bear, keeping a vigilant eye on the greed of the British, always eager to expand their empire at the cost of the Dutch. Kuyper was ahead of the other parties both in his 'ethical' colonial views and in his messianic nationalism. In his newspaper, *De Standaard*, one of the members of his party working in the East Indies was allowed to develop his ethical conceptions in great detail. In a series of articles published in the course of the 1880s this writer insisted on the necessity of granting financial independence to the East Indies, and of reducing the taxes payable by the indigenous population. The army and navy should be strengthened and vigorous action should be taken in Achin. He emphasized the need for railways, roads, irrigation works, the development of the Outer Provinces, for improved training of autochthonous civil servants.[3] So it followed that a Christian cabinet under Kuyper himself was the first to make the ethical colonial conception government policy and to proclaim in the speech from the throne (1901) that the Netherlands as a Christian nation had a moral obligation towards the colonies. It was logical too that A. W. F. Idenburg (1861–1935), who both as Colonial Secretary (1902–5, 1908, 1918–19) and as Governor-General (1909–16) best represented

[1] Furnivall, p. 230.
[2] Kuyper, *Ons Program*, pp. 955 ff. and *Antirevolutionaire staatkunde*, ii. 579 ff.
[3] D. M. G. Koch, *Batig slot. Figuren uit het oude Indië* (Amsterdam, 1960), pp. 70 ff. The author was called Teun Ottolander.

these policies, should have been a member of the Anti-
revolutionary Party. Ethical policy formed an integral part of
the Christian democratic system with its inclination towards
nationalism, militarism, and imperialism. Van Heutsz, who as
Governor-General loyally followed Idenburg, the Colonial
Secretary, Idenburg himself, and Van Heutsz's aide-de-camp
H. Colijn—in later years the leader of the Anti-revolutionary
party—all started their careers as soldiers. In the 1830's the
culture-system was introduced by Governors-General with a
military training; from 1841 to 1899 all Governors-General
with one exception were civilians. From 1899 to 1916 responsibility for the colonies was once again carried by men who at
some stage of their life had been professional soldiers.

Ethical policy had strong nationalist overtones. From 1901
until his death in 1933 the famous jurist C. van Vollenhoven
taught colonial public law and native customary (adat) law
at the University of Leiden. He was a member of the liberal
democratic party. In 1899 he felt deeply moved by Van
Deventer's *Gids* article on Indonesia.[1] In 1906 when Snouck
Hurgronje too came to Leiden the university developed into a
centre of Islamic and Indian studies and served as the main
school for training colonial civil servants who departed for
Indonesia imbued with precise knowledge, ethical conceptions,
and Dutch nationalism. In the pre-1914 years Van Vollenhoven was a fervent nationalist. He published a booklet in
1913 called *De eendracht van het land* (*The Concord of the Country*)
that made quite an impression. The Dutch people, as if
predestined by a higher power to greater things, had become
strong again through economic recovery and through the
magnificent development of its authority in the East Indies.
Now he called upon it to restore its seventeenth-century glory
by assuming an international task. The nation needed a 'central
mission'. This was easy enough to define: the Netherlands had
the duty to start building up an international police force,
the strong arm of international law fighting for peace. It was
obliged by its tradition to dare act as Jeanne d'Arc, La Fayette,
Saint Paul had done, and it was in a better position to do so
than the United States or France, which perhaps felt a kindred

---

[1] Henriëtte L. T. de Beaufort, *Cornelis van Vollenhoven, 1874–1933* (Haarlem, 1954),
p. 46.

messianic call. It was more prosperous than France and more disinterested than either nation. As a vital young people, Van Vollenhoven wrote, we want to resume our place in the first rank of nations; our inspiration must come from 'the knowledge that we can return to glory in an international role'.[1]

Although the general concept of ethical policy was not of course peculiar to the Netherlands, in its practical application the theory had to be adapted to the special situation in the Dutch colony and so it developed its own characteristic features. This was a complicated process. It was relatively easy to define Dutch obligations abstractly, but in practice, faced by everyday realities, it was by no means easy to determine them with any degree of precision. The uncertainties concerning Dutch educational policy are typical. Van den Bosch, the initiator of the culture-system, had taken the line as early as the 1830s that it was the duty of the Dutch to educate the Indonesian population—but there was no money for it then and probably it did not fit too well into the system as a whole anyway. The liberals who came to power in 1848 devoted more attention to the matter but at the end of the century education was still extremely restricted. No more than about 100,000 indigenous children attended a primary school. The higher forms of education were available to a tiny minority of Indonesians. The training-schools for Indonesian teachers had less than 150 pupils; those for Indonesian civil servants about 200, and the few secondary schools had practically no indigenous pupils at all. Van Deventer calculated that at the end of the century the educational situation in Java and Madura was dramatically worse than in British India where proportionately eight times as many children attended school.[2] Obviously the ethicals were faced by a grave challenge and they met it with the utmost seriousness. In 1907 Van Heutsz introduced a new type of school, the village school, providing basic education in a three-year course run by the village communities themselves. In 1915 these schools had more than 300,000 pupils; in the following years the numbers rose rapidly and reached nearly two million in 1940. The number

---

[1] C. van Vollenhoven, *De eendracht van het land* (The Hague, 1913), pp. 96, 56, and *passim*.
[2] Colenbrander and Stokvis, i. 289.

of pupils in ordinary primary schools offering a somewhat longer course trebled during the first fifteen years of the twentieth century.

But of course none of this was enough. It proved impossible to build up a comprehensive basic educational system for a population growing at such an alarming rate: neither the money nor the teachers were available. In 1815 Java had 4·5 million inhabitants, in 1880 nearly 20 million, in 1930 41·7 million. From 1900 to 1928 the number of children between the ages of six and eight increased by 1·9 million; the number of children attending school by only 1·3 million.[1] Moreover, Dutch educational policy was burdened with an insoluble problem, or one that nobody had the courage to solve: that of the language. The Dutch administration in Batavia was reluctant to spread the Dutch language. The mass of the Indonesian population, as far as it received any education, was taught in the regional language; the teachers too were kept ignorant of Dutch. The argument was that by teaching some Dutch one might develop a proletariat divorced from its own environment and class but without any chance of making a living elsewhere. Thus Dutch was handled as a language which was only to be permitted as a privilege to a small élite. Eventually, and in fact more rapidly than was expected, the indigenous aristocracy as well as the Indonesian civil servants in the lower ranks developed social ambitions that could only be fulfilled by better schooling. The authorities reacted with the greatest caution. No one denied that this was a phenomenon to be applauded and that some new facilities ought to be provided; in actual practice, however, the reluctance to offer decent large-scale teaching in Dutch severely restricted the opportunities available to the indigenous population. In this field various Dutch traditions were operative which could not immediately be overcome: the emphasis laid in the Netherlands itself on basic instead of secondary education; a certain scepticism regarding the usefulness of the Dutch language in a world which ignored it; the unlimited perfectionism of Dutch secondary and grammar schools with their overloaded teaching programmes especially in languages which

[1] I. Brugmans, 'Onderwijspolitiek', in H. Baudet and I. Brugmans (eds.), *Balans van beleid* (Assen, 1961), p. 157.

were rightly considered unsuited to Indonesian pupils.[1] Snouck Hurgronje, Idenburg, and others did what they could to break the barriers and to make Dutch available to larger groups. Undoubtedly they achieved something, but a clear decision was never taken and a rational system was not developed. It is true that De Kat Angelino also regarded Dutch educational policy as an element in a coherent whole of administrative principles, but the reader of the documents sees the improvisations, the hesitations, and the good intentions rather than the guidelines of a system.

This is natural enough. The problems were virtually unmanageable. Moreover, ethical policy was drafted for the benefit of a passive, backward people who were to be educated by the superior Dutch race to a measure of independence.[2] It was questionable whether such a policy would prove sufficiently flexible to be adapted to the first totally unexpected manifestations of Indonesian activity. In 1908 when the Javanese society for the elevation of the natives, Budi Utomo, was founded and some years later when a nationalist-religious movement, Sarekat Islam, emerged, Idenburg as Colonial Secretary and later as Governor-General allowed them, with the wisdom and tact that distinguished this eminent statesman, the opportunity to develop in relative freedom. Even so no adequate answer to their claims was forthcoming. The movements were studied seriously and their appearance was recognized as inevitable. They fitted, it was thought, into the pattern of 'the awakening of Asia'—brought about by the Chinese, the first activist group in the Dutch East Indies,[3] the Japanese,

[1] Interesting material in S. L. van der Wal (ed.), *Het onderwijsbeleid in Nederlands-Indië, 1900–1940* (Groningen, 1963). Cf. Snouck Hurgronje, *Ambtelijke adviezen* iii. 2000–13 and for a comparison with Chinese schools in British India see C. Smit (ed.), *Bescheiden betreffende de buitenlandse politiek van Nederland 1848–1919*, 3rd period, *1899–1919*, iii (The Hague, 1961), pp. 88 ff. See also P. L. Geschiere, 'The Education Issue in the Dutch East Indies in the Twentieth Century. Opinions on the Question of 'Western Education' versus 'National Education'', *Acta Historiae Neerlandicae*, vi (The Hague, 1973), 146 ff.

[2] See Kuyper's speech in the Second Chamber (1900) as quoted by H. A. Idema, *Parlementaire geschiedenis van Nederlandsch-Indië 1891–1918* (The Hague, 1918), p. 141.

[3] The situation of the Chinese was bad. In contrast to the few Dutchmen living in China who enjoyed extraterritorial rights, the 10,000 Chinese in Netherlands India were subjected to humiliating regulations by which they were virtually put on the same level as the native population. Cf. Van Dongen, op. cit., pp. 80, 108, 142.

and the Indians in the British Empire; they were related to the emergence of militant Muhammadanism in Turkey and ought not to be regarded, everyone agreed, as forms of transient, isolated unrest that could be rapidly eliminated.[1] However, the problem had little urgency in that before 1914 neither Budi Utomo nor Sarekat Islam strove for independence. There was only one group that did so: the Indian party started by the Indo-Europeans in 1912. These men wanted a completely independent East India in which the various races—Europeans, Chinese, and natives—would melt together into one unity. Before 1914 this was the only party the government took action against: it was forbidden and its leaders were banned. Its purposes later proved unrealistic. The Indonesian empire they were dreaming of, built up on the basis of a complete amalgamation of races and groups of people according to the pattern of South American republics, did not materialize. After the Second World War, when Indonesia became independent, only 18 per cent of the Indo-Europeans chose to remain in the new state now ruled by the natives.[2]

Until the 1920s the principles of ethical policy were universally accepted and did not come under discussion. Although Van Deventer's suggestion that 187 million guilders should be returned to the colony was not put into effect, government and Parliament were willing to help the East Indies financially. When Idenburg resigned as Colonial Secretary in 1905 his successor, a liberal, emphasized that his own policies would be inspired by the same ideas for there was no disagreement among the political parties as far as these were concerned.[3] This was perfectly true. During parliamentary debates on colonial affairs the various parties did not follow specific party lines. In 1906 the Second Chamber discussed a government proposal to expand the use of Dutch law in the East Indies. Both Idenburg and Van Deventer were in favour of this. But men like Van Kol, a socialist, and the liberal N. G. Pierson were against such a system of Westernization and unification. They wanted

---

[1] See the excellent reports published by S. L. van der Wal (ed.), *De opkomst van de nationalistische beweging in Nederlands-Indië* (Groningen, 1967); Snouck Hurgronje, iii. 2000 ff.; F. L. Rutgers, *Idenburg en de Sarekat Islam in 1913* (Amsterdam, 1939).

[2] P. W. van der Veur, 'De Indo-Europeanen: een probleem en uitdaging', in Baudet and Brugmans (eds.), *Balans van beleid*, p. 98.

[3] Idema, op. cit., p. 187.

to maintain as far as possible native customary law—the adat law.[1] They endorsed the thesis of Van Vollenhoven who in the same year began the publication of his systematic exposition of traditional Indonesian law. On this question too a discussion arose within the framework of ethical conceptions, a discussión of great importance but without consequences for party politics. In the long run both the government and public opinion came to accept Van Vollenhoven's point of view and encouraged the growth or the maintenance of a pluralistic system of law. For the Europeans, Indo-Europeans, and the Chinese a slightly modified form of Dutch law applied: for the native population Van Vollenhoven and his pupils systematized adat law. Yet the political parties did at least take the opportunity to enter into a long-drawn-out discussion about one point. From 1911 the liberal democrats and other parties of the Left considered it necessary to warn repeatedly against the government's tendency to concentrate on developing the Christian schools. Probably the criticism was unfounded.[2] In practice the result may have been to stimulate Sarekat Islam in the East Indies, where echoes of these debates naturally penetrated and this was not an anti-Dutch but by definition an anti-Christian movement.

It is really impossible to determine with any precision whether ethical policy was successful in improving the standard of living of the natives. At various times attempts have been made to calculate the average income of native families but estimates vary so widely that no reliable conclusions can be drawn. Despite repeated attempts to determine the percentage of income that had to be paid in taxes there is no agreement about this either.[3] Thanks to the introduction of income tax in the East Indies in 1908, which of course mainly concerned the Europeans, the state received considerably more income, but it is questionable whether the tax load carried by the indigenous population was much reduced after this. Ironically these uncertainties are partly due to the very thoroughness of the investigations. One of the first acts of the ethical statesmen was to establish in 1902 a committee to study the causes

---

[1] Snouck Hurgronje was the first to use this term in his book *De Atjehers* (1892–3). The word 'adat' is Arabic and means 'custom'.

[2] Rutgers, op. cit., p. 40.   [3] Ibid., p. 26; Furnivall, pp. 393 ff.

of what was called the diminished prosperity of the natives. The committee spent three years in collecting material; this then turned out to be so immense that it was not until 1920 that its publication in thirty-five volumes was completed. Despite the precariousness of all generalizations in this matter, however, it is generally considered probable that notwithstanding the rapid population growth the economic situation of the masses improved, at least between 1904 and 1914. If this development did not continue after the World War that can partly be explained by the gaps which clearly existed in the system of ethical policy, but on the other hand there were international factors at work for which the Dutch administration can hardly be held responsible. However one may wish to judge the ultimate results of ethical policy one thing is clear: though it may be true that the native population benefited from the greatly expanded state care for education, health, means of communication, credit banks, and agriculture, until 1920 the Dutch economy itself was making bigger profits from the colonies than it had ever done. Ethical imperialism was an economic success for the mother country. It is an unrealistic simplification to say, as has been done, that territorial imperialism was intended to open the Outer Possessions for capitalistic exploitation and that the attempt to raise the level of native prosperity served Dutch industry in need of a mass market, yet it would be equally naïve to deny that these phenomena were related to one another. It cannot be accidental that the transformation of the Dutch economy and the general acceptance of ethical colonial principles occurred simultaneously.

3. *The Dutch Economy*

In 1913 Van Vollenhoven, calling upon the Netherlands to make a bid for international greatness, declared that the nation had unique opportunities before it: 'in twenty years', he wrote, 'there has been born a new Netherlands'[1]—vigorous and healthy thanks to its own prosperity and no less to the unparalleled prosperity of the East Indies. The author had good reason to be optimistic. Apparently the growth of the Dutch

[1] *Eendracht*, p. 48.

economy during the 1890s had been so fast that it amounted to a fundamental structural change.[1] In the course of two decades the Dutch had at last succeeded in raising the level of their economy to that of their neighbours. But notwithstanding the relative rapidity of the process it cannot be called revolutionary. The Netherlands did not go through a period of over-hasty innovation and adventurous expansion followed by desperate collapse. Neither was it hit to the same extent by the social difficulties which accompanied industrialization elsewhere. The country owed this harmonious development to two main factors. Firstly, the economic and political conditions for development had been gradually established in a long period of adaptation; secondly, the state was already in possession of an apparatus with which to control social tensions. Perhaps two additional factors helped as well: as the economic renovation of the Netherlands took place forty years after Belgium and twenty years after Germany the mistakes made by the pioneers were known and could be avoided; moreover, the economic level of the country before it entered into the phase of dynamic growth was very much higher than it was, for example, in Belgium when the economy in that country began to be transformed.

The circumstances that made Dutch economic expansion possible form a complex whole difficult to analyse. It is obvious that Dutch willingness, apparent since 1890 in both the colonial and the economic field, to substitute for their wait-and-see policies a certain measure of aggressiveness was somehow related to the intellectual development of the 1860s and 1870s. The first protagonists of the ethical policy were born in the 1850s and grew up in an intellectual climate which was changing fundamentally. They belonged to the same generation as the leaders of the artistic and literary movement of the 1880s or were slightly older; they shared this generation's desire to establish for their nation a new and more honourable place in the world. During the 1880s the men of letters succeeded in relating Dutch culture to international developments; after 1890 Dutch colonial and economic expansion also began to be determined and accelerated by the international rhythm. Whereas earlier Dutch reactions to what was happening abroad

[1] I follow the interpretation of De Jonge, *De industrialisatie in Nederland tussen 1850 en 1914.*

had been distrustful and negative, there was now a much greater readiness to respond and to assume the initiative. The country was structurally mature enough to achieve the expansion it was now seeking.

As a result of the school reforms groups of people emerged during the 1880s and 1890s who were able to play an important role in society without having had to meet the severe classicist requirements of the traditional higher education. The so-called Higher Burgher Schools founded by Thorbecke in 1863 and gradually growing in size and numbers produced pupils with some knowledge of modern languages and science.[1] Towards the end of the century about 10,000 such people had found a place in society. Moreover, the professional training of the workers, totally neglected at the beginning of the century, was looked after more carefully. The number of pupils attending some sort of technical school rose from 4,000 in 1860 to 8,000 in 1880 and 18,000 in 1900. The drastic improvements in primary education enforced by the laws of 1857 and 1878— the modifications of 1889 did not lower the quality of the schools —must also have had an effect which made itself increasingly felt over the years. In this way education not only improved in quality but also became more differentiated and adaptable. Economically the situation of the masses became probably somewhat better in the period from 1850 to 1880. The abolition of some indirect taxes on foodstuffs and the agricultural boom seem to have led to such an improvement in the quality of food available to the masses that illnesses like tuberculosis claimed fewer victims and the death rate began to drop from the 1870s onwards. During the same decade structural unemployment seems to have been drastically reduced. In agriculture, a very prosperous business until 1880, and the crafts associated with it or developing because of it, there was reasonably high employment. In mid-century about 10 per cent of the adult men were unemployed over long periods; this figure was to drop to 5 per cent.

Holland's share in international shipping which diminished during much of the nineteenth century became more important

[1] The international prestige of Dutch science was emphasized by the fact that the first Nobel prizes for physics and chemistry went to Dutch and German scientists (1901 and 1902).

again in the late 1870s. The newly established connections with the sea and the modern harbour equipment at Amsterdam and Rotterdam enabled these ports to benefit from worldwide commercial activities, which continued to grow even during the depression from 1873 to 1896 and then increased enormously. From 1875 to 1885 trade in the Dutch ports merely kept pace with the growth of world trade; after 1885 it considerably surpassed this. Most of the ships cleared in Dutch harbours sailed under the Dutch flag. From 1890 to 1910 the Dutch merchant fleet grew by 200 per cent. This was mainly due to the huge development of navigation to the East Indies: the tonnage destined for the colonies grew by 350 per cent. But navigation on the Rhine expanded as well, multiplying by five during this period. Naturally the Dutch shipyards profited, and although many orders for new ships were placed abroad, their manpower increased between 1889 and 1909 by 166 per cent.

The textile industry, one of the few important industries earlier in the nineteenth century, expanded greatly, especially the cotton industry; textiles were excellent articles for export to the East Indies and to other markets, and these also contributed considerably to Dutch overseas trade. Between 1887 and 1910 the textile manufacturers in Twente, the oldest centre of the industry in the Netherlands, doubled their machine plant. But the development of the metallurgic industry was still more striking. Around 1850 some 21,000 men, that is only 7 per cent of the Dutch factory workers, were employed in all its various branches, engineering works, metalware factories, forges, etc. In 1889 the number had risen to 37,000, in 1909 to 65,000; at that date nearly 40 per cent of these men worked in engineering and electrotechnical works, indicating that the former major sectors of metallurgy, the forges and the manufacture of metal ware, had slipped from their prominent position. A similar expansion is to be seen in many other industries, from the tobacco, sugar, beetsugar factories to the printing trade. Of course new industries were developed in this period and in some branches the Dutch established enterprises which grew into worldwide concerns: the chemical industry, margarine production started by Jurgens in 1871 and Simon van den Bergh in 1872, Philips's electric bulb factory begun in 1892. Between 1889 and 1909

Dutch industry clearly underwent a radical structural transformation. From 1859 to 1889 the number of people employed
in industry increased yearly by 5,000, from 1889 to 1909 by
12,000 yearly, and most of them found work in the larger
factories. This whole evolution was of course dependent on the
development of industrial investment. Increasingly a larger
proportion of the national income was made available for
industry. It has been estimated that in 1880 5 per cent of the
national income was invested in industry, and that twenty
years later it was 10 per cent. National wealth, in 1850 perhaps
amounting to 6,000 million guilders, was in 1913 calculated to
be 14,300 million of which 2,000 million were invested in
industry and 3,000 million in agriculture. Obviously, the
Netherlands had become an industrial country although to a
lesser extent than Britain, Belgium, or Germany. How unrevolutionary and undramatic the development of industry in
the Netherlands was in comparison to other countries is shown
by the following figures. In the period from 1880 to 1910 the
proportion of employed persons in industry rose in the United
States from 25 per cent to 32·1 per cent, in Belgium from
38·7 per cent to 50·1 per cent, in Germany from 36·5 per cent
to 52 per cent, in Sweden from 14 per cent to 30·4 per cent. In
the Netherlands it grew from 30·8 per cent in 1890 to 33·4 per
cent in 1910.[1]

It was not only industry that succeeded in taking advantage
of the expanding world economy, agriculture and commerce
were thriving too. In a sense the 'agrarian revolution' may
even be called more radical than the industrial one.[2] In 1878
the agrarian crisis affecting the whole of Europe manifested
itself in the Netherlands with familiar symptoms. Huge grain
imports from the United States, Russia, and other countries
forced prices down disastrously. In spite of pressure from the
representatives of the agrarian provinces the government refused to take protectionist measures, partly on grounds of
principle but also because it wanted to keep the price of bread
low and rather hoped that the farmers would react by starting
to grow other crops. The only important step taken by the
government was to set up a committee in 1886 to study the

[1] De Jonge, op. cit., p. 237.
[2] Brugmans, *Paardenkracht en mensenmacht*, pp. 288–311.

whole agrarian situation in detail. This turned out to be a useful initiative and the proposals made by this committee in the course of the following years were gradually put into practice by the government. The farmers were helped by close inspection of the quality of agrarian products, by better agricultural education, by the creation of more credit facilities, and many other measures of this kind. However, they did more than just wait for state aid. They improved their situation by changing over to cattle-breeding, fruit- and vegetable-growing, by clearing waste land and, especially, by developing highly successful co-operative enterprises—for buying supplies for selling products (co-operative auctions) or processing them (co-operative dairy factories), as well as for expanding credit (co-operative rural credit banks). After agrarian world prices began to rise again in 1895 this process of renovation continued at a faster rate; a new period of agricultural expansion started. Of course this whole complex of economic development led to greater prosperity. In the period from 1860 to 1910 national income increased by about 120 per cent. It is assumed that the workers also benefited. Whereas the general rise in prosperity between 1850 and 1910 is estimated at between 30 and 50 per cent the mass of the people may have experienced a rise of between 50 and 70 per cent so that their situation not only improved in an absolute sense but perhaps also proportionately (although little enough) in comparison with the richer classes.[1]

The impact of the colonial factor on the development of the Dutch economy was vital. With the end of the Achin War in 1903 and the appointment of Van Heutsz to the post of Governor-General in 1904, the colonial economy throve more than ever before. This was not only due to the considerable expansion of the traditional crops such as sugar (after 1903 when European governments modified their protectionist policies towards national beetsugar industries, cane sugar became a very profitable product again), coffee, and tea, but also to the exploration and the exploitation of the Outer Provinces. In Sumatra tobacco and rubber plantations developed rapidly (the latter also in Java); there also the gigantic petroleum industry came into being with H. W. A. Deterding (1865–1939) as one of the leaders of the Koninklijke Petroleum

[1] De Jonge, p. 294.

Maatschappij, which in 1907 started collaborating with the
Shell Company of Borneo. The Dutch East Indies became a
favourite area for investment, and foreign capital, particularly
British capital, poured in. From 1900 to 1913 the value of
East Indian exports increased by 150 per cent. It is difficult
to assess to what extent Dutch national income was enlarged
by the colonial expansion but it seems reasonable to assume that
whereas between 1870 and 1890 2 or 3 per cent of the national
income came from profits made in the Indonesian plantations
and sent to Holland, from leave allowances, etc., this rose to
at least 5 per cent after 1890. If income from navigation and
the export of Dutch industrial products to the colony is added,
the percentage of the national income derived from the East
Indies was 5 per cent in 1890 and 10 per cent in 1913. This
steep rise was undoubtedly instrumental in pushing the Dutch
economy into a new phase.[1]

4. The Belgian Economy

By 1914 Belgian national wealth seems to have been larger than
the Dutch not only in an absolute sense but also proportionately,
although the difference was probably small.[2] National income
per head of the population was approximately the same.[3]
This represented a great success for Belgium. In 1850 or 1860
Belgium was a poorer country than the Netherlands in spite of
its modern industry.[4] If the figures used here are more or less

[1] De Jonge, pp. 355–6, 358.
[2] These figures are tentative and hypothetical. Baudhuin, 'Histoire économique
de la Belgique', *Histoire de la Belgique contemporaine*, i. 347 and *Histoire économique
de la Belgique 1914–1939* (2 vols., 2nd edn., Brussels, 1946), i. 28 thinks that in 1913
Belgian national wealth amounted to almost 51,000 million francs, that is 6,700 *per
capita*. According to his calculation France possessed a national wealth of 7,200 *per
capita*, Germany of 5,800. If Dutch national wealth amounted to 14,300 million
guilders in 1913, this would mean a *per capita* wealth of 5,100 francs. Calculations
quoted by E. Mahaim, *Le Secours de chômage en Belgique pendant l'occupation allemande*
(Paris and New Haven, n.d.), p. 8 do not lead to substantially different results.
[3] Belgian national income amounted to 6,500 million francs (approximately
850 francs *per capita*); Dutch national income was 2,346 million guilders (approximately 835 francs *per capita*).
[4] Belgian national wealth in 1846 is estimated at 10,750 million francs, in 1895
at 29,830 million francs, that is respectively 2,460 and 4,560 francs *per capita*
(Baudhuin, *Histoire de la Belgique contemporaine*, i. 337 ff.). Between 1850 and 1860
the figure for the Netherlands was probably approximately 4,200 francs *per
capita*.

correct, Belgian wealth *per capita* reached the Dutch level about 1890; after that it surpassed it. This means that notwithstanding the superiority of its modern economic equipment Belgium needed half a century to catch up with the Netherlands; thanks to the post-1896 boom it then overtook it. In both countries the population grew rapidly, in Belgium from 4·3 million inhabitants in 1846 to 7·6 million in 1913 (that is, by 77 per cent), in the Netherlands from 3 to 6 million.

Probably the most remarkable aspect of the Belgian economy in this period was its high degree of internationalization. Of course Belgian industry with its small home market had always been forced to work for export. What was new, however, was that Belgian concerns now started to build public works and to found factories abroad. In the 1870s and 1880s the Belgians were already building railways and tramways in France, Austria, Germany, and Italy, but the various governments eventually put a stop to this sort of activity. Thereafter Belgian interests were directed more towards countries like Spain, South America, and British India where foreign entrepreneurs had a much freer hand. Édouard Empain (1852–1929) was one of the most ambitious and successful business men in this field. He exported his tramcars and tracks to France, Egypt, Spain, Russia, and China and in 1900 started to build the Paris Métro. His interests and enterprises (Ateliers de constructions électriques de Charleroi, 1904; Compagnie minière des grands lacs, in the Congo) were scattered all over the world; in 1905 he began to construct Heliopolis, an extremely modern suburb of Cairo. From the 1890s onwards Belgian manufacturers engaged in still more ambitious and sometimes riskier projects. They founded important steelworks in southern Russia; and although these suffered many tribulations around the turn of the century and some disappeared altogether, Belgian participation in Russian industry remained important. In 1914 161 Russian enterprises were dependent on Belgian capital to the tune of 2,350 million francs. Leopold II also vigorously supported Belgian activities in China where the Belgians played a surprisingly large part in railway construction.

Later, another development, the origin of which stems from this period, turned out to be of supreme importance for the structure of Belgium generally: the beginning of the industrialization of Flanders, with certain indications that in the Walloon provinces decline was appearing in some sectors of the economy. This was a complicated phenomenon caused by a number of unrelated factors.[1] One of them was the increasing demand for coal for the expanding industries. The Walloon coal-mines were either old-fashioned or nearing exhaustion and could not be developed after 1900 to meet the demand. It was necessary therefore to import coal: one million tons in 1880, almost eleven million in 1913. It was clearly more economic to build coke-factories near the ports, and the new coke-plants, gas-works, and associated enterprises were constructed on sites near the Flemish coast; new chemical works soon followed in the same areas. Around Antwerp many other factories dependent on imports were built, lead, zinc, and chromium works, for example. Quite unconnected with these enterprises and when they were already well under way, rich coalfields were discovered in Belgian Limburg. In 1906 the first concessions were allotted but regular production started only in 1917. The prospects looked splendid. Whereas the Walloon mines were estimated to contain no more than another 1,000 million tons the new find promised at least ten times as much. Finally, there was a third factor which gave the Flemish provinces greater economic importance. The market for cotton which had been produced at Ghent for many years was greatly enlarged in this period and wool lost its place as the most important Belgian textile product. In 1896 15,709 workers were employed in the Belgian cotton industry; in 1910 this figure had risen to 34,208. Yearly imports of raw cotton more than doubled between 1900 and 1912. It was Flanders that benefited most from this. Thus gradually there came about the re-establishment of Belgium's economic centre in the Flemish-speaking areas where it had always been located before the nineteenth century and the first industrial revolution. It was certainly not a rapid or revolutionary process. It took some decades before Flanders reasserted its economic superiority; nevertheless, there were already indications before 1914 that this was going to happen.[2]

Belgium was hit as hard by the agrarian crisis as the Nether-

---

[1] For the following see M. Neirynck, 'Het economisch leven in België', *Algemene geschiedenis der Nederlanden*, xi (1956), 112–40.

[Footnote 2 at foot of opposite page]

lands and it reacted in roughly the same way. Dependent as it was on foreign markets, there was no question of Belgium turning to protectionist policies although in 1887 and 1895 imports of wheat, butter, oats, and some other products were restricted. But as in the Netherlands the government preferred other measures: better agricultural education, the introduction of more scientific methods of cultivation, and close inspection of the quality of agrarian products. The farmers themselves developed new organizations. They did not confine themselves, however, to the highly efficient and down-to-earth co-operatives that the Dutch were building up but tried to put the corporatist ideals of the Christian democrats and the priests who propagated them into effect by establishing (not without support from Catholic cabinets) an infinitely complicated and rather peculiar system of local farmers guilds united in the federated Farmers' Union (Boerenbond, 1890). Early in the twentieth century various co-operatives for selling and buying, and a credit bank (Middenkredietkas, 1903), were founded under the supervision of the Union, as a result of which the crisis could be overcome with relative ease. In actual fact the Belgian experiments did not differ essentially from the Dutch, but the religious inspiration was lacking in the Netherlands—apart from a comparatively unimportant Farmers' Union which a few Dutch Catholics, following the Belgian example, set up in 1896.

5. Dutch and Belgian Foreign Policy

Early in 1912 the Belgian Ambassador at The Hague wrote to his government that the Dutch had moved out of the twilight world in which they had been living for so long and made an appearance on the international scene. He was inspired to

[2] Ibid., p. 123:

	Per cent factory workers		Per cent population	
	1896	1919	1896	1910
Wallonia	57	51·4	38·2	36·1
Flemish provinces	26·4	31·5	43·1	43·7
Brabant (with Brussels)	16·6	17·1	18·7	20·2

make this remark after reading an article by J. de Louter (1847–1932), professor of international law at the University of Utrecht, in which he studied the factors enabling the Netherlands to become more active internationally and the consequences this had for Dutch foreign policy.[1] De Louter found two main causes. The British attack on the Boers had provoked bitter anger in the Netherlands but at the same time shown the Dutch how humiliating it was for a nation to be impotent, compelled to look on whilst British imperialism victimized her next of kin; clearly the Dutch had been unable to perform an obvious national duty. Secondly, the choice of The Hague as the seat for the first Peace Conference obliged the Dutch, he felt, to make a positive contribution to international affairs. De Louter did not think that Dutch foreign policy ought to depart from its traditional course; a small country must aspire to friendly relations with the whole world without binding itself. But such an attitude need not be humble or self-deprecating. A small Power could win universal respect by strengthening its defences, by supporting the development of international law, and by being ready to act as a mediator in the interest of peace. By such means it could obtain a major place among the nations. There is much similarity between De Louter's reflections and those of Van Vollenhoven, another expert in international law. In 1913 Van Vollenhoven enumerated Dutch activities since 1899: the Peace Conference (1899), the sending of a warship to carry President Kruger from Lourenço Marques to Marseilles (1900), the showing of the flag in Chinese waters (1900), the offer of mediation in the Boer War (1902), vigorous action against Venezuela which was threatening the West Indian colonies—all this, Van Vollenhoven thought, proved that the Netherlands had reawakened.[2]

This optimism is perplexing and was certainly not shared by everyone. Van Vollenhoven himself asserted that in 1899, when the Tsar called upon the World Powers to meet in The Hague and consider means to make war less probable and less

---

[1] C. Smit (ed.), *Bescheiden betreffende de buitenlandse politiek van Nederland 1848–1919*, 3rd period, *1899–1919*, vi (The Hague, 1968), pp. 623 ff.

[2] C. van Vollenhoven, 'Nederlands internationale rol, in het bijzonder ten aanzien van den bewapeningswedstrijd', *Verslagen der Marine-Vereeniging* (Den Helder, 1913), p. 120.

atrocious, only two Dutchmen outside the government were interested in the Tsar's initiative: the hall-porters of the best hotels at The Hague. Even within the government enthusiasm was limited. W. H. de Beaufort (1845–1918), the liberal Foreign Secretary, dreaded the trouble and the complications it would entail for him.[1] He had no confidence in the success of the conference and was not prone to messianic emotions. In fact the professional diplomats were probably right in claiming that the Netherlands ought not to try to catch the world's attention. The international position of the Netherlands could hardly be said to be improving at all. For the defence of its colonial empire the Netherlands depended entirely on British support; nobody, however, could predict what consequences the rapid development of Japan and the Anglo-Japanese Treaty of 1902 would have in South East Asia. In the Dutch colonies the Japanese threat was regarded as acute. In Europe the sharpening of Anglo-German hostility made the Netherlands more vulnerable than it had ever been in the nineteenth century. The naval development of Germany was inevitably prejudicial to the interests of a nation which had been largely dependent on British protection ever since it had to surrender its maritime supremacy at the beginning of the eighteenth century. It seems paradoxical, therefore, that men like De Louter, Van Vollenhoven, and others at this time should have believed that Dutch influence and independence were increasing and that they should have wished to take advantage of the fact with an idealistic foreign policy designed to enhance the nation's glory. Yet it is possible to understand their attitude for it is consistent with a general trend in European development. During the 1860s the unitary movements in Italy and Germany seemed to be anticipating a future in which small countries would be absorbed by the Great Powers or brought together into gigantic new entities. But in the 1890s it looked as if the small states were not only enjoying a new lease of life but were actually growing in status. The triumph of the democratic idea throughout the civilized world meant that the nineteenth-century view of a permanent hierarchy in

---

[1] C. Smit (ed.), *Bescheiden*, 3rd period, i (The Hague, 1957), p. 11; A. Vandenbosch, *Dutch Foreign Policy since 1815. A Study in Small Power Politics* (The Hague, 1959), p. 75.

international affairs which subordinated the small Powers to the greater Powers had to be abandoned. Moreover, the international situation itself, in which growing conflicts between the major nations forced them to seek for allies, however small, to maintain their influence, gave the small powers more room to manœuvre than they had enjoyed in the past.[1]

Dutch attempts to take part in world politics emphasized the limits rather than the importance of their actions. At the time of the Boxer crisis in 1900 the Dutch Government sent three cruisers into Chinese waters and, pressed on by Dutch public opinion, considered whether it should participate in the international punitive campaign against Peking. Finally it decided not to. This was not because the Dutch Cabinet was anti-imperialist. On the contrary, it associated itself with the policy of the imperial Powers, although without actually doing anything to further it. It was the concern for neutrality that limited Dutch freedom of action. The danger was not so much of getting involved in the Chinese troubles—there was little objection to that—but in the conflict of interests dividing the major Powers engaged in overpowering China. Moreover, even if the government had joined the action Dutch public opinion as expressed in the daily Press and Parliament would probably not have been satisfied. It was mainly Kuyper and his Christian democrats who insisted on a vigorous Dutch response. But if their wishes had been granted the Dutch Government would inevitably have been forced, for economic reasons, to support the British open-door policy. And Kuyper and his followers were vehemently anti-British. In this context it is interesting to see how fundamentally different Belgium's position was. For reasons of geography and because of their small size both countries favoured in Europe neutralist policies that were in many respects identical; but whereas the Dutch with their commercial and maritime tradition were always driven into the arms of Britain, Belgium, being to a much greater extent a real continental state, found itself in China dependent on France and Russia, helping to construct the railway with which these states hoped to cut through the British sphere of influence in the Yangtze area.[2]

[1] Cf. R. L. Rothstein, *Alliances and Small Powers* (New York, 1968), pp. 14 ff.
[2] For this see Van Dongen, *passim*.

Large sections of the Dutch population were made painfully aware of the country's total impotence when they were confronted with the South African crises; and how insoluble the dilemma of Dutch foreign policy was became apparent during the time of office of Abraham Kuyper (1901–5), who represented much of what was modern in the *fin de siècle* period: imperialism, militarism, nationalism, and an indomitable desire for action. It is easy to understand why the South African question should have attracted so much attention in the Netherlands. However, when the British annexed the Transvaal in 1877 Dutch reactions were cautious. Although the easily outraged conservative publicist G. W. Vreede sharply attacked British policy there was as yet no general outburst of public indignation. On the contrary, the coarseness of the Boers, their unreliability, their quarrelsomeness, the harshness of their policy towards the natives were criticized and their religious rigorism met with distinct disapproval. But suddenly Dutch sentiments changed. The Transvaal's resistance to Britain provoked a really surprising and spontaneous reaction. Their fight, it was thought, was proof of a revival of the true Dutch spirit. In South Africa the missed opportunities in the Dutch past could be made good. In the seventeenth century Holland had lost America to Britain; in the nineteenth century, Dutch commentators wrote, the Boers were reconquering South Africa for the Dutch race. Various political amateurs elaborated the wildest projects; it was proposed to cede Borneo or Surinam to Britain if the Netherlands were given mandatory power over South Africa to guide it into independence, and to find there what Britain possessed in North America—an inexhaustible market for its civilization and its language.[1] With the decision of the Boers, regarded as members of the Dutch race, not to submit to Britain, the Dutch began to develop a nationalistic fervour powerless in fact but potentially dynamic.

During the 1880s Dutch influence in the Transvaal increased considerably. A young Dutchman, W. J. Leyds (1859–1940), became Paul Kruger's confidant and highest civil servant. Kruger saw to it that the most important concessions at the

[1] P. J. van Winter, *Onder Krugers Hollanders. Geschiedenis van de Nederlandsche Zuid-Afrikaansche Spoorweg-Maatschappij* (2 vols., Amsterdam, 1937–8), i. 28–33. Cf. Fruin, *Verspreide Geschriften*, x. 402–18.

disposal of the Republic were given to Dutch people; a company founded by Dutchmen in 1887 constructed the important railways connecting the Transvaal with the neighbouring countries, Mozambique, the Orange Free State, and Natal. These Dutch entrepreneurs were not primarily moved by economic interests. Nationalist rather than commercial motives prompted them to try and collect the needed capital—much of it came from Germany—and to make the plans. There were many other projects besides the railways and they were closely studied without, however, being carried out: the founding of a National Bank, a steamship line to Delagoa Bay, mining firms, colonization. Dutch interest in the Transvaal seems to have reached its climax by about 1890.[1] But on the whole very little came of it. The Dutch economy was not sufficiently developed for imperialist ventures; no capital was made available and industry did not need such a market. The endlessly discussed idea of making Dutch farmers emigrate to the Transvaal turned out to be equally unworkable. Consequently, the relationship between the Netherlands and the Transvaal was rather one-sided. They were intimate in those fields where Kruger wanted to employ Dutchmen—in the schools, the state administration, and for his railways[2]—but outside these areas Dutch influence was incidental and small. Neither the Dutch economy nor Dutch traditions lent themselves to a coherent policy of economic penetration in South Africa. Still another factor would have made this difficult anyhow: the Dutch met with considerable antipathy both on the part of the Boers and of the Uitlanders.[3] The railway building turned out to be extremely expensive partly because of the lack of Dutch experience in this sort of business and partly because of the patriotic desire to use Dutch personnel and material without exploring the cheapest markets and looking for the best-trained people.[4] The Dutch working in state administration were often arrogant and fussy; their religious concepts, moreover, were not necessarily in harmony with those of the Boers. Thus in all fields there was disappointment

[1] Van Winter, op. cit. i. 241.
[2] Ibid. ii. 60.
[3] Ibid. 73 ff.
[4] J. S. Marais, *The Fall of Kruger's Republic* (Oxford, 1961), pp. 39–41.

and tension. By about 1898 Dutch influence in South Africa was already decreasing rapidly.[1]

Nevertheless, the Dutch remained loyal to their enthusiasm of the 1880s. They had identified themselves with the Boers to such an extent that British policy was felt as a national humiliation. At the outbreak of the Boer War in 1899 they passionately chose the South African side. Even Kuyper did so although earlier he had been deeply shocked by Kruger's refusal to rely exclusively on Kuyper's Calvinist adherents.[2] In 1899 when the Dutch Government was unwilling to insist on the Transvaal and Orange Free State being invited to the first Peace Conference at The Hague, Kuyper attacked the Cabinet in the most vehement terms. During the summer mass meetings were held in Amsterdam and The Hague and once again people exhausted themselves in making elaborate and fantastic plans to support the Boers. In the autumn of 1899 and in 1900 criticism by Press and public opinion of the government's inactivity rose to a dangerous point. It was of course the moral issue that was paramount, the Boers winning sympathy as the innocent victims of cynical imperialism. Nobody, incidentally, seems to have realized that in Achin the Dutch themselves were fighting an imperialist war in some respects comparable to the Boer War. Why this should have been forgotten is easy to see. For fundamentally the Dutch were, in both Achin and in the South African affair, inspired by a purely Dutch nationalism. Dutch anger at British policy was anger at a British attack on Holland itself, on a Dutch position abroad, a Dutch patrimony. Such nationalist fervour is rare in Dutch history and the Cabinet had to be very cautious in its handling of a difficult and unfamiliar situation. In September 1900 it found one way of briefly silencing criticism. A warship was sent to Lourenço Marques where Kruger had sought refuge, and the President was brought to Europe. For Dutch public opinion this represented a triumph. But the British were far from put out: they preferred to see Kruger in Europe rather than in Africa. And this was all the liberal Cabinet ventured to do. The Netherlands, so it was thought, was so dependent on Britain for its commerce and colonies that it would have been mortally dangerous to risk its wrath.

[1] Ibid., pp. 219–21.　　　　[2] Van Winter, i. 51; ii. 56, 65 ff.

In 1901 the 'confessionals'—Protestants and Roman Catholics—won a victory in the parliamentary elections and Kuyper was at last in a position to form a Cabinet. He took the Home Office, but the power of his personality was so overwhelming and the Foreign Secretary appointed on his advice so weak that foreign policy was also largely determined by him. This seemed a decisive moment in Dutch history. It will never become entirely clear what precisely Kuyper wished to do and actually did, but undoubtedly it was his ambition to alter in some way or another the traditional course of Dutch foreign policy based on neutrality and a reluctance to get involved in major international problems.[1] In practice this meant first of all that Kuyper should try to reduce Dutch dependence on Britain. Apparently, he expected that Germany would be successful in its attempts to break British supremacy outside Europe and would thus create more opportunity for the small Powers to move in. He was probably impressed by the idea propagated by many German imperialists that the Wilhelminian Reich had somehow been given the mission to shape, to the detriment of Britain, a new global balance of power, of which the smaller nations in particular would be able to take advantage. Other influences were also at work upon him. In the course of the preceding decades the Dutch economy had increasingly come to be orientated towards Germany. By 1900 Germany was by far the Netherlands' largest trading partner. Many German experts and technicians were employed in Dutch industry; German economic growth after 1870 greatly stimulated Dutch expansion. Thus, to put it in a very general and simplified way, the traditional emphasis in the Dutch economy on trade and trade capital, concentrated in the seaports and the maritime provinces and closely connected with Britain, had diminished as a result of this new economic development. Kuyper hated the conservative-liberal spirit of the capitalists in Holland and was anxious to use the new economic tendencies directed towards Germany as an element of his pro-German policy. Moreover, he felt more at home in the climate of the German

[1] The brilliant hypotheses about the nature of Kuyper's foreign policy put forward by A. S. de Leeuw, *Nederland in de wereldpolitiek van 1900 tot heden* (Zeist, 1936) find little support in the documents published later by C. Smit in his volumes of *Bescheiden*.

Empire with its Christian discipline and its state care for the weak and poor than in cynical Britain or frivolous and decadent France.[1]

Kuyper's foreign policy failed; in fact it did not become a foreign policy at all. It remained in the realm of theory, an idea which did not find much support in the Netherlands. For in spite of its anti-British attitude during the South African crises and the immense success of popular pro-Boer literature and children's books the Dutch public was also hostile to a closer association with Germany, as was shown time and again when the daily Press discussed the possibility of establishing a German–Dutch customs union or even a formal alliance. Some German publicists supported such projects (they were never officially backed by the German Government) but Dutch reactions remained cool although all observers agreed that Dutch feelings towards Germany had become much friendlier over the past decades.[2] Kuyper's initiatives were mistrusted by the civil servants in the Foreign Office and by the diplomats.[3] In 1905 Queen Wilhelmina went to the trouble of putting in writing her firm belief in the policy of neutrality.[4] She regarded an alliance with Germany as dangerous because the Empire was not yet capable of defending Dutch maritime interests in the event of war. But an alliance with Britain gave no guarantee for Dutch territorial integrity, and therefore the country ought not to make a choice until the very last moment when it might be forced to do so under attack or the direct threat of attack. In addition to such arguments, which the Queen was of course not alone in defending, the Dutch were considerably irritated by German attitudes towards South Africa. Notwithstanding his pompous promises the Emperor had

---

[1] The Belgian Roman Catholics shared this deep respect for the well-ordered Christianity of the German Empire that inspired much more confidence than atheistic France: R. Devleeshouwer, *Les Belges et le danger de guerre 1910–1914* (Louvain, 1958), pp. 93 ff.

[2] Much material in Smit (ed.), *Bescheiden* vi and cf. J. de Vries, 'De problematiek der Duits-Nederlandse economische betrekkingen in de negentiende eeuw', *Tijdschrift voor Geschiedenis*, lxxviii (1965), 46 ff.

[3] Cf. the memoranda written by S. Hannema who was appointed Secretary-General at the Foreign Office in 1902: C. Smit (ed.), *Bescheiden*, 3rd period, iii (The Hague, 1961), pp. 208, 465–6 n., 579–80.

[4] C. Smit (ed.), *Bescheiden*, 3rd period, ii (The Hague, 1958), pp. 465–7 (29 Apr. 1905).

finally refused the Boers effective support. As Kuyper himself was equally unable to help the Boers, he engaged instead in a burst of feverish activity, travelling to the Western capitals and in January 1902 offering Britain his services as a mediator. The British Government did not accept the offer but was able to make use of it. In the memorandum presented by the Dutch it was clear that they now accepted that the capitulation of the Boers had become the only practical solution. Of course the British made this defeatism known to the leaders in the Transvaal and undoubtedly Dutch despair about their cause rendered the Boers more pliant in the negotiations that ended in the Peace of Vereeniging of May 1902.[1] For Kuyper this could be represented as a success. Not only had a war that threatened the very survival of the Boer population come to an end, but the decisive peace negotiations had been started as a result of a Dutch initiative. But the success was a paradoxical and limited one. The profound impotence of Kuyper's foreign policy had been emphasized by the fact that only in this (from the point of view of the Boers totally negative) way could he contribute towards the solution of the South African problem.

In theory Belgian foreign policy was even more powerless but for an officially neutral country it was remarkably active. Leopold II's restless energy and the worldwide interests built up by Belgian industry kept the diplomats busy. Even so foreign policy generally was characterized by both a certain nervousness which rendered it hesitant and unpredictable and a lack of flexibility. The Belgian Foreign Office took little account of the major developments in international affairs. To a certain extent this was also true for the Netherlands but Dutch problems differed fundamentally from Belgian. Of course the Dutch view that foreign entanglements must be deferred until the moment when Dutch territory was being invaded or on the point of being attacked was unrealistic; it made some sense, however, because there was a reasonable chance that Dutch neutrality would be respected by the major European Powers. Strategic reasons alone explain why the Belgian situation was much more difficult. In 1870 Belgium

---

[1] De Leeuw, op. cit., pp. 36 ff. Cf. Smit (ed.), *Bescheiden* i, *passim* and *idem, Hoogtij der neutraliteitspolitiek. De buitenlandse politiek van Nederland 1899-1919* (Leiden, 1959), pp. 29-35.

was not involved in the Franco-German conflict; violation of its neutrality would have entailed British intervention as was explicitly stated in the Anglo-French and Anglo-German treaties of August 1870. After 1904 the threat of British intervention lost much of its effectiveness. Britain had come to an agreement with France and it was not unreasonable to suppose that, in the case of war between France and Germany, Britain would support France whether or not Germany respected Belgian territory.

This affected the heart of Belgium's traditional foreign policy. After 1904 British declarations that those who violated Belgian neutrality would be punished no longer afforded real protection.[1] Moreover, for several years Von Schlieffen, the head of the German General Staff, had been seriously considering the possibility of invading Belgium at the outbreak of Franco-German hostilities. In 1904 his plan of attack was made more precise; in 1905 and 1906 it was worked out in detail. The core of it was a massive invasion of Belgium. The Entente took account of this possibility; in 1906 British and Belgian military experts discussed means of defence. But the Belgian Government did not want to face the consequences of the radical changes which were taking place. It did not allow further consultations with the Entente and recognized but one duty: scrupulous maintenance of Belgian neutrality. The British Foreign Office realized what use it could make of this. A unilateral violation of Belgian neutrality would enable the British to enter the war as the protector of neutral Belgium. If they were unable to adopt this moral role British public opinion would perhaps make it more difficult for the government to give France the support it thought necessary and wished to provide.[2] In this way Belgian neutrality was denatured; it became a piece on a chess-board and lost its fundamental meaning. The Belgian politicians were not unaware of this as is shown by various elaborate memoranda written on behalf of their Foreign Office.[3] Yet it was impossible for them to draw

[1] Rothstein, op. cit., pp. 65 ff.

[2] G. Ritter, *Der Schlieffenplan* (Munich, 1956), *passim*. De Leeuw's hypotheses concerning the plan and the role of Kuyper in relation to it are wrong: De Leeuw, pp. 64–72 and cf. Ritter, 82 n. 3.

[3] For an exhaustive analysis of this material see H. Lademacher, *Die belgische Neutralität als Problem der europäischen Politik 1830–1914* (Bonn, 1971).

concrete conclusions from the change of circumstances. A total revision of Belgian policies, for example by concluding an alliance with one of the Great Powers, was not, and could not be, seriously considered. As a result, the only thing to be done was to strengthen defence. Only fear of a strong Belgian army might have made the Germans hesitate to attack the country. But the Belgian army was weak and neglected and when at last the government started reforming it, in 1913, it was much too late. Belgian diplomacy was just as helpless. It exhausted itself in civilities, apologies, reassurances, and appeasing noises but did not seem to possess a clear direction.[1] No thought was given to the meaning of Belgian neutrality in the twentieth century. During the 1860s Belgian Romantics had used neutrality as an argument on behalf of territorial expansion; this turned out to lead into an impasse and henceforth the colony conquered in Africa satisfied the rather weak messianic and imperialist impulses of the Belgians. In Europe Belgium behaved as a small satiated state without further ambitions, dependent on the goodwill of the Great Powers rather than on its own means of defence, averse from adventures but in moments of crisis turning always in the same direction— towards closer collaboration with the Netherlands.

The Dutch declined all Belgian suggestions and invitations. No Dutch Cabinet was prepared to support Belgium. The Belgians sometimes interpreted this as proof of vexing Dutch carelessness. It seemed to them that the Dutch gravely underrated the dangers and in reckless nonchalance failed to take the elementary precaution of associating themselves with Belgium. However, this view turned out to be wrong. During this whole period Belgium was in danger; the Netherlands was so to a much lesser extent. Support for Belgium would have exposed the Dutch to Belgian risks without any compensating advantages. There was in fact no place in the world, whether in Africa, Asia, or Europe, where the two countries, though on polite and even friendly terms with each other, found that they had enough in common for a real solidarity to emerge. In Europe this became very clear in 1887. As the tension between Germany and France looked like leading to another crisis

---

[1] Devleeshouwer, op. cit., p. 27.

Leopold II and the Beernaert Government grew extremely nervous. In January 1887 Beernaert proposed Belgian–Dutch talks about ways of countering a German attack on Belgium. The Hague refused.[1] In 1888 the Dutch even declined Belgium's request to appoint military attachés although the French and the Germans had had military attachés in Brussels since the 1870s. Some newspapers, however, reacted in quite a different way. Kuyper's paper, *De Standaard*, advocated an active foreign policy of collaboration with Belgium and Germany to parry the French threat seemingly made acute by the Boulangist adventure.[2] In this way Kuyper more or less associated himself with a campaign launched by the German, Austrian, and Italian governments to persuade the Netherlands and Belgium to join the Triple Alliance.[3] This did not really go beyond the stage of rumours and vague projects but the mere possibility that a Dutch–Belgian *rapprochement* could be brought about for such a purpose was probably enough to make the Dutch Government even more cautious than usual.

During his period of office from 1901 to 1905 Kuyper tried to give a new turn to this problem but again failed. He was suspected of personally discussing his plans in the capitals of the Triple Alliance and in Brussels without consulting the Cabinet or the Foreign Secretary. Improbable though this is, he did have an astonishing conversation with the Belgian minister at The Hague in July 1903. He then pointed out that British attacks on Leopold II's Congo policies had much in common with criticism of Dutch policies in the East Indies and heavily emphasized the need for solidarity between the two colonial states in the face of British imperialism.[4] Leopold was quick to invite Kuyper to Brussels and in January 1904 the visit took place. On this occasion Kuyper probably explained to Leopold once again the necessity of a close entente directed against Britain. The conversation had no visible consequences and indeed what could have been expected to result from such a proposition? In the same month Leopold

[1] Woltring (ed.), *Bescheiden* iv. 99 ff. Cf. A. de Ridder, 'La Belgique et les puissances européennes', *Histoire de la Belgique contemporaine*, i. 199 ff. and K. Hampe, *Belgien und Holland vor dem Weltkriege* (Gotha, 1918), pp. 22–3.

[2] J. A. van Hamel, *Nederland tusschen de mogendheden* (Amsterdam, 1918), p. 426.

[3] De Ridder, op. cit., p. 209.

[4] Smit (ed.), *Bescheiden* vi. 507–10.

went to Berlin where he was anxious to gain more sympathy for his adventures in the Congo. Wilhelm II despised his royal visitor as an incarnation of the devil, the personification of immorality and lust for money.[1] But he told him (on 28 January 1904) that in the event of a Franco-German war, which he thought imminent, Leopold must choose the German side: he would be rewarded by the restoration of the Burgundy of Philip the Good and Charles the Bold.[2] By this preposterous suggestion Wilhelm achieved what few other people were capable of—the complete bewilderment of the Belgian King. Some days later he caused similar consternation in the Dutch royal family. At the outbreak of war between Russia and Japan (8 February 1904) he wrote a letter to Queen Wilhelmina expressing his fear that Britain would support Japan and so make it impossible for the war to be localized. If in that case France came into conflict with Germany he advised the Netherlands to join Germany within twelve hours.[3] It is clear that after such daunting manœuvres Kuyper had little room for his policy of associating Belgium and the Netherlands with the Triple Alliance—assuming that this could truly be called a policy and that Kuyper was still in favour of it.

Notwithstanding all these setbacks Belgian diplomacy continued to hope for a closer association with the Netherlands. From 1903 to 1910 Belgium was represented in The Hague by the minister J. G. J. P. Baron Guillaume (1852–1918) who repeatedly discussed with members of the Dutch Government what he called the gaps in the Dutch defence system, the result of which made military co-operation with Belgium very difficult. Fundamentally, the defence systems of the two countries were identical. The Belgians thought of Antwerp as a fortress to which the army retreating from the frontier could eventually withdraw. The Dutch too did not plan to defend their frontier for any length of time and had a sort of natural fortress in the province of Holland that was surrounded by the water defence line and could be made inaccessible by inundation. However, under pressure from both France and Germany the Belgians started to build fortresses along the River Meuse

[1] J. Willequet, Le Congo belge et la Weltpolitik (1894–1914) (Brussels, 1962), pp. 95–6.
[2] Ibid., pp. 93, 103.   [3] Smit (ed.), Bescheiden ii. 215–16, 218–20.

during the 1880s. From a strategic point of view it was obviously desirable to connect them with similar constructions in Dutch Limburg but the Dutch did not want to build them. It was one of the aims of Belgian diplomacy to persuade the Dutch that they should defend Limburg against a possible German attack. They failed. More important, however, was the mouth of the River Scheldt. The Belgians were worried that the Dutch clearly lacked the resources to maintain the neutrality of the Scheldt and hoped for a gesture on the part of the Dutch which would show that the two governments were at one in their interpretation of neutrality.[1] In 1910 the Dutch Government at last asked Parliament for permission to build fortresses along the Scheldt. For a variety of reasons the introduction of the bill came at a particularly unfavourable moment. It looked as if the proposal was made under German pressure and thus constituted a remnant of Kuyper's despised pro-German policies. In fact this was not so. The plan was logically derived from the strict conception of neutrality the government adhered to and as such it was applauded by the Belgians who might, on the surface, well have been expected to consider it prejudicial because the Dutch fortresses would most probably serve to prevent British ships from coming to the aid of Antwerp.[2] Shortly after there appeared to be international repercussions. The French Foreign Minister criticized the bill publicly in January 1911, although he was soon persuaded that it was impossible to do much about it. Meanwhile the British had come to the conclusion that the Dutch initiative would not harm their interests. In the event the project was never carried out. After much heated discussion the bill was finally adopted in 1913 but in a very simplified form (the costs having been reduced from 40 to 13 million guilders) and when the war broke out Krupp, from which the Dutch bought all their military equipment, did not deliver the guns and other material they had ordered.

Belgium's slow and tentative attempts to establish some sort of military entente with the Netherlands were accompanied by the campaign of a young Belgian journalist, E. Baie

[1] Ibid. vi. 560–1 (1906), 586–7 (1909).
[2] In 1909 the Belgian minister at The Hague told Dutch members of Parliament that the bill which was being prepared was worth their support: ibid. 597.

(1874–1963), who may have acted in concert with members of the French Cabinet—he was at least loudly applauded by the French Press.[1] In the summer of 1905 Kuyper's Cabinet was succeeded by a liberal coalition government that could not be suspected of being pro-German. In October 1905 Baie published in *Le Petit Bleu*, a Brussels newspaper, an article advocating a customs union and military alliance with the Netherlands. In his view it was obvious that the two countries must lean on the Entente Powers and turn against Germany. He proposed[2] to establish an interparliamentary committee to examine means of realizing his project. Naturally this idea was unacceptable to the Dutch. In law there was only one possibility: the Dutch had the right to make an alliance with Belgium obliging them to come to the aid of the neutral Belgians if these were attacked. But they would receive nothing in return.[3] Moreover, there was a bitter and paradoxical element in the whole matter. In 1830 French revolutionary impulses had been instrumental in dividing the United Kingdom of the Netherlands and the establishment of a Belgian state had been interpreted as a French victory. Now France was supporting the conception of a reunited Netherlands which would bring no advantage to the northern part.[4] By some Belgians, Walloons as well as Flemings, the split of 1830 had repeatedly been deplored as a mistake, and now even some Frenchmen started seeing it that way. But the Dutch thought differently and, all things considered, this was less surprising than might at first appear. In 1830 the Dutch had in fact accelerated the Belgian departure and observed it with gratification in spite

---

[1] *The Times* too was in favour of the plan.

[2] In his book *L'Entente hollando-belge* (Brussels, 1906).

[3] Cf. the excellent memorandum of 14 Nov. 1905 written by N. W. Barnardiston, the British military attaché at Brussels and The Hague: Smit (ed.), *Bescheiden* vi. 224–30. On 30 Aug. 1906 the Belgian minister at The Hague wrote that the Dutch refused to be forced 'à devoir nous prêter un concours que nous pourrions nous refuser à leur accorder, en nous basant sur les obligations que nous impose notre position d'état neutre': ibid. 567.

[4] See Jules Cambon, French Ambassador at Berlin, to the French Foreign Secretary (21 June 1914): 'Cette conception de l'union militaire de la Belgique et de la Hollande est un singulier exemple de l'instabilité des choses de la politique. La France a jadis considéré comme un succès de rompre l'union hollando-belge que l'Europe de 1815 avait créée contre elle et aujourd'hui nous voudrions la rétablir en partie, parce que ce n'est plus de notre côté que l'équilibre est menacé': ibid. 488.

of their deep feeling of humiliation and defeat. At the beginning of the twentieth century they were proved right: they were more secure within the boundary of their own *raison d'État*. This was clearly pointed out in a *Gids* article by De Beaufort, a former Foreign Minister.[1] He rejected the idea that the split of 1830 was regrettable because it divided a powerful state into two small states, and from a reunion he expected only disaster. In his view it was very unattractive to exchange the status of a small Power for that of a middling one too weak to make itself felt and too strong to keep out of international complications. H. T. Colenbrander, the well-known liberal historian, entirely agreed with him. After reiterating the usual banalities about the unique service rendered to Europe by Belgium thanks to the synthesis of Germanic and Romanic civilizations established there and the equally customary condescending civilities to the Flemish brethren who—it was their charm and their weakness—were still living in a style dating from three hundred years ago, he declared that re-uniting the Netherlands would ruin the northern part.[2] Such reactions were typical.[3] They prevented all opportunities of serious discussion, and no such discussion ever took place.

Baie's initiative was welcomed with such acclaim by influential circles in Belgium that it was impossible for the Dutch to ignore it.[4] But the Dutch Government carefully withdrew from all responsibility for the negotiations that followed. They were treated by the Dutch as a private matter concerning a few individuals who established a Belgian–Dutch Committee and met in 1907 in Brussels, in 1909 in The Hague, and in 1910 once again in Brussels. Yet on both sides men of great authority were appointed to sit on the Committee. In 1907 Beernaert, the former Belgian Prime Minister, presided over the session and in his opening speech he did not conceal that he regretted the split of 1830.[5] Th. Heemskerk, the leader of the

---

[1] Reprinted in De Beaufort, *Nieuwe geschiedkundige opstellen*, i. 230.

[2] H. T. Colenbrander, 'Nederlandsch-Belgische droombeelden en werkelijkheid', *De Gids* (1907) iv, pp. 506 ff.

[3] Only very few Dutch publicists were in favour of Baie's plan. One of them was R. A. Klerck, *Nederland en België* (The Hague, 1907). Cf. Vandenbosch, op. cit., pp. 244–5.

[4] The leaders of the Flemish movement were in general indifferent or hostile to Baie's plan. Cf. Elias, *Vlaamse gedachte* iv. 282–4.

[5] Smit (ed.), *Bescheiden* vi. 577.

Dutch party—he was to become Minister of the Interior in 1908—reacted coolly. In the Dutch view, he said, the Committee ought not to discuss problems of international policy but should confine itself exclusively to considering ways of improving economic relations between the two countries. Naturally the discussions produced no results. Their effect was entirely negative, as was immediately realized by Belgian diplomats.[1] If there had been any willingness in the Netherlands to think about a cautious military *rapprochement*—and even this was doubtful—it was bound to disappear completely now the Dutch were asked to revise their foreign policy so radically. Moreover, some Dutch commentators suspected Baie of seeking Belgian expansion at the expense of the Dutch. This was easy to understand. The whole project was designed to serve Belgian political and economic interests and in fact the action group, thwarted in its initial ambitions, started to advocate Belgian annexation of Dutch Limburg and Flanders as well as French Flanders and Luxemburg.[2] Thus shortly before the World War Belgian expansionist impulses, defended in the 1860s with such lyrical warmth by Émile Banning, reappeared in a hard, business-like, totally unromantic form.

[1] Smit (ed.), *Bescheiden* vi. 556.

[2] Th. van Welderen Rengers, *Les Relations néerlando-belges considérées dans le cadre de la position politique internationale de la Belgique* (Leiden, 1931), pp. 12–13; C. A. van der Klaauw, *Politieke betrekkingen tussen Nederland en België, 1919–1939* (Leiden, 1953), p. 5.

VIII

SYNTHESIS, 1895–1914

1. *Culture*

IN 1892 P. J. Blok (1855–1929) published the first volume of his *Geschiedenis van het Nederlandsche volk* (*History of the Dutch People*); in 1900 appeared the first volume of *Histoire de Belgique* by Henri Pirenne (1862–1935).[1] Both books were an immediate success. In the Netherlands and in Belgium the authors were praised as courageous men who had admirably accomplished a truly national task. Edmond Picard, who had opened the debate on 'l'âme belge' some years before, spoke of the importance of Pirenne's work in the Senate at the time of its publication.[2] During the next few years when volumes were appearing regularly—Pirenne completed four before 1914—his work came to be admired as a national monument. It was studied by the members of the royal family, officers were made to read it in the military colleges, barristers in Brussels expounded it, schoolchildren received it as a prize for good examination results, for the bourgeoisie in town and country and the literary élite it was essential reading. On publication in the summer of 1911 the fourth volume sold seven hundred copies within three days.[3] This was partly but certainly not entirely due to the exceptional quality of Pirenne's insight and style. Blok's work, though scholarly and useful, was much inferior intellectually as well as stylistically, but it excited great interest in the Netherlands even if it never became quite so fashionable or attracted so much snobbish attention. The

---

[1] P. J. Blok, *Geschiedenis van het Nederlandsche volk* (8 vols., Leiden, 1892–1907. A German translation was published between 1902 and 1918; an incomplete version in English in five vols. between 1898 and 1912). H. Pirenne, *Histoire de Belgique* (7 vols., Brussels, 1900–32). The first volume of the German translation, which was not continued after 1914, was published in 1899. A Dutch translation came out at Ghent between 1902 and 1933.

[2] *Henri Pirenne. Hommages et souvenirs* (2 vols., Brussels, 1938), i. 132.

[3] Ibid. 182–4.

popularity of these two books is understandable: the fact that
they were conceived in the 1890s, the historical conception
which lay at their root, and the success they achieved were in
various ways characteristic of the culture of this decade.

In the 1880s an extremist group of men of letters had in their
struggle against tradition recklessly sacrificed most of the
standards of civilization and society in favour of an extravagant
individualism that destroyed, together with the ordinary forms
of language, essential elements of human contact. In the 1890s
the cultural style swung towards the other extreme. In the
previous nervous decade people had believed themselves to be
facing the deepest crisis of the century; they now sought with
comparable rashness an all-embracing synthesis. The conflict
between emotion and reason, spontaneity and tradition, individual and community—a perennial conflict, but seldom so
predominant as in this period[1]—could, it was hoped, be resolved on a new and higher level. In their quiet, academic
way Blok, who was a professor at Groningen, and Pirenne,
who was a professor at Ghent, expressed the needs of their
contemporaries and fulfilled their longing for the great synthesis which subsumes the particular in the universal, for the
historical vision which assigns the individual's place in the
continuity of general development, for the scholarly and
empirical which gives certainty where individualistic impressionism and subjectivism are rampant. Pirenne said: 'il n'y
a de science que de l'universel';[2] Blok maintained that there was
no difference between the methods of science and the humani-
ties, for both were founded on empiricism and sought after
natural laws.[3] Both Pirenne and Blok wrote from the premiss
that history is a history of communities, the development of
which is not ruled by the whims of individuals or by chance,
but by general economic and social facts.

By carefully assembling and sifting all the evidence at their
disposal—and they were both very learned men—they hoped
to uncover the inner meaning of their national histories. What

[1] J. Kamerbeek, jun., 'Huizinga en de beweging van tachtig', *Tijdschrift voor geschiedenis*, lxvii (1954), 147.

[2] *Henri Pirenne* i. 18.

[3] P. J. Blok, *De geschiedenis als sociale wetenschap* (Leiden, 1894), pp. 17-18. See also I. H. Gosses, 'Petrus Johannes Blok', *Verspreide geschriften* (Groningen, 1946), pp. 492-519.

the facts revealed was a kind of epic celebration of national grandeur. Pirenne, convinced that he studied history in a purely scholarly way without any patriotic or political prejudice, imagined that he had discovered a reality which was not only superficially but deeply and intrinsically beautiful. In the course of time Blok too became more and more alive to the fact that his learning served his country. Working on the volume which dealt with the Revolt of the Netherlands was for him, as he wrote in his preface, 'a source of indescribable pleasure, of exalting emotions'. Both men were nationalists and royalists. Throughout his life Pirenne remained convinced that Belgium was a synthesis of the Germanic and Romanic civilizations, that his generation had inherited a continuous history going back to the early Middle Ages, and that his nation must fulfil again the mission accomplished in the late Middle Ages and in early modern history and act as a link between the nations, a common fatherland, a crusader for right and justice in the tradition of Godfrey de Bouillon.[1] He thought in the same strain as Émile Banning, who had expressed similar sentiments in the 1860s. Blok was a loyal representative of the curious Dutch nationalism that found inspiration in the Boer War in the 1890s and like Pirenne, who according to his own account served King Albert with feudal loyalty—Leopold II he admired profoundly—Blok loved Queen Wilhelmina to whom he was privileged to teach national history in the 1890s. Of course, this uncomplicated nationalism made these books attractive to a wide circle of readers. Pirenne's nationalism was in a way more original than Blok's. In Belgium national feelings had remained very weak in spite of everything. Godefroid Kurth (1847–1916), who taught history at Liège and had been Pirenne's master, once wrote that in his youth the Belgians' indifference to their country had been so great that they did not even know their national anthem. During the 1880s, however—Kurth was a Christian-democrat and had been a fervent adherent of the Catholic regime since 1884—national pride had begun to grow.[2] Yet before 1914 there was nothing in

---

[1] This was how he formulated it in 1930 in an epilogue to his *Histoire de Belgique*, remained unpublished during his lifetime: *Henri Pirenne* ii. 546.

[2] G. Kurth, *La Nationalité belge* (Namur, 1913). This book contains lectures from 1905.

Belgium to compare with the nationalist agitations of the Dutch *fin de siècle* period.[1] Consequently, Pirenne's book was acclaimed as a welcome boost to the national consciousness. It had all the right qualities. The author had created, from the chaos of the regional and local history of the countries which were to form the Belgian state in 1830, an order which suggested that they had been united at a very early stage largely as a result of a natural economic necessity and that Belgium thus possessed a national existence of considerable antiquity.

Blok's work began to appear in a German translation in 1902 in the series *Geschichte der europäischen Staaten* edited by Karl Lamprecht. Lamprecht was also directly responsible for Pirenne's decision to write a history of Belgium; in 1894 the German historian invited him to do so and in 1899 the German version of the first volume was published in Lamprecht's series even before the original French text appeared in Brussels. Lamprecht himself was in the 1890s a very controversial figure in Germany. In his *Deutsche Geschichte*, the first volume of which saw the light in 1891, he tried somewhat impetuously to break through the framework of the narrowly philological, textually critical method of German historiography and to transform it into a social science. An unusually hard and bitter polemic with more cautious colleagues was the result. For Germany itself the consequences were disastrous. Lamprecht lost the battle and the German study of history lost its opportunity to develop a new historical method.[2] Through Pirenne, however, many of his ideas spread elsewhere. For Pirenne was considered by the French historians Marc Bloch and Lucien Febvre to be one of the patrons of the famous school of the *Annales*. By their friendship and co-operation with Lamprecht, Pirenne and Blok put themselves in the forefront of the historical debate and they could do so without much risk in their own countries, because there was not the commanding and self-confident philological tradition that prevailed in Germany where it had originated. What Lamprecht wanted, Pirenne and Blok tried to achieve in their much more sedate manner. Against the individualistic trend they set the collectivist ideal; positivism

---

[1] Cf. Devleeshouwer, *Les Belges et le danger de guerre*, pp. 12 ff.

[2] G. Oestreich, 'Die Fachhistorie und die Anfänge der sozialwissenschaftlichen Forschung in Deutschland', *Historische Zeitschrift*, ccviii (1969), pp. 320–63.

must make way for a psychological historiography; specialism must yield to universalism.[1] It is true that Blok, who had an active but at bottom very conventional mind, realized in the end hardly any of his original intentions. What is of concern here, however, is the original impulse, because this is characteristic of the whole culture of the Netherlands in the 1890s.

There were many ways of reaching the sought-for synthesis. Marxism, Spinozism, neo-Thomism, 'psychic monism', Hegelianism, anarchism, symbolism, to mention a few of the prominent systems of the time, could all offer a cure for what many came to look upon as the disease of the 1880s. The purpose of all of them was to free the individual from the isolation into which the experiences of the last decade had driven him and for this reason they sometimes assumed an almost religious character. In Dutch literature this was particularly noticeable in the emergence of what has been called the *vates*-type, the prophetic poetic figure, who tried to express in his poems an experience of that essential unity which underlies the incoherent diversity of existence. These writers belonged to that generation of European poets which included Alexander Blok, Stefan George, Rilke, and Yeats,[2] but perhaps nowhere were the aspirations of this generation so intensely experienced as in Holland. There was a vehemence and a passion about it all, and in the longing for synthesis and unity something extravagant. It was a poetry of extremes in both form and content; the debate on which it was centred seemed like a struggle between life and death. Herman Gorter (1864–1927) was probably the most heroic of them all. His lyric epos *Mei* (1889) with its supple, quick rhythms, its endless striving to capture in words the elusive beauty of sensory impressions, and the variety and wealth of its lyrical resources, was acclaimed from the moment of its publication as the greatest achievement of the movement of the 1880s. Yet destructive elements were lurking in it too, and they were soon to dominate Gorter's art. In the poetry he wrote between 1889 and 1892 he carried the impressionism of *Mei* to its furthest limits; free from all traditional

[1] In his masterly book *Op het breukvlak van twee eeuwen* (2 vols., Leiden, 1967) J. Romein places the discussion around Lamprecht in a broad historical setting (ii. 154 ff.).

[2] Th. Weevers, *Poetry of the Netherlands in its European Context, 1170–1930* (London, 1960), p. 189.

forms he tried to transmute the most fleeting sensations into language and sometimes he almost achieved his unattainable end. But, however splendid these verses might be, Gorter himself knew that he was spent and could not go any further in this style. In *Mei* he had complained of the loneliness of the poet who, when he becomes a God to himself, has nothing more to impart to his fellow creatures. Gorter took refuge in Spinozism as he understood it, translated the *Ethica* (he was a classical scholar), and tried to put his new tenets into poetry. His example was followed by contemporaries but it was a fashion which did not last long. Yet it characterized the intellectual atmosphere of the early 1890s. To a certain extent the choice of Spinoza as a guide was accidental, but he was known to the young literary men from the national tradition and when they came to study him he seemed to satisfy their needs: his mathematical method gave certainty, his pantheism and mysticism pointed to the great whole in which the individual still occupies a significant place.

This attempt by Gorter to reorganize his life on the basis of a philosophical system not his own was not a success.[1] But then he was converted to Marxism and in 1897 joined the Sociaal Democratische Arbeiders Partij which had been founded three years before. This was a decision of great importance not only for Gorter's poetry but also for the history of the SDAP. It was no small matter for a man of Gorter's calibre to join a party that so far had only a meagre following—it totalled 2,200 members in 1898, mainly among the agricultural labourers in Friesland and poor Amsterdam Jews.[2] Together with his pupil, the poetess and publicist Henriette Roland Holst (1869–1952), who enrolled herself as a member at the same time, he quickly acquired a leading position in the party.[3] Their passionate and untiring activity as theorists, propagandists, and poets raised the intellectual level of socialism in the

[1] Henriette van der Schalk, who some years afterwards married the artist R. N. Roland Holst, 25 Aug. 1893 to A. Verwey, in Mea Nijland-Verwey (ed.), *Kunstenaarslevens* (Assen, 1959), pp. 103–4.

[2] S. de Wolff, *En toch . . . ! Driekwart eeuw socialisme in vogelvlucht* (Amsterdam, 1951), pp. 108–9.

[3] For an exhaustive study of Gorter's political activities see H. de Liagre Böhl, *Herman Gorter. Zijn politieke aktiviteiten van 1909 tot 1920 in de opkomende kommunistische beweging in Nederland* (Nijmegen, 1973).

Netherlands to a point it had not known before. For them it was a truly international principle that went far beyond the trivial local problems of everyday life in the Netherlands. Gorter knew how to make a deep impression on his working-class audiences and with his gift for clear and compelling exposition was able to initiate them into Marxist doctrine: this, it was said, was propaganda 'exalted to the sphere of beauty'.[1] Henriette Roland Holst, the rich lady who devoted herself to relieving the oppressed, was also deeply respected far and wide. Yet curiously enough the party was in the long run damaged by this support. Gorter lacked a quality which the other great socialist poet of the Low Countries, Émile Verhaeren, who was nine years his senior, possessed to a high degree: a true love for the people and a deep concern about their living conditions.[2] In Gorter's socialism there was a detachment, an abstraction, which astonished and annoyed some of his partisans. His consistency was absolute but simplistic. When he and some others thought they noticed in the policy of the SDAP traces of revisionism—wrongly as it happened—they fought these elements without regard to persons or fear of the consequences. In 1909 Gorter, the panegyrist of unity and community, had to leave the party together with a group of like-minded people. The SDAP was one of the first socialist parties in Europe that split for doctrinal reasons: it had only happened before in Russia and in Bulgaria.

It was just such a split that the left-wing radicals in Germany, with whom Gorter, Henriette Roland Holst, and the young astronomer Anton Pannekoek (1873–1960) were closely associated, had always tried to avoid. Rosa Luxemburg and her group sought above all to maintain the unity of the socialist parties and in the last resort set a higher value upon party organization than did Gorter and his followers.[3] Yet Gorter and in particular the penetrating theorist Pannekoek, who from 1905 to 1914 taught at the socialist party schools in Berlin and Bremen where Rosa Luxemburg also worked, thought in other respects along much the same lines as their Polish-German

[1] S. de Wolff, *Voor het land van belofte* (Bussum, 1955), pp. 141–2.
[2] W. van Ravesteyn, *Herman Gorter* (Rotterdam, 1928), pp. 31–2.
[3] For these connections see H. M. Bock (ed.), *A. Pannekoek, H. Gorter: Organisation und Taktik der proletarischen Revolution* (Frankfurt, 1969). Bock reprints a number of their German writings dating from 1912 to 1921.

friend and arrived at similar conclusions. The so-called Dutch Marxist school, with Gorter, Pannekoek, and Henriette Roland Holst the chief representatives, can reasonably be described as 'Luxemburgist'.[1] But this did not imply a system.[2] The Dutch authors produced no great works in the field of politics. Pannekoek wrote books on astronomy, his political work consisting chiefly of articles, pamphlets, and lectures.[3] Gorter published some political brochures; so too did Henriette Roland Holst, but she also wrote what was probably the most lasting political publication to emerge from this group—an extraordinarily penetrating outline of Dutch history in the nineteenth century according to Marxist principles (1902). Rosa Luxemburg herself did not seek to frame a new system either, but she did write one political book of a wider import, her famous *Die Akkumulation des Kapitals* (1913).

In spite of such reservations it is still possible to indicate the two main points on which this Marxist interpretation deviated from the view the majority still held: the emphasis on the general strike as a necessary step in the revolutionary process and the faith in the spontaneous creative power of the revolutionary masses. Pannekoek and Gorter formulated these ideas in essentially the same way as Rosa Luxemburg. With them, too, we find the profound, and later almost desperate, confidence in the possibility of developing the proletariat's class-consciousness by urging them to participate in continuous revolutionary agitation and to disregard all failures.

---

[1] The term 'Dutch Marxist school' is in fact unjust. It is far from certain that some of the Dutch social democrats who were blamed for their revisionism by Gorter and his circle were wrong in maintaining that they too, were orthodox Marxists. Henriette Roland Holst much later wrote a biography, *Rosa Luxemburg. Haar leven en werken* (Rotterdam, 1935) that J. P. Nettl in *Rosa Luxemburg* (2 vols., London, 1966), ii. 919, calls 'impressionistic and somewhat romantic in political matters'. On the relative usefulness of the term 'luxemburgism' cf. Nettl, ii. 543-6, 787 ff.

[2] In philosophy they declared to rely on Dietzgen whose superficial attempt to blend idealism and materialism into cosmic monism made a deep impression on them: cf. F. Kool (ed.), *Die Linke gegen die Parteiherrschaft* (Dokumenten der Weltrevolution, iii, Olten, 1970), pp. 87-8 and C. H. Ketner, *Joseph Dietzgen, een socialistisch wijsgeer* (Amsterdam, 1919).

[3] Only much later did Pannekoek systematically expose his ideas, which, however, had hardly developed any further, in *Lenin als Philosoph* (pseudonym John Harper, Amsterdam, 1936) and *De arbeidersraden* (pseudonym P. Aartsz, Amsterdam, 1946).

In the long run the intellectual factor, the reform of the consciousness of the masses, became the central point of this
conception, though of course it was never disconnected from
its materialist basis. Naturally, propaganda was a very important element in the politics of all socialists. With the Dutch
Marxists it would sometimes appear—especially after 1919—
that politics was in essence only propaganda. Gorter's political
prose, simple, perfectly clear, if sometimes not exempt from
exaltation, has at times the rhythm of the catechism. It rouses,
instructs, produces effects by its patient and at the same time
restless repetitions. Pannekoek, a mathematician and an astronomer, used with skill the refined logic of Marxist polemics and
always seemed capable of reducing his opponents' arguments
to manifest nonsense. Needless to say, Gorter and Pannekoek
utterly failed in what was after all their principal objective.
The proletarian masses in Western Europe did not develop a
class-consciousness and did not listen to what was so passionately imparted to them.[1] After Rosa Luxemburg's death the
two Dutchmen played some part in the foundation of various
communist parties and splinter groups in Germany.[2] Inevitably, they came into conflict with Lenin, who made use of a
revolutionary élite and a rigidly organized party in order to
carry the revolution through. In his notorious pamphlet of
1920 *'Left-wing' Communism: an infantile Disorder,* he sharply
reproved Gorter and Pannekoek.[3] Gorter answered in the
same year with his *Open Letter to Comrade Lenin,*[4] an important
work written with insight but achieving nothing. Against the
authority of Lenin and Bolshevism such writings were of no
avail. Yet Gorter remained active till his death as the theorist
of a radical anti-Comintern, a fourth International, which

[1] The Leninist and the strictly organized communist parties with their leaders
and élite had no success in Western Europe either and thus their criticism of the
utopianism and individualism of Gorter *cum suis* was rather premature. For a
moderate and civilized Bolshevist attack on Gorter's political activity see J. and A.
Romein, 'Herman Gorter', *Erflaters van onze beschaving,* iv. 308 ff. Bock's book—
amongst others—proves that in the 1960s anti-Leninism and the belief in the
spontaneous power of the revolutionary masses was once more regarded as relevant
by left-wing socialists.

[2] Cf. Bock, pp. 26 ff. and W. van Ravesteyn, *De wording van het communisme in
Nederland, 1907–1925* (Amsterdam, 1948), pp. 168–9, 193, 206–8.

[3] The name of K. Horner, mentioned here with particular contempt, was a
pen-name used at the time by Pannekoek.

[4] *Offener Brief an den Genossen Lenin* (Berlin, 1920), reprinted in Bock, pp. 169–227.

had no more than a hundred or so adherents. In between all his struggles and debates he was engaged on what he considered his principal task, the great epic *Pan* (1907–16) which, though a failure, contains some fine passages and was certainly one of the most ambitious socialist attempts to express mankind's solidarity in poetry. For the last few years of his life Gorter retired to the seclusion of the dunes on the North Sea where he continued to write some accomplished poetry.[1]

In 1927, on Gorter's death, his old friend Albert Verwey (1865–1937) looked back on their common past in the 1880s and their subsequent estrangement. The greatness of that time, he wrote, 'does not lie in its Individualism, nor in its Socialism, but in the passion with which we lived through the struggle between them in our hearts and minds'.[2] Nowhere in the world, one of Verwey's followers reflected in 1907, was the clash between individualism and the longing for harmonious community so intensely felt as in the Netherlands, nowhere was the conflict more extreme.[3] In his own way Verwey was a part of that struggle throughout his life. In the 1880s he emerged as something of a young poetic genius in the revolutionary literary circles of Amsterdam. He became the favourite of Willem Kloos, to whom in 1885 he addressed a sonnet sequence of lyrical adulation.[4] On becoming engaged, however, Kloos broke with him and in 1890 Verwey retired to a house away from the centre of things at Noordwijk near Leiden, where he lived on with his large family till his death. From that isolated post he sought to guide Dutch cultural life through the periodicals which he edited. In the preface to the first issue of his *Tweemaandelijksch Tijdschrift* (1894) he wrote that a great revolutionary period was about to come; it would be religious, informed by Spinoza's conception of God; socially and politically it would be governed by an undogmatic socialism.[5] In the introduction to the third periodical he set up, *De Beweging*, he assumed the existence of a universal spiritual movement, of a

---

[1] From 1918 Pannekoek was attached to the University of Amsterdam where he became professor of astronomy in 1925.

[2] Nijland-Verwey, op. cit., p. 238.

[3] Is. P. de Vooys, 'Zedelijkheid en socialisme', *De Beweging*, III, iv, (1907), 91.

[4] M. Uyldert, *De jeugd van een dichter* (Amsterdam, 1948), pp. 214 ff.

[5] Cf. M. Uyldert, *Dichterlijke strijdbaarheid* (Amsterdam, 1955), pp. 55–6.

conscious spirit that gives guidance and order, a spirit of the age, which expresses itself in philosophy, art, learning, and poetry, and manifests itself politically in socialism.[1] It was in this spirit that Verwey tried to act. He was convinced that in essence it was the very spirit of poetry, the poetical dream, the inspiring idea, and with that extremism characteristic of the time which infected him too he propounded the thesis that poetry was the centre of the new socialist synthesis, so that he himself rendered society an essential service not as an individual but as a transmitter of poetic truth. Thus to Verwey and his followers socialism became a poetic vision of all that was harmonious and pervadingly beautiful, and as such it was clearly very remote from the sordid practices of party politics. Verwey could never understand why Gorter and Henriette Roland Holst should try to subordinate their poetry to their political beliefs and he was quite right when he said that they failed. But inevitably he failed too. *De Beweging*, his most ambitious periodical (1905–19), was too esoteric and too dull to attract much notice.[2] Important socialist politicians did publish in it occasionally, but they could count on a wider reading public elsewhere. Yet in spite of the isolated position in which he unhappily found himself, Verwey was an interesting figure; his studies on literary history, his judgement and taste, his abstruse poetry, which is still admired by some authorities for its grandeur and depth,[3] and the whole structure of his ideas seem to make him a central and highly representative personality, representative because of the ideal he strove after, the quality of his work, and the innate vagueness of his spiritual craving for synthesis.

Perhaps there is another reason why he may be considered representative. For all his modernity and his knowledge of international developments in the field of art, literature, and philosophy, he remained critical of the latest fashions. Nietzsche, whom he read in 1888, was not to his liking;[4] the triumvirate honoured by his German friends for having led the way to the Jugendstil—Nietzsche, Wagner, Böcklin—inspired him with

---

[1] *De Beweging*, I, i (1905), 7–8.

[2] The sad story of *De Beweging* has been described by Uyldert, *Dichterlijke strijdbaarheid* and *Naar de voltooiing* (Amsterdam, 1959).

[3] This is the way in which his disciple Weevers put it: op. cit., p. 187.

[4] Nijland-Verwey, pp. 8–9.

a certain aversion.[1] He felt such figures to be essentially foreign to the Dutch spirit. One of the best-known contributors to his periodicals and a loyal friend, the architect H. P. Berlage (1856–1934), shared this scepticism. Yet Berlage was not lacking in daring and revolutionary sense. He was a socialist. He wrote lengthy studies on the monumental, quiet, orderly architecture that he expected future generations of socialists to create. After the two cultural stages of civilization that European history had known, the classic and the feudal-Christian, after the uncultured stage of the bourgeois period, socialism would design a higher art based on the highest possible principle, that of equality.[2] The Art Nouveau of his Belgian colleague Henry van de Velde (1865–1957) he rejected in spite of his admiration for the latter's gifts; it seemed to him that the style was disorderly, a bad application of the principles of simple honest construction, and was doomed to an early failure.[3] This indicates a difference between Dutch and Belgian culture. Both were modern, but while the Belgian artists and literary men were at the centre of international fashion, the Dutch tended to remain aloof. They may not have reacted more slowly, but they were certainly more cautious when it came to putting their theories into practice. Their extremism was introverted, expressing itself as an inner struggle; they were not given to stylistic ostentation. The period of Art Nouveau was of short duration in the Netherlands; its individualism repelled and it gave way to the monumental, communal style, dedicated to the socialist ideal. The clearest expression of this artistic concept was the Exchange which Berlage built in Amsterdam. It is a nice paradox that in Belgium one of the first achievements of the new architecture was the socialist People's House (Maison du peuple) at Brussels, planned by Victor Horta (1861–1947), which was begun in

[1] A. Verwey to his wife, Berlin, 23 Oct. 1897: 'To say the truth, I did not like Böcklin at all. I did not tell George, for if I do not like Böcklin, nor Wagner, nor Nietzsche, what then is left?' Mea Nijland-Verwey (ed.), *Albert Verwey en Stefan George* (Amsterdam, 1965), p. 45.

[2] H. P. Berlage, 'Kunst en maatschappij', *De Beweging*, V, iv (1909), 166 ff., 235 ff.

[3] *Idem*, 'Beschouwingen over stijl', *De Beweging*, I, i (1905), 74. As early as 1898 Berlage wrote an article in *De Kroniek* in which he rejected Art Nouveau and warned his readers against Henry van de Velde. Cf. Romein, *Op het breukvlak* ii. 297 and W. Thys, *De Kroniek van P. L. Tak* (Amsterdam, 1956), p. 103.

1896 and finished in 1900. In the Netherlands it was Berlage's capitalistic Exchange, opened by the Queen in 1903, the year of the greatest strike the country ever saw. However individualistic Horta's art may have been it served socialism; Berlage's communal art served trade.

Berlage's views on cultural history were far from original, of course. It is easy to show Ruskin's and Morris's influence; indeed Dutch socialism often borrowed its aestheticism from Britain whilst drawing its economic and political currency from Germany. Without having much effect on literature and art, Germany was very largely responsible for the remarkable development of Dutch philosophy. In the nineteenth century philosophy was assiduously studied in the Netherlands, but did not pretend to be a creative discipline. The great schools of thought were taught in the universities each in their turn, but as Dutch liberalism itself was unsystematic, indeed averse to systems, no original national system of philosophy developed. Dutch liberals wrote essays and sketches and looked with scepticism and irony on what they regarded as over-ambitious and undesirable attempts to encapsulate life. In the 1890s the situation changed. The new quest for unity, order, and synthesis was a striking departure, when we consider that earlier the need for a system had seemed to the liberal bourgeoisie to be almost anti-liberal, a kind of lower-middle-class compulsion experienced by Calvinists, socialists, and the like. From this point of view the search for a coherent explanation of all problems and the reconciliation of all antinomies, a search begun at so many different levels and in so many different ways, can be seen as an aspect of the democratization of society. This impulse was certainly apparent in the field of philosophy. In the Netherlands, which had no nineteenth-century philosophical tradition of its own, two philosophers began to make their influence felt during this period— G. Heymans (1857–1930) and G. J. P. J. Bolland (1854–1922). Their methods were more original than those of their predecessors and they found incomparably more people willing to listen to them.

Heymans had the better mind. He was an influential empirical psychologist, and his theory of types in particular helped to establish his reputation. He wrote in German and his erudition was German. The metaphysics he sponsored, known as 'psychic monism', derived from the school of G. Fechner.[1] Heymans sought to eliminate the dualism of spirit and matter and to extend the concept of the individual self so indefinitely that it could be associated with or absorbed in a universal common consciousness.[2] Although he eschewed mysticism there was no doubt a semi-religious aspect to his philosophy. Heymans himself did not take part in Dutch debates but the problems with which he was concerned clearly related to those of his compatriots, and what he was trying to do on the metaphysical plane paralleled what many others were attempting in the fields of economics, sociology, or the arts.

This is equally true of Bolland, a totally different kind of man with very different ideas. He was one of the most obtrusive people of this period, an immoderate author and a relentless orator. Whilst Heymans was an accurate and conscientious scholar, Bolland remained something of the untrained amateur in spite of his encyclopedic knowledge. After a hard youth he worked his way up to be an English master at a school at Batavia; there he took up his study of philosophy. He discovered Eduard von Hartmann's work, explored it minutely, accepted its doctrines and defended them in innumerable publications. Then he lost his belief in them. Meanwhile he had renounced all certitude in religious matters too. He had been brought up a Catholic but already in his youth had drifted away from the Church. The more he occupied himself with religious history, the more hostile he became towards Christianity. It had neither dogmatic nor historical veracity, and was in his opinion no more than 'a craving for miracles and pious deceit'. By the time he had ceased to believe in anything, he was appointed professor of philosophy at Leiden.[3]

There he found a way out of his difficulties. He became a Hegelian. But he did so in his own way, like a prophet, like one possessed. Perhaps nobody in the Netherlands had ever been able to generate so much philosophical ardour before and it proved catching. Outside the Netherlands, too, his enthusiasm

[1] His *Einführung in die Metaphysik auf Grundlage der Erfahrung* was published in 1905 in Leipzig.

[2] T. J. C. Gerritsen, *La Philosophie de Heymans* (Paris, 1938), p. 251.

[3] W. N. A. Klever, *Jeugd en Indische jaren van G. J. P. J. Bolland* (Amsterdam, 1969), p. 64.

attracted attention. The Hegelian revival in the twentieth century cannot be understood without considering the influence of Bolland's propaganda. His philosophy was a form of mysticism; his reasoning brought his readers and hearers to a state of 'intellectual drunkenness'. His rhetoric was meant to have a releasing effect, to elevate man to the level at which he feels that all contrasts and differences have melted into a great synthetic experience of unity.[1] Such rhetoric, however, contained dubious and dangerous elements. Bolland's mysticism had a way of degenerating into total disdain for the non-elect, whether they were the muddle-headed common herd or intellectuals of an analytical bent. His contempt for socialists and Jews made him, a friend of the democratic Albert Verwey, a precursor of Fascism—though in that respect his influence was only slight.[2] His influence was not in fact political but religious. His followers felt a real craving for metaphysical certainty and truth, and this his oratorical and rhetorical skills supplied. This was even admitted by one of the sharpest adversaries whom Bolland came across in his lifetime, the remarkable J. A. dèr Mouw.[3] Dèr Mouw (1863–1919) was a brilliant man, a classical scholar, a Sanskritist, a linguistic philosopher. In his philosophy he was inexorably sober and exact; he despised Bolland's flight into mysticism. His own investigations did not lead to religious ecstasy but to a fear of utter loneliness in a world which was nothing but the delusion of the thinking individual. It would be nonsense to maintain that Dèr Mouw was representative of his times, he was much too eccentric for that. But he did share many of the current preoccupations and took a keen interest in mathematics and the natural sciences.[4] In 1913 he suddenly took to writing poetry. At his death he had finished two large collections. The title was *Brahman*; the pseudonym under which he published was Adwaita, 'he who transcends dualism'. It is superb poetry, the work of a man who has been delivered from his isolation by the

---

[1] H. J. Pos, 'Dèr Mouw versus Bolland', in J. A. dèr Mouw, *Verzamelde werken* (6 vols., Amsterdam, 1947–9), iii. 103 ff.

[2] Cf. A. A. de Jonge, *Crisis en critiek der democratie* (Assen, 1968), pp. 45–51.

[3] Cf. his *Kritische studies over psychisch monisme en nieuw-hegelianisme* (1906), reprinted in *Verzamelde werken*, v. 170–1.

[4] For some remarks on his place in Dutch literature see A. M. Cram-Magré, *Dèr Mouw-Adwaita* (Groningen, 1962), pp. 219 ff.

experience of an ecstasy completely controlled by his intellect.

Of course the Catholic *fin de siècle* philosophers did not follow the infidels in their search for the solution to the great dualistic dilemma, and the problems with which they were faced differed from those of the Marxists, Spinozists, and Hegelians. Yet from the point of view of cultural history they belong in the same category and they too felt compelled to pursue their meditations until a kind of synthesis had been attained or anyhow seemed attainable. The difficulties, however, were many, and only too conspicuous at the Catholic University of Louvain, which had been a centre of debate and conflict throughout the century. One of the most influential and prolific Louvain authors and professors was the priest G. C. Ubaghs (1800–75), born in Dutch Limburg. He published works in three languages—Latin, French, and Dutch—but the system he defended was in the end condemned by Rome (1866). It included elements which the Pope had already repudiated in other Catholic doctrines and it is not difficult to understand why Ubaghs's views were considered heterodox even in the form into which he had moulded them.

Ubaghs had started his career as a follower of Lamennais and Bonald. He opposed the emphasis placed upon the creative power of the individual and of reason and saw man bound by tradition and the community. After the knowledge of God had been revealed to the first man, the following generations did not acquire their knowledge by independent reasoning but by the instruction they received from their elders, which was handed on from one generation to the next. After a while, however, Ubaghs moved from this traditionalism towards a more ontological position: the first thing which the human spirit beholds is the essence of God, so that he has a direct knowledge of the Infinite. In Ubaghs's second phase tradition was only a means of widening the knowledge of the finite and of developing the intellect of the individual. The danger of such speculations was that they served the objective in view— the fight against rationalism and scepticism—by a devaluation of reason, which had been defended throughout the ages against Protestants and Jansenists by the orthodox Catholic doctrine and which, indeed, was thought to co-operate harmoniously with faith and—what Ubaghs denied—to be able to prove God's existence.[1] Although he did so with the utmost caution, it still meant that Ubaghs recognized in this manner the fundamental dualism of human nature. Moreover, his arguments were framed in such a way that they reduced the possibility of relating Catholic philosophy to the development of science. Naturally, in the nineteenth century this was something that might have serious consequences. But once this traditionalism and ontologism had been forbidden, once Ubaghs kept silent and his books gradually fell into disuse in the seminaries in the Low Countries where they had long been deeply admired, another system had to replace it. For the time being, however, no satisfactory solution was available.

It was not until the 1880s that one began to emerge in Louvain in the form of neo-Thomism. Already in 1879 Pope Leo XIII had recommended in his encyclical letter *Aeterni Patris* a renewed study of Thomas Aquinas's doctrine as a way out of the philosophical impasse. In 1880 he wrote to the archbishop of Mechlin that the institution of a chair of Thomism at the only Catholic university in Europe, at Louvain, would promote the restoration of Catholic philosophy. The Belgian bishops hesitated. They feared that such a resolution might be considered a Catholic offensive, a continuation in a new form of the ultramontane attack on the unchristian spirit of the time that had already failed so dismally.[2] In 1882, however, they gave in and D. F. F. J. Mercier (1851–1926) was appointed to the new chair, which he occupied until 1906 when he became archbishop of Mechlin. In 1894 he opened the building, spacious for the time, of his Institut supérieur de philosophie and before long he was drawing students from Belgium and other countries too. Its architect, George Helleputte (1852–1925), as well as being professor of architecture at Louvain, was an important Christian democratic statesman. In spite of serious conflicts with the university authorities Mercier succeeded in making his institute a centre where seminarists and others were initiated not only into Thomas's doctrine but also into the methods of modern

---

[1] H. A. C. M. van Grunsven, *Gerard Casimir Ubaghs* (Heerlen, 1933), p. 126 n. 2 and *passim*.

[2] A. Simon, *Le Cardinal Mercier* (Brussels, 1960), p. 45.

science, especially psychology. A well-appointed physiological-psychological laboratory was set up and some pupils were sent to Wundt at Leipzig to learn the latest views.[1] Mercier himself published continuously; the most important books were his works on psychology and epistemology.[2] He was indefatigable in studying not only scholasticism but modern, especially French, philosophy, in which he appreciated both Maurice Blondel's apologetics and the ideas of Bergson—that the latter's best pupils were converted to Catholicism could hardly-have escaped his notice.[3]

What Mercier found attractive in such ideas was not the anti-intellectualism to which they tended, but the anti-positivism which was their starting-point. It was, indeed, the greatest ambition of neo-Thomism too to attain a synthesis in which the antinomies of human existence would appear to have been solved. According to the whole tradition of scholasticism an important place had to be assigned to reason in such a synthesis. Mercier neither feared nor despised reason and science. He was convinced that scientific truth could not clash with religious truth; if it seemed to do so, then the way in which science had found its truth was wrong and the reasoning should be started all over again.[4] Just as a fundamental conflict between faith and science was impossible, so too was the divorce of spirit from matter propounded by Descartes and his followers. Mercier strove to demonstrate anew the essential unity of human nature which post-scholastic philosophy had denied or forgotten. Spiritualism and materialism, positivism and vitalism, all were equally dangerous because this unity was arbitrarily broken by such inevitably one-sided statements. In 1913 Mercier, then archbishop of Mechlin, expounded on a ceremonial occasion how far he and his school had gone in their work of restoration. He delivered

---

[1] A detailed history of the institute in L. de Raeymaeker, *Le Cardinal Mercier et l'Institut Supérieur de Philosophie de Louvain* (Louvain, 1952).

[2] *Les Origines de la psychologie contemporaine* (Louvain, 1897) and *Critériologie générale ou théorie générale de certitude* (Louvain, 1899).

[3] Cf. De Raeymaeker, op. cit., p. 174. Bergson, asked in 1920 whether he had ever met a true mystic, answered that he had once come across one: Cardinal Mercier had vividly impressed him as 'living mysticism' (ibid., p. 24 n. 8).

[4] A. Simon, *Position philosophique du Cardinal Mercier* (Brussels, 1962), p. 75. See also L. de Raeymaeker, *Dominanten in de philosophische persoonlijkheid van Kardinaal Mercier* (Brussels, 1952).

his speech in the Académie Royale de Belgique, of which he was chairman that year, in the presence of King Albert and the diplomats accredited at Brussels. He spoke with the double authority of a clerical leader and a scholar, as a man with great influence upon the whole life of the nation. His school, too, exercised much authority. His successor as director of the philosophical institute, Simon Deploige, advised and supported the Christian democratic statesmen in office.[1] Though Mercier attained his own worldwide fame during the First World War as a result of his resistance to the Germans, the impact of his philosophy on the cultural and political élite of his country was greatest before 1914.

Mercier called his speech 'Vers l'unité'.[2] Scholasticism, he said, is characterized by its desire to establish the synthesis of all seemingly contradictory elements which man finds when analysing his own spirit. In such a loftier view sense and reason, natural and supernatural, free will and grace, State and Church, and all those other opposites that seem to fragment life, appear to be only forms of one total experience, scraps of one total truth. But this knowledge is not only an act of faith; it is scientific knowledge which can be gained by careful study and accurate psychological analysis. Thus 'Vers l'unité' is the triumphant, almost official, manifesto of a philosophy which claimed to have drawn near to unity and harmony. In this respect neo-scholasticism is a very characteristic expression of the whole cultural atmosphere of these years. Politically, too, Mercier belonged to the *fin de siècle* period. In 1906, when he became archbishop, he spoke ardently about patriotism. The fatherland he held to be something holy. In 1910 he published a pastoral in which he defended Leopold II's memory and which he entitled: 'La piété patriotique.' He esteemed highly the King's Congo policy; in 1908 he called upon the faithful to perform by their work in the colony a communal act of love which a superior nation owed to the disinherited races. He wanted to increase the military strength of the country, unlike the traditional Belgian Catholics who had prided themselves on their antimilitarism. National service he praised as a

---

[1] On Deploige's influence see Rezsohazy, *Origines*, p. 154.
[2] Reprinted in *Revue néo-scolastique* (1913), pp. 253–79; analysed by De Raeymaeker, *Le Cardinal Mercier*, pp. 173 ff.

sacrifice to justice.[1] Thus Mercier did for the idea of the nation what he did for the idea of science. His predecessors had not known this form of patriotism and had reserved such feelings for the Catholics, whom they cherished and protected as a sort of nation within a neutral state. Mercier, who reconciled the Catholics to science, also disclosed to the faithful a general view of the nation in its wider sense. It was the first time in the history of Belgium that an archbishop identified himself— theoretically at any rate—with the people as a whole.[2] Both in its philosophy and in its political sentiment and ambition Belgian neo-Thomism concurred with Christian democracy. But in such a harmony of faith, unity, and patriotic duty there was no room for dissidents: Mercier had little sympathy with the Flemish movement. In the same year that he took up his post at Mechlin, 1906, the episcopacy condemned the use of Dutch as a teaching medium at the universities. By doing so, however, Mercier alienated Flemish intellectuals, non-Catholics as well as Christian democrats, and weakened the prestige of his patriotism.

Neo-Thomistic political theory was characterized as much as its scientific theory by the flexible way in which it could adapt to modern times without betraying its orthodox starting-points. But neither in Belgium nor in the Netherlands did it produce important results. Only rarely did Mercier's Louvain institute publish books on political problems. In the Netherlands the best representative of neo-Thomism, the priest J. Th. Beysens (1864-1945), delivered at Utrecht University a series of lectures on the state which he published, but they did not convey much that was new. What was far more striking about these neo-Thomists was the fact that they were so wide open to the concepts of totally different systems; after having seriously studied all conflicting systems—liberalism, socialism, communism, anarchism—they tried to set the bounds within which the necessary reforms had to be confined, but they showed some respect for revolutionary points of view and even derived a wide variety of ideas from them. These authors, moreover, decidedly rejected every attempt to construct a specific Catholic political theory which might be set against

[1] De Raeymaeker, *Le Cardinal Mercier*, pp. 25-6.
[2] Simon, *Le Cardinal Mercier*, pp. 117-18.

the unchristian doctrines as an antithesis. Neo-Thomism did not think in antitheses but in syntheses; it had an essentially different structure from ultramontanism and differed alike from the anti-revolutionary principle defended by the Dutch Calvinists who achieved a triumph in the field of learning when they founded a university of their own in 1880 (De Vrije Universiteit at Amsterdam) in order to develop an exclusively Christian learning as distinguished from the pagan scholarship of the state universities.

Pierre Harmignie, who was appointed to a senior position in the Institut supérieur de philosophie, thought that in politics as well as in ethics good and evil could not be defined in an abstract way because each judgement depended on the circumstances in which it was formed.[1] Beysens learned from history that there is no specifically Roman Catholic form of social organization: the Church had resigned itself to the most diverse arrangements and always pursued only one objective: replacing bad by better circumstances.[2] Neo-Thomistic sociology displayed similar tendencies. Simon Deploige published in 1911 his *Le Conflit de la morale et de la sociologie*—reprinted for the fourth time in Paris in the 1920s with an introduction by Jacques Maritain, who praised it highly—in which he fiercely attacked Durkheim and his school. It was not in fact his intention to dismiss modern sociology, though he had his doubts about the originality of the French, who were in his opinion too pretentious, and rejected certain consequences of their doctrine; the tenor of his argument was that in Thomas Aquinas's work can be found what the sociologists wrongly thought to be the latest discoveries of their own and that consequently neo-Thomism was able to absorb the whole of sociology. According to Deploige, the social sciences were the continuation or revival of Thomist philosophy:[3] now that sociology had demonstrated so clearly the emptiness of the seventeenth- and eighteenth-century rationalistic doctrine of natural law with its abstractions, its generalizations, and its dogmatic individualism, it was possible to come into contact again with the thirteenth-century

[1] P. Harmignie, *L'État et ses agents. Étude sur le syndicalisme administratif* (Louvain, 1911), p. 353.

[2] J. Th. Beysens, *Hoofdstukken uit de bijzondere ethiek* (3 vols., Bussum, 1917), i: *Eigendomsrecht*, pp. 76–7. See also ibid. ii: *Wijsgeerige staatsleer*.

[3] S. Deploige, *Le Conflit de la morale et de la sociologie* (Louvain, 1911), pp. 389 ff.

philosopher's cautious, undogmatic, and flexible *scientia prac-
tica* and *scientia moralis*.[1]

Whilst Deploige thought it worth while to devote a whole
book to a polemic against Durkheim without rejecting the
basis of his ideas, the first director of a sociological institute in
Brussels did not even think it necessary to go to the trouble of
criticizing Durkheim. In 1906 Émile Waxweiler (1867–1916)
published his *Esquisse d'une sociologie*. He observed parentheti-
cally that he did not intend to say anything further about the
burlesque idea that a social group forms an organic whole:[2] the
organic theory defended by Durkheim among others was dismissed without his deigning to refute it. While according to
Durkheim society had a life and soul of its own, independent
in a sense of the individuals which formed it, Waxweiler refused
to use the very word 'société'.[3] Waxweiler was a follower of
Solvay. The Institut de sociologie that he led had been established and paid for by Solvay and the doctrine which was
elaborated there was 'social energetics'.

Ernest Solvay (1838–1922) was a man of genius, as was often
and eagerly admitted. Thanks to the discovery and practical
use of a chemical process, he had built up an enormous industrial complex with numerous branches in Europe as well
as in the United States. In the course of the years the firm
developed into an empire in which investment trusts and
banks were incorporated. Solvay's mind, however, was always
probing new fields of activity. He was a self-confident thinker,
an autodidact, who had little leisure for pure research, but
much as he regretted this in one way he did not hesitate to
invite the best specialists to study his ideas closely and to
elaborate them, so important did he think them and so convinced was he that they were right. At the University of
Brussels he established affiliated institutions of physiology,
chemistry, and physics under strict orders to take his theories
as the basis for their research. He founded a higher commercial
school and an Institut de sciences sociales (1894) where he asked
leading socialists—among others Émile Vandervelde—to

[1] The Dutch neo-Thomist J. D. J. van Aengenent wrote a well-informed but
unoriginal *Leerboek der sociologie* (Leiden, 1909).

[2] É. Waxweiler, *Esquisse d'une sociologie* (Brussels, 1906), p. 262.

[3] Ibid., p. 270. Cf. D. Warnotte, *Ernest Solvay et l'Institut de Sociologie* (2 vols.,
Brussels, 1946), ii. 388–9.

develop his social views. The result of this was disappointing. The socialists proved to be too much committed to their own opinions to give Solvay's views a fair chance.[1] In 1900, however, he found young Waxweiler willing to take charge of a new institute. The Institut de sociologie was opened in 1902 and Waxweiler tried very diligently to make it a laboratory for investigating Solvay's social energetics.

Solvay was in search of total truth.[2] From about 1880 he was dominated by the at times agonizing desire to formulate just one simple law which would explain the working of the universe. He tried to find it in three spheres: in physics, in physiology, and in social reality. The solution he finally proposed was so rigorously monistic that it seemed not only extremely adventurous but almost mystical. Solvay was one of the most characteristic representatives of the *fin de siècle* period: typical in his capitalistic passion for expansion and his profound admiration for Leopold II's Congo policy, typical in his social ideas, typical in particular in his deep-felt need for a radical and more or less definitive interpretation of life and the world in a purely monistic sense. He had no time to study philosophy but it is by no means accidental that his ideas seem to be related to Bergson's. Nor is it accidental that they were developed further in 1909 by the German chemist Wilhelm Ostwald, Nobel prize winner and organizer of the German Monists' Association, in a book dedicated to Solvay, the founder of social energetics.[3] The pith of these ideas was apparently simple enough. The only reality in the world is energy. Materialism is a meaningless theory because matter is only a form of energy. Spiritualism also is unnecessary and one-sided because spirit too is in essence energy. Action is the conversion of energy. If we know the laws to which the transformation of energy conforms, then it is possible to explain man first as a biological being and next as a social being. As soon as this has been successfully done we can control society, which is after all nothing but a community of biological beings who transform energy. Then it is necessary to organize

[1] E. Mahaim, 'Notice sur Émile Waxweiler', *Jaarboek van de Koninklijke Belgische Academie*, civ (Brussels, 1938), 180; Warnotte, op. cit., 524.

[2] See *Notes, lettres et discours d'Ernest Solvay* (2 vols., Brussels, 1929) and Warnotte, op. cit.

[3] W. Ostwald, *Energetische Grundlagen der Kulturwissenschaft* (Leipzig, 1909).

society in such a way that all available energy, which cannot be lost according to the law of the conservation of energy, is converted in the way most useful to that society.

Consequently, social energetics is a science which explains and reforms society. Solvay belonged to the liberal party. He did not adhere to socialism because he thought its social ideas too static and at the same time too revolutionary. He was bound to liberalism by his rejection of religion and by the system that he called 'productivism' and deduced from social energetics. According to this the state must create or maintain the possibility of maximum productivity. This requires a highly trained scientific and technical élite. But by increased productivity the social problem, acute in Solvay's opinion, could be solved. Solvay also supposed that a drastic overhaul of the fiscal system would increase productivity as well as social equality: instead of direct and indirect taxes he wanted to introduce a new system of death duties that would guarantee revenue to the state and the removal of the caste of *rentiers* from society. In this way every individual would stand an equal chance and would be able to enjoy all the fruits of his labour in his lifetime. These and similar ideas are clearly related to Saint-Simonism, although Solvay does not seem to have known much about that.[1] The system was neither capitalistic nor socialistic; it was an attempt to regulate and to increase the dynamics of capitalism by state interference and a certain social levelling. Energy, inexhaustible and capricious like a god, could not be kept under strict control or added to; but by improving his social tools man could employ it more usefully than had been the case up till now.

2. *The Flemish Movement*

Lodewijk de Raet (1870–1914), Waxweiler's friend since 1896, frequented the sociological institute and collaborated in a number of its investigations. At the same time he was one of the leading figures in the Flemish movement. De Raet tried, not altogether successfully, to introduce the spirit of Solvay's energetic monism into a cultural and social movement which had

[1] Cf. G. Barnich, *Essai de politique positive basée sur l'énergétique sociale de Solvay* (Brussels, 1919), pp. 373 ff.

lived in an atmosphere of faded Romanticism for far too long. But the opposition in the Flemish movement itself was too great, and Solvay's system too limited and too abstract to serve as a starting-point for a new policy. It did appear possible, however, to derive certain impulses from it which could give the Flemish movement a more definite aim. In keeping with the principles of the Brussels institute De Raet thought that the revival of Flanders was dependent on an élite capable of raising the economic standards of the country. The first task of the movement, therefore, was to found a university with Dutch as a teaching-medium for the instruction of those who could lead the way in developing Flemish productivity. De Raet's vision was élitist, productivist, and biological. It was dominated by the Institut Solvay where biology—the combination of the natural and the social sciences—was thought to be the core of sociology. In this view the fact that the Flemish population was larger than the Walloon seemed of more importance than ever before.[1]

In 1903, a year after the opening of Solvay's institute, De Raet's campaign got well under way. He demanded that the medium of instruction at Ghent University, founded in 1817 by King William I, should be Dutch instead of French, which had replaced Latin in 1835. No one had previously dared to ask for this so bluntly. Again and again even the most convinced Flamingants had hesitated to claim that the Dutch language could be used for scientific purposes. Curiously enough they knew nothing about the situation in the Netherlands. They did not know that in Holland the most intricate scientific subjects were lectured on and written about in Dutch as a matter of course. It was a long time before the fact was brought home to them that there were numerous scientific textbooks in Dutch, numerous Dutch-language scientific journals, congresses, and organizations. And it must have been some sort of a revelation to them when they realized that between 1901 and 1914 five

[1] According to M. Lamberty, *Lodewijk de Raet* (Hasselt, 1961), pp. 71–2, De Raet was not directly influenced by Solvay and Waxweiler, although their ideas were similar. This, however, does not alter the fact that De Raet's conceptions did not become coherent enough to be acceptable before being put in the theoretical setting produced by Solvay and Waxweiler. De Raet shared the respect felt by the other two men for Leopold II's Congo policies (Lamberty, pp. 162–3). His frequent use of the term 'volkskrachten', 'popular forces' (Elias, *Vlaamse gedachte* iv. 78) is also significant; it reminds one of the *énergie* which was so popular in Solvay's school.

Dutchmen had been awarded Nobel prizes for their work in the field of the natural sciences while not a single Belgian had won such glory in spite of the much praised universality of the teaching language in Belgium. Once Belgium's relative backwardness in scientific research had been noted, the extreme and unprovable conclusion was immediately drawn that this was caused by the neglect of the popular language. It was said that in Flanders the reason why the bourgeoisie failed to make worthwhile contributions to science was because they were so passively dependent on France, and this one-sided respect for everything French had the further effect of cutting them off from Germany and England. The Netherlands, on the other hand, was open on all sides. However universal the French language might be, its use in Flanders led to claustrophobia, provincialism, and dangerous isolation.[1]

The French-speaking Walloon Waxweiler endorsed the view that higher education in Flanders must be in Dutch. He himself learned Dutch and was lecturing in it about 1900 in the University Extension at Ghent to students who regarded sociology as the science through which the new society would be created.[2] To his friend De Raet, the ideal of a Dutch university at Ghent became the body and soul of the Flemish movement. It would turn out the Dutch-speaking lawyers, doctors, and scientists who could develop Flanders; it would make the whole people more confident by creating an élite speaking and writing in Dutch; it would produce the teachers who could contribute to the training of agriculturists and technicians at every level of vocational training; it could strengthen the Flemish economy and raise productivity. This programme was a deliberate break with the tradition of the literary, historically minded, rather sentimental Flemish movement. Undoubtedly, earlier on, in particular during the great economic crisis of the 1840s, certain Flemish newspapers and authors had discovered a connection between the economic decline of Flanders, the prosperity of

[1] This argument was developed by J. MacLeod (1857–1919) as early as 1895. Cf. Elias, op. cit. iv. 42–3. MacLeod was a curious, attractive personality: biologist, sociologist, and anarchist, a thoroughly modern man whose ideas came often very near to some theses of the Institut Solvay.

[2] Cf. Karel van de Woestijne's testimony in the *Nieuwe Rotterdamsche Courant* of 1 July 1916 quoted by P. Minderaa, *Karel van de Woestijne. Zijn leven en werken* (Arnhem, 1942), p. 130.

the Walloon provinces, and the falling into disuse of the Dutch language in Belgium—in that respect it might be said that the Flemish movement had had an economic aspect from the beginning.[1] But only at this late date in the history of the movement were men like De Raet able to place the connection between the two phenomena in the framework of precise sociological arguments. It had been a mere impression; now it was presented as a scientifically proven fact. Obviously, it was no accident that De Raet's philosophy originated in the 1890s for it was then that there appeared the first signs for many years of economic growth, of a very gradual shifting of the balance of economic power in favour of Flanders. At the beginning of the twentieth century the trend may not have been obvious, but it was at least perceptible. From this it followed, according to De Raet's hard-headed way of thinking, that the Flemish struggle should be transformed into a struggle for political power. Through their university and their economic growth the Flemings were to seize in the unitary Belgian state the power which was their due.

For the time being De Raet's plans were not successful. Yet they were by no means the abstract speculations of an isolated scholar. They were widely supported in the Flemish movement and gave rise to mass agitation. The movement generally emerged during these years from the preparatory stage of banquets and literary coquetry into a movement of popular agitation. This was related to the introduction of universal suffrage in 1893 which greatly increased the influence of the very large number of people who spoke exclusively Flemish, and made it politically important to win them over. There were candidates for the Chamber who promised to use only Dutch in the House of Representatives; what is more, there were among them those who, once elected, kept their promise. In 1895 a bill was introduced in the Chamber to make the Dutch version of the laws legally valid—hitherto only the French version had been recognized as official. When the Second Chamber had passed this bill in 1896 by a great majority, Francophile circles and newspapers tried to influence

[1] See R. van Eenoo, 'Economische crisis en Vlaamse beweging: reacties uit de Brugse pers (september 1830-februari 1848)', *Tijdschrift voor sociale wetenschappen*, xiv (Ghent, 1969), 3–43.

the discussion that was to follow in the Senate. And in 1897 the Senate indeed mutilated the bill in such a way that little remained of it. Moreover, the senators showed themselves very inventive in formulating ingenious taunts in sonorous French directed against the Flemings and the Dutch language. At that moment the Flemish action became a truly popular action. Farmers, shopkeepers, workmen, parliamentarians, local authorities, professors, and many others protested each in his own way; in innumerable tumultuous meetings this indignation was given voice. The number of those who took part in these manifestations ran into tens of thousands. The action continued for many months (from February until June 1897) and afterwards it flared up time and again whenever the Chamber and the Senate considered the question anew.[1] Finally, the Flemings gained a decisive victory. In 1898 the bill was passed in its original form both by the Chamber and the Senate and received the royal assent. Evidently a Flemish movement that roused the masses was politically so important that its demands had to be met. This was the first time such a movement had taken shape.

The second time was when the university question was treated as a popular cause. In itself it was a curious development that De Raet's élitist programme in which little or no attention was paid to the greatly neglected primary schools—there was still no compulsory education—could become the signal for an agitation held to be democratic. But the movement was still deficient in general aims and a broad-based theory and it was far from coherently organized—it remained a politically heterogeneous movement of liberals, progressive Catholics, and socialists. In consequence, the solution of one single problem could appear as a panacea simply because it was brilliantly argued and seemed to be supported by scientific evidence. The general importance of the university was grossly exaggerated. According to the rhetoric of one of the Flemish leaders the university was 'the supreme teacher of a nation, the chief organ, the fountain-head of the moral national existence'.[2]

[1] M. de Vroede, *Juliaan de Vriendt in de politiek en de Vlaamse Beweging, 1889–1900* (Antwerp, 1960), pp. 96 ff., 121 ff.

[2] F. van Cauwelaert in an address read in September 1910: 'Universiteit en volksleven', partly reprinted in R. Roemans and H. van Assche (eds.), *Frans van Cauwelaert* (Hasselt, 1963), p. 50.

On 19 December 1910 a meeting was held at Antwerp in which over 5,000 people took part and representatives of three parties delivered addresses: the liberal Louis Franck, the Catholic Frans van Cauwelaert, and the socialist Camille Huysmans. Huysmans said that they would awake the people like three crowing cocks. Franck (1868–1937) had been a member of the House of Representatives for some years and belonged to the left wing of his party. He was a well-known Antwerp barrister and politician, who continued to concern himself with Flemish affairs even after his career took him into much wider fields: he was Minister of the Colonies from 1918 to 1924. Van Cauwelaert (1880–1961) went to school at one of those *petits séminaires* in Flanders where the boys were punished for talking Flemish to each other and so had long felt the need for reform. At Louvain he studied philosophy under Mercier and belonged there to the minority which opposed the enforced mastery of French. At the intercession of Mercier he became a teacher in experimental and pedagogic psychology at Freiburg in Switzerland in 1907, probably because, being pro-Flemish, he could not expect a chair at Louvain. But in 1909, when he was absolutely certain that Mercier would prevent him from ever getting a chair in Belgium, he came back, read law at Louvain, and set up as a barrister at Antwerp. In 1910 he became a member of the Chamber.

Van Cauwelaert was a combative and a pious man. The tone of his speeches and writings is not bitter, although he did have some personal reasons for bitterness, but a certain mildness characterizes the Flemish movement in general. In spite of its clamour and romantic excitement, in spite of the hard logic De Raet tried to introduce, the movement developed no doctrine of revolt and had no leaders driven by idealism, rancour, despair, or ambition—none of the makings of a guerrilla fighting force. In Belgian history of the nineteenth century street-fights were by no means unknown; indeed they had proved at critical moments to be a decisive factor in politics. The Walloon part of the country was ravaged by riots several times. As recently as the 1880s the liberals and Catholics had given battle in the Brussels streets. But Flanders, predominantly agrarian and intensely pious, remained very quiet at the time. The protest demonstrations kept a festive character, with flags, banquets, and speeches in which the Flemings were praised and the Walloons fraternally admonished. Though the Flemish movement became a movement of the masses during these years, it remained free from hatred and subordinated itself not only to the fact of the Belgian unitary state but also to Belgian national feeling. Even during this democratic phase it did not correspond to such virulent emancipation movements as those of the Czechs or the Irish. Van Cauwelaert could become one of the most celebrated orators of Flanders, delivering his florid and fluent sentences about the restoration of the national soul, and the self-respect, self-confidence, and self-sacrifice which would make the Fleming a superior man. It was not by a direct appeal to their aggressive instincts but by rhetorical, religious pedagogy that he kindled the public's enthusiasm.

His friend and colleague[1] Huysmans (1871–1968) acquired a reputation for being a master of sarcasm. His irony, however, was too whimsical and his socialist idealism too real to allow genuine bitterness. Huysmans studied philology at Liège and wrote a thesis about the figure of the devil in some Middle Dutch plays. After having been a teacher for some years, he gave up his career as a scholar—though later, even as a minister, he still found time to study and publish some Middle Dutch texts—and took up journalism and politics (1897). Since 1887 he had been a member of the Belgian Workers' party. In 1905 he became secretary of the Second International, a post which he retained until 1921. This put him in close touch with the big men of the socialist movement abroad. In such a context there was no room for the parochial self-sufficiency which sometimes characterized the Flemish movement. Huysmans could judge the importance of Flemish achievements and grievances against the background of the social and ethnic questions prevalent in Europe. Unlike most leaders of the Workers' party, who at heart distrusted the Flemish movement because it might distract attention from the social problem, he saw the imperative need for language reform and threw himself into the struggle whole-heartedly.

---

[1] Huysmans was a member of the Chamber of Representatives from 1906. From 1921 to 1933 he was Alderman for Education in Antwerp where at that time Van Cauwelaert was burgomaster. From 1933 till 1940 he was burgomaster himself.

In his opinion it would have been unnatural for a Flamingant not to be socialist and for a socialist not to be a Flamingant, so closely were the two emancipation movements related.[1] This was an unusual attitude. Many socialists were surprised at Flemish propaganda which, starting from the fact that French was the language of the bourgeoisie in Flanders, suggested that 'Dutchifying' Flanders would lead to a termination of the class struggle. In their opinion such a hypothesis was absurd because the class struggle was by no means absent in linguistically homogeneous countries. Moreover, they were looking for opportunities to impart some knowledge of French to the workers so as to improve their chances in life. Huysmans did not see it that way at all, but he did not dramatize the conflict. He did not maintain that the Flemish people were oppressed. As an internationalist and as a Belgian, Flemish separatism founded on the supposition of Flemish nationalism and a Flemish 'race' did not appeal to him. His ideal was cultural autonomy within the unitary state and the economic framework of the Belgian nation. Huysmans was no extremist. Though he made many enemies by his caustic but always witty irony, though he was averse from compromises and belonged to a theoretically revolutionary party—if, from an international point of view, to its right wing[2]—he was certainly not the man to exploit Flemish grievances for revolutionary ends.

After 1910 the *vernederlandsing* (Dutchification) of Ghent University remained the most important item on the Flemish agenda. Every Sunday the propagandists went into the country in order to rouse farmers and workers to fight for the Dutch-language university. In all the towns of Flanders big meetings were organized, attended by thousands. In 1912 a meeting at Ghent attracted an audience of more than 15,000 people. Over 100,000 people signed a petition to the Chamber. Yet for the time being all these efforts were unsuccessful. The opposition was very strong. Most Belgian statesmen had no sympathy at all for the cause, and even members of Parliament representing

[1] R. Roemans and H. van Assche (eds.), *Camille Huysmans* (Hasselt, 1961), p. 144.

[2] See Chapter IX below for his curious position during the First World War when in circles of Belgian socialists he could pass for an extremely left-wing politician.

Flemish districts were against this particular reform. According to a calculation of 1912, only 55 out of 105 Flemish representatives were in favour, and only 36 out of the 101 Catholic members of the Chamber, whose party was much more pro-Flemish than the socialists or the liberals, supported it.[1] The episcopacy, led by Mercier, declared strongly against it in 1906. In the episcopal *Instructions collectives* they wrote that by introducing Dutch as the university language 'la race flamande serait du coup réduite à des conditions d'infériorité dans la concurrence universelle'. Such an argument could not of course be used in connection with secondary education. But when in 1901 the bishops had to yield to Flemish pressure—particularly from the Christian democratic wing of the Catholic party[2]—and were obliged by law to use Dutch as a teaching-medium in some subjects in Catholic secondary education in Flanders (as had been the case in the state schools since 1883), at the top of the educational hierarchy the university continued to use French. At the outbreak of the First World War a bill proposed three years earlier by Franck and Van Cauwelaert for the gradual introduction of Dutch at Ghent University had still not been discussed in a general parliamentary debate. Nor were the Flemings successful in organizing special Dutch-speaking regiments in the army. In 1913 they did manage to obtain the guarantee that in future the Flemish recruits would receive their training in their own language; the officers, however, would continue to give their orders exclusively in French, even though most soldiers spoke only Dutch.[3]

Attempts to found a lasting Flemish political party failed. In the early 1890s a number of liberal Flemings at Brussels, whose demands found no response with the French-speaking party leaders in the capital, tried to start a party of their own; outside Brussels, however, their initiative was not supported.[4] At the very beginning of this ephemeral Vlaamsche Volks-

---

[1] Elias, iv. 168.

[2] On the relations between the Flemish movement and Christian democracy, cf. below, p. 634.

[3] According to the inquiry of 1910 the number of people in the Flemish provinces (Brussels not included) that could be regarded as bilingual was less than 13 per cent of the population. In Brussels about half the population also spoke French; in towns like Antwerp and Ghent perhaps one-quarter.

[4] De Vroede, *Juliaan de Vriendt*, pp. 25 ff.; Elias, iv. 233 ff.

partij (Flemish People's party) Lodewijk de Raet played an important part but afterwards he drifted away and reverted to the old well-worn tactic of trying to form Flemish pressure groups within the existing parties. To this abortive experiment the Flemish movement owes a remarkable pamphlet, namely the passionate criticism of it written by a friend and fellow student of De Raet's, August Vermeylen. Vermeylen (1872–1945) was born at Brussels of a lower-middle-class family. His father could speak good French as well as his Flemish-Brussels dialect but his mother hardly knew it. At grammar school he got to know De Raet; like him he became a convinced supporter of the Flemish cause, though at first the two boys exercised their literary muscles by composing French verses. In 1889 they founded a journal, *Jong Vlaanderen*, as a counterpart to *La Jeune Belgique*, though it did not survive for long. When De Raet took up politics, Vermeylen wrote his 'Kritiek der Vlaamsche Beweging' ('Criticism of the Flemish Movement') (1895). He criticized the pettiness of many a Flemish action, the silly tendency to consider all great problems only from the linguistic point of view, reducing, for instance, the colonial problem to the question whether legislation for the Congo should also be published in Dutch. The Flemings, he wrote, beg when they can take, ask or demand when they must act. They tinker at reforms, which are far too limited to make sense and far too dependent on the state to last. Vermeylen was an anarchist in these years and thought that State and Parliament were doomed. In the ecstatic manner of his generation and using the Dutch language as finely as it had even been used in Flanders, he prophesied the brilliant future of the free individual in a harmonious world without power, and he reproached the politicians among his friends that they did not inspire the Flemish movement—'the most sincere and honourable endeavour that ever originated in Belgium'—with his ideal.[1] His writing created a sensation. Here for the first time an essentially revolutionary doctrine was applied to Flemish affairs—though the article did not say how an anarchist had to act and offered no programme for Flemish action. Pretty soon, however, Vermeylen renounced the anarchist element in his

---

[1] A. Vermeylen, 'Kritiek der Vlaamse Beweging', *Verzameld Werk* (6 vols., Brussels, 1951–5), ii. 44–82.

study. Though he occasionally used revolutionary-sounding terminology,[1] in fact only the thesis remained that if Flanders created a civilization of its own, then it had a place in European culture. Vermeylen himself wrote in an autobiographical novel about someone much akin to himself that he was too weak 'for the heroic life, as we had conceived it'.[2] He was a man of letters and a scholar, no leader of the people or bitter extremist.

Together with some literary friends he edited a journal that played a part in Belgian literature written in Dutch comparable to that of *De Nieuwe Gids* in the Netherlands. Its curious title *Van Nu en Straks* (*Of Present and Future*) strikingly expressed the young editors' obsession with actuality and the dream of a new future. The outward appearance of the first volume, designed by Henry van de Velde in intricate Art Nouveau letters and decorations, was quite an event as well. From 1893 the journal appeared irregularly, whenever the editors thought they had collected enough brilliant copy; it was illustrated with original woodcuts and lithographs by such famous or rising artists as James Ensor and Jan Toorop. Dutchmen often contributed to it with great pleasure. *Van Nu en Straks* was deeply impressed by fashionable anarchism or communism. Henry van de Velde was a communist and was attempting to construct a new 'communal art', after reading Walter Crane and William Morris. In 1893 Élisée Reclus had taken up residence in Brussels; the young intellectuals who came to listen to him were quickly converted.[3] And the Flemish men of letters, who accepted anarchism, found with pride that they had overtaken the Dutch at last. While *De Nieuwe Gids* was still sticking to radical liberalism or socialism, *Van Nu en Straks* rejected all politics and penetrated, so these erudite young men thought, to the people's hearts directly, without the intercession of parties.[4] Although all this was of course an illusion, it was true that *Van Nu en Straks*—twelve years after *La Jeune Belgique*, eight years after *De Nieuwe Gids*—was strik-

---

[1] Elias, iv. 60.   [2] Ibid. 61.

[3] G. Schamelhout, 'Uit de jaren 1892–1901', *Gedenkboek A. Vermeylen* (n.p., 1932), p. 112. Vermeylen went beyond Reclus. He later declared that Nietzsche, Stirner, and especially Richard Wagner impressed him much more profoundly: cf. L. Sourie, *Inleiding tot de geschiedenis van 'Van Nu en Straks'* (Courtrai, 1942), p. 35.

[4] E. de Bom, 'De jonge Vermeylen', *Gedenkboek*, pp. 34–5 (letter from De Bom to J. Mesnil, 12 Feb. 1895).

ingly more modern than any of its rivals. It represented the opposition of the 1890s to the crisis of the 1880s. Vermeylen, who apparently knew Saint-Simon too, imagined that his generation in 1894 had passed from the critical period of the split soul to the organic period of a common belief and a new individualistic synthesis.[1]

In historical perspective, however, the significance of *Van Nu en Straks* lay in the fact that for the first time a whole group of Flemish literary men, and not just a solitary genius like Gezelle, were operating on as high a level as their Dutch colleagues. Intellectually, the work of Vermeylen and that of a great poet like Karel van de Woestijne (1878–1929) was equal to that of the Dutch and to that of the French-writing Belgians—of course, a judgement on their purely literary and aesthetic quality is more difficult. The fact that the Dutch-writing essayists, philosophers, poets, and novelists in Flanders could match the remarkable revival that the civilization of French Belgium and the Netherlands had known before was in itself extremely important. If Flemish literature, like that of the Netherlands, eventually remained provincial in as much as it did not radiate abroad, then here too the explanation is probably that it was to foreign impulses that it owed its best achievements. Internationally it was what has been called 'a second blooming, rather a result of fruitful movements started elsewhere than a really new and fertile contribution to the universal literary patrimony'.[2] Such a statement need not in the least detract from the intrinsic qualities of the works of art themselves.

3. *Political Developments*

The political history of the Low Countries was equally lively during the two decades before the First World War. Important decisions were reached. The Belgians annexed the Congo; the Dutch started their ethical policy in the Dutch East Indies. In both countries important laws were introduced after discussions of general issues had developed into philosophical debates of much greater depth than had been usual

[1] Vermeylen, 'De kunst in de vrije gemeenschap', *Verzameld Werk*, ii. 35.
[2] Lissens, *De Vlaamse letterkunde*, p. 96.

within the old technical and juridical framework of the parliamentary debating style. Bright young journalists covered parliamentary activities with sharp, well-written commentaries. In the Netherlands particularly political caricature was brilliantly developed into an artistic form of a high order, as well as into a lethal weapon. The parties, which by the extension of the franchise had become dependent on much larger groups in the nation, did their utmost to get at the masses and probably succeeded in doing so better than ever before. Through an intricate network of associations and Press organs their propaganda was spread and the population taught to think in political terms. Democracy apparently meant that all social development had its political aspects. It was now not only in Parliament but in the provincial and town councils, which had once restricted themselves to purely administrative matters, that political factors came to play a great part. And outside the representative bodies too, in the factories and in the streets, a fierce opposition was making itself felt. Strikes, organized on a large scale—in 1902 and 1913 in Belgium, in 1903 in the Netherlands—expressed the conflicts dramatically.

There is no doubt that this politicization of life was very largely due to the aggressiveness of a socialism dependent for its very existence on mass involvement in politics. This was probably an essential function of socialism. For years the socialists forced all political parties to follow their tactics, after their compelling appeal to the workers and the relatively swift success of their propaganda. But even so a victory of socialism did not follow. The confessional parties in particular contrived to mobilize their forces so efficiently that the socialists had drastically to revise their too simplistic hypotheses. It became increasingly clear that the socialist system was founded on arbitrary premises. It was not true that the masses, once awakened to political consciousness, automatically accepted socialist beliefs, as had been generally expected. The gulf between doctrinaire socialism and the expectations of the workers themselves grew ever wider in this period. With the help of German expedients such as revisionism and reformism an attempt was made to adapt socialism to the facts of society, but this was a rather hopeless undertaking and in the Low Countries must be considered a failure. The assumption—

gratuitous as it appeared afterwards—of a revolutionary class-consciousness of the masses was intellectually incompatible with the supposition—slightly less arbitrary, it is true—that the socialists could look after the workers' well-being better than the liberals or confessionals. Leaders such as Vandervelde and Troelstra, leaning more or less towards reformism, succeeded no better than Gorter and Pannekoek with their ultra-left 'Marxist' opposition verging on communism, in keeping their balance on the tightrope of dogma. The socialists appeared to be as inconsistent as all the other politicians, wavering between compromise and principle; despite their endless debates on the strategy of the revolutionary movement, they were often hopelessly uncertain about the policy to be pursued in real life. Nevertheless, socialism may have been changing gradually from an abstract intellectual alternative into a normal political party, prepared for the time being to accept things very much as they were, though without relinquishing its ambition of founding the true socialist society one day.

At the beginning of the century the socialists both in Belgium and the Netherlands tried to create an atmosphere of crisis and impending revolution by means of a number of big strikes. This, however, was virtually impossible in a society which was growing fast economically and in a cultural climate characterized by energetic monism and a faith in the power of synthesis. It was difficult to revive the excitements of the 1880s and to sustain the belief that a total break in history was imminent. Politics entered a period of relative quiet. People began to take long-term views and tried to calculate the consequences of their decisions for years ahead. In socialism too the tendency was to await events more calmly, still with the confidence that in a more distant future the revolution would eventually come. Even the ultra-left theory of the spontaneous, revolutionary strike—a theory eagerly propagated in times of crisis—had an element of resignation about it. The strike in practice could not after all be expected to bring about an immediate revolution: it could only be used to educate the workers and to consolidate the proletarian consciousness. In this spirited but essentially quiet political atmosphere politicians inevitably had to set aside attitudes they had acquired in the tenser periods of the past. The parties were less in need of charismatic leadership.

From 1884 to 1914 Belgium was governed by Catholic cabinets, but among the numerous ministers in office there was none who could or would rise above the group. In the Netherlands Kuyper as leader of a Protestant–Catholic Cabinet from 1901–5 tried to play the part of a political visionary. But not only did his policy fail, after 1905 he was more or less pushed aside by his own party and had no successor with comparable ambitions. And however much the Dutch socialist Troelstra wanted to dominate his party, he made no attempt at all to imitate the messianism that Domela Nieuwenhuis displayed in the 1880s.

The universal, if plural, suffrage that was introduced in Belgium in 1893 consolidated the Catholic party in the position of authority it had gained in 1884. After Beernaert's resignation in 1894 seven Catholic cabinets ruled the country until 1914, of which the most lasting held out nearly eight years and the weakest only a couple of months. Though, in the years from 1904 to 1910 especially, the majority on which these governments relied had a way of disintegrating, Catholic supremacy had by no means been undermined when the World War broke out in 1914. The party could still depend on a great many followers among the people and seemed to be vital and creative enough to bear the responsibility of government for a long time. Throughout this period the Catholics commanded an absolute majority in the Chamber. From 1894 to 1899 this majority was exaggerated by the electoral system. With 104 out of 152 seats in 1894, 110 in 1896, and 112 in 1898 Catholic supremacy was so overwhelming that even in the eyes of the victorious politicians themselves it was dangerous and in fact unrealistic. In 1894 the liberal party lost no fewer than 41 seats and in 1896 another 8. In 1899 it had only 12 members in the Chamber. The socialists maintained their position (28 seats in 1894). This meant, therefore, that in the long run the most important opposition to the government had to come from the socialists or from a coalition with the liberals dominated by the socialists. Such a perspective was so unattractive to the Catholics that in 1899 they accepted what they had refused their leader Beernaert in 1893, namely proportional representation in the constituencies. This gave the liberals, equally spread all over the country and nowhere in command of an absolute majority, some scope for recovery. However, the number of votes cast for them did not increase proportionately: in 1894 it was 29 per cent of the total, in 1900 22·5 per cent, in 1912 only 11·2 per cent, but by then a number of liberals had entered into a coalition with the socialists that polled heavily. The number of liberal seats, however, rose from 12 to 31 in 1900; when in 1902 the Chamber was extended to 166 members, the liberals obtained more new seats. In 1904 they had 42 out of 166 seats, in 1906 45 out of 166, but in 1914 only 45 out of 186. The Catholics, who obtained in 1900 48 per cent of recorded votes and 86 out of 152 seats, were in the same position in 1914 with nearly 50 per cent of the votes and 101 seats out of 186. The socialists obtained in 1894 19 per cent of the total number of votes and 28 seats (out of 152). In 1900 they won 22·4 per cent and 32 seats. But in 1902 they had only 33 seats out of 166, in 1914 40 out of 186. Evidently, there was no reason for them to expect that they could improve their position in the Chamber within the prevailing electoral system. On the contrary, they even seemed to grow somewhat weaker. While in the Chamber they were stronger than the liberals from 1894 to 1900 and as late as 1902 still had two seats more, between 1904 and 1914 their representation in Parliament was smaller than that of the liberals.[1]

In the Netherlands the situation was much less simple. After the reform of 1896 the suffrage remained more limited than in Belgium, though it was bound gradually to grow in reflecting advances in prosperity and popular education. The party structure, moreover, was more complicated. The Catholic party was faced by at least two Protestant parties; the liberal party was breaking up as well and even the socialists were experiencing a similar, though less serious, process of fragmentation. Thus it was by no means easy to determine just where the majority in the Chamber lay. As in Belgium the religious parties continued to be called 'right', and all the others, conservative though they might be, were known as 'left'. But the 'left' formed no kind of a unity, few liberals being prepared to work with the socialists. From 1901 to 1918 the Catholics held 25 out of 100 seats. Abraham Kuyper's Protestant party had a much more capricious fate: 24 seats in 1901, 15 in 1905, 23

[1] For complete figures see Luykx, *Politieke geschiedenis*, pp. 562 ff.

in 1909, and 11 in 1913. Including the members of the more moderate Christian Historical Union, the Christian (that is, Catholic–Protestant) coalition had 58 seats in 1901, 48 in 1905, 60 in 1909, and 45 in 1913. Thus in 1901 and 1909 it was possible to form cabinets that were more or less homogeneously 'right'. In 1905 and 1913, on the other hand, there were no corresponding cabinets that could be designated 'left'. The last undeniably liberal government ruled from 1897 to 1901, but in 1905 a Cabinet was formed which was liberal only in name, one which could find its way out of parliamentary politics only by eschewing most of the things that liberalism traditionally stood for. Again in 1913 a Cabinet of left-liberal stamp could not rely on a safe majority in the Chamber because the socialists, although they supported it in practice, did not want to be too closely associated with it in theory. The result of the poll of 1913 was dramatic indeed. The socialists gained 6 seats, giving them 15 in a Chamber of 100 members, which seemed to indicate the possibility of rapid expansion—for years they had failed to muster as many as 10. Admittedly, they were some way from matching the traditional strength of their Belgian brethren (15 per cent of the members as opposed to more than 20 per cent in Belgium), but at last the positions of the two socialist parties had become more or less comparable. Nevertheless, it is clear that the gradual extension of the suffrage was not automatically bringing about a decisive increase in the strength of the radical–liberal and socialist parties. In 1918 elections with universal, proportional manhood suffrage were held for the first time; the confessional parties then won exactly half the seats.

So the pivot of political development was the evolution of the confessional parties. To a considerable extent they were responsible for formulating political decisions though whether in reaching such decisions they can be held equally responsible for their contents remains an open question. How far their politics could and must differ materially from that of the 'left' parties was becoming a more and more difficult problem. Certainly, attempts were made to design policies on strictly confessional lines—for instance, in the period from 1908 to 1913, when some Protestants wanted to introduce a kind of corporatism. But these were a complete failure, not only because of opposition from outside the confessional parties, but because they themselves were divided. Moreover, it is probable that their social position was less strong than their political. Although a section of the economic and intellectual élite in Belgium undoubtedly voted Catholic, many influential bankers, industrialists, and merchants, to say nothing of artists and intellectuals, supported liberal or socialist programmes. In the Netherlands this tendency was much more pronounced. It may be assumed that generally speaking the Anti-revolutionary party, which continued to give political guidance to the Christian coalition, had less support among the upper classes than the Dutch liberals or Belgian Catholics.

Among the mass of the people, too, confessional politics encountered centres of resistance which could not be ignored. In the early years of the twentieth century the socialists had managed to organize their trade union movement on a somewhat sounder basis than before. The same sort of thing had been achieved in Germany as early as 1891 and in France in 1895; in 1898 the Belgian socialist party had set up a federation to co-ordinate the very disparate efforts of the various unions and to encourage the founding of new syndicates.[1] In 1906 the Dutch socialists at last followed suit, bearing the German example particularly in mind.[2] The Catholics and Protestants had not failed to take advantage of the tardiness of the socialists and had initiated a trade union movement of their own with undoubted success. But the socialist organizations, growing in numbers and effectiveness, now became a force to be reckoned with. By 1914 some 125,000 workers in Belgium had joined a socialist trade union while some 110,000 belonged to a Catholic organization.[3] In the Netherlands the Dutch federation of trade unions, which was socialist, had a membership of 84,000, the Catholic federation 29,000, and the Protestant 11,000; on the other hand, no fewer than 142,000 workers had joined the much more loosely organized and weaker unions which were not associated with any federation.[4] Though a great proportion

---

[1] Delsinne, *Mouvement syndical*, p. 14.

[2] Fr. de Jong Edz., *Om de plaats van de arbeid. Een geschiedkundig overzicht van ontstaan en ontwikkeling van het Nederlands Verbond van Vakverenigingen* (Amsterdam, 1956), p. 56.

[3] Chlepner, *Cent ans d'histoire sociale*, pp. 116, 118.

[4] *Zeventig jaren statistiek in tijdreeksen* (The Hague. 1970), p. 156.

of the industrial workers therefore remained outside any organization—in Belgium it is estimated at 80 per cent, in the Netherlands it must have been almost as many—it was necessary nevertheless for statesmen to take into account the opinion of the socialist trade union movement, if not of the socialist party itself.

Under the circumstances the Christian democrats, who had started a vigorous campaign among Catholics and Protestants, needed to adjust themselves to the existing capitalistic society, from which they claimed to be hardly less alienated than the socialists. They also had to adopt certain socialist techniques and methods, the theoretical foundations of which were to be found in the concept of the class war which they so much deplored. In effect, therefore, they no longer aspired to a 'new' society opposed both to the existing structure which they rejected, and to the socialist ideals they feared, but confined themselves to the ambition—large enough in itself—of organizing and directing the lower classes in such a way that they could resist the secularizing effects of the society in which they were doomed to live. A strong Catholic or Protestant labour movement and clear social legislation were in their opinion the best way of raising the people to an economic and intellectual level at which they would be less vulnerable to the revolutionary and supposedly atheistic propaganda of the socialists. Social legislation implied, however, not only a degree of state interference which roused the opposition of the conservative Catholics and old-style Protestants, to whom the state was still, as in the times of liberalism, the irreligious enemy of Christian society; it meant at the same time some acceptance of the prevalent political and social system. It is remarkable that this attempt to accommodate Christian democracy to the existing system, this 'reformism' for fear of revolutionary socialism, should take place at a time when the socialists themselves were tempering their revolutionary ideals and were rather more reluctant to put forward their 'socialist society' as a true alternative to the 'capitalist society' of their enemies.

In its first phase Belgian Christian democracy, if we may already call it by that name, was ultramontane, corporatist, and very much dependent on French ideas.[1] It sought a state and

---

[1] Above, pp. 248 ff., 363 ff.

a society the antithesis of liberal: a Catholic state and a society from which liberal individualism had been removed. This ultramontanism was very conservative indeed. The guilds, in which employers and employees should work together, were only conceivable in a society with no class conflicts, one in which not only the paternal guidance given by the employers but also their social position could be confident of acceptance. After the great eruption of social unrest in 1886, a group of ultramontane corporatists realized that their programme would have to be revised and they started examining Catholic social ideals abroad systematically. They were especially drawn towards those which had been developed in Austria and Germany.[1] Two elements engaged their attention most of all. Firstly, the discovery that even a conservative movement—and of course Christian democracy was a conservative movement—had to be supported by the masses.[2] Secondly, the awareness that even a corporatist reorganization of society in a conservative sense could only come about through state interference. In the late 1880s such ideas were summarized and particularized at Freiburg in Switzerland during the annual conferences of a select group of Catholic sociologists from several countries. One of the two Belgian representatives was the Louvain architect George Helleputte, who had already experimented a great deal with corporatist projects at home. In 1891 Leo XIII bestowed his papal blessing on the Freiburg system in his *Rerum Novarum*.

A month before this encyclical was published, the Belgian

---

[1] Monique Hensmans, 'Les origines de la démocratie chrétienne en Belgique', *Les Dossiers de l'action sociale catholique*, xxix (1952), 121–4. In 1890 an international Catholic congress was held at Liège where especially the Austrians and Germans made an enormous impression. I do not know whether the Belgian audience admired the virulent anti-Semitism of some of the theories they applauded. This point has not been systematically studied by Belgian historians. Some data in P. Gérin, *Catholiques liégeois et question sociale (1833–1914)* (Brussels, 1959), pp. 183–4: the Christian democratic paper *Le Pays de Liége* published in 1892 vehemently anti-Semitic articles and continued to do so after that year. According to Gérin anti-Semitism was a permanent feature of the Christian democratic programme at Liège (ibid, p. 278).

[2] The best mind among the Christian democrats, Léon de Lantsheere, wrote in his periodical *La Justice sociale* (10 Mar. 1895) that 'le parti catholique ne serait sérieusement et véritablement conservateur que lorsqu'il serait sincèrement et foncièrement démocratique'. Quoted by G. Hoyois, *Henry Carton de Wiart et le groupe de 'La justice sociale'* (Paris, Courtrai, 1931), p. 63.

social Catholics had started the Ligue démocratique belge (Belgische Volksbond) on Helleputte's initiative. Its programme appeared a couple of months after the encyclical and truly reflected the character of the movement. In comparison with the old ultramontane school as well as with liberal Catholicism it was radical because the necessity of social organization and the possibility of state interference were admitted and no special privileges for the guilds were stipulated. Much, however, remained as uncertain as in the encyclical itself. It was not established in what circumstances the state must intervene and how far that intervention might go. Nor was it clear whether the acceptance of Christian trade unions of which the employers were not members was meant to be more than a tentative concession to a passing reality, which would have to be reformed in due course—that is, by the restoration of the guilds in which employers and workers co-operated. On the crucial problems of social insurance—should the state make it obligatory for the employees?—no opinion was expressed. Yet the Ligue with all its limitations and hesitations was an important new development because it made a vigorous attempt not only to knit together the scattered Catholic unions, but also to impress upon them some common social ideas. The Ligue met with an immediate response. It was joined by a large number of associations, so that already by the summer of 1891 it could claim to have a membership of more than 60,000. This number rose over the years until by 1908 there were more than 200,000. More remarkable than the numbers, however, was the heterogeneity of the component parts of the Ligue; in fact often the main problem was to convince all these so-called members of the significance of any action in which the Ligue might be engaged and to persuade them to take part in it.

At Ghent, where much of the work was concentrated, the engineer and neo-Gothic architect Arthur Verhaegen (1847–1917) was active in many fields. In 1891 he established a newspaper, *Het Volk*, written in Dutch—a language he felt himself obliged to learn—of which after a difficult start 16,000 copies were published in 1910.[1] At Liège it was the priest Antoine Pottier (1849–1923) who radically broke with ultramontanism and liberal Catholicism and defended the consequences of the

[1] Rezsohazy, *Origines*, pp. 126 ff.

new doctrine with an ardent and at times rude impatience; he demanded fixed minimum wages and obligatory social insurance and, in later life, when he taught sociology at Rome more or less in exile (from 1902), he developed extreme ideas about the participation of the workers in running their own factories.[1] He and the newspaper Le Bien du peuple, founded in 1892, were joined by the historian Godefroid Kurth in 1893. Kurth, who came from Luxemburg and whose French, according to a good though over-sensitive witness, was coloured by local patois in form and pronunciation, brought into Christian democracy an intentionally plebeian, rustic, and German element, an enormous passion, and an immoderate, if unctuous, militancy.[2] The 'Liège school' soon became the most radical Christian democratic party in French-speaking Europe.

At Louvain Helleputte continued his experiments. At Brussels attempts were made in the 1890s to reconcile Christian democracy with contemporary culture. Besides the gifted writer Henry Carton de Wiart it was there that Léon de Lantsheere (1862–1912) in particular tried to incorporate the movement in the grand synthesis after which so many of his generation, in such different ways, aspired. He was one of Mercier's first pupils; as well as law and philosophy he also studied mathematics, design, and music.[3] The Brussels group turned away from neo-Gothic archaism, which Verhaegen and Helleputte espoused not only in their architectural style but in their social ideas, and was much more attracted by such trends as Symbolism and art social. The man of action in this community of young intellectuals was Jules Renkin (1862–1934), an agitator without literary pretensions, a radical but

---

[1] G. Legrand, Le Rôle de Mgr Pottier dans le mouvement social contemporain (Gembloux, 1924), p. 19. See Gérin, op. cit., passim. Gérin (pp. 471 ff.) supposes that King Leopold II, who did not at all like Christian democrats of Pottier's type, strongly insisted on his departure for Rome.

[2] M. Wilmotte, La Culture française en Belgique (Paris, 1912), pp. 140 ff.; idem, Mes Mémoires, pp. 24 ff. From 1890 onwards Wilmotte was Kurth's colleague at Liège after having been his favourite pupil. Wilmotte is considered to be the founder of Romanist philology in Belgium and was a warm friend of the Symbolists. His publications are distinguished by their light elegance and fine scepticism but at the same time by a near-total lack of knowledge of and understanding for all non-French culture. This has often led him to write surprising nonsense.

[3] Rezsohazy, Origines, p. 138; Hoyois, op. cit., p. 63.

like so many Belgian politicians also a professional barrister, and consequently inclined to curb the free expression of his principles and indignation by a certain realism. The Brussels group rejected many of the ideas that prevailed in Ghent and Louvain. They did not believe in the revival of the guilds and preferred Catholic workers' unions; they rejected the traditional antimilitarism that was still quite natural to a man like Helleputte and defended conscription; they saw before the others that social insurance had to be made obligatory if it was to be effective; they advocated proportional representation and they also originated a nationalism and imperialism that did not exist elsewhere in this form. But however modern they might be and however much success they might have, their journals *L'Avenir social* (1891–4) and *La Justice sociale* (1895–1904) were aimed at a highbrow audience and they had nothing like the close contact with the masses achieved by the groups in Liège or Ghent.

The Catholic politicians of the old style who supported Charles Woeste turned on the Christian democrats with extreme passion: 'Fuyez-les comme la peste' was the watchword that the 60-year-old leader gave,[1] though he claimed that *Rerum Novarum* was the programme on which his whole policy was based. This sharp-witted, frosty, ascetic man—his conservatism was unselfish: he had no interests in large landownership, industry, or banking—saw in Christian democracy a dynamism which he thought hateful and dangerous, a materialism he despised, and a Caesarism he was afraid of. In retrospect he does not appear to have been altogether wrong. In the twentieth century some Christian democratic assumptions degenerated too easily into Fascist caricatures. The way, however, in which he chose to fight was so bitter and his attitude so negative that he strengthened grudges and heightened tensions unnecessarily. His conflict with the priest Adolf Daens became particularly notorious. Adolf Daens (1839–1907) and his brother Pieter (1842–1918), who was a printer and journalist, founded the Christian People's party at Alost in 1893, which soon aroused a considerable response in other parts of the Flemish provinces too. In some respects it was related to the Meeting party which played an important part

[1] H. Carton de Wiart, *Beernaert et son temps* (Brussels, 1945), p. 19.

especially among Flemish Catholics in the third quarter of the century.[1] Both of them drew on the reservoir of aspirations and resentments that existed in Flanders. Though the Daensists had a much clearer programme than the men of the Meeting party—based upon more recent developments in Catholic thinking about society—they still relied upon the same kind of complicated and unripe discontent as their predecessors and that was why their policy quickly disintegrated. The combination of social idealism with the Flemish language problem and efforts to preserve Catholicism, however logical it might be in theory, again appeared to be sterile politically. On the one hand, the bourgeoisie was still strong enough to resist such adventures successfully; on the other hand, internal contradictions within the party turned out to be irreconcilable.

Daens's programme did not differ essentially from that of the Brussels Christian democrats, though the latter placed less emphasis on the linguistic demands of the Flemish, which they nevertheless supported. Yet Daens's own position was quite exceptional. Whereas a radical like Renkin might be inclined to detach Christian democracy from the broad Catholic party, he remained in it on condition that some autonomy was guaranteed to his group. This was possible after the introduction of proportional representation in 1899, when it was no longer essential to put forward at elections only those candidates who could be sure of a majority, which the Christian democrats never were. Still a young group held to be extremist, they had for the time being relatively few adherents among the electors entitled to more than one vote. The Christian democrats increased their representation in the Chamber from about eight members in 1894 to at least fifteen members in 1902. In 1907 Helleputte, Renkin, and Lantsheere, among others, took office; in 1908 Renkin, as a great advocate of the Belgian annexation of the Congo, became the first Belgian Minister of the Colonies; in 1911 Carton de Wiart also became a member of the Cabinet. In these triumphs and their preparation Daens took no part. True, his People's party became large enough for him and his brother to obtain seats in the Chamber of Representatives, but they had no influence there worth speaking of. The leaders of his party were socially much inferior to those

[1] Above, pp. 245 ff.

of the Catholic party and its Christian democrat wing and even to those of the socialist party. They were intellectually less well equipped and tactically very clumsy. Daens became a tribune of the people, a man whose popularity expanded into hagiolatry, a charismatic leader in a time which did not ask for one. His breach with the Catholic party and his estrangement from the Church weakened his position fatally. He was only two years younger than Woeste and in fact lost not only to this great adversary but to that generation which was about thirty years of age at the publication of *Rerum Novarum* in 1891. His tragedy was more than a personal one. With his party a popular movement perished which, if it had been given more scope by the Church and the Catholic party, might have played a useful part in the social and cultural-linguistic emancipation that was proceeding so tardily in Flanders. The whole affair left deep resentment against the Catholic party, its French-speaking leaders, and the episcopacy which, however Christian democratic and pro-Flemish it might claim to be, was always on its guard against dispersion of effort and uncompromisingly maintained the principle of a unitary party. But the main tragedy of course was that all those miserable petty-bourgeois people and totally unrevolutionary workers, who touched Daens's cassock as if he were a miracle-worker and placed flowers and clothes along the road where he went,[1] could not in the end be helped by him in any way.

Daensism went under. The strength and the flexibility of the Catholic party were large enough to suppress such separatism and Daens's tragedy consolidated its position. With consternation, indignation, and grudgingly admiring surprise its liberal and socialist adversaries analysed the methods by which it succeeded in keeping and strengthening its hold on society. In 1911 Barnich, an adept of Solvay's, published his *Le Régime clérical en Belgique*, introduced by the old progressive Paul Janson and the much younger liberal celebrity Paul Hymans.[2]

[1] K. van Isacker, *Het Daensisme. De teleurgang van een onafhankelijke Christelijke arbeidersbeweging in Vlaanderen, 1893-1914* (Antwerp, 1959), p. 101. This is an excellent book, not rendered out of date, in my view, by L. Wils's reflections in *De oorsprong van de Kristen-Demokratie. Het aandeel van de Vlaams-demokratische stroming* (Antwerp, 1963). Interesting material in L. Wils, *Her daensisme* (Louvain, 1969).

[2] G. Barnich, *Le Régime clérical en Belgique. L'organisation du parti catholique. La législation sociale et les œuvres* (Brussels, 1911).

In some six hundred pages the author sketched with bold outlines and a great many figures the infinitely complicated landscape he observed. The map of Belgium was black with Catholic strongholds especially in Flanders. Schools;[1] monasteries;[2] guilds; insurance companies; political clubs; trade unions; confessional, parochial, and philanthropic organizations; clubs for women, girls, soldiers, and schoolchildren; banks, credit banks; museums; farmers' unions—all in some way interconnected and hierarchically dependent on the bishops or on the state, and all of them led by priests, who as often as not had no time for their pastorate on top of all their organizing duties—this formed the impenetrable, unimaginably ingenious complex of Catholic power. The state subsidized the whole Catholic insurance system for workers and the lower middle classes; it helped the Catholic unions to pay sickness or unemployment benefits or old-age pensions and to found mortgage banks for the small farmers. Barnich tried to prove that the *liberté subsidiée* was a system which strictly speaking only the Catholics could use because they had at their disposal the organization necessary for it, or the capital to set up such an organization where it was lacking, and in particular the organizers who could be freed for these tasks—the priests and vicars, surely not less than 6,000 men, whose salary was paid by the state. Of course the Catholics had their answer ready. They for their part recited the petty-minded anticlerical actions of the Left in those municipalities where liberals and socialists held a majority. They worked out just how many liberals had infiltrated government departments, courts of justice, and other state institutions at the time of their supremacy.[3] But such arguments were hardly decisive; what counted in the end was the fact that from 1884 to 1914 the Catholic party successfully

---

[1] More than four-fifths of the approximately one million children between six and fourteen years followed around 1910 some form of confessional education either in private schools or in 'communal' schools in Catholic regions: Barnich, op. cit., p. 167.

[2] At the end of the eighteenth century Belgium had about 10,000 monks and nuns, in 1829 about 4,800, *c.* 1850 about 12,000, in 1866 18,200, *c.* 1900 38,000. Above, pp. 199 and 243 and Barnich, pp. 151 and 366. The growth in the early twentieth century can partly be explained by mass immigration of regular clergy from France.

[3] Cf., e.g., H. Carton de Wiart, *Le Parti libéral d'aujourd'hui. Ses contradictions. Son impuissance* (Brussels, 1902).

consolidated its position—and that was not only the position of a party but of a Church and of a view of society. As in the 1830s and 1840s the liberals and anticlericals now saw reform measures praised for their progressiveness—the revision of the constitution in 1893 like the revolt of 1830—serve only to advance the Catholic cause.

Dutch Catholicism never knew such triumphs. Neither culturally nor politically could it achieve in this period successes comparable with the Belgian ones. The Catholic share of the Dutch population continued to fall slowly.[1] One reason was that the growth of the population in North-Brabant and Limburg, provinces which were almost entirely Roman Catholic, was less than in the Protestant districts of the country with a lower death rate resulting from improved economic conditions. A second explanation is thought to be the migration of Catholics into the large towns of Holland where many of them lost contact with the Church, became Protestant by mixed marriages, or in exceptional cases came to join the group of people, small as yet, that insisted on being entered as 'irreligious' in the census (only 1·47 per cent in 1889, nearly 5 per cent in 1909). Politically the Catholics were far from strong. Only in 1897 did Schaepman at last succeed in drawing up a programme that could serve as a basis for a loosely organized political party.[2] But he himself was not widely respected in the party slowly taking shape. The moderate Christian democratic character of his ideas and his policies—he was for cautious social legislation, extension of the franchise, and personal conscription—frightened many among the highly conservative and patrician Catholic leaders, especially in the province of Holland. When in 1900 Schaepman as a member of the Second Chamber voted for the liberal bill by which compulsory education was introduced, conservative indignation ran so high that Catholic unity seemed broken. Yet it was maintained. The foundation in 1904 of the General League of Roman Catholic Electoral Associations confirmed the existence of a real and coherent Catholic party. From 1901 to

[1] It was 38·15 per cent in 1849; 35·38 per cent in 1889; 35·02 per cent in 1909. Not until 1920 did the Catholic section of the population begin to grow in proportion to the rest of the population: De Kok, *Nederland op de breuklijn Rome-Reformatie*, p. 292.

[2] Above, p. 353.

1905 the Catholics co-operated in Abraham Kuyper's Cabinet without playing an important part in it. Throughout the period the Catholic party could do little else but support Protestant Christian democracy, however reluctantly. They did not, in fact, contribute any ideas of their own to that policy.

Yet in social life itself some Catholic leaders not only tried to build up an original organization but to inspire it with fairly original ideas. The priest Alfons Ariëns (1860–1928) spent the greater part of his life on social work among the Catholic working classes in one of the oldest industrial centres in the Netherlands, the textile towns of Twente. In 1889 he founded a Roman Catholic Workers' Union at Enschede—a courageous act. Even in Belgium, where it was still fashionable to think of guilds as an ultimate solution to the social problem, the decision had not yet been taken to found unions exclusively intended for workers which the employers could not join.[1] In 1891 Ariëns also initiated true Catholic trade unions, thereby starting a system that in the Netherlands assumed curious ideological overtones. At the same time, under German influence, he allowed experiments with trade unions in which Protestant and Catholic syndicates joined. Dutch Catholicism, in fact, tended to look towards Germany even more than to Belgium.[2] Many Catholic families had come originally from Westphalia and Hanover; in Twente and Limburg, where the industrial centres of the Catholic population were, their dialect and the intensive frontier traffic—a great many Limburg people actually worked in Germany—led to many personal contacts with the neighbouring country. It is understandable, therefore, that the idea of a common Protestant–Catholic organization in defence of the material interests of the Christian, anti-socialist workers should find favour in these districts. In other parts of the country, however, such views met with unswerving opposition and the strictly denominational dividing lines were

---

[1] Schaepman and Ariëns maintained manifold connections with Belgian Christian democrats. Ariëns even tried to bring the Catholic workers from Enschede into contact with those of Ghent—a modest attempt to help develop the Catholic International which some people wanted to establish as a bulwark against the Socialist International. For his weekly founded in 1894 Ariëns liked borrowing articles from Pottier's *Le Bien du peuple* and *Het Volk* from Ghent: G. Brom, *Alfons Ariëns* (2 vols., Amsterdam, 1941), i. 306.

[2] Ibid., pp. 342 ff.

adhered to even at the trade union level. In Germany, too, the fight between interdenominational and denominational trade-unionism blazed up at the beginning of the twentieth century. In the Netherlands there was little else but the repetition and continuation of such debates.

Another centre of Catholic action against the propaganda of socialism was Limburg, where a new industrial proletariat was created in the space of a couple of years by the expansion of the mining industry. Here it was the priest H. A. Poels (1868–1948), hailing from this province, who led and justified the movement. Compared with the nervous, tense Ariëns with his tormenting introspection and his hankering after penitence—though these were a source of his strength as well as his weakness—Poels was a robust fighter who sought rather than evaded conflict. Though he turned out more learned work and had a reputation as an expert in Old Testament studies—after his doctoral thesis Ariëns wrote only rarely on scholarly matters—Poels nevertheless gave the impression of being less intellectual and of belonging to the type of the merry, corpulent priest from the South as opposed to the more ascetic, somewhat pietistic type characteristic of the northern part of the Netherlands from which Aërins came. After a tumultuous career as a scholar which ended in disaster because his biblical criticism met with too much resistance at Rome, in 1910 Poels was appointed priest in a small Limburg village. There he found a Catholic organization already in existence, but much still needed to be done. He was quick to make known his convictions. He wanted two things. Firstly, he wanted anti-socialist national, if need be, interdenominational trade unions, which would fight for the workers' material interests without intervention from the clergy. Secondly, he wanted and got a 'class organization', an organization of the Catholic population in local or diocesan clubs divided according to the different social classes. These were to be under the leadership of priests and to be subordinate to the episcopacy. The clubs for the workers would of course be the most substantial and the most important. In such clubs Poels saw the opportunity for that thorough reformation of the human soul, for that change of consciousness, for that reconversion by which alone the world could be saved. Poels and his men might almost be said to occupy in Catholicism the place which the left-wing Marxists occupied in socialism. Of course, they wanted first of all to alleviate the distress in which the workers found themselves; their inspiration, however, was the firm conviction that through propaganda and instruction in a strong framework of organization it was possible to bring about the much more essential work of spiritual reform. Such ideas are related to the extremism of Gorter and Pannekoek which represented the Dutch contribution to international Marxism. Before 1914 Poels's ideas met with no great success. After the war, however, his conception was exported to Belgium and Germany as the Dutch contribution to Catholic social doctrine. Again the ideal appeared difficult to realize.[1]

In addition to Twente and Limburg there was also a Christ-ian democratic school in the province of Holland that cheer-fully plunged into the debate. Its originators, resident at Leiden, were the sociologist J. D. J. Aengenent (1873–1935), who became bishop of Haarlem in 1928, and the lawyer P. J. M. Aalberse (1871–1948), who entered the Second Chamber in 1903. They were amiable but less striking characters than Ariëns and Poels. In their view Catholic trade unions could be justified if they were led by priests. This gave less scope to trade-unionism than Poels had intended and, moreover, de-prived Poels's conception of 'class organization' of its point.[2] The debate between what came to be called the Leiden and the Limburg schools was in itself neither dramatic nor interest-ing. It continued for years but lost much of its meaning as it became increasingly obvious that twentieth-century society could not be reorganized along such lines. From a cultural-historical point of view it is fascinating, however. It was, in-deed, an international phenomenon. Just as in the Netherlands the Leiden school was against the Limburg school, so in the French-speaking countries Angers was against Liège and in Germany Berlin against Cologne. Of course, all these schools

---

[1] J. Colsen, *Poels* (Roermond, 1955) gives a very detailed description of Poels's ideas and activities. On his influence in Belgium, see ibid., pp. 449 ff., 643. In 1927 Poels's *standen* organization became one of the materials used for the *Code social. Esquisse d'une synthèse sociale catholique*, begun under Mercier's supervision and published by the Union internationale d'études sociales at Mechlin (ibid., pp. 470–1).

[2] J. P. Gribling, *P. J. M. Aalberse, 1871–1948* (Utrecht, 1961), pp. 139–83.

did not defend the same doctrines. Between Leiden and Berlin, between Liège and Cologne there were considerable differences. But apparently Christian democrats were split in very much the same way as the socialists. Poels and his men belonged to the puritan, extreme wing of Christian democracy, and Aalberse and Aengenent were reformists.

Catholic reaction manifested itself elsewhere in the Netherlands. The so-called integralists, a curious phenomenon, launched a grim campaign against all that they considered modern. In the newspaper of which he became editor-in-chief in 1898 (*De Maasbode*) its Dutch spokesman, the priest M. A. Thompson (1861–1938), turned with the greatest possible vehemence against all Dutch leaders who had been praised elsewhere for their contribution to what was called Catholic emancipation. Pope Pius X, who succeeded the scholarly Leo XIII in 1903, furthered the fight against 'modernism' and in many respects again took as a starting-point Pius IX's *Syllabus Errorum*. But 'modernism' came to mean so many things that it could hardly be defined any longer. However, whatever it was, there was not much 'modernism' about either in the Netherlands or in Belgium. In Belgium the neo-Thomism of the Louvain school was still so vigorous and fresh that there was no room for 'modernistic' novelties. In the Netherlands the clergy, educated in the strict discipline of the seminaries and keenly aware that they represented a minority still on the defensive, shrank from adventures of that kind.[1] However, whereas in Belgium, where hardly any modernists were to be found, it followed that hardly any integralists attempted to persecute them, among the equally orthodox Dutch Catholics these keen hunters after modernistic game restlessly pursued their prey. Thompson was their leader. In spite of the tremendous noise he made and the fear he inspired in some of his victims, he remained a lonely man, out of place in the spiritual and political climate still dominated by the desire for synthesis. In any case, what purpose could such an agitation, related to the Action française, serve in the Netherlands where it could obviously not be grounded in Dutch-Catholic nationalism or Dutch megalomania? In 1912 the number of subscribers to *De Maasbode* had dropped to a point where the

[1] Rogier, *Katholieke herleving*, pp. 434 ff.

management of the paper decided to give up Thompson. In 1914 Pius X died. His successor Benedict XV lost no time in liquidating the power bloc the integralists had built up at Rome. Thompson quickly sank into oblivion.[1] But during the interwar years the integralist rancour appeared to be still smouldering in the Netherlands too: it was not unnatural for Thompson's followers to affiliate themselves with Fascism.[2]

In the Netherlands the Protestant version of Christian democracy was far more interesting than the Catholic but its efforts to realize its conceptions politically miscarried. Its history became a tragedy. Hardly any of the high-minded intentions of the Protestant leaders or the systems carefully and imaginatively developed by them were put into effect. This may be explained in at least three ways. As soon as the moment came for the Anti-revolutionaries to mould their social doctrine into concrete form, it was found to contain too many flaws and contradictions to be directly applicable. Even more serious was the fact that the power of the Anti-revolutionaries, even when in office, remained very limited indeed. They owed their important place in political life to their coalition with the Catholics. The Catholics supported them loyally but were understandably cautious when faced by the rather adventurous experiments on which the best Anti-revolutionaries were bent. Though they did not always oppose them, they were by no means enthusiastically in favour of them. In such situations it became all too clear that the Anti-revolutionaries represented in the end only a small part of the Dutch population, both as a political party and as a confessional community. In many respects the party formed the political framework in which the orthodox Calvinists were organized. But these were a small minority: 8·21 per cent of the Dutch population in 1889, 9·66 per cent in 1909. In itself it was a remarkable achievement to get so much influence in a more or less democratic state with such a small number of faithful followers—an achievement which can only be explained by the prestige of the

[1] This whole matter has been described in detail by Rogier, *Katholieke herleving*, pp. 425–88.
[2] L. M. H. Joosten, *Katholieken en fascisme in Nederland, 1920–1940* (Hilversum, 1964), *passim*.

Anti-revolutionary leaders and that of Protestantism in general. But for a truly creative policy this basis was too narrow.

Moreover, serious conflicts arose in the Anti-revolutionary party itself. When the Second Chamber had to decide on a far-reaching liberal proposal to extend the franchise, the Anti-revolutionary faction was divided. Kuyper was for it, though it did not conform to all his principles. De Savornin Lohman was against.[1] In the field of religion and scholarship too these forceful personalities clashed. In the end Lohman decided to break away from the firmly organized party and form a group which boasted the curious name of Free Anti-revolutionaries. It was not until 1898 that they actually became an independent party. In 1903 they began to co-operate with another small Protestant group that was also reluctant to follow Kuyper. After they had been joined by a third group in 1908 the Christian Historical Union was formed, which obtained twelve seats at the election of 1909. It has always remained smaller than the Anti-revolutionary party (ARP) but it became a lasting factor in Dutch political life all the same. Essential though the difference between both Protestant parties apparently was, it cannot easily be defined. There was a difference in sense of timing: the Christian Historicals were not in principle against the democracy championed by Kuyper but they thought he was proceeding too rapidly. There was also a difference in religious temper: the Christian Historicals were no less strict in their faith, but their religious experience was more pietistic and they attached less value to form. The essential point was that for the Christian Historicals politics meant something different: as a Christian democrat Kuyper aspired towards a total policy, one permeated with Calvinistic principles and active in all fields of public life, and therefore he needed a centrally led, firmly constructed party with a binding and fully elaborated programme. Lohman's policy was far more cautious and in point of fact defensive. In his opinion the only object of Christian party organization was to protect the Christian population. The Christian parties had to ensure that the Protestants could live quietly in social surroundings of their own making, could send their children to Protestant schools, and find protection for their workers in

---

[1] Above, p. 361.

Protestant trade unions. It was not their business to exercise power in the interest of comprehensive social and political reform. For him, therefore, party organization was of much less importance. Kuyper acted as the commander-in-chief of an army. Lohman did not need such discipline because he preferred to defend the interests of the Protestants in the Second Chamber as an individual. In consequence, the Christian Historical Union has had a curbing influence on Protestant policy and at critical moments has taken the edge of the ambitions of the Anti-revolutionaries.[1]

From 1901 to 1905 and from 1908 to 1913 the Protestant–Catholic coalition ruled the country, during the first period under Kuyper himself, during the second under Heemskerk. Kuyper achieved lasting results in only two fields. He introduced ethical policy into the Dutch East Indies[2] and he reformed education. In 1904 Kuyper's Higher Education Bill led to eloquent and erudite debates in the Second Chamber on whether the examinations at the Calvinistic Free University at Amsterdam founded by Kuyper in 1880 could or should grant the same rights as the diplomas of the State Universities and the municipal University of Amsterdam. In 1905 Kuyper got his way at last, though not before the recalcitrant First Chamber had been dissolved. This was a great success for him. The Free University, for the greater part financed by the contributions of the orthodox Protestant lower middle classes, was now in a better position to develop into a complete and fully recognized institution. But this stronghold of what may be called the antithesis, this symbol of the ambition to establish a Christian species of scholarship as a counterpart to heathen learning, was already out of date by the time Kuyper got his way. It owed its creation to a generation that was about to be replaced by the men who aspired after synthesis. The neo-Thomist conception of science was no longer based on the assumption that there was a necessary antithesis between Christian and pagan research. Though Kuyper's influence naturally continued to be felt for a long time in Calvinistic

---

[1] On all this cf. L. C. Suttorp, *Jhr Mr Alexander Frederik de Savornin Lohman* (The Hague, 1948), pp. 293–4 and *passim*. An excellent exposition also in J. Schokking, *Het voorname punt van verschil tusschen Antirevolutionairen en Christelijk-Historischen* (The Hague, 1938).

[2] Above, p. 405.

circles, there too in the next few decades attitudes were gradually changing. For denominational primary education Kuyper did little that was essential during his stay in office. He did manage to raise the state subsidies to the free schools but he did not seek complete equalization of free and state education, though his most fervent opponents, the socialists, were insisting on this at the time. Kuyper was not willing to accept what he too regarded as the logical consequence of fully grant-aided free schools: state supervision to guarantee the quality of their teaching.

It was clear, however, that each twentieth-century Cabinet would be judged on its social and not on its educational legislation. Kuyper knew this as well as the opposition. He had proclaimed time and again that he wanted to introduce a coherent system of social legislation, but there were two things that prevented him. First there was the legacy from the preceding Cabinet formed by N. G. Pierson in 1897 which held office until 1901. It was of a left-wing liberal persuasion, and extremely energetic. It succeeded in making it impossible at last for a conscript to hire a substitute (1898); introduced compulsory education (1900); reorganized the army (1901); drafted a public health service closely supervised by medical state inspectors (1901); and put the full responsibility for house-building on to the municipalities (1901). Rarely was radical liberalism more 'étatistic' than in this period and never was it more productive. This appeared most clearly during the discussion of the Workers' Compensation Bill, which was finally passed after a long debate in 1901. Accident insurance was made obligatory for a large group of workers and its administration was entrusted to a national insurance bank to be founded for the purpose. Not only was the principle of compulsory state insurance accepted, therefore, but also the principle that the workers could now rely on a public institution for the management of their affairs and to that extent be independent of their employers. Kuyper, who became the undisputed leader of the right-wing opposition during these years, rejected the system as un-Dutch, socialistic, and bureaucratic. In close consultation with the employers[1] he drafted an alternative that meant less centralization and more scope for private

[1] De Vries, *Schets eener parlementaire geschiedenis* ii. 183, 185.

enterprise, and was essentially an attempt to confine the responsibilities of the state so that it should be no more than a guide to those who must in the long run learn to look after themselves. This alternative proposal was defeated, so that when Kuyper came to office in 1901 he found a well-organized and popular system of social legislation already in operation that could not easily be replaced.

Kuyper's second problem was an outbreak of social unrest more serious than any that had occurred in the Netherlands before. Early in January 1903 the Amsterdam dockers came out on strike, incensed by the haughty way in which the employers thought they could ignore the trade unions, which had already existed for several years. At the end of January the railwaymen, who were naturally in close contact with the dockers at the Amsterdam goods station, joined them. There was a danger that other towns would follow suit, but the directors of the dock companies as well as of the two railway companies capitulated after only a few days and conceded almost all the demands. This made an enormous impression, for it had never happened in the Netherlands before that the public utility services, which, without being government undertakings, were subject to strict regulations, had been suspended on such a large scale. The socialists, and in particular the anarchists and their apostle, Domela Nieuwenhuis, rejoiced, the former because it demonstrated the power of the workers, the latter because it also demonstrated the value of a spontaneous strike, an unprepared manifestation of revolutionary consciousness, repressed, they suggested, rather than stimulated by the socialist leaders. The 'bourgeois' parties were hardly less extreme in their opinions; they considered the strike a crime, an attack on order and public interest, a form of intolerable violence. These reactions ·are understandable enough. On both sides the surprise was such that the tendency to exaggerate the affair needs no explanation. The government, however, was placed in a very awkward position. In January 1903 they had kept aloof as far as possible, partly because they thought this correct but largely because there was no obvious way in which they could act. Afterwards they were quick to point out that it was necessary to remedy the flaws in the system which the strike had made evident. Early in February they called up part of the militia. At the end of February they introduced bills to make strikes in public utility enterprises illegal. The proposals were neither unreasonable nor exceptional: all modern states were being faced with the same problem. Yet for Kuyper, who had always claimed to combine democratic progressiveness with respect for authority and religion, it was disastrous to be forced by circumstances and by his own followers and friends to restrict the right to strike—his first measure in the field of social law. Of course the socialists seized the opportunity with both hands to represent him as the leader of black reaction. Early in April when the bills were discussed in the Second Chamber they announced first a transport strike and shortly afterwards a general strike. On 10 April the failure of these strikes was so apparent that the socialist leaders in total disarray had to admit that their tactics had completely miscarried. On 11 April the bills were passed. The Cabinet triumphed but as a maintainer of order, not as a reformer of society.[1]

Yet Kuyper persisted in trying to realize part of his programme. At his office a great many social bills were prepared but none came under discussion in the Second Chamber.[2] It was now evident that Kuyper was not the man to lead a ministerial department; he had no administrative experience and too little juridical knowledge. With problems of a philosophical or theological nature he felt at home like a 'smuggler in the mountains',[3] technicalities he tended to dismiss in a perfunctory fashion. In his own circle too his prestige dropped to such an extent that to his great annoyance he was supplanted by Heemskerk as leader of the Coalition Cabinet which in 1908, after a three-year liberal interlude, took up the reins of government.

Th. Heemskerk (1852-1932), son of the conservative statesman responsible for the revision of the constitution of 1887, underwent a religious conversion on completing his studies and then joined the Anti-revolutionary party. He led the government with insight and good humour but was not the most

---

[1] On this cf. the very detailed work by Rüter, *De spoorwegstakingen van 1903*.

[2] E. E. B. F. Wittert van Hoogland, *De parlementaire geschiedenis der sociale verzekering, 1890-1940* (2 vols., Haarlem, 1940), i. 124 ff.

[3] Van Deventer in *De Gids*, quoted by Vermeulen, *Schets eener parlementaire geschiedenis* iii. 91.

important man in it. This was the vicar A. S. Talma (1864–1916). Talma had ideas of Christian social order that he tried to realize by some ambitious legislation. His views on trade-unionism resembled those which the priests Ariëns and Poels were developing at the same time. There should be Protestant trade unions concerned solely with the workers' economic interests, and in addition a general association closely related to the Church, the task of which would be wider—instruction, moral reform, extensive social care. Like Poels he wanted on the one hand to help the workers to organize themselves independently for the improvement of their economic position; on the other hand, he tried to bring them together for the benefit of their spiritual welfare in a very firm religious association that could regulate their moral life and state of mind far more strictly than the Church itself.[1] Such ideas met with much resistance in Catholic and Protestant circles. To many it still seemed unacceptable that Christian workers should be advised to organize themselves and to fight for material gain on their own initiative. The belief that God's ordering compelled the lower classes to obedience was generally current at the time, not only among the Christian middle classes but also among the Christian workers themselves.

The bills which Talma framed and defended with such reckless energy that he completely exhausted his great physical strength, aroused a great deal of opposition within his own circle as well as outside. Talma tried to make a start with the realization of a system that, had it worked, could have been called corporatist. He attempted to do so on several levels but his most important bill was that creating Boards of Labour (1910). The state should erect Boards of Labour, tied to town and country, consisting of employers and employees, entrusted with the enforcement of social legislation, for instance in relation to social insurance, and equipped with some corporate, legislative competence of their own. The chief importance of the bill was that state interference was no longer confined to the protection of the weaker and more vulnerable sections of the population but could now order and reform social relations in a much wider sense. It was entirely in accordance with the Christian democratic system that the state should not exercise

[1] J. M. Vellinga, *Talma's sociale arbeid* (Hoorn, 1941), pp. 29 ff.

a lasting and preponderant function but create the framework of rights, duties, and finances within which a corporatist order could gradually be brought about. Talma had so little support in the Second Chamber, however, that he was forced to temper his policies until little remained of the self-governing bodies in which all parties interested in conditions of employment were to be represented. The Boards of Labour became no more than auxiliary organs concerned with social insurance.[1] In this mutilated form the bill was finally passed in 1913. Talma was no more successful with his other social bills. True, his disability insurance bill and his sickness insurance bill were passed, but only years later were the initial steps taken to put them into operation.[2]

Yet at the outbreak of the First World War social legislation in the Netherlands was no longer notably inferior to that in other Western European countries. It could also stand comparison with Belgium. In Belgium such legislation had got under way at about the same time as in the Netherlands. As a reaction to the great strikes of 1886 all sorts of social measures were introduced during the next three years which showed at least that Parliament now recognized the need to act. After the foundation of a separate Ministry of Industry and Labour (1895) far-reaching bills were passed in rapid succession designed to improve the workers' negotiating position with their employers, in their factories, and in cases of accidents or illness. In 1899 a Frenchman, who made a close study of Belgian legislation for a juridical doctoral thesis, wrote that not a single country in the nineteenth century was developing such a complete and coherent social system as Belgium after 1886, a system that was neither individualistic nor socialistic, but what he called 'associationist'.[3] This was undoubtedly too generous. The Boards of Industry and Labour, for which he expressed deep admiration—they dated from 1887 but had been reformed several times—had too little authority to be really effective, though their foundation was interesting.

[1] T. de Ruiter, *Minister A. S. Talma. Een historisch-ethische studie over de corporatieve gedachte in de christelijk-sociale politiek van Nederland* (Franeker, 1946), pp. 110, 115.

[2] The Disability Insurance Act in 1919, the Sickness Insurance Act in 1930. Wittert van Hoogland, op. cit., i. 209.

[3] F. Payen, *Une Tentative récente d'organisation du travail. Les conseils de l'industrie et du travail en Belgique* (Paris, 1899), pp. 17, 192–3.

They had been created by royal decree, were bound to the place where they were established, and consisted of representatives of the employers and employees of the various industries. No doubt it was hoped that they would help to reconcile class antagonisms, but as they were not granted any legislative power, their usefulness was relatively slight.[1]

It is remarkable that in the Netherlands a moderate-liberal government in 1897 copied this first attempt at social organization in a bill which Kuyper thought much too cautious: the Christian democrat leader claimed for these Boards (called Chambers of Labour in the Netherlands) the right to make their own regulations. But he was refused, and consequently these institutions were not much of a success in the North either. Obviously, neither in the Netherlands nor in Belgium was the time ripe for a truly corporate organization of labour; when Talma tried again in 1910 he too failed. Although in 1903 Belgian legislation came near to a fundamental revision of the foundation and justification of social policy in general, this certainly did not mean the development of a corporative system. Two years after the Netherlands passed a Workers' Compensation Bill in 1901, obligatory on both employers and employees, the Belgian Parliament also decided on such a fundamentally important step.[2] True, the Belgian Workers' Compensation Act was far less 'étatistic' than the Dutch—there was no question of a national insurance bank—but for the state to compel employers to insure their workers meant an infringement of two essential elements of the capitalist system, namely the freedom of employers and employees when concluding labour contracts, and the employers' omnipotence within the framework of the stipulations of the contract agreed upon. It also meant an infringement of the system of the *liberté subsidiée*, which from then on gradually fell into disuse.

In the eyes of the socialists these laws, however welcome in some respects, naturally fell short of what was required. They were accepted for the time being as emergency measures or provisional palliatives. Though the Belgian socialists pursued

---

[1] The indeed clearly corporatist element in the project thus remained limited. It was developed somewhat further in 1895 by granting representatives of these councils seats in the borough councils.

[2] Rezsohazy, *Origines*, pp. 313–14.

in practice a reformist policy, they remained confident that capitalist society would eventually be replaced by a socialist one, and that the state, which they served by the mere fact of their membership of the Second Chamber, would finally disappear. Social democracy was faced with the insoluble emotional and intellectual dilemma of whether it would be possible in the long run—thus it might best be summarized—to be at the same time reformist or revisionist, and Marxist or revolutionary. This was, indeed, the paradoxical situation in which Belgian as well as Dutch social democracy found itself. With words and theories they defended the revolutionary ideal; by force, however, they tried time and again to seize the means by which the ideal could be realized in a peaceful way. The social democrats were reformists because they no longer entertained much hope of a spontaneous revolution, instantaneously renewing the whole of society, and so they adapted themselves to the leisurely pace of parliamentary reform. Revolutionary, nevertheless, they remained, not only in relation to the ultimate end but also in their attempts to obtain by political strikes and demonstrations what they still considered the elementary condition which had to be fulfilled before the ideal came within reach—that is, universal suffrage. When once, if need be by force, all citizens were enfranchised, parliamentary means could be used to reform society radically.

The socialist leaders in Belgium always pretended to have a short-range and a long-range policy. Later this proved to be an illusion. What men like Vandervelde and Destrée formulated as their ultimate aim was in fact unattainable by the chosen means; it has not been brought any nearer by the introduction of universal suffrage. For Émile Vandervelde (1866–1938), who was of a French-speaking bourgeois family and whose father was a friend of Paul Janson's,[1] socialism was not a weapon to free the workers as rapidly as possible from distress and oppression, as it was for working-class leaders like Bertrand and Anseele. Nor was it a system to explain all life and reality, as it was to such poetical natures as Gorter and Henriette Roland Holst. In a parliamentary debate Vandervelde's friend Destrée once let out the remark: 'Les systématiques sont des gens néfastes.'[2] Socialism was something natural for them.

[1] Vandervelde, *Souvenirs*, pp. 16 ff.   [2] Destrée, *Discours parlementaires*, p. 202.

Vandervelde's father and his friends were radical-liberal, irreligious, and Freemasons; it needed no conversion for the son to become a socialist. Consequently, the socialism Vandervelde defended was quiet and stable, without the crude aggressiveness of that of men like Anseele, 'le virtuose de la brutalité'[1] (who, on the other hand, were in a far greater measure 'reformist' in their theories, in so far as they theorized, than the intellectuals of the party), and without the somewhat fanatical emotion of some Dutch preachers of the socialist gospel. What gave Vandervelde and Destrée such a unique position in the Belgian movement was the mere fact that they, bourgeois intellectuals, became leaders of a party founded by workers and deeply influenced by the pragmatism of those who wanted to improve the lot of the proletariat as quickly as possible.

The political objective of Belgian socialism until 1914 was a struggle for the vote, that is to say for the abolition of the plural vote of 1893 and the electoral privileges of the higher classes. In 1899, 1902, and 1913 the opposition tried to force the pace: not only did they fail but after 1899 the effect of increasing violence and revolutionary threats actually diminished. In 1893 outside action had forced Parliament into revising the electoral law. In 1899 the opposition achieved another similar success. A curious attempt of the Catholic government, led by Jules Vandenpeereboom, to introduce certain changes into the electoral law which would have still further strengthened the parliamentary position of the Catholics led to passionate demonstrations by liberals and socialists inside as well as outside the Chamber. This may have been the most dangerous moment in the history of Belgium during this period, for the liberal party also gave the impression of being ready to accept the risk of a revolution.[2] The Catholics, however, themselves deeply divided, gave in very quickly. Vandenpeereboom resigned and his successor, Paul de Smet de Naeyer, introduced a form of proportional suffrage that satisfied the liberals for some time to come. The opposition was triumphant. In spite of its hopeless weakness in Parliament it had extorted a reform of great moment by pressure from outside. The socialists, however, concluded from this that they could obtain much more

[1] M. Wilmotte, *La Belgique morale et politique (1830–1900)* (Paris, 1902), p. 341.
[2] Van Kalken, *Commotions populaires*, p. 182.

far-reaching concessions even without liberal support. This turned out to be a serious overrating of their own strength. In 1902 and 1913 the state machinery was equal to the sort of outside actions which had been successful in 1893 and 1899. The reasons are obvious. In 1893 and 1899 the party then in power was itself divided. In 1902 and 1913 that was not the case. The Catholics were stronger than ever before. Moreover, the elections after 1893 showed no spectacular growth of socialist support, and it seemed justifiable to conclude that the danger of revolution was past, if it had ever existed.

In 1902 the disturbances themselves were in fact more serious than in 1893 and 1899. In March Janson and Vandervelde proposed the abolition of plural voting. In April socialist demonstrations were organized in Brussels and they soon got out of hand. In a desperate attempt to make themselves masters of the situation and to prevent bloodshed—some had been killed already—the socialist leaders decided to call a general strike. The strike movement, which had already got under way in the Borinage, quickly spread and impressed even its opponents by its dignity and its discipline. Yet lamentable incidents occurred, and there were further victims. On 18 April the Chamber rejected Janson's and Vandervelde's motion, refusing a debate on electoral reform. It was all over then. The strikers—on 18 April some 300,000 industrial workers—could not possibly keep up their agitation for long in the economically hard circumstances of that year of depression. The *gendarmerie* and the army took drastic and efficient action and the socialist leaders, most of whom had agreed to the adventure reluctantly under the influence of the foolhardy faith in revolution of romantic extremists, hurriedly called the strike off (20 April). It was a total defeat. The impossibility of an improvised, spontaneous revolution seemed to be demonstrated once and for all. In 1903 a similar adventure in the Netherlands, which had apparently learned nothing from the Belgian experiences of 1902, ended in an equally complete failure. In both countries this led to a victory of the 'reformists' within the socialist parties and socialists as well as non-socialists found that the romantic period had come to an end.

But correct though this may be up to a point, neither in the Netherlands nor in Belgium did the socialists resign themselves entirely to the fact that they could be little more than a normal democratic party. The revolutionary sentiment from which the parties originated, and the social isolation of the socialist leaders which lasted until 1914, were still palpable and at times decisive factors. In this context the form of co-operation which the socialists found with the radical-liberal party was interesting. This co-operation was intimate in both countries, but it was regarded by the socialists as a means of creating the conditions which would render possible the overthrow of the bourgeois society, of which the liberals, radical though they might be, were according to socialist principle also a part. This was more than a theory. Though usually the Belgian and Dutch socialists were, indeed, 'reformists', they remained revolutionaries at the same time. Just before the World War the Belgian Workers' party once more took the initiative in declaring a general political strike in order to obtain universal suffrage. But while still cherishing their hopes of revolutionary renewal, they united with the liberals to wage war against clericalism. It was a complicated situation: in socialist theory society was divided horizontally into proletariat and bourgeoisie; in socialist practice it was divided vertically into clericals and anticlericals.

Not surprisingly the Marxists found such impurities highly objectionable. The young Hendrik de Man (1885–1953) and Louis de Brouckère (1870–1951), from Antwerp and Wallonia respectively, published in 1911 two articles in Kautsky's authoritative Marxist weekly *Die Neue Zeit* in which they explained as well as condemned Belgian reformism and the coalition with the liberals.[1] The explanation was simple. Nowhere, they thought, was the proletariat physically and psychologically so weak as in Belgium, where capitalism had started its systematic exploitation of the workers as early as the Middle Ages and where in the nineteenth century industrialization had developed earlier and more quickly than elsewhere on the Continent. Without much resistance the workers, who had for the greater part remained Catholic, still allowed themselves to be exploited; in Belgium wages were lower and working

---

[1] Hendrik de Man, 'Die Eigenart der belgischen Arbeiterbewegung', *Ergän-zungshefte zur Neuen Zeit*, ix (10 Mar. 1911), 1–28; Louis de Brouckère, 'Die politische Krise in Belgien', ibid. 28–72.

hours longer than in any other industrial country in the world. In such a situation the Parti Ouvrier Belge (POB) knew of no other expedient than unmethodical revisionism. Everything of which the party was proud was ruthlessly criticized: the federal nature of the party, the trade unions, and most of all the powerful co-operatives. De Man much preferred the German model. The Belgian socialists did not even develop a revisionist theory one could discuss; they had only a revisionist practice. Moreover, this revisionism came from one centre only, from Flanders, from Ghent. In Wallonia the situation was in a sense more desperate for a sound theorist, for there reigned a sort of petty-bourgeois republican radicalism derived from backward France, which had a shackling influence on the industrially highly developed Belgian society with its more strongly marked class contrasts. But neither De Man nor De Brouckère could think of anything else to suggest by way of remedy other than razor-sharp reflection on theory and propaganda. This did not mean a great deal. Yet it aroused consternation among the Belgian leaders, whose party was criticized so passionately in a paper that had much influence with the international socialist intelligentsia.[1] Vandervelde retorted in *Die Neue Zeit*, not in a Belgian journal. For these debates of the Belgian intellectuals did not penetrate into Belgium: the socialist publishing house refused to have the articles translated and to circulate them.[2] Discussion of principles did not belong there. But that was not because, as De Man asserted, Belgian socialism was petty bourgeois and reformist, it was because the stresses in Belgian socialism were emotional and not doctrinal.

This was apparent very soon after the articles in *Die Neue Zeit* had been published. In Belgium revolutionary temper flared up more militantly than in Germany, as a result of the education issue which was still a serious problem. The unwise Primary Education Act of 1884[3] was replaced in 1895 by a system that guaranteed better education but at the same time made Catholic authority in the primary schools even stronger than it already was.[4] In the twentieth century the government

[1] H. de Man, *Après coup* (Brussels, Paris, 1941), p. 99.
[2] Mieke Claeys-Van Haegendoren, *25 jaar Belgisch socialisme* (Antwerp, 1967), p. 37.   [3] Above, p. 367.
[4] Mallinson, *Power and Politics in Belgian Education*, pp. 108–11.

went one step further. It was at last accepted that compulsory education, which the Catholic conservatives had always been against, could be avoided no longer: the Christian democrats were defending it and the numbers of Belgian illiterates remained inexcusably large compared to those in neighbouring countries; in 1900 it was still 19 per cent of the population.[1] In 1911 the government proposed its introduction—perhaps also under some pressure from King Albert, who was in sympathy with the social liberalism of the Institut Solvay.[2] However, the Cabinet added to it a very drastic extension of the state grant to the free Catholic schools. This raised the suspicion of anti-étatistic Catholics like Woeste; it also drove the liberals and socialists together and in the end the bill was thrown out.[3] The liberal–socialist agitation was sharp and violent. Once more demonstrations and meetings were organized; once more revolution was threatened. The liberals and socialists united in a 'cartel' on the basis of a common programme, and at the municipal elections of October 1911 they achieved encouraging successes. They anticipated victory in the general elections to be held in June 1912, and declared that they would propose the liberal Paul Hymans as leader of a liberal–socialist Cabinet. That was the reformist POB all over.

But the result of the poll was a bitter disappointment: it increased the Catholic majority. At once serious riots broke out in the old Walloon centres of socialism. The government reacted sharply: again several men were killed. At the end of June an extraordinary congress of the POB assembled at Brussels, at which the party leaders tried to soothe highly strung nerves and to prevent a repetition of the mistake of 1902. Against the will of a man like Destrée—a refined man of letters, who was suddenly set aglow with revolutionary fire—the executive committee managed to prevent a strike being called without any adequate preparation. But in the circumstances and given their own revolutionary emotions they were compelled to threaten a strike unless the single vote were introduced

[1] M. de Vroede, 'De weg naar de algemene leerplicht in België', *Bijdragen en mededelingen betreffende de geschiedenis der Nederlanden*, lxxxv (1970), 160–1.

[2] L. de Lichtervelde, *Avant l'orage (1911–1914)* (Brussels, 1938), pp. 19, 23.

[3] In 1914 at last a new, more careful, and less challenging proposal was accepted with the result that at any rate the principle of compulsory education was legalized before the World War. Cf. Mallinson, op. cit., pp. 114–17.

at very short notice. In October 1912 Paul Hymans drafted in the name of the left and right wings of the liberals—they were called 'les gauches libérales' to include all shades—a statement demanding compulsory education, the protection of the state schools, universal suffrage for men over 25, and workers' pensions, but explicitly rejecting a political strike.[1] The ways of the liberals and the socialists diverged again. In February 1913 the socialists decided that the general strike should begin on 13 April. The circumstances were excellent, wages higher than ever before. Although men like Huysmans, Vandervelde, and Bertrand questioned the sense of the undertaking, they could not control the revolutionary impulses of the party. The strike in itself was a success: 450,000 workmen stopped work.[2] But was it in fact anything more than a gesture, a concession to naive impatience? As early as June 1912, shortly after the Catholic victory over the left cartel, the leader of the Cabinet, Charles de Broqueville, had informed King Albert in a letter that he wished to reform the franchise. In February 1913 Broqueville gave this letter to Vandervelde to read.[3] On 24 April 1913 the Chamber made a propitiatory gesture, and at once the POB resolved to call off the strike. Never before had reformism and revolution co-operated in a more curious way. Vandervelde, in whom the Catholic minister placed such confidence that he showed him his correspondence with the King, was chairman of the Second International and leader of a party which sought to disrupt state and society by a general strike.

The Dutch socialist movement in many respects resembled the Belgian. The Sociaal-Democratische Arbeiders Partij was founded in August 1894.[4] It was hostile to the anarchist and anti-parliamentary element that had come to dominate Domela Nieuwenhuis's old movement. Naturally, the sensational successes of the Belgian socialists, who had extorted a form of universal suffrage in 1893, inspired the Dutch; the result of the Belgian poll of October 1894, when 28 socialists were returned,

---

[1] Hymans, *Mémoires*, i. 47.

[2] The events are analysed in detail in É. Vandervelde, L. de Brouckère, and L. Vandersmissen, *La Grève générale en Belgique (avril 1913)* (Paris, 1914). As in 1902 about half the industrial workers went on strike.

[3] Vandervelde, *Souvenirs*, p. 58; Luykx, *Politieke geschiedenis*, p. 252.

[4] Above, p. 347.

convinced them that their decision to establish a new party was correct. It seemed that also in a small country it was possible for the proletariat to make its voice heard in Parliament. For the time being, however, the SDAP remained a group of little importance compared to the POB. The membership was very small: it did not reach a thousand until 1896, and only in 1897 were two socialists elected members of the Second Chamber. Early in 1914 the SDAP numbered about 25,000 members, considerably less than the POB. By the 1930s, with the membership of the SDAP swiftly growing until it reached about 89,000 in 1938, membership of the POB was about 600,000. But this was because in Belgium a member of a socialist trade union was automatically made a member of the POB. In the Netherlands such an arrangement was totally unacceptable[1] and there the reformist federation of trade unions, which was founded in 1906—the NVV with a membership of 294,000 in 1938–stood aside from and politically to the right of the party. But though in consequence the SDAP was weaker, the rhythm of its development up to the First World War was comparable with that of the POB. The important events and the crises fell on broadly the same dates. The Belgian strike of 1902 was followed in the Netherlands by the railway strike of 1903. In 1909 in both countries the essence of Marxist theory was discussed in dramatic terms. In 1913 the POB and the SDAP expressed their revolutionary sentiments, the one by means of another strike and the other by refusing to take office.

Yet there were curious and rather paradoxical differences. In 1909 the SDAP expelled part of its Marxist wing from the party; the POB with its much smaller Marxist minority never did so. For all that the SDAP sometimes reacted in a less 'reformist' way than the POB. Whereas in 1912 the POB aspired to a liberal–socialist coalition government, in 1913 the SDAP turned such a possibility down. That was partly because it felt much weaker than its Belgian sister and thought the risk of losing its independence too great—the Belgian leaders and Vandervelde most of all dissuaded the SDAP from following the Belgian example.[2] It was also partly because such a compromise seemed irreconcilable with the revolutionary theory to

[1] Troelstra, *Gedenkschriften*, ii. 224–5. [2] Ibid. iii. 220.

which it remained true. On the other hand, the SDAP was more cautious when it came to political strike action. A lot of words were written about this and a lot of talk was spent on it. The socialist leaders in the Netherlands were keenly aware of the need for revolutionary mass demonstrations, outbursts of violence, manifestations of iron determination which gave them the sense of being elevated high above the petty workaday life of compromising, wrangling political drudges. When the SDAP decided to put new life into the campaign for universal suffrage which had languished after the Election Act of 1896, the political strike was always thought of as a weapon to bring the bourgeoisie to their knees. The idea appealed to some leaders of the SDAP, but the trade union movement thought it far too dangerous after the débâcle of 1903 when some 5,000 workers lost their jobs. In 1911 and 1912 things did not go beyond big demonstrations on the day that Parliament was ceremoniously opened—grandiose shows at which the leaders, members of the Chamber themselves, enormously enjoyed one day's revolutionary enthusiasm. Apart from that there was only a petition of the people and the strike in disguise of 1913 when the socialist workers went out into the streets to demonstrate instead of working on election day. Compared to the socialist action of 1913 in Belgium these were rather trivial deeds. Probably it is no mistake to say that the POB was more deeply rooted in the masses than the SDAP and consequently more erratic and thus more revolutionary, as well as less insistent on 'principle', intellectually less 'pure' and thus more reformist. Moreover, it was much more self-confident. This may help to explain why it was not long before the POB was shouldered with government responsibility, albeit in exceptional circumstances, whereas the SDAP had to wait until 1939.

The relative immaturity of the SDAP also appears from the nature of its leadership. Though undoubtedly Vandervelde became the most important political figure in the Belgian party, his authority was less personal than that of his Dutch colleague, P. J. Troelstra. Troelstra was no charismatic leader after the manner of Domela Nieuwenhuis; he tolerated fellow workers by his side, he respected the opinion of the party congresses, and for years he tried to give the Marxist intellectuals ample scope to express their criticisms. Yet he was always aware of himself as the leader and indeed the creator of the movement, whose vision should not only command respect but serve as a guide and inspiration to party members. If during the first twenty years of its existence the history of the SDAP was marked by sharp conflicts and a serious schism, this was certainly in part due to Troelstra's lack of emotional balance which influenced the policy of a party still in its infancy. The strife within the party can often be interpreted as the inner conflict of its leader. Troelstra (1860–1930) came from a lower-middle-class Frisian family, studied law at Groningen, and seriously took to politics only when he was thirty. He belonged to the radical and social-ist Friese Volkspartij and hoped to find a home in Domela Nieuwenhuis's SDB.[1] In the early 1890s he saw both parties fail. Thus his starting-point was different from Vandervelde's. Vandervelde, six years Troelstra's junior, joined the POB when it was achieving quick and unexpected successes; Troelstra's career started amidst ruins. Troelstra, moreover, was an impecunious provincial. His love of the Frisian language, in which he wrote reputable poetry, and his dislike for the Dutch literature of the 1880s in which Gorter, four years younger, excelled, gave him an outlook upon the world essentially different from the French-speaking and well-to-do Vander-velde and Destrée with their élitist preference for the latest thing in the fields of science, belles-lettres, and the fine arts. Troelstra never tried to belong to the cultural *avant-garde*.

To begin with it was mostly Frisian agricultural labourers and Jewish diamond-cutters from Amsterdam who enrolled as members of the party he helped to found in 1894. Its agrarian character was apparent from the readiness of the party to support the small farmers. By the turn of the century this attempt to unite farmers and industrial workers in one socialist movement was being attacked as fundamentally un-Marxist. It still remains an open question whether this was so. After all, in 1917 Lenin re-enacted Troelstra's policy of the 1890s on a gigantic scale. In any case Troelstra could not possibly have acted otherwise at the start because the SDAP was dependent on its Frisian following and, indeed, on the rural population in general. The Election Act of 1896 was framed in such a

---

[1] On this period see A. F. Mellink, 'Het politiek debuut van Mr. P. J. Troelstra (1891–1897)', *Tijdschrift voor Geschiedenis*, lxxxiii (1970), 38–58.

way that the small farmers and agricultural labourers were enfranchised to a greater degree than the lower middle classes and the industrial proletariat of the big towns. This situation gradually changed, however, and in the early twentieth century the SDAP went through the first stage of an urbanization process that transformed it into the party of skilled workmen.[1] This consolidated the position of the Jewish diamond-cutters, who supported the SDAP in its fight against anarchism and had always been attracted by the English socialist movement. They infused into the SDAP a strong element of Fabianism, sometimes difficult to reconcile with the German Marxism of the party. Thus the SDAP tended to move in curious directions. The controversy about reformism, revisionism, and Marxism, which began in the Netherlands comparatively late in 1902— the outstanding revisionist Eduard Bernstein had been a controversial figure in Germany since 1896—was indeed a rather ephemeral phenomenon compared to the fundamental conflicts that had characterized the SDAP after 1894.

Yet it was to all appearances this controversy that led to a schism in 1909. At the party congress in Deventer the majority resolved to expel the group of Marxist dissidents who were offering such stout resistance to Troelstra's leadership. The dissidents promptly founded a new party, the Sociaal Democratische Partij (SDP), which had a membership of under two hundred but could later boast that it was the first real communist party in Western and Central Europe. In 1918 it called itself Communistische Partij Holland (CPH). In itself it was strange that it was Dutch socialism (so weak in 1909— the SDAP had not yet 9,000 names on its books) that was vulnerable to such a dramatic split, and it would be difficult to hit upon a fitting explanation for it in terms of historical determinism. Curiously enough one of the most controversial issues was education. For various reasons Troelstra thought it sensible to gratify the Catholics' and Protestants' desire for their schools to be state-aided. He thought this just and, moreover, he shared the illusion of many liberals that state aid would cause the confessional parties, which in his opinion owed their cohesion to the conflicts about the school, to disintegrate. The doctrinaire Marxists in the party thought Troelstra's

[1] Cf. De Wolff, *En toch . . . !*, pp. 102 ff., 122, 174.

tactics objectionable. It seemed to them that Troelstra was deviating from the traditional line of the International by introducing Dutch variations and departing from the 'principle' in a quite unjustified and parochial way.

Troelstra found himself in a more and more difficult position. During the big strikes of 1903, as a revolutionary parliamentarian, he was unable to define his point of view with sufficient clarity. The few true reformists in the party reproached him for having rashly supported a strike doomed to failure; the revolutionaries criticized him equally violently for the hurry with which he called off the strike. He lost much of his prestige and his impotence was seen as a symbol of the hopelessness of his position: a choice between reform and revolution seemed inevitable.

A new generation of extremists appeared on the scene, with characteristics and tactics notably different from those of the generation born in the 1860s. Troelstra's relations with his contemporaries, Gorter and Henriette Roland Holst, were bad enough—the latter once described him to Lenin as a 'hundsgemeiner Kerl';[1] his relations with the new generation, D. Wijnkoop, W. van Ravesteyn, and others, were worse. If Troelstra felt little sympathy for Gorter's and Henriette Roland Holst's poetry he still had some respect for their achievements. He did not appreciate their exercises in Marxist theory but was willing to justify them as errors of the poetic imagination. Wijnkoop and Van Ravesteyn, on the other hand, did not inspire him with awe nor did they wish to. They were genuine extremists and in their periodical *De Tribune*, founded in 1907, they permitted themselves a kind of criticism that Troelstra thought intolerable. He himself was denounced as a reformist and pragmatist. But Wijnkoop (1876–1941), who was to be the Dutch communist leader for many years, followed the example of the activist Lassalle rather than of Marx. It was the learned Van Ravesteyn (1876–1970) who preferred to play the part of the Dutch Marx,[2] but his mind, very impressionable and burdened with an encyclopedic knowledge, lacked depth and originality. There was something tragic in their fate. Their predecessors in Marxist extremism, the demigods of the Dutch

---

[1] A. J. Koejemans, *David Wijnkoop* (The Hague, 1967), p. 87.
[2] Ibid., p. 94.

Marxist school, had been failures politically but had excelled as intellectuals. Wijnkoop, Van Ravesteyn, and their followers limited their life-work to fruitless political agitation. They assigned to themselves the function of full-time professional revolutionaries and propagandists but in practice achieved nothing. Eventually some of them, including Van Ravesteyn, rejected communism altogether, so their pretensions to special political skills as well as to Marxist orthodoxy vanished into thin air. In 1909 Troelstra had no difficulty in expelling them from the party. Four hundred members followed them, and some of the older generation left the party too, though others remained in the SDAP. It was only during the World War that the SDP, which they founded, managed to gain some influence; before 1914 it was without importance.

The SDAP itself, however, grew surprisingly rapidly, from some 10,000 members in 1911 to 25,000 in 1914. The party also readjusted its programme. This was not because it now represented a revisionist party hostile to the Marxist SDP— for the SDAP was by no means revisionist—but because reality forced it to revise the 1894 programme. In 1894 the founders of the party had chiefly copied the famous Erfurt Programme, in which the whole Marxist system as explained at the time had been summed up. In 1912 it appeared impossible to abide by the programme in its entirety. It was rewritten in such a way that it could still claim to be Marxist but at the same time allow for somewhat wider interpretations. A formula was found to which 'left' and 'right' in the party could agree.[1] It was significant that this should be possible after all the doctrinaire squabbling that had gone on.

Yet the problems had not finally been solved. The election results of 1913 presented the SDAP with an agonizing and almost impossible decision. The Dutch party structure had not become any simpler during the past decade, for all parties except the Catholic had suffered by disruptions: the anti-revolutionaries, the socialists, and the liberals. Under the stress of circumstances the parties of the Left had tried to bring about a certain unity, and the adventurous corporatism defended by the anti-revolutionary minister Talma stimulated

---

[1] De Vrankrijker, *Het wervende woord*, p. 169. In fact it did not differ fundamentally from the SDP programme also redrafted in 1912: De Liagre Böhl, *Gorter*, p. 61.

them most of all to close the ranks. The liberals succeeded in doing so. They were a long time in giving their party a firm shape and a binding programme. In 1884 the Liberal Union had been founded but it was only in the 1890s that it resigned itself to the necessity of drafting a programme. In 1899 it began to take up a well-defined position by declaring itself in favour of universal manhood suffrage. In 1901 the executive council of the party tried to translate this statement into practical terms by giving priority to the electoral question. But it failed and consequently decided to resign and to found a new party, the Vrijzinnig Democratische Bond (VDB), which was joined by all sorts of radical liberals of a former period.[1] To the right of the Liberal Union were some conservatives who called themselves Free- or Old-Liberals, and they were spiritedly independent of the rest of the party, often taking a line quite remote from anything the great mass of the liberals were willing to accept. Between the Liberal Union and the VDB the differences were difficult to define. The schismatic character of the Dutch party structure cannot be accounted for by an obsession with niceties of principle. The anti-revolutionary and the socialist parties split because they fell out on the practice, the pace, the general character of political action. This was the case with the liberals too. A general agreement could be reached on principles but not on the order of priorities. But this meant that in an emergency they could come together again with no great difficulty. So they did in 1912. The Liberal Concentration, in which the three liberal groups united for the elections, demanded universal manhood suffrage and free national pensions. The SDAP was demanding them as well.

The elections of 1913 were a débâcle for the confessional parties which lost 15 seats, a disappointment for the VDB and the Liberal Union, but a success for the Free-Liberals and in particular for the socialists, who won 11 seats.[2] The confessional

---

[1] E. van Raalte, *Dr. D. Bos. Leven en werk van een Nederlands staatsman* (Assen, 1962), pp. 108–10.

[2] Since some candidates were elected in more than one district at the same time new elections were necessary. The SDAP thereby lost 3 of its 18 seats. Account should be taken of the fact that the distribution of seats did not represent the opinion of the electorate correctly. At the first election the confessional parties obtained more votes than the liberals and the SDAP but—just as had been the case at all elections since 1897—they lost their prominence as a result of the district system.

Cabinet which had held 60 seats since 1909 resigned because only 45 supporters survived. It was obvious that the Left should try to form a government. Consequently, the liberal-democratic premier designate immediately applied to Troelstra asking whether the SDAP was prepared to join a Cabinet. It is remarkable that all the newspapers, including those of the Right, thought this step entirely acceptable; neither among the denominationals nor among the liberals was there any fear of a theoretically revolutionary party entering the government buildings.[1] The SDAP hesitated, however. For a few dramatic weeks it tried to find an honourable way out. There were in the party forceful and highly capable persons who were not only willing but anxious to take office. Troelstra was not one of them. Like the great mass of the party members he instinctively disliked a policy which would compel the socialists to compromise themselves by submitting to all the fuss and bother of a bourgeois monarchy. Moreover, though universal suffrage was ready to hand now, he was afraid that the party was too divided amongst itself to venture upon such an adventure, unparalleled in Europe. After vehement debates the SDAP finally chose isolation and refused to take office. This was a proof of weakness, division, and irresolution rather than of a truly revolutionary spirit or a well-thought-out orthodoxy. But in one respect the decision could be justified: as was hoped, a Cabinet of a radical-liberal hue was actually formed that relied on the left parties without being bound to their programme, and it was this that succeeded in introducing universal suffrage in 1917.

[1] G. B. van Dijk, 'De kabinetscrisis van 1913 in de Nederlandse pers', *Bijdragen voor de geschiedenis der Nederlanden*, xxi (1966), 36–57.

IX

WAR

1. *Belgium, 1914–1918*

FOR several decades Belgian statesmen had found it almost impossible to analyse the defence problem in an objective and practical fashion. Experts from the Foreign Office continued to put their faith in the traditional guaranteed neutrality, realizing too late that international developments had weakened Belgium's security.[1] Although the Christian democrats began to take a lively interest in military matters and wanted to strengthen Belgian defence, the Catholic party then in power generally retained its moral reservations towards the army and refused to expose what they considered the best part of Belgian youth to the degrading life of the barracks. Military reforms, moreover, were risky from a political point of view. The population was not interested in the army; anyone who dared to plead for a greater effort was soon denounced by public opinion as a militarist. Apart from these subjective considerations the problem may have been insoluble anyhow, for even with a well-organized army the Belgians could not have held out against German troops for very long. Essentially the problem was a political, not a military, one. Generations of Belgian theorists had praised neutrality as something morally and practically satisfying. It was inconceivable that Belgian statesmen should abandon this system in order to join the Entente. Such a psychological and diplomatic revolution was quite impossible in the climate of those years and hardly anybody advocated it.

The Belgians, moreover, had no sense of belonging 'ideologically' to the Entente. In the years just before the First World War Belgian statesmen and Belgian public opinion were well disposed towards Germany. In Brussels the French minister felt his isolation, for Belgian high society as well as the Foreign

[1] Above, p. 431.

Minister himself gave all their attention to the German minister.[1] By about 1910 Germany had succeeded in ousting France as Belgium's main trading partner. In his well-known book of 1910, *La Belgique moderne*, the French author Henri Charriaut repeatedly shows his consternation at the successes of the Germans and their swift penetration into Belgian life. The Flemish Catholics in particular were impressed by the seriousness of the Germans, their discipline and morality. But also in the small circle of intellectuals German prestige was considerably higher than that of the French. Belgian students, although educated in the French language, went to study in Germany far more regularly than at the Sorbonne.[2] Only one category of the population was and remained outspokenly pro-French: the army officers who proudly cultivated the French language of their caste and its French style of living—in an army that consisted mainly of Flemish country boys totally ignorant of French and including 10 per cent illiterates. From these circles came frightened warnings—well founded as was proved by events—of the danger of a German attack. But not until 1912 did the leader of the Catholic government, Charles de Broqueville, who had entered Parliament in 1892 as an antimilitarist and had not supported the bill of 1909 introducing general conscription, at last decide that radical military reforms were necessary. The expansion of the German army in 1912 as well as secret information received in Brussels apparently tipped the scales.[3] In 1913 a new Defence Bill was passed which did indeed mean a break with traditional policy.

Relatively the Belgian army had been on the decline since 1839. According to military specialists it had then been in excellent shape and was still adequate in 1870 both in quality and size. But after that, when everywhere in Europe general conscription strengthened national defence, the Belgian army rapidly deteriorated. The nadir was reached in 1902 with the Defence Law, by which the nation's defence was mainly entrusted to volunteers whom, as it turned out, it was impossible to enrol in sufficient numbers. While the army was visibly

---

[1] Devleeshouwer, *Les Belges et le danger de guerre*, p. 47.

[2] *La Belgique et la guerre* (4 vols., Brussels, 1920–3), ii, J. Cuvelier, *L'Invasion allemande*, p. 7.   [3] De Lichtervelde, *Avant l'orage*, p. 74.

declining. Parliament decided in 1909, after discussions which dragged on for a year, to make military service compulsory for one son in each family. This increased the annual quota of recruits (13,300 in 1902, 19,000 in 1909) but the effect was undone because by way of compensation the term of service was reduced to fifteen months. In 1913 the annual contingent was raised to 33,000 recruits by abolishing the exemption for younger sons. It was the intention to increase the total strength of the army as soon as possible from the 180,000 men projected in 1902 and 1909 to 340,000 men. In 1914, of course, this number had nowhere near been reached. When the army was called up, it totalled just over 200,000 men of whom about 120,000 served in the field army. In comparison with 1839 when it numbered 100,000 men out of a population half that of 1914, when it was well trained and well equipped and confronted with much smaller foreign armies, Belgian military strength was very considerably reduced.[1] Fundamental disagreement between De Broqueville and King Albert on strategy and the structure of the supreme command further weakened Belgium's military position, slowing down the process of decision-making to such a degree that the strategy to be followed in the event of a German invasion had still not been determined at the time of mobilization.

Until the very last moment the Belgian Government kept to a strict interpretation of neutrality. In this it went so far that the Entente Powers did not really know what to expect from it in the event of a German attack. As it refused to commit itself, simply reiterating that the country's forces would be used against any invader, there was, so it seemed, a possibility that the army—generally known to be very weak—would be instructed to make some appropriate gestures and then to withdraw or to capitulate. Remarkably enough, the government had not yet made up its mind about such a possibility. It

---

[1] *La Belgique et la guerre*, iii, M. Tasnier and R. van Overstraeten, *Les Opérations militaires*, pp. 8–16. Statisticians have calculated that the Belgian army at full war strength represented in 1840 2 per cent of the population, in 1910 2·4 per cent (Wanty, *Milieu militaire*, p. 235). In France the proportion between army and population was 1 : 8, in Austria and Germany 1 : 13, in the Netherlands 1 : 31, and in Belgium 1 : 41 (Devleeshouwer, *Danger de guerre*, p. 79). In France defence costs amounted to 31·10 francs per head of the population, in Germany to 23·52 francs, and in Belgium to 8 francs (Wanty, op. cit.).

refused to consider the problem of what exactly would happen
if the guarantees given in 1839 proved worthless, and a French
or a German army invaded Belgian territory. On 31 July
1914 the Belgian Government mobilized the troops. It did
so at 7.00 p.m., after three hours of deliberation in the presence
of the King, on hearing the news of Germany's proclamation
of the *Kriegsgefahrzustand*, of French army transports moving
east, and, most of all, of the mobilization of the Dutch army
which had taken place at 1.30 p.m. that same day.

The mobilization was orderly and satisfactory. On 1 August
the ministers were informed that the Germans were about to
invade Luxemburg. On the evening of 2 August, a Sunday, the
German minister handed the Belgian Foreign Minister an
ultimatum demanding the right of way for the German army
on the pretext that the French were planning to march through
Belgian territory. One hour later the Cabinet unanimously
rejected this. The so-called Crown Council consisting of the
King, the Cabinet, the Ministers of State, and some high army
officers met shortly after. A heated discussion seems to have
taken place.[1] Only then were the vital questions asked. Apparently the influential Catholic leader Woeste, a Minister of
State, was prepared to protest against the ultimatum but not to
reject it. When it became clear that a large majority of the
meeting categorically refused to accept it, he insisted on a
merely symbolic defence. But when it was shown that on this
point as well he was virtually isolated, two generals began to
discuss their disagreement about the strategy to be followed.
The Council also considered what attitude to take towards the
Entente Powers but the point was not elaborated. As a result
of the deliberations the German ultimatum was rejected but
an agreement on the military and international political
consequences was not reached.

Early in the morning of 3 August the German minister was
informed of the Belgian refusal. On 4 August in the morning
he answered that the German army would march into Belgium
that same day. Shortly afterwards King Albert addressed

---

[1] Those who were present and reported on it give contradictory evidence: cf.
Devleeshouwer, *Danger de guerre*, pp. 299 ff. and the excellent exposition by J.
Bartier, 'België tijdens de Eerste Wereldoorlog', *Algemene geschiedenis der Neder-
landen*, xii (1958), 9–10.

Parliament. His brief, powerful speech was listened to in silence and applauded in thrilled harmony. It was perfectly clear by now that the Belgians intended to defend their territory, although the Germans still entertained the hope that they would not go beyond a patriotic demonstration. But Belgian determination was complete. At the meeting of the Crown Council the liberals had shown themselves the most strongly opposed to the German claims. In Parliament the socialists, too, loudly applauded the King on 4 August. Vandervelde, who was President of the Second International, agreed to being appointed a Minister of State and thus accepted, on behalf of his party, moral responsibility for the policies of the Catholic government. It is not remarkable in itself that this should have happened. But it is remarkable that it needed no discussion. Apparently the Belgian socialists were unable to keep aloof from the patriotic emotions coming to the surface during the first days of August. The nationalist rhetoric of the socialist newspapers differed in no way from that of the liberals and Catholics.

The German attack started in the early morning of 4 August. Their troops rapidly marched to the Liège fortifications which formed an obstacle on the way to France. The Belgians could not prevent Liège falling but they succeeded in defending the city one day longer than the German strategists had expected, and they held on to the fortifications on the Meuse for a few days more. This had palpable effects on the development of the German campaign and was of course psychologically of great importance. But the main body of the Belgian army was concentrated near Louvain, both to protect Brussels and to safeguard the connection with Antwerp. It hardly went into action, and when it was attacked by a German army of some 200,000 men it withdrew on 20 August to the fortifications of Antwerp, with some losses and against the wishes of the French Supreme Command. On that same day the Germans marched into Brussels. After the brief initial success the débâcle came as a bitter shock. During the first fortnight the population in those regions and towns where no fighting took place had enthusiastically celebrated the heroic actions of the Belgian army—the Belgian General Staff sent out most optimistic bulletins—and put out the flags. But the costly fortifications

of Antwerp where the complete Belgian army—of which
90,000 field troops and 60,000 garrison troops were left—took
refuge were both out of date and unfinished.[1] For the time
being the Germans, heading for Paris, left Antwerp alone and
were unable to prevent some Belgian sallies. But on 27 September, after their defeat on the Marne, they attacked the
town. Resistance soon proved fruitless and catastrophic. Support from England arrived too late and was insufficient. On
7 October the King withdrew the bulk of his troops from the
fortress. During the days that followed the rest, including
2,000 British marines, left the town; 30,000 men fled to the
Netherlands where they were interned. On 10 October Antwerp surrendered to the Germans.

The German military machine which rolled through Belgium
was responsible for much brutality. In August nervous German
soldiers had reacted with pathological distrust and extreme
reprisals to any unexpected movement from the civilian population, any inexplicable incident, any suspicion. Belgian military resistance was proving more tenacious, the civilians more
hostile, than the Germans had anticipated. In the German
army as well as in the irresponsible German Press the black
legend of Belgian *francs-tireurs*—an echo of what had happened
in France in 1870—was already being heard in the first days
of August, with horror stories about systematically planned
attacks on German soldiers and atrocious tortures. From 6
August onwards the *Kölnische Volkszeitung* published articles
under such titles as 'The Beast in Belgium', 'Ferocious Belgium',
'Horrors in Liège', containing the most unbelievable reports on
the unbridled sadism of the Belgians.[2] The punitive measures
taken by the German soldiers, alarmed by unexpected shootings,
were excessively severe. Without trial or close examination
they shot arbitrarily chosen or arbitrarily accused civilians and
set fire to countless houses. In the province of Liège the civilian
population suffered some 1,200 casualties, in the province of
Luxemburg 842, in the province of Namur as many as 2,000.
In the province of Brabant—where the centre of Louvain and
its ancient library went up in flames—839 people died from
German bullets, and in Hainaut about 350. In these provinces

[1] Tasnier and Van Overstraeten, op. cit., pp. 128 ff.
[2] Cuvelier, op. cit., pp. 55 ff.

nearly 16,000 houses and public buildings were burned.[1] The reign of terror was wild and unneccessary; it was not systematic in the sense of being planned or prepared or made subservient to war aims.[2] However, it is understandable that allied propaganda depicted it as such. It is understandable, too, that it caused sheer panic in Antwerp when the town was attacked early in October, although by then the Germans had considerably mitigated their policy of terror. At least half a million civilians, including many refugees who had found a temporary shelter in the town, left it precipitately. Hundreds of thousands sought safety in the Netherlands.[3]

What was left of the Belgian army was led by King Albert to posts behind the River IJzer. There they withstood a strong German offensive which started on 18 October for eight days, suffering heavy losses. When the Belgians opened the lockgates at Nieuwpoort and rendered the IJzer valley virtually impassable, the Germans stopped their attacks for the time being. But the roads to the ports on the Straits of Dover remained cut off and the Belgian army had dwindled to a mere 60,000 men. It was years before its numerical strength was back to that of early 1914. New recruits were found in the small region along the IJzer left unoccupied by the Germans, and they were joined by volunteers who had successfully escaped from the occupied territory, as well as by people who had fled from Antwerp to an allied country and returned to assist in the defence. Early in 1918 the army totalled 170,000 men.[4] But this was still a modest force, and in fact the number

---

[1] All these data in the very detailed report by Cuvelier, *passim.*

[2] German historians have long maintained that the conduct of the German troops was justified as a reaction to a systematic attack on German soldiers by the civilian population. The German Whitebook of 10 May 1915 was used as a source for this thesis. Its credibility is denied by Peter Schöller, *Der Fall Löwen und das Weissbuch. Eine kritische Untersuchung der deutschen Dokumentation über die Vorgänge in Löwen vom 25. bis 28. August 1914* (Cologne, Graz, 1958; Dutch trans. Louvain, 1958). In 'Zur Bereinigung des Franktireurproblems vom August 1914', *Vierteljahrshefte für Zeitgeschichte*, ix (1961), 234–48, F. Petri and P. Schöller support the thesis put forward by the Belgians shortly after the events that there had never been *francstireurs* and that the shots at German soldiers, usually the reason for reprisals, were fired by nervous Germans themselves.

[3] Altogether probably some 1,400,000 Belgians, that is almost one-fifth of the population, left the country in this period. Of course, many returned rather soon: H. Pirenne, *La Belgique et la Guerre Mondiale* (Paris, New Haven, n.d.), pp. 64–5.

[4] Tasnier and Van Overstraeten, p. 282.

of volunteers remained relatively small. Even in August 1914, when on the spur of the moment young men volunteered to take revenge for the German outrages, their number remained under 20,000, which was small in proportion to the available resources. As a result of the curious military system in force before 1913, most young men had been kept out of the army. Moreover, nearly all volunteers came from the towns; the peasant population proved immune to patriotic idealism.[1] During the following years an estimated total of 30,000 men took the admittedly risky but far from impossible step of leaving the occupied parts of Belgium[2]—not even the equivalent of one class according to the law of 1913. Belgium did not have to sacrifice a whole generation to the war.

From October 1914 the whole of Belgium with the exception of the small part along the IJzer was occupied by the Germans. The Belgian Government had gone into exile and taken up residence in Le Havre. King Albert, on the other hand, stayed with the army on Belgian territory and refused to leave it. The occupied area was divided into two zones, one constituting the so-called *étape*, close to the front and under military rule (East-Flanders, Western Hainaut, Southern Luxemburg), the other (about two-thirds of Belgian territory) governed by the German Governor-General: from December 1914 until his death in April 1917 this was the aged Prussian officer Von Bissing. In both zones German rule was strict and severe. But generally it was correct and the standards of the German civil service were high. There was no question of any active resistance to the occupying forces. The Belgian civil servants continued their work and on the advice of the Belgian government-in-exile signed a declaration that they were prepared to meet their obligations loyally in accordance with the laws of war. Even after the war Belgian patriots praised the patience and discipline of the population during the occupation most emphatically. The situation was different from the French occupation or from the Second World War and provoked different reactions. Relations with the occupying authorities were more business-like,

[1] Pirenne, *Guerre Mondiale*, p. 53. Cf. Devleeshouwer, *Danger de guerre*, p. 277 n. 2.

[2] Pirenne, *Guerre Mondiale*, p. 80; cf. the interesting notes in the book by Georges Rency (pen-name of Albert Stassart, 1875–1951), permeated with patriotic complacency, *La Belgique et la guerre*, i, *La Vie matérielle de la Belgique durant la Guerre Mondiale* (Brussels, 1920), p. 80.

more aloof, and not dominated by ideological feelings. Whatever the intentions of the Germans towards Belgium may have
been, no individual German had a new political and social
programme at his disposal to inflict upon the peoples defeated
by force of arms.

In Belgium, therefore, the German occupation did not lead
to a guerilla movement; it brought stagnation. In the small
industries and of course in agriculture work was continued,
but the big industries either stopped or considerably reduced
their production. The tendency to limit all work to a minimum
was quite general. A large number of newspapers ceased to
appear because the directors refused to apply for publication
permits. Notwithstanding urgent requests by the occupying
authorities, university teachers were unwilling to resume their
lectures and examinations. Not only was free scholarship impossible, according to them, in an occupied and isolated
country, they also considered it improper to teach young men
who were only able to follow university courses by shirking
their patriotic obligation to leave the occupied zone and
enlist in the Belgian army.[1] Of course, the whole machinery of
political activity also came to a halt. In this exceptional situation the old forces which had seemed to dominate public life
were paralysed. The government had gone into exile; neither
Parliament nor the provincial councils assembled. The political
parties virtually stopped their activities. The pre-war problems
lost their urgency, the pre-war contrasts their edge. The conflicts between Right and Left, between confessionals and anti-
confessionals, between conservative and democratic Catholics,
between doctrinaire and progressive liberals, although not
settled, were postponed until better days. Suddenly politics
and ideology ceased to dominate society.

This pervasive stagnation, which for many hundreds of
thousands of Belgians turned the four war years into a long and
extremely dull vacation, cannot be explained as the outcome of
a conscious and well-considered gesture on the part of the Belgian people, a form of large-scale passive resistance. It did,
however, sometimes have that effect. For all sorts of reasons
neither the economic and intellectual élites nor the masses of the
population assisted the Germans in their occasional efforts to

[1] Th. Heyse, *Index documentaire*, i: *L'Université flamande* (Ghent, 1919), p. 204.

break through the stagnation and to get life going again. The passivity with which the occupation was endured could develop into a form of resistance at moments when the Germans required active aid for their war efforts. German policies, however, were rather difficult to understand. Superficially they seemed whimsical, for aims and methods were repeatedly altered. Nobody knew the deeper-lying causes of these oscillations since the details of German intentions with regard to Belgium were of course not brought into public discussion. Officially it was only known that the German Government wanted guarantees against a repetition of the events of 1914 when—according to their version—the aggressive policies of the Allies in collaboration with Belgium had forced it to start a defensive war. Generally speaking, the German authorities agreed that Belgium ought to be brought permanently into the German sphere of influence. The assertion, spread by extreme Flamingants, that the Belgian state had slavishly followed the French before 1914—which was untrue—suited German purposes very well and it was considered to be self-evident that Belgium needed to be disengaged from France. This could be achieved by annexation. Governor Von Bissing saw this as the best solution and military circles and pan-Germanist societies, such as the *Alldeutscher Verband*, supported it, too. On the other hand, the German Foreign Office, the Chancellor Bethmann-Hollweg, and the political department of the government-general at Brussels tended to favour more cautious policies which would bind Belgium to Germany without permanently occupying it or incorporating it in the Reich.[1]

In practice, however, this difference of opinion was of no importance. Whichever attitude was adopted the same problem arose—whether the country that was to be connected with Germany in some way or another should be a strong or a weak Belgium. It was difficult to judge whether a Belgium which had regained its full economic potential would be a valuable addition to German power or a serious competitor. It was no

[1] On this whole matter see F. Wende, *Die belgische Frage in der deutschen Politik des Ersten Weltkrieges* (Hamburg, 1969) and F. Petri, 'Zur Flamenpolitik des Ersten Weltkrieges', in R. Vierhaus and M. Botzenhaft (eds.), *Dauer und Wandel der Geschichte. Festgabe für Kurt von Raumer* (Münster, 1966), pp. 513–36. Petri slightly modifies the well-known theses of F. Fischer, *Griff nach der Weltmacht. Die Kriegszielpolitik des kaiserlichen Deutschlands, 1914–1918* (Düsseldorf, 1961).

more clear whether the relative independence which the German civil authorities wanted to grant the Flemings and the Walloons would facilitate relations with Germany or rather impede the penetration of German power. On the basis of these considerations there were two conceivable policies. The Germans could leave Belgium unimpaired as much as possible so that the whole potential of the country would be available for the Germans after their final victory. Or they might break up the Belgian unitary state, intensify the tensions between groups and classes within its population, and destroy the big industrial plants in order to dislocate the country and prevent it from resisting German exploitation after the war. The Germans, in fact, pursued neither policy with any consistency. The first policy, which Von Bissing appears to have preferred, was abandoned on essential points because the military and economic specialists demanded Belgian goods and workers. The second policy was not tried until 1917, and then did not work properly, being improvized and self-contradictory. The administrative separation of Flanders and Wallonia was indeed effected, Flemish separatism was encouraged, and the economic infrastructure was for the greater part destroyed. But this took place at a time when the war was going badly for Germany and the Germans had reverted to brute force, with the inevitable result that they could not rely on the Flemings or the workers whose help they needed if they were effectively to divide the nation.

As a consequence of this uncertainty the Germans kept falling between two stools. They did not want to go beyond practical administrative measures in a region near the front line where unrest could be dangerous, and Von Bissing's aloofness was characteristic of this policy. He hardly sought contact with the population and administered the country as far as possible within the framework of Belgian pre-war legislation. But at the same time he was forced to take measures which ran counter to this policy in order to promote either the German war effort or Bethmann-Hollweg's ideas. He was supposed to collect war contributions, machines, goods, and workers, to win the Flemings over to the German cause, and prepare the dissolution of the Belgian state, which meant inflicting severe damage upon the economy and carrying out far-reaching changes in the political structure. On the whole the Belgian population reacted negatively to the sudden and incoherent German initiatives of which they were the victims. At such moments the people's attitude of passive waiting, carefully and systematically controlled by the bourgeois élite, developed into a form of resistance. This was true of Flanders too, and whatever may be thought of the German policy towards Flanders and the so-called 'activists', it is beyond doubt that this had already failed before the Germans were defeated on the battlefield. It did not win the support of the masses of the Flemish population on which it was ultimately dependent.

The two main problems which confronted Belgian society immediately after the establishment of the German regime were food supplies and unemployment. The big industries were forced to reduce their production. They were no longer able to obtain raw materials from abroad—ore for the steelworks, cotton and wool for the textile industry—and could not sell a substantial part of their goods since foreign markets were closed to them. Only rarely did the Belgian entrepreneurs consider production for the German army—for which they might have obtained the necessary raw materials—an acceptable alternative. On the whole even strong German pressure did not succeed in persuading Belgian industry to co-operate.[1] Patriotism was always advanced as the main reason for this refusal. It is not clear whether other factors also played a part, and no systematic research on this subject has been carried out.[2] Over the years the Germans proceeded to put a number of factories under German management and got them operating again.[3] Moreover, they succeeded in keeping some thousands of mostly small enterprises going since closure would have meant total ruin for the employers. But among the big industries it was only in the collieries that work continued as far as possible with the special consent of the Belgian government-

---

[1] Ch. de Kerchove de Denterghem, *L'Industrie belge pendant l'occupation allemande, 1914–1918* (Paris, Yale, n.d.), pp. 73 ff.

[2] De Kerchove, who strongly stresses patriotism as the major explanation, also mentions the insecurity of labour conditions, the instability of circumstances, and the *malaise* caused by the continual interventions by the Germans in industrial questions (ibid., p. 58). Of course, collaborating industrialists seriously risked prosecution in case of an allied victory (ibid., p. 160).

[3] Ibid., p. 90.

in-exile, which feared that otherwise although the German war industry might lack fuel the Belgian population would be the first to suffer. The social consequences of the situation were disastrous. An average of some 650,000 workers were unemployed during the war, that is more than half the number of factory- and office-workers who had remained in occupied Belgium.[1] From a Belgian point of view this entailed the serious danger that these people would be tempted by favourable labour conditions to take up jobs with the Germans, either in Belgium or in Germany itself where labour shortages became increasingly damaging to the war economy. It was therefore most urgent for the Belgian patriots to organize a system of relief in order to keep the working classes under control.[2]

Although Belgian agriculture and cattle-breeding were highly developed and productive, at least for wheat and to a lesser extent for oats, the country was dependent on imports. In 1913 more than four million tons of foodstuffs were imported, two-thirds of which was grain.[3] In reply to the Allied blockade of their coasts the Germans declared that they would take no responsibility for food supplies in the occupied territories. As the Belgian Government had failed to lay in stocks, it was at once apparent that there were serious difficulties ahead. The refusal of the Germans to provide food themselves meant that the problem had to be solved by the Belgians and that the Germans were morally bound to allow them to do so. In this way they granted the Belgians elbow-room and responsi-bilities quite incompatible with the principles of the occupation regime. This was to their advantage economically but detri-mental politically. The organization set up by the Belgians consisted of a Comité national de secours et d'alimentation and a Commission for Relief in Belgium, the first established in Brussels, the second in London, with offices in many other places, including Brussels. It developed into an enormous enterprise with its own finances, its own connections abroad, and, although in principle neutral, with its own political significance. The innumerable civil servants, politicians,

---

[1] Mahaim, *Le Secours de chômage en Belgique pendant l'occupation allemande*, pp. 140–2.
[2] Ibid., pp. 47–8.
[3] A. Henry, *Le Ravitaillement de la Belgique pendant l'occupation allemande* (Paris, 192, p. 134).

industrialists, professors, business men, and bankers who found little to do in their regular jobs spent most of their energy on this organization. Supplying food became a patriotic duty.

The initiative to set up the Comité was taken by the aged Ernest Solvay in September 1914. He himself made one million Belgian francs available for the purpose. His example was followed by numerous private persons and enterprises. The Brussels bankers especially contributed generously. The Société générale not only provided money but also allowed the Comité to make use of its offices and staff. Before long the Brussels Relief Committee developed into a national committee. Émile Francqui (1863–1935), director of the Société générale, a man of inexhaustible energy and broad international experience, became chairman of the committee's executive. One of his connections, Herbert Hoover, set up the Commission for Relief which saw to the importation of foodstuffs and, at a later stage, of other goods like clothing and footwear. Both the Allied Powers and the Germans supported these initiatives. The Comité, moreover, was placed under the patronage of those neutral states which still had their representatives in Brussels: the United States, Spain, and the Netherlands. A special arrangement was made for financing the relief programme for it soon became clear that voluntary gifts from Belgium and abroad, although large (in Great Britain, the United States, and other countries over 100 million francs was collected) were insufficient to meet the demands. The main problem was that the Comité itself was unable to make any purchases abroad because the Germans did not allow the profits of the food sales to be exported. In November 1914 a member of the board of the Société générale, who had been dispatched to Le Havre, found a solution. The Belgian Government undertook to provide the Commission with 25 million francs monthly (later on 37·5 million) for buying victuals and transporting them into Belgium. The Comité distributed and sold these. The income was used to pay off Belgian government debts and to meet obligations which the government-in-exile, unable to send money to Belgium, could not meet directly. The Comité also helped in various ways many people who had suffered as a result of the war, the unemployed in the first place. The organization developed on a massive scale with more than

125,000 virtually unpaid collaborators.[1] Altogether the Comité—not including provisions for the population in the areas of northern France occupied by the Germans—spent in Belgium over 2,000 million francs to supply the needy with money, food, clothing, and so on,[2] and the goods it imported and distributed were worth nearly 2,500 million francs.[3] How enormous these sums are in the Belgian perspective is clear if one considers that the whole state budget over the year 1912 did not surpass 895 million francs.

Notwithstanding its growth the Comité national remained essentially unchanged. It was led first of all by the élite among Belgian managers and bankers. Although it opened many provincial and local offices it was highly centralized. Each Thursday members of the Comité from all over Belgium met at Brussels in the office of the Société générale to discuss how to carry out Francqui's decisions. Many members of Parliament had been nominated for the Comité; after the meeting they used to have lunch together and undoubtedly felt like an illegal rump parliament guaranteeing the continuity of public life. Francqui and his staff ruled as enlightened despots an organization which they took pride in building up as a large commercial enterprise. It was their ambition to show how efficiently, carefully, and business-like such an institution for public welfare could be if it were administered by experienced managers instead of politicians. They wanted to prove that business men were better equipped to manage the national estate than the statesmen whom they held in little regard, and that a private enterprise could be run more efficiently than a government undertaking.[4] Of course they did this work not only because it was necessary but also because they now had time to spare. In small countries—it was the same in the Netherlands—politics is not normally considered to be an occupation of the highest order. Not only are the salaries considerably higher in trade and industry, the power wielded by the directors within and outside their enterprises seems larger. To be a director of a big Brussels bank with many international branches and interests seems to provide more responsibility and influence than a post in the Cabinet. But now that business

[1] A. Henry, op. cit., p. 186.   [2] Rency, op. cit., p. 232.
[3] Henry, op. cit., p. 61.   [4] Mahaim, op. cit., p. 17.

had come to a standstill and statesmen had withdrawn from
public life, the big bankers and industrialists occupied themselves in an activity which—all outward appearances notwithstanding—became inevitably a political one, and they did
so in their own characteristic way. The spirit of the enterprise
was liberal and religiously neutral—no effort was made to
bring the numerous Catholic charitable institutions into it—
and if not outspokenly authoritarian at least paternalist; it was
national and expressed itself in French. For four years the
French-speaking élite of the Brussels bourgeoisie supported,
fed, and patronized Belgian society in the national spirit of
the traditional Belgian unitary state. In a period when politics
and ideology were dormant and unable to conceal the concrete
distribution of power, the real character of this still thoroughly
bourgeois society seemed to come to light again.

The Comité attained its ends. This was not always easy.
Not only did the occupying authorities sometimes stand in the
way; more serious still was the fact that Belgian agricultural
production itself was left outside the Comité's distribution
system. There was a thriving black market and apparently
important supplies of foodstuffs were sometimes in spite of
everything sold to Germany.[1] Nevertheless, the Comité on
which half the population came to depend was able to prevent
disaster. Although sometimes there was not enough food for
the urban masses, there was no famine. As far as the Comité's
patriotic preoccupations were concerned, there is no doubt
that the relief procured for the poor and unemployed helped
to prevent large-scale collaboration with the Germans. However, German policy in this respect too was very arbitrary.
On the one hand, they profited from the fact that the Comité
neutralized the most serious effects of massive unemployment
resulting from the war itself and from deliberate German interference. For in doing so it vigorously helped to maintain order.
On the other hand, the German war economy needed more
labour. When it proved impossible to enrol a large number of
Belgian workers for Germany or for Belgian industries producing for Germany on a voluntary basis—there were no more than
some tens of thousands of such workers—the German Government decided in October 1916 forcibly to deport masses of

[1] Henry, p. 149.

people, and not only the unemployed, from the occupied territory to Germany, against the emphatic advice of Governor Von Bissing who feared grave disturbances.[1]

The Belgian population did not as it happened rise in revolt; without active resistance but in a mood of bitter hostility and under the most humiliating conditions about 120,000 men and boys allowed themselves to be sent off to Germany—only slightly more than a quarter of the number the German General Staff had counted upon. In February 1917, however, this systematic massive deportation was stopped. From October 1916 Cardinal Mercier had denounced the German action in the sharpest possible terms. Many Belgian authorities followed suit. The neutral Powers associated themselves with these protests: the Vatican, Spain, the Netherlands, Switzerland, and the United States declared in November and December 1916 that deportations were against the rules of war. In face of this heavy pressure, combined with strong opposition by the socialists in the Reichstag, Wilhelm II gave way. By the summer of 1917 most of the deported men had been sent back to Belgium.[2] But at the very moment when they recognized the total failure of this experiment, the Germans decided to close the Belgian factories unless the directors applied for permission to continue production. Most of them refused. Then the Germans started systematically to ransack their factories. During the first years of the war the Germans had already requisitioned thousands of engines and machines; in the summer of 1917 they began to dismantle Belgian industry almost completely. The best machinery was taken to Germany, the rest was turned into scrap-iron. The damage was incalculable. It was, however, intended to compensate the proprietors and for that purpose detailed inventories were drawn up and the ravages were painstakingly registered. But circumstances prevented any payment being made. As a result Belgian losses, estimated by Bissing at nearly 7,000 million francs already in the autumn of 1915, were immensely increased. Nevertheless, the Germans did not go the whole hog. The collieries were left undamaged and of the rest enough survived for three-quarters

[1] F. Passelecq, *Déportation et travail forcé des ouvriers et de la population civile de la Belgique occupée (1916–1918)* (Paris, New Haven, n.d.), p. 93.
[2] Ibid., pp. 311–12.

of the number of workers employed in 1914 to be again at work in the factories by December 1919.[1]

This sad but banal story of war and plunder was complicated by the fact that the deportations and the destruction of industry from which the Flemings too suffered coincided with German efforts to win over the Flemish movement. This was indeed a coincidence. There was no question of the Germans trying to force the Flemings by terror to collaborate. The contradiction between the two policies carried out simultaneously was strong and repugnant. In October 1916 one old Flemish dream came true and the Flemish University at Ghent was solemnly opened, but it was at the very moment when the Germans started to deport large groups of men from the town. In March 1917 the decision to split up the administration of the country into autonomous Flemish and Walloon departments and thus to grant Flanders a long-wished-for independence, was made public just before the Germans started systematically to dismantle the Belgian factories. It was bizarre and reckless for the Germans to encourage Flemish separatism and to give it an institutional shape without offering any material advantages to the Flemish community, which in fact remained subject to the German Government. Of course, the Germans continued to rule over the whole country. The policy of the Germans would have been understandable if they had wanted to weaken Belgium by destroying the unity of the state. In that case German support of Flemish separatism could have been interpreted as an element in a broad attack intended simultaneously to undermine the Belgian state in every way, economically, intellectually, and administratively. But the proceedings of the Germans were not as simple and coherent as that. On the contrary, they seem to have hoped that their Flemish policy would win them permanent support. Within the inevitably strict limits of a war policy, by definition self-interested, their interference in Flemish affairs was determined by a sort of sympathy rather than by sheer selfishness and cynicism.

At the time of their invasion of Belgium the Germans had no clear understanding of the Flemish question and were little interested in it. They considered Belgium important from a strategic and political point of view and were hostile to it

De Kerchove, op. cit., p. 265.

because they regarded it as an appendix of France. There was no plan, no outline, however sketchy, of a policy with regard to the Flemings. It had hardly occurred to the Germans that they might claim to be liberating, or at least to be in the presence of, an oppressed Germanic population. This idea was first put forward after the outbreak of the war by some German politicians and by small groups of Flemings who helped the German authorities to develop both theories and plans.[1] At the start, however, the activities of these groups seemed to be quite unimportant. In the autumn of 1914 a Dutch clergyman who worked in Ghent, J. D. Domela Nieuwenhuis Nyegaard (a nephew of the formidable anarchist), formed a circle of idealists called Young Flanders (Jong-Vlaanderen) which was outspokenly pro-German. He drew up a programme in which he put forward the conception of a Kingdom of Flanders to be established under German patronage. He published a daily paper, financed by the Germans, which restricted itself more cautiously to advocating 'administrative separation', and composed intolerably rhetorical dissertations on the excellence of the Germanic race, reducing the whole agitation of these people, who called themselves 'activists',[2] to a level both intellectually and politically inferior to that of the pre-war Flemish movement.[3] The voluble prose emerging from these first Ghent activists was, with some exceptions, unattractive, provincial, naïve, and egocentric. After the political realism of De Raet and Vermeylen's brilliant style this meant a relapse into the worn-out attitudes and phraseology of late Flemish Romanticism.

When the Ghent activists started their campaign they had no connections with the Germans, although they were passionately pro-German. In their eyes the war had an ideological significance. It was a Germanic struggle against the Roman south in which Flanders naturally took the side of the Germans.[4]

---

[1] On the following cf. Lode Wils, *Flamenpolitik en activisme* (Louvain, 1973).

[2] In November 1915 the term was first used in Belgium. It was derived from Swedish political jargon; Swedish 'activists' were people who wanted the country to enter the war on the German side. A. W. Willemsen, *Het Vlaams-nationalisme. De geschiedenis van de jaren 1914–1920* (2nd edn., Utrecht, 1969), p. 30; H. J. Elias, *Vijf-entwintig jaar Vlaamse Beweging 1914/1939* (4 vols., Antwerp, 1969), i. 14 n. 1.

[3] Above, pp. 462–73.

[4] Much material in M. van de Velde, *Geschiedenis der Jong Vlaamsche Beweging, 1914–1918* (The Hague, 1941).

The German authorities were not unwilling to give some
financial support to Young Flanders but had no use for its
political aims. Neither in Bethmann-Hollweg's schemes nor
in those of the army was there room for an independent
Flanders, totally severed from south Belgium, with a king
and a policy of its own. Such a disruption of the Belgian state
would, after all, weaken their grip on the country as a whole
rather than strengthen it. Domela Nieuwenhuis's activities
were carefully watched and, whenever it seemed desirable,
drastically thwarted.[1] For the Germans had other plans. As
early as January 1915 they persuaded Young Flanders to
ask them to Dutchify the University of Ghent and to split
the Belgian state, without breaking it up, into two separate
administrative unities, Wallonia and Flanders.[2] When they
thought the time ripe they complied with these requests but
it took some years. For the time being the Flemish question was hardly taken into consideration. The large majority
of Flamingants avoided connections with the Germans and did
not seek German help for a solution of the Flemish problem.
They looked upon the Germans as the national enemy, refusing
to believe that they could win the war. Only in the second half
of 1915 did some of them begin to feel doubts about what they
had hitherto taken for granted and then activism won a few
more adherents.

This can partly be explained as a reaction to the attitude of
some Walloon publicists and the far from clear pronouncements
on the subject by the Belgian Government at Le Havre. From
August 1914 onwards the Flemish movement as such was
sometimes bitterly criticized by the French-speaking Belgian
Press in exile and by some of the papers still published in
Belgium. These authors represented the war as a struggle of
Latin civilization against Teutonic barbarism. Through the
victory of the Allies Belgium, the proud saviour of Latin principles, would gain a place of honour in a new Europe where

[1] Petri, 'Flamenpolitik', pp. 534–5. Domela found support with the Alldeutscher
Verband which was pan-Germanist and thus played into the hands of an extreme
annexionist group.
[2] Elias, *Vlaamse Beweging* i. 26. According to Domela, as has been said before,
the second claim did not go nearly far enough. It was, however, an extreme claim
compared with the aims of the pre-war Flemish movement of which only a small
radical wing wanted this.

Flemish of course would play no part.[1] Their plans for the future of the country differed greatly from anything thought of before the war. At Le Havre the journalist Fernand Neuray (1874–1934), in his influential Catholic daily paper *Le Vingtième Siècle* which had been moved from Brussels to France and was loyally supported, financially as well, by the Prime Minister De Broqueville,[2] launched a campaign for a radical revision of Belgian foreign policy. Starting from ideas that were romantic in Banning's writings but had turned hard and business-like in Baie's pre-war prose,[3] he propagated an active annexationist policy relying on France. Luxemburg, Dutch Limburg, the Dutch part of Flanders, and the left bank of the Rhine should be absorbed in a new Belgium, united by deep nationalist feeling and no longer divided by linguistic or religious conflicts. It would be Roman Catholic, anti-socialist, a strong and heroic new nation.[4] Baie, too, expressed such thoughts but without bringing in religion.[5] In the circles of the Flemish movement all this made a most unfavourable impression. Such exalted nationalism not only seemed stupid and politically dangerous, it relied so strongly on France that it had outspokenly anti-Flemish overtones. Moreover, it was rightly supposed that the Le Havre government tended to find these views acceptable.

At the end of December 1915 Von Bissing announced that he wanted to reopen the University of Ghent, with Dutch as the teaching-medium. This confronted the Flemings with a painful choice. They themselves had made a Dutch-language university the centre of their pre-war aspirations. However, they deeply disliked the prospect of collaborating with the Germans and were doubtful whether it was morally permissible to accept the realization of this ideal as a gift from the enemy. Moreover, they knew that the mass of the population was inspired

---

[1] Elias, *Vlaamse Beweging* i. 17; Willemsen, op. cit., p. 29. Much material also in R. de Schrijver (ed.), *Uit het archief van Frans van Cauwelaert*, i: *Geschriften over Vlaamse Beweging en Belgische politiek, 1895–1918* (Antwerp, 1971). It should be stressed that this type of thesis was certainly not frequently put forward in the emigrant Press either. They remained exceptional: Wils, *Flamenpolitik*, pp. 108 ff.

[2] Wils, *Flamenpolitik*, p. 145.

[3] Above, pp. 436 ff.

[4] A selection of his articles in F. Neuray, *La Belgique nouvelle* (Brussels, 1918).

[5] See his pamphlet written as early as March 1915 but published in 1916: *La Belgique de demain* (Paris, 1916).

by an unsophisticated form of patriotism which, although before the war it was scorned by the socialists, disparaged by the Flemings, and thought irrelevant by the conservative Catholics, was a spontaneous response to the war as well as being positively recommended as a moral duty by all Belgian civil and ecclesiastical authorities. This sentiment was so strong, straightforward, and widespread that even the activists recognized that founding a Dutch-language university at this time could never be the popular issue they had thought it to be before 1914. Nevertheless, there seemed to be objective reasons for taking the chance. In the event of a German victory the future of the young university would be safe enough. If the Allies won, it was of vital importance to possess, as a last refuge, a Dutch-speaking university representing the best in Flemish civilization. After a total German defeat a vehement attack on the Dutch language in Belgium was to be expected, even if the Flamingants continued to refuse to collaborate with the Germans, and so, it was argued, it was necessary to seize the opportunity of building a permanent safeguard for it as quickly and as resolutely as possible. In 1916, moreover, many people thought a compromise peace the most probable outcome of the war: this would be the most satisfactory solution for the Flemings, who could then expect to preserve some autonomy within the framework of the Belgian state with the help of German pressure, whilst allied pressure would save them from annexation by the Germans. For the development of a Dutch-speaking university this was by far the best prospect.[1]

It was with such considerations in mind that Flemish intellectuals of widely divergent backgrounds accepted appointments in the new University of Ghent. The University was opened in October 1916. During the two years of its existence it developed into an institution of some significance, with some hundreds of students and some dozens of professors, most of them Belgians, the others Dutch and German. But its success remained limited. It proved very difficult to find the teachers needed. In the Netherlands sympathy with Flemish activism

---

[1] See the intelligent, sober, and tormented argumentations which led a very pious and unselfish man like Dosfel to accept a chair in the Flemish University: A. de Bruyne, *Lodewijk Dosfel, 1881–1925. Kultuurflamingant, aktivist, nationalist* (Wilrijk, 1967), pp. 176 ff.

was rare; among the Belgians most leaders of the Flemish movement—among them, August Vermeylen at Brussels and Frans van Cauwelaert who had taken refuge in the Netherlands—condemned this form of collaboration with the German authorities as unpatriotic. For the Roman Catholics the situation was extremely delicate. Cardinal Mercier, the archbishop of Mechlin, had for many years opposed all encroachments on the supremacy of French, and now during the war he emerged as the most courageous and outspoken representative of uncompromising Belgian patriotism. In his pastoral messages he gave the impression of virtually identifying piety with loyalty to the French-speaking Belgian unitary state.[1] Although members of the lower clergy in Flanders totally disagreed with his views, the entire episcopate followed Mercier's line.

To the younger generation all this looked much less relevant than to their parents. Among the grammar school pupils at Antwerp and the students at Ghent there was much sympathy for the activists, with their radicalism and spirited resistance to the essentially bourgeois tradition of Belgian patriotism. Many of the best Flemish writers in the period between the world wars had in their youth participated in 'activism' or at least showed positive appreciation of it.[2] To them activism did not mean prostrating oneself before imperial and militaristic Germany or cheapening oneself with pan-Germanist rhetoric; it meant getting out of the rut of bourgeois French, and the possibility of new intellectual explorations. During the war they adopted Expressionism as the new artistic style. Even in a social and political sense activism showed a tendency to go far beyond prewar ideals. While those who had been active in the movement

---

[1] In a letter which he sent to Pope Benedict XV on 5 August 1917 and which he showed to the Belgian clergy he wrote: 'Le patriotisme que, dans une Pastorale bien antérieure à la Guerre . . . j'appelais, à la suite de Saint-Thomas d'Aquin, la 'piété patriotique' lie les consciences. . . . M'inspirant de ce principe, j'ai déclaré . . . que ceux-là seraient traîtres à la patrie, qui seconderaient les tentatives de rupture de notre unité nationale . . .', F. Mayence (ed.), *La Correspondance de S. Em. le Cardinal Mercier avec le gouvernement allemand pendant l'occupation, 1914–1918* (Brussels, 1919), p. 377.

[2] e.g. Urbain van der Voorde, Felix Timmermans, Paul van Ostayen, Willem Elsschot, Richard Minne, Wies Moens, Achilles Mussche, Marnix Gijsen. The woodcut artist and sculptor Jozef Cantré designed a bronze commemoration medal on the occasion of the opening of the Flemish University and became the technical assistant of the Dutch professor of art history, André Jolles: W. Thys, 'Uit het leven en werk van André Jolles (1874–1946)', *De Nieuwe Taalgids*, xlvii (1954), 204.

before 1914 were experimenting with a Flemish university, and some months later with peculiar forms of Flemish autonomy, that is limiting themselves to academic culture and politics, in some Flemish towns there were groups of young activists inspired by Bolshevist ideals, admittedly of a very immature kind. Although these groups had no practical significance their appearance is interesting all the same, for it shows that activism could serve as an expression of deep dissatisfaction with society generally. Notwithstanding the lower-middle-class character of activism when it first developed in 1914 there was always an anti-bourgeois element in it. J. D. Domela Nieuwenhuis who had no sympathy with the socialism of his famous uncle—his own pan-German rhetoric differed widely from it—bitterly criticized the Flemish bourgeoisie and capitalist industry. He passionately hated the French-speaking industrialists and merchants flaunting the prosperity they owed to the labour of the miserably paid Flemish proletariat. Thus it was not by accident that activist sentiment was associated with a sort of revolutionary Marxism hostile to the nationalist attitude of the Belgian Workers' party. These young people were as much opposed to the romanticism of the Flemish movement as to Vandervelde's extreme anti-German policy. They dreamt of a peace by compromise and of autonomy for Flanders in a better society.[1]

In 1917 the activists managed at last to give political shape to their movement. This was a long and difficult process and finally it was the international situation that induced them to put aside the endless controversies they had been pursuing among themselves. Towards the end of 1916 and at the beginning of 1917 when apparently serious efforts were made to end the war, the activists thought that they had better create an organization which would enable them to stand for some form of Flemish separatism during the peace negotiations. To this end the Council of Flanders was set up in February 1917. Its first session lasted until January 1918. When the prospect of peace vanished, its ambitions altered accordingly. Efforts were made

[1] Data on these groups in M. Claeys-Van Haegendoren, *25 jaar Belgisch socialisme*, pp. 94, 103–4 and in her article 'De antwerpse socialistische federatie van 1914 tot 1921', *Res Publica*, ix (1967), 42 ff.; C. Renard, *Octobre 1917 et le mouvement ouvrier belge* (Brussels, 1967), pp. 44–5, 72–3, indicates the influence exercised by the publications of the Dutch Marxists in these circles.

to give it the character of a parliament responsible for the government of the Flemish provinces. The Germans seemed to be preparing the ground for this in March 1917 when they decreed that Belgium would henceforth be administered by two different groups of civil servants, the Flemish civil servants, residing at Brussels and their Walloon colleagues, for whom offices were found in Namur. This was a significant moment. The integrity of the Belgian state was threatened: it is debatable whether this was an advantage for the Flemings, but there can be no doubt that it was a great blow to the French-speaking civil servants who were of course not allowed to take part in the administration of Flanders and, if they were Walloons, were banished to the provincial town of Namur. The measure was therefore sharply resisted. But after long deliberations the members of Parliament, who regularly saw each other in connection with the meetings of the Comité national, decided to discourage civil servants from handing in their resignations. In accordance with the policy to which the patriots had committed themselves from the start of the war a way of expressing Belgian anger was sought that would not disrupt the state administration. For that reason only a limited number of high officials were advised to resign. The harsh measures taken by the Germans against these men ensured that their courageous opposition had the desired effect.[1]

The administrative separation was a failure. The new system operated badly under the desperately difficult circumstances of the time. The theoretically autonomous regional administrations were in fact totally dependent on the German Government in Belgium, which was of course not divided into Flemish and Walloon sections. The new arrangement was highly unpopular. Although before 1914 some Walloons and a small group of radical Flamingants had tinkered with the idea of administrative separation, its enforcement by the Germans strengthened the loyalty of the majority of the population to the strictly unitarian and centralized administration that had existed since 1830. This loyalty was increased by the peculiar behaviour of the Council of Flanders. Deeply divided over the policy to be followed and practically without any support from

[1] J. Levie, *Michel Levie (1851–1939) et le mouvement chrétien social de son temps* (Louvain, 1962), pp. 441–2.

the population, entirely dependent on the Germans in their search for independence, the Council wasted week after week in endless and fruitless, often very naïve, discussion. They produced no manifesto, no single document, no idea, no investigation that was of more than transitory significance.[1] In December 1917 the failure of the Council was so glaring that ways were sought to give it a better foundation. The Council proclaimed Flanders independent—a political separation following the administrative one—and dissolved itself. A new council, somehow elected or nominated by the people, was to take over its task in a new capacity: as a sovereign representative body based on a new constitution.[2] From February 1918 onwards a 'consultation of the people' was organized which lasted for weeks and was in fact no more than a series of sometimes relatively well-attended meetings at which the public expressed its solidarity with the new council. Both the character and the method of the procedure were revolutionary enough. The Council indeed collected some tens of thousands of signatures and then considered it could legitimately act as the chosen representative of the Flemish population. But it was to no avail. This council had no more effective power or authority than its predecessor: all the Germans did was to lavish money on it—paid of course by the Belgian taxpayer—for making propaganda. In a way this propaganda was probably successful, not because it converted many people to activism but because it created a situation which continued after 1918: the Flemish question developed into one of the most important political problems that divided the country. Before 1914 it had never been quite so serious.[3]

Compared with the activities of the activists, who may have risked their future but for the time being benefited financially from their choice, the history of a pro-Flemish party among the

[1] My judgement is not only based on the strongly anti-activist edition of part of the documents of the Council (*Les Archives du Conseil de Flandre*, Brussels, n.d., and *Het archief van den Raad van Vlaanderen*, Brussels, 1929; cf. P. Geyl in his *De Groot-Nederlandsche gedachte*, Antwerp, 1930, ii. 151–69), but also on the works of Willemsen, *Vlaams-nationalisme* and Elias, *Vlaamse Beweging*, which are certainly not hostile to activism.

[2] Not before October 1918 was a draft for a Flemish constitution at last completed. Much in it was taken from the Belgian constitution of 1831 and the Dutch of 1887. Texts in *Archives*, pp. 267 ff.

[3] Elias, *Vlaamse Beweging* i. 87–105.

soldiers on the IJzer front—the so-called Front movement—
is of a more serious, indeed an almost tragic, character.[1]
The higher ranks in the army were not only pro-French and
French-speaking but decidedly anti-Flemish. Within the army
though the majority of the soldiers were Flemings; their
number grew from 60 per cent to 80 per cent and most of them
of course knew no other language than their own. For that
very reason they were not qualified for promotion or service
behind the front and were doomed to stay in the trenches
without much hope of being relieved. Some Flemish intellectuals in the army interested themselves on their behalf and
started study-circles, and there were other strictly Roman
Catholic and outspokenly pro-Flemish unions which sought to
raise their morale and improve them spiritually. At first the
commanders-in-chief tolerated this, although grudgingly and
with deep disdain. But in February 1917 the study-circles were
banned. This was unwise, for the leaders of the circles continued
their work which, having thus acquired an illegal character,
tended to become more radical. Emphasis from now on was
laid much less on morals and religion than on general politics.
In July 1917 the leaders published an open letter to King
Albert in which they listed their grievances and cautiously
defended the activists in the occupied parts of Belgium against
the accusation of treason levelled against them by the government. They declared themselves willing to continue to fight
against the Germans provided that Flanders could after the
war count on a fairer deal. Although this sounded provocative,
in comparison with the serious sedition in the French army in
April and May 1917 the unrest behind the IJzer front was
fairly moderate and expressed itself mainly in words. The army
commanders acted with the same restraint: they restricted
themselves to exercising an imperfect censorship and imposing
some relatively mild penalties.

But in the atmosphere of deep *malaise* and defeatism that had
penetrated into the allied armies, even this was sufficient to
radicalize Flemish propaganda. In an authoritative document,
drafted in October 1917, the leaders of the Front movement
demanded that after the war Flanders be granted full self-
government. In the spring of 1918 a delegate of the movement

[1] On the following see ibid. 106-55 and Willemsen, pp. 82-108.

crossed the front, together with some others who had not been instructed to do so, and was allowed by the Germans to get in touch with the Council of Flanders and the activists in the occupied region. This caused a lot of confusion. The delegate went far beyond his instructions when in his conversation with the Council of Flanders he intimated that at least 50,000 Flemish on the IJzer would be willing to support activism if they survived a large-scale German attack. A Flemish revolution seemed at hand and there was much talk of soviets and Bolshevists. At the front the Flemish leaders were far removed from this sort of thinking. They preferred to believe that as a result of their triumphs over the Germans and of an allied victory, Flemish soldiers would play a decisive part in post-war Belgium, able to realize their desire for Flemish autonomy either through the benevolence of a grateful nation or, if this was not forthcoming, through violence. In June 1918 the leaders of the Front movement decided on their line of action. If the Germans did launch a large-scale offensive, Flemish soldiers were to put up serious resistance but do everything possible at the same time to avoid being slaughtered. With the end of the war in sight it was as important to save Belgian honour as to keep unimpaired the newly developed Flemish strength—the leaders, too, counted on 50,000 militant Flamingant soldiers. Of course, this somewhat subversive statement ran counter to military discipline, but it was not apparently widely circulated and it remained without practical significance. The German offensive did not come and when in September the Belgian army itself went into the attack the Flemish soldiers obeyed their orders. The triumphant Belgian army in no way backed the activists who were either put into prison or hastily fled abroad. The 50,000 militant Flamingant soldiers who had played such a heroic role in the dreams of the activists proved obedient soldiers. They longed for home and had no interest in an activist revolution. To the deep disappointment of the leaders of the Front movement most of them were unable and unprepared to embark upon any action in defence of the Flemish cause. It had all been illusion, vanity, intellectual speculation. It was not the activists who triumphed after the war, nor the IJzer soldiers, nor even the Belgian government-in-exile, but the bankers and managers of the Comité national.

2. *The Netherlands, 1914–18*

In the Netherlands public opinion did not look upon the First World War as an ideological conflict in which every responsible human being was morally obliged to take sides. In the eyes of the Dutch the war was caused by the ambition of the Great Powers and there was no good reason for trusting one side more than another. When the United States joined in the war in 1917 nobody was really surprised that a country which had until then emphatically supported the rights of neutral Powers now disregarded them as cynically as, in the opinion of the Dutch, the Entente Powers and the Central Powers had done since 1914. The neutrality the Dutch Government tried to maintain[1] meant a refusal to take sides in conflicts in which the Dutch did not want to get involved and which they felt were no concern of theirs. 'Our self-esteem', an excellent commentator wrote, 'told us that we were too good to fatten other people's ambitions with our blood.'[2] Neither the propaganda of the Germans nor of the Allies influenced Dutch public opinion. This does not mean that in general the Dutch considered themselves morally superior to the Great Powers, although it is true that they derived a certain complacent sense of virtue from their neutrality. They were too painfully aware, however, that their fate depended on the policy of the belligerents to be able easily to maintain a spirit of moral self-exaltation. Of course they realized that the outcome of the war would affect the future of the Netherlands, and it was fairly widely recognized that a peace imposed by the Allies would constitute less of a threat to Dutch independence than a German victory. But it was still such a short time since the Boer War that doubts were entertained even on this point. Probably Dutch public opinion preferred on the whole a compromise peace. Wilson's declarations of April 1917 concerning a world made 'safe for democracy' and the 'rights and liberties of small nations' may have sounded fine in Dutch ears, but the

---

[1] The Netherlands did not belong to the nations guaranteeing Belgian neutrality in 1839. But it had signed the London Treaty of 1867 which guaranteed the neutrality of Luxemburg: since this was a collective guarantee, it lapsed at the moment one of the signatories, in this case Germany, violated it.

[2] H. T. Colenbrander, *Studiën en aanteekeningen over Nederlandsche politiek (1909–1919)* (The Hague, 1920), p. 145.

proposition that these ends could only be reached through the total defeat of Germany was decidedly less attractive and less self-evident.[1]

In August 1914 the Netherlands was no better equipped to counter a German attack than Belgium. Its army was about the same size. But it fitted German strategy to respect Dutch neutrality, a neutrality which the British Cabinet thought to be more advantageous to the enemy than to the Allies.[2] In September 1914 the Dutch were made to understand by London that in the event of an allied victory they would pay for their neutrality by losing Dutch Flanders to Belgium.[3] The Dutch Government refused to be intimidated and stuck to its policy of strict neutrality. In general it knew that, if only for the sake of Dutch colonial interests, it would have to opt for the allied rather than the German cause if such a choice were ever forced upon it; nobody, however, doubted for one moment that for many reasons—of a political, economic, and moral nature—neutrality was incomparably more satisfactory than any alliance.[4] Early in October 1914 a discussion took place in the Cabinet which can serve to illustrate the curious predicament in which the Dutch found themselves. The situation was dangerous. The Germans were laying siege to Antwerp and the risk of Dutch neutrality being infringed grew as the fighting approached their frontier. If neutrality were to be strictly maintained it might be necessary for Dutch troops to take action against allied armies pursuing German soldiers across the Belgian border into Dutch territory. In that case a Dutch

[1] There is no good analysis of Dutch public opinion during the First World War. Th. H. J. Stoelinga, *Russische revolutie en vredesverwachtingen in de Nederlandse pers maart 1917–maart 1918* (Bussum, 1967) has interesting data on the attitude of the periodical Press.

[2] C. Smit (ed.), *Bescheiden*, 3rd period, iv (The Hague, 1962), p. 22: conversation between the British Foreign Secretary and the Dutch minister in London, 5 Aug. 1914.

[3] Ibid. 122. Even if the Netherlands should join England, the Dutch Foreign Minister expected in October 1914 that Dutch Flanders would become Belgian: ibid. 156. Cf. J. de Vries (ed.), *Herinneringen en dagboek van Ernst Heldring (1871–1954)* (3 vols., Groningen, 1970), i. 197.

[4] Only one minister, M. W. F. Treub, passed for a convinced champion of the Entente. Minister F. E. Posthuma who joined the Cabinet at the end of October 1914 was pro-German. The other ministers had less pronounced opinions. The Dutch ministers in the United States, Germany, China, Russia, and Rumania were considered to be pro-German by the Entente diplomacy, probably not always correctly.

decision to fight the Allies would be entirely dependent on the actions of other people and in no way a considered policy to further Dutch interest. A number of Cabinet ministers sought ways of reducing this element of pure chance in Dutch decisions and proposed making it known to Germany that if the Dutch got involved in the war, no matter how or why, they would always side with the Allies. It would be absurd, they argued, to allow the nation to be drawn by circumstances and the logic of neutral principle into supporting Germany when a German victory would lead to the annexation of Belgium and might well put an end to the independence of the Netherlands, which would be exposed to Germany from the east and the south. According to these ministers Dutch interests demanded that what they called the 'idealistic' policy of neutrality should be abandoned.

The majority in the Cabinet, however, disagreed. The Prime Minister, Cort van der Linden, stressed the moral value of strict neutrality. 'Whereas all who take part in the war', he said, 'are bound to become disastrously one-sided in their opinions and driven by hatred and passion, the neutral states are able to keep their moral and intellectual powers unaffected [for the benefit of the whole of Europe].' But this was not the main argument. To the majority, the decisive consideration was the prospect that, if the Dutch made it clear to the Germans that they intended to maintain their neutrality but that this neutrality was of a pro-British disposition, this might lead to a German invasion which they could not resist.[1]

The problem, however, was much more complicated than the ministers then realized, for the commander-in-chief of the army and navy, General C. J. Snijders, had ideas on the matter that were flatly opposed to those of the majority as well as the minority in the Cabinet. In February 1915 he asked the government whom they regarded as a potential future enemy so that he could take the necessary precautions. The government answered that they intended to oppose any deliberate breach of Dutch neutrality; but so absolute was this neutrality, so unlimited Dutch freedom of action, that the government could not even guarantee in case of war to join the enemies of the

[1] 'Notulen van de ministerraad van 3 oktober 1914', Smit (ed.), *Bescheiden* iv. 145–59.

aggressor it was fighting against.[1] Snijders was not satisfied. In March 1916 Cort van der Linden had to repeat to him the government's standpoint. He added that the government would not make the mistake, which had ruined Belgium, of joining the opposing party as soon as a breach of neutrality had taken place.[2] In January 1917 Snijders put the problem still more pungently when he asked what the government would do if both parties were to violate the Dutch frontier at the same time.[3] Once more the Cabinet maintained that the principle was simple enough: both aggressors were to be opposed if necessary, although it would depend on circumstances what measures were actually taken.[4] The Minister of War repeated the Cabinet's criticism of Belgian policy in August 1914. The fact that the Belgians had given up their neutrality as soon as the Germans invaded their territory had in his opinion weakened Belgium's position.[5]

Quite understandably Snijders got increasingly irritated by such an excess of academic theorizing. But how paradoxical his own attitude was became apparent in April 1918. Relations with Germany were tense at the time and The Hague had seriously to reckon with a German attack. Snijders then went to the trouble of pointing out that opposing such an attack would be meaningless. Even though the army had more than doubled since 1914 it would still be impossible to resist the German troops for any length of time. The situation was different as far as the Entente was concerned. If the Netherlands in spite of everything was drawn into the war, she should opt for an alliance that gave her a reasonable chance of victory—in other words, join the Germans.[6] The Minister of War and the whole Cabinet were deeply shocked by Snijders's philosophy.[7] His defeatism and his political preferences were quite contrary to the spirit of Dutch neutralism. In 1918, moreover, the Minister of War had a more optimistic view than

---

[1] *Bescheiden* iv. 306–10. Cf. C. T. de Jong, 'De Nederlandse neutraliteit tijdens de Eerste Wereldoorlog', *Tijdschrift voor Geschiedenis*, lxv (1952), 259–60.

[2] P. H. Ritter, jun., *De donkere poort* (2 vols., The Hague, 1931), ii. 19 ff.

[3] C. Smit (ed.), *Bescheiden*, 3rd period, v. i (The Hague, 1964), pp. 1–4.

[4] Ibid. 14–21.   [5] Ibid. 50.

[6] Ibid. 534–46. Cf. De Jong, 'De Nederlandse neutraliteit' 268–9.

[7] See also S. L. van der Wal (ed.), *Herinneringen van Jhr. Mr. B. C. de Jonge* (Groningen, 1968), pp. 40–8.

Snijders about the possibilities of holding out against a German attack, and he was not prepared to regard the many millions of guilders Snijders had spent on defence as wasted. But when the Queen was asked to dismiss Snijders, she refused. For various reasons she was annoyed with the Cabinet, which in her opinion had done too little to ensure food supplies.[1] Moreover, her dynastic pride was deeply offended by the decision of the United States and the Allied Powers to seize the Dutch merchant fleet (20 March 1918), an act which the Dutch Government had done nothing about.[2] Rather than dismiss Snijders she would have preferred to see the whole Cabinet quit office. But with general elections due in July 1918 the Cabinet chose to stay on, arguing that it would be irresponsible to expose the country to a political crisis in such threatening circumstances. From a constitutional point of view the situation was of course impossible. The Cabinet ought to have acted the moment the Commander-in-Chief first expressed his divergent views on the nature of Dutch neutrality, that is as long ago as early in 1915. It failed to do so. Perhaps this was understandable for Snijders was undoubtedly an accomplished soldier and he would have been difficult to replace as commander-in-chief. Practical considerations governed the Cabinet's attitude.

This was also true in a more general way. Dutch statesmen tried to accommodate the belligerent nations as best they could, allowing both parties to profit in equal measure from the advantages Dutch neutrality could offer. But to achieve such a policy the Dutch were bound to make far-reaching concessions. Although they were undoubtedly right in doing so, it meant that despite all their statements of principle they were not

---

[1] G. Puchinger, *Colijn en het einde van de coalitie. De geschiedenis van de kabinetsformaties 1918–1924* (Kampen, 1969), pp. 27 ff.

[2] Cf. *Herinneringen en dagboek Heldring* i. 237, 682. The indignation caused by the seizure of the Dutch ships—it concerned 135 ships with a net tonnage of about 500,000—was in the Netherlands general and unusually vehement: Charlotte A. van Manen, *De Nederlandsche Overzee Trustmaatschappij* (8 vols., The Hague, 1935), iv. 247 ff. The Dutch sailors refused to enter American service and left their ships (ibid. 255). In fact, the requisition was favourable for Dutch politics. The Dutch could not be accused by Germany of putting their means of transportation at the disposal of the United States and the Allies and thus violating their obligations as neutrals. Queen Wilhelmina thought the Foreign Minister too pro-Entente: Puchinger, op. cit., p. 31.

really defending Dutch neutrality. At an early stage they had already allowed the Entente substantially to curtail neutral rights. The problem was that for food and raw materials the Netherlands was as dependent as Belgium on foreign markets and had to do everything within its power to keep open its overseas trade. Naturally the Entente Powers were unwilling to allow neutral ships full freedom of navigation. They demanded a guarantee from the Dutch Government that contraband goods transported in neutral ships would not be sold to Germany. This the Dutch Government did not see fit to give; it would not, they thought, be consistent with Dutch neutrality and would undoubtedly irritate the Germans. Then some leading commercial figures intervened after close consultation with the British commercial attaché.[1] In November a number of Dutch shipowners, merchants, and bankers founded a joint stock company, the Netherlands Overseas Trust Company (NOT) which was organized in such a way as to be able to provide the required guarantee.[2] Its director was C. J. K. van Aalst (1866–1939), the president of the Nederlandsche Handel-Maatschappij (Netherlands Trading Company). It is noteworthy that the NOT, which developed into a state within a state and did much to ensure food supplies in the Netherlands and Belgium, was run by a banker just as the Belgian Comité national was led by the director of the Société générale. The fact that both the Netherlands Trading Company and the Société générale were founded by King William I during the years of the United Kingdom is also worth noting.

The Netherlands Overseas Trust succeeded in keeping Dutch trade going. But as early as April 1915 the company had gone beyond what was legally permissible. When Britain decided to intensify its economic war against Germany in March she asked the NOT to guarantee that no goods whatever, contraband or otherwise, imported in Dutch ports should be sold to the Central Powers. The NOT gave such a guarantee, wrongly.[3] In the first place the British demand was difficult to justify

---

[1] He even claimed in his autobiography to have taken the initiative and to have designed the whole plan: Sir Francis Oppenheimer, *Stranger within* (London, 1960), pp. 244 ff.

[2] Van Manen, op. cit. i. 74.

[3] Ibid. ii. 54 ff.; *Herinneringen en dagboek Heldring* i. 197 ff. In July 1915 NOT became still more dependent on Britain: Van Manen, ii. 134.

from a legal point of view and for the sake of sound international relations it would have been better if the NOT had at least voiced a protest. Moreover, the NOT assumed a responsibility it was far beyond its capacity to fulfil. Until the beginning of 1917, when its influence began to diminish, the organization expanded into an extremely powerful institution with a personnel of about 1,000 men—whereas the Dutch Foreign Office had only 45 civil servants in 1914. It controlled the entire foreign trade of the Netherlands. But notwithstanding the government's support it could not prevent large-scale and often very efficiently organized smuggling across the eastern border. On the one hand, the NOT acted as an instrument of the Entente; on the other, its success as well as its influence caused illegal imports into Germany to assume enormous proportions. There was little the government could do about it. By its narrow interpretation of the principle of neutrality it had in fact abandoned its responsibilities.

Even so Dutch foreign policy was not all bad. It was a flexible and sober policy solely intended to serve Dutch interests, very different from the high-pitched messianism which before 1914 had characterized the vision of some Dutchmen of their country's place in the world.[1] Domestic policy, too, was calm and cautious. The Cabinet remained in office until the autumn of 1918; although not tied to a party programme, it had a progressive liberal character. The main task it had assumed in 1913 was the introduction of universal suffrage which required a revision of the constitution. It also had a programme of social legislation, with the introduction of old age pensions as its most important item. Essential though these reforms were, however, they were certainly not meant to promote a thorough reconstruction of society. The Cabinet wished to adapt the state's institutions to social developments which had already taken place; its policy was not subordinate to any intellectual system. The same pragmatic attitude prevailed in its treatment of the war crisis. Innumerable problems forced it to intervene in social life and it was sufficiently progressive to do this without reservations. At the same time it was so essentially liberal that it never tried to take advantage of circumstances to give society a new direction and a new shape. The

[1] Above, pp. 421 ff.

government reacted whenever there was an injustice to be
repaired, misery to be prevented, a danger to be controlled;
it withdrew as soon as the situation seemed to permit it. But
circumstances inevitably obliged it to increase its activities and
as a result the number of civil servants and government offices
in the Netherlands grew enormously during the war.

Legislation dealing with the crisis started in 1914 but it was
very restricted during the early years.[1] There was no reason for
haste. Unemployment was not high and food supplies were
sufficient—although the government had to intervene in order
to prevent large quantities being sold to Germany at high
prices. In 1914, 1915, and 1916 Dutch industry, agriculture, and
navigation did very well. As had been the case so often in
Dutch history, the country benefited from its neutrality. Not
only the big firms and the farmers prospered but all sorts of
private persons as well—from shopkeepers to soldiers garrisoned
on the eastern border, who engaged in the highly profitable
smuggling trade. The national income rose from 2,346 million
guilders in 1914 to 3,202 million in 1917 which meant a real
increase even though the purchasing power of the guilder fell.[2]
The government never attempted to take advantage of profits
made in such extraordinary circumstances in order to meet
its own rapidly increasing expenditure. During one of the
few dramatic parliamentary debates of this period it rejected a
proposal from liberals and socialists both in Parliament and
outside for a capital levy on private persons and enterprises.
Despite a well-organized, large-scale agitation the government
stuck to its own policy of issuing a loan.[3] It turned out to be an
extremely successful policy and in the years that followed the
government continued to finance its extraordinary expenses
through loans with interest and redemption covered through
temporary increases in direct and indirect taxes. From 1914 to
1919 the public debt doubled in size but the yield from taxes
increased even more.[4]

[1] See C. W. de Vries, *Schets eener parlementaire geschiedenis van Nederland* iv (The
Hague, 1955), pp. 248–52.
[2] According to Brugmans's calculations in *Paardenkracht en mensenmacht*, p. 454.
[3] M. W. F. Treub, *Oorlogstijd* (Haarlem, 1916), pp. 351 ff.
[4] De Vries, *Schets* iv. 254. However, some new taxes amounted to the capital levy
rejected in 1914. Very important was also the 30 per cent levy on war profits
introduced in 1916 which produced 161 million guilders in 1917 and 157 in 1918.

In 1917 and 1918 the situation became more critical. The economy stagnated to such an extent and supplies became so scarce that the government was forced to ration an increasing number of articles. At the same time the purchasing power of the population diminished because of rapidly spreading unemployment in industry and trade and the high cost of living. This led the government to fix prices for the goods it distributed that were lower than those it had paid when purchasing them. There was no principle involved here. Although it was after all moving in a new direction the Cabinet felt no need to justify the notion that in such a period of scarcity the state is responsible for providing each subject with the means to buy essential foodstuffs and the other necessities of life. Of course the system was by no means perfect or equitable. The well-to-do could go on buying on the black market at exorbitant prices. But the government was forced to intervene in agriculture as well. It ordered the farmers to grow crops that were indispensable for the supply of food to the population and took over practically the whole harvest. When the farmers, tempted by the high prices for meat, butter, and cheese in the export market, began to neglect crop-growing, the government ordered them to reduce their cattle and to grow more corn and potatoes.

Notwithstanding all these measures the situation became each day more critical. By the end of the war the condition of the workers, badly clothed, underfed, miserably housed, was desperate. Although most of them were not revolutionary-minded they were doubtless full of resentment against the still ostentatious luxury displayed by the individuals who had made huge profits, and against the Dutch bourgeoisie generally— the shipowners, bankers, and merchants—who had done very well during the first years of the war and behaved with due caution during the last. 'In no other country', wrote the famous revolutionary poetess and historian Henriette Roland Holst, 'did the bourgeoisie make capital out of the catastrophe of the war with such shameless cynicism, by all possible means, even the lowest and most despicable.'[1] Her statement is arbitrary because it cannot be proved, and probably incorrect because at least in 1917 and 1918 life was difficult for all

---

[1] Henriette Roland Holst–Van der Schalk, *Kapitaal* ii. 118. The quoted sentence was written in 1926.

sections of the Dutch population: dividends and bonuses dropped too.[1] But even so it clearly indicates the apparent widening of the gulf between rich and poor in a period during which the bourgeoisie seemed to triumph. And in a way it did triumph. This, in any case, is strongly suggested by the fact that the NOT, a company of bankers and shipowners, managed to acquire enormous power and entered autonomously into negotiations with foreign legations, conducting its own foreign policy. In the Netherlands, just as in Belgium, the bourgeois élite apparently still dominated society; its influence manifested itself when party politics ceased and gaps appeared in the administrative apparatus which only this élite was able to fill.

In August 1914 the political parties decided to suspend their contests until better days. On 3 August Troelstra stated in the Second Chamber that the SDAP sided with the government and that the national idea prevailed over any conflicts within the country. He approved of the mobilization and the defence expenses. This remained the policy of the SDAP throughout the war, in spite of strong opposition from some in the ranks of the party, and even though Troelstra himself modified his basic principle to some extent. To him it was essential for the Netherlands not to sacrifice her proletariat in a senseless imperialist slaughter. There were moments when he pushed his interpretation of the situation so far that he seemed to abandon his original standpoint. Thus in April 1918 he was of the opinion that the Netherlands should passively allow the Germans to invade the country—such an invasion was feared at the time—and avoid at all costs getting involved in the war.[2] If developed further, this would have led him to oppose not neutrality itself but the government's policy of armed neutrality and would have brought him closer to those in his party who from 1914 onwards were against giving any support to the national defence and sometimes advocated massive refusal of military service.[3] However, Troelstra could not quite accept these consequences. Others again, mainly inspired by the attitude of the Belgian socialist party, wanted the Netherlands,

---

[1] Brugmans, *Paardenkracht*, p. 455.

[2] Troelstra, *Gedenkschriften*, iv. 91 ff.

[3] Ibid. iii. 303 ff.; W. H. Vliegen, *Die onze kracht ontwaken deed* (3 vols., Amsterdam, 1926–38), iii. 32 ff.

if the country were forced to give up neutrality, to join the democratic Entente against autocratic Germany and thus, unlike Troelstra, no longer interpreted the war as a struggle between imperialists all equally inimical to the proletariat.[1] But although in heated discussions strongly divergent points of view were defended in the SDAP, in practice the party faithfully supported the government's defence policy, which was a policy of national self-interest. Ideologically Troelstra's arguments seemed perhaps purer than those of the 'chauvinist' socialists in the belligerent countries; this apparent purity, however, he owed not to a fundamentally different attitude towards the problem of war but to the fact that the Netherlands remained neutral.[2]

To the other parties the problem was far less complicated; as a result there were hardly any important parliamentary debates on defence and foreign policy. With regard to home affairs the situation was different. In the autumn of 1915 the Prime Minister Cort van der Linden started the procedure needed to revise the constitution. It soon became apparent that Parliament was prepared to accept almost unanimously both the immediate introduction of universal male suffrage and the financial equalization of state and private primary schools. Nobody seemed to feel like continuing the pre-war debates on those subjects. In December 1917 the revised constitution was promulgated. The process of formally democratizing the state was nearly completed—women's suffrage was introduced in 1920, and private secondary schools too were some time later given the same financial advantages as state schools. In July 1918 the new democracy came into operation with the first elections under universal male suffrage and proportional representation. Given the precarious circumstances the election campaign was understandably rather dull. The confessional parties saw no need to revise their traditional programmes, rightly calculating that universal suffrage would not harm

---

[1] Troelstra, op. cit., iii. 311; Vliegen, *Onze kracht* iii. 26 ff.

[2] Troelstra, together with Camille Huysmans, the Belgian secretary of the Executive Committee of the International Socialist Office which in 1914 moved from Brussels to The Hague, tried to maintain the Second International. Within the international movement they steered a sort of middle course between the 'chauvinist' socialists and the internationalist revolutionaries who in 1915 met in Zimmerwald.

them for the time being. However, they did change the style of their electoral campaigns. Before 1917 there was no proportional representation in the Netherlands and parties that felt more or less congenial were forced to co-operate closely and to support each other's candidates if they wanted to obtain the majority in the constituencies for themselves or their political friends. Proportional representation made this unnecessary and enabled the parties to march independently. The great disadvantage of this was, of course, that it was no longer necessary before the elections to start negotiations about the possibility of future co-operation, which made it much more difficult to form a Cabinet than it had been. At the same time proportional representation inevitably led to a considerable increase in the number of parties represented in Parliament—in 1918 there were no less than 17 parties in the Second Chamber, of which 8 had only one seat. In 1918 the laborious job of constructing a Cabinet powerful enough to hold out against a strongly divided Parliament, in which no single party constituted a majority, began only after the elections. It had to be done by the confessionals. Both the Catholics and the anti-revolutionaries had benefited from the system of universal suffrage to such an extent that, together with the Christian-Historicals who had done slightly less well, they held 50 seats in a chamber of 100.

For the liberals the elections were disastrous. In 1913, although divided among three parties, they obtained 40 seats of which in 1918 only 15 were left. The SDAP made considerable progress but less than expected. At the first ballot of the 1913 elections they had obtained 18 seats of which 3 had been lost at the second ballot. In 1918 they got 22 seats. But although it was of course significant that they proved so much more powerful than the liberals, it was obvious that neither universal suffrage nor the miseries of the war had brought about a political landslide towards the Left. For the first time the communist party entered the Chamber in the persons of Wijnkoop and Van Ravesteyn, who in November 1918 rebaptized their SDP—founded in 1909—Communistische Partij Holland (CPH). During the war they had campaigned for extreme state intervention to control food supplies and total demobilization. Naturally they interpreted the successes of the

Bolshevist. revolution in Russia as the proof of their being theoretically right.[1] During the last few years they had displayed much energy, much demagogy and hysterical eloquence, and specialized in the roughest abuse—copied from the style of the radical pamphleteers of the 1780s and 1790s. Now they saw their diligence and doctrinal purity rewarded by seats in a Chamber dominated by the confessionals. They claimed to be able to understand the deepest causes of world events by their scientific methods, and personally to participate in such. events as a result of their internationalism. They must have felt strangers in the Dutch political arena, in which even the urgent drama of the war in its last phase could not disturb the leisurely pace at which those responsible chose to form a new Cabinet. Not until September 1918 did the parties at last succeed, after complicated consultations amongst a tiny group of political leaders and confusing interventions from the Queen.[2] A Catholic nobleman from the province of Limburg, Ruys de Beerenbrouck, became Prime Minister in a Cabinet of confessionals.

In November 1918 the new Cabinet found itself in a curious position. Throughout the year there had been signs of restiveness in the country. The orthodox Marxists of the SDP and the revolutionary anarchists, who were still drawing on the themes of Domela Nieuwenhuis dating from the 1880s, had been trying hard and in close co-operation with each other to exploit the economic difficulties in order to provoke numerous wildcat strikes and demonstrations. The SDAP was put in the uncomfortable position of having to oppose this movement and ensure that efforts to organize a general strike should meet with no success. The socialist leaders were of the opinion that revolutionary action against a government that might be held responsible for the way in which scarce victuals were distributed but not for the scarcity itself was senseless and harmful. Not even the reformist members of the party board, however, denied that there was something profoundly unsatisfactory in the situation in which they found themselves.[3] In 1918 the

---

[1] As editors of the daily *De Tribune* they took pride in the fact that their paper, 'the only maximalist daily in the whole of Western Europe', acted as early as 1917 as 'an official outpost, a sort of organ of the Russian Revolution': Van Ravesteyn, *Wording*, p. 168.

[2] Puchinger, pp. 42–161.   [3] Vliegen, *Onze kracht*, iii. 368.

feeling of national solidarity which had manifested itself in 1914 and made support for the government appear quite natural had completely disappeared. The contrast between rich and poor had become too deep. But although it was distressing for the socialist leaders in such circumstances to continue their cautious policies they still felt obliged to do so, and the result of the July elections did nothing to ease their position. The various revolutionary parties had won nearly 50,000 votes, and although this was only one-sixth of the total number of votes cast for the socialists as a whole, it was disagreeable that they should have won considerable support in Amsterdam. There was reason to expect that the tendency in the labour organizations to adopt more radical views would increase, whereas national policy in general clearly moved in a conservative direction.

Shortly after the government had taken office a wave of disturbances took place which caused grave concern. On 25 October 1918 soldiers in an army camp on the Veluwe started rioting. After an inquiry the suspicion that this was inspired by a revolutionary programme and had a political motive was invalidated; if the revolt, caused by the soldiers' anger at not getting leave and the bad food, demonstrated anything at all, it was that army discipline was seriously undermined by the long years spent in idleness and useless training. Following the riots Troelstra asked on 5 November for the dismissal of Snijders, which indeed followed within a few days. The Cabinet's decision to dispense with his services was far from elegant. He ought to have been discharged much earlier for his political views, but it was improper to send him away now at the very end of the war because of a relatively unimportant incident. But to Troelstra the decision represented a success. Troelstra lived during these days under great nervous tension. He was an extremely emotional man whose nature was split by irreconcilable conflicts, a most capable member of Parliament as well as a romantic revolutionary, a cautious tactician as well as a brilliant popular orator profoundly moved and influenced by the enthusiasm of the response which he found in mass meetings. All his life it had been Germany that had provided the models for his policies and his judgements. The revolt in the German army, breaking out shortly after the riots in the Netherlands, apparently convinced him that the Dutch soldiers, too, were ripe for revolution. Some socialist leaders in Rotterdam, a town badly stricken by the stagnation in shipping, confirmed his opinion that the German revolution would be continued in the Netherlands. On 9 November the burgomaster of Rotterdam, Zimmerman, asked these leaders to help maintain public order in the event of a revolutionary outbreak. Zimmerman was a haughty, resolute pessimist, profoundly interested in the classics, who with stoical calmness wanted to ensure that the collapse of civilization as he knew it would at least run an orderly course.[1] Troelstra and his adherents immediately jumped to the conclusion that the bourgeoisie was ready to surrender its power. In a speech at Rotterdam, on 11 November, Troelstra proclaimed that this would soon happen. On 12 November he delivered a brilliant speech in Parliament lasting for hours, in which he repeated his announcement.

The government was well informed of what had been going on in Rotterdam since 9 November. The Roman Catholic trade unions and other Catholic organizations had immediately launched a large-scale appeal to the public. Troops were dispatched to Amsterdam, Rotterdam, and The Hague, and the voluntary militia was called up. On the advice of a small group of active Protestant politicians the British Government was persuaded to declare on 12 November that it would not allow any transport of food into the Netherlands if the monarchy were abolished. The demonstrations of loyalty to the Cabinet and the Crown, the publications and meetings, assumed enormous proportions. On 14 November Troelstra told the Second Chamber that he no longer foresaw a revolution. The week ended with a long series of increasingly massive manifestations of loyalty to fatherland, monarchy, and government. The socialist workers mounted no countermeasures at all, apart from a few badly planned and unpopular activities by the Amsterdam communists which proved only that they were noisy but ineffective. Troelstra himself never tried to make the working classes participate in events nor to lead them in any concerted action. The revolution he had expected

[1] H. J. Scheffer, *November 1918. Journaal van een revolutie die niet doorging* (Amsterdam, 1968), p. 254.

would essentially have been a voluntary abdication of what he called the 'bourgeoisie'.

Troelstra's 'error' had an important effect on developments during the period between the world wars. It took the SDAP many years to recover some of the prestige lost in November 1918. But the party itself had been in no way responsible for the unhappy affair. Only a few members of the party's executive board and a few parliamentarians had condoned Troelstra's adventure. The leaders of the labour unions and the party were quite convinced that the Dutch workers had no revolutionary ambitions, and that whatever Troelstra might say, the army and police forces were generally loyal to the government. But they could not keep him quiet, nor do anything to counterbalance the expectations he had raised. Although his role inside and outside the party was almost finished, the party itself had for a long time to live with the reputation so acquired of being dangerous and unreliable. Moreover, the reaction provoked by Troelstra's threats greatly strengthened the position of the government and the monarchy, emphasizing the conservatism which had characterized the Netherlands during the war. On the other hand, the unrest created by Troelstra enabled the confessional government quickly to carry its Christian democratic programme of social measures into effect. Both in the eyes of the frightened masses and of the higher classes this social policy was a guarantee against a repetition of what had seemed for one tense week the start of revolution.

3. Belgian–Dutch Relations in 1919

In Belgium there were two groups of a revolutionary disposition: Flemish extremists and German soldiers. The hope of the former that unrest in the Belgian army would lead to the formation of Flemish soldiers' councils had proved totally unrealistic. But in the German army the revolutionary movement continued. With amusement and not without some uneasiness the inhabitants of Brussels observed the revolutionary antics of the German soldiers, with their councils and their actions against the officers. But when the German soldiers attempted to involve the Belgian workers in their revolution and to set up workers' councils, the socialist leaders in Brussels hurried to make it clear to them that there was not a shadow of solidarity between the Belgian proletarians, cruelly oppressed by the occupying forces for four long years, and the German army. The only thing the Belgians wanted was that the Germans should leave Brussels immediately and in good order.[1] The last troops left in fact on 17 November 1918; they carried home with them not only booty of all sorts but the revolution as well.

The Belgians had their own ways of reforming society and political life, and it was during these November weeks that rapid and radical political developments began, the details of which are still not quite clear. On 11 November King Albert received at his headquarters in Loppem—a village near Bruges —several Belgian politicians who had lived in Belgium during the war and knew well the feelings of the people. On 13 November the King was given a reception by the town of Ghent. There he and his cabinet—the Le Havre Cabinet—had a long interview with the president of the Comité national, Francqui. During the evening of that day the ministers decided to resign and on 17 November they handed in their resignation to the King. On 21 November it was announced that a new Cabinet had been constituted. This was led by a Catholic Prime Minister and had six Catholic, three liberal, and three socialist ministers—a cabinet of national solidarity, far more progressive than its predecessor. On 22 November King Albert addressed Parliament and announced radical reforms: straightforward universal male franchise without additional votes for specific categories, equal rights for the various national languages, the foundation of a new Flemish university at Ghent, and the repeal of Belgium's obligatory neutrality.

Several factors determined the course of events. The government-in-exile, divided over various issues and during the past few years repeatedly changed, was anxious to hand over its responsibilities at the earliest opportunity. It could do this even sooner than it had expected once it was clear that in Belgium itself some fundamental political decisions had already been taken. Within and around the Comité national it was agreed that only a three-party government would be able to

[1] L. Bertrand, *Souvenirs d'un meneur socialiste* (2 vols., Brussels, 1927), ii. 309 ff. Cf. Renard, op. cit., p. 76.

organize the country's reconstruction. This meant that the Catholics must volunteer to give up their supremacy and to make the vital concessions with regard to the franchise they had always refused to make in the past. The Christian democrats were indeed willing to do so. It was they who opened the way for the Loppem government by winning over the Catholic party, with the exception of Woeste and his followers, and it was the liberals and the socialists who profited most from this situation.[1] There are two points which deserve some emphasis. In the first place it is clear that Francqui's influence on the course of events was important, although it is difficult to say exactly how decisive it was. In all probability it was Francqui who suggested to the King that Delacroix should be the new Prime Minister. Since early 1917 there had been regular meetings at Brussels in connection with Solvay's and Francqui's Comité national, both in the office of the Société générale and at the Institut Solvay (remarkable for its ambition to reform society on the basis of the theory of radical-liberal productivism). Hundreds of politicians from all parties had met there and taken decisions on the programme of the first post-war Cabinet. The second point is that from 1917 onwards various influential men had been repeatedly and emphatically warning the authorities against the dangers of a post-war revolution. There can be no doubt that the speed with which the statesmen acted was at least partly caused by their fear that the profound discontent which had taken root in Belgium beneath the surface of seemingly unanimous patriotism (discontent with the desperate social conditions and misery of the proletariat, even before 1914 amongst the lowest-paid in Europe; discontent in Flanders with cultural discrimination) would have unpredictable, and quite likely violent, consequences.

Only three members of the old Cabinet took part in the new. One of these was the Foreign Minister, Paul Hymans, liberal, Protestant, a man of fine taste and erudition who was nominated on 1 January 1918. He was to be responsible for giving Belgian foreign policy a new direction. This policy was inherited from the Le Havre Cabinet; it had not been devised

---

[1] C. H. Höjer, *Le Régime parlementaire belge de 1918 à 1940* (Uppsala, 1946), pp. 81–90; cf. G. Vanloubbeeck, 'L'Activité politique à Liège pendant la guerre 1914–1918', *Revue belge d'histoire contemporaine*, ii (1970), 126–30.

by the leaders of the Comité national. Naturally, at Le Havre the international position of Belgium had been frequently discussed. At the beginning of the war the King and the government held that Belgium, although she was forced to participate in the battle, must maintain the neutral status on which her independence had been based since 1839. Belgium was resisting aggression and fighting for freedom, but she ought not to conclude an alliance with France and Britain or endorse the war aims of the Allies. Besides purely juridical arguments in favour of a policy of isolation, moral and practical motives also played a part. Belgium was seen as the victim of injustice and not as a belligerent in the ordinary sense of the word. By this the tragedy of her fate and the value of her heroic resistance against the violator of rights and treaties were emphasized, for, the reasoning went on, notwithstanding her independence, defended by force of arms, her soldiers contributed more to the salvation of mankind than anyone could reasonably have expected.

On the strength of such rhetorical but not altogether un-justified considerations it was argued that Belgium would be able to capitalize on its policy of non-alignment once the war had been won—an outcome that at times seemed doubtful, the King initially being fairly pessimistic. Since the system of 1839 with its compulsory and guaranteed neutrality had failed to work, Belgium ought to be granted full power to shape her own policy in the case of an allied victory; and new measures should be taken to improve the strategic position from which she had to defend her territorial integrity. From 1916 the Le Havre Cabinet repeatedly expressed such demands without, however, specifying the nature of the measures intended to guarantee national safety. Some Belgian publicists in exile were more outspoken on the subject. In their eyes the abroga-tion of Belgium's guaranteed neutrality, which implied a re-vision of the treaties of 1839, opened the way to a revision of the territorial regulations defined in these treaties as well. The Dutch province of Limburg should be added to Belgium, and the same applied to Dutch Flanders since the whole course of the River Scheldt should be within Belgian territory. The same authors also had their eyes on Luxemburg. Long before 1918 the Dutch knew that such ideas were circulating in Le Havre and finding support among Cabinet ministers. It soon became apparent that Paul Hymans, whose political thinking was deeply influenced by the writings of Banning,[1] was by no means hostile to expansion. But not until January 1919 did the government put its ambitions in writing in a memorandum addressed to the Allied and Associated Powers. There is something profoundly romantic in this paper, the bombast and pathos reminding one at times of the atmosphere of 1830.[2] There was a strong element of nostalgia in Hymans's policy. It expressed, he wrote, not the fantasy of a conqueror but a desire to recover the Belgium visualized by the creators of her national independence in 1830.[3] Pierre Orts, one of his most intimate collaborators, was imbued with Banning's romanticism.[4] Another supporter, Pierre Nothomb, who was the most extreme propagandist for territorial expansion in Belgium itself, fed his poetic and extravagant patriotism, according to Hymans, on the memories of 1830.[5] But between 1919 and 1830 there was this essential difference: the territories Belgium claimed, still thankful for the neutrality they had enjoyed, had no desire to join Belgium.[6] For this reason alone Belgian policy was quite unrealistic in the ideological climate of 1919.

But the Netherlands was out of favour with the Allied Powers. They suspected, perhaps justifiably, that the arrival of Wilhelm II in the Netherlands on 10 November 1918 came as less of a surprise to some Cabinet ministers and members of the court than was officially reported;[7] it coincided to the displeasure of the Allies with the government's decision to allow 70,000 German soldiers to make their way home through Dutch Limburg and so avoid being made prisoners of war. For one moment the Belgians seemed to have a positive chance of

---

[1] Hymans, *Mémoires*, i. 286 ff. See above, pp. 220 ff.

[2] O. de Raeymaeker, *België's internationaal beleid 1919–1939* (Brussels, 1945), p. 47.

[3] Hymans, *Mémoires*, i. 294, 373–4.

[4] Ibid. 334.   [5] Ibid. 301, 380.

[6] Van der Klaauw, *Politieke betrekkingen*, p. 28. In April 1919 a declaration of loyalty was addressed to Queen Wilhelmina by practically the complete adult population of Limburg: Smit (ed.), *Bescheiden* v. ii, 1034.

[7] The Foreign Minister Van Karnebeek who was considered to be pro-German was probably informed and in favour of Wilhelm's plan to take refuge in the Netherlands. It is also far from improbable that Van Heutsz, the former Governor-General of the Netherlands East Indies who was attached to the Military House of Queen Wilhelmina as aide-de-camp, helped prepare the Emperor's escape: see Scheffer, op. cit., pp. 266 ff.

realizing their ambitions. But the situation changed rapidly. Dutch diplomacy was tactful and authoritative, and succeeded in checkmating Hymans. Fundamentally, in any case, the Belgian position was weak. For reasons of principle the government had refused to specify the demands which it intended to make after the war, apart from such obvious ones as the restoration of Belgian independence and the payment of war damages. Thus Hymans had no firm commitment on which to base his case, and nothing to offer himself. The prestige Belgium had won during the war turned out to be insufficient for such an ambitious policy. Even the French, who wanted to include Belgium in their sphere of influence and military system, had their reservations about Belgian aspirations since they themselves hoped to win the Grand Duchy of Luxemburg. The Dutch, supported by the United States and Britain, refused to discuss the cession of any territory. In June 1919 the Allied Powers accepted their point of view and decided that an international committee on which Belgium and the Netherlands were represented should make proposals for a revision of the treaties of 1839, without considering a transfer of territory.

Of course the whole matter had an unhealthy effect on Belgian–Dutch relations. The Dutch were deeply irritated by the fact that the Belgians had addressed their demands and their memorandum directly to the Great Powers without informing the Dutch Government about their contents. Nevertheless, the Dutch acted with extreme caution during the negotiations which followed, realizing pretty well that although the foreign policy of the Belgians was regarded by many diplomats in Paris as unreasonable and immature, and was indeed rather clumsy, they still enjoyed far greater prestige with the big Powers than the neutral Netherlands. The Belgian position was weakened, however, by the indifference of the Belgian people and the outspoken hostility of most socialists and all Flemings towards any expansionist policy.[1] It was only amongst a small minority that Belgian patriotism, revived during the war, took such a curiously romantic shape. No

---

[1] R. Devleeshouwer, 'L'Opinion publique et les revendications belges à la fin de la première guerre mondiale 1918–1919', *Mélanges offerts à G. Jacquemyns* (Brussels, 1968), pp. 207–38.

doubt the hesitations of many Catholics also curbed enthu-siasm. No less a person than Cardinal Mercier warned the King against a policy of annexation which he thought to be unworthy of Belgium and also dangerous, because if successful it would increase the number of Dutch-speaking Belgians.[1] In the end, Belgium obtained only a minor technical adjust-ment of its eastern frontier by the annexation of Eupen and Malmédy. Even in Africa, where Hymans had asked for an extension of the colony, nothing was gained. Belgium was only granted the mandate over two former German provinces: Ruanda and Urundi.

[1] Smit (ed.), *Bescheiden* v. ii, 1021, 1031.

X

STABILITY, 1919-1939

1. *The Character of the Period*

IN the course of the nineteenth century the opposition to the liberal state took new forms and changed its character. It was most vigorously attacked by those Christians who sought to strengthen the position of the Churches, and who insisted on the absolute rigidity of their dogma. In their view the nineteenth-century liberal state was opposed to any such ends. Its very neutrality implied that the state could never support the ambitions of the dogmatic Christians. Moreover, it was felt to be in the nature of such a state to do everything possible to further the process of social secularization. As long as the opposition was confident that it could preserve the Christian character of society by restricting the influence of the state, it was able to adopt an attitude of strict conservatism, and even to participate in, and take responsibility for, the limited number of activities to which the state was thought to be entitled. But in the last decades of the century the situation changed and conservatism alone proved inadequate. For various reasons it became impossible to bridle the state's power, far less to push it back. As soon as the opposition accepted this fact, they developed the doctrine of the so-called 'antithesis'. In principle at least, they now refused to bear responsibility for the actions of the neutral state, which in all its functions and appearances they depicted as a monstrous Leviathan. As a consequence the denominational parties, both Roman Catholic and Protestant, had to be transformed into strong, combative mass organizations whose overriding purpose was the Christianization of the state.

Meanwhile the state continued to expand its power, but in the 1880s and 1890s it became clear that in liberal countries such as Belgium and the Netherlands this expansion was to be accompanied by democratic reforms. The mid-century state, with a small bourgeois élite bearing all responsibility, no longer seemed to have the power and authority needed to perform the tasks now thrust upon it. Decisions on social legislation, military service, tax reform, and mass education involved so much that important sections of the higher middle classes themselves recognized the need for much wider electoral support than the political élite of the liberal era had ever enjoyed. To large groups of the population the democratic reforms of the period meant, of course, political and sometimes also social emancipation. At the same time they served to make acceptable to the citizen his increasing dependence on, or even subjection to, the steadily growing power of the state, the 'freedom' which as an individual he had to give up being in a sense compensated by the 'power' he won as an elector.

This extension of the franchise provided the denominational parties with more political influence than they had ever had before. But it was not the sort of influence they needed to put the doctrine of the antithesis into practice. Neo-Thomism, moreover, the philosophy of the Catholic version of Christian democracy, explicitly abandoned the antithetic way of thinking. As a result the religious parties had to look for solutions fundamentally different from the doctrine of the antithesis. They experimented with the *liberté subsidiée*, studied the possibilities of corporatism, and in fact looked in all directions for some realistic conception of the relationship between state and society. They hoped that by interposing or maintaining an intermediate layer between the state and its subjects the secularizing effect of state power could be checked. Where the state's influence on daily life was most apparent—in schools, social work, etc.—it was allowed to act only indirectly, to do no more than lay down general rules and provide the necessary finances for the institutions set up by the Churches, political parties, and other groups.

During the period between the world wars this process continued and amounted in the end to something approaching to a coherent system. It was a system indeed that survived the Second World War and in the 1940s and 1950s developed even further. In Dutch parlance it was called *verzuiling* (pillarization), the various religious, philosophical, or political conceptions, and the corresponding groups solidly organized with the state's help, being considered the pillars that together supported the dome of Dutch nationhood. Some political scientists have come to use it as the *terminus technicus* for a most peculiar type of democracy—in American publications also called 'pacificatory democracy' or 'consociational democracy'—which occupies a place of its own amongst the various types of democratic organization that have been developed.[1] At first sight this form of democracy suggests dramatic and disruptive inner contradictions. *Verzuiling* means that the state enables all the main groups of the population, Catholics, Protestants, socialists, humanists, etc., to organize their everyday life entirely as they wish: to have their own schools, youth associations, universities, sport's clubs, trade unions and employers' unions, their own social security organizations, and, for the cultural benefit of the masses, their own theatres, choirs, reading clubs, and, in the Netherlands, even their own broadcasting associations. The theory behind this segmentation was not originally conceived as peaceful pluralism but as a theory of conflict. The ideas and ways of life of a Roman Catholic and a Protestant, of a liberal and a socialist, were represented as so totally dissimilar, their aims so hostile to each other, that it was assumed they were not only quite unable to co-operate but were bound to be forever at each other's throats. Such a heroic if disastrous picture was far from the truth, however. In comparison with the large Powers of continental Europe, in the Netherlands and, to a lesser degree, in Belgium also democracy was in fact characterized by great stability.

Political scientists were fascinated by the paradox. The problem, moreover, was even more intricate than has been suggested. For the social system not only appeared to be divided from top to bottom and fragmented into independent groups between which contact was virtually impossible, the Dutch statesmen were also plagued by the unbridled urge of this democracy to embody all nuances of political opinion in separate political parties. Proportional representation, introduced in the Netherlands in 1918, made it possible for relatively small groups of dissidents to get a seat in the Second Chamber,

[1] H. Daalder, 'The Netherlands; opposition in a segmented society' in R. A. Dahl (ed.), *Political opposition in Western Democracies* (New Haven, 1966), pp. 188–236; A. Lijphart, *The Politics of Accommodation: Pluralism and Democracy in the Netherlands* (Berkeley, 1968); Luc. Huyse, *Passiviteit, pacificatie en verzuiling in de Belgische politiek* (Antwerp, 1970).

less than one per cent of the votes cast being sufficient for a party to have the right to representation. The result was at times laughable. In 1933, apart from the already numerous 'old' parties—there were seven of them: the Roman Catholic party, two Protestant, two socialist, and two liberal parties—47 smaller groups took part in the elections and 7 of them succeeded in getting a seat. As a result the new Cabinet was confronted with no less than 14 groups in the Second Chamber.[1] None the less, the basic stability was not affected. Despite this unchecked fragmentation, Dutch parliamentary history remained harmonious and calm during the interwar years. Although there were 10 cabinets in twenty-one years, continuity was greater than such figures indicate, the same ministers often staying on in their old posts under the same leadership. Ruys de Beerenbrouck led the Cabinet for ten years, Colijn for seven, and D. J. de Geer for four years.

In some respects the situation in Belgium differed considerably from that in the Netherlands. Proportional representation did not lead to a proliferation of an ever-increasing number of parties. Alongside the nineteenth-century parties of liberals, Catholics, and socialists only three new parties of more than transient importance were formed in the interwar period: an extremist Flemish party, a communist party, and a Fascist party.[2] This meant that until 1925 the governments had to contend with 4 groups in Parliament, from 1925 until 1936 with 5, and from 1936 to 1939 with 6; in the Netherlands the number oscillated between 10 and 14. Meanwhile neither in Belgium nor in the Netherlands were there any important changes in the composition of Parliament. Belgium, where normally around 40 per cent of the electorate voted for the Catholic party, was less strongly attached to the religious *zuilen* than the Netherlands with its constant majority of Catholic and Protestant members.[3] Liberalism was equally important in both

[1] P. J. Oud, *Het jongste verleden. Parlementaire geschiedenis van Nederland* (2nd edn., 6 vols., Assen, 1968), v. 26.

[2] In the Netherlands all the splinter groups together, (the communist and Fascist parties excluded) averaged in this period 6 to 7 per cent of the seats in the Second Chamber; in Belgium the percentage was under 1 per cent.

[3] The fact that in Belgium women not yet had the vote was certainly of influence. In 1946, at the first elections in which women took part, 42·53 per cent of the votes were cast in favour of the Catholic party.

countries (15 to 16 per cent). Socialism remained stronger in Belgium where it kept about 35 per cent of the seats compared with about 22 per cent in the Netherlands. In Belgium it was more difficult to form a Cabinet than in the Netherlands. Three possibilities were tried: for nine years the Catholics governed the country together with liberals and socialists; for one year they shared power with the socialists; and for eleven years with the liberals alone. In the Netherlands only Catholics and Protestants held governmental responsibility, except for one brief period when a few liberals entered the Cabinet.

The stability which characterized the composition of Parliament in Belgium was not, surprisingly, reflected at government level. From 1831 to 1894, under the system of limited suffrage based on the *cens*, there were 17 cabinets; from 1894 to 1919, under the so-called multiple male franchise, there were 9; but from the introduction of ordinary male suffrage in 1919 until 1940 there were no less than 17. The lifespan of cabinets thus became too short by any standards. This unrest was not caused by Parliament, which was never particularly troublesome. Cabinets were not brought down by the Chambers; they fell apart because agreements made between the partners when they decided to co-operate in the Cabinet were no longer felt to be binding, or because new problems arose about which there had been no preliminary understanding. It is not surprising that many contemporaries considered the instability of government a mortal danger to the parliamentary system, the more so because it seemed to get worse as time went on: none of the six cabinets formed between 1936 and 1940 remained in office for more than nine months. Commentators were deeply worried by the apparent similarity between conditions in Belgium and in France, where the 40 cabinets between 1919 and 1940 were clear symptoms of crisis.

But the situation was much less serious in Belgium than in France. The main difference was that in the latter the parties were not as solidly and coherently organized as in Belgium and their programmes were less articulate. Whereas in Belgium the lifetime of the cabinets was shortened by the difficulty of improvising *ad hoc* compromises between the coalition partners, in France Parliament itself with its fluctuating majorities and its impatience with each Cabinet formed was the real source of instability.[1] In Belgium the crisis of the parliamentary system was therefore far less fundamental. Indeed it has been claimed with some justification that it is wrong to talk about a crisis in Belgium at all.[2] Although each Cabinet remained in office for too short a period, the Cabinet ministers stayed on much longer.

It can easily be shown that the differences between Belgium and the Netherlands were in fact only relative, less a question of structure than of organization. In Belgium ministers regularly shifted from one department to another, in the Netherlands they did so much less frequently.[3] The figures show that for an average of 10 Cabinet posts available in the Netherlands some 50 persons were needed during this period, whereas in Belgium about 80 ministers were needed to fill an average of 13 Cabinet posts.[4] There can be little doubt that such figures, arranged in this way, take the sting of drama out of Belgian instability, those for Great Britain, for example, being roughly the same. Whereas in the Netherlands 5, and in Belgium and England about 6, persons sufficed for one Cabinet seat during these twenty years, France needed at least 13.[5]

If Belgian and Dutch democracy may be assumed to have been relatively stable throughout this period, the question of how such stability could be achieved in countries which were both intellectually and organizationally so deeply divided still needs to be answered. Why did the system work as adequately as it did? The explanation cannot be found in any conscious effort on the part of the political leaders to moderate their high principles and the tensions they ostensibly generated: they did nothing of the kind. Until the late 1930s the Dutch socialist party, the SDAP, remained faithful to the doctrine of the class struggle and the coming of the new society. In Belgium the

[1] Cf. F. Périn, La Démocratie enrayée. Essai sur le régime parlementaire belge de 1918 à 1958 (Brussels, 1960), p. 100.

[2] See also A. Philippart, 'Analyse statistique de la stabilité ministérielle en Belgique de 1918 à 1961', Res Publica, iv (1962), 275–96; W. Verkade, Democratic Parties in the Low Countries and Germany. Origins and historical developments (Leiden, 1969), pp. 90–4.

[3] Belgium had 16 different Ministers of Home Affairs, 11 Finance Ministers, 9 Foreign Ministers against 5 of each in the Netherlands.

[4] The Defence Ministers are not included in these figures.

[5] In Great Britain some 120 persons took office in cabinets averaging 17 members, in France some 260 persons in cabinets averaging 20 members.

Flemish movement gained force and so did its separatist wing. In no respect did the differences between religious and non-religious people give the impression of narrowing; controversy was frequently even more acerbic than it had been in the last years before 1914. The *verzuiling* and strong party organization enabled the participants in the debates effectively to consolidate their positions. Discord seemed to be getting worse all the time. Discussion was loud; this was a period of portentous and solemn utterances. Politicians and publicists never tired of pointing to the formidable and exceptional features of the era— first in a tone of hope and idealism, later in one full of fear and gloom. But the public did not react and was not even supposed to. It was entrenched in its own organizations on which it was becoming more and more dependent, so that it took hardly any part in the public political debate. Both the Dutch and the Belgians were politically passive; generally they voted faithfully for the party their parents had supported or for the one popular in their region or amongst their fellow workers, feeling secure within the institutions created for them by the parties or the Churches. At party congresses or the manifold other manifestations organized on a massive scale to increase the solidarity within the *zuilen*, they were addressed by their leaders and reminded of the vital importance of their loyalty, their faith, their idealism, and their activity. They listened gravely and approvingly and felt deeply satisfied with what they heard. Nobody expected more from them. Thus the leaders were free to act as they thought fit. On the whole they did so with a strong sense of responsibility and a high degree of efficiency. They formed a small group of men capable of taking Cabinet posts and leading the parties. They knew one another well and, negotiating with each other about political matters, they were prepared, not to betray their principles—they were far from cynical or opportunist—but for the sake of the country's stability to declare if necessary that their principles did not bear directly upon the urgent problems that happened to be under discussion. In this way they created a level of consultation that was, one might say, somehow out of reach of their principles. This procedure, as necessary as it was curious, made it possible for their peculiar form of democracy to function relatively well, but at the same time it undermined democracy in two ways.

First, the whole system depended on the political passivity of the people. Had the Catholic, Protestant, or socialist masses insisted on their leaders fully implementing their doctrines and the principles on which the *verzuiling* was based, there would not have been much room for the prevailing policy of compromise and co-operation. In the second place, only a few of the politicians who governed the country really approved of parliamentary democracy in the form it was then taking. Apart from the liberals, all the big parties in Belgium and the Netherlands had serious doubts about whether, all things considered, parliamentary democracy was a workable form of government, and in fact none of them ever concluded that it was really satisfactory. In the 1930s in particular the 'crisis of democracy' became a favourite theme for debating societies in both countries and the various parties worked out all sorts of projects for reorganizing the state along corporatist lines. Neither in Belgium nor in the Netherlands did Fascism have more than a fleeting success with the masses, but in both countries the religious as well as the socialist parties solemnly pondered over a reform of public institutions in some ways akin to the organizational principles of authoritarian regimes.

2. *Belgian and Dutch Foreign Policy*

The essential aims of Belgian and Dutch foreign policy were identical. Whatever ambitions and aspirations either country entertained, they were always subordinate to the search for security and stability. The means they chose to realize these aims were, however, strikingly different. The Netherlands kept to its policy of independence or neutrality which, it was argued, had been so eminently successful in 1914. In Belgium, on the other hand, the events of 1914 were seen as proof of the inadequacy of neutrality and of the necessity for securing the country's safety by treaties or military agreements—that is, by associating with the victorious Powers. Only in 1936 when, after bitter disappointments and humiliations, this policy led to excessive tensions within the country, did Belgium opt for the foreign policy that the Netherlands had been pursuing since 1918. Neutral, badly defended, morally unprepared, in 1940 both countries succumbed helplessly to German aggression.

In 1919 Belgian diplomacy had applied itself to a series of tasks, each of them as it turned out impracticable. The Belgians wanted to obtain better strategic frontiers by means of an extension of their territory; they wanted colonial expansion; they wanted total compensation for all the damage they had suffered and, instead of the 1839 guarantee of their neutrality, binding agreements with France, Britain, and the Netherlands obliging these countries to give immediate support in the event of another German attack. Realization of these ambitions was dependent on some far from negligible conditions: the willingness of the Netherlands to abandon part of its territory, the willingness of the Allied Powers, and France in particular, to subordinate their own claims for reparation payments to the Belgian demands, and, finally, the willingness of Britain and France to co-ordinate their foreign policies. As early as 1919 it was obvious that none of these conditions could be fulfilled. The Dutch refused to cede Zeeuws Vlaanderen and Limburg.[1] France claimed priority for its own reparation payments, and on many issues the Entente was sharply divided. The Belgians, who had not allowed for the possibility that their demands might not be met in full, were deeply offended. The very fact that they were unable to offer more modest alternatives plainly shows the character of their diplomacy. It was romantic in its insistence on re-establishing frontiers Belgium had briefly held after 1830 and in failing to appreciate the extravagance of its own demands; it was legalistic because it saw all this as a matter of 'right', to discuss or oppose which was intolerably unjust; and it was sentimental since it took for granted that gratitude for Belgium's war effort would move the Great Powers to support this 'right'.

After the disappointments at the hands of the Great Powers on nearly all points—including reparation payments and war debts—the Belgians tried to attain at least some success in their negotiations with the Netherlands. In March 1920, however, the international committee which had been negotiating in Paris since June of the previous year in an attempt to revise the treaties of 1839 between Belgium and the Netherlands broke up without having reached a single decision on any vital issue. The deadlock was a result of the complete divergence of Dutch

[1] Above, p. 565.

and Belgian foreign policies at the time. Not only did the Dutch categorically refuse to give up any part of what they considered to be their ancient rights, they also refused to accept any political or military obligation towards other states, thus rejecting proposals to set up in collaboration with Belgium a new defence system with regard to Limburg. The only result of the conference was an agreement on certain specific economic and fiscal problems, but in May 1920 the Belgian Government, deeply offended by Dutch stubbornness over anything that in their view really mattered, decided not to ratify it. This put an end to the Paris negotiations which had been held under the supervision of the Great Powers. Nothing had been achieved by Belgium. Belgian statesmen could no longer lean on the support of their wartime partners, should they later choose to resume negotiations with the Netherlands.[1] In its relation with its northern neighbour Belgium had lost the initiative and, far from being able to put forward imperative demands, was forced to seek concessions instead.

The Belgian position deteriorated still further. The British attitude was extremely reserved; when in 1919 Britain declared its willingness to guarantee Belgium's territory against enemy attacks provided the Belgians returned to neutrality, this came as a most painful shock.[2] The Belgians looked upon neutrality as humiliating for so brave a country, and now released from the ties of 1839 they refused to risk being forced into the same situation as in 1914 when neutrality had failed so abysmally. Under these circumstances the Belgian diplomats saw no other solution than to seek the support of France and to subscribe to France's sharply anti-German policies. Since France was in danger of becoming isolated herself, she greatly appreciated Belgium's approval as a prop both to her morale and her strategy.[3] From 14 April to 17 May 1920 500 Belgian soldiers joined the French in the occupation of Frankfurt, thus helping to the great annoyance of Britain to bring pressure upon the

[1] Van der Klaauw, *Politieke betrekkingen*, pp. 52–75.

[2] Belgian consternation is clearly visible in the material published by Ch. de Visscher and F. Vanlangenhove (eds.), *Documents diplomatiques belges, 1920–1940* (5 vols., Brussels, 1964–6), i. 57, 60 ff., 78, 83, 86, 92.

[3] Belgian compliance also served to make France give up its far-reaching plans with regard to Luxemburg. Belgium was given the opportunity to conclude an economic union with Luxemburg in 1922.

German Government.[1] In September 1920 a Franco-Belgian military agreement was signed that brought Belgium into the French alliance system.[2] Although for a short time in 1922 an agreement with Britain, one of Belgium's aims since 1919, still seemed possible, the negotiations were once more thwarted by Britain's demand that Belgium should become a neutral country again. This was a fundamental point. Once more England turned out to be willing to guarantee the territorial integrity of a neutral Belgium against attack; but feeling little sympathy for Belgian foreign policies, she did not want to become involved with the activities of Belgian diplomacy. The Belgians, for their part, tried to maintain, or restore, unity within the Entente, but their influence was far too slight. When the Franco-British negotiations which had included the *pourparlers* between Belgium and Britain were discontinued, the Anglo-Belgian draft treaty found its way into the waste-paper basket.[3]

At that moment new ties with Britain held little attraction for a France wanting a free hand in her policy towards Germany. Exasperated at Germany's unwillingness or inability to pay the agreed reparations, the French Government decided to occupy the Ruhr area (11 January 1923). Once again Britain was hostile and Belgium co-operative. The Belgians, however, did not significantly benefit from their participation in the Ruhr adventure, either in terms of financial rewards or of prestige. On the contrary, it undoubtedly damaged the international position of the country, now apparently a mere satellite of France, completely dominated by one big Power. On domestic grounds also the action was dangerous and ill advised. The socialists were opposed to its 'militaristic' aspects, whilst in Flanders such total dependence on France was highly

---

[1] *Documents diplomatiques belges* op. cit. i. 107–301. Cf. F. Vanlangenhove, *La Belgique en quête de sécurité* (Brussels, 1969), pp. 23–4.

[2] The treaty had virtually no military consequences, although it contained several agreements on the strategy to be followed in case of a new German attack. It was secret and was not published before 1936 (reprinted in *Documents diplomatiques belges* i. 405–8). France saw it as a treaty of alliance; Belgium did not accept this interpretation but was careless in its treatment of the agreement. There is an extensive bibliography on the treaty. Cf. De Raeymaeker, *België's internationaal beleid*, pp. 110–32; Jane K. Miller, *Belgian Foreign Policy between two Wars, 1919–1940* (New York, 1951), pp. 181–4 and D. O. Kieft, *Belgium's Return to Neutrality* (Oxford, 1972), pp. 1 ff.

[3] *Documents diplomatiques belges* i. 448 ff. Cf. Vanlangenhove, op. cit., pp. 29–40.

unpopular, and not only in the more extreme Flemish nationalist circles. But the opposition, though angry, was not directed
against the aims of Belgian diplomacy in general. The majority
of Belgians subscribed to the main purposes of a policy that
sought to implement the Versailles Treaty as fully as possible,
to obtain from Germany as much compensation for the damage
suffered as it possibly could and from France and Britain the
strongest possible guarantees against renewed German aggression. There was considerable doubt, however, whether the
means chosen by the government were right. It is therefore not
surprising that the Belgians should have tried to repair the
detrimental effects of their Ruhr policy without damaging their
excellent relations with France. In the course of 1923 and 1924
they supported developments finally leading to the general
acceptance of the Dawes Plan (summer 1924) and its more
realistic approach to the problem of German reparation payments. When in February 1925 the Germans started trying to
reduce international tension by negotiating the agreements
that ultimately resulted in the Locarno Pact of October 1925,
the Belgians, at first hesitant, eventually decided to accept this
as the best way of achieving what they had been seeking since
1919: both a French and a British guarantee. From this perspective it did not seem to matter much that the form of these
guarantees was radically different from what had been originally asked—through the Locarno Treaty, Great Britain, France,
Italy, Belgium, and Germany guaranteed Germany's western
frontiers.[1]

During these same years the Dutch too were faced with some
interesting problems of foreign policy. One of them was the
question whether the Netherlands ought to accept the invitation to join the League of Nations. In the end government and
Parliament decided that this was indeed necessary (1920).
Refusal would have led to dangerous isolation, and they would
have lost the opportunity of supporting an organization which,
although to their minds too much a result of the allied victory

---

[1] See, e.g., how the influential politician Jaspar interpreted the treaty in an
article in the *Revue belge* (De Raeymaeker, op. cit., p. 190 n. 68). Hymans saw the
treaty as an improvement of the system of permanent neutrality adopted in 1839
(ibid. 192). The dangerous implication of the treaty was seen only at a later
stage: the fact that Belgium would not be in a position to remain neutral in a
French-German war (ibid., p. 194).

and too closely linked with the unjust and unwise Treaty of Versailles, might yet have the vitality to reach out towards broader and nobler ideals. With this in view the Dutch were willing, though without much enthusiasm, to abandon their rigorous principle of neutrality and even, according to some, a part of their sovereignty. But hardly anybody represented this as a real turning-point in Dutch foreign policy; although joining the League to some extent diminished their independence, the Dutch could argue that they were on the side of what they had always claimed was the ideological *raison d'être* of their foreign policy generally—the maintenance of international law. Thus Dutch public opinion was deeply gratified when the League of Nations decided to establish its International Court of Justice in The Hague (1921). This indicated that Dutch prestige, seriously undermined in 1918 and 1919, had recovered and also that the Dutch contribution to the establishment of international law was at last appreciated.[1] Yet, although the Dutch participated *con amore* and most conscientiously in the activities of the League, there were reservations about what was actually achieved. This was particularly clear in connection with the Geneva Protocol covering the peaceful settlement of international conflicts (October 1924). As opposed to the Belgians, who supported it largely because it promised to promote their own security, the Dutch thought that it would commit them too far. In fact it seemed to them that it merely served to strengthen France's position *vis-à-vis* Germany, and they were well pleased when Britain's refusal to accept it deprived it of all significance.[2]

The Netherlands took no part in the negotiations leading to the Treaty of Locarno, nor was it included in the Treaty itself.[3] The 'Locarno spirit', however, affected Dutch policies: such grave international problems having been settled in an atmosphere of general reconciliation, the time seemed ripe for seeking a solution to the problems still dividing the Netherlands and

[1] Vandenbosch, *Dutch Foreign Policy since 1815*, pp. 173–81; Oud, op. cit. i. 259–67.

[2] De Raeymaeker, pp. 157 ff.; Miller, op. cit., pp. 186–7; Vandenbosch, op. cit., pp. 181–3; Oud, ii. 209.

[3] The French and the Belgians would have liked this. Hymans realized, however, that joining the Treaty would have been at complete variance with traditional Dutch policy (*Documents diplomatiques belges* ii. 145, 167, 170). For that reason neither France nor Belgium invited the Netherlands to join. (De Raeymaeker, pp. 179–81.)

Belgium. Little had happened since the failure of the negotiations in 1920, and it was not until the summer of 1924 that the
Belgian Foreign Secretary Hymans took the matter up again.
He decided to reactivate the proceedings by no longer asking
for what he had so tenaciously insisted upon in 1920, 1921, and
1922: a military agreement on the defence of Limburg against
a German attack. Belgian statesmen were apparently feeling
much more secure since the end of the Ruhr adventure, so
Dutch strategic support seemed less vital than before.[1] In this
more relaxed frame of mind, negotiations should have proved
easier. In April 1925 the Belgian and Dutch governments did
sign a treaty, though it did not substantially differ from the
draft treaty which the Belgians had rejected in May 1920. It
was undoubtedly favourable to Belgium. The clauses of 1839
concerning the rivers and some economic provisions detrimental
to Belgium were replaced by friendlier arrangements. The Belgian Parliament accepted the treaty in 1926. So did the Dutch
Second Chamber, but the First Chamber rejected it on 24 March
1927 and this decision was final. It proved impossible to modify
the treaty in such a way as to make it acceptable to both parliaments before the outbreak of the Second World War.

That the treaty was, after all, unacceptable to the Netherlands is understandable. The First Chamber probably reflected
the opinions of the majority of the Dutch people interested in
the matter. In 1919 and 1920 it had been feared that the Allies
would support some of Belgium's political claims and so it had
seemed prudent to be conciliatory at least on the economic
front. In 1925 Belgium was no longer politically dangerous.
Nevertheless, the Belgian Foreign Minister Hymans, not without some justification perhaps, was believed still to harbour
romantic political illusions: consequently, even seemingly innocent and obvious measures were suspect. The article stipulating
that the end of Belgian neutrality implied the nullification of
the 1839 agreement that Antwerp should not be a naval port
worried the Dutch who embarked upon searching inquiries
whether the treaty allowed the Belgian navy to pass through
the Dutch part of the Scheldt in the event of war. The fact that
Belgium did not possess a single warship and had no intention

---

[1] Van der Klaauw, op. cit., pp. 82 ff.

of building a navy[1] rendered the matter academic, but the Dutch opponents to the treaty feared that if the point were not cleared up the Dutch claim to complete sovereignty over their part of the river might lose some of its credibility, and that the Belgians would immediately exploit this to realize their further-reaching pretentions, for instance co-sovereignty.[2] Although suspicions of this kind were characteristic of Dutch–Belgian relations, they may well have been over-emphasized to avoid concentration on matters of strictly economic interest that were no less influential. One of the main concessions on the part of the Dutch was to allow the construction of a canal between Antwerp and the Rhine delta and, probably, to pay part of the costs. Serious opposition to this came first from Rotterdam and then from Amsterdam. A number of powerful firms provided funds for a national campaign against the treaty because the new canal, so was the main argument, would enable Antwerp, already favoured by France, to ruin Rotterdam. Only the most modern means to influence public opinion were considered appropriate to achieve the desired result, such as a propaganda campaign in the Press by a publicity agency that had had success in promoting Blue Band margarine.[3]

Opposition to the treaty was fed by anxiety about the interests not only of the employers but also of the dock-workers in the big ports, by profound puritanism with regard to Dutch neutrality and fear that it should be jeopardized if the Scheldt became accessible for Belgian warships, by the recollection of Belgian annexationism, and, of course, by the traditional Dutch disdain for Belgium. As a result there were strong opponents to the treaty in nearly all parties. This was a national opposition to an indeed unsatisfactory and ill-balanced proposal. However, there were other aspects to it. A short-lived political group— the National Union—formed in 1925, threw itself into the fight with vigour and efficiency: it was an extreme nationalist group with conservative doctrines tending towards a form of Fascism.[4]

---

[1] In time of war, the Dutch opposition thought, the French, closely associated with Belgium, would be able to send their warships under the Belgian flag to Antwerp: Oud, iii. 118.

[2] Van der Klaauw, pp. 91 ff. Cf. Heldring, *Dagboek* i. 661.

[3] Heldring, *Dagboek* i. 669.

[4] Van der Klaauw, pp. 103–4. On the Nationale unie see esp. A. A. de Jonge, *Crisis en critiek der democratie*, pp. 94–102.

One of its leaders, F. C. Gerretson, was in close contact with Flemish activists of the First World War who had taken refuge in the Netherlands and with the radical wing of the Flemish movement that wanted to destroy the Belgian unitary state completely. Amongst these Flemish extremists he found support for his thesis that any treaty favouring Belgium was a victory for the anti-Dutch, French-dominated Belgian Government and thus for the oppressors of Flanders.[1]

It is also remarkable that the campaign was largely organized by a National Committee of Action against the Treaty with Belgium,[2] which was led with considerable passion by its secretary, A. A. Mussert—a graduate from the Delft Technical High School and a highly specialized civil servant attached to the Department of Public Works of the province of Utrecht. This was Mussert's first step into politics and enough to encourage a belief that he possessed political genius as well as a political mission. In 1930 he tried (in vain for the time being) to found a national socialist party. In a letter soliciting support, he wrote that the Netherlands was being made impotent by party feuds and was neglecting her defence, although the danger coming from abroad ought to be clearly visible to anybody 'at this alarming time, with a neighbour on the southern frontier building up strong military forces, at the same time allied to France through a secret military treaty, and in such a state of internal commotion that our country will before long be threatened with most serious problems'.[3] Belgium in the role of the enemy menacing the Netherlands! However improbable such a suggestion may have been, it was undoubtedly an echo of the violent reactions to which the draft treaty of 1925 had given rise in right-wing circles.

To what depths of distrust Belgian–Dutch relations had sunk became apparent in 1929 when a Dutch newspaper published a document showing that in 1920 the Belgians and the French had agreed upon invading the Dutch province of Limburg in case of war with Germany. This was a cheap and gross falsifica-

[1] Nevertheless, the Flemish extremists did not vote against a treaty which was so favourable to Antwerp and Flanders: they just abstained.

[2] For this see the careful study by R. L. Schuursma, *Het onaannemelijk tractaat: Het verdrag met België van 3 april 1925 in de Nederlandse publieke opinie* (Groningen, 1975).

[3] L. de Jong, *Het Koninkrijk der Nederlanden in de Tweede Wereldoorlog* (The Hague, 1969), i: *Voorspel*, Pl. 51: facsimile of Mussert's circular of 15 Dec. 1930.

tion. Yet suspicion of the Belgians was so general and so virulent that business circles in Rotterdam, the government which had seen the false documents before publication, and the press, were all convinced that they were genuine. For days the Dutch newspapers, and not only those of the Right, spent themselves on denouncing the cynical lack of scruple shown by the Belgian and French authorities.[1] But greater than the fear of Belgium was the fear of France. After the rejection of the Belgian treaty in 1927 a sum of money was raised in the Netherlands for journalists of the French daily Press, which was much read in Belgium, with a view to ensuring their objectivity, or in other words a spirit friendly to the Netherlands.[2]

Of course this hostility between the Netherlands, irritated by Belgian ambition, and Belgium, exasperated by Dutch pride, was not a new phenomenon. Many times in the past relations between the two kingdoms had deteriorated in a period of European *détente*. As long as neither felt threatened the emphasis inevitably fell on those things that divided them: national sentiment, economic rivalry, conflicts over the control of the big rivers and over frontiers. In their bilateral relations they could afford a degree of stubbornness and bitterness that could not conceivably be allowed in their dealings with their stronger neighbours. In the 1920s, moreover, the situation was, for the first and the last time, complicated by the Flemish question. The cause of Flemish nationalism directed against the Belgian state was vociferously advocated by some of the activists who had fled to the Netherlands in 1918 and been provided there with a modest livelihood. Both in the agitation against the treaty of 1925 and in the aftermath of the falsifications of 1929 Flemish nationalists and their Dutch friends played an important part. But the Dutch Government never in any way sought support from these people or their ideas. Like all their predecessors since 1848 the Dutch authorities took the stand that Belgium should remain a strong state, a bulwark at the Dutch frontier, and they carefully avoided getting mixed up in the

---

[1] The falsification had been produced by the Belgian security service itself and was in a devious way delivered to a Flemish nationalist. Apparently the idea was to compromise this man and through him his movement. Cf. G. Provoost, 'Het Frans-Belgisch militair accoord van 1920 en de zaak der Utrechtse documenten in 1929', *Res Publica*, xi (1969), 327–49.

[2] Heldring, *Dagboek* i. 691, 695.

Flemish–Walloon conflict. This implies that the deterioration in official relations between Belgium and the Netherlands in the 1920s was caused by conflicting interests that were largely traditional. As a result it was possible for the two countries to come together again, as they had so often done in the past, as soon as the European *détente* was over and wars again threatened. Then the fundamental similarity of their constitutions and their aspirations as well as of the problems both had to face prevailed over their rivalry—not that the rivalry itself was consciously put aside or solved by some compromise, for before the Second World War the statesmen did not succeed in coming to an agreement on the questions which had led to the painful crisis of the 1920s.

The new friendship of the thirties did not produce concrete results. Both countries tried, partly in collaboration with the Scandinavian countries, to extend their economic horizons, which were being dangerously reduced by the protectionism of the big nations, by stabilizing or even lowering their tariffs on their mutual trade, but they were not successful. The agreement of 1932 between Belgium, Luxemburg, and the Netherlands to scale down reciprocal import and export duties by 50 per cent in the course of four years (the Treaty of Ouchy) could not be put into effect because of British and American opposition. The economic crisis of 1929, the victory of the German national socialists in 1933, and the impotence of the League of Nations narrowed the scope of the small Powers catastrophically, with the inevitable result that they withdrew as best they could into the sanctuaries of their own independence, avoiding participation in international politics whenever possible. For the foreign policy of the Netherlands this entailed no change considered fundamental; Dutch loyalty to the now disintegrating League of Nations had always been interpreted as in no way inconsistent with an independence that allowed no measurable infringement of Dutch sovereignty. From 1933 any ambiguity gradually disappeared. The Netherlands reverted completely to the position it had been in before the First World War. In the 1930s there was more support for such a policy than there had been before 1914, when, for reasons of principle, the socialists had always refused to accept the vital condition on which it was dependent—the building-up of a strong national defence. Both the socialists and the other political parties had felt that the system of collective security in the post-war years allowed and even morally obliged the Netherlands to disarm unilaterally; now they began to see national defence as a political and ethical duty.

For Belgium the problem was less simple. The country was tied to the covenant of the League of Nations, to a military agreement with France (1920), and to the Treaty of Locarno. The Belgian statesmen responsible for this complicated situation maintained that such an accumulation of treaty obligations, while increasing the country's security, had not added to its burdens or impaired its autonomy. In their view the purpose of the treaties was to provide French and British guarantees of Belgian independence. To interpret them as an obligation on Belgium's part to open its frontiers to French troops whenever and for whatever reason France might get involved in a war with Germany would be clearly contrary to the spirit of the undertaking for in that case Belgium would be far from independent, indeed a mere satellite of France. Even so, there were French soldiers and statesmen who took the view that such an interpretation was not only correct but really went without saying, and from time to time high French authorities said so openly.[1] In the thirties the issue became even more important for Belgium because well-informed observers were arguing that the Germans would never re-enact the campaign of 1914 and if they decided to attack France would prefer to stay out of Belgian territory. On the other hand, the whole organization of the French defence system seemed in effect to make it impossible for the Germans not to violate Belgian territory. In 1929 the French had decided to reinforce their German frontier, but the Maginot Line was to stop at the Belgian–Luxemburg frontier and not to be extended to the Channel. This, it was feared, would force the Germans once more to invade Belgium in the event of war with France and once again make Belgium the great European battlefield.[2] Whichever way the Belgian authorities looked at the problem, however persistently they tried to wrest assurances from France, however emphatically they

[1] Kieft, op. cit., pp. 12 ff.
[2] *Documents diplomatiques belges* iii. 35–6, 230–1. Cf. Rothstein, *Alliances and Small Powers*, pp. 101 ff.

repeated that the whole point of their foreign policy was to strengthen their independence and security, there was no satisfactory answer to the essential dilemma—whether France's strategic intentions, not to mention the ambiguities in the texts of the treaties themselves, did not point to a radically different conclusion, the certainty that Belgium would be involved in any Franco-German conflict unless Britain were to force France to take a more moderate course.

The whole system of alliances, however unsatisfactory it might be, did have some attraction for its Belgian architects. To a much greater extent than the Dutch, Belgian foreign policy had been characterized ever since 1831 by their desire to act on the international scene and to take part in the great decisions of European diplomacy. For the Dutch the nineteenth-century tradition was to withdraw from international diplomacy as best they could, it being considered a privilege of small countries not to be obliged to participate in power politics. In contrast, the Belgians tended to emphasize their presence on the ground that this added to their prestige and thus to their security. At least two factors may explain the difference. In the 1830s and 1840s, when the Belgian tradition of diplomatic activity originated, there was some reason for the Belgians and their king to suppose that a state so young and vulnerable needed unremitting alertness on the part of its diplomats and its Foreign Department, faced as they might be by all manner of challenges. The Dutch in the nineteenth century had no reason for such nervousness. As an ancient maritime and colonial power, they were inclined to adopt the British style in international politics; the Belgians, however, followed the French example. In the Belgian Foreign Office and in its Foreign Service the French language was supreme, and although their national interests differed, the Belgians were inevitably attracted by the French diplomatic style formed in the centuries of its power. This, of course, does not mean that Belgian diplomats and the leading personalities in the Foreign Office supported France under all circumstances. On the contrary, most of them in the 1930s were exasperated by French attitudes. Without realizing it clearly, the French hurt Belgian feelings deeply by simply assuming that the interests of Belgium were identical with those of France, and by dismissing all opposition to French policies as the result of Flemish Franco-phobia.

So in time the Belgian Foreign Office came to realize that unintentionally its policy had grown far too dependent on France and needed to be carefully reformulated. It should be emphasized that the new definition of the purposes of Belgian foreign policy was not intended as a break with the past. Even the greatest advocate of Belgian–French friendship, Paul Hymans—with some interruptions Foreign Minister for more than ten years and retiring from office only in 1935—always represented Belgian foreign policy as a policy of independence. His intention was to increase Belgian security by associating with the Great Powers, but only so that they would come to its support in the event of a new German attack. Hymans's way of achieving this ideal was to participate actively in international negotiations. However, he did not succeed in achieving his aim. The help Belgium might expect in emergencies was uncertain and ambiguous; the obligations it accepted were equally ill defined and were indeed interpreted in a number of contradictory ways. In the thirties the Foreign Office was aware of this fact. Consequently, though its objects remained the same, it sought other means of achieving them. Belgium chose to withdraw from the chaos of international politics and to declare itself no longer bound by what remained of the collapsing system of alliances it had helped to build. In a way this meant a return to the position of the pre-1914 period. On the other hand, it was tantamount to abandoning the tradition of diplomatic involvement that had been characteristic of the Belgians since 1831.

Domestic circumstances caused the Belgian authorities to present their decision in a somewhat dramatic way. After 1918 for the first time in Belgian history foreign policy became a subject of heated discussion. This was surprising for in the nineteenth century it had been normal practice to keep such matters out of party controversies and conflicts, in order to present to the outside world the picture of a homogeneous and united country. Possibly this tradition might have been continued even after 1918 if Belgian diplomacy had not, in the critical years just after the peace, created the impression of being anti-Dutch in its annexationism, pro-French in its search for security, and, as part of general government policies, anti-Flemish. This impression was not entirely unjustified. The situation was unfortunate. There was no essential difference of opinion as to what Belgian foreign politics ought to be about. In general the Flemish too supported the Treaty of Versailles; they too were in favour of trying to obtain as much as possible from Germany by way of reparation payments; they too desired that France and Britain should formally promise to come to the country's rescue if Germany were to attack it again. However, Belgian participation in the occupation of Frankfurt, the Franco-Belgian military agreement, and the occupation of the Ruhr suggested that Belgian foreign policy was being controlled by France to such an extent that it was becoming positively dangerous for Flanders. The Flemish were seriously perturbed by these developments which confirmed their worst expectations. Their nervousness increased, a nervousness induced by the contemptuous dismissal of their aspirations by the French-speaking Belgians, which had become more noticeable during the war, and by the tendency of these people, apparent after 1918, to look upon the whole problem of Flemish cultural and, to a certain extent also political, autonomy as a matter artificially worked up by the German occupation and thus thanks to the allied victory removed from the political agenda. To the Flemish Belgium's foreign policy revealed the full extent of the myopia and stupid prejudices under which the post-war governments in Brussels were labouring. It was not only the extremists: the more moderate elements among the Flemish leaders felt equally strongly. They found support among the socialists who, while insisting no less than the Flemish on gigantic reparation payments, nevertheless condemned Franco-Belgian policies in relation to Germany as militaristic. The first success of this curious collaboration of pro-Flemish and socialist leaders came when Parliament rejected a Franco-Belgian commercial treaty (1924) and by so doing expressed also its moral disapproval of the military agreement, which had never been discussed in Parliament, and of the Ruhr policy.[1]

The secretiveness with which the responsible authorities surrounded the military agreement of 1920 was cleverly exploited

[1] Cf. Th. Luykx, *Dr Alfons van de Perre en zijn tijd (1872–1925)* (Antwerp, 1972), p. 265.

by Flemish propagandists. In fact, the agreement was relatively innocuous and its effect negligible—there never were army consultations between the French and Belgian general staffs and the defence systems of the two countries remained uncoordinated. Yet it served excellently as the major target of a pro-Flemish, anti-French, and antimilitarist campaign, organized in the grand style in which hundreds of thousands of people took part.[1] The damage thus caused by the agreement was out of all proportion to the benefits that accrued. After 1931, therefore, the Belgian authorities tried to extricate themselves from it in some way acceptable to France.[2] At first they were unsuccessful; it was not long, however, before the urgency of the situation became manifest even to the French. Realizing that sooner or later their partners would be forced to cancel it unilaterally, they accepted that the accord had ceased to exist and made an announcement to that effect on 6 March 1936.[3] There were two reasons why Belgian pressure had built up so strongly. The most important was undoubtedly that from 1933 onwards successive Belgian governments were increasingly aware of the imperative need for a much higher expenditure on defence. Since the main objective of antimilitarist propaganda had come to be the cancellation of the military agreement, it was logical to argue that only after this had been achieved could Parliament as well as public opinion be expected to give sufficient support to the efforts required in this field. Moreover, a large number of Belgians were horrified by the Franco-Russian Treaty of 1935, and almost equally by the emergence in 1936 of the French Popular Front, which by June of that year became the government of the day. It was not only among the Catholics and Flemings that suspicion of France became even more intense: considerable doubts came to be felt among the liberals, once the most loyal advocates of Belgium's pro-French policies. Just how thoroughly conservative, anti-communist, and even anti-democratic public opinion had become by 1936 was shown by the surprising victory of the Belgian Fascist party at the polls of 24 May: participating in the elections for the first time it won no less than 11·5 per cent of the votes cast.

---

[1] Cf. Willemsen, *Vlaams-nationalisme*, pp. 184, 290.
[2] Kieft, pp. 12 ff.   [3] Ibid., p. 55.

The day after it was officially confirmed that the military
agreement had been cancelled, the Germans renounced the
Treaty of Locarno and sent their troops into the Rhineland.
That same day the Dutch minister in Brussels told the Belgian
Premier that in his opinion this regrettable development might
have one favourable aspect: it would allow Belgium to be rid
once and for all of its obligations towards France.[1] Belgium,
indeed, seized the opportunity thus offered. In July 1936 Paul
Spaak, then Foreign Minister, told representatives of the international Press that nothing would make Belgium take up arms
but the necessity to defend its own interests and its own frontiers. In October King Leopold III expounded the same principle in a powerful speech which he personally delivered at a
Cabinet meeting.[2] The German violation of the Treaty of Versailles, he said, had put Belgium back into a situation comparable with that of 1914. It was now Belgium's task, not to
prepare for a coalition war against Germany, but to build up
a strong defence system to protect its own territory. That such
a policy was realistic was shown, in his opinion, by 'the proud
and unflinching example of the Netherlands and Switzerland'.
The ministers were so impressed by this speech that they had it
published immediately: it was, of course, largely their concern
with domestic issues that prompted them to rush so precipitately into print. They expected that the 'new policy', represented as truly 'national', would be appealing enough to
persuade the Flemish and the Walloons, the socialists and
the Catholics, as well as the Fascists, to support a considerable
increase in Belgium's military effort, and in this they were
right. In December 1936 national service was extended from
12 to 17 months. Reactions in the neighbouring countries were
predictable: strong criticism in France, resignation in Britain,
satisfaction in Germany, and joy in the Netherlands, where the
fact that Belgium had decided to follow the example of Dutch
foreign policies seemed to confirm their wisdom and enhance
their significance.

The novelty of Belgium's foreign policy after 1936 was somewhat extravagantly stressed. The Belgian leaders overstated
their aims in terms felt to be challenging and shocking to
France. On the other hand, the French had never properly

---

[1] *Documents diplomatiques belges* iv. 114.   [2] Ibid. 323 ff.

understood how narrow the limits were which the Belgians had always set to the friendship that had existed between them. Moreover, the revision of Belgian policy was accompanied by a campaign of rare violence on the part of the Belgian right-wing Press which condemned the Franco-Russian Treaty and the Popular Front as a conspiracy of Jews, Freemasons, and communists against the peaceful *Third Reich*.[1] Such reactions gave rise to unfortunate misunderstandings. In fact the change in foreign policy can hardly·be described as fundamental; still loyal to the aims it had pursued for years, Belgium merely adopted a new diplomatic method. But errors of judgement in presenting the Belgian case gave the impression that in a spirit of complete defeatism, or perhaps even out of a certain respect for the German New Order, they had suddenly given up the role they had been playing until 1936 and, instead of being a symbol of wise and responsible internationalism, had defected to the ranks of the wretched and selfish *sauve-qui-peut* Powers which abounded in Europe.[2]

According to this reading of the facts Belgium's defection seriously impaired the ability of France, Britain, and the Soviet Union to counter German aggression, the Belgian position being vitally important both strategically and morally. Indeed, the Belgian Government put a ban on all official contacts with the British and French staffs; it stated time and again that it intended to defend its territory against any foreign country, even France; and in January 1939 when the British and the French thought that Germany was preparing an attack on the Netherlands and that this ought to be for them a *casus belli*, the Belgians were still determined to remain neutral—as the Dutch had been in 1914—and to refuse to allow French troops to march northwards through their territory whatever happened.[3] This stark policy of complete abstinence—it did not by the way prevent the Belgians from taking part in military consultations with the Netherlands, Britain, and France early in 1940, but these served mainly to show that the various national defence systems were entirely incompatible[4]—was not relieved by any useful initiative. Leopold III's pathetic appeal for peace in

---

[1] Cf. M. H. Jaspar, *Souvenirs sans retouche* (Paris, 1968), p. 173.
[2] Rothstein, op. cit., p. 113.   [3] *Documents diplomatiques belges* v. 152 ff.
[4] De Jong, *Koninkrijk* ii. 252–68.

August 1939 was meant to rally all the small countries of Europe, but in fact only the President of Finland and the Kings and Queens of Belgium, the Netherlands, and the Scandinavian countries supported it, and it had no effect at all. Nor had the clumsy offer made in November 1939 by Leopold and Queen Wilhelmina—originally a Dutch initiative—to mediate between the belligerents.

Belgian diplomacy has always justified its neutralist policy by pointing to domestic tensions, claiming that it was the only way to prevent a desperately divided country from falling apart at a time when war was imminent. Part of its explanation was therefore the Flemish opposition to pro-French policies. Although this interpretation is not, of course, entirely wrong, it is one-sided and leaves far too much room for blaming one group of the population for a policy that in May 1940 turned out to be disastrous. The policy of 1936 was unmistakably a policy desired and approved by some influential and very conservative people—those people in fact who after reluctantly accepting economic sanctions against Italy in 1935 were not sorry to see them fail, and who, opting for Franco in 1936, were greatly relieved to find that Belgium was only being asked to subscribe to the doctrine of non-intervention.[1] Thus in 1936 the question was not only whether or not to pursue pro-French policies but also whether to take sides in a conflict that was interpreted by the conservatives as a struggle between communism and national socialism. Many Belgians undoubtedly thought that the real significance of the so-called revision of their foreign policy in 1936 was that Belgium was able to refuse this choice.

3. Domestic Developments

During the interwar years the Netherlands was ruled by confessional cabinets. In Belgium the Catholics participated in all governments formed during the period and played an important part in them; the Prime Minister was usually a member of the Catholic party. Thanks to the universal suffrage the

---

[1] There was much discussion in left-wing circles about non-intervention. The number of Belgian volunteers for the International Brigade is estimated at between 2,000 and 3,000 among whom were at least 750 Flemings, which is high in comparison with the approximately 800 Dutchmen who joined: A. de Smet, 'Les partis politiques belges et la guerre civile espagnole (1936–1939)', Res Publica, ix (1967), 699–713 and De Jong, Koninkrijk i. 483.

power of the confessional parties penetrated more deeply than ever into society. Nevertheless, there were vital internal and external limitations to that power. The leaders of the religious parties spent more energy on protecting the Christian way of life than on reforming society or on converting their compatriots. Although there were Catholic authors and politicians in the Low Countries who developed theories similar to those of Mussolini, Salazar, or Franco, in practice they always started from the assumption that the modern culture they were concerned with was pluralistic and that the population of Belgium or the Netherlands was not sufficiently homogeneous to accept the sort of institutions and social conceptions then fashionable in Southern Europe. In these democratic countries the Christian parties have never aimed at uniting the people under a comprehensive political philosophy: on the contrary, they used their power in order to organize the segmentation of the people —a segmentation which they may have regretted but were willing to accept as inevitable.

After the great creative period of the late nineteenth century the interwar years were for the confessional parties a time of intellectual sterility. This was an era not of invention but of stabilization and organization. Immediately after 1918 the heavy task of reconstruction, particularly urgent in Belgium, required practical insight and resolution. During the war a considerable amount of power which might be characterized as parapolitical had, as a result of an apparently compulsive social process, reverted to the leaders of the most important business concerns. Although after 1918 most of them hurried to surrender it in order to devote themselves wholly to business once more, the leading business men remained none the less more closely connected with politics than they had been before 1914. Two well-known and important Catholic Prime Ministers of Belgium—Theunis and Van Zeeland—were bankers; the most influential statesman in the Netherlands, the anti-revolutionary Colijn, had been a director of the Royal Dutch. In Belgium, Francqui was twice called in by Catholic Prime Ministers to join the Cabinet and to use his technical skill as well as his considerable prestige in an attempt to solve the desperate financial problems facing the country. Throughout the period, in fact, technical aspects of politics—most of them understandably determined by the economic situation, the only other big problem being the Flemish question—were of more pressing concern than matters of theory or principle. Still, theorists found themes to improvise upon, though the improvisations were rather less fundamental than they appeared in the inflated style of contemporary publicity. Typical in this respect was the organization of the so-called *standen*, and the social system developed by Veraart.

Early in the century the Roman Catholic priest H. A. Poels had begun to organize the Catholics in what he called 'estates', or in Dutch *standen*, a cautious and nicely old-fashioned term for what socialists usually described as classes.[1] For each of the four groups into which, according to Poels and others, the population was naturally divided—farmers, workers, middle classes, and upper classes—it was his intention to develop cultural and religious diocesan societies which would do more even than Church services to deepen the Christian faith of their members. In 1916 the Dutch episcopate adopted the system, after deciding that each worker joining a trade union in order to protect his material interests should at the same time join his class organization for the benefit of his soul. After the war day-to-day reality seemed less amenable to Poels's aspirations. In 1921 the Dutch episcopate recognized the organization of Roman Catholic employers as a *stand* organization, and by so doing conceded that these organizations had not developed into spiritual and religious associations attached to the various dioceses but had become national interest groups. And in fact it was as interest groups that they played their part during the interwar years, forming the constituent elements of the political parties of the Roman Catholics in the Netherlands[2] and even more so in Belgium.

In Belgium they served to give the party a more flexible structure. This was due to a Flemish initiative. During the war some young Flemish intellectuals had discussed the possibility of reforming the Catholic party in such a way that it would become a real Flemish and 'popular' party.[3] In order to break the power

[1] Above, p. 490.

[2] Cf. J. A. Veraart, 'De standsorganisatie en de politieke organisatie', *Opstellen over politiek* (Amersfoort, n.d.), pp. 141–51.

[3] Ph. van Isacker, *Tussen staat en volk. Nagelaten memoires* (Antwerp, 1953), pp. 46 ff.

of the old, established party leadership—a leadership which was mainly French-speaking and thoroughly conservative—the party was divided into four groups. A large variety of existing associations, those of farmers, workers, employers, and others, some pursuing political aims, some mainly acting as social insurance offices or clubs, were incorporated into the four *standen*, each of these *standen* being entitled to nominate candidates for the local, provincial, and national elections. In this way the *stand* of the workers, too, obtained its own representatives. The effects of this reform, officially sanctioned in 1921, were not altogether fortunate. The Belgian party became a rather weak federation of virtually autonomous sections with totally different views on fundamental matters. It could certainly not be claimed that all Catholics belonged together in one exclusively Catholic political organization. In the thirties it became increasingly apparent that the system was not working, and consequently in 1936 the party was once again thoroughly reconstructed. Instead of a Union catholique belge, a federation of the *standen*, there was a Bloc catholique belge, which was also a federation, but this time formed by a Flemish and a Walloon Catholic party. In this new form the party was undoubtedly more coherent than its predecessor, as is shown by the fact that the Bloc succeeded in drawing up a programme that was binding on all its members, something that the Union had never managed to do. Needless to say, by that time the principles of the *standen* organization, once upheld by Poels and his followers with such deep conviction, had lost most of their significance. In the end Poels's system turned out to have been no more than an improvisation, unsatisfactory and transient despite the earnestness with which it had been set up.

The history of the *standen* organization seems to be a case of practice lagging behind a lofty but incoherent theory dating from before the First World War. The history of the Veraart system and the whole complex of social reforms connected with it is rather different. Immediately after 1918 a debate began in the Netherlands between socialists and Roman Catholics on the theme of 'socialization' versus 'industrial organization'. One or the other must be the over-all remedy for the ills of the time. In some respects the two systems were not unlike: both aimed at well-organized economic growth and were based on the assumption that to establish social justice it was necessary radically to reform the structure of the economy. In 1920 the Dutch Socialist party (SDAP) published a lucid, well-written report,[1] advocating centralization and nationalization of industry, through which, it was thought, greater productivity and a more balanced structure of society could be achieved. Trade and industry should be forced to accelerate the process of monopolization and major sections should be brought under state control. Efficiency and rationalization were the catchwords, not democracy or co-partnership of the workers, although these of course were also mentioned and recommended, albeit in moderate terms and with a proper emphasis on their inevitable limitations. The socialization report is a severe, puritanical piece of work, hostile to revolutionary violence, but nevertheless more radical and systematic than any earlier programme drafted by the SDAP. It was never subjected to serious discussion and had no practical effect at all. But the fact that the SDAP had shown itself capable of elaborating such a system strengthened to some degree the self-confidence of the socialists, so deeply shocked by the débâcle of November 1918.[2]

This type of socialization was completely unacceptable to the religious parties. They had a system of their own: that of J. A. Veraart. During the war Veraart had successfully mediated in the printing trade: at a time when fierce competition was causing disastrous wage cuts he had managed through collective wage and price agreements to set the industry on its feet again. In effect membership of the employers' unions and of the trade unions became necessary for enterprises wanting to survive.[3] However, this was enforced not by law but by binding mutual agreements between the employers and workers in the printing trade. In this way there came into being, without any basis in law, a sort of corporation possessing to a large degree autonomous legislative power and jurisdiction.[4] Yet the history of the printing trade[5] itself showed that these corporations were

[1] *Het socialisatie-vraagstuk. Rapport uitgebracht door de commissie aangewezen door de S.D.A.P.* (Amsterdam, 1920).   [2] Above, pp. 558 ff.

[3] J. A. Veraart, *Vraagstukken der economische bedrijfsorganisatie* (2nd edn., 's-Hertogenbosch, 1919), pp. 40–57.

[4] Ibid., pp. 121 ff.

[5] J. A. Veraart, *Beginselen der economische bedrijfsorganisatie* (Bussum, 1921), pp. 27–36.

far from stable, dependent as they were on mutual understanding and the assumption of a fraternal common interest.
Veraart, having been appointed to a chair in the Technical
High School at Delft, nevertheless devoted the whole of his life
to substantiating the thesis that this system, if applied to the
economy as a whole, would solve all the social problems of the
time. Here, he argued, was a truly Catholic principle, a corporatist doctrine originating from a new school of economic
research. Moreover, the system would cut the state down to its
proper size. It is true that the state had to legalize the system.
It had to give the boards representing the various branches of
industry the necessary legislative powers and recognize them
as organic parts of the state itself. But once this was done, the
various branches of industry could themselves be made responsible for most of the intricate fabric of social insurance, and
labour legislation could be limited. Consequently, it would be
possible drastically to reduce the number of civil servants.
Veraart dreamt of an economy controlled by a large number
of industrial boards, with equal representation of employees
and employers within each branch of industry, and with an
executive nominated by the government. These boards would
meet regularly to take binding decisions on labour conditions,
prices, the organization of the individual enterprises, their
expansion or contraction. But given such deeply democratic
solidarity in industry as a whole, there was no reason for
workers in particular factories or enterprises to ask for co-
partnership, nor was there for the employers to grant it. From
this perspective strikes and lock-outs were equally inadmissible.
Solidarity of the classes, the unity of capital and labour, the
profound calm and harmony of a society that had recovered its
organic structure were the foundations of Veraart's vision, con-
jured out of his experience in just one branch of industry over
a brief period.

Between the wars discussion of this system of what was called
public-legal industrial organization (*publiekrechtelijke bedrijfsorganisatie* or PBO) assumed enormous proportions in the
Netherlands, but led to no concrete results of much importance.
In 1919, a year full of social tension and wild rumours about
the danger of revolution, Veraart managed to bring together
the four *standen* of the Roman Catholics and induced them to

accept a programme, known as the Easter Manifesto.[1] The gist
of it was that the Catholics undertook to introduce in their own
enterprises the system which Veraart considered the ideal solution for the Dutch economy as a whole. In other words, a single
religious group—quite numerous, admittedly, but still a
minority of the population: 35·6 per cent in 1920—adopted on
behalf of its own community a reform of the economic system
held to be fundamental and comprehensive—in fact, a sort of
corporatism—without the rest of the nation being asked to take
part in the experiment. It is not at all surprising that it should
have failed. The Catholics themselves were bitterly divided,
and when it came to the point a number of Catholic entrepreneurs were reluctant to risk such an adventure at a time of
economic depression. Consequently, this extraordinary initiative, characteristic both of the segmentation of Dutch society
and of the immoderate presumptions of socio-political theory,
was never given a real chance.[2]

It was only in the legal field that some steps were taken to
put the theory into practice. The revision of the constitution in
1922 and 1938, for example, made it possible to grant a measure
of legislative authority to industrial boards. In 1938, however,
the idea of industrial organization was no longer exclusively
Catholic. Gradually and hesitantly the socialists had abandoned
their own ideal of socialization and drawn closer to Veraart's
point of view than anybody could have foreseen in 1920.
Though not accepting the wholesale corporatism of the Catholics, and insisting on a degree of state power that allowed
Veraart to accuse them of still seeking state socialism,[3] they
nevertheless made it possible for a bill to be passed much later—
in 1950—on industrial organization along lines suggested by
Veraart and intended radically to reform the economy. The
act, however, almost totally failed to come up to expectations.
At this stage in its development it was clearly impossible to
reorganize the Dutch economy in a corporatist manner. Both
on the level of academic economics and on that of human

---

[1] Printed in ibid., pp. 67–8.

[2] Cf. F. J. H. M. van der Ven, *Economische en sociale opvattingen in Nederland*, in
De Nederlandse volkshuishouding tussen twee wereldoorlogen (Utrecht, n.d.), pp. 44 ff.

[3] Veraart, *Beginselen der publiekrechtelijke bedrijfsorganisatie* (Bussum, 1947), pp.
145 ff.

psychology the underlying theory turned out to be far too restricted.

Veraart was a staunch champion of parliamentary democracy with nothing but contempt for all forms of Fascism. His own progressive socio-economic corporatism had nothing in common with political corporatism, which he regarded as by definition conservative. The attitude of the Dutch and Belgian Catholic parties, in contrast, sometimes seemed a little ambiguous. Mussolini's understanding with the Pope and the papal concordat with Hitler might well seem to indicate that it would be wrong to reject these new political forces out of hand. At the same time it was one of the major concerns of the Catholic parties as well as of the episcopate to maintain unity among their co-religionists and to prevent defections to other parties. Not until 2 February 1934, however, did the Dutch episcopate issue a warning to the faithful joining Fascist or national socialist groups on the grounds that that would weaken Roman Catholic unity. On 20 November 1935 the Belgian episcopate forbade priests to attend meetings of the Fascist party Rex, arguing that this movement which had grown up within the framework of the Catholic party had now become entirely independent of it. On 24 May and 24 December 1936 respectively the Dutch and Belgian bishops at last issued straightforward declarations directed against right-wing totalitarianism as such—the Belgians going further by including left-wing totalitarianism as well.[1]

The main purpose of the Dutch Roomsch-Katholieke Staats Partij (RKSP: Roman Catholic State party) in those years was to take part in all cabinets and to use this basis of power to protect and strengthen the Catholic community and its steadily increasing interests in schools, associations, trade unions, and so on. This could only be achieved on two vital conditions. Aided if necessary by the episcopate, the party had to maintain the unity of the Catholics, assembled in one political organization, and, in order to stay in office, to avoid at all costs serious conflicts with its political partners, that is the Protestant parties and one of the liberal groups. Though occasionally embarrassed

---

[1] On the Netherlands see L. de Jong, *Koninkrijk* i. 348, 355 ff.; on Belgium see, Cardinal Ernest van Roey, *Au service de l'Église* (6 vols., Turnhout, 1939–48), ii. 182–4 and iii. 124.

by obstinate secession movements and involved in some disputes with the Protestants, the party achieved its aims without too much trouble. At the elections the majority of Catholics remained faithful to the party (the number of Roman Catholics voting for the Catholic party only dropping under 80 per cent in 1933)[1] and over one-third of the Roman Catholic voters were party members—as against the 10 per cent of socialist voters who were members of the SDAP.[2] The drawback of this policy was of course that the party was left with little scope for vigorous action. In its relations with the Protestants this was shown specifically and rather painfully when it had to accept Parliament's decision to close the Dutch diplomatic post at the Vatican in 1925, and again during the 1930s when it was obliged to accept the anti-revolutionary Colijn as the national leader. Internally, too, the RKSP had to move with great caution, avoiding any semblance of extremism that might upset the Catholic voters. In fact, it owed its success to its own colourlessness.

This caused a number of young men of letters and theorists to revolt. In 1922 they founded a literary, cultural, and political periodical, *Roeping*, and in 1925 another one, *De Gemeenschap*, in which they expressed with a kind of nervous acerbity their disgust with modern society and with the Roman Catholic party's policy of compromise. Deeply impressed by the Action française and Léon Bloy, admired for his heroic absolutism, as well as by purely Fascist literature and examples, they bombastically proclaimed Roman Catholicism as the God-willed principle of order in a degenerated world, and ascetic puritanism as the ethics of the younger generation. With bitter invective they demolished democracy, the parliamentary system, and capitalism, while praising the monarchy, the principle of leadership, and corporatism as the only hope for a better future.[3] There was no originality either in their criticism or in their concrete plans. After 1933 the most talented among them began to turn against national socialism. These groups, though enjoying con–

---

[1] *De R.-K. Staatspartij. Maandblad ter voorlichting van de leden en organen der partij, uitgegeven door het dagelijks bestuur*, iv (1935), 109; vi (1937), 136–7.

[2] Ibid. i (1932–3), 162. In 1933 the RKSP had 374,377 members, the SDAP 81,914.

[3] On all this see L. M. H. Joosten, *Katholieken en fascisme in Nederland 1920–1940* (Hilversum, 1964).

siderable popularity among young intellectuals, probably had
no direct influence on politics. Still, the RKSP seems to have
made some allowance for right-wing authoritarian ideas notwithstanding its faithfulness to parliamentary democracy. The
party's official periodical praised the corporatist state;[1] it com-
mented quite favourably on the Austrian corporatist constitution of 1934;[2] and not long before the Germans invaded the
Netherlands it mentioned the Portuguese form of government
as the one corresponding most closely to the ideals of the Dutch
Roman Catholics.[3] Some years before the war one of the most
prominent young politicians among the Catholics, C. P. M.
Romme, wrote repeatedly about the need to grant the Queen
a larger measure of personal responsibility so that she might
play a leading part in the state, if need be against the wishes of
Parliament.[4] It is not to be wondered at that after the capitulation in May 1940 there were some from these circles who
thought that now at last, after the dismal collapse of the old
order, they could realize at least some of their ideals.

The authoritarian movement among young Roman Catholics in the Netherlands was too immoderate and vehement to
be taken altogether seriously. A comparable development in
Belgium, on the other hand, had greater significance. In 1919
young Catholics in Louvain founded *La Jeunesse nouvelle*, a
literary periodical of the *avant-garde* which soon began to address
itself to political matters. To this group political reform was
synonymous with the restoration of law and authority. In 1923
the group formally created a Ligue de Jeunesse nouvelle, with
a bimonthly called *Pour l'autorité*. After three years the Ligue
was rechristened the Ligue pour la restauration de l'ordre et de
l'autorité dans l'État. As in the Netherlands, but even more so,
the influence of the Action française was decisive. In the Ligue's
opinion the over-optimistic and misleading democratic axiom
of equality had led to nothing but chaos and misery. These

---

[1] *De R.-K. Staatspartij*, ii (1933), 262 ff. and *passim*. See also *R.-K. Staatspartij. Een
onderzoek omtrent wijziging van ons staatsbestel* (1936) which contains the outspokenly
corporatist views of a committee led by the chairman of the RKSP, C. M. J. F.
Goseling.

[2] *De R.-K. Staatspartij. Maandblad* iii (1934), 113–17.

[3] Ibid. ix (Jan. 1940), 4.

[4] Ibid. vi (1937), 39–42, criticizing Romme's views and cf. De Jonge, *Crisis en
critiek der democratie*, pp. 305 ff.

young intellectuals sneered at the democratic power of the greatest number and championed 'l'autorité de l'intelligence'. Since man is by nature imperfect, he is in need of authority, tradition, hierarchy, and the eternal truth of the Church. By strengthening royal authority and governmental power, shortening parliamentary sessions, revising the electoral law—with the franchise restricted to family fathers who would have the right to cast as many votes as they had children under age—and by making Parliament representative not of individuals but of social groups, the state would gradually be transformed and become capable of solving the great social problems of the day. Again, nothing in these suggestions was original, most of them having been put forward in vain before the World War. In 1926, when the Action française was condemned by the Church, the group began to lose momentum; early in the thirties it collapsed. For a few years it had nevertheless expressed the ambitions of a whole generation of nationalist, Catholic students.[1] The spirit of these ideals was, of course, in some respects very close to that of Fascism. When Léon Degrelle, the founder and leader of the Fascist movement in Belgium, was a pupil at the Jesuit College in Namur in the early 1920s he idolized Léon Daudet and Charles Maurras.[2] However, it was by no means inevitable for people enraptured by Catholic authoritarian theories to become Fascists. In Belgium such ideas exercised a positive influence in the late thirties under the clearly anti-Fascist governments of the Catholic leaders Van Zeeland and Pierlot, two politicians held in great respect by the young as men with enough authority and energy to save the country from anarchy.[3]

In the Netherlands nobody expected a Catholic to provide this sort of leadership. Yet in Holland in the thirties there was an equally urgent call for a strong personality to emerge from one of the traditional parties, a leader who could bring order to a chaotic era by a display of power, resolution, and fortitude. Such a man, helped by circumstances and appropriate backing

---

[1] See J. W. Serruys, *Sous le signe de l'Autorité* (Brussels, 1935), and E. Weber, *Action Française. Royalism and Reaction in Twentieth-Century France* (Stanford, 1962), pp. 487 ff.

[2] J. M. Étienne, 'Les origines du rexisme', *Res Publica*, ix (1967), 88.

[3] H. Davignon, *Souvenirs d'un écrivain belge, 1879–1945* (Paris, 1951), p. 331; Jaspar, op. cit., p. 186.

and publicity, would have the authority to stop the growth of Fascism and the flight of the masses into the arms of a Fascist leader. This end was achieved in the Netherlands as well as in Belgium, albeit in different ways. In 1936 Fascism had suddenly become a mass movement in Belgium, claiming 11½ per cent of the votes at the elections. In 1937 its leader Degrelle, whose outspoken, personal attacks on respected politicians were designed to discredit the parliamentary system, ventured to put his popularity to a decisive test. After forcing through an election, he himself stood for the Chamber of Representatives in the district of Brussels. The Prime Minister Paul van Zeeland, who was not a member of Parliament, took up the gauntlet and put himself up for nomination on behalf of the Catholics, the socialists, and the liberals. On 9 April 1937 the archbishop of Mechlin, Cardinal Van Roey, advised the faithful to vote for Van Zeeland. They obeyed: Degrelle obtained 19 per cent, Van Zeeland 76 per cent of the votes, with 5 per cent abstentions. In 1936 about 75,000 inhabitants of Brussels had voted for Rex and another more or less Fascist party which had joined forces with it. This time Degrelle got 69,000 votes. It was a triumph for parliamentary democracy made possible by two decisive factors: the political choice of the episcopate and the personal prestige of Van Zeeland. This prestige was based on the generally recognized superiority of his intelligence and of his financial expertise, as well as on his will to reform the political and economic system. Although he cultivated an unctuous, gently didactic oratory, his dynamism, his relative youthfulness, and his lively mind were his main attractions. These, however, proved unsteady supports. Half a year after his victory over Degrelle Van Zeeland was forced to resign because of a relatively trivial incident.

The Dutch Protestant Hendrik Colijn (1869–1944) owed his prestige as a leader to his calmness, his experience, and his sence of tradition. His personal influence far surpassed that of his own anti-revolutionary party, which went through hard times under the impact of universal suffrage. Like the Catholic party, the anti-revolutionaries recruited their followers from all classes of the population. But whereas the Roman Catholics were sure, especially in the virtually homogeneous Catholic provinces south of the big rivers, of the loyalty not only of the employers but also of the workers who had obtained the vote in 1917, the anti-revolutionaries continued to rely almost exclusively on the orthodox members of the lower middle classes. After the introduction of universal suffrage the ARP consequently lost seats, dropping from an average of 18 seats in the period 1901–18 to 14 in 1918–39, while the RKSP was growing from 25 to an average of 30 seats. Occasionally, however, the ARP achieved considerable successes at the elections, particularly in 1937 when it suddenly obtained 17 seats: this was a personal triumph for Colijn whose image as the strong, national leader upholding the nation's Christian traditions without subordinating them to party interests had been built up with much effect during the election campaign.[1] These same elections put an end to the optimistic expectations of the Dutch national socialists. At the elections for the Provincial States in 1935 the Dutch National Socialist movement had fared extraordinarily well, winning nearly 8 per cent of the votes at its first appearance before the electorate. The elections for the Second Chamber in 1937, however, were a disaster: the party now obtained only slightly over 4 per cent. The Dutch history of Fascism and national socialism differs considerably from that of Belgium, but its rhythm is practically identical.

In this period Protestant policies were unassuming and deeply pessimistic. Although in the thirties some anti-revolutionaries and Christian-Historicals, and the Protestant trade unions as well, showed some sympathy for the Roman Catholic idea of corporatism,[2] the Protestant parties remained in general profoundly sceptical about all projects of systematic social reform. The main reason for this was, of course, the social structure of the ARP itself. At the time when Christian democracy was first being developed, one of the great issues had been the emancipation of the Calvinist community and the lower middle classes, where orthodoxy was most strongly represented. Once this emancipation had been realized, what mattered was to consolidate the achievement rather than embark on an ambitious reform programme in an inevitably futile attempt to make the party attractive to the working class generally—

---

[1] Oud, vi. 1 ff.

[2] Van der Ven, op. cit., p. 92; Fr. de Jong Edz., *Om de plaats van de arbeid*, p. 235.

a class that had become estranged from Protestant orthodoxy. The Protestant workers, solidly organized in the Christelijk Nationaal Vakverbond (Christian-National Trade Union) with some 60,000 members in the 1920s and some 100,000 in the following decade, and relying heavily on the ARP, had never raised any serious objections to this policy of considered reserve. Not until 1931 did a representative of the Protestant trade union gain one of the anti-revolutionary seats in the Second Chamber; in one of his speeches he quite correctly observed that the corporatism then being advocated closely resembled the ideals put forward by Kuyper in the late nineteenth century, and went on to say that it would be most unwise to precipitate such innovations or to try to make them compulsory.[1]

Colijn's personality, too, helped to determine the character of anti-revolutionary politics. He came from a strictly Calvinist peasant family in the province of North-Holland. Not wanting to be a farmer and equally uninterested in the careers then open to clever boys of his class—those of schoolmaster or parson—he became a professional soldier. From 1893 he served in the Dutch East Indies where Van Heutsz noted his organizing ability, his capacity for hard work, and his shrewdness. The leaders of the ARP followed his career with interest; in 1909 he was earnestly requested to return to Holland and accept a safe place on the list of anti-revolutionary candidates for the Second Chamber. So he did and two years later he was appointed Minister of War. After his term of office he became a director of the Royal Dutch, a post he held from 1914 until 1922, his intention being to make enough money to allow him to be free from financial worries when he returned, as he intended to do, to the ill-paid role of politician. During the war he was actively and variously engaged in efforts to support Dutch neutrality, and in 1920 he became chairman of the ARP although he continued for a while to live in London. One of the things that persuaded him in 1920 to return to full-time politics was highly characteristic of the attitude he was to adopt during the next twenty years. He explained in a personal letter[2]

---

[1] Oud, iv. 286.
[2] London, 30 July 1920, to C. Lulofs, quoted by G. Puchinger, *Colijn. Momenten uit zijn leven* (Kampen, n.d.), p. 111.

that he felt obliged to take this step because of the alarming economic situation: he wanted to be there to fight back were the great crash eventually to come. To Colijn the developments that threatened the European economy were irreversible. There was, firstly, the disastrous Treaty of Versailles; and secondly, the rapid exploitation of the enormous economic potential of the non-European countries during the war when hardly any European products had been available for export. Now Europe had to adapt itself to a permanent reduction of its exports and, as a result, to a permanently lower level of prosperity. Some apparent improvement in 1925 he attributed to pure accident. The crash of 1929 was, according to him, an inevitable consequence of decreasing prosperity; that it came so dramatically and suddenly was because in the preceding years blind optimism and reckless speculation had created an artificial prosperity, in sharp contrast to the true underlying tendencies of the European economy.[1] Quite unlike either the Roman Catholics or the socialists, whose answer was increased productivity by means of socialization or by industrial organization, Colijn remained convinced throughout the whole period that it was the statesman's main task to teach society how to come to terms with a permanently reduced standard of living.

It has often been said that the policies of Colijn, the former director of a big international concern, tended to be liberal rather than anti-revolutionary. Undoubtedly, his objections to the over-ambitious policies of regulation then fashionable, to a corporatism of which he dreaded the 'totalitarian' aspects,[2] and to the growth of officialdom, echoed many of the fears of the liberals. They shared his aversions, but on the other hand he was too deeply pessimistic about all human endeavour and too militant a pragmatist in times of crisis when he was prepared to adopt quite drastic measures for the term 'liberal', whatever its precise meaning may be, to seem altogether appropriate.

[1] In 1920 Colijn started a long series of pessimistic speeches on this theme. Cf. the reprints in *Geen vergeefs woord* (Kampen, 1951), pp. 214 ff. (1920), pp. 230 ff. (1921), pp. 295 ff. (1931), pp. 308 ff. (1933); in H. Colijn, *Voor het Gemeenebest*, ed. L. W. G. Scholten (Utrecht, 1938), p. 132 (1935), p. 229 (1927) and esp. his speech in the Chamber on 10 November 1932, published in the form of a pamphlet *Van heden en toekomst*. See also his revealing letter to Governor-General De Jonge, Aug. 1933: De Jonge, *Herinneringen*, p. 207.

[2] Cf. Colijn's speech in the Chamber on 10 November 1933: Scholten (ed.), *Voor het Gemeenebest*, pp. 65 ff.

The liberals had of course been seriously weakened in both countries by the introduction of universal suffrage. After 1904, thanks to the plural-vote system combined with proportional representation, the liberal members of Parliament in Belgium had continued to outnumber the socialists. After the first elections in 1919, however, held under the straightforward universal manhood franchise which no longer allowed additional votes to the higher classes, the liberals found themselves outnumbered by the socialists by more than two to one. From 1904 to 1914 the liberals had averaged 44 seats:[1] from 1919 until 1939 they averaged 28.[2] The socialists, on the other hand, had an average of 35 seats in the first period and of 70 in the next. In the Netherlands the various liberal parties together held an average of 35 seats under the limited suffrage system between 1901 and 1918, and an average of 15 from 1918 to 1939,[3] as against the socialists' 10 and 22 seats respectively. After the war, therefore, the liberals had to adjust themselves to a fundamentally new distribution of power, and they did so with remarkably little trouble. Although losing much of their political influence, as representatives of the leading groups in industry and trade they retained considerable authority among civil servants and the daily Press. What the liberal élite really wanted in these years of unrest, crisis, and planning, was to preserve the *status quo*, to retain the social power that it had so clearly wielded during the war. To this extent the eclipse of their political strength mattered little to them, for both in the Netherlands and in Belgium the confessional parties provided the political and social stability that most liberals regarded as the prime objective in confused times. This does not mean that they had turned conservative. It was for just this desired stability that they supported the laws by which in both countries the condition of the working classes substantially improved after 1918. What it did mean, however, was that they themselves were unable and unwilling to initiate further reforms.

The mood and policies that had directed Belgian liberalism before the war were more or less exhausted after 1918. Some of the reforms advocated by the progressive wing came into

[1] After 1904 the total number of seats in the Chamber was 166, after 1912 186.
[2] From 1919 to 1925 the total remained 186 seats, from 1925 to 1936 it was 187, after 1936 202.   [3] In a Chamber of 100 seats.

effect before 1914, the rest after the war. However, all those
cherished aims—national military service, straightforward universal male suffrage, and compulsory education—were realized
not by the liberals themselves but by the other parties. The
popular anticlericalism, which had been a binding force
throughout the nineteenth century, faded in the interwar years.
Although some liberals, especially in the country districts,
remained staunch anticlericals, as a political device it became
obsolete when the Catholics no longer had a majorty in the
Chamber, and when the non-confessional parties decided in
1919 to grant large state subsidies to the Roman Catholic
schools.[1] It was then that the liberal party adopted a new programme. The *laissez-faire* principles to which the right wing had
clung for so long disappeared, but what took their place could
in fact also be found in the programmes of other parties: limita-
tion of working hours, fixed minimum wages, social insurance,
progressive income tax, etc.[2] As early as 1920, however, it was
clear that the liberals were tending to interpret these aims with
the utmost caution,[3] and in the course of time they were virtually forgotten. As was to be expected the younger members
of the party reacted against this political and intellectual lassi-
tude,[4] but there were no conflicts or schisms as there had been
so often in the nineteenth century. In 1935 an elaborate new
programme was approved, in which various general pronouncements on current problems were made; these showed that the
liberals were in principle willing to support reforms proposed
by other parties but not inclined to add many of their own.
Liberalism had no 'doctrine'; liberals distinguished themselves by
their temperament. They were politically and socially cautious,
pragmatic, and, if such a generalization is helpful, they protected
the 'bourgeoisie'; they were loyal to the party but hated strict
party discipline; they belonged to the type of Belgian patriots
that had emerged during the war and emphasized the need for
a strong army. With regard to the vital Flemish question, their
attitude was on the whole antagonistic. During the war liberals
had been active in the Flemish cause and this had done their

[1] F. van Kalken, *Entre deux guerres. Esquisse de la vie politique en Belgique de 1918 à
1940* (2nd edn., Brussels, 1945), pp. 30–1.
[2] Höjer, *Régime parlementaire belge*, pp. 47–8.
[3] Chlepner, *Cent ans*, p. 353.
[4] Jaspar, pp. 70 ff.

reputations no good. As a result, little attention was paid to Flemish politicians and Flemish ideals for a long time to come.

Dutch liberalism had been divided between several parties,[1] even more so after 1918. But in 1921 five liberal groups at last joined together to form a new party, the Vrijheidsbond (Freedom League), also known after 1924 as the Liberale Staatspartij. Apart from that, there was only one other important liberal party left: the Vrijzinnig-Democratische Bond (VDB: Liberal Democratic League). It was necessary for both of them to stress the differences between them in order to justify such dispersal of effort. On some issues the VDB could be more radical than the Vrijheidsbond, coming close in fact to conceptions put forward by the progressive wing of the Catholic party. It did not disagree, for instance, with Catholic policies concerning worker participation in management and the granting of legislative authority to industrial councils.[2] Yet it categorically rejected corporatism, which to many Catholics was the logical end of such reforms. The supporters of the Vrijheidsbond strongly disapproved of all this. Despite the quality of the party's leadership and the number of their representatives in Parliament, which was larger than that of the VDB, they played a lesser role than the liberal democrats. On two points the VDB took the lead, although in the end its policy failed.[3] The first was a tactical mistake, for it was assumed that before long the RKSP must collapse from its own inner tensions. The policy of the liberal democrats therefore was to prepare for close co-operation with the Catholic left wing when the split came and so to bring about a concentration of non-socialist 'progressives'. But the RKSP did not split, repeatedly bringing all separatist small groups and parties back into the fold. The second mistake concerned defence. From 1924 to 1936 the VDB held strictly to the principle of unilateral national disarmament, promoting it and publicizing it in every way it could—though at the same time allowing that participation in military actions initiated by the League of Nations was a possibility. The motivation was mainly ethical and originally without a religious base. But it is

---

[1] Above, p. 515. [2] Oud, iii. 22 ff.

[3] See O. Vries, 'De Vrijzinnig-Democratische Bond als factor in de Nederlandse politiek (1917–1933)', *Bijdragen en Mededelingen betreffende de Geschiedenis der Nederlanden*, lxxxviii (1973), 444–69.

interesting to see how the party tended to conform to the spirit
of the Dutch interwar years by increasingly adopting religious
views as a justification for its political options; as would seem
natural in the case of a liberal party, it was the liberal form
of Protestantism called 'remonstrant' that had the greatest
influence. But in 1936 the party felt obliged to abandon the call
for disarmament—one year before the socialists, who had included disarmament in their party programme since 1921, did
the same.

There were major differences between Belgian and Dutch
socialism during this period. The Dutch SDAP got off to a bad
start with its 'revolutionary' error of November 1918 but the
Parti Ouvrier Belge, as an ultra-patriotic and reformist party,
shared government responsibility with Catholics and liberals
from 1918 until 1921 and exercised a real influence. For most
of the time the SDAP was to the left of the POB. It stood for
unilateral national disarmament, whereas the POB never did:
the latter advocated a shorter period of national service and
army reforms but thought national defence essential. The SDAP
was opposed to the policies of the victors of 1918; the POB felt
no qualms about accepting the Treaty of Versailles or even
praising it. Even with regard to Belgium's annexationism of
1918 and 1919 the attitude of the POB was not always uncompromising; some important Belgian socialists sympathized with
this exasperated nationalism.[1] Again, the SDAP was much more
interested in the theory of social reform than the thoroughly
pragmatic POB and there was nothing in Belgium comparable
to the Dutch reports on socialization (1920), on industrial
organization and co-partnership (1923), or on the reorganization of the state (1931).

By far the most important difference between the two parties,
however, was the fact that the POB participated in various
coalition governments,[2] whereas it was not until August 1939
that the SDAP managed to gain two seats in the Cabinet. The
cause was obvious. For one thing, the POB was stronger than
the SDAP. Moreover, thanks to their complete identification
with the nation and the national tradition during the war, they

[1] Claeys-Van Haegendoren, *25 jaar Belgisch socialisme*, pp. 63–6, 165–6.
[2] From 1918 to 1921, from 1925 to 1927, from 1935 to February 1939, and from
September 1939 to 1940.

were much more fully integrated into the parliamentary and economic system than the SDAP. On the other hand, the rhythm of socialist popularity was strikingly similar in both countries. In 1921 the POB suffered a serious election defeat; the SDAP did so in 1922. In 1925 both parties won brilliant victories,[1] but in 1929 the POB was already beginning to lose votes and the decline continued. For the SDAP it was in 1933 that the decline, which came as a bitter disappointment, began. Hitherto the socialists had been convinced that in a period of industrial expansion the system of parliamentary democracy would ensure for them a solid majority and thus the means for changing society. Time and again this turned out to be wrong. For the Belgian socialists, moreover, it was an extremely bitter experience when the decidedly progressive government they had formed in 1925 in collaboration with the Christian democrats with a large majority in Parliament was reduced to impotence by the leaders of the Belgian banks and industry. Parliament apparently had far less power than constitutional theory prescribed. As for the trade unions, even there the growth of the socialist organizations was less satisfactory than had been expected, for the growth of the smaller confessional unions took away much of the potential support. In the Netherlands in 1919 the socialist NVV had 191,000 members as opposed to the 138,000 in the Catholic and Protestant unions; in 1939 it was about 306,000 as against 291,000. In Belgium the socialist unions benefited spectacularly from the war and the high expectations aroused by the peace. In 1914 they had totalled only about 125,000 members; in 1920 there were 677,000. But that was the peak and during the thirties their number vacillated around 550,000. Meanwhile the Catholic unions, which before the war had some 100,000 members and which suffered dramatic losses after the war, had recovered: in 1939 their membership had risen to 340,000.[2]

For the socialists in both countries the 1920s were years of

---

[1] The POB obtained 39 per cent of the votes, the SDAP nearly 23 per cent.

[2] Compared with other European countries these figures are not very high. In 1925 the number of organized workers taken as a percentage of the total population amounted in Austria to 17·1, in Germany to 15·3, in Great Britain to 13·3, in Belgium to 9·9, and in the Netherlands to 7·3. Cf. J. P. Kruyt, *België. Boeren en arbeiders sedert den Wereldoorlog* (Groningen, 1932), p. 88.

dispiriting stagnation[1] despite the brief moment of success in 1925 when, after a period of very conservative government, the electorate expressed more sympathy for the opposition. The great economic depression plunged them deeper into despondency and uncertainty. They were by no means sure that Marxist socialists ought to oppose the policies devised by the 'bourgeois' governments in the Low Countries to try and overcome the crisis by deflation and the preservation of free trade and the gold standard. There were, it seemed, only two possibilities: either the depression was not essentially different from nineteenth-century precedents, in which case it could indeed be handled in this way, or it was a new phenomenon which, if allowed to run its course unhindered, might bring the capitalist era to an end. As many reformist party leaders had continued to think in terms of orthodox Marxism, they found it difficult to brush such conclusions aside. The trade unions were in a different position. In Germany they had never totally identified themselves with Marxism and were, as a result, much more open to the idea of economic planning as a way out of the depression. This idea, of course, was not socialist in origin; Rathenau had been one of its early advocates and the liberal report, *Britain's Industrial Future*, dating from 1928, to which Keynes contributed, had made a strong impression. In 1932 the German trade unions launched their project, drafted by Woytinski, Tarnow, and Baade (the WTB-Plan), to create more work and enlarge the purchasing power of the masses by means of state credit.[2]

It was only after the ugly débâcle of German socialism in 1933 that the socialist parties in Belgium and the Netherlands began to consider such ideas. The ways and means they then adopted were very similar, though the style was different. In Belgium the new policy was dramatized as a radical break with the past, a revolutionary initiative by the younger generation

---

[1] Cf. Claeys-Van Haegendoren, *passim* and the far less valuable work by H. van Hulst, A. Pleysier, and A. Scheffer, *Het roode vaandel volgen wij. Geschiedenis van de Sociaal-Democratische Arbeiderspartij van 1880 tot 1940* (The Hague, 1969), pp. 88 ff. See also H. F. Cohen, *Om de vernieuwing van het socialisme. De politieke oriëntatie van de Nederlandse sociaal-democratie 1919–1930* (Leiden, 1974).

[2] Mieke Claeys-Van Haegendoren, *Hendrik de Man. Een biografie* (Antwerp, 1972), pp. 159 ff.; R. Wagenführ and W. Voss, 'Trade Unions and the World Economic Crisis', in H. van der Wee (ed.), *The Great Depression Revisited* (The Hague, 1972), pp. 259 ff.

which after a deep inner crisis had abandoned the obsolete doctrines of the old. In the Netherlands the revision of the programme was treated far more calmly. The Belgian *Plan du
travail* adopted by the Christmas Congress of the POB in 1933
and published by the party's Institute of Social Research,
founded to promote the Plan, in a fuller version in 1935, was
something fundamentally new for that country: such a precise
programme of action and such a detailed vision of the future
had never been drafted by the POB before. When in April 1934
the SDAP decided to follow the Belgian example and set up its
own research institute for the preparation of a Labour Plan,
it started work on a document—published in 1935—which drew
on a whole series of earlier studies.[1] Given such precedents, it
was much easier for the Dutch than for the Belgians to present
the Plan as a logical step in a long party tradition. From the
point of view of propaganda, however, both parties adopted the
same methods. By means of mass meetings, demonstrations, a firm
display of solidarity with flags, songs, and rhymed plays to be performed by hundreds of party members, they tried to get across
their message not only to the socialists themselves but to all those
who had shown themselves responsive to Fascist propaganda.

The Belgian Plan was based on the theories of Hendrik de
Man who was also responsible for the histrionics that went with
it. De Man felt and showed a close affinity with the passionate
intellectualism of the leaders of the so-called Dutch Marxist
school. He was a more learned man than Gorter and had a more
constructive mind than Henriette Roland Holst—both of whom
he admired[2]—but he shared their need for a 'total and all-
demanding faith', a faith the contents of which he might be
prepared to change, but never the intensity.[3] He liked sharp
contours; transitions between one phase of his life and the next
he refused to regard as gradual; indecision or error he tended
to interpret as sudden conversion. In his *Zur Psychologie des
Sozialismus* (1926) he described his alienation from Marxist

---

[1] The Chairman of the SDAP, Albarda, did not omit immediately to stress the
point: *De Socialistische Gids*, xix (1934), 250–1. Hilda Verwey-Jonker, 'Vijf en
twintig jaar socialistische theorie', in *Ir J. W. Albarda. Een kwart eeuw parlementaire
werkzaamheid in dienst van de bevrijding der Nederlandse arbeidersklasse* (Amsterdam,
1938), pp. 341–4, also situated the Plan in the continuous development of Dutch
socialism and pertinently refused to regard it as a break with the past.

[2] De Man, *Après coup*, p. 66. [3] Ibid, p. 147.

dogmatics not in terms of a well-considered reassessment but as a complete break with all forms of Marxism. It had been a 'new birth', an inner liberation, and it could be sociologically generalized as the alienation of the younger generation from everything that characterized the previous one.[1] In *Die sozialistische Idee* (1933) he tried to place his socialist views in the context of the intellectual revolutions brought about by psychoanalysis, quantum mechanics, and relativity theory, revolutions described by him in most dramatic terms. It may not be unjust to qualify much in these passages as rhetorical and to dismiss them as over-ambitious academic exercises reminiscent of the cultural-historical excesses of his former Leipzig master, Lamprecht, and of Spengler, whom he quoted as well as criticized at length. Yet the main impression left by his book is the sense of haste, of urgency, and of distress which despite the over-emphatic German style and the abuse of the superlative is both serious and genuine.

So the liquidation of the Marxist revolutionary ideal could be represented as a new revolution and the form of socialism advocated by De Man as the most radical one conceivable. Social democracy had tried, as De Man rightly put it, to reconcile the irreconcilable, to link a short-term reformist policy which had served the workers well with an ultimate revolutionary objective which could in no way be regarded as its logical consequence. With this purely theoretical ultimate aim in mind, however, the socialists had continued to cling to the dogma of the class struggle and international class solidarity, together with all those trite hypotheses about the upsurge of the proletariat and of a militant proletarian consciousness which were required to support it, however often they had been proved wrong in the past. Proportionately the 'middle class' was growing more quickly than the working class, and neither before nor after 1914 had anyone been able to perceive the stirring of a proletarian consciousness; quite the contrary, the workers were seeking the protection of the nation and aspiring to the cosiness of petty-bourgeois life. But while such simple observations entailed the repudiation of the Marxist scheme, they did not make it necessary to abandon socialism. Socialism, in De Man's view, was an ancient historical phenomenon, the

[1] De Man, *Psychologie*, pp. 3–4.

most noble idea conceived by mankind, the product of no particular economic system or social class. The consequence was clear. The socialists should give up both their reformism and their revolutionary idealism, together with the myths on which the latter rested; they should closely co-operate with the middle classes, some of whom—as De Man saw happening in Germany —were in danger of being proletarianized and opting for Fascism by way of escape. With such new allies and such new ideas socialists should carry out radical structural reforms for the benefit of society as a whole.

This was the purpose of the *Plan du travail*. Émile Vandervelde personally invited Hendrik de Man, then a guest lecturer in social psychology at Frankfurt University, to return to Belgium in order to bring new inspiration to the POB. In March 1933 he settled in Brussels and immediately formulated his Plan, initially a short sketch of only eight pages, later worked out in detail in a book of more than 400 pages, which was published in 1935.[1] Although much in it was derived from the German WTB-Plan,[2] it retained a strong personal flavour. It is strategic in character, a plan of attack written by a man who had immensely enjoyed military life. But if the reader can easily see how the attack on capitalism was to be mounted, the true nature of the society which was to emerge after the victory is likely to remain beyond his grasp. In this respect the Plan differs fundamentally from the 1920 SDAP report on socialization: there the vision of a community of industrious workers operating in the largest possible and most rationally organized state-controlled monopolies was plain to see. Such an ascetic and well defined future was not at all what De Man was seeking. He appears to have disliked the centralizing and monopolistic tendencies in contemporary society; he accepted them as facts but wanted to mitigate their effects wherever possible and to prevent their future development.

De Man's proposal to nationalize in some way or another the banks and credit institutions as well as the monopolistic heavy industries, particularly in the energy sector, was intended to

[1] H. de Man (et l'équipe du Bureau d'Études Sociales), *L'Exécution du Plan du Travail* (Antwerp, 1935). On the Plan see also Dodge, *Beyond Marxism: The Faith and Works of Hendrik de Man*, pp. 124–46.
[2] Claeys-Van Haegendoren, *De Man*, p. 166.

provide the state with the resources it needed to put the economy on its feet; it was primarily a strategic move. Monopolistic enterprises as such, whether private or state-owned, had no particular charm for De Man, but he needed them as central institutions to provide the necessary credit and energy to protect the freedom of the smaller enterprises and of agriculture in particular. Private property should be preserved. It was precisely because the Plan was a plan of attack against the banks, first of all, that the state had to be made strong in order to realize it. Therefore provision was made for the establishment of a number of state institutions which would grant the executive far more independence than it had ever had before, and also for the nomination of permanent economic directors who, although Cabinet members, would be independent of Parliament and entitled to serve their full terms of office—three years—even in the event of a government crisis. So the Plan left room for a private sector on the one hand, subject only to over-all economic planning, which may be described as representing a policy of differentiation and decentralization; and on the other, for a concentration of economic and political power in semi-autonomous councils, with civil servants beyond the reach of party politics and by virtue of their control of banking and credit more powerful than any state officials in Belgian history. There was in this an element of paradox inasmuch as De Man had repeatedly and emphatically declared his dislike of all forms of étatism.

It is interesting to compare the Dutch Plan with De Man's proposals.[1] Both assumed that the economy, strangled by the government's ill-conceived deflationary policies, could be revived by large scale state-financed public works which, by increasing the number of well-paid workers, would augment the purchasing power of the nation. De Man needed 5 milliard francs (that is, almost 350 million guilders) to accomplish this; the Dutch proposed to spend an amount of 200 million guilders in each of three consecutive years. Significantly, both projects were designed to further the interests not only of the industrial workers but also those of the farmers and the middle classes. Both, in other words, were meant to show that the socialists,

[1] *Het plan van de arbeid. Rapport van de commissie uit N.V.V. en S.D.A.P.* (Amsterdam, 1935).

faced with the threat of Fascism, were willing to widen their basis beyond a single class in order to become broad popular parties.

There were, however, striking differences of style in the way the Dutch and Belgians approached their problems. To start with, the Dutch book setting forth the Plan was at once more pedantic and more balanced than its Belgian counterpart. The authors consider the various possibilities in measured tones and then put forward their proposals. It is not a plan of attack but a long-term project of which the consequences are studied in detail. The Dutch socialists, unlike the Belgians, did not see themselves as standing before a capitalist stronghold of banks to conquer which was the most urgent priority. In the Netherlands the influence of the banks on industry and trade was not nearly so formidable. Thus the Dutch Plan confined itself to a proposal to nationalize the Nederlandsche Bank and to make possible some control over private banks. Secondly, it was more emphatic about the need to rationalize and organize the economy with explicit reference to the Socialization Report of 1920.[1] Moreover, the Dutch were concerned with the orderly development of industry in ways that did not apply to Belgium, where the process of industrialization had started much earlier. The Dutch Plan dealt not only with the current economic crisis but also sought to indicate how economic growth generally could be stimulated by structural reform. This element was lacking in the Belgian Plan which was exclusively one for immediate recovery. As a Dutch writer put it in 1934, the ideal seemed to be to achieve a 'frozen society, a society without opportunity for further development',[2] whereas the Dutch Plan foreshadowed the dynamic developments that followed the Second World War.

The centralizing tendency which seems inherent in De Man's conception was quite alien to the Dutch who preferred a system of decentralization with corporatist features. The first elaborate description of this is to be found in a Report of 1931,[3] which launched the Plan's political programme. The intention was to

---

[1] Ibid., p. 125.
[2] Hilda Verwey-Jonker, 'Kanttekeningen bij het Plan-De Man', *De Socialistische Gids*, xix (1934), 382.
[3] *Nieuwe Organen* (Amsterdam, 1931).

organize economic activity into so-called *productschappen* (literally, 'productships') for particular branches of industry, agriculture, transport, etc., each governed by a board of its own. These boards would consist of the experts and representatives of the interested parties and also of men representing the general and the consumers' interests, and they should be given legislative authority as well as autonomy under state supervision. This, of course, is not far removed from the corporatism which, as interpreted by the Roman Catholics, had been so strangely prominent in Dutch discussions ever since 1919.

Both plans buried a lot of socialist dogmatics. If revolutionary Marxism is to be called 'left-wing', then *planisme* moves even further to the right than reformism. Yet in the Netherlands the reformist leaders of the socialist party, which had once been far more left-wing than the POB, found it acceptable, and a younger generation of non-Marxist socialists enthusiastically expounded it. In Belgium De Man's personality became a symbol of the Plan and by his dramatic tactics he was able to win over the ultra left-wing elements. The old, reformist leadership of the party, however, was not so easily persuaded to abandon its familiar blend of reformism and Marxism.[1] It was mainly due to the support of Paul-Henri Spaak, then spokesman of the rebellious left-wing formed by the younger generation—towards the end of his life Spaak wrote that De Man was one of the few people in whom he had recognized a spark of genius[2]—that the extreme Left became the most faithful promoter of the Belgian Plan.

All this shows only one thing clearly: that under these circumstances the division of socialism into a left-and a right-wing no longer made much sense. Spaak and his group adopted ultra-left and revolutionary attitudes but they were hardly interested in theory. Vandervelde and his generation clung to orthodox Marxism, but they invited De Man to start his

---

[1] Claeys-Van Haegendoren, *25 jaar Belgisch socialisme*, pp. 319 ff. Louis de Brouckère (b. 1870) is a characteristic example. He was De Man's Marxist companion in arms in 1911. Without correctly understanding the problems with which De Man was wrestling he simply denied the reality of the new 'middle classes', the *embourgeoisement* of the workers, the materialism of the reformists, and all other premisses of De Man: Louis de Brouckère, 'Lutte de classe du prolétariat ou concentration nationale?', *Œuvres choisies* (4 vols., Brussels, 1954–62), ii. 29–76.

[2] P. H. Spaak, *Combats inachevés* (2 vols., Paris, 1969), i, 25–6.

campaign for *planisme*. The Dutch SDAP came to the ineluctable but painful conclusion that it must draft a new programme making no reference to the class struggle but stressing the need to fight, even by arms if necessary, for what it now believed to be the best Dutch traditions of intellectual freedom and toleration. This programme, adopted in 1937, was serious and realistic; compared with its 1912 predecessor it was, however, extremely uncertain about fundamental principle. What was lacking in socialism in all its shades during the late thirties was a consensus about, as well as confidence in, the direction in which society was moving.[1]

The Dutch Plan met with a cool reception from the other political parties and could make little headway in the climate of these years. The pragmatism of the political leaders was so innate and the political stability resulting from the *verzuiling* so reliable that any theory, no matter by whom it was promoted, could in the end be safely ignored. But the fate of the Belgian Plan took a more dramatic turn. In 1935 De Man himself joined the Cabinet formed by Paul van Zeeland, which though committed to limited economic reforms was under no obligation to carry out the Plan as a whole. The Cabinet was undoubtedly successful in its economic policies—the economic situation improved rapidly—but its success owed nothing to the Plan. In 1936 however, De Man was persuaded to join Van Zeeland's second Cabinet as Finance Minister, and Spaak and Vandervelde also became members. Soon the latent tensions between the ageing Vandervelde, still backed by a large group of the POB membership, and the younger generation came into the open. But it was not the Plan itself which occasioned the break, it was foreign policy. Spaak and De Man championed the recently introduced policy of neutrality with eloquence and tenacity; Vandervelde, who admired the French Front populaire, felt that he could not take responsibility for such a policy and in January 1937—on his seventy-first birthday—he resigned. It now looked as if there were a radical split in the POB between the internationalist Marxism which an older generation refused to give up and the national *planisme* advocated by De Man and Spaak, of which the policy of neutrality was

---

[1] I quote, with a small alteration, Hilda Verwey-Jonker, 'Vijf en twintig jaar', p. 338.

represented as a logical corollary. Although the formal unity of the POB was preserved, it turned out to be impossible to reach real agreement on these matters. Embittered by the failure of his *planisme*, little interested in administrative routine, and probably painfully inadequate as head of a government department, full of disgust, moreover, with parliamentary intrigues and the sterility and mediocrity of parliamentary debate, De Man became more and more convinced of the need for a fundamental revision of state institutions. In 1938 he resigned from the Cabinet of P.-E. Janson to spend the last months before the German invasion advocating an authoritarian democracy led by the one man he still had faith in, King Leopold III. Within the POB his prestige had steadily declined. And when Belgium was invaded in 1940, the POB was in total disarray not only on the matter of fundamental principle but even on the immediate question of their relations with the German conqueror.

The integration of the socialist movement into the political and social life of the interwar years is probably one of the reasons why in the Low Countries it lost the considerable cultural influence it had had before the war. Socialism had become a *zuil*. No doubt for its adherents it still offered a distinctive way of life, the 'conscious' socialist manifesting himself by his clothes, his style of speaking, the architecture of the house built for him by a socialist building society, by his songs, his hobbies, and by the customs and ritual of his youth movement. In the Netherlands, particularly, much was done along these lines to raise aesthetic standards but it was for party members only. Socialism had become a little world of its own, existing alongside the worlds of Protestants and of Roman Catholics, an autonomous community of citizens catered for by its own organizations. It had ceased to be an impressive intellectual system or a passionately affirmed doctrine of salvation, although the socialist leaders spoke with the ponderous grandiloquence popular in those years. Understandably enough, artists were no longer attracted to a movement which in the fields of belles-lettres and of art had become sadly listless. The socialists' willingness to accept the *zuilen* system may well explain also why the socialist parties were never in this period threatened by really dangerous schismatic movements despite the divisive forces which sometimes seemed as if they ought to be tearing them apart. In 1932 a group of some 2,000 members left the Dutch SDAP to found the Onafhankelijke Socialistische Partij (Independent Socialist party). This was to prepare for the revolution which they assumed would be the inevitable result of the economic crisis. But in the general elections of 1933 the consciousness of the proletarian masses which the new party claimed to represent failed to express itself as expected and the party did not win a single seat. It quickly disappeared amidst the ritual squabbling customary on these occasions about theoretical subtleties and the practical conclusions to be drawn from the true doctrine.

Communism remained politically and culturally a marginal phenomenon in the Netherlands though it was there that the first communist party in Western Europe had been formed under the leadership of Wijnkoop and Van Ravesteyn, men who prided themselves on their long experience and expertise.[1] The party grew but remained small, with 1,089 members in 1918 and probably about 11,000 in 1940. Before 1940 it never won more than 3·4 per cent of the votes at general elections and never held more than four seats in the Second Chamber. The history of the party was enlivened by furious internal conflicts. In spite of fierce competition Wijnkoop and Van Ravesteyn managed to cling to power for a good many years but in 1925 the opposition, supported by the Comintern, succeeded in overthrowing these men who had presumed to assert their independence of Moscow. From then on Russian influence increased rapidly and by 1930 was dominant. The party specialized in attacks on the social democrats, but these were outlawed everywhere in 1935 when the Comintern saw a chance of socialist–communist collaboration in an anti-Fascist popular front. In the Netherlands there was no such chance. There was no advantage at all for the SDAP in an alliance with the marginal CPN.

The political failure of communism in such a stable community was only to be expected, but in a country quick to follow international and especially German intellectual fashion

[1] In 1909 it was called Sociaal Democratische Partij, in 1918 Communistische Partij Holland, and since 1935—the period of national communism—Communistische Partij Nederland (CPN).— A. A. de Jonge, *Het communisme in Nederland. De geschiedenis van een politieke partij* (The Hague, 1972) gives an excellent survey, putting the published memoirs of many party members in their true perspective.

the cultural sterility of the movement was surprising. The end-less series of internal troubles, the bitter polemics and the ritual invectives, the relentless attacks on the SDAP, the schisms, reconciliations, revisions—none of them provided either a workable theory or even an entertaining discussion. True, a small number of novelists and poets explored communist themes in their work but contemporary critics, probably correctly, did not rate this literature very highly. There were no doubt some intellectuals of communist persuasion, not necessarily party members, but they did nothing to inject Marxist-Leninist visions into Dutch culture generally. From this small, peripheral group only one author merits special attention: the historian Jan Romein (1893-1962). From 1922 till 1925 he was on the editorial board of the communist daily *De Tribune*, a position he lost in 1925; in 1927 he was suspended as a party member. Yet he remained a Marxist and a communist and in 1934 he published in collaboration with his wife Annie Romein-Verschoor *De Lage Landen bij de zee* (*The Low Countries near the sea*). In this book he tried to apply the method of historical materialism to Dutch history. Its success was undoubtedly due to its lively style, and to its author's intelligence and patriotism, rather than to historical materialism. The series of short bio-graphies of great Dutchmen, also written in collaboration with Annie Romein—*Erflaters van onze beschaving* (*Testators of our civilization*)[1]—appealed even more strongly to a national con-sciousness tenaciously resisting all the world's evil. Together with the Bible, this national portrait gallery, moderate in tone, up to date in its use of modern psychological insights, and per-meated with a warm feeling of Dutch self-confidence, was able to provide support and consolation to many readers before the war and during the German terror.[2]

Before 1914 there had been no orthodox Marxist party in Belgium, though during the war there emerged in Antwerp, Ghent, and Louvain groups of activists who sympathized with Bolshevism and called themselves communist. These had almost no contact with the labour movement, however, and disap-peared with the restoration of Belgian independence. After the

[1] 4 vols., Amsterdam, 1938-40.
[2] Annie Romein-Verschoor, *Omzien in verwondering* (2 vols., Amsterdam, 1970-1), i. 267.

war it was the socialist youth sections of the POB in Wallonia and Brussels who reacted against their party's participation in the government and the betrayal of the revolution. But at higher party levels, too, there was dissatisfaction with the purely reformist character of socialist policy. This was not an opposition—as had been the case in the Netherlands in 1909 and in Belgium in 1911—arising out of the dogmatic puritanism of some intellectuals. J. Jacquemotte (1883–1936), spokesman of the malcontents, was a Walloon trade-unionist. He had started his career in Brussels as a shop assistant and then became an office clerk; in 1910 he became secretary-general of the Syndicat des employés. He was not given to theoretical subtleties. During the war he had loyally supported the policy of the POB but after 1918 he was anxious that his party should find a way to resume the class struggle. At that time Jacquemotte's group was certainly not communist or Bolshevist.[1] Transposed into the Dutch situation they would have resembled the SDAP rather than the CPH. They received no support from intellectuals, the Marxist left wing of the POB which De Man had led before the war having changed its mind. None the less, the POB started a campaign to isolate Jacquemotte and his friends that in the end forced them to leave the party. On 29 May 1921 they founded the Communist party of Belgium. Meanwhile the activities of the rebellious youth had already led to the establishment of the Walloon Communist Federation (26 May 1920), which was considerably more articulate in its Bolshevist doctrines. Under supervision of the Comintern the two parties joined forces in September 1921, but the difference in their origins made full collaboration difficult.[2]

Belgian communism was never very popular. The party grew from about 1,000 members at the start to about 9,000 in 1939, but it was slightly more successful in elections than the Dutch party. After obtaining less than 2 per cent of the votes at the general elections in 1925 and 1929, the percentage rose to nearly 3 per cent in 1932 and to over 6 per cent in 1936. It was therefore not until the initiation of national communism that the movement achieved some degree of success in Belgium,

[1] Claeys-Van Haegendoren, 25 jaar Belgisch socialisme, p. 128; see also Une Grande Figure du mouvement ouvrier belge: Joseph Jacquemotte. Articles et interpellations parlementaires, 1912–1936 (Brussels, 1961).

[2] Claeys-Van Haegendoren, 25 jaar socialisme, pp. 149–54.

especially in Wallonia and Liège. Yet it only found support for popular front policies among the extreme left wing of the POB, then led by Spaak who, however, was soon to be converted to De Man's *planisme*. When Spaak became in 1936 one of the most ardent champions of neutrality, communist anti-neutralist and anti-Fascist propaganda was hurled at him as well. However, the German–Russian Pact of August 1939 forced the Belgian communists to espouse neutrality too, and—after September—to interpret the war as a struggle between German and British imperialism from which Belgium should keep aloof. They give the impression of having been some twenty-five years behind the times for this was exactly the interpretation which Dutch socialists had fabricated in relation to the war of 1914. But apparently this series of abrupt changes of attitude did not unduly confuse the small and well-disciplined membership which the party commanded.[1]

Fascism and national socialism, too, were essentially ephemeral phenomena in the Low Countries, although they posed a more concrete challenge than communism. Apart from the fact that after May 1940 there was the all too obvious presence of the Germans, even in the thirties Fascist elements had to some extent put the traditional parties on the defensive, being the representatives of a large, international, and increasingly aggressive movement. It was just possible to dismiss communism as no more than an objectionable system in a distant and barbarous country.[2] Fascism, however, represented a challenge that demanded a response on different levels. The electorate had to be protected from Fascist propaganda which might go to its head; the socialist campaign for the Labour Plan was an attempt to put forward alternatives attractive to the masses. Moreover, it was necessary to rewrite one's own party programme in such a way that, although visibly hostile to Fascism, it satisfied the apparently widely felt need for energetic social and economic controls and the strengthening of state authority.

---

[1] J. Gérard-Libois and José Gotovitsch, *L'An 40. La Belgique occupée* (Brussels, n.d.), pp. 51–62.

[2] This was no longer possible after 1945 but communist popularity was short lived even then. The Belgian communists won 12·68 per cent of the votes in the parliamentary elections of 1946, 7·48 per cent in 1949, 4·74 per cent in 1950, 3·57 in 1954, and 1·89 in 1958. The Dutch figures are 10·57 per cent in 1946, 7·74 per cent in 1948, 6.16 per cent in 1952, 4·75 per cent in 1956, and 2·41 in 1959.

Both Van Zeeland's and De Man's policies and the party programme which the Dutch Roomsch-Katholieke Staats Partij
adopted in 1936 are characteristic of this general trend. In such
a way Fascism and national socialism could be made to seem
superfluous, mere caricatures of the much more sensible
conceptions of the traditional parties. But whereas it was taken
for granted by the overwhelming majority of the population in
the Low Countries that communism was no more than an
isolated aberration, it took some effort to manœuvre Fascism
into a similar position and the result was only partially satisfactory. Communism, in spite of its bewildering changes of
policy, nevertheless appeared as a closed and coherent system
that could be attacked in its totality. For the established parties
one of the alarming features of Fascism was its ability—an
ability which it owed to its lack of consistency—to hover in the
borderland between radical reform within the national framework which was just acceptable and revolutionary foreign
importations which were not.

How very difficult it was to draw this line became particularly clear in Belgium where Fascist or national socialist movements were associated with both the Flemish nationalist parties
and the Catholic party. To a much greater extent than in the
Netherlands, where national socialism would have counted for
nothing without the German influence,[1] these movements were
indigenous and would have emerged in one form or another
even without Italian or German intervention. They were a
result of strictly national problems, depended on a good deal
of improvisation, and could not be precisely defined. Moreover,
the Fascism of Brussels and Wallonia which appealed to the
Catholic bourgeoisie was of a different variety from the Flemish
version although the latter sought adherents from among the
Catholic population as well. The Brussels–Walloon brand of
Fascism exploited lower-middle-class rancour in the then
familiar fashion to prepare the way for strong authoritarian
government: the Flemish Fascists drew upon their historic
grievances of oppression and neglect to demand a new form
of Flemish independence; social reforms, though touched upon,
were quite clearly of only secondary importance. This is why

[1] I. Schöffer, *Het nationaal-socialistische beeld van de geschiedenis der Nederlanden*
(Arnhem, 1956), p. 58.

Flemish Fascism and national socialism can only be studied in the context of the Flemish problem as a whole.[1]

Dutch and Belgian Fascism, whatever its pretension to being a 'popular' movement, was originally the product of intellectuals, as its pompous nomenclature suggests. The first short-lived Fascist party in the Netherlands, founded in 1922, called itself League of Actualists; the first really Fascist organization in Belgium (1931) was called League of Dutch-speaking (*Dietsche*) National Solidarists. The silliness of Dutch Fascism[2] is also apparent in its immoderate passion for organization: during the twenties and early thirties there were dozens of Fascist parties, each consisting of a handful of people devoted to some ephemeral 'leader'. Only the Nationaal-Socialistische Beweging in Nederland (NSB: National Socialist Movement in the Netherlands), founded by A. A. Mussert, became a political party of some importance with its 1,000 members in 1933, rising to 52,000 in 1936—outnumbering not only all other Fascist groups but also the communists. In 1935 it looked like becoming a real danger to parliamentary democracy when it obtained nearly eight per cent of the votes at the provincial elections. But in 1937 membership dropped to 48,000 and at that year's general elections the number of votes was nearly halved. The elections for the Provincial States in 1939 were even more disastrous; the NSB was reduced to less than 4 per cent of the votes and had become just as insignificant as the CPN, although with its 32,000 members early in 1940 it still commanded a larger group of fanatical supporters.

Compared with the bizarre Dutch Fascist leaders of the twenties, Mussert (1894–1946) was a man who inspired confidence: an excellent civil servant attached to the department of Public Works in the province of Utrecht, who had won fame as organizer of the National Committee against the treaty with Belgium in 1925.[3] He set up the movement with care, at first as a somewhat exclusive association to which only reliable idealists were admitted. His attitude was sufficiently firm and his programme sufficiently vague to attract the kind of people

[1] Below, pp. 638 ff.
[2] There is an extensive literature on these movements in the Netherlands, expertly summarized by A. A. de Jonge, *Het nationaal-socialisme in Nederland. Voorgeschiedenis, ontstaan en ontwikkeling* (The Hague, 1968).
[3] Above, p. 582.

who thought that only the most grandiose measures could cope with the economic and political crisis which parliamentary democracy seemed unable to do anything about. In its first phase the NSB revived the ideal of the absolute state, which disciples of the famous philosopher Bolland sought solemnly to define in abstract Hegelian terms. Compared with the crazy slander campaigns launched by the Belgian Fascist Degrelle, the propaganda of the NSB was relatively civilized and evidently in 1935 a significant part of the electorate felt inclined to give it a chance. However, this chance was rapidly lost by the party's leaders who totally misinterpreted their success. Inspired by events in Germany they deluded themselves into believing that the time was ripe for the most extreme forms of radicalism. They became increasingly anti-Semitic and the concept of the absolute Hegelian state was replaced by revolutionary doctrines. The party enthused over Italian and German adventures in foreign policies. From being an extreme right-wing nationalist party within the Dutch political framework, the NSB became a revolutionary movement totally outside the Dutch tradition. The established parties and the Churches quickly closed ranks. In 1936 the faithful were forbidden by the Roman Catholic bishops and the Calvinist Reformed Churches to join the NSB. The SDAP launched a full scale anti-Nazi propaganda campaign. And since its criticism of party politics had been one of the NSB's most successful gambits—it called itself a 'movement' and not a 'party'—a counter-movement emerged (June 1935) operating outside the parties and taking no part in elections. It called itself Unity through Democracy (Eenheid door Democratie, EDD); although far from developing into a mass movement (its membership never rose above 25,000), its numerous publications and demonstrations certainly helped to strengthen opposition to Nazism. Finally, the Dutch section of the Comité de vigilance des intellectuels antifascistes, although set up rather belatedly in June 1936—the Paris Committee dated from March 1934—also exercised some influence on Dutch intellectuals, not on the whole deeply interested in political matters, before it was wholly taken over by the communists.[1]

---

[1] L. R. Wiersma, 'Het comité van waakzaamheid van anti-nationaal-socialistische intellectuelen (1936–1940)', *Bijdragen en Mededelingen betreffende de geschiedenis der*

The NSB was a solidly organized party; Rex, its Belgian counterpart representing Brussels–Walloon Fascism—with probably never more than 20,000 members[1]—was disorderly and chaotic. Mussert, in spite of his heroic posturing, remained a petty bourgeois totally devoid of oratorical gifts; Degrelle's eloquence could throw thousands of people into rapture. Although at moments, when it suited its purpose, the NSB flirted with religious feelings, it was in fact from the start completely indifferent to all forms of religion; Rex tried to lead a Catholic crusade. Both groups, however, drew their main following from amongst the middle classes, from those who saw in corporatism and authoritarian reform a better chance of gaining influence than was available to them in a democracy consisting of a well-organized working class and increasingly powerful big enterprises. Whereas the NSB hardly found any support among the upper middle classes, Rex was remarkably enough subsidized at one time by big banks and industries.

Degrelle (born in 1906), after failing to complete his studies at Louvain University, took on the task of expanding the Catholic publishing house which went by the name of Rex, its purpose being to bring about the victory of Christus Rex. Before long he turned the house into an independent firm, particularly active in the field of politics. Immensely ambitious and aggressive, with a great talent for invective and eloquent malice—important assets in these years, as also was his power to simulate indignation on all sorts of abuses—he needed a public and in his search for one he began by excoriating the Catholic party for its decrepitude and by launching a vehemently puritanical campaign amongst the young to root out political immorality. In 1936 the Catholic party understandably broke with him, but it was then that success began to assume formidable proportions. He could always command a large and enthusiastic audience, for he was a handsome young man, with dreamy but searching eyes, and a voice that could be impressively thunderous or tender when he spoke (as he

Nederlanden, lxxxvi (1971), 124–50.—In 1938 the committee had between 1,000 and 2,000 members. In France Vigilance had about 8,000, in Belgium about 1,000 members.

[1] J. Willequet, 'Les Fascismes belges et la seconde guerre mondiale', *Revue d'histoire de la deuxième guerre mondiale*, xvii (1967), 103. Cf. J. M. Étienne, *Le Mouvement rexiste jusqu'en 1940* (Paris, 1968), pp. 79–80.

almost always did) about small children and his own aged
mother.[1] He presented himself as an undaunted crusader
fighting for law and order, decency and selflessness, and his
attacks on party leaders who had important interests in banks
and industries made a deep impression and indeed were not
always without justification. After his victory in the 1936 elections followed by defeat the next year, he became more overtly
national socialist, introducing the theme of anti-Semitism and
advocating dictatorship. Then Rex was overtaken by the same
destiny that wrecked the NSB; initially an extreme right-wing
party within the national framework, it became a revolutionary
party whose daemon was Nazi Germany. When it became clear
that Degrelle was personally striving after a sort of Fascist-
rexist dictatorship, he soon lost the confidence of the unadventurous bourgeoisie of Brussels and Wallonia—in Flanders his
following had always been more restricted.[2] Even in spite of
generous support from Mussolini rexist finances were in complete chaos and at the outbreak of war the party, which got
hardly more than 4 per cent of the votes in 1939, had become
a bankrupt and marginal phenomenon.

It is difficult to determine the effect of the economic crisis
on the relative, albeit short lived, success of the Fascist parties.
At the general elections of 1932, when the Belgian economy
was at its lowest ebb, the electorate took no risks. When it did
show itself ready to entertain new ideas in 1936, the economy
was already rapidly recovering. The success of the NSB, on the
other hand, coincided with a year of continuous depression;
not until 1936 did the Netherlands begin to benefit from the
rising trend in the world's economy. In spite of this, the Fascist
cycle in both countries was much the same. It was shortly after
the worst was over that Fascism appealed to people as a policy
that could protect or restore social stability, and perhaps prevent another collapse. But as soon as Fascism developed into
a revolutionary movement that threatened this stability, it lost
all its appeal. And there was a further factor. In both countries

---

[1] See the comments in *La Dernière Heure* (30 May 1936), quoted by Renée
Grabiner, 'La montée du Rexisme: étude de la presse bruxelloise non rexiste,
octobre 1935—mai 1936', *Res Publica*, xi (1969), 744–5.

[2] In the elections of 1936 he obtained 7 per cent of the votes cast in Flanders,
15·1 per cent in Wallonia, and 18·5 per cent in the district of Brussels: Étienne,
op. cit., p. 57.

the monarchy, treated with respect by the Fascists, was so essential and indispensable a part of the national existence that there was really no room for any ideology advocating dictatorship.

4. *The Flemish Problem*

During the interwar years the Flemish question was the fundamental political issue in Belgium. All other political problems—corporatism and the radical revision of the parliamentary system in the first place—seemed to disappear fairly rapidly after 1940 and were left unsolved after 1944. But the determination of the Flemings to achieve greater independence and influence was a constant in Belgian politics in the twenties and thirties and it continued to be one after the Second World War. This proves that a large proportion of the Flemish population remained dissatisfied with its place in the Belgian state. How can this be explained? Allowing for the fact that the population of Flanders was greater than that of the Walloon provinces and growing at a greater rate,[1] and that universal male suffrage had been introduced in 1918, one might have thought a definitive solution possible. Most Flemings did not understand French (88 per cent in 1930) and to many others who did it was still a foreign language, so taking this in account too it would seem reasonable to suppose that in a democratically governed country nothing could have prevented the Dutch-speaking population from achieving its demands if once they were pressed with sufficient determination. Putting it in its broadest and simplest terms, the people who stood for Flemish interests wanted to make sure that Dutch-speaking Belgians did not, either in their daily life or in their careers or their social opportunities, suffer from their inability to speak French fluently any more than the French-speaking Belgians did from their ignorance of Dutch. But there was in fact no broad and simple solution. All efforts to bring about the desired result were jeopardized not only by

[1] Between 1921 and 1939 the population of the Flemish provinces increased by some 17 per cent, that of Wallonia by less than 4 per cent, that of the district of Brussels by about 14 per cent. The electorate increased during this period in these areas by 26 per cent, nearly 10 per cent, and over 20 per cent respectively. In 1939 the Flemish provinces had 4,157,661, the Walloon provinces 2,960,768, and the district of Brussels 1,277,847 inhabitants.

the prejudices of some francophones but by a whole complex of elements closely associated with the structure and history of the Belgian kingdom.

When the kingdom was founded in 1831 there was no Flemish question.[1] All power was firmly in the hands of the nobility and higher middle classes who in both the Flemish and the Walloon provinces spoke French. No doubt they expected that the Flemish population would soon adopt French as the language of their administration, their schools, and their culture generally, just as the Walloons had done. The Germanic dialect of Flanders and the Romance dialect of Wallonia would live on as warmly cherished relics of a rich past, but no longer with a genuine function of their own in modern society. A generation later it was clear that this expectation had been totally unrealistic. In 1866 still fewer than 10 per cent of the Flemish population knew French. In Flanders opposition arose to the use of French in the law courts, in the administration, and in secondary education, and Parliament was forced to face the fact, and even to some extent legally to endorse it, that for the time being Flanders was a province in which both languages were being used.[2] This represented a success for the Flemish movement. It was, however, a most ambiguous success, not because the laws Parliament had been obliged to pass were insufficiently enforced—although this was the case—but because the principle that Flanders was a bilingual province was in itself ambiguous. It was a good thing for the Flemings that administrative and legal business could now be conducted in a language people understood; on the other hand, it apparently meant that the Flemish society should be permanently split into a French-speaking élite and the masses who could be regarded as simply incapable of grasping or of assimilating French culture. In a sense, however, this development seems inevitable. The romantic rhetoric used by the petty bourgeois of the Flemish movement, glorifying the Dutch language and the Flemish people, shows their limitations. Too often they give the impression of not quite believing themselves that the Dutch language was no less estimable than French, for they of course were creatures of Belgian culture, itself wide open to French influence.

---

[1] Above, pp. 170 ff.   [2] Above, p. 256.

Moreover, they had not fully absorbed the mentality of the Dutch, to whom their language was naturally the equal of any other civilized tongues, perfectly well equipped to serve as a means of communication in the sophisticated modern world. Thus it would never have occurred to these representatives of the Flemish movement that French-speaking people might be forced to learn Dutch. In the last resort this meant that the only way left for the Flemish to make Flanders a linguistically homogeneous area was by driving the social and intellectual élite of the francophones away, that is by starting a revolution. But the relatively small group of Flemish romantics knew only too well that this was out of the question, and that even in pursuit of their modest ambitions they could not count on little understanding and still less enthusiasm from the devout and passive Flemish masses.

Not until the early twentieth century was the problem of the élite tackled more seriously. It was then that some people ventured to suggest that the only way of changing the situation radically was by forming a Dutch-speaking élite.[1] How well the significance of this challenge was grasped by the French-speaking population in and outside Flanders is apparent from their refusal to allow Ghent to become a Dutch-language university. For decades they had shown a willingness to compromise on many other points, but here they drew the line. But how weak, on the other hand, this challenge still was is shown by the fact that the advocates of a Dutch-language university refused to consider suggestions that, alongside the French University of Ghent, there should be founded a second, Dutch-speaking one either in Ghent or in Antwerp: they were afraid that parents would prefer to send their sons to the 'French' university because its certificates would provide better opportunities than 'Dutch' ones. The conclusions to be drawn are evident. In the democratic state which Belgium was gradually becoming, any government was obliged to recognize that in principle the Dutch language was equal to the French. The leaders of the Flemish movement also realized that this principle could only bear fruit in Flanders provided that its élite could be forced to exchange French for Dutch. The refusal from the francophone Flemings to accept this was supported so

[1] Above, pp. 462 ff.

powerfully by the French-speaking population in Brussels and Wallonia that the Chamber never even discussed the proposal that Ghent should be turned into a Dutch-speaking university, and thus no start was made.

So it remained impossible in Belgium to have a university education in the language daily used by the majority of the Belgian people. In a society developing into a democracy, where the universities were gradually drawing students who did not belong to the French-speaking élite, this situation was so patently absurd that few seriously thought that it could last for long. But there is another factor that should always be emphasized. Although the Flemish movement gathered strength and was increasingly supported by those seeking greater social opportunities, there was no vehement struggle between the two nationalities. The emancipation of the Dutch-speaking lower middle classes in Flanders—for it was this layer of the population that continued to be the driving force of the movement— was no more dramatic than that of the working classes. In the same way as the idea of a class struggle was essentially alien to the reality of Belgium's supple social development, so the idea of a struggle between two nationalities hardly clarified the Belgian situation. This became evident during the First World War when the activists and their striving for Flemish autonomy met with practically no support.[1] It was as evident during the inter-war period. .

The euphoria of the French-speaking Flemings after the German defeat was appreciably dampened by the first post-war speech from the throne. When on 22 November 1918 King Albert announced that his government wanted to bring about the complete equality of the two national languages as well as the foundation of a Dutch-language university at Ghent— leaving undecided how that should be done and what was to happen to the 'French' university—these people were bewildered and deeply indignant. How was it conceivable that Flanders should be deprived of the French language at the very moment when the Latin spirit had shown itself triumphant? The French language not only associated Belgium with its most faithful friend but also with universal civilization, and in Belgium itself, famous for its heroic patriotism during the war, it

[1] Above, pp. 535 ff.

served as the instrument of national unity.[1] Had not the experiments of the activists during the war with their university at Ghent and with Flemish autonomy been clear proof of the treacherous character of the whole Flemish movement?

The mentality which made such interpretations possible was not confined to a small group of fanatics, as is shown by the reaction against the activists and by their prosecution in court. A large number of Flemish activists and others who were wrongly taken for activists were put in internment camps or prisons, hundreds of them were prosecuted, and at least as many were kept under arrest without being brought to trial. Thousands of state, provincial, or urban civil servants lost their jobs. Thirty-nine persons were sentenced to death—most of them in their absence—though not one sentence was carried out. Compared with the purges after the Second World War when about 100,000 people were arrested and some 50,000 brought into court—1,247 death sentences were then passed of which 242 were carried out—the hunt for activists after 1918 may seem to have been mild, but contemporaries judged differently. The fact that only a few Walloons were prosecuted, the arbitrariness of many arrests, the rigour of some measures—university entrance was forever forbidden to young people, some of them not yet of age, who had studied at the Flemish university of 1917—all this, and the whole atmosphere in which the persecution took place, suggested that this was not to be regarded as administering justice but as wreaking vengeance upon the Dutch-speaking majority of the population in general.[2]

In contrast to many French-speaking Belgians who may have thought the Flemish question over and done with in the new era, the King and his cabinets after 1918 always admitted that it remained of real importance though for the time being they did little to solve it. It was Parliament's role to initiate measures in this field and the Cabinet's role to adopt them in diluted form. The group of Flemish Christian democrats in the Chamber had become so large—in 1921 out of the 80 Catholic seats 46 belonged to them—that no Cabinet in which the Catholics participated (and they joined all of them) could risk ignoring their wishes. On the other hand, this Flemish bloc was counter-

---

[1] Heyse, *Index documentaire*, i, pp. xviii ff., xxii–xxiii, 291 ff.
[2] Willemsen, op. cit., pp. 155–7, Elias, *Vijfentwintig jaar* i. 180–5.

balanced by the Catholic members from Wallonia and Brussels, on the whole more conservative and naturally more indifferent towards Flanders. Though smaller in number than the Flemings they drew strength from the support which they received from the episcopate led by Cardinal Mercier, who had little sympathy for the Flemish movement. Mercier's patriotism was religious in the full sense of the word; he feared that by making Flanders a province where only Dutch was used as the official language, Belgian unity would be undermined and this was for him reason enough to oppose such a policy consistently. After his death in 1926 he was succeeded as archbishop of Mechlin by Van Roey, who though certainly less biased also considered it his major political duty to preserve Belgium as a unitary state. Some of the lower Flemish clergy, however, were both passionately Christian democrat and Flemish nationalist.[1] Under such circumstances it is understandable that the various cabinets, subject as they were to contradictory Catholic points of view, treated with the utmost caution a problem it was impossible for them to brush aside.

It was the more difficult to neglect it because the economic development of the Flemish provinces, which had been evident since the beginning of the century,[2] continued after 1918. While industry in Wallonia was stagnating, the industrialization of Flanders—concentrated in Antwerp, Brabant (especially Brussels), and Limburg—made rapid progress. There were as many industrial workers in Flanders as in Wallonia and partly as a result of social legislation wages, which until 1914 had been considerably lower in Flanders than in Wallonia, increased. In the late thirties Flanders had some 400,000 workers employed in industry. The agrarian sector, too, which gave work to about 300,000 people, prospered from the modernization of its methods, improvements in marketing, and the excellent Lease Act of 1929, which allowed the peasants and their farm-hands to live far more comfortably than before 1914. So the economic and cultural backwardness of the Flemish population as compared with that of Wallonia gradually ceased to be a relevant factor. This was also partly due to compulsory education,

[1] Willemsen, pp. 120-3.
[2] Above, p. 420. There is an extensive literature on this subject, partly summarized by Willemsen, pp. 144 ff. and Elias, ii. 10 ff.

introduced at last in 1914 and strictly enforced after 1918, and to the use of Dutch in secondary education. As a result the representatives of the Walloon provinces, who realized quite well what was going on, had step by step to abandon what had in the past seemed the self-evident, and until 1914 not entirely unrealistic, premiss that the supremacy of their language was the logical consequence of the supremacy of their culture and their economy.

Although appreciating the importance of Flanders's economic growth for the attainment of their political objectives, the Flemish leaders were nevertheless apprehensive about some of its effects. As in Flanders the language of banking and industry also used to be French, it was not unreasonable to suppose that the linguistic requirements of business men and their office clerks would obstruct Flemish efforts to transform the upper classes into a Dutch-speaking élite. Moreover, the Flemish economy was dependent on the financial centre of Belgium, that is on Brussels and its banks. In the strange jargon employed by the Flamingants it was said that Belgian capital had been 'Frenchified', and by infiltrating into Flanders had had a denationalizing effect. The size of Brussels itself also presented problems. From 1846 to 1947 the Brussels agglomeration grew from 211,634 to 955,929 inhabitants. Whereas in 1846 66·65 per cent of its population was Dutch-speaking, by 1910 it was 51·27 per cent and by 1947 29·39 per cent. Some of the immigrants were of course Flemings who settled in Brussels and its environments and apparently changed their language without difficulty within a few generations. To the Flamingants it was infuriating that the Flemings, who in their own provinces were slowly and strenuously establishing the supremacy of Dutch, should have to stand helplessly by while the ancient capital became a 'Frenchifying machine'.[1] One way in which they sought to mitigate these side-effects of economic progress was by founding Flemish banks and credit institutions, which seemed to meet with some success in the twenties. Most of them, however, were still not strong enough to survive the depression of the early thirties and had to be wound up. The spectre of what an authoritative Flemish nationalist called 'the colonization of Flanders by Frenchified Brussels capital, based on

[1] Elias, *Vijfentwintig jaar*, i. 202.

Brussels and Walloon political power',[1] helps to explain the anxiety and extremism that characterized Flemish reactions during the interwar years.

There was always disagreement amongst the Flamingants about the tactics to be followed and even about the aims of their campaign. On one issue, however, all were agreed: Flanders should become an exclusively Dutch-speaking area. Considering the enormous complexity of the problem it is not surprising that the Flamingants differed vehemently about the best way of achieving this aim. Was it sensible to stick to traditional methods, to continue to use the national parties as channels through which the urgent Flemish pleas for reform should pass, in the sure knowledge that no power in Belgium could long prevent the emancipation of Flanders? Or were more drastic methods needed, of whatever nature? There was a world of difference implicit in such questions. The advocates of gradual reform wanted to maintain the Belgian state and the parliamentary system. The advocates of radicalism strove for a form of Flemish autonomy that would entail the demolition of the state's old structure and possibly even the collapse of the state as such.

Since the first group's point of departure was what it described in 1919 as a minimum-programme, it came to be called the party of the 'minimalists' and blamed by the 'maximalists' for pursuing half-hearted policies. In this respect, too, the vocabulary used by the Flemish movement was highly individual and extreme. It was in the first place absurd to describe the minimum-programme, considering the situation of 1919, as one of excessive caution; it was, secondly, impossible for the self-styled maximalists to produce a coherent programme themselves. If maximalism may nevertheless be regarded as an interesting phenomenon, this is because it expressed the frustrations as well as the uncertainties under which a not inconsiderable group of Flemish intellectuals was labouring. Whilst the minimalists restricted themselves to Belgian problems and looked for solutions within the Belgian framework, the maximalists inclined to participate in European literary, artistic, and political fashions, although they remained intellectually

---

[1] Ibid. ii. 16.

as well as emotionally part of a thoroughly provincial movement.

Maximalism had its origins in the Front party of the war years.[1] Early in 1919 a number of young ex-servicemen who had been active in that movement founded a new political party called Het Vlaamsche Front (the Flemish Front) committed to continuing the struggle despite the bitter disillusionment of November 1918, when they saw the Flemish soldiers, free at last to leave the trenches, meekly returning home instead of devoting themselves, if necessary arms in hand, to the great fight for Flanders' rights. The programme of the Flemish Front was not essentially different from that of the minimalists. Both wanted legislation to ensure that in Flanders Dutch would be the only language permitted in the law courts, in the administration, and in all educational institutions. But whereas the minimalists—both the Catholics and the socialists among them —continued to be members of the big national parties for whom the Flemish question was of course only one of Belgium's many problems, the Front party claimed absolute priority for it and rejected in advance all proposals which did not include some form of self-government—what form precisely was left for further discussion. The party met with little success. Badly organized, disrupted by interminable conflicts between its leaders, dependent on the goodwill of the Catholic population and thus seriously weakened by the obstruction of the episcopate, it obtained no more than 6 per cent of the votes in Flanders at the elections of 1919 and 1921.

The Vlaamsche Front defined itself as nationalist, left-wing, and antimilitarist. It is possible to justify this definition but not easy. The intellectual confusion in which the party found itself was the more confounded when former activists who had not themselves fought in the war began to join in. Many came from abroad, particularly from the Netherlands to which they had fled in November 1918 to escape prosecution. The nationalism of the Flemish party implied in the first place that there was no Belgian nation. Whether there was a Flemish nation, however, was still open to question, for some considered Flanders to be part of a greater Dutch-speaking nation which also included the Netherlands. As for being left-wing, there were

[1] Above, p. 543.

the usual grandiloquent claims to democratic progressiveness, but underneath there seems to have been just a feeling of disgust for the French-speaking upper classes and an honest desire for a better society rather than anything that could be called a political programme. The antimilitarism reflected the humiliating misery of the war. But at the party congress of 1921 a proposal to include unilateral disarmament in the party programme (as the Dutch socialists did in the same year) was rejected by an overwhelming majority.[1] The ceremonies at the IJzer where the various organizations of Flemish ex-servicemen gathered each year to honour the Flemish dead became, instead of a protest against war, a mass protest by the radical wing of the Flemish movement against the failure to compensate Flanders for its sacrifices during the war.

The ideology of the Vlaamsche Front was so capricious that left-wing sentiments and democratic convictions could be transmuted into Fascist authoritarianism without too much intellectual tension being experienced. The most extreme example of this development was Joris van Severen (1894–1940).[2] He was the most complicated personality among Flemish politicians, the son of a well-to-do West Flemish notary public and educated in a strict Catholic, French-speaking Jesuit college at Ghent. As a soldier he loathed the way Flemish soldiers were treated but he was a passionate reader of French literature, Marcel Proust being his most admired author in later life. In his youth a dandy among his somewhat rustic political associates, with a taste for Surrealism and Dadaism, he became a proud and austere man as he grew older, stressing the great distance separating him from the sentimentalism of the Flemish movement by the cool, severely intellectual style of his speeches and the extremely correct cut of his clothes, even his Fascist uniform. Until 1931 he supported the Vlaamsche Front, for some time even as a member of Parliament; however, during the 1920s Mussolini and Salazar replaced Lenin and Trotsky as his models and he began to call himself an antidemocrat and a traditionalist, equally disgusted by disorder, humanitarianism, socialism,

[1] Elias, *Vijfentwintig jaar*, ii. 40.
[2] On him see the uncritical but informative works by A. de Bruyne, *Joris van Severen. Droom en daad* (Zulte, 1961) and Rachel Baes, *Joris van Severen. Une âme* (Zulte, 1965).

and communism.[1] His thoroughly undisciplined mind sought order and discipline in the external world without finding it, least of all in the graceless garrulity of the Vlaamsche Front. In 1931 he formed the Verbond van Dietsche Nationaal-Solidaristen (Verdinaso: League of Dutch-speaking National Solidarists) which was to embody all the artistocratic and military virtues under his ascetic leadership and enforce strict political and social discipline. In 1934, still more exasperated by the romantic theories about the Flemish or Great-Netherlandish national soul, he astonished his followers by announcing that Verdinaso was not seeking to establish a Dutch-speaking state, consisting of Flanders and the Netherlands, but aimed to restore the sixteenth-century Burgundian state in which the French-speaking nobles and officers had had such an enormous influence. In the nineteenth century too various Belgian statesmen, among them liberals such as Rogier and Frère-Orban, had cherished the hope that the split of 1830 between the Netherlands and Belgium might somehow be repaired. Van Severen continued this tradition, but what had formerly been the thesis of French-speaking liberals now became the thesis of a Dutch-speaking 'solidarist', whose great model was Salazar and who wanted a Belgian–Dutch federal state, organized on corporative lines, strong enough to defend its independence even against Hitler's Germany.

Verdinaso had only a few followers in Belgium and even fewer in the Netherlands.[2] But the Flemish Front party fell into a state of permanent crisis. After an electoral success in 1929—when it obtained the support of 11·65 per cent of the Flemish voters—it lost two seats in 1932, though not only because of the foundation of Verdinaso. In 1933 it was decided to reorganize the party radically, to call it Vlaamsch Nationaal Verbond (VNV: Flemish National League), and to adopt an entirely new programme. The break with the past was complete. In its rather peculiar fashion the Vlaamsche Front had been left-wing and democratic; the VNV was right-wing and authoritarian. The humanitarian ideals of 1919, with which the Vlaamsche

---

[1] Quoted from a letter from 31 Jan. 1925 by Baes, op. cit., p. 81.

[2] In Flanders Verdinaso had less than 3,000 members, in the Netherlands no more than some hundreds. Precise figures are not available, cf. Willemsen, p. 412 and Elias, *Vijfentwintig jaar*, iv. 152 n. 8.

Front had, in theory at least, associated itself by claiming kinship with the great movements of socialism or Bolshevism or Expressionism, these ideals had gone. The fashionable colour was no longer red, but black. But whereas left-wing extremism had had some sort of cultural impact, despite its political insignificance, in so far as some outstanding Flemish men of letters had been deeply influenced by it, right-wing fashion was both politically and intellectually sterile. The VNV did not go as far as Van Severen; some of its members continued to favour the system of parliamentary democracy. But even they accepted the *Führerprinzip*—although the new Flemish leader, Staf de Clerq (1884–1942) was little suited for the part. As to the future of Flanders itself, they remained strangely undecided. The moderates were perfectly aware of the unreality of the proposal to unite Flanders with the Netherlands—despite all the argument the Dutch had never taken the idea seriously—yet this reappeared in the new programme as one of the party's aims, in preference to the view that Belgium should be reshaped as a federal state with a large degree of autonomy for Flanders. In spite of these contradictions the new-style Flemish nationalists were far more successful than their predecessors had been in 1933.[1] In 1936 they obtained 16 seats, and 17 in 1939. From these figures two conclusions may be drawn: first, that Flemish nationalism did not become a mass movement—in 1936 it had only 12·7 per cent of the Flemish vote—and second, that its success during the period in which it opted for Fascist ideas and abstained from showing real hostility towards Germany was at least more enduring than that of Rex and the NSB, which collapsed after 1936.

This may be because in spite of its hopeless intellectual disorder it was expressing ideas that were also popular outside the party: the ideas of Flemish autonomy and of a corporatist reorganization of society. When in October 1936 the Catholic Union was divided into a Walloon section (the Parti Catholique Social) and a Flemish one (de Katholieke Vlaamsche

---

[1] The number of party members remained restricted. During the war, when the VNV collaborated with the Germans—in November 1940 it declared to be national socialist—it increased from 25,000 in May 1940 to 70,000 in 1943 (Gérard-Libois, *L'An 40*, p. 301). Compared with the NSB, which of course covered a larger area—a whole country, not half of it—this was rather high. In 1941 the NSB had a membership of 80,000.

Volkspartij—the KVV: Catholic Flemish People's party), the latter[1] at once made overtures to the VNV with a view to some sort of collaboration. The initiative came from a group of professors at Louvain University, founders in 1934 of the weekly *Nieuw Vlaanderen* (*New Flanders*) which stood for federalism and corporatism. One of the best minds among them was Gaston Eyskens (b. 1905). How difficult it was in those years to distinguish clearly between Fascism and 'solidarist' federalism or—if the case arose—'solidarist' Great-Netherlandish conceptions, appears from the fact that the first offer of collaboration with the VNV by members of the Katholieke Vlaamsche Volkspartij was made a few days after the VNV had formally come to terms with Rex (6 October 1936). The KVV itself came to an agreement with the VNV a couple of months later. Although these agreements remained without practical consequence—they were soon either cancelled or forgotten—they do show the depth of Flemish despair. In the very year in which the Belgian Government under Flemish pressure severed its links with France and returned to a policy of neutrality, it seemed possible that all political parties in Flanders inspired by Catholic ideas were unanimously opting for a policy diametrically opposed to the traditions of Belgian democracy, envisaging only extreme measures to solve the national and economic crisis. There were several reasons for this. One was the fear of infection from the French Popular Front, which persuaded the intellectuals of *Nieuw Vlaanderen* that the Catholics should concentrate all their energies on the threat. Corporatism had also become the Catholic patent remedy for all the ills of the period. And the only way to stop Brussels and the central administration promoting the hegemony of the French language, and also to protect the interests of students now beginning to graduate from the Dutch-language universities at Ghent and Louvain, seemed to be to make Belgium a federal state.

In the end all these ambitions were frustrated. The overwhelming majority of the Catholic party, even in Flanders, was unwilling to fight with such allies for a 'new order'; on the contrary, together with the socialists and liberals they successfully organized the resistance to Fascist and semi-Fascist movements

---

[1] The fact that the KVV did not appoint an executive committee before March 1937 proves how provisional all this was.

to save parliamentary democracy, although many loyal members of the Catholic party probably did not rate its chance of survival much higher than the socialists of De Man's school.

Yet, however negative one's final judgement on Flemish nationalism may be,[1] one aspect had a long-term effect on historiography. The Dutch historian Pieter Geyl (1887–1966) had come into contact with the Flemish movement as a student before the First World War. After 1918 he found friends in the circle of the Vlaamsche Front and tried to give direction to the party's policy, always offering advice and criticism, and publishing under various pen-names innumerable articles about it in Dutch and British dailies and weeklies.[2] He was a passionate man, an agnostic, and a liberal, but in the eyes of his excited Flemish friends he was a moderate and remarkably down-to-earth. The idea increasingly popular with the Vlaamsche Front that Flanders should be united with the Netherlands he dismissed as folly. Flemish nationalism's turn to the right he despised and resisted. In his view the only satisfactory long-term solution of the problem was to reorganize Belgium as a federal state. It amused him to help draft a bill containing such a proposal which one of his Flemish-nationalist friends introduced in the Chamber of Representatives in 1931, not because he considered it had any real chance of success but because he vainly hoped to raise the dismal level of discussion to a slightly higher plane.[3] Meanwhile in articles and after 1930 in his multi-volume *Geschiedenis van de Nederlandse stam*[4] Geyl was working on an interpretation of history which was to prove fruitful. In his opinion people speaking the same language should form one nation; the fact that all Dutch-speaking people did not form one nation was the result of a tragic accident in the history of the Low Countries. Thanks to Geyl's sometimes drastic

---

[1] Willemsen's judgement is on the whole positive. In his *Vijfentwintig jaar*, Elias, one of the VNV leaders, warmly defends it: cf. iv. 100–1. I am inclined to follow M. de Vroede in his dispassionate review of both works: 'De betekenis van het Vlaams-Nationalisme', *Bijdragen en Mededelingen betreffende de geschiedenis der Nederlanden*, lxxxv (1970), 337–45.

[2] See P. van Hees, *Bibliografie van P. Geyl* (Groningen, 1972).

[3] R. de Nolf, *Federalisme in België als grondwettelijk vraagstuk* (Antwerp, 1968), pp. 233 ff.

[4] i (1930); ii (1934); iii (1937); continued in 1959. The book suddenly stops in 1798.

simplifications and his passionate defence of the theses that he propounded so intelligently, his systematic reinterpretation of nationalism in the Low Countries made a deep impression, although nowadays there may be only a few historians left who accept it with all its implications. Remarkably enough, however, its influence was stronger in the Netherlands, where there was little interest in Flemish matters, than in Belgium confronted daily with the problem. Such even among Flemish intellectuals was the impact left by the monumental glorification of the Belgian nation in Pirenne's *Histoire de Belgique*.

The so-called minimalists did not believe that either a Dutch-Flemish political union or a Belgian federal state was feasible; they thought that the interests of Flanders could be sufficiently served within the existing framework of government. It was Frans van Cauwelaert in the Catholic party, and Camille Huysmans among the socialists, who championed the minimalist programme and expounded it in the Chamber of Representatives, simultaneously attacking the Vlaamsche Front. There was one weakness in their position: if transforming Flanders into an area where only Dutch was used was a minimum demand, what could be the maximum, given that the unitarian structure of Belgium was to be maintained? Be that as it may, despite its name the minimalist programme was radical enough.[1] All education, university education included, all jurisdiction, and the whole administration should be in Dutch wherever the language of the majority of the population was Dutch. The army should be split up into French-speaking and Dutch-speaking units. And finally, the central administration should be arranged in such a way that regional matters were dealt with in the language of the region concerned. To realize these aims there were three possibilities. All civil servants could be required to have a perfect knowledge of both French and Dutch: or for every French-speaking civil servant in the central administration there should be a Dutch-speaking colleague: or the central administration could be divided into two parts—the last no doubt was the simplest solution but it was coming close to federalism. Consequently, the reforms demanded by the minimalists had far-reaching implications at

[1] For the best analysis of the minimum programme see the work of the Swedish political scientist Höjer, op. cit., pp. 15 ff.

the level of central government. They sought not only to exclude French-speaking Flemings but also to provide Dutch-speaking Belgians with far more influence at the centre than they had ever had before. It is characteristic of the aggressiveness and the ambitions of the post-war Flamingants that the Katholieke Partij in Flanders only accepted candidates for election to Parliament who were willing to subscribe to this programme.

During the interwar years their aims were largely realized. There were three phases: the first a period of hesitation and compromise (1919–28), the second characterized by a series of rapid and thorough reforms, and the third starting about 1935, during which a few gaps in the recent legislation were filled but which was largely distinguished by the state of disarray that followed the fulfilment of the minimalist programme, when it seemed as if the whole country were in the throes of a profound political crisis. It is interesting to study this development in the perspective of Belgian parliamentary and political history generally, for there, too, it is possible to distinguish three phases: one of reconstruction before 1925, one of consolidation until about 1935, followed by a time of crisis. Each of these phases opened with socially progressive policies and ended with a more conservative type of government. The remarkable thing is that nearly all laws furthering the emancipation of Flanders were finalized in the later years of each phase and after the socially progressive impulses had given way to more conservative tendencies. The reason may be that the more conservative cabinets got the vital support they needed from the Flemish Christian democrats, not themselves conservatives, on the condition that certain Flemish demands were met.[1]

In 1921, after much delay and in the face of bitter protests from the French-speaking inhabitants of Wallonia and Flanders, a bill was passed which, in contrast to the act of 1878 it replaced, made Dutch and Dutch alone the official language of Flanders for administrative purposes. There were still, however, too many loopholes and no effective sanctions to enforce the law. Equally unsatisfactory were developments with regard to the transformation of Ghent into a Dutch-language university. Again it was the Flemish Catholic members of Parliament who

---

[1] Cf. F. Maes, 'De democratie tegenover de economische en financiële problemen en structuren', *Res Publica*, iv (1962), 380–1.

took the initiative, insisting that the King's promise to found a Dutch-language university made in his speech from the throne in November 1918 should be honoured. After two years of discussion, accompanied by the customary demonstrations organized by the French- and the Dutch-speaking population, the government forced Parliament to accept a compromise. In principle the University of Ghent was to become Dutch-speaking, but in practice it was to be divided into two sections: a Dutch-language one in which two-thirds of the lectures were to be given in Dutch and one-third in French, and a French-language counterpart where the proportions were reversed. With regard to still another item on the Flemish list of grievances—the language problem in the army—in 1929 a bill was at last passed which made far-reaching concessions to the Flemings but again failed to provide the necessary sanctions. And in the same year something was finally done about the painful problem of the activists who had suffered after 1918. With the passing of time it had become clear that the whole persecution had been a mistake; in Flanders it was remembered with increasing uneasiness and its effects were deeply deplored even by people who had considered activism as at best a blunder and had categorically refused to participate in it. Flemish politicians of all persuasions demanded an amnesty. This was never actually granted but activists still in prison were set free and those condemned in their absence were allowed to return to Belgium.

The legislation of the twenties was disappointing to the Flemish leaders; at the same time for the extremists among the French-speaking Belgians it was a defeat. The depth of Flemish disappointment was illustrated by an incident in Antwerp. The death of a liberal member of Parliament from that city necessitated a by-election. In such cases it was traditional that only the party that had lost its member of Parliament should put forward a new candidate. The socialists and Catholics respected this custom, the Front Partij did not. It entered Dr. August Borms as a candidate, an activist originally condemned to death who had spent the last ten years in prison. As he had, of course, lost his political rights he could never have been admitted into the Chamber, yet he got 83,000 votes against 44,000 for the liberal candidate and 53,000 abstentions. This sensational result did not indicate a sudden rise in the popularity of the Flemish Front;[1] but it did show that the resentment felt in Flanders for the slowness of Flemish emancipation and the refusal to restore civil rights to the former activists was beginning to assume dangerous proportions. As a result the French-speaking Belgians realized that they were rapidly losing ground in Flanders and they began to wonder whether it might not be wise to give up the struggle. The second period in the history of language legislation was affected by this change of attitude on the part of the francophones outside Flanders. By withdrawing their support from the French-speaking Flemings, they would be better able to maintain the integrity of Wallonia. By 1930 all parties had come to the same conclusion; the socialists even laid it down in a solemn agreement between the Walloon and the Flemish members of the party, the Compromis des Belges, prepared by Destrée on behalf of the former and by Huysmans on behalf of the Flemings.

Things began to move more rapidly. It was now the government which took the initiative and no longer Parliament. By the act of 5 April 1930 the university of Ghent became a wholly Dutch-language institution. Opposition remained, of course, but on nothing like the scale of before the war and it soon faded away as the university proved perfectly equal to its scholarly and social tasks.[2] On 28 June 1932 a new act was passed concerning the language of the administration; as a matter of course the principle that in each region only one language was to be used was confirmed and this time instruments were provided to enforce it. Moreover, the central administration too was reorganized; some sections were split up, in others Dutch-speaking officials were appointed alongside high-placed French-speaking civil servants in Brussels to ensure that Flemish matters could indeed be dealt with in Dutch, Walloon matters in French. At the same time an act on primary and secondary education came into effect, by which the use of Dutch as a teaching-language in private schools was made

---

[1] In the general elections of 1929 the party obtained in Antwerp only 16,524 votes.

[2] As early as 1930 the free Catholic University of Louvain started a considerable number of courses in Dutch; later Dutch was put on an equal footing with French.

obligatory in Flanders; subsequently certificates of French-language private schools in Flanders would no longer have legal validity.

Then legislative activity died down for a few years. Not until June 1935 was it enacted that all lawsuits in Flanders should be heard in Dutch only, although exceptions were made that alarmed the Flemings. After that the Flemish question apparently came to seem less urgent in the eyes of the government and of Parliament. The Flemish demand that full amnesty should be granted to all prosecuted activists and that the fines they had paid should be returned to them was not conceded. After fierce demonstrations by French-speaking patriots and counter-demonstrations by Flemings an Amnesty Act was passed in June 1937 which gave nobody satisfaction. Again, after endless bickering, a new act in July 1938 tried to settle the language problem in the army, but for the Flemings the solution was still disappointing. Obviously Flanders' linguistic homogeneity could be enforced by law but it was difficult to come to terms with all its ramifications. Both amnesty and the army debate were sensitive issues that affected the nation as a whole. To recognize that the activists were wrongly punished might be taken to mean that Belgian patriotism, as it had emerged during the World War, had been meaningless and in vain. To split the army into a Flemish and a Walloon section might be regarded as a weakening of Belgian national unity and perhaps even of the will to fight as one nation against foreign aggression.

The extremism of VNV and Verdinaso, the growing support of representative groups and persons in the Katholieke Vlaamsche Partij for the principle of federalism, the many incidents and demonstrations of the late thirties, not to mention the entire history of Belgium during the Second World War and after, show that the inter-war years did not finally solve the Flemish problem. Enormous difficulties remained, the most complicated of all being the position of Brussels. Nevertheless, the interwar period witnessed a radical change in the distribution of power between Flanders and Wallonia; in the 1920s and 1930s the aims that King William I had sought to achieve in the 1820s were at last realized. What he failed to bring about in his autocratic way after the defeat of the French Empire,

Belgian democracy was able to accomplish after the French victory of 1918.

5. *Economic Developments*

Naturally at the end of the First World War the Netherlands was in a far better condition economically than Belgium. Though the economy had been upset during the war years this had no lasting consequences. Industry had continued to produce the same articles as before. The merchant fleet had been enlarged. Agriculture and cattle-breeding had not suffered long-term damage. The gold reserves of the Bank of the Netherlands had risen from 289 million guilders in 1915 to 635 million in 1920.[1] Although the situation had been extremely critical in 1917 and 1918, in 1919 it became clear that the economy as a whole had not been seriously affected. Economic development interrupted in 1914 could, so it seemed, continue without fundamental changes. The whole system of controls and rationing set up during the war was dismantled as quickly as possible. Of the 197 offices established for that purpose which still existed in November 1918 only 59 were left one year later and these too disappeared before long. They left no traces, sometimes even no archives or reports[2]—so definitive was the end of government intervention considered to be.

The extent of the damage suffered by Belgium during the war was analysed at great length in order to demonstrate the amount of reparations to be demanded from Germany. The Louvain economist F. Baudhuin, who thought the official calculations excessive, concluded that Belgium had sustained a material loss in buildings, factories, railways, and so on amounting to between $3\frac{1}{2}$ and 4 milliard francs at their 1913 value; another 2 or $2\frac{1}{2}$ milliard francs were lost by war contributions and by German confiscation of stocks. The country's national wealth therefore had been reduced by 12 per cent, or even by between 16 and 20 per cent if the loss of Belgian investments in Russia and Central Europe were also taken into account.[3]

[1] Brugmans, *Paardenkracht en mensenmacht*, p. 459.

[2] F. A. G. Keesing. *De conjuncturele ontwikkeling van Nederland en de evolutie van de economische overheidspolitiek, 1918–1939* (Utrecht, n.d.), pp. 9, 12.

[3] Baudhuin published these figures in the late twenties; see his *Histoire économique de la Belgique, 1914–1939* (2 vols., 2nd edn., Brussels, 1946), i. 74 ff.

Obviously, these losses were by no means compensated for by the reparation payments. The 3 milliard goldmark which Belgium received until 1931—it had hoped for more than 10 milliard—had a purchasing power equivalent to 2 milliard pre-war francs.[1]

Their relative situations in 1918 explain the divergent developments of the Dutch and Belgian economies during the inter-war years. Until 1928 Belgium went through a phase of reconstruction. Real *per capita* income was considerably lower than it had been in 1913, in 1929 by no less than 9 per cent.[2] In the Netherlands it soared[3] in spite of the fact that the population grew far more rapidly than in Belgium. From 1913 to 1930 the Belgian population increased by less than 6 per cent, the Dutch by 28 per cent,[4] but Dutch real *per capita* income went up by 35 per cent. However, as a result of the economic crisis of the thirties, combined with the permanently high growth percentage of the Dutch population—more than 11 per cent from 1930 to 1939 as against less than 4 per cent in Belgium—the great difference in the level of prosperity was considerably reduced. Compared with 1913, real *per capita* income between 1937 and 1939 had gone up by nearly 22 per cent in Belgium and by 25 per cent in the Netherlands.

The first post-war governments in Belgium—there were three of them between November 1918 and December 1921, all formed by Catholics, liberals, and socialists—adopted with popular approval financial and economic policies based on the wrong premises, just as their foreign policy was based on a defective analysis of international relations. As Germany was expected to pay the bills there was no need for Belgium to be thrifty. And since the much devalued Belgian franc would, it was wrongly thought, somehow return to its pre-war value in

---

[1] Baudhuin, *Histoire économique*, i. 151.

[2] According to Baudhuin: cf. his 'Les conditions générales de l'évolution des finances publiques dans l'entre-deux-guerres', *Histoire des finances publiques en Belgique* (3 vols., Brussels, 1950–5), ii. 75.

[3] See *Het nationale inkomen van Nederland, 1921–1939* (Centraal Bureau voor de Statistiek, Utrecht, 1948), p. 52.

[4]   *Population (in thousands)*

	Netherlands	Belgium
1913	6,163	7,639
1930	7,884	8,092
1939	8,781	8,396

the near future, it was profitable to float large loans in Britain, the United States, and elsewhere: repayment would be made in much stronger francs and thus at a lower rate.[1] From 1919 to 1925 the national debt, both abroad and at home, rose from about 22 milliard to 54 milliard francs,[2] with a currency constantly depreciating and prices going up rapidly. The index of retail prices in Belgium rose from 100 in 1914 to 501 in 1924,[3] in the Netherlands to 152.[4] These difficulties were greatly aggravated by disappointing tax yields. During the war several research groups, of which the most important sprang from the Solvay Institute and was associated with the Société générale, had prepared plans for a revision of the tax system, now generally recognized to be totally obsolete. Naturally the main innovation proposed was the introduction of a graduated income tax. This had been considered more than once before 1914 but had always been put off; in the socially progressive climate of 1919 it was readily accepted. However, neither the population nor the tax-collectors' offices were prepared for this new form of taxation, with the result that in the beginning it produced far less than had been expected. Since import duties were not adjusted to meet rising prices, state income decreased in purchasing power to less than it had been in 1913.[5] Only when at the end of 1921 the socialists had left the government and a Catholic–liberal coalition had taken over, was a serious effort made to restore financial order: as a result of repeated tax increases it became possible to cover expenses more satisfactorily. In 1913 the total tax burden per head of the population amounted to 45 gold francs; in 1919 it rose to 57, in 1920 to 50, in 1921 to 65, in 1923 to 109, and in 1925 to 125.[6] The burden of taxation, calculated as the proportion between taxes and gross national income, increased by 70 per cent in the period from 1913 to 1924 and by 29 per cent from 1924 to 1938.[7]

From 1918 to 1925 all efforts in Belgium were directed towards

---

[1] Baudhuin, *Histoire économique*, i. 85 ff.

[2] F. Vrancken and E. Seulen, 'Financement et liquidation de la première guerre mondiale', *Histoire des finances publiques*, ii. 26–7.

[3] Baudhuin, 'Conditions générales', ii., 75.   [4] Keesing, op. cit., p. 39.

[5] Baudhuin, *Histoire économique*, i. 107. Cf. M. Masoin, 'Les Recettes publiques de 1919 à 1939', *Histoire des finances publiques*, ii. 121.

[6] Masoin, op. cit., p. 150.

[7] Max Frank, *Analyse macroéconomique de la fiscalité belge* (Brussels, 1960), p. 72.

restoring the situation of 1914. The ambition was to rebuild the economy, not to reform it. Nevertheless, all political parties agreed that it was necessary to ensure that within the old economic system working conditions should be radically improved. On the one hand, therefore, the state was to provide funds for rebuilding the railways, the factories, and other means of production which had been destroyed, so that the pre-war development, interrupted in 1914, could continue within the old framework; on the other hand, it was expected to assume social responsibilities not required of it in the years before the war. Even so, social policy after 1918 still derived very largely from the pre-war aspirations of radical liberals, Christian democrats, and reformist socialists, and was kept strictly within the limits set by the élite of the early twentieth-century bourgeoisie —an élite which had convincingly shown during the war where real power lay in Belgian society. Reform was not intended to destroy the old economic system but to correct some of its evil side-effects. Even the socialist party and the trade unions were content simply to restore if possible the pre-war economic system.

In reality, however, more was changing than was allowed for in theory. More or less improvized measures turned out to have unforeseen implications, as is shown by the proliferation of the so-called *commissions paritaires* set up in 1919.[1] Early that year discontent among the workers and lower-grade office-clerks, including civil servants, became widespread. They asked for wage increases, the eight-hour working day, and recognition of the trade unions as equal partners in negotiations over conditions of employment. As strikes spread, especially among the miners and metal-workers, the government tried to mediate. It set up two committees whose task was to study working hours in these branches of industry. The committees consisted of an equal number of representatives of the employers and of the workers, that is to say of the trade unions. Between 1919 and 1922 another 23 *commissions paritaires* were instituted by royal decree, most of them at the request of the trade unions, and after a lull until 1936 their number once more increased fairly rapidly. The responsibilities of these committees steadily

[1] M. Gottschalk, 'Le travail', *La Belgique restaurée*, ed. E. Mahaim (Brussels, 1926), pp. 320–3; Chlepner, *Cent Ans*, pp. 316–25.

broadened until they included all matters relating to labour conditions: although their decisions were not binding, they certainly carried weight.

In this way, on the initiative of socialist ministers, consultative bodies were created on a national level, and came to possess a more or less independent function. They helped to negotiate collective labour contracts, acted as advisers to the government, and sometimes were granted the right not only to advise but to take decisions with regard to the application of social laws. Although formally without legislative authority, they were well on their way to acquiring it, and in 1945 they did. Consequently, a system meant to provide practical solutions to practical problems and initiated by the state became unintentionally something that might be called 'corporatist', had it been the outcome of corporatist principles. But it was not: everyday practice was more fertile than theory. It was partly due to these committees that the eight-hour day was introduced—in most enterprises it had been ten hours in 1914: the act of 1921 making this obligatory generally only confirmed an existing situation.[1] Naturally, the committees were especially active where wages were concerned. It was partly due to them that these not only kept up with rising prices but sometimes surpassed them.

The history of social insurance also underwent significant changes in the first years after the war, although pre-war principles were maintained. The system of the *liberté subsidiée* was upheld, but even more than at the turn of the century it was without the idealistic and practical content it had once possessed.[2] It had been introduced to limit state power by directing government money not to individuals in need of support but to the insurance institutions founded by the trade unions, political parties, or ecclesiastical bodies. During the war the National Committee had not made use of the system and after 1918 it proved difficult to get it working again. In 1920 unemployment benefit regulations became an unsatisfactory kind of compromise between pre-war practice and complete government control. There was, in principle, a system of voluntary insurance against the consequences of unemployment. The workers paid a small premium to unemployment funds, most of which were controlled by the trade unions, and the state contributed a

[1] Gottschalk, op. cit., pp. 343, 348 ff.   [2] Above, p. 501.

subsidy equal to half the total premium yield on condition that it was allowed carefully to verify the accounts. If in a period of prolonged unemployment the funds were to dry up recourse could be had to the Fonds national de crise,[1] which was financed and administered by the state. This mixed system also applied to disability and sickness benefits. Thanks to large state subsidies the number of sickness insurance funds—socialist, Catholic, neutral, and liberal—was extended and the number of insured persons increased enormously. Yet there was no question of making social insurance obligatory, except in the case of old age pensions. Under the act of 1924 each worker had to pay a monthly premium which was supplemented by the employer by the same amount and by the state by another 50 per cent. Although in most of these types of insurance responsibility remained with the administrators of the funds, in practice the grip of the state on the whole system increased to such an extent that there was not much freedom left in the *liberté subsidiée*. Here, in other words, developments would seem to have contradicted corporatist theories.

It is generally agreed that by 1925 Belgium had recovered from its material losses and that the economic structure of 1913 had by and large been restored to its old form. It is also agreed that the standard of living of the workers had reached a higher level than in 1913 when wages were lower and working hours longer than in the other industrialized countries. In a study written in 1925 and published in 1926, *La Belgique restaurée*, this was demonstrated with a wealth of statistical material. Nevertheless, the excellent editor of the volume, E. Mahaim, in his matter-of-fact and optimistic contribution on national income, stated: 'La Belgique d'aujourd'hui n'est pas heureuse.'[2] Apparently, neither material recovery nor the expectation of an international *détente* following the treaties of Locarno had been able to remove Belgium's sense of insecurity. In a country where electoral landslides were rare, the elections for the Chamber on 5 April 1925 showed that there was widespread unrest: the liberals lost 10 of their 33 seats, the Catholics lost 2, the socialists won 10 seats, making them equal with the Catholics with 78 seats each. This was a defeat for the Catholic–liberal coalition that had been in office since 1921. It also seemed to

---

[1] Gottschalk, pp. 369–71.   [2] *La Belgique restaurée*, p. 610.

imply that socialism, which had made headway in England at the elections of December 1923 and in France at those of May 1925—and was to do so in the summer of 1925 although less spectacularly in the Netherlands—was rapidly gaining strength. The liberals, convinced that it would be profitable for them to go into opposition for a while, decided for the first time since 1917 not to take part in the new Cabinet. Influenced by the failure of MacDonald's experiment in 1924 the socialists rejected the idea of forming a minority government. They turned instead towards the progressive elements in the Catholic party, in an effort to come to terms with them without getting involved with the rest of the party. They met with some success for the Catholic–socialist government formed in June 1925 drew its support both from the socialists and from the mainly Flemish Christian democratic bloc inside the Catholic party, not from the twenty-five or so conservative and mainly Walloon representatives. Even though the socialists had not succeeded in splitting the Catholic party, they had undoubtedly shown how deeply divided it was.[1]

The new government, led by Prosper Poullet with Vandervelde as Foreign Minister, remained in office for nearly a year in an atmosphere of permanent political and financial crisis, without being able to realize any of its socially progressive and pro-Flemish aims. The powerful, French-speaking, conservative Press and the forces of high finance gave it no rest. In Parliament support was adequate, but when it came to implementing its policies the government was powerless. This was a purely political matter. Socially there was no difference between the leading ministers and high society. Poullet (1868–1937) came from an old aristocratic family, his wife belonged to the nobility. His reputation as a scholar was based upon a detailed study of the history of Belgian institutions and not on any flights of ideological fancy. During the war, however, he had become convinced that the main task for the future was careful social reform and Flemish emancipation.[2] A. E. Janssen (1883–1966), whose role as Minister of Finance soon turned out to be of vital importance, was no dangerous upstart either: a Louvain professor with an international reputation as a financial expert, he

---

[1] Höjer, p. 158.
[2] Poullet knew Dutch but not well enough to lecture in it.

was director of the National Bank and had been brought into the Cabinet as a non-political specialist. Nor was there anything sensational about Catholics and socialists working together in one Cabinet; they had already done so between 1917 and 1921.

Nevertheless, the Brussels *salons* were closed to Poullet and his ministers and on one public occasion a high nobleman even spat in Poullet's face.[1] Janssen's financial projects, which were intended only to stabilize the Belgian franc, were undermined by financiers and assaulted by both the liberal and right-wing Press for no other reason than that success would set these 'tristes démagogues' more firmly in the saddle.[2] The reason for the persecution is clear enough. For the first time the left wing of the Catholic party had allied with the socialists.[3] If the socialists supported the Flemish policy of the Christian democrats, the latter would reciprocate by helping the socialists raise wages, improve social security, and reduce working hours. As far as defence was concerned the partners were generally antimilitarist, in an ill-defined sort of way. It was a different situation from that of 1917 to 1921 when the socialists in the government had been pinned down by their liberal and Catholic colleagues, and this was a point that the socialist Press was only too ready to emphasize. In 1925 the socialists undoubtedly interpreted their electoral success as a major step forward in the evolution of a socialist society. But the conservatives and the centre reacted promptly by using all the means at their disposal to prevent any modification of the restored free-market economy, any precipitate steps towards Flemish emancipation, and any reduction in the strength of the army.

The weakest point in the economy was the position of the

[1] L. Moyersoen, *Prosper Poullet en de politiek van zijn tijd* (Bruges, 1946), pp. 284, 286.

[2] Quoted by Moyersoen, op. cit., p. 319, from *La Libre Belgique* (12 Mar. 1926).

[3] Moreover, the affair was complicated by personal elements. The evil spirit behind the campaign was thought to be the Brussels financier Charles Fabri (1874-1938) who in 1937 is supposed to have launched an even more venomous campaign against Van Zeeland. Fabri was a solitary, slightly mysterious person. His reputation for being a great financier evaporated after his death when it became known that he had invested irresponsibly large sums of money in the affairs of the strange Amsterdam banker Dr. F. Mannheimer whose firm, the House of Mendelssohn, in 1939 went bankrupt in a sensational way.—On Fabri see Baudhuin, *Histoire économique*, ii. 260-6 and on his role in 1925-6 see Moyersoen, p. 311. On Mannheimer see Heldring, *Herinneringen*, ii. 1383 ff.

franc, which had lost much of its value and in 1924 and 1925 slumped still further. Nobody had expected this. It had been thought that the franc would become stronger as the Belgian economy expanded and as the financial affairs of the state improved. But the Belgian franc, the currency of a country that by 1925 had put its economy in order, was regarded abroad as dependent on the French franc, the currency of a country with a disappointing economic record. The electoral victory of the French left-wing parties in May 1924 over Poincaré further diminished confidence in the French franc, and the socialist gains in Belgium in April 1925 had immediate repercussions in the money-market. Poullet's government was desperately anxious to dispel the impression that the future of the Belgian franc was linked to that of the French and the remedy was evident: the Belgian franc should return to the gold standard (as the guilder had ironically enough in the same month of April 1925 which was to be so disastrous for the franc). The government, however, was faced with a most delicate situation. Its predecessors had borrowed money on a large scale by issuing treasury bills repayable in six months. The withdrawable debt of the National Bank had risen as a result to no less than one milliard francs monthly. After 5 April 1925 countless Belgians and foreigners hastily cashed in their bills, if possible in exchange for foreign currency. It was an unhappy coincidence that in this year the Americans began to press for the repayment of Belgium's war and post-war debts. Although this was arranged in a manner not unsatisfactory to Belgium, the Belgian public, still fondly believing that Germany would pay all these debts, was thoroughly disillusioned. From the start, therefore, Poullet had to accept that his Cabinet was in no position to assume additional responsibility for the poorer sections of society; it had to prove that by cutting expenses drastically and by increasing taxes it was entitled to sufficient confidence abroad to obtain the large loans it needed to solve the problem of the floating debt.

This policy failed. The French monetary crisis of 1925 and 1926—France had twelve Finance Ministers within eleven months—had a malign effect on the situation in Belgium. In May 1926 Poullet's government gave up the struggle without having been defeated in Parliament. The Belgian franc had then slumped lower than ever. The new government was led by a conservative Catholic. It was a Cabinet of national unity with Catholic, socialist, and liberal members whose only task was to find a way out of the monetary morass. Its main personality was Émile Francqui who in July, after Parliament had given the government full powers for six months, could set to work undisturbed by political distractions. He managed to solve the basic problem of the floating debt in an ingenious and radical fashion. The state surrendered its ownership of the railways to a new company in exchange for shares totalling 10 milliard francs, of which one-half remained in the possession of the state and the other half was put at the disposal of the holders of treasury bills which were no longer convertible into money. The confidence inspired by this, the work of a Cabinet clearly conservative despite its socialist ingredients, together with the personal prestige of Francqui and some tax increases, were sufficient to ensure the success of the operation. In October 1926 the government fixed the rate of the franc at 175 to one pound sterling (in early 1925 the pound had returned to the gold standard). This represented a depreciation of the franc to one-seventh of its pre-war value. Although the rate turned out to be too low, the monetary respite which followed upon the return to gold undoubtedly stimulated the remarkable growth of Belgium's economy in the period before 1930. Nevertheless, the whole episode had a negative effect. Much of the deep distrust felt by the socialists against the *haute finance* which, they thought, had proved more powerful than the electorate, dates from their experiences in these years. Hendrik de Man's *Plan du travail* of the thirties was in the first place intended as a frontal attack on the bankers.[1]

In the Netherlands the return to the gold standard on 28 April 1925 was triumphantly claimed by Colijn, the Finance Minister, to be the result of the wise and thrifty policies of the confessional government. In 1914 the Netherlands had forbidden the export of gold; this was now permitted again at the pre-war price in guilders. The decision was taken in concert with the British Government and published on the same day. But whereas the British decision to restore the pound's pre-war gold value was a result of an over-evaluation of the currency, the

[1] Above, p. 616.

Dutch measure was realistic. The situation in the Netherlands was highly favourable. Although the depression between 1920 and 1923 had caused difficulties there too—growing unemployment, a substantial drop in profits and investment—it had not led to a genuine crisis and had not affected real *per capita* income. The Dutch balance of payments which had been adverse in 1919, only half the imports being compensated for by exports, slowly improved; in 1925 nearly three-quarters of the imports bill was covered.[1] Over the years budgetary problems too were solved along more or less classical lines, although there was understandably a good deal of opposition. In this respect the situation was less favourable. By 1922 total state expenditure had risen to five times the amount of 1913 and although the tax yield increased from 28 guilders *per caput* in the first decade of the century to 107 guilders in 1921, it had been necessary to borrow enormous sums, especially during and just after the war, to cover costs of defence as well as of unemployment and other welfare benefits. During the depression that began in 1920 the tax yield was of course reduced but expenses increased. This was dangerous because it was difficult to get long-term state loans subscribed on the overstrained capital market and the only alternative was to increase the floating debt; this was possible in the Netherlands because surplus capital which had fled Germany was available for short-term loans. It was not until 1922 that the government embarked on a policy of drastic retrenchment; Colijn, Finance Minister in two cabinets from August 1923 to March 1926, was always ready to adopt radical measures to achieve his aims. By economizing on education, defence, and civil servants' salaries, by reducing the government's participation in house-building, and by raising a number of indirect taxes, he managed to balance the budget and to reduce the floating debt to normal proportions.[2]

Under far less difficult circumstances the Dutch cabinets pursued economic policies not fundamentally different from those of Belgium. And in the same way as in Belgium this policy, the culminating success of which was thought to be the return to the gold standard, was coupled with efforts to improve conditions among the mass of the workers while preserving the old economic structure. In the Netherlands, too, a more

[1] Keesing, p. 53. [2] Ibid., pp. 54–64.

constructive social policy seemed compatible with the liberal economic system of before 1914. The effective contacts between government and trade unions established during the war to cope with the problems of unemployment and food supplies helped to persuade the Cabinet and Parliament not to neglect social affairs at the time when they were dismantling most of the machinery through which they had controlled the economy during the war. The confessional government taking office in September 1918[1] made its intentions clear by establishing a separate Ministry of Labour. Led by the Catholic Christian democrat Aalberse, this ministry was very active especially in 1919 when the Labour Act made the eight-hour working day obligatory in factories. The Disability Insurance Act of 1913, which included an old age insurance scheme for wage-earners but was only partly put into force during the war, was extended and made fully operative. The major part of the insurance premiums was to be paid by the employers. In order that all aged and disabled workers could draw their pensions from the moment the act took effect, the state promised to provide the money until such time as the insurance institutions had accumulated funds. The state also promised to help in the case of the voluntary old age pension scheme (act of 1919) which was applicable to other categories than wage-earners.[2] The state therefore agreed to finance old age pensions for the time being; in due course, however, the insurance institutions would be able to draw on their own resources and state help could be gradually withdrawn.

The most characteristic and most important achievement of Aalberse's social policy was the establishment of the Supreme Labour Council (1919). This was a permanent advisory committee of between 40 and 50 members appointed by the Minister of Labour, consisting of representatives of employers and unions in equal numbers, with some independent experts and higher civil servants. The Council did the same sort of work as the *commissions paritaires* in Belgium, but whereas the latter appeared as it were without premeditation, in the Netherlands the Council was carefully planned and fitted into a neat theoretical framework. Yet circumstances in the Netherlands and in Belgium did not differ fundamentally. In both countries

[1] Above, p. 557.   [2] Oud, i. 125.

the advisory committees were allowed to represent a corporatist element in the state; for planning and executing the social insurance system no such corporatism was allowed, contrary to Talma's wishes in 1910.[1]

The depression starting in 1920 caused the government to cut expenditure and employers to refuse to accept further responsibility for their workers' welfare with the result that social legislation came to a halt. Undoubtedly the electoral success of the socialists in 1925 was largely due to widespread dissatisfaction with the way in which priorities had been chosen. But in the Netherlands the gains of the socialists were not sufficient for them to achieve even the limited and thwarted power possessed by their Belgian counterparts. Moreover, the rapid recovery of the economy after 1925 was also to the advantage of the workers. Belgium enthusiastically participated in the boom that characterized the world economy, and once the franc had been stabilized confidence in the future was even exuberant. The Netherlands reacted with greater restraint. Between 1927 and 1930 *per capita* income in Belgium rose far more rapidly than in the Netherlands but still remained at a considerably lower level.[2] What was essential, however, was that for the first time since the war real income surpassed the level of 1913. Moreover, after 1926 the state had sufficient income at its disposal not only to finance urgently needed improvements in roads, canals, and railways, but also to stimulate industrial concentration and the establishment of new industries, first of all in chemicals. Yet the period of expansion was too short to allow a thorough structural reform and rationalization of an industry rebuilt in its pre-war image. In the Netherlands, still less industrialized than Belgium, it was easier to rationalize production, as was shown by the merger of Dutch and British enterprises in the enormous Unilever (1929), the expansion of Philips's glow-lamp factory into a worldwide concern, the establishment of a petrol refinery near Rotterdam by the rapidly growing Royal Dutch, the concentration of the rayon industry (AKU), and the merger of the shipbuilding yards of Wilton and Feyenoord (1929).

---

[1] Above, p. 499.

[2] Estimated *per capita* income around 1929: the Netherlands £66, Belgium £48·4, Great Britain £90.

In 1930 the effects of the world crisis were not yet clearly apparent in the Low Countries. Belgium celebrated its centenary as a national state and taxes went down. Not until 1931 did the situation worsen. World taxes dropped sharply but production costs did not. In September 1931 the fall of the pound sterling, dragging other currencies along with it, added to the difficulties. From 1931 until 1935 the pound lost some 43 per cent of its value against the franc and about 40 per cent against the guilder. Neither in the Netherlands nor in Belgium, countries with a stable currency, did it seem reasonable to follow the pound in its dramatic and painful humiliation. As in 1931 nearly everybody in the Low Countries regarded devaluation as unnecessary, unjust, and dangerous, governments had to embark on a strict policy of deflation in order to keep production costs down. Quite apart from the question of whether such policies would succeed, in some branches of industry conditions were already critical. The Dutch shipping-trade, naturally suffering great losses because of the contraction of world trade, earned its income mostly in depreciated pounds and paid its costs in expensive guilders. In the course of 1931 more than one-third of the Dutch merchant fleet tonnage was laid up. In all branches of industry unemployment grew, from 18,000 in the middle of 1929 to over 100,000 at the end of 1930, 300,000 in 1933, and at least 500,000 in 1935—in percentages of the working population and calculated on a yearly average, from 3·4 (1930), 12·8 (1933), 15·6 (1935), to 17·5 in 1936. These are dramatic figures, although not until 1936 did they compare unfavourably with those in Great Britain, where in fact the situation had been considerably worse. In Belgium, too, unemployment assumed disquieting proportions: the number of totally unemployed grew from 76,000 at the end of 1930 to 200,000 in 1931, 340,000 in 1932, and 350,000 in 1934, when more than one-third of the insured workers were totally or partly unemployed. Then the figures dropped, although until the Second World War they remained much higher than they had been in the twenties. In both countries nominal national income in 1934 had fallen by about one-quarter since 1930. Thanks to the drop in prices, however, real *per capita* income was maintained at a level well above that of 1913. Even in these years of crisis it was still much higher in Belgium than in the difficult period of recovery after 1918. In the Netherlands the situation was different; throughout the thirties incomes remained lower than in the preceding decade.

The policy of deflation failed. On 13 March 1935 Belgium abandoned the gold standard with the result that the franc lost 28 per cent of its value; on 26 September 1936 the Netherlands were the last among the gold bloc countries to give up the fight, and the result was a 20 per cent devaluation of the guilder. Neither in Belgium nor in the Netherlands, however, did the disasters forecast by the champions of the gold standard occur: there was no flight of capital, no price rise, no uncontrolled inflation which would have made it impossible to balance the budget. On the contrary, thanks to the devaluation the economies of both countries were able to profit from the rising world trend. Understandably, the policy of deflation has in retrospect been severely condemned as the policy of parties wishing to shift the burden of necessary sacrifices on to the shoulders of the unemployed in order to spare the interests not only of the big capitalists but also of the lower middle classes with some money in the bank, who from an electoral point of view were so important to the confessional parties. It was condemned as the policy of people imprisoned in the obsolete orthodoxy of liberal economic theory. In short, to later critics it was socially unjust and scientifically wrong. Such criticism, however, is too severe.[1] Neither economic theory nor economic practice in the early 1930s provided a workable alternative. If the decision not to devalue the guilder was justified—as it certainly was—then lowering production costs must seem the only possible way of keeping a foothold in the export market. Given that liberal methods for systematically manipulating the economy had not yet been clearly defined at the time—even in the admittedly radical Labour plans the orthodox thesis that the state's budget should be balanced was not questioned—it is difficult to see what other options the governments had, apart from the choice between a disorderly flight into devaluation with unforeseeable consequences and the determination to survive a difficult period by a careful and austere policy of deflation.

[1] Interesting reflections on this question in P. W. Klein, 'Depression and Policy in the Thirties', *Acta Historiae Neerlandicae*, v (The Hague, 1975), 123–58, and J. de Vries, *De Nederlandse economie tijdens de 20ste eeuw* (Antwerp, 1973), pp. 139 ff.

As it turned out, this policy had in fact extremely radical effects on the organization of the economy, especially in the Netherlands. It is easy to see why. Deflation was an attempt to get through the depression while keeping the economy fundamentally unimpaired; it followed that the state had to be ready to intervene wherever there was danger of permanent damage being done. Thus the state had to provide a livelihood for hundreds of thousands of unemployed, and to support those sectors of the economy that could not survive the depression by cutting down production and reducing their staff—agriculture, in the first place, which in the Netherlands was mainly organized in small enterprises with little or no room for economies. In time the double paradox of this policy became increasingly clear. Whereas according to orthodox deflationist theory the state had to reduce its responsibilities and expenses (and did so, for instance, by lowering salaries of civil servants), in fact it came to be burdened with increasingly heavy and costly ones. At a time of strongly reduced tax yields the proportion of state expenditure in the national income taken as a whole went up in Belgium from 19·8 per cent between 1926 and 1930 to 23·4 per cent between 1930 and 1934,[1] and in the Netherlands from 17·4 per cent in the twenties to 23·5 per cent in the thirties.[2] Secondly, although deflationist orthodoxy entailed lowering prices, the government could save agriculture only by supporting prices. In other words, the policy of deflation did not fail only because foreign currencies which had remained loyal to gold finally collapsed, so that the Low Countries were forced by external circumstances to devalue too, but also because the various aims pursued by government turned out to be contradictory.

As in most democratic states the Dutch and Belgian systems of government functioned less than adequately during the crisis. Cabinets were expected to act quickly on a variety of different matters, and this could not be compatible with the principle of parliamentary control. As a consequence in both countries the influence of Parliament diminished. In 1932 the Belgian Government was given full powers to fight the economic crisis and these were renewed from year to year. Circumstances

[1] Calculated from *Histoire des finances publiques en Belgique*, ii. 75, 206, 220.
[2] Klein, op. cit. 128.

forced the legislature to abandon so much of its power to the executive that Parliament, or so it seemed, was left with nothing but the right to vote on the budgets[1]—budgets, moreover, based on admittedly unreliable estimates, themselves at the mercy of constantly changing and unforeseen circumstances. In the Netherlands the governments did not demand such a general delegation of power but in the course of the years the crisis legislation provided them with far-reaching authority in such matters as limiting imports (1931), concluding treaties on payments (1932), and regulating agriculture (1933).[2] In the Netherlands, too, the governments were unable to draw up realistic budgets, with the result that not only parliamentary control over the executive but also discussion of actual policy became extremely difficult.[3]

On the whole Belgian economic policy did not substantially differ from the Dutch. Both countries tried to protect their own production not by raising high tariff barriers but by setting temporary restraints on the import of certain goods. Both countries made some attempt to provide the unemployed with low-paid jobs by starting new public works, but the scale they thought admissible was so small that unemployment relief remained by far the most important way of assuring the hundreds of thousands a minimum livelihood. And in both countries the attempt was made to save certain industries from disaster. But there were also some remarkable differences. In 1932 wage cuts justified by the falling level of prices caused a strike in the Borinage which spread throughout Belgium. The government acted as mediator and brought pressure to bear on the employers to stabilize wages for the time being. So to avoid unrest it was prepared to abandon its policy of deflation in one fundamental respect.[4] In the Netherlands there was no such social unrest and no digression from the principle of deflation. Nor did the Dutch experience one of the most peculiar symptoms of the depression in Belgium, the vulnerability of the banks. Traditionally banks played a larger part in the industrial life of Belgium than in the Netherlands. It was the 'mixed

---

[1] H. Speyer, *Corporatisme ou parlementarisme réformé* (Brussels, 1935), pp. 37 ff.

[2] H. M. Hirschfeld, *Actieve economische politiek in Nederland in de jaren 1929–1934* (Amsterdam, 1946), pp. 64, 76 ff., 130; Oud, iv. 197 ff.

[3] Klein, p. 130.   [4] Baudhuin, *Histoire économique* i. 245.

banks' in particular—deposit banks providing long-term loans for industry and attending to the issue of shares and bonds— that ran into difficulties which were sometimes catastrophic. The bankruptcy of the Banque belge du travail, established in 1913, and of the General Bank Society, associated with the Farmers' League, caused widespread alarm: the first was a socialist, the second a Catholic enterprise and for both a great deal of political and social prestige was involved. These and other failures prompted the Rexists to launch vociferous campaigns against politicians whom they accused of dishonest financial practices; in the lawsuits that followed it was sometimes possible to prove negligence and greed, but there had been no malversation comparable with that which occasioned the French scandals of the same period, which had doubtless inspired the Rexists in the first place.

The fundamental difference between the policy of the Netherlands and of Belgium lay in their treatment of the agricultural problem. In both countries this was serious, but in the Netherlands where more people were occupied in agriculture than in Belgium (20·6 per cent against 17 per cent of the working population in 1930), and the share of agriculture in the national product was greater, the effects of the depression were probably more severe. The fall in agricultural prices on the world market caused unprecedented difficulties. But the greater importance of agriculture in the Dutch economy does not alone explain why Dutch agricultural policy took a form that would have been inconceivable in Belgium. In a series of measures culminating in the comprehensive Agricultural Crisis Act of 1933, the Dutch Government pursued a policy which had far-reaching consequences, and one which, although by no means based on them, had affinities with current theories about the reorganization of free market capitalism. In Belgium, as was clear from De Man's Plan, other problems were thought to have priority. When Paul van Zeeland, on the strength of his commitment to economic reform and his financial expertise, became minister for the first time in June 1934, he quickly set about reorganizing not agriculture but banking, one of his measures being the 'splitting up' of the mixed banks. And when in 1935 he became Prime Minister in an explicitly reformist Cabinet the problem of financial power was once again uppermost in his mind.

Quite different, too, was the style in which the two countries ultimately surrendered the autonomy of their currencies. Belgium treated devaluation as part of a new economic policy but in the Netherlands Prime Minister Colijn's government saw it as a capitulation into which the Dutch were forced by the lack of stamina of the other gold bloc countries. Belgium gave way in March 1935, France and Switzerland on 26 September 1936, and thus towards midnight on that same day the Netherlands, last bulwark of the gold standard, had to follow suit. In Belgium the decision to devalue came from a Cabinet led by Van Zeeland, with Hendrik de Man as Minister of Labour, which had been formed for the specific purpose of carrying through a far-reaching programme of economic recovery, to which devaluation was only incidental. Ironically, the beneficial consequences of devaluation diminished the need for radical economic reform. Indeed, to De Man's great annoyance only a fraction of his plan was carried out. The fate of the Office de redressement economique (OREC) is symbolic. It was set up in 1935, at De Man's request, as a central council for guiding economic growth by means of a systematic policy of subventions: it was turned into a permanent institution in 1937 and abolished in 1939.[1] On the other hand, in 1936, for the first time since 1919, serious efforts were made to improve the conditions of the workers by introducing a 40-hour week and making paid holidays obligatory. But such measures were not intended as part of a radical reorganization of the economic system.

6. *The Colonial Problem*

The economic crisis caused many difficulties in the colonies too. The post-war experiences of the Congo, closely linked to Belgium since the annexation in 1908,[2] were very similar to those of the mother country, the depression being followed by the exuberant optimism of the late twenties. The setbacks in the early thirties hit the industry of the Congo dramatically. The total value of exports fell from over 2 milliard francs in 1929 to less than 1 milliard in 1932; imports which in 1929 approximately equalled exports were reduced to less than 5 million. Many thousands of African workers had to be dismissed and many

[1] Baudhuin, *Histoire économique* i. 342–3.   [2] Above, p. 397.

Europeans returned to Belgium. As a result colonial policy for
a time attracted the attention of Parliament—a rather exceptional situation in a country where neither public opinion nor
Parliament had shown much concern for the colony since the
excitement caused by the annexation problem had faded away.[1]
Yet discussion even now was restricted to the economic aspects
of the colonial relationship. It was now realized that the rapid
and expensive industrialization that had begun with the foundation of the Union minière du Haut Katanga in 1906, and
which had been energetically pursued by the government after
the war, had not been without harmful side-effects. In fact the
exploitation of the rich Congolese mines—copper, diamonds,
etc.—had come under the control of the Belgian banks of which
the powerful Société générale was by far the most important. In
many cases it was difficult to distinguish clearly between the
responsibilities of the state and those of the big financial concerns. When the influence of the banks was being severely
criticized in the mother country itself, the near stranglehold
they had on Congolese industry was bound to become a serious
issue.

The results of these debates were insignificant and it is not
difficult to see why. When the Belgian state annexed the Congo
in 1908 it had no colonial policy and it never attempted to work
one out. The Belgian state in fact restricted itself to exploiting
the colony in the most responsible way it could envisage. Certain forms of indirect rule were introduced, and a system of
comprehensive social and medical care was rapidly developed
in the twenties and thirties by the big enterprises closely connected with the state. The system of primary education was
extensive in comparison with other African colonies and mainly
in the hands of Catholic missionaries who received strong
government support. These were important innovations, most
of them introduced after 1918, and they helped to make the
Congo one of the best-run colonies in Africa. They were not,
however, part of a clearly thought-out plan for the future of
colonial government. The pragmatism of the Belgians and their
commitment to day-to-day problems did not encourage reflections on the nature or purpose of colonialization. Nor did the

[1] R. Anstey, *King Leopold's Legacy. The Congo under Belgian Rule, 1908–1960*
(Oxford, 1966), pp. 109 ff.

native population force them to reconsider their points of view. It was possible for a small body of under two thousand civil servants and a small army to govern a population of more than ten million people, spread over an enormous area. Only the occasional messianic religious movements gave expression to what has been called a proto-national spirit,[1] but there was no serious reason for the government to worry about the possibility of nationalist resistance. Consequently, the depression did not lead to fundamental changes, although it persuaded the authorities that agriculture, badly neglected as a result of the heavy emphasis on industrial development, should be given much more attention. But the predominant influence of Brussels capital was in no way broken. No more than in Belgium itself was the depression in the colonies deep and lasting enough to sustain the reformist zeal of the early thirties. After a period of uncertainty it turned out that the essential stability had not been disturbed.

The history of the Dutch East Indies—with a population six times larger and a body of European civil servants ten time as great[2]—can hardly be compared with that of the Congo. Nor can the economy, for the value of East Indian exports in 1929 was ten times that of the Congo. But the exports were agricultural products, such as sugar, tobacco, and tea, and the price of these fell more steeply than the price of industrial products. Rubber, an important export, became unmarketable. As a result the Dutch East Indies were more seriously hit by the depression than the Netherlands itself or the Congo. While Congolese exports were halved in the period from 1929 till 1932, exports from the Indies fell by two-thirds. The effect on the economy of the mother country was probably more painful in the Netherlands than in Belgium, because the Dutch were more closely associated economically with their eastern colonies. It has been calculated that Dutch investments in Indonesia rose from 750 million guilders around 1900 to 1,500 million in 1915 and about 4,000 million in 1929; in 1935

---

[1] J. Schipper, *Koloniale opinies over Kongo* (Leiden, 1970), p. 31; cf. Anstey, op. cit., pp. 122–42.

[2] In 1930 the Netherlands–Indies authorities employed some 20,000 Dutchmen. The whole administration, partly Indonesian, consisted of over 100,000 people.

23 per cent of Dutch national wealth was invested there.[1] The share of the East Indies in the Dutch national income rose rapidly: in 1938, after the depression, under circumstances which were only slowly improving, it was still estimated to amount to 13·7 per cent.[2]

The colonial government used the same instruments as the Dutch when faced with the task of mitigating the consequences of the depression. Civil servants' salaries, soldiers' pay, and old age pensions were drastically cut and all plans for extending education and other government services to promote the interests of the native population were hastily abandoned. After 1933 the East Indian administration was constantly obliged to move in the direction of a planned economy. In some cases it intervened in business in a most radical way, regulating and restricting, for instance, the production of sugar and rubber, limiting the import of specifically Japanese products that had become extremely cheap after the devaluation of the yen, and establishing a native Indonesian industry, albeit on a small scale. There was no doubt that this policy was intended first of all to restore a 'profitable basis for big enterprise', as Governor-General De Jonge later put it.[3] Although the interests of the Indonesian population were not neglected, it is beyond dispute that they were subordinated to those of the major European concerns, as was shown by the regulation of rubber production. The depression and the excessive exchange value of the guilder, maintained for too long, damaging the Indian economy even more than it did the Dutch, were not only bad for business, but also for the native population which suffered serious impoverishment.[4]

During his period of office from 1931 to 1936 Governor-General De Jonge pursued his crisis policies energetically and haughtily: he had no precise ideas about the future of the colony but of one thing he was certain—the 'ethical' policy was

[1] Furnivall, *Netherlands India*, p. 312; Gonggrijp, *Economische geschiedenis van Indonesië*, p. 167; D. Crena de Iongh, 'Nederlandsch-Indië als beleggingsgebied van Nederlandsch kapitaal', in C. Gerretson *et al.*, *De sociaal-economische invloed van Nederlandsch-Indië op Nederland* (Wageningen, 1938), p. 110.

[2] See H. Baudet, 'The Dutch Retreat from Empire', in J. S. Bromley and E. H. Kossmann (eds.), *Britain and the Netherlands in Europe and Asia* (London, 1968), p. 228. Cf. above, p. 418.

[3] De Jonge, *Herinneringen*, p. 187.   [4] Gonggrijp, op. cit., p. 185.

finished.[1] He was not alone in this view. In itself it is not surprising that the ethical policy, which was a component of 'imperialistic' expansion and intended to promote the prosperity and well-being of a passive native population, should have become obsolete in the twenties when the impulses of imperialism had subsided and native intellectuals were disturbing the calm of paternalism. Yet the erosion of the policy and the conceptions that replaced it were interesting. It is impossible to say when exactly ethical policy was given up. All Governors-General up to 1931 accepted it, even if the policy of one of them, ruling during the economic difficulties of the early twenties, was distinctly conservative and hostile to the Indonesian nationalist movement. However, there were already some Colonial Ministers who were deeply irritated by what they considered to be the expensive sentimentality of the 'ethicals'; after 1929 the Ministry was dominated by such sceptics. Nevertheless, the main elements of ethical policy were preserved in their original form; during the depression of the early thirties considerable care was taken not to economize on public education for the native population and even university education, begun in 1920, was expanded. Ethical policy in this and other fields was by no means fundamentally changed, far less were its results undone.

In the field of politics too the so-called 'Indianization' of the civil service progressed rapidly, and strictly along ethical lines. In 1918 the Volksraad (People's Council) was installed. This was intended as a representative body consisting at the start of 39 persons, 15 of them Indonesian. Although for the time being the Council was only advisory it was evidently thought that it would eventually develop into a real Parliament. After 1925 it was indeed allowed a share in legislation, and the composition of its membership changed radically: after 1931 it had 25 Dutch, 30 Indonesian, and 5 Arabian and Chinese members. Notwithstanding resentment in some circles and hostility of influential statesmen such as Colijn, who publicly and forcefully rejected the principles on which the Volksraad was based, it was impossible to change the course of events. As Colijn himself found during his period as Colonial Minister from 1933 to 1937, the only thing he could do was to retard developments.

[1] Above, pp. 401 ff.

At a time when the value of parliamentary democracy was widely questioned in the Netherlands this was relatively easy, and the Volksraad did not object any more strongly than the Dutch Parliament to the fact that during the great depression the all-important economic policy was for the most part beyond parliamentary control.

But although some elements of ethical policy were maintained, the nature of the colonial relationship changed. For a number of interrelated but diverging reasons the system was slowly but ineluctably collapsing. First of all there was an innate weakness in the system itself. Ethical policy was first planned during the heyday of late-nineteenth-century imperialism. Its first champions, although convinced that the colonial relationship—a relationship of guardian and ward—would eventually come to an end, calculated the process of emancipation in terms of hundreds of years rather than of decades. When some Indonesians in the 1920s began to demand a measure of independence and proceeded to revolutionary action to achieve this, the ethicals were faced with a problem to which they had no answer. Indonesian nationalism did not fit into the system, despite the willingness of some ethicals to make room for it. Their ideal of emancipation was undoubtedly the assimilation of the Indonesian élite with Western culture and the co-operation of Indonesians and Dutch as equals in a common society. The incompatibility of ethical and nationalist ends caused the nationalists either to turn sharply against ethical policy or to try to transform it into something quite different. Dutch reactions, even those of progressives, were ambiguous. There was a group of Dutch civil servants and professors at the Indonesian institutes for higher education who in 1930 founded a periodical called *De Stuw* (*Weir*) and pleaded for a neo-ethical policy of emancipation leading towards an independent Indonesian commonwealth.[1] Pressure from the authorities, however, forced them to stop publishing in 1934. The group never fixed a firm date for Indonesian independence, nor had it wished to, for it expressed an essentially paternalistic point of view and was in some respects as conservative in approach as the ethicals of the early days. It never considered the possibility of develop-

---

[1] E. B. Locher-Scholten, 'De Stuw: tijdstekening en teken des tijds', *Tijdschrift voor Geschiedenis*, lxxxiv (1971), 36–65.

ing Indonesian industry so as to strengthen and modernize the economy. Notwithstanding its considerable sympathy for the nationalists and understanding of their impatience, it kept within the bounds of a careful and gradual policy of development and refused to put its vision of the future into concrete terms.

The history of Indonesian nationalism—there is no need to go into details here[1]—is confused and difficult to interpret. Its origins were various but it learned to reconcile standpoints that at first might seem irreconcilable. Marxism, Muhammadanism, Pan-Islamism, nationalism were all fused together in a complex of ambitions to which—so it seems—the Indonesians themselves added very little. They failed indeed to provide a coherent theory that would explain how all these doctrines could in some way or another be used for the same purposes. Perhaps this is one of the many reasons why in this period the way in which the political movements or parties of the Indonesians sprang up, split up, were abolished, and reinstituted, was so incomprehensible. Yet the movement as a whole showed remarkable continuity and resilience, even in the face of the government's severely repressive measures. It is true that the government had little difficulty putting down or preventing revolutionary actions. Communist revolts on Java and Sumatra in 1926 and 1927 were short-lived and no serious repercussions followed the arrest of such nationalist leaders as Sukarno in 1929 and 1933 and Hatta, Shahrir, and others in 1934, or their expulsion from Java—some of them were sent to Upper Digul on New Guinea, an internment camp built in 1927 and destined to become legendary in the history of Indonesian nationalism. Yet such measures were not enough to suppress the nationalist movement entirely. Even in the thirties the movement survived although the East Indies administration watched and controlled its activities closely. Numerically it was weak. The various political parties counted their followers by some tens of thousands at the outside. Only Sarekat Islam developed for a couple of years into a genuine mass party. But whatever its weakness and limitations nationalism was a permanent problem in the thirties, and the administration did little to resolve it.

[1] On this see, J. M. Pluvier, *Overzicht van de ontwikkeling der nationalistische beweging in Indonesië in de jaren 1930 tot 1942* (The Hague, 1953).

It might even be legitimate to say—it has at any rate been said—that the government actually turned down a reasonable plan to find a way out of the difficulties. In 1936 the People's Council petitioned the authorities to organize an Indonesian–Dutch conference which should draft as quickly as possible a new constitution granting autonomy for a democratically ruled Indonesia.[1] Both at the Governor-General's residence in Indonesia and in The Hague the petition was studied with suspicion and in 1938 it was refused by royal decree. It was a tragic decision. The petition was inspired by the desire to bring about a form of government allowing Dutch and Indonesian democratic forces to collaborate in the fight against Fascism.[2] Yet on the other hand the decision was inevitable in view of the weakness of the nationalist movement and the feelings of the Dutch in the East Indies who would have found the granting of autonomy totally unacceptable. In the course of the 1920s and 1930s the Dutch population there had become strongly conservative. At the end of the World War political parties were formed which increasingly tended to stress the need for defending purely Dutch interests, passing over or even condemning the old ideals of assimilation and association. When in 1917 the Dutch Protestants in the Indies formed a political party they proudly proclaimed it the Christian Ethical party. In 1929, however, they felt obliged to change the name to Christian Political party, because to them too ethical policy had become synonymous with weak and sentimental leniency.[3] Ethical policy was a thing of the past. A new system was needed.

The new system which gradually emerged in the late twenties has no name and no distinct features, or rather it does not fit into the usual categories of left and right, of progressive and conservative. Colijn adhered to this new school. He was opposed to the Volksraad which in his view had the impossible task of representing a vast and mostly illiterate population and symbolizing the unity of a country that was in fact held together only by the Dutch administration. He was in favour of a federal-

[1] See the documents in S. L. van der Wal (ed.), *De Volksraad en de staatkundige ontwikkeling van Nederlands-Indië* (2 vols., Groningen, 1964–5), ii. 219 ff.

[2] Pluvier, op. cit., p. 118.

[3] B. J. Brouwer, *De houding van Idenburg en Colijn tegenover de Indonesische beweging* (Kampen, 1958), p. 132.

ist structure and of the development of more or less representative bodies from below, functioning in much smaller areas
than the Volksraad and slowly growing to more authority. He
spurned Indonesian nationalism as the error of an exiguous
group of men confused by their Western education, who presumed the existence of an Indonesian nation when in reality
there was only an agglomeration of backward peoples with
very little in common. This was an outspokenly conservative
view. It is not surprising that Colijn was attracted by the spirit
of the training-school for overseas civil servants at the University of Utrecht which opened in 1925 with the help of subsidies
from various big concerns: it was meant to be a counterpart
and rival to the Faculty of Indology at Leiden University which
still cherished ethical ideas.[1] But in Leiden ideas were changing
too. If it is correct to assume that until the twenties the Leiden
school had never clearly distinguished between the ideal of
Westernization and Europeanization on the one hand and the
care for and institutionalization of the venerable Indonesian
native traditions—like the adat[2]—on the other, then the change
is obvious: from the twenties onwards the emphasis was on the
pluralistic character of Indonesian society and on the dualism
of its economic system, native and Western, instead of on assimilation and association.[3] Nevertheless, the leaders of the
Leiden school, Snouck Hurgronje and Van Vollenhoven, were
bitterly opposed to views like those of Colijn and they denounced
his opinion of Indonesian nationalism as narrow-minded and
disastrous.

Oddly enough the 'ideologist' of the new system, a Leiden
graduate called A. D. A. de Kat Angelino, was a great admirer
of Colijn, believed in federalism, and thought Indonesian
nationalism meaningless and objectionable.[4] De Kat (1891–
1969) published in 1929 and 1930 an enormous book in three
volumes, commissioned by the Minister for the Colonies (a
shortened version appeared in English under the title *Colonial
Policy*),[5] The style is baroque and rhetorical, underlining that

---

[1] Ibid., p. 99.   [2] Above, p. 411.

[3] R. van Niel, *The Emergence of the Modern Indonesian Elite* (The Hague, 1960),
pp. 244 ff.

[4] Cf. his letter to Colijn, 22 Dec. 1927, in Van der Wal, *Volksraad* ii. 36–45.

[5] The original work has 2,158 pages and is entitled *Staatkundig beleid en bestuurs-
zorg in Nederlandsch-Indië* (3 vols., The Hague, 1929–30).

the scholarship of this man who was both Indologist and Sino-
logist is overwhelming. But nowhere else can one find so eloquent a plea for Holland's mission, a mission to create in her
colonies a great synthesis of East and West through wise and
expert leadership and a passionate concern for the spiritual
welfare of the native inhabitants. De Kat displays a grasp of the
inner unity of this whole complex of messianism, idealism,
Dutch nationalism, and an absorbed interest in the East itself—
the object of meticulous study and sympathy, the subject of
innumerable publications. The ideals of twentieth-century conservative colonialism were here explored and explained in the
most comprehensive way. But hardly was the book off the press
when the colonial administration had to start radically cutting
expenditure in the face of harsh reality. In the late thirties when
there once more seemed to be scope for some constructive work
the Second World War intervened to render all such theories
irrelevant. After 1945 it was too late for them to serve any useful
purpose.

7. A Note on Literature

For the general historian of the Low Countries in the nineteenth
century a study of the culture and more specifically the
literature of the epoch may help his analysis of social and
political change. Not only did Romanticism, positivism,
liberalism, socialism, and many other movements penetrate
into literature, they sometimes started as literary before
becoming political movements. Consequently, it is possible
for the historian to treat a number of authors or of literary
trends as pivotal phenomena in his general description of the
period. For the interwar years, however, such an approach
is not so fruitful. In the Low Countries none of the great
literary and artistic innovations in Europe had much influence
on events, except perhaps—but in a confused and sterile
way—the humanitarian Expressionism of the Flemish Front in
its first stage.[1] The great nineteenth-century poets—Bilderdijk,
Potgieter, Verwey, or Gorter—held definite views about
society and although they did not necessarily use their poetry

---

[1] Above, pp. 637 ff.

to disseminate their personal message their poetic vision was undeniably and intentionally part of their total vision of God, man, and society, of what was happening in the world, and of what ought to be changed. The most important poets between the wars did not have the same comprehensive vision. Of. course their work also proceeds from an interpretation of contemporary reality and is closely associated with the period in which it was written—because in this poetry the individual is in search of a place within or against society, because he expresses himself in a language meaningful for his contemporaries, or because in the thirties he is attacking national socialism. Yet the poetry of the prominent writers—A. Roland Holst, J. C. Bloem, Martinus Nijhoff—was only vaguely connected with the philosophical or political movements of the period. It did not try to find a solution to any but individual problems, it had no ambition to serve a specific purpose; politically, socially, and philosophically it did not aspire to be constructive. In this negative sense their poetry may well have been representative of the period, a period of carefully organized stability. In another sense it certainly was not. In contrast with the grandiloquent and rhetorical style used in politics, the best poets achieved after long years of practice a conciseness and precision probably never equalled in Dutch literature.

Naturally the international threats of the thirties deeply impressed Dutch and Belgian authors and radically influenced the work of some of them. For the most famous author in these years, the historian Johan Huizinga (1872–1945), his interpretation of European cultural history was profoundly marked by the tragic circumstances of the 1930s. His *The Waning of the Middle Ages* (first Dutch edition in 1919) and his *Erasmus* (1924) which established his reputation, owed their origin to purely personal interests. His *In the Shadow of tomorrow* (first Dutch edition in 1935) was a fierce attack on what he saw as the barbarization of European civilization, a barbarization that had generated the monstrous systems of Marxism and Fascism. In his extraordinary and daring *Homo Ludens* (first Dutch edition in 1938) themes that had fascinated him since the 1890s were brought together and shaped into his theory of what he called the play-character of culture: it was a condemnation of the times in which he was living and a plea for the restoration of noble traditions and unselfish morality.

Confronted by national socialism Dutch literature resumed its nineteenth-century role and once again began to present a message. This is abundantly clear from the career of two men of letters, who were intimate friends, E. du Perron (1899–1940) and Menno ter Braak (1902–1940). After an early period during which their critical minds expressed little more than cynical nihilism, they emerged in the thirties in what, at least as far as Ter Braak was concerned, may well be called their true colours. They showed themselves as passionate moralists. But once their main concern became the fight against Fascist ideologies they were forced to adopt an essentially defensive or, if that word is preferable, a conservative attitude. They did not pretend to represent a new vision. On the contrary, they wished to rescue from the past all that they felt to be valuable and relevant. Studied from this angle it is obvious that their work did not disrupt the stability of the period. But this does not imply that these polemicists and essayists felt at home in their national environment and praised it. They were iconoclasts by nature. They despised the commonplaces of the national tradition, they fought the complacency of the Dutch establishment, and took Stendhal, Multatuli, Nietzsche as their models. They were sceptical individualists who regarded metaphysics and religion, aesthetics and scholarship, as illusions, seemingly venerable masks hiding stupidity or self-interest. The brilliance of Ter Braak's argumentation, the subjectivity of Du Perron's literary judgements shocked and astonished readers accustomed to a more ponderous and more cautious style.

In his last great book, *Van Oude en Nieuwe Christenen* (*Old and New Christians*, 1937), Ter Braak embarked once again on a long polemic against Christianity, Marxism, and Fascism; he went to great trouble to show the relativity of the idea of equality; he analysed the levelling of culture in the era of the masses and exposed, as he had done so many times before, the false pretensions of scholarly objectivity and detachment. But that was not the reason why he wrote this tragic work. The whole book is the report of the author's long and almost tormented debate with himself about the meaning of the democratic and humanist idea; the whole argument is intended to show that even a man who had abandoned all illusions and all dogma can still defend 'liberal' democracy and its system of values with perfect honesty and without cant. On 14 May 1940, the day of the Dutch capitulation, Du Perron died from a heart attack and Ter Braak committed suicide.

EPILOGUE
1780–1880–1980

THE Dutch population, 2 million in 1780, had doubled by
1880; in 1973 it was 13·5 million. The Belgian population, 3 million in 1800, was 5·5 million eighty years
later and 9·7 in 1973. In the Netherlands the mortality rate of
26 per thousand in the middle of the nineteenth century fell
to 22 only thirty years later; in the middle of the twentieth
century it was 8. In Belgium during the same period it was
reduced from 22 to 21 and to 12 in the 1950s. The Dutch birth-
rate rose from 34 per thousand in the 1850s to 36 in 1880; in the
1950s it was 21. In Belgium it remained 31 in the first period
but fell to 17 in the middle of the twentieth century. In both
countries the number of people living in towns of over 5,000
inhabitants was large and rapidly growing: in Belgium from
35 per cent of the population in 1850 to 51·5 in 1910, in the
Netherlands from 37 to 69 per cent.

At the end of the eighteenth century the only big town in
the Low Countries was Amsterdam with more than 200,000
inhabitants. In 1880 Brussels (421,000) had pushed Amsterdam
(317,000) into second place; it had become one of the major
cities in continental Europe, bigger than Marseilles, Madrid,
Rome, or Hamburg. Antwerp (169,000) and Rotterdam
(148,000), although rapidly growing ports, were still much
smaller and The Hague, residence of the royal family and
seat of the government with the cosmopolitan appearance
of a capital, had 113,000 inhabitants, less than industrial
towns such as Ghent (131,000) or Liège (123,000). In 1973 the
conurbation of Brussels was equal to that of Rotterdam, both
with over one million inhabitants, and The Hague was with
its nearly 700,000 no longer the quiet city of the nineteenth
century.

When Eugène Fromentin, the renowned French painter and
author, made in July 1875 a journey through Belgium and the
Netherlands to collect material for his brilliant book on
Les Maîtres d'autrefois (1876), he found Brussels a nice capital,

Mechlin a big, gloomy city, dead, empty, silent in the shadow of its churches and monasteries; he enjoyed Amsterdam which apparently came up to his expectations but his big surprise was The Hague: the least typically Dutch town in Holland, he thought, one of the most original in Europe, aristocratic, wealthy, elegantly dignified. Walking in silence along the small lake in the heart of the city, next to the ancient building where Oldenbarnevelt had climbed the scaffold and John de Witt had been lynched, he meditated, after a long day spent in studying the glory of Dutch seventeenth-century painting, on the troubled history of the country he visited and the statesmen who had controlled its destiny, and he asked himself why it is that of all life and all greatness only beauty is spared by the passing of time.

As so many other travellers of that age, Fromentin arrived by train from Paris. What he wanted to see were museums and what he saw outside them were reminiscences: the skies, the canals, the colours, even the people of seventeenth-century paintings. Looking today at paintings or prints of late nineteenth-century towns and comparing them with those of the late eighteenth century (there is an overwhelming number of eighteenth-century prints illustrating with accomplished skill all aspects of Dutch town life) what strikes us is how little seems to have changed from 1780 to 1880. It all looks so calm to modern eyes, so neat, so beautifully adapted to the human size, and so modest even in what then seemed extravagant. Of course there were trains, but what the prints show us are coaches, hooded carts, and innumerable boats of all sizes and forms in the canals and on the rivers. Dutch towns were still silent. Travellers from the south, accustomed to the hullabaloo and dirt of Italian and French town life, had since the seventeenth century been surprised by the quietness of even the busiest Dutch cities where the climate did not permit people to spend much time in the streets. Yet Dutch towns were not dull. Even in the second half of the nineteenth century clothing was still greatly diversified, with the higher classes in their black suits, the officers in elaborate uniforms, the students in semi-bohemian clothes, the maid-servants wearing their traditional cornets, white stockings, and aprons, and the peasants coming to the market or the shops each in their local dress and often expensively decorated with golden casques (*oorijzers*). It was feared by some perspicacious observers that the diversity which was still real might disappear in the 'uniformity which is the curse of modern life' (as Abraham Kuyper put it in 1869), but no one could have predicted that even the smells which distinguished countries and cities and parts of cities would come under the attack of modern development. 'Ici', Fromentin wrote in Amsterdam, 'plus encore qu'à Rotterdam, l'air est imprégné de cette bonne odeur de Hollande . . . Une odeur dit tout . . .' The distance between 1780 and 1880 is very much shorter than that between 1880 and 1980.

The history of the Low Countries during the Second World War and the period of reconstruction shows an amazing continuity. In 1940 the inhabitants were ill prepared for the ordeal awaiting them but the majority were convinced that at some time in the future they would be allowed to perpetuate their independent existence and regain in some form the stability of the interwar years. One of the paradoxes of the post-war period is that they largely succeeded in this despite the entirely different framework in which they lived. Up to the 1960s it is as if the war and its aftermath had changed their external conditions while leaving their internal circumstances intact. Their international position changed radically. The pre-war neutral colonial states lost their empires—the Dutch in 1949, the Belgians in 1960—and abandoned their neutrality; moreover, they joined forces in the organization of the Benelux which served as an inspiration for the idea of European unification. In an endeavour to make up for the losses incurred in the East Indies the Dutch started a process of industrialization which was far more systematic and radical than that which had occurred in the 1890s; after their Congo disaster the Belgians also embarked on a policy of planned economic reorganization which, however, met with serious resistance and had dramatic repercussions both socially and politically. Yet up to the 1960s and notwithstanding the nearly total revision of so many aspects of their life, the inhabitants of both countries kept to the systems and ways of thinking which had guided them through the crisis of the 1930s and the 1940s. Their economic recovery was fairly rapid. The Belgians, who had lost 55,000 men and women during the war and 8 per cent of their national wealth, were in 1945 in a much better position than the Dutch whose personal and material losses were four times as great. Thanks to American help and the expansion of the world economy the Dutch managed to heal many of their wounds and to renew their economy drastically with the result that they achieved in the 1950s a level of prosperity never reached before.

On 28 October 1957 the burgomaster of Brussels announced that his city wished to become the capital of a United Europe and the seat of the organizations of the Common Market and Euratom; it was prepared to reserve the sites where the World Exhibition was going to be held in 1958 for buildings to house the new European bureaucracy. Exactly one month later the municipal council of Rotterdam unanimously accepted the proposal to build Europoort, the large harbour and industrial complex which has provided the means for the town to become the biggest port of Europe. Thus after the catastrophe of 1940 and the problems of reconstruction Belgium and the Netherlands had recovered to such an extent as to be able to resume, and enlarge, traditions which in the past had often been looked upon as deeply national: the central economic function of the North, the political aspiration of the South destined, in the view of Pirenne and his predecessors, to act as the pivot of Europe. But in both cases the vision of a greater European unity transcending national boundaries and perhaps absorbing national identities lent the new initiatives a character adapted to radically altered circumstances.

⸱ Shortly after these ambitious decisions the climate of opinion in the Low Countries began to change. During the 1960s it became possible for generations which had not experienced the war, or only as children, to raise doubts on many matters which their elders had generally preferred not to challenge. If the men who after 1945 exerted themselves to reconstruct the ruined economy had retained their pre-war political organization and continued to profess their belief in pluralistic stability—perfectly suited, they discovered, to serve as a framework for economic expansion on an unprecedented scale—the young men and women of the 1960s, after economic success had been achieved, felt embarrassed by those relics.

They eagerly participated in the drive for renewal, reform, or even revolution which characterizes so much of European civilization in that period and they indeed succeeded in undermining some of the structures and attitudes of the past. While it is still impossible to see whether the Belgians and the Dutch were, and are, sufficiently inventive to put on developments which are global the stamp of their national idiosyncrasies, so much, however, is clear: not the Second World War but the prosperity of the 1960s made younger generations aware of the discrepancy between the traditional organization and stability controlling their life and the wholly untraditional environment which had emerged.

CHRONOLOGICAL TABLE

Netherlands	Belgium
1780–4 Fourth Anglo-Dutch War. The humiliating defeat incurred by the Dutch Republic strengthens the opposition of the anti-Orangist Patriots to the existing form of government.	1780–93 The sister of Emperor Joseph II, Marie Christine, acts as regent in the Austrian Netherlands.
1781, 26 Sept. Publication of an anonymous pamphlet, *To the People of the Netherlands*, written by J. D. van der Capellen and containing the political programme of the Patriots.	1781 Protestants obtain religious liberty.
1782 Patriot activity increases. The States General recognize American independence.	
1783 Tension increases as a result of the newly created Free Corps and of pro-Orangist disturbances caused by the lower strata of the population.	1783 Disestablishment of the contemplative orders.
1784 First congress of Patriot Free Corps at Utrecht.	
1785 The States of Holland curtail Stadtholder William V's power; he leaves the province of Holland for Gelderland. The States sign a defensive alliance with France.	
1786 Orangist disturbances at The Hague. William V, who on the advice of his brother-in-law, the Prussian King Frederick William II, acts against a number of Patriot town administrations in Gelderland, is by some provinces deprived of his authority as captain-general.	1786 'Enlightened' reforms in the administration and in the ecclesiastical seminars.
1787 William V's troops beaten by the Patriot army of Utrecht. In June William's wife, Wilhelmina, is prevented by a Patriot Free Corps	1787 The total reform of the general administration and the administration of justice leads to massive opposition. The government i

s

Netherlands

from entering Holland, and then asks the King of Prussia for help. In Sept. Prussian troops occupy Dutch territory. The States of Holland withdraw anti-Orangist measures. Restoration of Orange regime. Many Patriots flee to France. L. van de Spiegel becomes Grand Pensionary.

Belgium

forced provisionally to withdraw all measures.

1789 At Breda, in the territory of the Dutch Republic, the conservative followers of Van der Noot join forces with the liberal Vonck with intent to conquer the Southern Netherlands and to establish a national government. The conservative 'Manifesto to the People of Brabant' proclaims independence.

1790 In Jan. the States General decide to call a *Congrès souverain des États belgiques unis* but in Dec. Emperor Leopold II, Joseph's successor, reconquers Brussels and the Congress is dissolved.

1792 After the French victory in the Battle of Jemappes the Austrian troops leave Belgium. The French welcomed as liberators.

1793 The French declare war on Britain and the Dutch Republic.

1793 The incorporation of Belgium into the French state is provisionally suspended thanks to the French defeat in the Battle of Neerwinden near Louvain.

1794 In Dec. French troops march over the frozen rivers into the Northern provinces.

1794 As a result of their victory in the Battle of Fleurus the French are able to reconquer Belgium (June).

1795 Stadtholder William V flees to Britain. In Amsterdam and other towns Patriot revolutionaries take over government. In May the Republic and France sign the Treaty of The Hague.

1795 The Treaty of The Hague between the Dutch Republic and France puts an end to the closure of the Scheldt. In Oct. the French annex the Austrian Netherlands and Liège.

1796 First meeting of the National Assembly.

1797 In a plebiscite the moderate constitution drafted by the National Assembly is rejected.

1797 The Austrian Emperor cedes the Southern Netherlands to France (Peace of Campo Formio). Actions

Netherlands

A second National Assembly fails to achieve results.

1798 *Coup d'état* by demcoratic Patriots and introduction of first Dutch constitution replacing the ancient federal structure by a unitary model. A second *coup d'état* leads to a less democratic government.

1799 The invasion of British and Russian troops in North-Holland fails.

1801 As a result of a new *coup d'état*, inspired by Napoleon, the government system becomes more autocratic.

1802 Following the Peace of Amiens the British return the colonies, except Ceylon, to the Dutch.

1805 The constitution is altered once more. Schimmelpenninck becomes Grand Pensionary. Gogel reforms the tax system.

1806 Primary Education Act. Napoleon forces Schimmelpenninck to resign. Louis Napoleon becomes King of Holland. Enforcement of the Continental System.

1810 Abdication of Louis Napoleon and annexation of the Republic by France.

1813 After the Battle of Leipzig the French troops and civil servants start to leave the country. In Nov. three leading personalities at The Hague take up government and ask the Prince of Orange to return. In Dec. William VI, son of William V who died in 1806, is inaugurated as Sovereign Prince William I.

1814 New constitution.

Belgium

against the priests and conscription cause the so-called Peasants' War in Flanders, Brabant, the Campine, and Luxemburg.

1801 Thanks to the Concordat the problem of the 'prêtres réfractaires' is solved.

1813 Bitter opposition to conscription, taxation, censorship, etc.

1814 The French troops leave Belgium.

The eight London articles (July) determine the shape of the United Kingdom of the Netherlands and Belgium.

Aug. Treaty with Britain. Most of the Dutch colonies returned.

Aug. William I becomes Sovereign Prince of Belgium.

	Netherlands	Belgium

1815 After the Battle of Waterloo William I takes the title of King.
New constitution with a Parliament of two Chambers and equal
representation of North and South.

> Beginning of a long-drawn-out
> conflict between the government
> and the Bishop of Ghent.

> 1819 It is decided that from 1823
> Dutch will be the only official
> language in the Flemish provinces.

1822 The King organizes his Amortization Syndicate and creates the
Société générale des Pays-Bas pour favoriser l'industrie nationale.

> Further conflicts with the Belgian
> clergy.

> 1825 Foundation of the Collegium
> Philosophicum at Louvain.

> 1828 Alliance of Romantic liberals and
> Roman Catholics to acquire more
> freedom.

> 1830 Disturbances at Brussels and Liège
> escalate into a revolutionary move-
> ment. A provisional national
> government in Brussels proclaims
> independence. Election of a Na-
> tional Congress. In Nov. the Great
> Powers start negotiations in Lon-
> don to solve the Belgian problem.

1831 The London Protocols of Jan. accepted by William I but
rejected by the National Congress.

> 7 Feb. Proclamation of the new Belgian
> constitution.
> 4 June Leopold of Saxe-Coburg elected
> King of Belgium (1831–65).

New proposals by the London Conference accepted by the
Belgians but rejected by William I.
2–12 Aug. Invasion of Belgium by Dutch troops. The Dutch
withdraw when the French come to the rescue of the Belgians.

> 1836 Municipal Corporations Act.

1838 New legal codes to replace those
imposed by Napoleon.

1839 Final agreement between Belgium and the Netherlands.

> The Great Powers guarantee Bel-
> gian neutrality.

1840 Following Belgian secession the
constitution is partially revised.
Abdication of William I.

Netherlands

1840-9 King William II.

1844 F. C. van Hall reorganizes state finances.

1848 William II decides to have the constitution radically revised. A commission headed and inspired by the liberal leader J. R. Thorbecke drafts a new one.

1849-90 King William III.

1851 Municipal Corporations Act.

1853 The re-establishment of the R.C. hierarchy leads in April to vehement Protestant opposition and the resignation of the Thorbecke Cabinet.

1857 Primary Schools Act.

1863 Slavery abolished in the West Indies.

1864 The collaboration of Roman Catholics and liberals inaugurated in 1848 is made more difficult by the encyclical *Quanta Cura*.

1867 Conflict about Luxemburg.

1868 Conflicts between conservative Cabinet and the Second Chamber end in conservative defeat. The Dutch bishops declare themselves to be opposed to religiously neutral schools.

1870 Abolition of the culture-system in the East Indies.

1873-1904 War in Achin (Sumatra).

1878 Organization of the Anti-revolutionary party (Calvinist). Primary Schools Act favouring liberal principles.

Belgium

1842 Education Act favouring Roman Catholic influence in primary schools.

1846 Liberal Congress at Brussels.

1850 Secondary Schools Act favouring liberal principles.

1862 The Flemish Meeting party at Antwerp.

1863 First Roman Catholic Congress at Mechlin. The Roman Catholics start cautiously to build up a political party.

1865-1909 King Leopold II.

Netherlands	Belgium
	1879 Primary Schools Act favouring liberal principles.
1881 Foundation of the Sociaal Democratische Bond (Social Democratic League).	
	1884 Foundation of the Fédération des cercles et des associations, i.e. a Roman Catholic political party. Primary Schools Act in accordance with Roman Catholic principles.
1885 Foundation of the Liberal Union.	1885 Foundation of the Parti Ouvrier Belge (Belgische Werklieden Partij). Congo Conference at Berlin. Leopold II allowed by the Belgian Parliament to become sovereign of the Congo.
1886 Disturbances in Amsterdam suppressed by the army. Parliament decides to set up an inquiry into labour conditions in factories.	1886 Serious social disturbances starting in Wallonia lead to decision of Parliament to undertake an inquiry into the conditions of the workers.
1887 Constitution revised so as to allow alteration of electoral qualifications.	1887 Liberal party disrupted by break with Progressives.
1889 Primary Schools Act allowing the state to subsidize Roman Catholic and Protestant schools. Labour Act based on material of the parliamentary inquiry.	1889 Labour Act based on material of parliamentary inquiry.
1890–1948 Queen Wilhelmina.	1890 Establishment of the Catholic Farmers' League.
	1891 Foundation of Belgian Popular League (R.C.).
1892–3 Revision of the tax system.	
	1893 Daens creates the Christian Popular party. Revision of the constitution introducing general male suffrage with additional votes for qualified electors.
1894 Foundation of Social Democratic Workers' party (Sociaal Democratische Arbeiders Partij: SDAP).	
	1895 Primary Schools Act strengthening the Church's influence and allowing state subsidies to Roman Catholic schools.

Netherlands	Belgium
1896 Electoral Act increasing the number of electors. Beginning of a Roman Catholic party organization.	
1898 Abolition of possibility to take a substitute for doing military service.	1898 Dutch text of laws and royal decrees declared to possess same legal validity as French text.
1900 Introduction of compulsory education.	
1901 Foundation of Vrijzinnig Democratische Bond (Liberal Democratic League).	
	1902 Failure of general strike organized by socialists to abolish plural votes system.
1903 Failure of railways strike.	
1906 Foundation of the Dutch League of Trade Unions (Nederlands Verbond van Vakverenigingen: NVV).	
	1907 King Leopold II forced to give the Congo to the Belgian state.
	1908 The Congo accepted as Belgian colony.
1909 Foundation of the Christian Historical Union (Christelijk Historische Unie: CHU). Split in SDAP and foundation of the left-wing Social Democratic party.	1909–34 King Albert.
	1913 Abolition of possibility to take a substitute for doing military service.
1914 Aug. General mobilization. Nov. Foundation of the Netherlands Overseas Trust (NOT).	1914 Introduction of compulsory education. 4 Aug. German invasion. 7 Aug. Fall of Liège. 9 Oct. Fall of Antwerp. Foundation of Comité national de secours et d'alimentation. Foundation of Young Flanders, a pro-German party.
1915 Income tax.	1916 Declaration of Sainte-Adresse containing British and French guarantee to restore Belgian independence. Opening of Dutch-language university at Ghent.

Netherlands	Belgium
1917 Revision of constitution: general male suffrage, proportional representation, financial equality of state and free schools.	1917 Council of Flanders founded by the Germans.
1918 Nov. Abortive revolution. Social Democratic party adopts the name of Communist party of Holland.	1918 Oct. German troops start to leave Belgium. Nov. Roman Catholics, liberals, and socialists form a new national government.

1919 Belgian claims relating to part of the Scheldt and of Limburg.

Introduction of women's suffrage.	First elections with general male franchise without plural votes.
	1920 Secret Military Accord with France.
1921 Foundation of Liberal Freedom League (Vrijheidsbond).	1921 Revision of the constitution to legalize new electoral regulations and alter composition of Senate. Foundation of Belgian Catholic Union. Economic Union with Luxemburg.
1922 Revision of the constitution.	
	1923 Belgian participation in the occupation of the Ruhr area by France.
	1924 The Flemish persuade the Chamber to reject a commercial treaty with France.
1925 Second Chamber adopts draft treaty with Belgium providing for canal through North-Brabant.	1925 Belgium signs Locarno Treaty and adopts draft treaty with the Netherlands (rejected by Dutch First Chamber in 1927).
	1926 Devaluation of Belgian franc.
1927 First Chamber rejects Belgian treaty.	
1931 Foundation of National Socialist Movement (Nationaal Socialistische Beweging: NSB). Economic depression and increasing unemployment.	1931 Foundation of Verdinaso. Dutch recognized as only official language in Dutch-speaking provinces. Economic depression and increasing unemployment.
1933 Mutiny on the cruiser *Zeven Provinciën* in East Indies.	1933 *Plan du travail* (H. de Man). Foundation of Flemish National League (Vlaams Nationaal Verbond: VNV).
	1934–51 King Leopold III.
1935 Dutch Labour Plan.	1935 Devaluation of Belgian franc. Strengthening of position of the Dutch language in legal matters.

Netherlands	Belgium
9136 Devaluation of Dutch guilder.	1936 Return to policy of strict neutrality.
1938 Revision of the constitution.	
1939 General mobilization.	1939 General mobilization.
1940 10 May. German invasion.	1940 10 May. German invasion.

APPENDIX II

BELGIAN AND DUTCH CABINETS, 1815–1940

WHEREAS from 1830 it is possible to indicate with some precision the party to which a politician in Belgium belongs this is not so in the Netherlands where political parties developed later. Until the end of the nineteenth century it is often risky to determine the standpoint of a Dutch Cabinet minister in terms of party adherence. The indications given below should be taken as rather rough attempts to define the political views of men who did not want to be categorized in this way. In some cases I have considered it wiser not to mention a party at all.

Both in Belgium and the Netherlands various departments—especially Defence—were sometimes led by experts who did not wish to express an articulate political opinion but served as mere technicians.

Abbreviations

Agric.: Agriculture
AR: Anti-Revolutionary (Calvinist)
C: Conservative
CHU: Christian Historical Union (Protestant)
Christ. Dem.: Christian Democrat (Roman Catholic)
CL: Conservative Liberal
Dom. Trade: Domestic Trade
Ind.: Industry
L: Liberal
LC: Liberal Conservative
Lib. Dem.: Liberal Democrat
S: Socialist

THE UNITED KINGDOM OF THE NETHERLANDS, 1815–1830

For. Af.: on 16 Sept. 1815: A. W. C. van Nagell van Ampsen; on 1 Jan. 1824: J. G. Reinhold; on 16 May 1824: W. F. van Reede; on 23 June 1825: P. C. G. de Coninck; on 1 Dec. 1825: J. G. Verstolk van Soelen, until 13 Sept. 1841

Home Af.: on 16 Sept. 1815: W. F. Röell; on 21 Feb. 1817: P. C. G. de Coninck; on 19 June 1825: P. L. J. S. van Gobbelschroy; on 1 Jan. 1830: E. C. G. G. de la Coste, until 22 Oct. 1830

Education: on 16 Sept. 1815: O. Repelaer van Driel; on 19 Mar. 1818: A. R. Falck; on 30 Mar. 1824: P. C. G. de Coninck, until 5 Apr. 1825

Religious Af. (*Prot.*): on 16 Sept. 1815: O. Repelaer van Driel; on 19 Mar. 1818: F. W. F. T. van Pallandt van Keppel, until 28 Feb. 1841

Religious Af. (*RC*): on 16 Sept. 1815: J. F. G. Goubau d'Hovorst, since 1 Aug. 1826 under Home Affairs

Justice: on 16 Sept. 1815: C. F. van Maanen, until 3 Sept. 1830

Finance: on 16 Sept. 1815: C. C. Six van Oterleek; on 11 Apr. 1821: F. A. Noël Simons; on 1 May 1821: C. T. Elout; on 30 Mar. 1824: J. H. Appelius; on 12 Apr. 1828: P. A. Ossewaarde; on 10 June 1828: A. W. N. van Tets van Goudriaan, until 5 Jan. 1837

Public Works: on 16 Sept. 1815: C. J. van Ursel; on 1 July 1819: O. Repelaer van Driel, since 1 Jan. 1820 under Home Affairs

Defence: on 16 Sept. 1815: F. A. van der Goltz; on 1 Mar. 1818: M. Piepers; on 1 Mar. 1819: A. C. J. G. d'Aubremé; on 1 July 1826: Prince Frederik; on 1 Jan. 1830: D. J. de Eerens, until 1 Oct. 1834

Navy or Navy and Colonies: on 16 Sept. 1815: J. C. van der Hoop; on 13 Mar. 1825: A. A. Stratenus; on 5 Apr. 1825: C. T. Elout; on 1 Oct. 1829: J. J. Quarles van Ufford, until 1 Jan. 1830

Colonies: on 16 Sept. 1815: J. Goldberg; on 19 Mar. 1818: A. R. Falck; on 30 Mar. 1824: C. T. Elout, until 5 Apr. 1825

BELGIUM

Cabinet Goblet (26 Feb.–23 Mar. 1831)

For. Af.: S. van de Weyer (L)
Home Af.: J. F. Tielemans (L)
Justice: A. Gendebien (L)
Finance: Ch. de Brouckère (L)
Defence: A. Goblet d'Alviella (L)

Cabinet E. de Sauvage (23 Mar.–21 July 1831)

For. Af.: J. Lebeau (L)
Home Af.: E. de Sauvage (L)
Justice: A. Barthélemy (L)
Finance: Ch. de Brouckère (L)
Defence: C. d'Hane de Steenhuyse (L)
Without Portfolio: P. Devaux (L)

Cabinet F. de Muelenaere (26 July 1831–17 Sept. 1832)

For. Af.: F. de Muelenaere (RC)
Home Af.: E. de Sauvage (L); on 3 Aug. 1831: Ch. de Brouckère (L);
   on 16 Aug. 1831: Th. Teichmann; on 12 Nov. 1831: L. Fallon
   (L); on 21 Nov. 1831: B. T. de Theux de Meylandt (RC)
Justice: J. Raikem (RC)
Finance: J. Coghen (L)
Defence: V. de Failly (L); on 3 Aug. 1831: C. d'Hane de Steenhuyse
   (L); on 16 Aug.: Ch. de Brouckère (L); on 15 Mar.: F. de Mérode
   (RC); on 20 May: L. A. F. Évain
Without Portfolio: J. Lebeau (L): from 2 to 22 Aug. 1831; F. de
   Mérode since 12 Nov.; B. T. de Theux (RC) from 12 to 21 Nov.

Cabinet Goblet–Lebeau–Rogier (20 Oct. 1832–1 Aug. 1834)

For. Af.: A. Goblet (L); on 27 Dec. 1833: F. de Mérode (RC)
Home Af.: Ch. Rogier (L)
Justice: J. Lebeau (L)
Finance: A. Duvivier
Defence: L. A. F. Évain
Without Portfolio: F. de Mérode (RC)

Cabinet B. T. de Theux (4 Aug. 1834–6 Apr. 1840)
For. Af.: F. de Muelenaere (RC); on 13 Dec. 1836: B. T. de Theux
   (RC)
Home Af.: B. T. de Theux (RC)

THE NETHERLANDS 1830–1848

For. Af.: on 1 Dec. 1825: J. G. Verstolk van Soelen; on 13 Sept.
1841: H. van Zuylen van Nijevelt; on 6 Oct. 1841: J. W. Huyssen
van Kattendijke; on 21 Sept. 1843: W. A. Schimmelpenninck
van der Oye; on 15 Oct. 1843: J. A. H. de la Sarraz; on 1 Jan.
1848: L. N. van Randwijck, until 25 Mar. 1848

Home Af.: on 22 Oct. 1830: H. J. van Doorn van Westcapelle; on
1 Dec. 1836: H. M. de Kock; on 1 June 1841: W. A. Schimmel-
penninck van der Oye; on 15 Feb. 1846: J. A. van der Heim van
Duivendijke; on 1 June 1846: C. Vollenhoven; on 12 Oct. 1846:
L. N. van Randwijck; on 1 Jan. 1848: J. A. van der Heim van
Duivendijke, until 25 Mar. 1848

Religious Af. (Prot.): on 19 Mar. 1818: F. W. F. T. van Pallandt van
Keppel; on 28 Feb. 1841: H. van Zuylen van Nijevelt, until
25 Mar. 1848

Religious Af. (RC): on 1 Jan. 1830: F. J. M. T. de Pélichy; on 24 Nov.
1844: J. C. Willemse; on 15 Jan. 1845: J. B. van Son, until
25 Mar. 1848

Justice: on 3 Sept. 1830: F. W. F. T. van Pallandt van Keppel; on
5 Oct. 1830: C. F. van Maanen; on 1 Apr. 1842: F. A. van Hall;
on 7 Mar. 1844: M. W. de Jonge van Campens Nieuwland, until
19 Mar. 1848

Finance: on 10 June 1828: A. W. N. van Tets van Goudriaan; on
5 Jan. 1837: A. van Gennep; on 1 June 1837: G. Beelaerts van
Blokland; on 9 Jan. 1840: A. van Gennep; on 31 July 1840: J. J.
Rochussen; on 25 June 1843: J. A. van der Heim van Duivendijke;
on 22 Sept. 1843: F. A. van Hall; on 1 Jan. 1848: W. L. F. C. van
Rappard, until 25 Mar. 1848

Public Works, Trade, and Colonies: on 1 Jan. 1830: P. L. J. S. van
Gobbelschroy; on 4 Oct. 1830: G. G. Clifford, until 1 Oct. 1831

Defence: on 1 Jan. 1830: D. J. de Eerens; on 1 Oct. 1834: H. R. Trip;
on 1 Jan. 1840: A. Schuurman; on 1 Nov. 1840: F. C. List, until
25 Mar. 1848

Trade and Colonies: 1 Oct. 1831–1 Jan. 1834: G. G. Clifford

Colonies and Navy: 10 Aug. 1840–1 Jan. 1842: J. C. Baud

Navy: 1 Jan. 1830–10 Aug. 1840: J. C. Wolterbeek; 1 Jan. 1842–
15 Sept. 1849: J. C. Rijk

Colonies: on 1 Jan. 1834: A. Brocx; on 30 May 1834: J. van den
Bosch; on 1 Jan. 1840: J. C. Baud, until 10 Aug. 1840; on 1 Jan.
1842: J. C. Baud, until 25 Mar. 1848

BELGIUM

Justice: A. N. J. Ernst (L); on 4 Feb. 1839: J. B. Nothomb (L); on 8 June 1839; J. Raikem

Finance: É. d'Huart (L); on 4 Feb. 1839: F. de Mérode (RC); on 18 Feb. 1839: J. Wilmar (L); on 5 Apr. 1839: L. Desmaisières (RC)

Public Works: J. B. Nothomb (L), department created 13 Jan. 1837

Defence: L. A. F. Évain; on 19 Aug. 1836: J. Willmar (L)

Without Portfolio: F. de Mérode (RC)

Cabinet J. Lebeau (18 Apr. 1840–13 Apr. 1841)

For. Af.: J. Lebeau (L)

Home Af.: Ch. Liedts (L)

Justice: M. Leclercq (L)

Finance: E. Mercier (L)

Public Works: Ch. Rogier (L)

Defence: G. Buzen (L)

Cabinet J. B. Nothomb (13 Apr. 1841–19 June 1845)

For. Af.: F. de Muelenaere (RC); on 5 Aug. 1841: C. de Briey (RC); on 16 Apr. 1843: A. Goblet (L)

Home Af.: J. B. Nothomb (L)

Justice: C. van Volxem (L); on 14 Dec. 1842: J. B. Nothomb (L); on 16 Apr. 1843: J. d'Anethan (RC)

Finance: C. de Briey (RC); on 5 Aug. 1841: J. Smits (RC); on 16 Apr. 1843: E. Mercier (L)

Public Works: L. Desmaisières (RC); on 16 Apr. 1843: A. Dechamps (RC)

Defence: G. Buzen; on 6 Feb. 1842: H. de Liem; on 5 Apr. 1843: L. Desmaisières (RC); on 16 Apr. 1843: P. Dupont

Without Portfolio: on 5 Aug. 1841: F. de Muelenaere (RC)

Cabinet S. van de Weyer (30 July 1845–7 Mar. 1846)

For. Af.: A. Dechamps (RC)

Home Af.: S. van de Weyer (L)

Justice: J. d'Anethan (RC)

Finance: J. Malou (RC)

Public Works: C. d'Hoffschmidt (L)

Defence: P. Dupont (L); on 27 Feb. 1846: J. d'Anethan (RC)

Without Portfolio: F. de Muelenaere (RC); É. d'Huart (L)

BELGIUM

Cabinet De Theux–Malou (31 Mar. 1846–12 Aug. 1847)

For. Af.: A. Dechamps (RC)
Home Af.: B. de Theux (RC)
Justice: J. d'Anethan (RC)
Finance: J. Malou (RC)
Public Works: G. de Bavay (RC)
Defence: A. Prisse (RC)
Without portfolio: F. de Muelenaere (RC); É. d'Huart (L, later RC)

Cabinet Ch. Rogier (12 Aug. 1847–28 Sept. 1852)

For. Af.: C. d'Hoffschmidt (L)
Home Af.: Ch. Rogier (L)
Justice: F. P. de Haussy (L); on 12 Aug. 1850: V. Tesch (L)
Finance: L. Veydt (L); on 18 July 1848: H. J. W. Frère-Orban (L);
    on 17 Sept. 1852: Ch. Liedts (L)
Public Works: H. J. W. Frère-Orban (L); on 18 July 1848: H. Rolin
    (L); on 12 Aug. 1850: E. van Hoorebeke (L)
Defence: P. Chazal (L); on 12 Aug. 1850: M. Brialmont (L); on
    13 June 1851: V. P. E. Anoul (L)

THE NETHERLANDS

Cabinet G. Schimmelpenninck (25 Mar.–21 Nov. 1848)

P.M.: G. Schimmelpenninck (C)

For. Af.: G. Schimmelpenninck (C); on 17 May: A. A. Bentinck van Nijenhuis (C)

Home Af.: L. C. Luzac (L); on 13 May: J. M. de Kempenaer (L)

Religious Af. (Prot.): L. C. Luzac (L); on 30 June: S. van Heemstra (L)

Religious Af. (RC): L. A. van Lightenvelt (RC)

Justice: D. Donker Curtius (L)

Finance: G. Schimmelpenninck (C); on 17 May: P. A. Ossewaarde; on 3 June: P. P. van Bosse (L)

Defence: C. Nepveu; on 22 May: J. H. Voet

Navy and Colonies: J. C. Rijk

Cabinet D. Donker Curtius (21 Nov. 1848–1 Nov. 1849)

For. Af.: L. A. van Lightenvelt (RC)

Home Af.: J. M. de Kempenaer (L)

Religious Af. (Prot): S. van Heemstra (L)

Religious Af. (RC): J. A. Mutsaers (RC)

Justice: D. Donker Curtius (L); on 4 June 1849: H. L. Wichers (L)

Finance: P. P. van Bosse (L)

Defence: J. H. Voet

Navy: J. C. Rijk; on 15 Sept. 1849: E. B. van den Bosch

Colonies: G. L. Baud (CL); on 18 June 1849: E. B. van den Bosch

Cabinet J. R. Thorbecke (1 Nov. 1849–19 Apr. 1853)

For. Af.: H. van Sonsbeeck (L); on 16 Oct. 1852: J. P. P. van Zuylen van Nijevelt (LC)

Home Af.: J. R. Thorbecke (L)

Religious Af. (Prot.): J. T. H. Nedermeyer van Rosenthal (L); on 15 July 1852: P. P. van Bosse (L)

BELGIUM

Cabinet H. de Brouckère (31 Oct. 1852–2 Mar. 1855)

For. Af.: H. de Brouckère (L)
Home Af.: F. Piercot
Justice: Ch. Faider
Finance: Ch. Liedts (L)
Public Works: R. van Hoorebeke (L)
Defence: V. P. E. Anoul (L)

Cabinet P. de Decker (30 Mar. 1855–30 Oct. 1857)

For. Af.: Ch. Vilain XIIII (RC)
Home Af.: P. de Decker (RC)
Justice: Alph. Nothomb
Finance: E. Mercier (L)
Public Works: A. Dumon (L)
Defence: J. Greindl

Religious Af. (RC): H. van Sonsbeeck (L); on 16 Oct. 1852: M. P. H.
Strens (LC)
Justice: J. T. H. Nedermeyer van Rosenthal (L); on 15 July 1852:
M. P. H. Strens (LC)
Finance: P. P. van Bosse (L)
Defence: J. T. van Spengler; on 15 July 1852: H. F. C. Forstner van
Dambenoy (AR)
Navy: E. Lucas; on 20 Apr. 1851: J. T. van Spengler; on 1 Nov.
1851: J. Enslie
Colonies: C. F. Pahud (LC)

Cabinet F. A. van Hall (19 Apr. 1853–1 July 1856)

For. Af.: F. A. van Hall (CL)
Home Af.: G. C. J. van Reenen (CL)
Religious Af. (Prot.): E. C. U. van Doorn (C); on 20 Jan. 1854:
A. G. A. van Rappard (C)
Religious Af. (RC): L. A. van Lightenvelt (RC); on 31 Dec. 1853:
J. A. Mutsaers (RC)
Justice: D. Donker Curtius (LC)
Finance: E. C. U. van Doorn (C); on 6 Jan. 1854: F. A. van Hall
(CL); on 1 May 1854: A. Vrolik (C)
Defence: H. F. C. Forstner van Dambenoy (AR)
Navy: J. Enslie; on 16 Dec. 1854: H. F. C. Forstner van Dambenoy
(AR); on 8 Feb. 1855: A. J. de Smit van den Broeke
Colonies: C. F. Pahud (LC); on 1 Jan. 1856: P. Mijer (C)

Cabinet J. J. L. van der Brugghen (1 July 1856–18 Mar. 1858)

For. Af.: D. T. Gevers van Endegeest (C)
Home Af.: G. Simons (C); on 19 Jan. 1857: A. G. A. van Rappard
(C)
Religious Af. (Prot.): A. G. A. van Rappard (C); on 19 Jan. 1857:
M. Wiardi Beckman (C)
Religious Af. (RC): J. A. Mutsaers (RC); on 1 Aug. 1856: J. W. van
Romunde (RC)
Justice: J. J. L. van der Brugghen (C, AR)
Finance: A. Vrolik (C)
Defence: H. F. C. Forstner van Dambenoy (AR); on 31 Dec. 1857:
C. T. van Meurs
Navy: A. J. de Smit van den Broecke; on 1 Aug. 1856: J. S. Lotsy
(CL)
Colonies: P. Mijer (C)

BELGIUM

Cabinet Rogier–Frère–Orban (*9 Nov. 1857–21 Dec. 1867*)

For. Af.: A. de Vrière (L); on 26 Oct. 1861: Ch. Rogier (L)

Home Af.: Ch. Rogier (L); on 26 Oct. 1861: A. Vandenpeereboom (L)

Justice: V. Tesch (L); on 12 Nov. 1865: J. Bara (L)

Finance: H. J. W. Frère-Orban (L)

Public Works: J. Partoes (L); on 14 Jan. 1859: J. Vanderstichelen (L)

Defence: E. Berten; on 6 Apr. 1859: P. Chazal; on 13 Dec. 1866: A. Goethals

THE NETHERLANDS

Cabinet J. J. Rochussen (18 Mar. 1858–23 Feb. 1860)

For. Af.: J. K. van Goltstein (CL)
Home Af.: J. G. H. van Tets van Goudriaan (C)
Religious Af. (Prot.): C. H. B. Boot; on 3 Apr. 1858: J. Bosscha (C)
Religious Af. (RC): J. W. van Romunde (RC)
Justice: C. H. B. Boot
Finance: P. P. van Bosse (L)
Defence: C. T. van Meurs; on 1 Sept. 1859: E. A. O. de Casembroot
Navy: J. S. Lotsy (CL)
Colonies: J. J. Rochussen (LC)

Cabinet F. A. van Hall (23 Feb. 1860–14 Mar. 1861)

For. Af.: F. A. van Hall (CL); on 8 Mar. 1860: J. P. J. A. van Zuylen
  van Nijevelt (AR); on 14 Jan. 1861: L. N. van der Goes van
  Dirxland
Home Af.: S. van Heemstra (L)
Religious Af. (Prot.): J. Bosscha (C)
Religious Af. (RC): J. A. Mutsaers (RC)
Justice: M. H. Godefroi (CL)
Finance: F. A. van Hall (CL); on 23 Feb. 1861: J. S. Lotsy (CL)
Defence: E. A. O. de Casembroot
Navy: J. S. Lotsy (CL)
Colonies: J. J. Rochussen (LC); on 1 Jan. 1861: J. S. Lotsy (CL); on
  9 Jan. 1861: J. P. Cornets de Groot

Cabinet J. P. P. van Zuylen van Nijevelt (14 Mar. 1861–1 Feb. 1862)

For. Af.: J. P. P. van Zuylen (C); on 10 Nov. 1861: M. P. H. Strens
  (C)
Home Af.: S. van Heemstra (L)
Religious Af. (Prot.): J. A. Jolles (L)
Religious Af. (RC): M. P. H. Strens (C)
Justice: M. H. Godefroi (CL)
Finance: J. G. H. van Tets van Goudriaan (C)
Defence: E. A. O. de Casembroot
Navy: W. J. C. Huyssen van Kattendijke
Colonies: J. Loudon (L)

BELGIUM

Cabinet H. J. W. Frère-Orban (3 Jan. 1868–16 June 1870)
For. Af.: J. Vanderstichelen (L)
Home Af.: E. Pirmez (L)

THE NETHERLANDS

Cabinet J. R. Thorbecke (1 Feb. 1862–10 Feb. 1866)

For. Af.: A. J. L. Stratenus; on 12 Mar. 1862: P. T. van der Masen de Sombreff (L); on 2 Jan. 1864: W. J. C. Huyssen van Kattendijke; on 15 Mar. 1864: E. J. J. B. Cremers (L)
Home Af.: J. R. Thorbecke (L)
Religious Af. (Prot.): J. A. Jolles, until 1 July 1862
Religious Af. (RC): K. A. Meeussen (L, RC), until 1 July 1862
Justice: N. Olivier (L)
Finance: G. H. Betz (L); on 27 Nov. 1865: N. Olivier (L)
Defence: J. W. Blanken
Navy: W. J. C. Huyssen van Kattendijke; on 6 Feb. 1866: J. W. Blanken
Colonies: G. H. Uhlenbeck (L); on 3 Jan. 1863: G. H. Betz (L); on 2 Feb. 1863: I. D. Fransen van de Putte (L)

Cabinet I. D. Fransen van de Putte (10 Feb. 1866–30 May 1866)

For. Af.: E. J. J. B. Cremers (L)
Home Af.: J. H. Geertsema (L)
Justice: C. J. Pické (L)
Finance: P. P. van Bosse (L)
Defence and Navy: J. W. Blanken
Colonies: I. D. Fransen van de Putte (L)

Cabinet Mijer–van Zuylen–Heemskerk (1 June 1866–4 June 1868)

For. Af.: J. P. J. A. van Zuylen (C, AR)
Home Af.: J. Heemskerk (CL)
Religious Af. (Prot.): C. T. van Lynden van Sandenburg (AR) (15 Jan. 1868–4 June 1868)
Religious Af. (RC): A. F. X. Luyben (RC) (15 Jan. 1868–4 June 1868)
Justice: E. J. H. Borret (RC); on 10 Nov. 1867: J. Heemskerk (CL); on 4 Jan. 1868: W. Wintgens (C)
Finance: R. J. Schimmelpenninck (C)
Defence: J. A. van den Bosch (C)
Navy: G. C. C. Pels Rijcken (C)
Colonies: P. Mijer (C); on 17 Sept. 1866: N. Trakanen; on 20 July 1867: J. J. Hasselman (C)

Cabinet van Bosse–Fock (4 June 1868–4 Jan. 1871)

For. Af.: T. M. Roest van Limburg (L); on 12 Dec. 1870: J. J. van Mulken (L)
Home Af.: C. Fock (L)

BELGIUM

Justice: J. Bara (L)
Finance: H. J. W. Frère-Orban (L)
Public Works: A. Jamar (L)
Defence: B. Renard

Cabinet J. d'Anethan (2 July 1870–1 Dec. 1871)

For. Af.: J. d'Anethan (RC)
Home Af.: J. Kervyn de Lettenhove (RC)
Justice: P. Cornesse (RC)
Finance: P. Tack (RC); on 3 Aug. 1870: V. Jacobs (RC)
Public Works: V. Jacobs (RC); on 3 Aug. 1870: J. d'Anethan (RC);
    on 12 Sept. 1870: A. Wasseige (RC)
Defence: H. L. G. Guillaume
Without Portfolio: J. Malou (RC) (24 July–5 Dec. 1870)

Cabinet De Theux–Malou (7 Dec. 1871–11 June 1878)

For. Af.: G. d'Aspremont Lynden (RC)
Home Af.: Ch. Delcour (RC)
Justice: T. de Lantsheere (RC)
Finance: J. Malou (RC)
Public Works: F. Moncheur (RC); on 23 Oct. 1873: A. Beernaert
    (RC)
Defence: H. L. G. Guillaume; on 25 Mar. 1873: S. Thiebauld
Without Portfolio: B. T. de Theux (RC), died 21 Aug. 1874

THE NETHERLANDS

Religious Af. (Prot.): P. P. van Bosse (L), until 29 July 1870 when the department was abolished
Religious Af. (RC): F. G. R. H. van Lilaar, until 29 July 1870 when the department was abolished
Justice: F. G. R. H. van Lilaar (L)
Finance: P. P. van Bosse (L)
Defence: J. J. van Mulken (L)
Navy: L. G. Brocx
Colonies: E. de Waal (L); on 16 Nov. 1870: L. G. Brocx

Cabinet J. R. Thorbecke (4 Jan. 1871–6 July 1872)
For. Af.: J. L. H. A. Gericke van Herwijnen (L)
Home Af.: J. R. Thorbecke (L); on 5 June 1872: P. P. van Bosse (L)
Justice: J. A. Jolles (L)
Finance: P. Blussé van Oud Alblas (L)
Defence: G. P. Booms; on 28 Jan. 1871: A. Engelvaart; on 23 Dec. 1871: L. G. Brocx; on 5 Feb. 1872: F. A. T. Delprat (L)
Navy: L. G. Brocx
Colonies: P. P. van Bosse (L)

Cabinet De Vries–Geertsema (6 July 1872–27 Aug. 1874)
For. Af.: J. L. H. A. Gericke van Herwijnen (L)
Home Af.: J. H. Geertsema (L)
Justice: G. de Vries (CL)
Finance: A. van Delden (L)
Defence: M. D. van Limburg Stirum; on 15 Sept. 1873: L. G. Brocx; on 6 Oct. 1873: A. W. P. Weitzel
Navy: L. G. Brocx; on 18 Dec. 1873: I. D. Fransen van de Putte (L); on 16 May 1874: W. F. van Erp Taalman Kip (CL)
Colonies: I. D. Fransen van de Putte (L)

Cabinet J. Heemskerk (27 Aug. 1874–3 Nov. 1877)
For. Af.: P. J. A. M. van der Does de Willebois (L, RC)
Home Af.: J. Heemskerk (C)
Justice: C. T. van Lynden van Sandenburg (AR)
Finance: H. J. van der Heim (C)
Defence: A. W. P. Weitzel; on 29 Apr. 1875: H. J. Enderlein; on 1 Jan. 1876: W. F. van Erp Taalman Kip (CL); on 1 Feb. 1876: G. J. G. Klerck; on 30 Sept. 1876: H. J. R. Beyen
Navy: W. F. van Erp Taalman Kip (CL)

BELGIUM

Cabinet Frère-Orban–Van Humbeeck (*18 June 1878–10 June 1884*)
For. Af.: H. J. W. Frère-Orban (L)
Home Af.: G. Rolin-Jaquemyns (L)
Justice: J. Bara (L)
Finance: Ch. Graux (L)
Public Works: Ch. Sainctelette (L); on 5 Aug. 1882: X. Olin (L)
Education: P. van Humbeeck (L)
Defence: B. Renard; on 8 Sept. 1879: J. Liagre; on 6 Nov. 1880: G. Gatry

Cabinet Malou–Jacobs–Woeste (*16 June 1884–26 Oct. 1884*)
For. Af.: A. De Moreau (RC)
Home Af.: V. Jacobs (RC)
Justice: Ch. Woeste (RC)
Finance: J. Malou (RC)
Public Works, Agric., Ind.: A. Beernaert (RC)
Railways, Post: J. Vandenpeereboom (RC)
Defence: C. Pontus

THE NETHERLANDS

Colonies: W. van Goltstein van Oldenaller (C); on 11 Sept. 1876: F. Alting Mees

Cabinet J. Kappeyne van de Coppello (3 Nov. 1877–20 Aug. 1879)
For. Af.: W. van Heeckeren van Kell (L)
Home Af.: J. Kappeyne van de Coppello (L)
Justice: H. J. Smidt (L)
Finance: J. G. Gleichman (L)
Public Works and Trade: J. P. R. Tak van Poortvliet (L)
Defence: J. K. H. de Roo van Alderwerelt (L); on 29 Dec. 1878: H. O. Wichers (L); on 1 Feb. 1879: J. C. C. den Beer Poortugael (L)
Navy: H. O. Wichers (L)
Colonies: P. P. van Bosse (L); on 12 Mar. 1879: O. van Rees

Cabinet C. T. van Lynden van Sandenburg (20 Aug. 1879–23 Apr. 1883)
For. Af.: C. T. van Lynden van Sandenburg (AR); on 15 Sept. 1881: W. F. Rochussen (CL)
Home Af.: W. Six (CL); on 10 Feb. 1882: C. Pijnacker Hordijk
Justice: A. E. J. Modderman (L)
Finance: S. Vissering (L); on 13 June 1881: C. T. van Lynden van Sandenburg (AR)
Public Works and Trade: G. J. G. Klerck
Defence: A. E. Reuther
Navy: W. F. van Erp Taalman Kip (CL)
Colonies: W. van Goltstein van Oldenaller (C); on 1 Sept. 1882: W. M. de Brauw (AR); on 23 Feb. 1883: W. F. van Erp Taalman Kip (CL)

Cabinet J. Heemskerk (23 Apr. 1883–21 Apr. 1888)
For. Af.: P. J. A. M. van der Does de Willebois (L, RC); on 1 Nov. 1885: A. P. C. van Karnebeek (L)
Home Af.: J. Heemskerk (C)
Justice: M. W. du Tour van Bellinchave (C)
Finance: W. J. L. Grobbee; on 5 May 1885: J. C. Bloem
Public Works and Trade: J. G. van den Bergh (RC); on 11 July 1887: J. N. Bastert (C)
Defence: A. W. P. Weitzel
Navy: F. L. Geerling (C); on 19 Apr. 1884: W. F. van Erp Taalman Kip (CL); on 5 Aug. 1885: W. L. A. Gericke; on 26 Jan. 1887: F. C. Tromp (L)

BELGIUM

Cabinet A. Beernaert (26 Oct. 1884–17 Mar. 1894)

For. Af.: J. de Caraman-Chimay (RC); on 29 Mar. 1892: A. Beernaert (RC); on 31 Oct. 1892: de Mérode-Westerloo (RC)

Home Af.: J. Thonissen (RC); on 24 Oct. 1887: J. Devolder (RC); on 6 Nov. 1890: E. Mélot (RC); on 2 Mar. 1891: J. de Burlet (RC)

Justice: J. Devolder (RC); on 24 Oct. 1887: J. le Jeune (RC)

Finance: A. Beernaert (RC)

Public Works, Agric., Ind.: A. de Moreau (RC); on 26 Aug. 1888: L. de Bruyn (RC)

Railways, Post: J. Vandenpeereboom (RC)

Defence: C. Pontus; on 4 May 1893: J. Brassine

Cabinet J. de Burlet (26 Mar. 1894–25 Feb. 1896)

For. Af.: de Mérode-Westerloo (RC); on 25 May 1895: J. de Burlet (RC)

Home Af.: J. de Burlet (RC); on 25 May 1895: F. Schollaert (RC)

Justice: V. Begerem (RC)

Finance: P. de Smet de Nayer (RC)

Public Works, Agric.: L. de Bruyn (RC)

Railways, Post: J. Vandenpeereboom (RC)

Ind., Labour Af.: A. Nyssens (RC)

Defence: J. Brassine (RC)

Cabinet P. de Smet de Nayer (25 Feb. 1896–24 Jan. 1899)

For. Af.: P. de Favereau (RC)

Home Af.: F. Schollaert (RC)

Justice: V. Begerem (RC)

Finance: P. de Smet de Nayer (RC)

Public Works, Agric.: L. de Bruyn (RC)

Railways, Post: J. Vandenpeereboom (RC)

Ind., Labour Af.: A. Nyssens (RC)

Defence: J. Brassine; on 11 Nov. 1896: J. Vandenpeereboom (RC)

THE NETHERLANDS

Colonies: F. G. van Bloemen Waanders; on 25 Nov. 1883: A. W. P.
Weitzel; on 27 Feb. 1884: J. P. Sprenger van Eyk (L)

Cabinet A. E. Mackay (21 Apr. 1888–21 Aug. 1891)

For. Af.: C. Hartsen (C)
Home Af.: A. E. Mackay (AR); on 24 Feb. 1890: A. F. de Savornin
Lohman (AR)
Justice: G. L. M. H. Ruys de Beerenbrouck (RC)
Finance: K. A. Godin de Beaufort
Public Works and Trade: J. P. Havelaar
Defence: J. W. Bergansius (RC)
Navy: H. Dijserinck; on 31 Mar. 1891: G. Kruys
Colonies: L. W. C. Keuchenius (AR); on 24 Feb. 1890: A. E.
Mackay (AR)

Cabinet G. van Tienhoven (21 Aug. 1891–9 May 1894)

For. Af.: G. van Tienhoven (L); on 21 Mar. 1894: J. C. Jansen
Home Af.: J. P. R. Tak van Poortvliet (L)
Justice: H. J. Smidt (L)
Finance: N. G. Pierson (L)
Public Works and Trade: C. Lely (L)
Defence: A. L. W. Seyffardt (L)
Navy: J. C. Jansen (L)
Colonies: W. K. van Dedem van Vosbergen (L)

Cabinet J. Roëll (9 May 1894–27 July 1897)

For. Af.: J. Roëll (L)
Home Af.: S. van Houten (L)
Justice: W. van der Kaay
Finance: J. P. Sprenger van Eyk (L)
Public Works and Trade: P. W. van der Sleyden
Defence: C. D. H. Schneider
Navy: H. M. van der Wijck (L)
Colonies: J. H. Bergsma

Cabinet N. G. Pierson (27 July 1897–1 Aug. 1901)

For. Af.: W. H. de Beaufort
Home Af.: H. Goeman Borgesius (L)
Justice: P. W. A. Cort van der Linden (L)
Finance: N. G. Pierson (L)
Public Works and Trade: C. Lely (L)

BELGIUM

Cabinet J. Vandenpeereboom (24 Jan. 1899–31 July 1899)

For. Af.: P. de Favereau (RC)
Home Af.: F. Schollaert (RC)
Justice: V. Begerem (RC)
Finance: J. Liebaert (RC)
Public Works, Agric.: L. de Bruyn (RC)
Railways, Post: J. Vandenpeereboom (RC)
Ind., Labour Af.: G. Cooreman (RC)
Defence: J. Vandenpeereboom (RC)

Cabinet P. de Smet de Nayer II (5 Aug. 1899–12 Apr. 1907)

For. Af.: P. de Favereau (RC)
Home Af.: J. de Trooz (RC)
Justice: J. van den Heuvel (RC)
Finance: P. de Smet de Nayer (RC)
Agriculture: M. L. van der Bruggen (RC)
Railways, Post: J. Liebaert (RC)
Ind., Labour Af.: J. Liebaert (RC); on 5 Feb. 1900: A. Surmont de
   Volsberghe (RC); on 9 Aug. 1902: G. Francotte (RC)
Defence: A. Cousebant d'Alkemade

THE NETHERLANDS

Defence: K. Eland; on 1 Apr. 1901: A. Kool
Navy: J. C. Jansen; on 22 Dec. 1897: K. Eland; on 12 Jan. 1898: J. Roëll (L)
Colonies: J. T. Cremer (L)

Cabinet A. Kuyper (1 Aug. 1901–17 Aug. 1905)

For. Af.: R. Melvil van Lynden (AR); on 19 Mar. 1905: A. G. Ellis; on 22 Apr. 1905: W. M. van Weede van den Beren-Camp (AR); on 7 Aug. 1905: A. G. Ellis
Home Af.: A. Kuyper (AR)
Justice: J. A. Loeff (RC)
Finance: J. J. I. Harte van Tecklenburg (RC)
Public Works and Trade: J. C. de Marez Oyens (AR)
Defence: J. W. Bergansius (RC)
Navy: G. Kruys; on 12 Dec. 1902: J. W. Bergansius (RC); on 16 Mar. 1903: A. G. Ellis
Colonies: T. A. J. van Asch van Wijck (AR); on 10 Sept. 1902: J. W. Bergansius (RC); on 25 Sept. 1902: A. W. F. Idenburg (AR)

Cabinet T. H. de Meester (17 Aug. 1905–12 Feb. 1908)

For. Af.: D. A. W. van Tets van Goudriaan
Home Af.: P. Rink (L)
Justice: E. E. van Raalte (L)
Finance: T. H. de Meester (L)
Trade: J. D. Veegens (L); on 1 July 1906: J. Kraus
Public Works: J. Kraus
Defence: H. P. Staal; on 7 Apr. 1907: W. F. van Rappard (L)
Navy: W. J. Cohen Stuart; on 5 Aug. 1907: J. Wentholt
Colonies: D. Fock (L)

BELGIUM

Cabinet J. de Trooz (1 May 1907–31 Dec. 1907)

For. Af.: J. Davignon (RC)
Home Af.: J. de Trooz (RC)
Arts and Sciences: É. Descamps (RC)
Justice: J. Renkin (Christ. Dem.)
Finance: J. Liebaert (RC)
Agriculture: G. Helleputte (Christ. Dem.)
Public Works: A. Delbeke (RC)
Ind., Labour Af.: A. Hubert (RC)
Railways, Post: G. Helleputte (Christ. Dem.)
Defence: J. Hellebaut

Cabinet F. Schollaert (9 Jan. 1908–8 June 1911)

For Af.: J. Davignon (RC)
Home Af.: F. Schollaert (RC); on 5 Sept. 1910: P. Berryer (RC)
Arts and Sciences: É. Descamps (RC); on 5 Aug. 1910: F. Schollaert (RC)
Justice: J. Renkin (Christ. Dem.); on 30 Oct. 1908: L. de Lantsheere (Christ. Dem.)
Finance: J. Liebaert (RC)
Agriculture: G. Helleputte (Christ. Dem.); on 30 Oct. 1908: F. Schollaert (RC); on 5 Aug. 1910: G. Helleputte (Christ. Dem.)
Public Works: A. Delbeke (RC); on 5 Aug. 1910: G. Helleputte (Christ. Dem.)
Ind., Labour Af.: A. Hubert (RC)
Railways, Post: G. Helleputte (Christ. Dem.); on 5 Sept. 1910: Ch. de Broqueville (RC)
Defence: J. Hellebaut
Colonies: J. Renkin (Christ. Dem.), department created 30 Oct. 1908

Cabinet Ch. de Broqueville (18 June 1911–1 June 1918)

For. Af.: J. Davignon (RC); on 18 Jan. 1916: E. Beyens (RC); on 4 Aug. 1917: Ch. de Broqueville (RC); on 1 Jan. 1918: P. Hymans (L)
Home Af.: P. Berryer (RC)
Arts and Sciences: P. Poullet (RC)
Justice: H. Carton de Wiart (RC)
Finance: M. Levie (RC); on 28 Feb. 1914: A. Vande Vyvere (RC)
Public Works, Agric.: A. Vande Vyvere (RC); on 11 Nov. 1912: G. Helleputte (Christ. Dem.)

THE NETHERLANDS

Cabinet T. Heemskerk (12 Feb. 1908–29 Aug. 1913)

For. Af.: R. de Marees van Swinderen

Home Af.: T. Heemskerk (AR)

Justice: A. P. L. Nelissen (RC); on 11 May 1910: T. Heemskerk
(AR); on 7 June 1910: E. R. H. Regout (RC); on 18 Jan. 1913:
T. Heemskerk (AR)

Finance: M. J. C. M. Kolkman (RC)

Agric. and Trade: A. S. Talma (AR)

Public Works: J. G. S. Bevers (RC); on 21 Jan. 1909: L. H. W.
Regout (RC)

Defence: F. H. A. Sabron; on 27 July 1909: W. Cool; on 4 Jan.
1911: H. Colijn (AR)

Navy: J. Wentholt; on 14 May 1912: H. Colijn (AR)

Colonies: T. Heemskerk (AR); on 20 May 1908: A. W. F. Idenburg
(AR); on 16 Aug. 1909: J. H. de Waal Malefijt (AR)

BELGIUM

Ind., Labour Af.: A. Hubert (RC)

Railways, Post: Ch. de Broqueville (RC); on 11 Nov. 1912: A. Vande Vyvere for Railways and P. Segers (RC) for Post; on 28 Feb. 1914: P. Segers for the whole department

Defence: J. Hellebaut; on 23 Feb. 1912: Ch. de Broqueville (RC); on 3 Apr. 1912: V. Michel; on 11 Nov. 1912: Ch. de Broqueville; on 4 Aug. 1917: A. de Ceuninck and É. Vandervelde (S)

Colonies: J. Renkin (Christ. Dem.)

Economic Af.: P. Hymans (L) on 12 Oct. 1917; on 1 Jan. 1918: P. Poullet (RC)

National Recovery: Ch. de Broqueville (RC) on 1 Jan. 1918

Without Portfolio: E. Beyens (30 July 1915–18 Jan. 1916); J. Davignon (RC) (18 Jan. 1916–12 Mar. 1916); E. Goblet d'Alviella (L) on 18 Jan. 1916; P. Hymans (L) (18 Jan. 1916–1 Jan. 1918); É. Vandervelde (S) (18 Jan. 1916–4 Aug. 1917); É. Brunet (S) (1 June 1918–1 Jan. 1919)

Cabinet G. Cooreman (1 June 1918–21 Nov. 1918)

For. Af.: P. Hymans (L)

Home Af.: P. Berryer (RC)

Arts and Sciences: P. Poullet (RC)

Justice: H. Carton de Wiart (RC)

Finance: A. Vande Vyvere (RC)

Public Works, Agric.: G. Helleputte (RC)

Ind., Labour Af.: A. Hubert (RC)

Railways, Post: P. Segers (RC)

Defence: A. de Ceuninck and É. Vandervelde (S)

Colonies: J. Renkin (RC)

Economic Af.: G. Cooreman (RC)

Cabinet L. Delacroix I (21 Nov. 1918–17 Nov. 1919)

P.M., Finance: L. Delacroix (RC)

For. Af.: P. Hymans (L)

Home Af.: Ch. de Broqueville (RC)

Arts and Sciences: A. Harmignie (RC)

Justice: É. Vandervelde (S)

Agric.: A. Ruzette (RC)

Public Works: E. Anseele (S)

Ind., Labour Af., Food: J. Wauters (S)

Railways, Post: J. Renkin (RC)

Defence: F. Masson (L)

THE NETHERLANDS

Cabinet P. W. A. Cort van der Linden (29 Aug. 1913–9 Sept. 1918)
For. Af.: J. Loudon
Home Af.: P. W. A. Cort van der Linden (L)
Justice: B. Ort
Finance: A. E. J. Bertling; on 24 Oct. 1914: M. W. F. Treub (L);
on 8 Feb. 1916: A. van Gijn (L); on 22 Feb. 1917: M. W. F.
Treub (L)
Agric. and Trade: M. W. F. Treub (L); on 19 Nov. 1914: F. E.
Posthuma
Defence: N. Bosboom; on 15 May 1917: J. J. Rambonnet; on 15 June
1917: B. C. de Jonge
Navy: J. Rambonnet; on 28 June 1918: B. C. de Jonge
Colonies: T. B. Pleyte (L)
Public Works: C. Lely (L)

Cabinet C. J. M. Ruys de Beerenbrouck I (9 Sept. 1918–18 Sept. 1922)
For. Af.: H. A. van Karnebeek (L)
Home Af.: C. J. M. Ruys de Beerenbrouck (RC)
Education: J. Th. de Visser (CHU) since 25 Sept. 1918 when the
department was created
Justice: T. Heemskerk (AR)
Finance: S. de Vries (AR); on 28 July 1921: D. J. de Geer (CHU)
Agric. and Trade: H. A. van Ysselsteijn
Public Works: A. A. H. W. König (RC)
Labour Af.: P. J. M. Aalberse (RC)
Defence: G. A. A. Alting von Geusau (RC); on 5 Jan. 1920: C. J. M.
Ruys de Beerenbrouck (RC); on 31 Mar. 1920: W. F. Pop; on
28 July 1921: J. J. C. van Dijk (AR)
Navy: W. Naudin ten Cate; on 20 Feb. 1919: C. J. M. Ruys de
Beerenbrouck (RC); on 17 Apr. 1919: H. Bijleveld (AR); on
5 Jan. 1920: H. A. van Ysselsteijn; on 31 Mar. 1920: W. F. Pop;
on 28 July 1921: J. J. C. van Dijk (AR)
Colonies: A. W. F. Idenburg (AR); on 13 Nov. 1919: S. de Graaff

BELGIUM

Colonies: L. Franck (L)
Economic Af.: H. Jaspar (RC)

Cabinet L. Delacroix II (2 Dec. 1919–3 Nov. 1920)

P.M., Finance: L. Delacroix (RC)
For. Af.: P. Hymans (L); on 28 Aug. 1920: L. Delacroix (RC)
Home Af.: J. Renkin (RC); on 2 June 1920: H. Jaspar (RC)
Arts and Sciences: J. Destrée (S)
Justice: É. Vandervelde (S)
Agric.: A. Ruzette (RC)
Public Works: E. Anseele (S)
Ind., Labour Af., Food: J. Wauters (S)
Railways, Post: P. Poullet (RC)
Defence: F. Masson (L); on 4 Feb. 1920: P. E. Janson (L)
Colonies: L. Franck (L)
Economic Af.: H. Jaspar (RC); on 2 June 1920: F. de Wouters d'Oplinter (RC)

Cabinet H. Carton de Wiart (20 Nov. 1920–20 Nov. 1921)

P.M., Home Af.: H. Carton de Wiart (RC)
For. Af.: H. Jaspar (RC)
Arts and Sciences: J. Destrée (S); on 24 Oct. 1921: X. Neujean (L)
Justice: É. Vandervelde (S); on 24 Oct. 1921: A. Vande Vyvere (RC)
Finance: G. Theunis
Agric.: A. Ruzette (RC)
Public Works: E. Anseele (S); on 24 Oct. 1921: A. Ruzette (RC)
Ind., Labour Af., Food: J. Wauters (S); on 24 Oct. 1921: E. Mahaim
Railways, Post: X. Neujean (L)
Defence: A. Devèze (L)
Colonies: L. Franck (L)
Economic Af.: A. Vande Vyvere (RC)

Cabinet G. Theunis (16 Dec. 1921–5 Apr. 1925)

P.M., Finance: G. Theunis (RC)
For. Af.: H. Jaspar (RC); on 11 Mar. 1924: P. Hymans (L)
Home Af., Public Health: P. Berryer (RC)
Arts and Sciences: E. Hubert (L); on 16 Oct. 1922: L. Leclère (L); on 8 Nov. 1922: P. Nolf (L)
Justice: F. Masson (L)
Agric., Public Works: A. Ruzette (RC)

THE NETHERLANDS

Cabinet Ruys de Beerenbrouck II (18 Sept. 1922–4 Aug. 1925

For. Af.: H. A. van Karnebeek (L)
Home Af.: C. J. M. Ruys de Beerenbrouck (RC)
Education: J. Th. de Visser (CHU)
Justice: T. Heemskerk (AR)
Finance: D. J. de Geer (CHU); on 11 Aug. 1923: H. Colijn (AR)

BELGIUM

Ind., Labour Af.: R. Moyersoen (RC); on 11 Mar. 1924: P. Tschoffen (RC)
Railways, Post: X. Neujean (L)
Defence: A. Devèze (L); on 6 Aug. 1923: P. Forthomme (L)
Colonies: L. Franck (L); on 11 Mar. 1924: H. Carton (RC)
Economic Af.: A. Vande Vyvere (RC); on 10 Sept. 1924: R. Moyersoen (RC)

Cabinet A. Vande Vyvere (13 May 1925)

governed only a few weeks

Cabinet P. Poullet–É. Vandervelde (17 June 1925–19 May 1926)

P.M., Economic Af.: P. Poullet (RC); on 10 Dec. 1925: P. de Liedekerke (RC)
For. Af.: É. Vandervelde (S)
Home Af., Public Health: É. Rolin-Jacquemyns (L)
Arts and Sciences: C. Huysmans (S)
Justice: P. Tschoffen (RC); on 10 Dec. 1925: P. Poullet (RC)
Finance: A. Janssen (RC)
Agric.: A. Vande Vyvere (RC); on 24 Feb. 1926: P. de Liedekerke (RC)
Public Works: A. Laboulle (S)
Ind., Social Af.: J. Wauters (S)
Railways, Post: E. Anseele (S)
Defence: P. J. M. Kestens; on 16 Jan. 1926: P. Poullet (RC)
Colonies: H. Carton (RC)

Cabinet H. Jaspar I (20 May 1926–21 Nov. 1927)

P.M., Home Af., Public Health: H. Jaspar (RC); *Home Af. and Public Health* on 18 Jan. 1927: M. Vauthier (L)
For. Af.: É. Vandervelde (S)
Arts and Sciences: C. Huysmans (S)
Justice: P. Hymans (L)
Finance: M. Houtart (RC)
Agric., Public Works: H. Baels (RC)
Ind., Social Af.: J. Wauters (S)
Railways, Post: E. Anseele (S)
Defence: Ch. de Broqueville (RC)
Colonies: M. Houtart (RC); on 15 Nov. 1926: E. Pécher (L); on 18 Jan. 1927: H. Jaspar (RC)
Without Portfolio: É. Francqui

THE NETHERLANDS

Public Works: G. J. van Swaay (RC)
Agric. and Trade: C. J. M. Ruys de Beerenbrouck (RC) (until 1 Jan.
  1923 when *Agric.* was absorbed by *Home Af.* and *Ind.* and *Trade*
  by *Labour Af.*)
Labour Af.: P. J. M. Aalberse (RC)
Defence: J. J. C. van Dijk (AR)
Navy: E. P. Westerveld
Colonies: S. de Graaff

Cabinet H. Colijn I (4 Aug. 1925–8 Mar. 1926)
For. Af.: H. A. van Karnebeek (L)
Home Af. and Agric.: D. J. de Geer (CHU)
Education: V. H. Rutgers (AR)
Justice: J. W. Schokking (CHU)
Finance: H. Colijn (AR)
Public Works: M. C. E. Bongaerts (RC)
Ind., Trade, and Labour Af.: D. A. P. N. Koolen (RC)
Defence: J. M. J. H. Lambooy (RC)
Navy: J. M. J. H. Lambooy (RC)
Colonies: C. J. I. M. Welter (RC)

Cabinet D. J. de Geer I (8 Mar. 1926–10 Aug. 1929)
For. Af.: H. A. van Karnebeek (L); on 1 Apr. 1927: F. Beelaerts
  van Blokland (CHU)
Home Af. and Agric.: J. B. Kan
Education: M. A. M. Waszink (RC)
Justice: J. Donner (AR)
Finance: D. J. de Geer (CHU)
Public Works: H. van der Vegte (AR)
Ind., Trade, and Labour Af.: J. R. Slotemaker de Bruïne (CHU)
Defence: L. A. van Rooyen; on 24 Apr. 1926: J. M. J. H. Lambooy
  (RC)
Navy: L. A. van Rooyen; on 24 Apr. 1926: J. M. J. H. Lambooy
  (RC); on 1 Sept. 1928 absorbed by *Defence*
Colonies: J. C. Koningsberger

BELGIUM

Cabinet H. Jaspar II (22 Nov. 1927–21 May 1931)

P.M.: H. Jaspar (RC)
For. Af.: P. Hymans (L)
Home Af., *Public Health*: A. Carnoy (RC); on 19 Oct. 1929: H. Baels (RC); on 18 May 1931: H. Jaspar (RC)
Arts and Sciences: M. Vauthier (L); on 18 May 1931: R. Petitjean (L)
Justice: P. E. Janson (L)
Finance: M. Houtart (RC)
Agric., *Public Works*: H. Baels (RC); *Public Works* on 19 Oct. 1929: J. A. C. van Caenegem (RC)
Ind., *Social Af.*: H. Heyman (RC)
Railways, *Post*: M. Lippens (L); *Post* on 19 Oct. 1929: P. Forthomme (L); on 20 May 1931: F. Bovesse (L)
Defence: Ch. de Broqueville (RC)
Colonies: H. Jaspar (RC); on 19 Oct. 1929: P. Tschoffen (RC); on 27 Feb. 1930: H. Jaspar (RC); on 18 May 1931: P. Charles

Cabinet J. Renkin (5 June 1931–18 Oct. 1932)

P.M., *Home Af.*, *Public Health*: J. Renkin (RC); *Home Af.*, *Public Health* on 27 Feb. 1932: H. Carton (RC)
For. Af.: P. Hymans (L)
Arts and Sciences: R. Petitjean (L)
Justice: F. Cocq (L)
Finance: M. Houtart (RC); on 27 Feb. 1932: J. Renkin (RC)
Agric.: E. J. van Dievoet (RC)
Public Works: J. A. C. van Caenegem (RC); on 23 May 1932: G. Sap (RC)
Ind., *Social Af.*: H. Heyman (RC)
Transport: P. Van Isacker (RC); on 23 May 1932: P. Forthomme (L)
Post: F. Bovesse (L)
Defence: L. Dens (L); on 23 May 1932: P. Crokaert (RC)
Colonies: P. Crokaert (RC); on 23 May 1932: P. Tschoffen (RC)

Cabinet Ch. de Broqueville (22 Oct. 1932–13 Nov. 1934)

P.M., *Agric.*, *Middle Classes*: Ch. de Broqueville (RC); on 17 Dec. 1932: G. Sap (RC); on 12 June 1934: F. van Cauwelaert (RC)
For. Af.: P. Hymans (L); on 12 June 1934: H. Jaspar (L)
Home Af.: P. Poullet (RC); on 10 Jan. 1934: H. Pierlot (RC)
Education: M. Lippens (L); on 12 June 1934: V. Maistriau (L)
Justice: P. E. Janson (L); on 12 June 1934: F. Bovesse (L)

THE NETHERLANDS

Cabinet C. J. M. Ruys de Beerenbrouck III (10 Aug. 1929–26 May 1933)

For. Af.: F. Beelaerts van Blokland (CHU); on 20 Apr. 1933:
C. J. M. Ruys de Beerenbrouck (RC)

Home Af. and Agric.: C. J. M. Ruys de Beerenbrouck (RC)

Education: J. Terpstra (AR)

Justice: J. Donner (AR)

Finance: D. J. de Geer (CHU)

Public Works: P. J. Reymer (RC)

Ind., Trade, and Labour Af.: T. J. Verschuur (RC); on 1 May 1932
called *Economic Af. and Labour*

Defence and Navy: L. Deckers (RC)

Colonies: S. de Graaff

BELGIUM

Finance: H. Jaspar (RC); on 12 June 1934: G. Sap (RC)
Public Works: G. Sap (RC); on 12 June 1934: P. Forthomme (L)
Ind., Social Af.: H. Heyman (RC); *Ind. and Labour Af.* on 17 Dec.
  1932: P. van Isacker (RC); *Social Af. and Public Health*: H. Carton
  de Wiart (RC); *Ind., Middle Classes, and Dom. Trade* on 10 Jan.
  1934: F. Van Cauwelaert (RC); *Labour and Social Af.*: P. Van
  Isacker (RC)
Transport: P. Forthomme (L); on 12 June 1934: O. Dierckx (L)
Post: F. Bovesse (L); on 17 Dec. 1932: P. Poullet (RC); on 10 Jan.
  1934: F. van Cauwelaert (RC); on 12 June 1934: O. Dierckx (L)
Defence: G. Theunis (RC); on 17 Dec. 1932: A. Devèze (L)
Colonies: P. Tschoffen (RC)
Without Portfolio: L. Ingenbleek and P. van Zeeland on 12 June 1934

Cabinet G. Theunis II (20 Nov. 1934–19 Mar. 1935)

P.M.: G. Theunis (RC)
For. Af.: P. Hymans (L)
Home Af.: H. Pierlot (RC)
Education: J. Hiernaux (L)
Justice: F. Bovesse (L)
Finance: C. Gutt
Agric.: F. van Cauwelaert (RC); on 13 Mar. 1935: A. de Schrijver
  (RC)
Public Works: F. van Cauwelaert (RC); on 13 Mar. 1935: P. van
  Isacker (RC)
Labour and Social Af.: E. Rubbens (RC)
Economic Af.: P. van Isacker (RC)
Transport, Post: Ch. du Bus de Warnaffe (RC)
Defence: A. Devèze (L)
Colonies: P. Charles
Without Portfolio: E. Francqui

Cabinet P. van Zeeland I (25 Mar. 1935–26 May 1936)

P.M., For. Af.: P. van Zeeland
Home Af.: Ch. du Bus de Warnaffe (RC)
Education: F. Bovesse (L)
Justice: E. Soudan (S)
Finance: M. L. Gérard
Agric.: A. de Schrijver (RC)
Employment: H. de Man (S)
Social Af.: A. Delattre (S)

THE NETHERLANDS

Cabinet H. Colijn II and III (26 May 1933–24 June 1937)

For. Af.: A. C. D. de Graeff

Home Af.: J. A. de Wilde (AR)

Education: H. P. Marchant (Lib. Dem.); on 17 May 1935: J. R. Slotemaker de Bruïne (CHU)

Justice: J. R. H. van Schaik (RC)

Finance: P. J. Oud (Lib. Dem.)

Public Works: J. A. Kalff (L); on 13 Jan. 1935: H. Colijn (AR); on 15 Mar. 1935: O. C. A. van Lidth de Jeude (L)

Social Af.: J. R. Slotemaker de Bruïne (CHU) since 12 June 1933 when the department was created; on 31 July 1935: M. Slingenberg

Economic Af.: T. J. Verschuur (RC); on 17 Apr. 1934: H. Colijn (AR); on 25 June 1934: M. P. L. Steenberghe (RC); on 6 June 1935: H. C. J. H. Gelissen (RC); on 2 Sept. 1935 the department was divided into the two following sections:

   Trade, Ind., and Navigation: H. C. J. H. Gelissen (RC)

   Agric. and Fishery: L. N. Deckers (RC)

Defence: L. N. Deckers (RC); on 2 Sept. 1935: H. Colijn (AR)

Colonies: H. Colijn (AR)

BELGIUM
Economic Af.: P. van Isacker (RC)
Transport, Post: P. H. Spaak (S)
Defence: A. Devèze (L)
Colonies: E. Rubbens (RC)
Without Portfolio: P. Poullet (RC), P. Hymans (L), and É. Vandervelde (S)

Cabinet P. van Zeeland II (13 June 1936–25 Oct. 1937)
P.M.: P. van Zeeland
For. Af.: P. H. Spaak (S)
Home Af.: A. de Schrijver (RC)
Education: J. Hoste (L)
Justice: F. Bovesse (L); on 14 Apr. 1937: V. de Laveleye (L); on 13 July 1937: V. Maistriau (L)
Finance: H. de Man (S)
Agric.: H. Pierlot (RC)
Public Works, Employment: J. Merlot (S)
Social Af.: A. Delattre (S)
Transport: M. H. Jaspar (L)
Economic Af.: P. van Isacker (RC)
Post: D. Bouchery (S)
Defence: Lt.-Gen. Denis
Colonies: E. Rubbens (RC)
Public Health: É. Vandervelde (S); on 28 Jan. 1937: A. Wauters (S)

Cabinet P. E. Janson (23 Nov. 1937–13 May 1938)
P.M.: P. E. Janson (L)
For. Af.: P. H. Spaak (S)
Home Af.: O. Dierckx (L)
Education: J. Hoste (L)
Justice: Ch. du Bus de Warnaffe (RC)
Finance: H. de Man (S); on 12 Mar. 1938: E. Soudan (S)
Agric.: H. Pierlot (RC)
Public Works: J. Merlot (S)
Social Af.: A. Delattre (S)
Economic Af., Middle Classes: P. de Smet (RC)
Transport: H. Marck (RC)
Post: D. Bouchery (S)
Defence: L. Denis
Colonies: E. Rubbens (RC)
Public Health: A. Wauters (S)

THE NETHERLANDS

Cabinet H. Colijn IV (24 June 1937–25 July 1939)

General Af.: H. Colijn (AR) on 8 July 1937
For. Af.: H. Colijn (AR); on 1 Oct. 1937: J. A. N. Patijn
Home Af.: H. van Boeijen (CHU)
Education: J. R. Slotemaker de Bruïne (CHU)
Justice: C. M. J. F. Goseling (RC) .
Finance: J. A. de Wilde (AR); on 19 May 1939: H. Colijn (AR)
Public Works: J. A. M. van Buuren
Social Af.: C. P. M. Romme (RC)
Economic Af.: M. P. L. Steenberghe (RC)
Defence: J. J. C. van Dijk (RC)
Colonies: C. J. I. M. Welter (RC)
Agric. and Fishery: M. P. L. Steenberghe (RC); on 15 July 1937 to
  Economic Af.

BELGIUM

Cabinet P. H. Spaak (15 May 1938–9 Feb. 1939)

P.M., For. Af.: P. H. Spaak (S); *For. Af.*: on 21 Jan. 1939: P. E. Janson (L)

Home Af., Public Health: J. Merlot (S)

Education: O. Dierckx (L)

Justice: J. Pholien (RC); on 21 Jan. 1939: E. van Dievoet (RC)

Finance: M. L. Gérard; on 6 Dec. 1938: A. E. Janssen

Public Works, Employment: A. Balthazar (S)

Social Af.: A. Delattre (S)

Agric., Economic Af., Middle Classes: P. Heymans (RC); *Economic Af.*: G. Barnich on 21 Jan. 1939; *Agric.*: Ch. d'Aspremont-Lynden (RC) on 21 Jan. 1939

Transport, Post: H. Marck (RC)

Defence: L. Denis

Colonies: A. de Vleeschauwer (RC)

Public Health: A. Wauters (S); on 6 Dec. 1938: Jennissen (L); on 21 Jan. 1939: Eeckelers (S)

Cabinet H. Pierlot I (21–7 Feb. 1939)

P.M., Agric.: H. Pierlot (RC)

For. Af.: E. Soudan (S)

Home Af.: W. Eeckelers (S)

Education: E. Blanquaert

Justice: A. de Schrijver (RC)

Finance: C. Gutt

Public Works, Transport: H. Marck (RC)

Social Af.: A. Wauters (S)

Economic Af., Middle Classes: Richard

Defence: L. Denis

Colonies: Heenen

Cabinet H. Pierlot II (18 Apr.–3 Sept. 1939)

P.M., For. Af.: H. Pierlot (RC)

Home Af.: A. Devèze (L)

Education: Duesberg

Justice: P. E. Janson (L)

Finance: C. Gutt

Agric.: Ch. d'Aspremont-Lynden (RC)

Public Works, Employment: A. Vanderpoorten (L)

Social Af.: A. Delfosse (RC)

Economic Af., Middle Classes: G. Sap (RC)

THE NETHERLANDS

Cabinet H. Colijn V (25 July 1939–10 Aug. 1939)
General Af.: H. Colijn (AR)
For. Af.: J. A. N. Patijn
Home Af.: H. van Boeijen (CHU)
Education: B. J. O. Schrieke
Justice: J. A. de Visser (CHU)
Finance: C. W. Bodenhausen (L)

BELGIUM
Transport, Post: H. Marck (RC)
Defence: L. Denis
Colonies: A. de Vleeschauwer (RC)
Public Health: M. H. Jaspar (L)

Cabinet H. Pierlot III (3 Sept. 1939–10 May 1940)

P.M.: H. Pierlot (RC)
Vice P.M.: H. de Man (S), until 5 Jan. 1940
For. Af.: P. H. Spaak (S)
Home Af.: A. Devèze (L); on 5 Jan. 1940: A. Vanderpoorten (L)
Education: Duesberg; on 5 Jan. 1940: E. Soudan (S)
Justice: E. Soudan (S); on 5 Jan. 1940: P. E. Janson (L)
Finance: C. Gutt
Agric.: Ch. d'Aspremont-Lynden (RC)
Public Works: A. Vanderpoorten (L); on 5 Jan. 1940: L. Matagne (L)
Social Af.: A. Balthazar (S)
Economic Af., Middle Classes: G. Sap (RC); on 25 Mar. 1940: A. de Schrijver (RC)
Transport, Post: H. Marck (RC); on 5 Jan. 1940: A. Delfosse (RC)
Defence: L. Denis
Colonies: A. de Vleeschauwer (RC)
Public Health: M. H. Jaspar (L)
Food and Employment: A. Delfosse (RC) on 5 Jan. 1940
Information: A. Wauters (S) on 5 Jan. 1940
Without Portfolio: P. E. Janson (L) on 5 Jan. 1940

THE NETHERLANDS

Public Works: O. C. A. van Lidt de Jeude (L)
Social Af.: M. H. Damme
Economic Af.: H. Colijn (AR)
Defence: J. J. C. van Dijk (AR)
Colonies: C. van den Bussche

Cabinet D. J. de Geer II (10 Aug. 1939–10 May 1940)
General Af.: D. J. de Geer (CHU)
For. Af.: E. N. van Kleffens
Home Af.: H. van Boeijen (CHU)
Education: G. Bolkestein (Lib. Dem.)
Justice: P. Gerbrandy (AR)
Finance: D. J. de Geer (CHU)
Public Works: J. W. Albarda (S)
Social Af.: J. van den Tempel (S)
Economic Af.: M. P. L. Steenberghe (RC)
Agric. and Fishery: A. A. van Rhijn on 8 May 1940
Defence: A. Q. H. Dijxhoorn
Colonies: C. J. I. M. Welter (RC)

BIBLIOGRAPHY

In the following pages I mention some of the main works without any pretension of being exhaustive. A far greater number of titles can be found in the footnotes of this book but even these form only a tiny fraction of the total of books and printed source material available.

I. GENERAL

A. *Bibliographical tools*

A general bibliography of the history of the Netherlands including the nineteenth and twentieth centuries is H. de Buck, *Bibliografie der geschiedenis van Nederland* (Leiden, 1968). Since 1907 appears at irregular intervals the *Repertorium van boeken en tijdschriftartikelen betreffende de geschiedenis van Nederland*. It gives a complete inventory of all Dutch publications on Dutch history. From 1954 to 1965 E. and J. Kossmann wrote in the *Revue du Nord* (Lille) an annual 'Bulletin critique de l'historiographie néerlandaise'. Since 1973 *Acta Historiae Neerlandicae* (The Hague) publishes each year a short and critical survey of Dutch and Flemish historiography.

Current research in Belgium is summarized in a publication by Ghent University: *Bulletin critique d'histoire de Belgique*, since 1967. Before that date the same authors under the direction of the late Professor J. Dhondt published their material in a somewhat shorter version in *Revue du Nord* (Lille). Since 1967 another group of Belgian historians have been compiling the *Revue du Nord* chronicle. In both the *Revue belge de philologie et d'histoire* and the *Revue d'histoire ecclésiastique* there appears each year an extensive bibliographical survey of work on Belgian history.

H. Pirenne, *Bibliographie de l'histoire de Belgique* (3rd edn., Brussels, 1931) is rightly famous but not very useful for the modern period. Historians are greatly helped by three volumes published by the excellent Centre interuniversitaire d'histoire contemporaine:

P. Gérin, *Bibliographie de l'histoire de Belgique, 1789–1831* (Louvain, 1960).

S. Vervaeck, *Bibliographie de l'histoire de Belgique, 1831–1865* (Louvain, 1965).

J. de Belder and J. Hannes, *Bibliographie de l'histoire de Belgique, 1865–1914* (Louvain, 1965).

An informative essay on the achievements and the direction of research and on the gaps in our knowledge and understanding of the period was contributed by R. Aubert to J. A. van Houtte (ed.), *Un Quart de siècle de recherche historique en Belgique, 1944–1968* (Louvain, 1970), pp. 425–566.

B. *General works*

A general survey of Belgian and Dutch history is to be found in J. A. van Houtte *et al.* (eds.), *Algemene geschiedenis der Nederlanden* (12 vols., Utrecht, Antwerp, 1949–58). Volumes ix–xii deal with the period 1795–1945. The quality of the chapters written by many different authors is uneven; the bibliographical information is good. The major weakness of the book is that Belgian and Dutch developments are treated in separate sections virtually without any cross-references.

Th. Luykx, *Politieke geschiedenis van België van 1789 tot heden* (2nd edn., Amsterdam, Brussels, 1969) is a strictly factual but informative and reliable compendium of Belgian political history. It has extensive bibliographies. There is nothing comparable on Dutch history.

Even nowadays volumes vi and vii of H. Pirenne, *Histoire de Belgique* are still impressive and enlightening in parts despite the author's optimistic nationalism and his underestimation of the importance of the Flemish movement.

In H. Brugmans (ed.), *Geschiedenis van Nederland* (8 vols., Amsterdam, 1935–8) L. G. J. Verberne summarized in volumes vii and viii Dutch history from 1813 to the 1930s. This competent work was reprinted in the 1950s in a four-volume paperback edition (Utrecht).

C. *Parliamentary history*

The Dutch are in possession of an excellent parliamentary history written by several authors:

W. J. van Welderen baron Rengers, *Schets eener parlementaire geschiedenis van Nederland van 1849 tot 1901* (4th edn. in 2 vols., edited and annotated by C. W. de Vries, The Hague, 1948–9). W. H. Vermeulen continued the series under the same general title with a third volume treating the years 1901–1914 (The Hague, 1950). Volume iv (The Hague, 1955) written by C. W. de Vries and W. H. Vermeulen deals with the First World War and colonial affairs since the nineteenth century. The events from 1918 to 1940 are described in great detail by P. J. Oud in his masterly *Het jongste verleden* (6 vols., 1948–51; reprinted Assen, 1968).

The Belgians are not so well served but L. Hymans, P. Hymans, and A. Delcroix, *Histoire parlementaire de la Belgique, 1831–1910* (10 vols., Brussels, 1877–1913) is helpful.

Verbatim reports of parliamentary discussions:

Netherlands

Dagverhaal der handelingen van de Nationale Vergadering, representeerende het Volk van Nederland, 7 Maart 1796–4 Mey 1798 (9 vols., The Hague, 1796–8).

Dagverhaal van het Vertegenwoordigend- en Intermediair Wetgevend Lichaam des Bataafschen Volks (13 vols., The Hague, 1798–1801).

Dagverhaal van het Wetgevend Lichaam (The Hague, 1802).

J. J. F. Noordziek *et al.* (eds.), *Verslag der handelingen van de Staten-Generaal 1814/5–1830/1* (19 vols., The Hague, 1862–89).

W. van Erkelens and J. A. Jungmann (eds.), *Verslag der handelingen van de Staten-Generaal 1831/2–1838/9* (11 vols., The Hague, 1891–9).

J. A. Jungmann (ed.), *Verslag der handelingen van de Staten-Generaal 1839/40 en 1840* (2 vols., The Hague, 1902–3).

A. L. H. Ising (ed.), *Verslag der handelingen van de Staten-Generaal 1840/1–1845/6* (7 vols., The Hague, 1889–92).

Verslag der handelingen van de Staten-Generaal published since 1846 as a separate 'Bijblad' of the *Nederlandsche Staatscourant*.

Belgium

Émile Huyttens (ed.), *Discussions du Congrès national de Belgique* (5 vols., Brussels, 1844–5).

From 8 Sept. 1831 to 31 Dec. 1844 reports were published in the *Moniteur belge*. Since 1844 stenographic reports of all discussions appear in a separate publication *Annales Parlementaires* or *Parlementaire Handelingen*.

The parliamentary speeches of various statesmen were published in useful editions. For the Netherlands see for instance:

G. Groen van Prinsterer, *Adviezen in de Tweede Kamer der Staten-Generaal* (2 vols., Utrecht, 1856–7).

A. Kuyper, *Parlementaire redevoeringen* (4 vols., Amsterdam, 1908–12).

J. R. Thorbecke, *Parlementaire redevoeringen 1840–1866* (6 vols., Deventer, 1856–70) and C. G. van der Hoeven (ed.), *De onuitgegeven parlementaire redevoeringen van J. R. Thorbecke* (6 vols., Groningen, 1900–10). An Index to both publications appeared in 1912.

Strangely enough no such collections are available for leading Belgian statesmen such as Rogier, Frère-Orban, Woeste, Beernink, or Van Zeeland. But one can mention:

J. Destrée, *Discours parlementaires* (Brussels, 1914).

P. Janson, *Discours parlementaires* (2 vols., Brussels, 1905–6).

D. *Political parties*

Belgium

The history of the Belgian Catholic party is particularly well known thanks to the labour of the late Chanoine A. Simon. For a short synthesis see his *Le Parti catholique belge (1830–1945)* (Brussels, 1958) which has a good bibliography.

There is as yet nothing comparable on the Belgian Liberal party but see P. Hymans, *L'Œuvre libérale d'un siècle (1830–1930)* (Brussels, 1930).

On the Belgian labour movement see the work of one of its leaders: L. Bertrand, *Histoire de la démocratie et du socialisme en Belgique depuis 1830* (2 vols., Brussels, 1906–7) and two books by É. Vandervelde, *Le Parti ouvrier belge (1885–1925)* (Brussels, 1925), and *Le Cinquantenaire du parti ouvrier belge (1885–1935)* (Brussels, 1936).

The first attempt at scholarly analysis was made in J. Dhondt (ed.), *Geschiedenis van de socialistische arbeidersbeweging in België* (Antwerp, 1969). This is an uneven and perhaps somewhat disappointing book with some excellent and original contributions.

Netherlands

J. H. J. M. Witlox, *De Katholieke Staatspartij in haar oorsprong en ontwikkeling geschetst* (2 vols., 's Hertogenbosch, 1919–27) and *De staatkundige emancipatie van Nederlands Katholieken, 1848–1870*, ed. L. Rogier and F. Pikkemaat ('s Hertogenbosch, 1969) are anachronistic and parochial in their approach, yet thanks to the information they contain are indispensable. In a quite different way also L. J. Rogier and N. de Rooy, *In vrijheid herboren. Katholiek Nederland, 1853–1953* (The Hague, 1953) is rather idiosyncratic. This is the history of Dutch Catholicism rather than of the Catholic party, written in a most lively style, baroque, critical, and informative: an excellent but highly personal book.

There is an authoritative concise book on Dutch liberalism by K. E. van der Mandele, *Het liberalisme in Nederland. Schets van de ontwikkeling in de negentiende eeuw* (Arnhem, 1933).

The Protestants have not yet produced a good history of their parties. We must make do with memorial volumes such as *Schrift en Historie. Gedenkboek bij het 50–jarig bestaan der georganiseerde Antirevolutionaire partij, 1878–1928* (Kampen, 1928), or J. A. de Wilde and C. Smeenk, *Het volk ten baat. De geschiedenis van de A. R. partij* (Groningen, 1949)

Dutch scholarly research on the socialist movement is still in its infancy. It would not be possible for the Dutch to compose a work comparable to that of Dhondt mentioned above. F. Domela

Nieuwenhuis wrote his memoirs under the title *Van Christen tot Anarchist* (Amsterdam, 1910); P. J. Troelstra, *Gedenkschriften* (4 vols. and Index, 1927–32), is fundamental but should be used with caution. The best general survey is still W. H. Vliegen (one of the reformist leaders of the SDAP), *De dageraad der volksbevrijding. Schetsen en tafreelen uit de socialistische beweging in Nederland* (2 vols., Amsterdam, 1905). Vliegen continued his narrative in *Die onze kracht ontwaken deed. Geschiedenis van de SDAP in Nederland gedurende de eerste 25 jaren van haar bestaan* (3 vols., Amsterdam, 1924–38) but this is, it seems to me, a less well-written and less distinguished work than the former.

Meanwhile much work is being undertaken. G. Harmsen published in 1972 *Idee en beweging. Bekommentarieerde bibliografie van de geschiedenis van socialisme en arbeidersbeweging in Nederland* (Nijmegen) which is only a short and provisional version of the gigantic bibliography he is preparing. His *Historisch overzicht van socialisme en arbeidersbeweging in Nederland*, i: *Van de begintijd tot het uitbreken van de eerste wereldoorlog* (Nijmegen, n.d.)—a most informative survey—is equally intended as a first step towards a more definitive work.

H. van Hulst, A. Pleysier, and A. Scheffer. *Het roode vaandel volgen wij. Geschiedenis van de Sociaal Democratische Arbeiderspartij van 1880 tot 1940* (The Hague, 1969) is useful but superficial.

The socialist trade union movement has been studied by Fr. de Jong Edz., *Om de plaats van de arbeid. Een geschiedkundig overzicht van ontstaan en ontwikkeling van het Nederlands Verbond van Vakverenigingen* (Amsterdam, 1956). M. Ruppert, *De Nederlandse vakbeweging* (2 vols., Haarlem, 1953) studies also the Christian trade unions.

E. *Economic history*

The economic history of the Netherlands is admirably described by I. J. Brugmans, *Paardenkracht en mensenmacht. Sociaal-economische geschiedenis van Nederland* (The Hague, 1961). This is a dispassionate account, in many places descriptive rather than analytical and for that reason criticized by historians of a younger generation. It has an excellent bibliographical apparatus.

See also the exemplary *Geschiedenis van de Nederlandsche Bank* by A. M. de Jong (4 vols. in 5 parts, complete edn. Haarlem, 1967). The author describes the history of the bank from 1814 to 1914 and prints a large number of interesting documents.

For a first step towards a comparative study of the Belgian and the Dutch economies see J. A. van Houtte, *Economische en sociale geschiedenis van de Lage Landen* (Zeist, 1964) in which the period from 1795 to 1960 is treated on pp. 215–332.

Brugmans's work has no Belgian equivalent. As the title indicates, the emphasis of the work by the late B.-S. Chlepner, *Cent Ans d'histoire sociale en Belgique* (Brussels, 1st edn. 1956, reprinted 1972) is on social rather than economic history. The period studied is *c.* 1850–1960. This is not a textbook and it has no adequate bibliography but it is a perceptive and personal analysis of the major developments in economic and social history, a minor classic.

In his *Histoire économique de la Belgique, 1914–1939* (2 vols., 2nd edn., Brussels, 1946) F. Baudhuin provides important information over the period preceding his main subject. See also his contribution ('Histoire économique de la Belgique') to the work of J. Deharveng (ed.), *Histoire de la Belgique contemporaine, 1830–1914* (3 vols., Brussels, 1928–30).

F. *Foreign affairs*

The second volume of C. Smit, *De buitenlandsche politiek van Nederland* (2 vols., The Hague, 1945) deals with the period after the establishment of the monarchy. See also the same author's *Diplomatieke geschiedenis van Nederland inzonderheid sedert de vestiging van het Koninkrijk* (The Hague, 1950). The American historian A. Vandenbosch wrote a most useful introduction to the subject: *Dutch Foreign Policy since 1815. A Study in Small Power Politics* (The Hague, 1959). Although Belgian foreign policy has been studied more extensively there is no such survey covering the whole period. For a short exposition, however, see A. de Ridder, 'La Belgique et les puissances européennes' in J. Deharveng (ed.), *Histoire de la Belgique contemporaine, 1830–1914* or J. Garsou, *Les Relations extérieures de la Belgique, 1839–1914* (Brussels, 1946). An important aspect has been treated in great detail by H. Lademacher, *Die belgische Neutralität als Problem der europäischen Politik, 1830–1914* (Bonn, 1971). M. Suetens studied the *Histoire de la politique commerciale de la Belgique depuis 1830 jusqu'à nos jours* (Brussels, 1955).

As far as edited source material is concerned the historian of the Netherlands is much better served than the historian of Belgium. I refer here to the series *Bescheiden betreffende de buitenlandse politiek van Nederland, 1848–1919* in the Rijks Geschiedkundige Publicatiën, grote serie, The Hague. The series is divided into three periods. The first goes from 1848 to 1870 and is edited by C. B. Wels who published as yet only his first volume (RGP, grote serie, cxxix, 1972). The second period, 1871–1898, is edited by J. Woltring and is complete in 6 volumes (RGP, grote serie, cvii, cxviii, cxxii, cxxvi, cxxxii, cxxxviii, 1962–72). The third period, 1899–1919, edited by C. Smit (10 vols., RGP, grote serie, c, cii, cvi, cix, cxvi, cxvii, cxxviii, cxxxvii, cxlv, cxlvi, 1957–74), is also complete.

The historian of Dutch commercial policy is helped by N. W. Posthumus (ed.), *Documenten betreffende de buitenlandsche handelspolitiek van Nederland in de 19e eeuw* (6 vols., The Hague, 1919–31).

G. *Colonies*

For the Netherlands see W. Ph. Coolhaas, *A critical survey of studies on Dutch colonial history* (The Hague, 1961). There is an immense bibliography concerning the Dutch East Indies but no general work adequately covering the modern period. See, however, H. Baudet and I. J. Brugmans (eds.), *Balans van beleid. Terugblik op de laatste halve eeuw van Nederlands-Indië* (Assen, 1961). The West Indies, which I have not dealt with in this book because they hardly played a role in Dutch domestic policies, are much less studied.

Belgian research into the history of the Congo is impressive but there is, as far as I know, no general synthesis that could be recommended.

H. *Flemish question*

The output of books and articles on the Flemish problem is stupendous and likely to make the general historian feel desperate. The most important contribution on the history of the Flemish movement generally is undoubtedly H. J. Elias, *Geschiedenis van de Vlaamse gedachte, 1780–1914* (4 vols., Antwerp, 1963–5) who gives in his notes an extensive bibliography. Although the book is too long and confined to the study of ideas this will remain an indispensable work. The author continued it in his *Vijfentwintig jaar Vlaamse Beweging, 1914/1939* (4 vols., Antwerp, 1969) which is less satisfactory.

In his *Geschiedenis van de Vlaamse en Grootnederlandse Beweging* (vol. i, 2nd edn., 1942; vol. ii, 1959, Antwerp) Leo Picard is more than Elias concerned to take account of the effect of economic and social change; although this lively book is not always a sure guide it is generally enlightening and has brilliant passages.

Th. Coopmans and J. Broeckaert, *Bibliographie van den Vlaamschen taalstrijd* (10 vols., Ghent, 1904–14) is an edition of source material relating to the period from 1781 to 1886.

II. REVOLUTION, 1780–1813

In both Belgium and the Netherlands the interpretation of this period is clearly changing but one has the impression that no coherent new view has as yet been worked out. For a long time Dutch historiography has been dominated by the enormous work of

H. T. Colenbrander, *De Patriottentijd, hoofdzakelijk naar buitenlandse bescheiden* (3 vols., The Hague, 1897–9), a brilliantly written and well-documented book in which the author—himself a nationalist liberal—bitterly criticized the Patriots of the 1780s for their insufficiencies. Obviously, Colenbrander deplored in what he saw as the weakness of the Patriots the decline of Holland and of Dutch energy generally. The same critical tone can be discerned in his edition of source material relating to the period 1795–1840: *Gedenkstukken der algemeene geschiedenis van Nederland van 1795 tot 1840* (10 vols. in 22 parts, The Hague, 1905–22; Rijks Geschiedkundige Publicatiën, grote serie, i–vi, xi–xiii, xvi–xviii, xxv, xxvii, xxx, xxxvii, xl, xlii, xliv, xlvi, l). With all its faults—such as arbitrary selection of documents and innumerable misprints—this remains an absolutely indispensable work composed by a man whose knowledge of the period has never been surpassed.

Colenbrander's lack of sympathy with the Dutch revolutionaries of the 1780s and 1790s was implicitly criticized by M. de Jong whose biography of *Joan Derk van der Capellen. Staatkundig levensbeeld uit den wordingstijd der moderne democratie in Nederland* (Groningen, 1921) is much more positive. In 1947 P. Geyl started in his small book *De Patriottenbeweging, 1780–1787* (Amsterdam, 1947) an offensive against Colenbrander (who died in 1945) which he continued in several polemical articles. In Geyl's view the Patriot movement must be admired for its courageous attempt to reform the state; the whole period was according to him important and creative. In the last volume of his *Geschiedenis van de Nederlandse stam* (iii, Amsterdam, 1959) he also reinterpreted the so-called French period from 1795 onwards in a much more favourable way than Colenbrander and his followers allowed. The Batavian Revolution was not, as Colenbrander suggested, a mere copy or rather a caricature of the great French Revolution but an original, characteristically Dutch way of striving for fundamental change. To achieve this interpretation Geyl drastically simplified matters by rejecting the ideas and actions of the radical democrats as both antinational and ridiculous and by selecting the moderate party as the standard-bearer of the true Dutch revolution. In his stimulating but rather inconsistent *De strijd tussen aristocratie en democratie in Nederland, 1780–1848* (Heerlen, 1965) C. H. E. de Wit protested against Geyl; he himself opted for the radicals. But where does all this leave us? Nowhere, in fact. What is urgently needed is a much more dispassionate approach, a much clearer definition of the problems and an effort somehow to put the development of political ideas in the context of the economic situation and the social circumstances of which we know little. It would seem that the main conclusion to be drawn from recent discussions is that the period still deserves serious study.

In Belgium the situation is different because in contrast with the inclination of the Dutch to put forward general interpretations not based on original research the Belgians tend to specialize in exhaustive studies of small subjects, sometimes, however, inferring from their microscopic research conclusions which may be somewhat surprising by their boldness There is a second difference. It was Geyl's ambition to vindicate for Patriots and moderate reformers a place in the national development; in other words, he wanted to nationalize a reform movement regarded by Colenbrander as a foreign import. The older major works on the period in Belgium, however, were written by nationalist authors who emphasized the resistance of Belgian public opinion to the tyranny of French ideas and French rule. They regarded this resistance as 'national' and therefore applauded it. The most characteristic example is the standard work by P. Verhaegen, *La Domination française en Belgique* (5 vols., Brussels, 1922–9) dealing with the period from 1792 onwards. It was written before the First World War and is bitterly hostile to the Enlightenment and the French Revolution. For Verhaegen it was Van der Noot, the States of Brabant, and the clergy who represent true Belgian patriotism. This was unacceptable to Pirenne and Mrs. S. Tassier who in her books *Les Démocrates belges de 1789* (Brussels, 1930) and *Histoire de la Belgique sous l'occupation française en 1792 et 1793* (Brussels, 1934) opted for the Vonckists. A more systematic criticism of Verhaegen was made by R. Devleeshouwer in his *L'Arrondissement du Brabant sous l'occupation française, 1794–1795* (Brussels, 1964) in which the French appear in a much less sinister guise than in Verhaegen's book and in which the author points out the 'progressive' consequences of their activities during that year. Obviously, Verhaegen's interest in nationality has lost its appeal; the criterion nowadays is whether a policy is 'progressive' or 'conservative'. Meanwhile research into economic history developed rapidly and in 1967 J. Craeybeckx was able to write a learned and stimulating article 'De Brabantse Omwenteling: een conservatieve opstand in een achterlijk land?' (*Tijdschrift voor Geschiedenis*, lxxx, 1967, 303–30) in which he totally rejected the traditional view that the conservatism of the Brabant Revolution corresponded with the economic, social, and intellectual backwardness of the Austrian Netherlands. In Craeybeckx's opinion the Austrian Netherlands were in no sense backward; on the contrary, they may well in many respects have been further developed than France. Y. Vanden Berghe supported this view enthusiastically in an enormously detailed book on Bruges from 1780 to 1794: *Jacobijnen en Traditionalisten. De reacties van de Bruggelingen in de Revolutietijd (1780–1794)* (2 vols., n.p., 1972). He emphasizes the importance of the progressive democrats while demonstrating that it was the traditionalists who retained the upper hand. This now seems to have become one of the main problems: how was it possible for the Brabant Revolution to become so reactionary or for the position of the democratic revolutionaries to be so feeble in a town like Bruges if indeed the country was economically and intellectually highly advanced? It remains to be seen whether this will turn out to be a fruitful question.

III. UNITED KINGDOM AND BELGIAN REVOLUTION, 1813–1830

Colenbrander's *Gedenkstukken* are also for this period the most important collection of documents. The same editor devoted two large volumes of documents to the *Ontstaan der grondwet* (2 vols., The Hague, 1908–9, Rijks Geschiedkundige Publicatiën, kleine serie, i, vii). For the discussions in Parliament see above, section I c.

General surveys of the period are unsatisfactory although the *Algemene Geschiedenis der Nederlanden* (see above, sect. I b) has some good chapters in vol. ix. For a short and stimulating essay which, however, despite its title concentrates on the Belgian opposition to William I's policy see A. J. Vermeersch, *Vereniging en revolutie. De Nederlanden 1814–1830* (Bussum, 1970).

The economic development of the new state has been well studied in R. Demoulin, *Guillaume Ier et la transformation économique des provinces belges, 1815–1830* (Liège, 1938); H. R. C. Wright, *Free Trade and Protection in the Netherlands, 1816–1830* (Cambridge, 1955); and H. J. M. Witlox, *Schets van de ontwikkeling van welvaart en bedrijvigheid in het Verenigd Koninkrijk der Nederlanden* (Nijmegen, 1956). Very important is W. M. F. Mansvelt, *Geschiedenis van de Nederlandsche Handel-Maatschappij* (2 vols., Haarlem, 1924–6); naturally it also covers the period after 1830. So does the classic work on social history by I. J. Brugmans, *De arbeidende klasse in Nederland in de 19e eeuw, 1813–1870* (1st edn., The Hague, 1927, reprinted at various times).

Important for the history of political thought in Belgium in this and the preceding period is the lively and profound book by H. Haag, *Les Origines du catholicisme libéral en Belgique (1789–1839)* (Louvain, 1950). In the same context see K. Jürgensen, *Lamennais und die Gestaltung des belgischen Staates. Der liberale Katholizismus in der*

Verfassungsbewegung des 19. Jahrhunderts (Wiesbaden, 1963) and A. Simon, *Rencontres mennaisiennes en Belgique* (Brussels, 1963). Dutch political thought has not been systematically studied.

A. de Jonghe published in 1943 an excellent analysis of *De taalpolitiek van Koning Willem I in de Zuidelijke Nederlanden* (reprinted Bruges, 1967). Of course the primary school was an important instrument to improve the knowledge of Dutch in the Southern provinces. A large proportion of M. de Vroede's book on the training of primary school teachers, *Van schoolmeester tot onderwijzer. De opleiding van leerkrachten in België en Luxemburg van het einde van de 18e eeuw tot omstreeks 1842* (Louvain, 1970), is devoted to developments in this period.

There is relatively little on William I's religious policy. Ch. Terlinden, *Guillaume Ier, Roi des Pays-Bas, et l'Église catholique en Belgique, 1814-1830* (2 vols., Brussels, 1906) is old-fashioned and one-sided but most informative. P. Geyl gives in his article 'De oorsprongen van het conflict tussen Willem I en de Belgische Katholieken' (1948, reprinted in his *Studies en Strijdschriften*, Groningen, 1958) a new and balanced view of this decisive issue. For theological developments in the Netherlands see M. E. Kluit, *Het protestantse Réveil in Nederland en daarbuiten 1815-1864* (Amsterdam, 1970).

Few Dutch and Belgian professional historians practise the art of biography. H. T. Colenbrander, who used to accompany his editions of source material with surveys written for the general public, published a biography of *Willem I. Koning der Nederlanden* (2 vols., Amsterdam, 1931-5) which is, of course, extremely well documented but in no sense definitive. Since then no serious attempt has been made to study the character and career of this most remarkable man. Cf. H. T. Colenbrander (ed.), 'Gesprekken met Koning Willem I', *Bijdragen en Mededeelingen van het Historisch Genootschap*, xxxi (1910), 258-313 and C. Gerretson (ed.), 'Gesprekken met den Koning, 1826-1839', ibid. lvii (1936), 110-226.

Gijsbert Karel van Hogendorp has not found a modern biographer either. L. G. J. Verberne confined himself to *Gijsbert Karel's leerjaren* (Amsterdam, 1931) and Mrs. H. L. T. de Beaufort, *Gijsbert Karel van Hogendorp. Grondlegger van het Koninkrijk* (1st edn., Rotterdam, 1948) produced an elegant volume but had no scholarly ambition. Source material in G. K. van Hogendorp, *Brieven en Gedenkschriften*, ed. F. and H. van Hogendorp (7 vols., The Hague, 1866-1903).

A. R. Falck's life is well documented by the edition of his *Brieven, 1795-1843*, ed. O. W. Hora Siccama (2nd edn., The Hague, 1861), his *Ambtsbrieven, 1802-1842*, ed. O. W. Hora Siccama (The Hague, 1878), and his *Gedenkschriften*, ed. H. T. Colenbrander (The Hague,

1913; Rijks Geschiedkundige Publicatiën, kleine serie, xiii). Yet there is no modern biography.

C. F. van Maanen's career during the French Revolution has been described by M. E. Kluit, *Cornelis Felix van Maanen tot het herstel der onafhankelijkheid, 9 Sept. 1769–6 Dec. 1813* (Groningen, 1953) but there is little about his life under William I.

The life of Johannes van den Bosch was written by J. J. Westendorp Boerma, *Een geestdriftig Nederlander. Johannes van den Bosch* (Amsterdam, 1950). The same author studied *Johannes van den Bosch als sociaal hervormer* (Groningen, 1927).

Generally speaking, the period is not well known despite our abundant documentation. To arrive at a dispassionate account of the achievements and the failures of the United Kingdom it is necessary (among many other things) to take up again the problem of Belgian national feeling, to examine in detail whether it is true that Belgium was in advance of the Netherlands and if so in what sense precisely, and to study the Belgian civil servants and advisers who supported William I. One should at any rate try to consider the period more objectively by no longer interpreting all matters to which sections of the Belgian population were opposed as a foreign Dutch import alien to the Belgian nation.

The Belgian Revolution has been the object of endless debate and we are still very far from a consensus about its causes, its development, and its purpose. As a result of much research it is relatively easy to say what the Revolution was not: it was not a French conspiration; it was not the revolt of the French-speaking bourgeoisie against Dutch autocracy; it was not a spontaneous rising of Liberal and Roman Catholic nationalists against despotic oppression; neither was it a proletarian revolution. All such simplifications have been shown to be unsatisfactory. But how the Revolution should be defined in more positive terms is much more difficult to decide. A. Smits has in his *1830. Scheuring in de Nederlanden*, vol. i (the only one published): *Holland stoot Vlaanderen af* (Bruges, 1950) tried to prove that Flanders was fundamentally loyal to William I but was betrayed by the Dutch. J. Dhondt convincingly demonstrated that this was too narrow a view: see the discussion between Smits and Dhondt in *De Vlaamse Gids*, xxxv (1951), 181–6, 235–54, 664–73, 717–24. Perhaps the best guide at the moment is the chapter which Elias (*Vlaamse gedachte*, i. 357 ff.; see above, sect. I H) devoted to Belgian national consciousness in the 1830 Revolution.

As far as source material is concerned, see also apart from the *Gedenkstukken* C. Gerretson (ed.), *Muiterij en Scheuring* (2 vols., Leiden, 1936) and A. Smits (ed.), 'Instructies aan en rapporten van gouverneurs uit 1830', *Bijdragen en Mededelingen van het Historisch Genootschap*, lxvii (1948), 157–358. About the Belgian constitution cf. W. van den Steene, *De Belgische grondwetscommissie oktober–november 1830. Tekst van haar notulen en ontstaan van de Belgische grondwet* (Brussels, 1963).

IV. 1830–1848

Colenbrander's *Gedenkstukken* stop in 1840; they have no successor. Other material in A. J. C. Rüter (ed.), *Rapporten van de gouverneurs in de provinciën, 1840–1848*; this edition has remained incomplete (3 vols. published, Utrecht, 1941–50; Werken uitgegeven door het Historisch Genootschap, 3rd Ser., lxxiii, lxxvii, lxxviii, with an Index by G. A. M. Beekelaer, 1973). See also the highly informative book by J. de Bosch Kemper, *Geschiedenis van Nederland na 1830* (5 vols., Amsterdam, 1873–82).

A. Simon published in various books a large number of documents about the relations between Church and State in Belgium: *La Politique religieuse de Léopold Ier. Documents inédits* (Brussels, 1953); *Catholicisme et politique. Documents inédits, 1832–1909* (Wetteren, 1955); *L'Hypothèse libérale en Belgique. Documents inédits, 1837–1907* (Wetteren, 1956); *Aspects de l'Unionisme, 1830–1857. Documents inédits* (Wetteren, 1958); and *Réunions des éveques de Belgique. Procès-verbaux (1830–1867)* (Louvain, 1960).

B. Gille published most interesting *Lettres adressées à la maison Rothschild de Paris par son représentant à Bruxelles, 1838–1840, 1843–1853* (2 vols., Louvain, 1961–3).

For source material relating to Belgian social history see H. Wouters (ed.), *Documenten betreffende de arbeidersbeweging (1831–1853)*, (3 vols., Louvain, 1963), a publication of the Centre interuniversitaire d'histoire contemporaine.

The Belgian-Dutch conflict in the 1830s is documented in contemporary publications such as *Recueil des pièces diplomatiques relatives aux affaires de la Hollande et de la Belgique en 1830 et 1831* (3 vols., The Hague, 1831–3) and *Papers relative to the affairs of Belgium* (2 vols., London, 1833). C. Smit studied *De conferentie van Londen. Het vredesverdrag tussen Nederland en België van 19 April 1839* (Leiden, 1948).

H. W. von der Dunk wrote an interesting book on German opinion about the new state of Belgium: *Der deutsche Vormärz und Belgien, 1830–1848* (Wiesbaden, 1966), whereas H. Th. Deschamps studied *La Belgique devant la France de juillet. L'Opinion et l'attitude françaises de 1839 à 1848* (Paris, 1956).

For 1848 see A. de Ridder (ed.), *La Crise de la neutralité belge de 1848: le dossier diplomatique* (2 vols., Brussels, 1928). J. C. Boogman's great book on *Nederland en de Duitse Bond 1815–1851* (2 vols., Groningen, 1955) gives far more than diplomatic history; it contains much information about internal Dutch affairs. The same author made a bold attempt to compare the mentality inspiring Dutch and Belgian foreign policy in a challenging article of 1962 translated as 'Background and General Tendencies of the Foreign Policies of the Netherlands and Belgium in the Middle of the 19th Century', *Acta Historiae Neerlandicae*, i (Leiden, 1966), 132–58. C. W. van Santen, *Het internationale recht in Nederlands buitenlands beleid 1840–1850* (The Hague, 1955) printed a mass of source material.

It is astonishing that no more has been written on Belgian economic history in this period if it is taken into account that developments in the 1830s and 1840s have probably pushed the economy into the modern phase. However, P. Schöller published an enlightening study of 'La transformation économique de la Belgique de 1832 à 1844', *Bulletin de l'Institut de recherches économiques et sociales*, xiv (Louvain, 1948), 525–96. The decline of Flanders is analysed by G. Jacquemyns in his excellent *Histoire de la crise économique des Flandres (1845–1850)*, (Brussels, 1929).

The lack of modern biographies is most annoying. Even Thorbecke whose life was sketched in a judicious short book by I. J. Brugmans, *Thorbecke* (1st edn., Haarlem, 1932), has never been honoured with a large-scale biography. A selection of his private papers was published by J. Brandt-Van der Veen (ed.), *Het Thorbecke-Archief* (3 vols., Utrecht, 1955–67; Werken uitgegeven door het Historisch Genootschap, 4th Ser. iii, vii, viii). This publication is continued by G. J. Hooykaas (ed.), *De briefwisseling van J. R. Thorbecke*, i: *1830–1833* (The Hague, 1975; RGP, kleine serie, xlii). Older publications of his letters include *Brieven 1830–1832*, ed. G. Groen van Prinsterer (Amsterdam, 1873) and *J. R. Thorbecke. Brieven aan zijn verloofde en aan zijn vrouw* (Amsterdam, 1936). For his speeches in Parliament see above, section I c.

Studies of aspects of Thorbecke's activities are fairly numerous. W. Verkade gave in his *Overzicht der staatkundige denkbeelden van Johan Rudolph Thorbecke (1798–1872)* (Arnhem 1935) a helpful, systematically arranged survey of his political ideas without, however, analysing or testing them. K. H. Boersema, *Johan Rudolf Thorbecke* (Leiden, 1949) is an unsatisfactory book but it contains interesting views and material. J. B. Manger, *Thorbecke en de histoire* (Amsterdam, 1938) remains one of the best analyses of Thorbecke's thought although some of the author's hypotheses have turned out to be wrong. L. W. G. Scholten collected some good essays in his book *Voetstappen van Thorbecke* (Assen, 1966). See also the recent articles in *Acta Historiae Neerlandicae*, vii (The Hague, 1974), by J. C. Boogman, 'J. R. Thorbecke, Challenge and Response' and J. A. Bornewasser, 'Thorbecke and the Churches'.

With the other original statesman and thinker G. Groen van Prinsterer whose international reputation among historians rests on his edition of the *Archives de la Maison d'Orange-Nassau* the situation is not better. In the Rijks Geschiedkundige Publicatiën some instalments have appeared of the edition of his *Schriftelijke Nalatenschap* (started in 1925) but the series is far from complete. G. J. Vos Az., *Groen van Prinsterer en zijn tijd, 1800–1876. Studiën en schetsen op het gebied der vaderlandsche kerkgeschiedenis* (2 vols., Dordrecht, 1886–91) and T. de Vries, *Mr. G. Groen van Prinsterer in zijne omgeving* (Leiden, 1908) are informative. C. Tazelaar, *De jeugd van Groen 1801–1827* (Amsterdam, 1925) and J. L. P. Brants, *Groen's geestelijke groei. Onderzoek naar Groen van Prinsterer's theorieën tot 1834* (Amsterdam, 1951) study his early years. P. A. Diepenhorst's *Groen van Prinsterer* (Kampen, 1932) is an eulogy but well-informed. Some of the articles collected in *Groen's Ongeloof en Revolutie. Een bundel studiën* (Wageningen, 1949) are excellent. See also H. Smitskamp's good book on *Groen van Prinsterer als historicus* (Amsterdam, 1940).

In Belgium the only large-scale life of a leading statesman is E. Discailles, *Charles Rogier (1800–1885) d'après des documents inédits* (4 vols., Brussels, 1892–5), an indispensable but uncritical book. Some popular biographical sketches such as E. van Turenhoudt, *Un Philosophe au pouvoir. Louis de Potter, 1786–1859* (Brussels, 1946), C. Bronne, *Joseph Lebeau* (Brussels, 1944), F. Daxhelet, *Joseph Lebeau* (Brussels, 1945), and J. Ruzette, *J. B. Nothomb* (Brussels, 1946) are welcome since more profound studies are lacking. Of a radically different standard is A. Simon's excellent biography, *Le Cardinal Sterckx et son temps* (2 vols., Wetteren, 1950).

For King Leopold I see apart from the well-known book by E. Corti and C. Buffin, *Léopold Ier, oracle politique de l'Europe* (Brussels, 1927) also A. Simon, *Léopold Ier* (Brussels, 1962).

The interpretation of Dutch history in the 1840s has changed. Whereas they were traditionally seen as a period during which the liberal victory of 1848 was being gradually prepared Rüter and Boogman described them as years of great uncertainty, even of crisis; in this perspective the revision of the constitution in 1848 was an accident rather than the outcome of a slow development which was logically to be expected. See A. J. C. Rüter, 'De grondwet en het Nederlandse volkskarakter' (1948), reprinted in his collected *Historische studies over mens en samenleving* (Assen, 1967), pp. 342–84 and J. C. Boogman, 'The Dutch Crisis in the Eighteen-Forties', in

J. S. Bromley and E. H. Kossmann (eds.), *Britain and the Netherlands* (London, 1960), pp. 192–203.

We are not well informed about the growth and structure of the political groups and parties in both countries. In her *Politieke machtsstrijd in en om de voornaamste Belgische steden 1830–1848* (2 vols., Brussels, 1973) E. Witte studies the matter on the local level and reaches conclusions which prove this to be a promising approach.

For Catholic opinion in Belgium see H. Haag, *Les Droits de la cité. Les catholiques-démocrates et la défense de nos franchises communales 1833–1836* (Brussels, 1946) and R. Rezsohazy, *Origines et formation du catholicisme social en Belgique 1842–1909* (Louvain, 1958).

For the Flemish movement see M. de Vroede, *Bibliografische inleiding tot de studie van de Vlaamse Beweging, 1830–1860* (Louvain, 1959, published by the Centre interuniversitaire d'histoire contemporaine). Both De Vroede himself and L. Wils have written important studies relating to this period, for which see the Bibliographical Index. An interesting edition of source material is Ada Deprez (ed.), *Brieven van, aan en over Jan Frans Willems, 1793–1846* (6 vols., Bruges, 1965–8).

V. 1848–1879

Neither the structure and social background of the liberal parties nor the development of their ideas and mentality have been systematically studied. This is true for both Belgium and the Netherlands. Perhaps A. Erba, *L'Esprit laïque en Belgique sous le gouvernement libéral doctrinaire, 1857–1879, d'après les brochures politiques* (Louvain, 1967) clarifies some aspects. P. Hymans started in the beginning of the century a biography of Frère-Orban of which he completed two volumes (Brussels, 1905–10); J. Garsou continued this work with his *Frère-Orban de 1857 à 1896* (2 vols., Brussels, 1946–54). For his second volume he had the collaboration of H. van Leynseele. However, this work, although useful, is not the modern scholarly biography we need to understand the man, his policy, and his mind.

The only Dutch attempt in this field is a book by G. M. Bos, *Mr. S. van Houten. Analyse van zijn denkbeelden voorafgegaan door een schets van zijn leven* (Purmerend, 1952). S. van Houten himself made a contribution to the study of parliamentary history with his *Vijfentwintig jaar in de Kamer (1869–1894)* (5 vols., Haarlem, 1903–15). The sometimes bitter commentaries by the liberal Dutch professor J. T. Buys on current affairs are often most enlightening about what was going on in his party: *Studies over staatkunde en staatsrecht*, ed. W. H. de Beaufort and A. R. Arntzenius (2 vols., Arnhem, 1894–5).

Our knowledge of Belgian Catholic conservatism and the origins

of Christian democracy has been both extended and deepened by
K. van Isacker, *Werkelijk en wettelijk land. De katholieke opinie tegenover
de rechterzijde, 1863–1884* (Antwerp, 1955). The progress made is seen
when this work is compared with G. Guyot de Mishaegen, *Le Parti
catholique belge de 1830 à 1884* (Brussels, 1946). In the interpretation
of Lode Wils the history of the so-called Meeting party must be
situated in the development of Catholic opinion: *Het ontstaan van de
Meetingpartij te Antwerpen en haar invloed op de Belgische politiek*
(Antwerp, 1963). C. Woeste, *Vingt Ans de polémique* (3 vols., Brussels,
1885) and *Mémoires pour servir à l'histoire contemporaine de la Belgique*
(3 vols., Brussels, 1927–37) are well known and in spite of their
highly personal character important books.

Some of the leaders of the Catholic party were discredited in
1870 by the collapse of the financial empire built by Langrand-
Dumonceau who had won much popularity by his claim that he
endeavoured to 'christianiser les capitaux'. G. Jacquemyns devoted
an erudite and many-sided book to *André Langrand-Dumonceau,
promoteur d'une puissance financière catholique* (5 vols., Brussels, 1960–5).

The study of the Dutch confessional parties has not reached the
Belgian level. None of the biographies of Kuyper satisfies modern
scholarly needs: J. C. Rullmann, *Abraham Kuyper. Een levensschets*
(2nd edn., Kampen, 1937), P. A. Diepenhorst, *Dr. A. Kuyper*
(Haarlem, 1931), P. Kasteel, *Abraham Kuyper* (Kampen, 1938); nor
is there any book drawing together the different threads in the
thought of this complicated man, but see S. J. Ridderbos, *De
theologische cultuurbeschouwing van Abraham Kuyper* (Kampen, 1947) and
J. D. Dengerink, *Critisch-historisch onderzoek naar de sociologische
ontwikkeling van het beginsel der 'souvereiniteit in eigen kring' in de 19e en
20e eeuw* (Kampen, 1948). J. C. Rullmann composed an enormous
Kuyper-bibliografie (3 vols., Kampen, 1937). There are various collections of Kuyper's speeches and articles, *inter alia Starrentritsen* (Kampen, 1915). Late in life Kuyper tried to give a survey of his political
theory in *Antirevolutionaire staatkunde. Met nadere toelichting op 'Ons
Program'* (2 vols., Kampen, 1916–17).

For the founder of the Christian Historical Union see the biography by L. C. Suttorp, *Jhr Mr Alexander Frederik de Savornin
Lohman, 1837–1924* (The Hague, 1948).

As to the Catholic party, J. Persijn, *Schaepman* (3 vols., Utrecht,
1912–27) is useful although it has remained unfinished. J. van Wely,
Schaepman. Levensverhaal (2nd edn., Bussum, 1954) is very much
shorter but complete. See also J. Witlox, *Schaepman als staatsman*
(3 vols., Amsterdam, 1960), old-fashioned and one-sided but well
informed. All this work, both on Kuyper and Schaepman, was

written by authors who share the ideas of their leaders and admire their policies. This does not detract from their value but it has narrowed the perspective. One of the major weaknesses in the study of Dutch Christian democracy is that no one has tried to analyse Dutch developments in an international context and so to determine their originality.

Research into the beginning of the socialist movement, often concentrating on Belgian and Dutch participation in the First International, has not yet made possible the writing of a new synthesis but one finds numerous data in Th. van Tijn, *Twintig jaar Amsterdam. De maatschappelijke ontwikkeling van de hoofdstad van de jaren vijftig der vorige eeuw tot 1876* (Amsterdam, 1965)—an important work on Dutch social history generally—and in J. J. Giele, *De Eerste Internationale in Nederland* (Nijmegen, 1973).

The historian of the Belgian labour movement has for this period too the help of source material edited by H. Wouters for the Centre interuniversitaire d'histoire contemporaine: *Documenten betreffende de geschiedenis der arbeidersbeweging, 1853–1865* (Louvain, 1966) and *Documenten betreffende de geschiedenis der arbeidersbeweging ten tijde van de I^e Internationale, 1866–1880* (3 vols., Louvain, 1971). In the same series were published J. Bayer-Lothe (ed.), *Documents relatifs au mouvement ouvrier dans la province de Namur au XIXe siècle* (2 vols., Louvain, 1967–9) and Catherine Oukhow (ed.), *Documents relatifs à la Iere Internationale en Wallonie* (Louvain, 1967). Denise de Weerdt studied *De Belgische socialistische arbeidersbeweging op zoek naar een eigen vorm, 1872–1880* (Antwerp, 1972) as did K. van Isacker, *De Internationale te Antwerpen, 1867–1877* (Antwerp, 1964).

C. A. Tamse compares in his enlightening and excellently documented *Nederland en België in Europa (1859–1871). De zelfstandigheidspolitiek van twee kleine staten* (The Hague, 1973) the foreign policy of the two countries and their mutual relations. C. Gerretson (ed.) published *De Tusschenwateren 1837–1867. Diplomatieke documenten* (Haarlem, n.d.).

For Dutch economic history see J. A. de Jonge, *De industrialisatie in Nederland tussen 1850 en 1914* (Arnhem, 1968) and for the situation in the East Indies R. Reinsma, *Het verval van het cultuurstelsel* (The Hague, 1955).

King William III has had no modern biographer but see the rather eccentric book by C. W. de Vries, *Overgrootvader Willem III* (Amsterdam, 1952). In contrast, the works on King Leopold II who was of course an incomparably more influential person are innumerable. Neal Ascherson's *The King Incorporated: Leopold II in the Age of Trusts* (London, 1963) is fair and readable.

VI. 1879–1914

There is relatively little to add to the titles already mentioned. An important source for the history of liberalism as well as for Belgian history generally is P. Hymans, *Mémoires*, ed. F. van Kalken and J. Bartier (2 vols., Brussels, n.d.). R. Fenaux's *Paul Hymans. Un Homme, un temps, 1865–1941* (Brussels, n.d.) preceded this publication but is not without value. The life of the radical Janson has been described by a devoted and well-informed relative: L. Delange-Janson, *Paul Janson 1840–1913* (2 vols., n.p., 1962).

H. T. Colenbrander and J. E. Stokvis, *Leven en arbeid van Mr. C. Th. van Deventer* (3 vols., Amsterdam, 1916–17) contains valuable documentation on this Dutch liberal democrat. Another liberal democrat was the object of a book by E. van Raalte: *Dr. D. Bos. Leven en werken van een Nederlands staatsman* (Assen, 1962).

Information about Dutch radical liberalism can be found in J. Meijer, *Het levensverhaal van een vergetene. Willem Anthony Paap 1856–1923. Zeventiger onder de Tachtigers* (Amsterdam, 1959), G. Stuiveling, *De Nieuwe Gids als geestelijk brandpunt* (Amsterdam, 1935), and W. Thys, *De Kroniek van P. L. Tak* (Amsterdam, 1956). G. W. B. Borrie wrote the life of *Pieter Lodewijk Tak (1848–1907)* (Assen, 1973). Tak started as a radical but then became a socialist leader.

K. van Isacker studied aspects of Catholic political and social opinion in his excellent books *Averechtse democratie. Gilden en Christelijke democratie in België, 1875–1914* (Antwerp, 1959) and *Het Daensisme. De teleurgang van een onafhankelijke Christelijke arbeidersbeweging in Vlaanderen, 1893–1914* (Antwerp, 1959).

For right-wing Catholic politics see C. Woeste, *A travers dix années (1885–1895)* (2 vols., Brussels, 1895) and *Échos des luttes contemporaines (1895–1905)* (2 vols., Brussels, 1906). A. Simon published *Réunions des Évêques de Belgique 1868–1883* (Louvain, 1961).

Important material was made known by É. Vandersmissen, *Léopold II et Beernaert, d'après leur correspondance inédite* (2 vols., Brussels, 1920).

Three Dutch Catholic leaders were honoured by substantial and informative biographies in which their virtues are extolled: G. Brom, *Alfons Ariëns* (2 vols., Amsterdam, 1941); J. Colsen, *Poels* (Roermond, 1955); and J. P. Gribling, *P. J. M. Aalberse 1871–1948* (Utrecht, 1961). J. M. Vellinga, *Talma's sociale arbeid* (Hoorn, 1941) and T. de Ruiter, *Minister A. S. Talma. Een historisch-ethische studie over de corporatieve gedachte in de Christelijk-sociale politiek van Nederland* (Franeker, 1946) provide information about the Protestant version of Christian democracy.

Two major works by A. J. C. Rüter clarify the history of Dutch socialism during this period: 'Hoofdtrekken der Nederlandse arbeidersbeweging in de jaren 1876 tot 1886' (1938–9) reprinted in his *Historische studies over mens en samenleving* (Leiden, 1967), pp. 36–165 and *De spoorwegstakingen van 1903. Een spiegel der arbeidersbeweging in Nederland* (Leiden, 1935). The origins of Dutch communism are described in a rather egocentric manner by W. van Ravesteyn, *De wording van het communisme in Nederland, 1907–1925* (Amsterdam, 1948) and more objectively by A. A. de Jonge, *Het communisme in Nederland. De geschiedenis van een politieke partij* (The Hague, 1972). For Hendrik de Man's opposition within the Belgian socialist party see the biographies by P. Dodge, *Beyond Marxism. The Faith and Works of Hendrik de Man* (The Hague, 1966) and M. Claeysvan Haegendoren, *Hendrik de Man* (Antwerp, 1972).

It is unnecessary to print here the titles of books on colonial affairs quoted in Chapter VII but add W. R. Louis and J. Stengers (eds.), *E. D. Morel's History of the Congo Reform Movement* (Oxford, 1968). Aspects of Belgian economic expansion have been explored by J. P. McKay, *Pioneer for Profit. Foreign Entrepreneurship and Russian Industrialization, 1885–1913* (Chicago, 1970) and by G. Kurgan-van Hentenryk, *Léopold II et les groupes financiers belges en Chine. La Politique royale et ses prolongements (1895–1914)* (Brussels, 1972).

VII. 1914–1940

In the international series on the economic and social history of the First World War the section on Belgium contains a number of excellent books: C. de Kerchove de Denterghem, *L'Industrie belge pendant l'occupation allemande 1914–1918* (Paris, n.d.); E. Mahaim, *Le Secours de chômage en Belgique pendant l'occupation allemande* (Paris, n.d.); A. Henry, *Le Ravitaillement de la Belgique pendant l'occupation allemande* (Paris, n.d.); F. Passelecq, *Déportation et travail forcé des ouvriers et de la population civile de la Belgique occupée (1916–1918)* (Paris, n.d.); J. Pirenne and M. Vauthier, *La Législation et l'administration allemandes en Belgique* (Paris and New Haven, n.d.). These works were intended to serve the national historian of Belgium, Henri Pirenne (who was during the war himself deported to Germany) as material for his *La Belgique et la guerre mondiale* (Paris, n.d.) in the same series. Pirenne's synthesis is as brilliant as his *Histoire de Belgique*. The author's at times rhetorical and excessive patriotism did not make him lose sight of the less exalted aspects of reality. His treatment of the Flemish question, however, is totally inadequate.

The work on *La Belgique et la guerre* published in Brussels in four enormous volumes from 1920 to 1923 has many characteristic illustrations and a most informative text: i, G. Rency, *La Vie matérielle de la Belgique durant la Guerre Mondiale*; ii, J. Cuvelier, *L'Invasion allemande*; iii, M. Tasnier and R. van Overstraeten, *Les Opérations militaires*; iv, A. de Ridder, *Histoire diplomatique (1914–1918)*. The tone and purpose of this work are highly patriotic and emphatically opposed to the Flemish activists described in vol. i (p. 99) as 'des professeurs et des fonctionnaires besoigneux, chargés de famille, dont la mauvaise économie domestique en faisait, avant la guerre, la proie habituelle des usuriers. Certains étaient tout simplement des vicieux que l'alcool ou la débauche avaient prédisposés aux capitulations honteuses, mais lucratives.' There is no recent and more dispassionate work on the period as a whole. In his unhesitatingly pro-Flemish but scholarly work on *Het Vlaamsnationalisme. De geschiedenis van de jaren 1914–1940* (2nd edn., Utrecht, 1969) the Dutch historian A. W. Willemsen devotes much space to the war years. Mieke Claeys-van Haegendoren surveys the war period too in her major book on *25 jaar Belgisch socialisme. Evolutie van de verhouding van de Belgische Werkliedenpartij tot de parlementaire democratie in België van 1914 tot 1940* (Antwerp, 1967).

There has been virtually no scholarly discussion on Dutch history during the war years. P. H. Ritter, jun., *De donkere poort* (2 vols., The Hague, 1931) is a well-written and well-informed survey of events and situations. C. Smit, *Nederland in de Eerste Wereldoorlog* (3 vols., Groningen, 1971–3) is despite its ambitious title a straightforward narrative of events and moves relating to the international position of the Netherlands; it is almost exclusively based on the documents published by this author in the series of *Bescheiden betreffende de buitenlandse politiek van Nederland* (above, sect. I F). H. Brugmans (ed.), *Nederland in den oorlogstijd* (Amsterdam, 1920) is a collective work which contains useful material. C. A. van Manen's *De Nederlandsche Overzee Trustmaatschappij. Middelpunt van het verkeer van onzijdig Nederland met het buitenland tijdens den Wereldoorlog 1914–1918* (8 vols., The Hague, 1935) is too magnificent a monument to be manageable but is nevertheless a mine of information.

The study of the interwar years is not yet sufficiently advanced to provide fruitful controversies among scholars. Interesting speculations about the structure and politics in this period have been produced by a number of Dutch political scientists who, however, concentrated their attention on developments since 1945. But even so, their analysis of the so-called *verzuiling* in the Netherlands and in a less extreme way in Belgium too has considerably clarified some aspects of the interwar years. See H. Daalder, *Leiding en lijdelijkheid in de Nederlandse politiek* (Assen, 1964); A. Lijphart, *The Politics of Accommodation: Pluralism and Democracy in the Netherlands* (Berkeley,

1968); and L. Huyse who tried to apply the concepts developed by his Dutch predecessors to the Belgian situation in *De niet-aanwezige staatsburger* (Antwerp, 1969) and *Passiviteit, pacificatie en verzuiling in de Belgische politiek* (Antwerp, 1970).

Apart from the short, lucid, but necessarily somewhat superficial book by F. van Kalken, *Entre deux guerres. Esquisse de la vie publique en Belgique de 1918 à 1940* (2nd edn., Brussels, 1945) there are no general histories of Dutch and Belgian history between the wars. The first volume of L. de Jong's magisterial *Het Koninkrijk der Nederlanden in de Tweede Wereldoorlog* (The Hague, 1969) is for the major part (pp. 72–724) a history of the interwar period. As this volume served as an introduction to De Jong's main theme which is the Second World War the author tends to stress the fact that militarily, morally, and politically the conservative Dutch society of the 1920s and 1930s was unaware of the dangers besetting it and unprepared for the war that followed.

A reliable analysis of Belgian–Dutch diplomatic relations is C. A. van der Klaauw, *Politieke betrekkingen tussen Nederland en België 1919–1939* (Leiden, 1953). Belgian foreign policy has been studied by a Belgian author, O. de Raeymaeker, *België's internationaal beleid 1919–1939* (Brussels, 1945), by the American Jane K. Miller, *Belgian Foreign Policy between two Wars, 1919–1940* (New York, 1951)—a rather unsatisfactory book—and by D. O. Kieft, *Belgium's Return to Neutrality* (Oxford, 1972). Ch. de Visscher and F. Vanlangenhove edited a number of documents which are not particularly revealing: *Documents diplomatiques belges 1920–1940* (5 vols., Brussels, 1964–6). F. Vanlanghenhove's *La Belgique en quête de sécurité* (Brussels, 1969) is based on these documents and reflects the point of view of the Belgian Foreign Office. Dutch foreign policy during these years has not been studied in detail.

For economic history see Baudhuin's *Histoire économique de la Belgique, 1914–1939* (above, sect. I E) and for the Netherlands the collective work *De Nederlandse volkshuishouding tussen twee wereldoorlogen* (3 vols., Utrecht, 1952) which contains, among many others, distinguished studies such as F. J. H. M. van der Ven, *Economische en sociale opvattingen in Nederland* (written from a Catholic point of view) and F. A. G. Keesing, *De conjuncturele ontwikkeling van Nederland en de evolutie van de economische overheidspolitiek, 1918–1939*. See also J. de Vries, *De Nederlandse economie tijdens de 20ste eeuw* (Antwerp, 1973) and P. W. Klein, 'Depressie en beleid tijdens de jaren dertig', *Lof der historie* (Rotterdam, 1973), pp. 289–335.

In the field of political history some important titles must be added to those already mentioned in previous sections. C. H. Höjer, *Le*

Régime parlementaire belge de 1918 à 1930 (reprinted Brussels, 1969) is an excellent short analysis by a Swedish political scientist. In an enormous tome J. Beaufays made an interesting comparative study of *Les Partis catholiques en Belgique et aux Pays-Bas 1918–1958* (Brussels, 1973). The book is a mine of reliable information systematically arranged and carefully analysed.

The Director of the Koninklijke Nederlandsche Stoomboot-maatschappij E. Heldring left a diary of immense proportions in which he noted down his personal reactions to the events of the day and to people he met as well as all sorts of information and rumours: J. de Vries (ed.), *Herinneringen en dagboek van Ernst Heldring (1871–1954)* (3 vols., Groningen, 1970).

A curious document on the Dutch intellectual scene is the correspondence of Menno ter Braak and E. du Perron edited by H. van Galen Last: *Briefwisseling 1930–1940* (4 vols., Amsterdam, 1962–7).

BIBLIOGRAPHICAL INDEX

(References are to first citations)

The research for and the first draft of this book were completed by September 1975. Books and articles published since then may not be included in this index

GENERAL INDEX

Belgian R.C. politician, 508, 518–19, 537.

Brouckère, Charles de (1796–1860), Belgian liberal politician, 147–8.

Brouckére, Louis de (1870–1951), Belgian socialist, 505–6.

Bruges, medieval economy, 6, 9; 15; in 18th century, 23; population, 6, 50; 49.

Brumaire, *coup d'état* of: effect in Belgium, 77; effect in Netherlands, 92.

Brussels, Spanish court at, 14; inhabitants in 18th century, 16; cotton industry, 23; 24–5; 51; 55; and Brabant Revolution, 59, 61–3; Francis II in, 71–2; in 1830, 152–5; Université libre at, 199; Université nouvelle at, 321–2; Institut Solvay at, 460–1, 463, 507, 562, 651; Flemish leaders on, 636–7; inhabitants, 680.

Budi Utomo, 409–10.

Burgundian circle (1548), 8, 13.

Burgundy, duchy of, 8.

Burke, Edmund, 26, 87, 263, 294.

Busken Huet, Cd. (1826–86), Dutch writer, 260, 296, 309.

Buys, J. T. (1828–93), Dutch publicist, 260.

Calvin, J., 290.

Calvinism, during Revolt of the Netherlands, 11, 13–14; Calvinist immigrants into Dutch Republic, 15–16.

Cambrai, archbishopric, surrendered to France, 10.

Capellen, Joan Derk van der (1741–84), Dutch Patriot leader, 43.

Carolingian Empire, 4, 5.

Carton de Wiart, Henry (1869–1951), Belgian R.C. writer and politician, 365, 483, 485.

Casement, Roger, 392.

Castlereagh, H. R. S. Viscount, 140.

Cauwelaert, Frans van (1880–1961), Flemish leader, 467–8, 470, 539, 644.

Charlemagne, 4, 8.

Charles V, Emperor, 8–10, 13–14, 112, 118.

Charles VI, Emperor, 19.

Charles II, King of Spain, 18.

Charriaut, Henri, 518.

China, Belgian and Dutch policy towards, 424.

Christelijk Nationaal Vakverbond (Christian National Trade Union), 605.

Christelijk-Historische Unie, Dutch political party, 478, 494–5, 556.

Christian democracy, (i) Belgian, R.C., 365–7; on franchise, 371; on colonies, 390, 395, 401; between 1890 and 1914, 480–6; in 1921, 634; and Poullet's cabinet, 655–6.

(ii) Dutch, Prot.: on colonies, 401, 405–6; on foreign policy, 424; in early 20th century, 493–4, 499–500.

(iii) Dutch, R.C.: in Twente, 489; in Limburg, 490; in Leiden, 491.

Church, Dutch Reformed, 295–6, 303.

Church, R.C., (i) Belgium: Joseph II and, 54; under French rule, 73–4, 76, 78–9, 81; in United Kingdom, 126–8, 140–1, 144; in 1830s and 1840s, 199; in 1850, 236–7; between 1850 and 1875, 243.

(ii) Netherlands: re-establishment of hierarchy, 277–8.

Clercq, Gerrit de (1821–57), Dutch publicist, 183.

Clercq, Staf de (1884–1942), Flemish Fascist leader, 641.

Clergy, (i) Belgium: in Austrian Netherlands, 48; under French rule, 74, 77, 81; in United Kingdom, 126–8, 144.

(ii) Netherlands: 144.

Coal industry (Belgian), in Austrian Netherlands, 23; in bishopric of Liège, 24; in United Kingdom, 134; in 1830s, 176–7; *c*. 1900, 420.

Cobden treaty, 232.

Cobenzl, Count Charles of (1712–70), 25.

Cobet, C. G. (1813–89), Dutch classical scholar, 259.

Cockerill, John, 79.

Colenbrander, H. T. (1871–1945), Dutch historian, 437, 545.

Colijn, H. (1869–1944), Dutch politician, 406; 570; 593; 600; career, and nature of his policy, 603–6; and gold standard, 658, 667; 659; and colonial policy, 671, 674–5.

Collegium Philosophicum, 128, 149.

Cologne, Christian democratic school of, 491–2.

Colonies, Dutch, taken by Great Britain, 97; and partly restored, 110. *See also* East Indies, Dutch.

Comité d'études du Haut-Congo, 381–2.

Comité de vigilance des intellectuels antifascistes, 627.

Venlo, 224.

Veraart, J. A. (1886–1955), Dutch R.C. theorist, 595–9.

Verbond van Actualisten, Dutch Fascist party, 626.

Verbond van Dietsche Nationaal-Solidaristen (League of Dutch-speaking National Solidarists: Verdinaso), Flemish Fascist party, 626, 640, 648.

Vereeniging, peace of, 430.

Verhaegen, Arthur (1847–1917), Belgian architect and Christian democrat, 482–3.

Verhaegen, P., Belgian historian, 78, 331.

Verhaeren, Émile (1855–1916), Belgian poet, 312, 333, 445.

Verlooy, J. B. C. (1746–97), 56, 168.

Vermeylen, August (1872–1945), Flemish writer, 471–3, 535, 539.

Versailles, treaty of: approved in Belgium, 578, 588, 610; criticized in Netherlands, 579; 590; 606.

Verstolk van Soelen, J. G. (1776–1845), Dutch politician, 113.

Verviers, 25, 33, 79, 134.

Verwey, Albert (1865–1937), Dutch writer, 314, 448–9, 453, 676.

Verzuiling (Pillarization), 304, 568–70, 573–4, 620.

Vesdre, River, 23, 25.

Veth, P. J. (1814–95), Dutch scholar and publicist, 268.

Villiers de l'Isle-Adam, P. A. M. de, 329.

Vingtième siècle, Le, Belgian newspaper, 537.

Vissering, S. (1818–88), Dutch economist, 260, 263.

Vlaamsch Nationaal Verbond (Flemish National League), Flemish Fascist party, 640–2, 648.

Vlaamsche Front, Het, Flemish political party, 638–41, 643–4, 647.

Vlaamsche Volkspartij (Flemish People's party), 470–1.

Vlissingen, P. van (1797–1876), Dutch entrepreneur, 133.

Vloten, Johannes van (1818–83), Dutch historian, 206–7.

Volk, Het, Flemish newspaper, 482.

Volksraad (People's council), in Dutch East Indies, 671–2, 674–5.

Vollenhoven, C. van (1874–1933), Dutch teacher of Indonesian law, 406–7, 411–12, 422–3, 675.

Voltaire, 25.

Volunteers, Belgian, in 1914–18, 523–4.

Vonck, J. F. (1743–92), Belgian Patriot leader, 58, 60–4.

Vooruit, Flemish socialist newspaper, 343.

Vooruit, Ghent co-operative, 343.

Vree, F. J. van (1807–61), Dutch priest, 187.

Vreede, G. W. (1809–80), Dutch historian and publicist, 280–2, 425.

Vreede, Pieter (1750–1837), Dutch Patriot leader, 90, 92.

Vrijheidsbond (Freedom League), Dutch political party, 609.

Vrij-liberalen (Free-Liberals), Dutch political party, 515.

Vrijzinnig - Democratische Bond (Liberal Democratic League), Dutch political party, 404, 515, 609–10.

Vrolik, A. (1810–94), Dutch scientist and politician, 281 n.

Waal, E. de (1821–1905), Dutch politician, 273.

Wagner, Adolf, 359.

Wagner, Richard, 258, 403, 449.

Wallonia, 2; economy in 18th century, 22–3; under French rule, 76–7; in United Kingdom, 146; in 1830, 155; decline of (c. 1900), 420; separated from Flanders (1917), 527, 534, 536, 541.

Wallonie, La, Belgian periodical, 329, 332.

War of Independence, American, 42.

Waxweiler, É. (1867–1916), Belgian sociologist, 460–2, 464.

Weber, Max, 217.

West Francia, 5.

West Indies, Dutch, 270.

Weyer, Sylvain van de (1802–74), Belgian politician, 155 n.

Wijnkoop, D. (1876–1941), Dutch communist leader, 513–14, 556, 621.

Wilhelm II, Emperor, 434, 533, 564.

Wilhelmina, Queen of the Netherlands (1880–1962), 360, 429, 434, 441, 549, 592.

Willems, J. F. (1793–1846), Flemish writer, 120–1, 171.

William I, Prince of Orange (1533–84), 11, 13, 118.

William II, Prince of Orange (1626–50), 20.

William III, Prince of Orange (1650–1702), 20–1, 45.

William IV, Prince of Orange (1711–51), 20.

William V, Prince of Orange (1748–1806), 39, 40, 42, 46–7, 58, 82, 88, 102–3, 106.

MAP I. Belgium and the Netherlands as parts of Napoleon's Empire

MAP 2. The United Kingdom of the Netherlands, 1815–1830

NORTH

SEA

Schiermonnikoog
Ameland
Terschelling
Vlieland
Texel
Leeuwarden
Groningen
Assen
Zwolle
Almelo
Amsterdam
Apeldoorn
Hengelo
Enschede
Leiden
The
Hague
Amersfoort
Utrecht
Arnhem
Rotterdam
Nijmegen
's Hertogenbosch
Middelburg
Breda
Tilburg
Flushing
Eindhoven
Ostend
Bruges
Antwerp
Ghent
Mechlin
Alost
Maastricht
Brussels
Louvain
Liège
Namur
Mons
BORINAGE
Dinant
Luxemburg

0 20 40 60 80 100 km

0   20   40   60 miles

MAP 3. Belgium, the Netherlands, and Luxemburg, 1839–1940

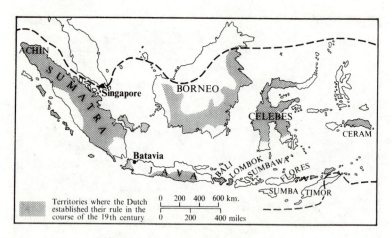

MAP 4. The East Indian Archipelago

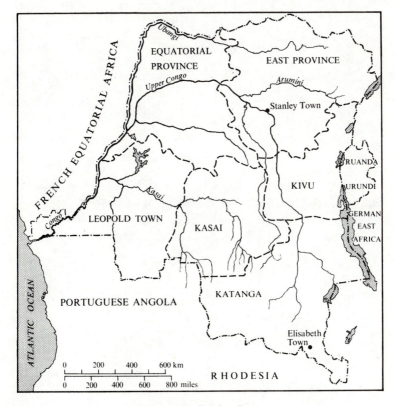

MAP 5. The Belgian Congo